# Preface

In the preface to the first edition published in 2006, we asked the question why it should be thought necessary to have a book devoted to a single, and somewhat old, piece of legislation.

The answer to our rhetorical question remains as valid as it was four years ago; in the 25 years since the Police and Criminal Evidence Act came into force, and despite the 'hailstorm' of criminal legislation enacted over the last decade, PACE and its Codes of Conduct retain a central position of importance. Other statutes are hastily enacted only to be repealed bit by bit, but PACE always remains; it is constantly adapted, constantly evolving, but still the foundation stone upon which police powers are built, the guardian of suspects' rights and, in s 78, the source of what is arguably the single most important provision in criminal evidence and procedure.

Timing a second edition of this work has not been easy. Shortly after the publication of the first edition the then Labour government issued a public consultation paper in March 2007 as a precursor to what was intended to be a review of both the Act and the Codes. In August 2008, a PACE Review Board was established and a revised consultation paper issued; we waited to see what the results would be. More time went by, and it was not until March 2010 that the summary of responses was eventually published. Two months later, and the general election intervened returning a new Government with new priorities. It seems that we shall have to wait some time yet to see whether there will be a wholesale reform of PACE or further episodes of piecemeal amendments.

Some changes, actual and proposed, we do know, and those changes are reflected in this book. The Crime and Security Act 2010 – the last piece of legislation enacted by the outgoing Labour government – contains provisions to reduce the amount of information to be recorded when a Stop-and-Search takes place. The Coalition Home Secretary, Theresa May, also pledged in her first speech to the Police Federation after taking Office that she would reduce the 'burden' of the Stop-and-Search procedures, and that the Stop-and-Account form would be scrapped in its entirety.

The powers of the police to Stop and Search under s 44 of the Terrorism Act will also be reviewed as a result of the decision of the European Court of Human Rights in the case of Gillan and Quinton v United Kingdom [2010] ECHR 28. Pending that review, interim guidance has been issued by the Home Office which requires a search to be 'necessary'¬ – not merely 'expedient' – for the prevention of terrorism, and which restricts the use of s 44 powers to searches of vehicles rather than persons (for which officers will have to rely on s 43 which requires 'reasonable suspicion' that the person is a terrorist as a condition precedent to a search).

A further ECHR ruling that has affected PACE is that in S and Marper v UK [2008] ECHR 1581. In a response to that ruling (stating that the retention of fingerprints and DNA samples from those suspected but not convicted of offences was a breach of A.8), the Crime and Security Act 2010 imports into PACE a framework for the retention and destruction of biometric material (fingerprints and DNA samples or profiles) taken from individuals in the course of an investigation into a recordable offence. The Crime and Security Act further amends PACE to give the police further powers to take fingerprints and DNA samples from people who have been arrested, charged, or convicted in the UK, and from those convicted overseas of serious sexual and violent offences, and to require a person to attend a police station for the purpose of taking that data, with a power of arrest if they fail to comply.

Other new amendments to PACE since the first edition reflect the rapid change in technology available to the Police. There are provisions allowing the police to interview suspects using digital media, the introduction of live link bail, and proposals to amend Code D of the Codes of Conduct to institute new identification procedures to deal with ever more frequent occurrence of identification by recognition of a suspect on CCTV.

What further changes may take place between now and a third edition can perhaps only be guessed at, although the early indications are that the Government will seek to reduce bureaucracy and put more power back into the hands of the police; whether they succeed in this, and whether any such reforms improve policing or merely help to redress budget deficits remains to be seen.

As with the last edition, our intention in writing this book has been to produce a straightforward practical guide to the Act and Codes and to the common problems that can arise in day to day practice; the emphasis is very much on the practical rather than on the academic. Even so, as any author-practitioner knows, combining a busy practise with authorship is difficult if not impossible without help. We therefore gratefully acknowledge the invaluable research skills and assistance provided by Holly Webb, Elena Elia, and Paddy Duffy of 23 Essex Street, and of Morag Ofili and Abigail Bright, pupils at QEB Hollis Whiteman. Last, but by no means least, we extend our thanks to Lucy Alexander and all in the Police Law and Criminology team at OUP for their encouragement and inexhaustible patience.

# PACE

## A Practical Guide to the Police and Criminal Evidence Act 1984

Second Edition

Paul Ozin

Heather Norton

*and*

Perry Spivey

OXFORD
UNIVERSITY PRESS

# OXFORD

UNIVERSITY PRESS

Great Clarendon Street, Oxford OX2 6DP

Oxford University Press is a department of the University of Oxford.
It furthers the University's objective of excellence in research, scholarship,
and education by publishing worldwide in

Oxford New York

Auckland Cape Town Dar es Salaam Hong Kong Karachi
Kuala Lumpur Madrid Melbourne Mexico City Nairobi
New Delhi Shanghai Taipei Toronto

With offices in

Argentina Austria Brazil Chile Czech Republic France Greece
Guatemala Hungary Italy Japan Poland Portugal Singapore
South Korea Switzerland Thailand Turkey Ukraine Vietnam

Oxford is a registered trademark of Oxford University Press
in the UK and in certain other countries

Published in the United States
by Oxford University Press Inc., New York

Cover photos: © ImageSource / Punchstock; Jorge Delgado / iStockphoto.com; dra_schwartz /
iStockphoto.com; loopa / iStockphoto.com; Up The Resolution (uptheres) / Alamy; Brand X Pictures /
Punchstock; Fabrizio Balestrieri / iStockphoto.com; Chris George / Alamy; David Coder /
iStockphoto.com; Dominic Harrison / Alamy; Up The Resolution (uptheres) / Alamy; Photodisc /
Punchstock

First published 2006

Second Edition published 2010

British Library Cataloguing in Publication Data

Data available

Library of Congress Cataloging in Publication Data

Data available

Typeset by Glyph International, Bangalore, India
Printed in Great Britain
on acid-free paper by
Clays Ltd, St Ives plc

ISBN 978-0-19-959524-2

10 9 8 7 6 5 4 3 2

# Contents

# Table of Cases

# Table of Legislation

# Table of Statutory Instruments

# Table of International Conventions

# Powers to Stop and Search: Part I

**Law and Commentary**

**Practical Guidance**

# Law and Commentary

## 1.1 Introduction

Part I provides the police with powers to stop and search persons and vehicles for stolen or prohibited articles without first exercising their powers of arrest. Code A 1.1 emphasizes that the powers must be used 'fairly, responsibly, with respect for people being searched and without unlawful discrimination'. Accordingly, the Act also provides safeguards (s 2) and imposes duties (s 3) upon those using those powers. Sections 4 and 5 of Part I set out similar powers and duties governing road checks.

Part I must be read in conjunction with Code A, updated as of 1 January 2009, which expands and explains the main provisions. Of particular importance in Code A are paragraphs 2.2–2.11, which provide important guidance about what can, and more importantly, cannot amount to reasonable grounds for suspicion justifying the use of these powers.

Before long, major revisions to stop and search powers and requirements will be necessary as a result of: amendments under the Crime and Security Act 2010 (not yet in force), the government's pledge to scrap the 'stop and account' form and to 'reduce the burden of the stop and search procedures', and the decision of the European Court in *Gillan and Quinton v United Kingdom* [2010] ECHR 28, that s 44 TACT breaches Art 8. In respect of the latter, interim guidance was issued on 8 July 2010 restricting the use of s 44 TACT to searches of vehicles rather than people and only where such searches are 'necessary'.

## 1.2 Powers to Stop and Search (Section 1)

### 1.2.1 Who may be stopped?

Under s 1(2), a constable may detain and search any person or vehicle, or anything which is in or on a vehicle for:

- stolen or prohibited articles (as defined in s 1(7)–(8));
- a bladed article to which s 139 of the Criminal Justice Act relates (s 1(8A)); or
- any firework which a person possesses in contravention of a prohibition imposed by fireworks regulations (s 1(8B)–(8C)).

However, the power to detain and search can only be exercised where the constable has reasonable grounds for suspecting that he will find such articles (s 1(3)).

### 1.2.2 Who may carry out the stop?

Only a 'constable', that is, a police officer, may carry out a stop and search. There is no requirement for the constable to be in uniform, save where the stop and search is carried out under the provisions of s 60 of the Criminal Justice and Public Order Act 1994, or under s 44 of the Terrorism Act 2000.

It follows from the above, that a Police Community Support Officer (PCSO) cannot carry out a stop and search under PACE, although they may carry out a 'stop and account'.

### 1.2.3 **Where may the power be exercised?**

The power to stop and search is one which can only be exercised in a public place. What is capable of constituting a public case has, in the context of other Acts such as the Road Traffic Act or the Prevention of Crime Act 1953, given rise to a substantial amount of case law with the courts' conclusions influenced by the purposes for which a person sought or was granted permission to enter a particular place and whether a place was open to the general public or restricted to a specified class of people. Section 1(1) does away with the need to make judgments on such considerations insofar as s 1 stop and search powers are concerned, as it specifies that a constable may exercise the power:

(a) in any place to which at the time when he proposes to exercise the power the public, or any section of the public has access on payment or otherwise, as of right or by virtue of express or implied permission; or,

(b) in any place to which people have ready access at the time when he proposes to exercise the power but which is not a dwelling.

'Dwelling' extends to land occupied with and used for the purpose of a dwelling. Accordingly, a constable could not carry out a search, whether of a person or a vehicle, in the garden or driveway of a private house. There is an exception to this prohibition, however, and that is where the officer has reasonable grounds to believe that the person or (in the case of a proposed search of a vehicle) the person in charge of the vehicle, does not reside in the dwelling, and that the person or vehicle is not on the land with the express or implied permission of the person who does (s 1(4)–(5)).

### 1.2.4 **What are 'stolen or prohibited articles'?**

These are set out in s 1(7)–(9). They are:

- an offensive weapon—ie any article made or adapted for use for causing injury to persons, or intended by the person having it with him for such use by him or by some other person;
- an article made or adapted for use or intended to be used in the course of:
  - burglary,
  - theft,
  - taking a motor vehicle or other conveyance without authority,
  - fraud,
  - destroying or damaging property.

Under s 1(8A) an officer may also search for an article to which s 139 of the Criminal Justice Act 1988 applies, that is:

- a bladed article.

And under s 1(8B) and (8C):

- a firework (where possessed in contravention of a prohibition imposed by firework regulations).

### 1.2.5 What are 'reasonable grounds' for suspicion?

Whether reasonable grounds for suspicion exist depends on the circumstances in each situation. In each case, however, there will be both subjective and object-ive factors. The officer must in fact himself suspect that stolen or prohibited articles will be found on the person or in the vehicle (simply being told by a superior officer to stop and search an individual will not of itself suffice—see *O'Hara v Chief Constable of the RUC* [1997] AC 286 applied in *Metropolitan Police Comr v Raissi* [2008] EWCA Civ 1237), but there must also be an objective reason or reasons upon which that suspicion is based. In *Samuels v Metropolitan Police Comr* CCRTF 98/0410/2, March 3 1999, CA, the court held that whether a sus-picion is reasonable, 'has to be determined as an objective matter from the information available to the officer'. The officer will need to be clear about the reasons for the stop and able to justify it; he must tell the individual at the time of the stop and prior to the search the grounds for the exercise of the power, and will have to make a written record detailing those grounds.

Code A 2.2–2.6 provides comprehensive guidance on what would or would not suffice to constitute an objective basis. Under the Code 'objective' means based on relevant facts, information, or intelligence. 'Relevant facts' could include a person's behaviour and/or the locality in which that behaviour is witnessed, for example a person seen late at night close to an area where a burg-lary has taken place apparently trying to conceal an item similar in size or gen-eral description to the type of item stolen in that burglary. Information or intelligence may be specific to an individual or to a specified group; Code A 2.6 provides the example of a gang known to habitually carry knives or other unlawful weapons. Code A 2.2 however states that: 'Reasonable suspicion can never be supported on the basis of personal factors, or on generalizations or stereotypes.' A person's race, age, appearance, antecedent history or religion cannot therefore provide an objective basis for reasonable suspicion, whether alone or in combination unless linked to other reliable information or intelli-gence—for example, where the appearance of the person stopped matches the description of a suspected offender.

### 1.2.6 Can reasonable grounds be established through questioning?

All officers routinely have contact with and speak to members of the public in the normal exercise of their duties. The Act is not intended to prevent what is a desirable and useful everyday occurrence. If, in the course of such contact, reasonable grounds for suspicion emerge, even though none had existed before, the officer may exercise his powers to detain and search that person under this part of the Act. Moreover, an officer who has reasonable grounds for suspicion to stop and search an individual may, prior to carrying out that search, ask questions about that person's behaviour, presence, or other factors that gave rise to the grounds for suspicion. What is not permitted, however, is the questioning of a person in order to find reasonable grounds. The power conferred on officers is one of stop and search, not stop and question. Accordingly, there is no power to detain a person for questioning under this part of the Act if no reasonable grounds exist to suspect that he is in possession of a stolen or prohibited article, and the person must be allowed to leave at will. Neither can reasonable grounds be provided retrospectively by a person's subsequent behaviour. In *Samuels v Metropolitan Police Comr* CCRTF 98/0410/2, March 3 1999, CA, the police wanted to stop and search Samuels, a black man in a high-risk burglary area who looked suspicious. Samuels was asked where he was going but he refused to tell them (although he was in fact on his way home). The police then asked to see his hands, but he refused and walked away. The police then tried to forcibly detain and search him. Finding that no reasonable grounds for suspicion existed prior to the stop, the court held that the fact that Samuels had then walked away could not turn an unreasonable suspicion into a reasonable one.

### 1.2.7 Can a person voluntarily consent to a search?

Code A 1.5 makes it clear that even where a person is prepared to submit to a search, an officer must not carry out a search unless there is a legal power to do so; therefore, if no reasonable grounds exist to carry out a search of a person under this part of the Act then no search may be carried out. Moreover, where a legal power does exist, the person may only be searched in accordance with the relevant provisions and the Code; a person cannot 'volunteer' to circumvent the Act or Codes. The only exception, set out in this part of the code, applies to persons entering sports grounds or other premises where it is a condition of entry that they should agree to a search being carried out.

## 1.3 Search Safeguards (Section 2)

### 1.3.1 Does an officer *have* to search a person or vehicle stopped under section 1?

An officer who detains a person or vehicle, whether under s 1 of Part 1 of the Act, or in pursuance of any other power to search a person or vehicle without first making an arrest, need not carry out such a search if it appears that a search is no longer required or is impracticable (s 2(1)).

A person who has been lawfully detained may be asked questions by the officer about the circumstances which have given rise to the reasonable suspicion that he may be in possession of a stolen or prohibited article. If, as a result of that questioning, or for any other reason, there cease to be reasonable grounds for such suspicion then the legal basis for the search has been lost and no search can take place. In these circumstances a record must be made of the circumstances of the stop, and the person detained must be informed that he is free to leave (Code A 2.10).

Where a person is lawfully detained but no search in fact takes place, the original detention is not thereby rendered unlawful (Code A, Note for guidance 3).

### 1.3.2 What are the officer's duties prior to undertaking a search?

Under s 2(2), if the officer is not in uniform, he must produce documentary evidence to show that he is a constable, and, whether in uniform or not, must inform the person that he is being detained for the purpose of a search and notify the appropriate person of:

- the officer's name (or warrant number if the officer reasonably believes that giving his name might put him in danger), and the name of the police station to which he is attached;
- the object of the proposed search;
- the grounds for the proposed search;
- his entitlement to a copy of the record of the search, unless it appears to the officer that it will not be practicable for such a record to be made, and how he can obtain such a copy (s 2(3); s 3(7), (8)).

In giving the above information, the appropriate person must be given a clear explanation of the powers that are being exercised, the purpose of the search in terms of the article(s) for which there is a power to search, and the grounds for the reasonable suspicion that has given rise to the stop and search (Code A 3.8).

Section 2(2)(b) makes it clear that the officer 'shall not' commence a search (other than that of an unattended vehicle) before such information has been given. Failure to comply with the requirements of s 2(2) and (3) may lead to evidence obtained as a result of the search being excluded: see *R v Bristol* [2007] EWCA Crim 3214 (searching officer, who was known to the person stopped, failed to identify himself or his station. The Court of Appeal held that however technical the error, a failure to comply with the requirements of s 2(3) rendered a subsequent search unlawful.) Applied in *Michaels v Highbury Corner Magistrates Court* [2009] EWHC 2928 (Admin).

If it appears that the appropriate person may not understand what is being said, for example, because of a language barrier or through disability, the officer must take reasonable steps to bring to his attention information about his rights and the powers to be exercised (Code A 3.11). This may include seeking the help of a person able to act as an interpreter.

The 'appropriate person' referred to above is the person to be searched, or in the case of a search of a vehicle, the person in charge of that vehicle (s 2(5)). Only an officer in uniform may stop a vehicle (Code A 3.9).

### 1.3.3 Does an officer have any duties in respect of a search of an unattended vehicle?

Where the search is of an unattended vehicle, the officer must leave a notice:

- stating that he has searched it;
- giving the name of the police station to which he is attached;
- stating that any application for compensation for any damage caused may be made to that police station;
- detailing his entitlement to a copy of the search record (if any was made) (s 2(6)).

The notice should be left inside the vehicle unless it is not reasonably practical to do so without damaging the vehicle (s 2(7)).

### 1.3.4 For how long may a person or vehicle be detained for the purposes of a search?

A person or vehicle may only be detained for the minimum amount of time reasonably necessary for the search to be carried out (s 2(8)). What is reasonable will depend on the circumstances pertaining to that particular stop and search and the extent and degree of thoroughness required. For example, where a person has been seen trying to conceal an item in a coat pocket, then in the absence of any reasonable grounds for suspicion that there are other items concealed elsewhere, the search should be confined to that pocket (Code A 3.3).

### 1.3.5 Where should the search be conducted?

The search must be carried out at or near the place where the person or vehicle was first detained (Code A 3.4). Code A 3.1 states that any search must be carried out 'with courtesy, consideration and respect' with every reasonable effort made to minimize embarrassment for the person being searched. Depending upon the nature and degree of the search, this may necessitate moving to a different area from that in which the person was originally detained—for example, somewhere quieter or more private. Such a place, whether a police station or otherwise, must be located nearby and within a reasonable traveling distance (whether by car or on foot) (Note 6).

### 1.3.6 Can the officer require the removal of clothing to facilitate the search?

Under s 2(9) an officer exercising powers under ss 1 and 2 only has power to conduct a superficial search requiring the removal of an outer coat, jacket, or gloves in public, although a person may be asked to voluntarily remove other items of clothing. Where a more thorough search extending beyond that of the outer clothing is required, that search must be conducted out of public view (Note 6). 'Public view' means both actual and potential public view; therefore a street, albeit deserted, would nevertheless be classed as a place within the public view. A search involving the removal of more than the outer clothing can only be conducted by an officer of the same sex as the person being searched and may not take place in the presence of anyone of the opposite sex unless the person specifically requests it (Code A 3.6).

Searches involving the exposure of intimate parts of the body may only be carried out at a nearby police station or other place out of public view, but not in a police van (Code A 3.7). It should be noted, however, that an intimate search (that is a search of the body orifices other than the mouth) cannot be carried out under the stop and search provisions, and that any search involving the removal of more than outer clothing (including shoes and socks) is regarded as a strip search and must therefore be carried out in accordance with the provisions of paragraph 11 of Annex A to Code C.

## 1.4 Search Records (Section 3)

### 1.4.1 When must a record of a search be made?

Under s 3(1) and (2), an officer who has carried out a search, whether of a person or a vehicle, must make a written record of that search unless not practicable to do so, either at the time of the search, or as soon as practicable thereafter. The emphasis is, however, firmly on contemporaneity; Code A 4.1 makes it clear that the record must be completed at the time of the search 'unless there are exceptional circumstances that would make this wholly impracticable'; examples provided by the Code are where there is a public disorder at the time, or the officer's presence is urgently needed elsewhere; another commonly encountered example might include the detainee's conduct at the scene, such as the use of violence.

The Crime and Security Act 2010 will bring in amendments to s 3(1) and (2), notably, that where an arrest follows the stop and search, then the record must be made as part of the custody record. In any other case however, the requirement for contemporaneity remains; the new s 3(2)(b) states that, save where it is not practicable to do so, the record must be made, 'on the spot'.

### 1.4.2 What must the search record contain?

The information required to be included within the search record is set out at s 3(3)–(6) and Code A 4.3, however certain subsections are due to be repealed when the amendments to this part of the Act brought about by the Crime and

Security Act 2010 come into force. At present, s 3(3)–(6) state that the record of search shall include:

- the name of the person searched if he is willing to provide it—s 3(3);
- where the name of the person being searched is not known, a description of the person or description of the vehicle (including registration number) being searched as appropriate—s 3(4) and (5);
- the object of the search—s 3(6)(a)(i);
- the grounds for making it—s 3(6)(a)(ii);
- the date and time when it was made—s 3(6)(a)(iii);
- the place where it was made—s 3(6)(a)(iv);
- whether anything, and if so what, was found—s 3(6)(a)(v);
- whether any, and what, injury to a person or damage to property resulted from the search—s 3(b)(a)(vi).

Code A 4.3 repeats some of these requirements and supplements them; so whereas s 3(6)(a)(iii) requires a record to be made of the date and time when the record itself was made, Code A 4.3(iv) states that the record must include details of the date, time and place where the person or vehicle was first detained, and in Code A 4.3(v), the date, time and place that the person or vehicle was searched; and although the requirement to record the outcome in terms of what if anything was found is set out in the Act (s 3(6)(a)(v)), the requirement to record the action taken as a result of the search—for example, arrest—is found in the Codes in para 4.3(viii) Code A.

Section 3(3) to (5) and s 3(6)(a)(v) and (vi) are however due to be repealed when the Crime and Security Act 2010 comes into force—perhaps surprisingly, given the obvious importance of the basic facts which those subsections cover: the name or description of the person or vehicle searched, the outcome of the search and a record of any injury or damage caused. There are proposals to incorporate similar amendments to Code A in line with these changes.

Conversely, the requirement set out in Code A 4.3(ii) and Note 18 to record details of the person's ethnicity will now be incorporated into the Act itself in a new s 3(6)(a)(v) and a new s 3(6A), the purpose being, as explained in Note 18 to Code A, 'to obtain a true picture of stop and search activity, help improve ethnic monitoring, tackle discriminatory practice, and promote effective use of the powers' (Code A 4.3(ii); Note 18).

Where a person is detained for the purposes of a search but where in the event no search is in fact carried out a record must still be made in the same terms as above (Code A 4.7).

Where the search is of an unattended vehicle (or anything in or on it), an officer must leave a notice recording that it has been searched and including the name of the police station to which the searching officer is attached, and explaining where a copy of the search record may be obtained and any application for compensation directed. Where practicable, the vehicle must be left secure (Code A 4.8–4.10).

### 1.4.3 **When must a record be provided?**

Where a record has been made at the time, a copy of that record must be given to the person who has been searched immediately (Code A 4.2). These days, many areas utilize hand-held electronic recording devices. If the officer has recorded the stop and search electronically and is able to print off a copy of the record at the time, he should do so (Code A 4.10A).

An electronically produced receipt may be given to the person searched rather than the full record, provided that it states how the full record can be accessed (Code A 4.2A). The same information must be given orally to the person concerned who has the right to request a full copy of the record in either electronic or hard copy format within 12 months (due to be amended downwards to three months) from the date of search (s 3(9)).

Where it is not practicable in the circumstances to provide the person searched with either a full written or electronically produced record, Code A provides two further alternatives. Code A 4.10B states that a receipt should be provided containing:

- a reference number;
- guidance on how to obtain a full copy of the record;
- the name of the searching officer; and
- the power used to carry out the stop and search.

Note 21 to Code A, however, states that where it is not practicable to provide either a written or electronic record or a receipt, the person should simply be given written details of the station from which he can obtain the record, endorsed with the date of the stop and search.

When the search is of an unattended vehicle (or anything in or on it), an officer must leave a notice recording that it has been searched, including the name of the police station to which the searching officer is attached, and explaining where a copy of the search record may be obtained and any application for compensation directed. Where practicable, the vehicle must be left secure (Code A 4.4–4.10).

## 1.5 **Stop and Account**

Although the only power (short of arrest) to detain a person is provided where the requirements for a stop and search are fulfilled, as noted above there may be other circumstances where the police and/or police community support officers (PCSOS) do have occasion to stop a person and ask them to account for their presence in a particular place, their behaviour, or the objects in their possession.

### 1.5.1 **What record must be made of a Stop and Account?**

Unless exceptional circumstances exist rendering it wholly impracticable to do so, a record must be completed at the time. Prior to the latest revision of

Code A, which came into force on 1 January 2009, the record had to include the same details as those required in a stop and search record. Those requirements resulted in an enormous increase in arguably unnecessary paperwork as a result of which the Government accepted the recommendation that the recording requirements should be eased where a stop and account had taken place as opposed to a stop and search. From 1 January 2009, therefore, the only details that the record must include are:

- the identity of the officer who made the stop and recorded the encounter (Code A 4.12);
- the person's self-defined ethnic background, or, where that is refused, a description of the person's ethnic background (Code A 4.12A, 4.17, 4.18).

Note 24 to Code A additionally suggests that the officer 'may consider' recording the date, time and location of the encounter where the record is not made electronically.

In a speech made to the Association of Chief Police Officers on 29 June 2010, the Home Secretary (Theresa May) pledged to scrap the stop and account form in its entirety; whether this means that there will in due course be no requirement at all to make a record where such an encounter takes place, or whether the use of electronic recording will replace 'form filling' remains to be seen.

There is no requirement for a record or separate record to be made where the encounter comprises:

- a general conversation with a member of the public;
- questioning to establish the background to incidents in which officers have intervened to keep the peace or resolve a dispute (Code A 4.13);
- stopping a vehicle when an HORT/1, a vehicle defect rectification scheme notice, or a fixed penalty notice have been issued, or when a breath specimen has been required under the Road Traffic Act (Code A.14);
- stopping a person who has been issued with a penalty notice for an offence (Code A.14).

There is no requirement to provide a copy of the record to the person stopped, but the person must be informed of their entitlement to a receipt (Code A 4.12, 4.15, 4.19)

## 1.6 Road Checks (Section 4)

### 1.6.1 What is the purpose of a road check?

For the period of a road check, all vehicles or classes of vehicles selected by any criteria may be stopped in the locality in which the road check is being conducted, in order to ascertain whether the vehicle is carrying:

- a person who has committed an offence (other than a road traffic or vehicle excise offence), where the authorizing officer has reasonable grounds

to believe that the offence is an indictable offence, and that the person is, or is about to be, in the locality of the proposed road check (s 4(1)(a), s 4(4)(a));
- a person who is witness to such an offence (s 4(1)(b), s 4(4)(b));
- a person who is intending to commit such an offence where the authorizing officer has reasonable grounds for suspecting that that person is in or about to be in the locality of the proposed road check (s 4(1)(c), s 4(4)(c));
- a person who is unlawfully at large where the authorizing officer has reasonable grounds for suspecting that that person is, or is about to be, in the locality of the road check (s 4(1)(d), s 4(4)(d)).

### 1.6.2 Who can authorize a road check?

Subject to one exception, a road check can only be carried out if it is authorized in writing by an officer of the rank of superintendent or above. The exception is where a road check is required as a matter of urgency for one of the reasons set out above (s 4(5)). Then, an officer below the rank of superintendent may authorize a road check provided that, as soon as it is practicable to do so, he makes a written record of the time at which he has given the authorization and causes an officer of the rank of superintendent or above to be informed that it has been given (s 4(6), (7)). The officer so informed may either:

- authorize the road check to continue in writing, or if he does not so authorize it,
- record in writing the fact that the road check took place and the purpose for which it took place (s 4(8), (9)).

### 1.6.3 What must the authorization contain?

The authorization must detail:

- the name of the officer giving the authorization (s 4(13)(a));
- the purpose of the road check, including specifying the relevant indictable offence (s 4(13)(b), s 4(14));
- the locality in which vehicles are to be stopped—(s 4(10), s 4(13)(c)).

Where the authorization is given by an officer of the rank of superintendent or above, the authorization shall in addition:

- specify the duration of the road check (not to exceed 7 days) (s 4(11)(a));
- direct whether the road check is to be continuous or to be conducted at specified times (s 4(11)(b)).

### 1.6.4 Can the period of authorization be extended or renewed?

Where it appears to an officer of the rank of superintendent or above that the period of the road check ought to extend beyond that originally authorized, he may in writing specify further periods not exceeding seven days during which it may continue (s 4(12)).

### 1.6.5 What are the safeguards?

The person in charge of a vehicle at the time it was stopped is entitled to obtain a written statement of the purposes of the road check on request where that request is made within 12 months of the day upon which the vehicle was stopped (s 4(15)).

# 1.7 Additional Powers of Stop and Search

Stop and search powers can be found in numerous other pieces of legislation, however specific provisions can be found in Code A relating to the powers provided for by:

* the Criminal Justice and Public Order Act 1994, ss 60 and 60AA; and
* the Terrorism Act 2000, s 44.

Code A 2.27 also extends the provisions of Code A to searches conducted in school premises under s 139B of the Criminal Justice Act 1998 for bladed or pointed articles or offensive weapons, and to searches of persons found on premises being searched under a warrant issued under the Misuse of Drugs Act 1971 where the warrant so provides.

Section 6(1) provides constables employed by statutory undertakers with powers to stop and search.

### 1.7.1 Powers attaching to statutory undertakers

By s 6(1) a constable employed by statutory undertakers (persons authorized by any enactment to carry on any railway, light railway, road transport, water transport, canal, inland navigation, dock, or harbour undertakings) is empowered to stop, detain, and search any vehicle before it leaves a goods area (area used wholly or mainly for the storage or handling of goods) included in the premises of the statutory undertakers. By definition, the power can be exercised in places to which the public do not normally have access and no grounds for reasonable suspicion are required. This extension of powers applies only to vehicles and not to persons.

### 1.7.2 Powers under section 60 of the Criminal Justice and Public Order Act 1994

An officer of the rank of inspector or above may give written authorization for a constable in uniform to stop and search where the authorizing officer reasonably believes:

- that incidents involving serious violence may take place in any locality in the officer's police area, and it is expedient to use these powers to prevent their occurrence; or
- that persons are carrying dangerous instruments or offensive weapons without good reason in any locality in the officer's police area (Code A 2.12).

Where the authorization has been given by an inspector, he must inform an officer of or above the rank of superintendent as soon as practicable (Code A 2.14).

These powers, which are separate from and additional to the normal powers that exist under the stop and search provisions, exist to prevent serious violence or the carrying of weapons which might lead to serious injury. They are not intended to be used to deal with routine crime problems. The authorizing officer must have a reasonable objective belief which will generally be based on intelligence.

The authorization must specify the grounds upon which it was given, the locality in which the powers may be exercised, and the period of time for which they are in force. That period shall be no longer than appears reasonably necessary to prevent or deal with the risk of violence or carrying of weapons, and shall in any event not exceed 24 hours (Code A 2.13). An officer of the rank of superintendent or above may, in writing, extend the period of authorization by a further 24 hours but may do so only once. Further periods will require a separate authorization (Code A, Note for guidance 12).

The locality specified in the authorization must similarly be restricted to an area no wider than that believed necessary for the proper exercise of the powers. If the area straddles different police force areas, an authorization must be obtained from an officer in each one (Code A, Note for guidance 13).

Code A applies to searches under this power.

### 1.7.3 Powers under section 60AA of the Criminal Justice and Public Order Act 1994

An officer of the rank of inspector or above may in writing authorize the removal and seizure of face coverings worn or intended to be worn wholly or mainly to conceal someone's identity, where the authorizing officer has reasonable grounds to believe that activities may occur in the officer's police area that are likely to involve the commission of offences, and it is expedient to use these powers to prevent or control such activities. The authorization must specify the grounds upon which it has been made, the locality in which the powers may be exercised, and the period of time for which they are in force. The period specified must be for no longer than reasonably necessary to prevent the commission of offences and may in any event not exceed 24 hours. An officer of the rank of superintendent or above may in writing extend the period by a further 24 hours.

There is no power to stop and search for disguises, although if an authorization under this section or s 60 is in force, and an item is found when exercising a search for something else (eg a weapon), the officer may seize it if he reasonably believes it is intended to be used to conceal someone's identity.

Code A, Note for guidance 4 sounds a note of caution to be applied where the head or face covering may be worn for religious reasons. Such an item should be removed out of public view and, where practicable, out of the sight of anyone of the opposite sex. Even so, an officer cannot order the removal of the item unless there is reason to believe that the item is being worn wholly or in part in order to disguise identity and not merely because it in fact does so.

Code A applies to searches under this power. See especially Code A 2.15–2.18.

### 1.7.4 Searches under s 44 of the Terrorism Act 2000

Section 44 TACT provides that where expedient for the prevention of terrorism, an officer of the rank of assistant chief constable or above may give authority providing powers for a constable or Community Support Officer in uniform to:

- stop and search any vehicle, its driver, any passenger, and anything in or on the vehicle or carried by the driver or any passenger; and/or
- stop and search any pedestrian and anything carried by the pedestrian (Code A 19)

for the purpose of searching for articles that could be used in connection with terrorism.

The primary distinction between Stop and Search powers exercised under s 44 TACT, and those carried out under s 1 PACE, is that there is no requirement, for reasonable grounds for suspicion (whether about the individual stopped or articles that he might be carrying) prior to the search. Consequently, s 44 presents what has been described as 'an extremely wide power to intrude on the privacy of members of the public' and amounts to an interference with the person's Art 8 rights of privacy.

The lawfulness of s 44 was considered by the European Court of Human Rights in *Gillan and Quinton v United Kingdom* [2010] ECHR 28. Gillan and Quinton, who were a photographer and journalist, had been searched under s 44 TACT when attending an arms fair. The European Court found that the use of s 44 was a clear interference with a person's Art 8 rights, and that the safeguards contained within Code A of PACE did not provide adequate protection against that interference being applied in an arbitrary manner as they only governed the *manner* in which the search was carried out and did not restrict the officer's decision to stop and search. The broad discretion afforded to an officer who required neither objective nor subjective grounds for suspicion before carrying out a stop and search led to a clear risk of arbitrariness. Accordingly, they found that the powers of authorization, and confirmation as well as those of stop and search under s 44 TACT were neither sufficiently circumscribed nor subject to adequate legal safeguards against abuse, were not in accordance with the law and violated Art 8.

This decision has prompted the coalition government elected in May 2010, to include the use of s 44 stop and search powers in a 'rapid review' of counter-terrorism powers. Pending that review, interim guidance was announced by the Home Secretary on 8 July 2010 as follows: 'The test for authorization for the use of section 44 powers is, therefore, being changed from requiring a search to be "expedient" for the prevention of terrorism, to the stricter test of its being "necessary" for that purpose; and, most importantly, I am introducing a new suspicion threshold. Officers will no longer be able to search individuals using section 44 powers; instead, they will have to rely on section 43 powers, which require officers to reasonably suspect the person to be a terrorist. And officers will only be able to use section 44 in relation to searches of vehicles. I will only confirm these authorizations where they are considered to be necessary, and officers will only be able to use them when they have "reasonable suspicion".'

Proposals to amend Code A to take account of this guidance are currently being considered.

### 1.7.5 **Powers to search in the exercise of a power to search premises**

A person not under arrest may be searched in the course of:

- a search of school premises under s 139B of the Criminal Justice Act 1988 for any bladed or pointed articles or offensive weapons (Code A 2.27(a)); or
- a search authorized by a warrant issued under s 23(3) of the Misuse of Drugs Act 1971 to search premises and persons found on those premises for drugs or documents (Code A 2.27(b)).

There is no requirement in either case for specific grounds to suspect that the person to be searched is in possession of an item for which there is an existing power to search (Code A 2.29). In all other respects, Code A applies.

# **Practical Guidance**

## 1.8 **Case Study 1 (Section 1)**

PC Brown is on foot patrol at 3am in a suburban street. He sees a youth carrying what appears to be an electrical item that is partially hidden under the youth's jacket. PC Brown calls after the youth who ignores him and quickens his step. PC Brown follows, but before he can reach him the youth turns into the garden of a private house and runs to the front door and goes inside. PC Brown knocks on the door which is answered by a middle-aged female. PC Brown explains what he has seen and asks to speak to the youth who he can see immediately behind the woman. The woman tells PC Brown that the youth is her son who has not done anything wrong and asks the officer to leave her premises. PC Brown then pushes past the woman, takes hold of the youth, and escorts him back to the street where he carries out a search under s 1 of PACE.

*Did PC Brown have the power to carry out a search under section 1 of PACE when he first saw the youth in the street?*

When PC Brown first saw the youth, he was in a place to which the public had access, and an objective assessment of the circumstances would give rise to a reasonable suspicion that the youth was carrying a stolen article because:

- he is seen during the early hours of the morning;
- he is carrying what appears to be an electrical item under his jacket;
- he ignores the officer;
- he quickens his step.

A search under section 1 of PACE at this point would have been justified.

*Had PC Brown stopped the youth in the driveway before he reached the house, would there be a power to search under section 1 of PACE?*

Although at this point the youth is not in a place where the public have access as of right, he is in a place where there is ready access. The power to search in this situation depends upon PC Brown having reasonable grounds to believe the person does not reside in the house and is not there with the express or implied permission of the occupier. Clearly, as the youth does reside there and would be able to show this to be so, it is unlikely that any such reasonable grounds would exist. Therefore, once the youth reached the sanctuary of his front garden he was no longer susceptible to a search under s 1. Had this been a case where the youth had simply walked into the garden of a stranger's house then the ready access part of s 1 would have been relevant and would have enabled PC Brown lawfully to carry out a search.

*Did PC Brown have the right to enter the house under section 1 of PACE?*

The provision is quite clear: the s 1 power can only be exercised in a place to which the public have access and other places where the public has ready access which is not a dwelling. Section 1 gives no power of entry in these circumstances.

*Once PC Brown returned to the street with the youth, did he have the power to search under section 1 of PACE?*

The youth was now in a place to which the public had access and, providing PC Brown had reasonable grounds to suspect he was still carrying a stolen article, technically, the power to search would exist. However, the route taken by the officer in unlawfully entering the premises and taking the youth back to the street would almost certainly result in any evidence obtained being excluded by the court. In addition, the flagrant breach of the requirements of the Act could well result in PC Brown facing misconduct proceedings.

## 1.9 **Case Study 2 (Section 1)**

PC Brown is on patrol in a busy high street when he receives information over his personal radio that a female is attempting to use a stolen credit card. He is given a full description of the suspect. PC Brown begins to make his way to the store and is then further informed that the female had become suspicious and has now left with the credit card. As PC Brown approaches the location he sees a female who exactly matches the description of the suspect walk out of the store in question.

*May PC Brown search the female suspect under section 1 of PACE?*

In this scenario, the officer has a full description of the suspect and the female seen leaving the store exactly matches that description. The offence occurred only a few minutes before and it is known that the suspect retained possession of the credit card. An objective assessment can only lead to the conclusion that there are reasonable grounds to suspect that the female may be carrying a stolen credit card. The female suspect is in a public place and PC Brown would therefore be able to exercise the power under s 1.

*Who should carry out the search?*

In this case the suspected stolen article could easily be concealed and a more thorough search would be justified. As such a search would invariably involve the removal of more than outer jacket, coat, gloves, and footwear, the search should be carried out by an officer of the same sex as the suspect. Whilst not required for less intrusive searches, it is good practice whenever possible to use an officer of the same sex to carry out the search.

*Where should any search be carried out?*

The search must be carried out where the suspect was first detained or nearby. There is no definition of 'nearby', but moving a person a few yards to a more private place or perhaps to a police van would not be unreasonable. As this case will involve the removal of more than the outer clothing, the search must be carried out away from public view. In this case, arranging for a police van to attend the scene would be appropriate and ensure privacy for the person being searched.

*How should the search be conducted?*

The nature of the circumstances and the item sought will determine the extent to which the search should be carried out. For example, if PC Brown was looking for a large item such as a car radio, the search would be restricted to that which is necessary to reasonably find such an article. In this case, a credit card can be easily concealed and a much more thorough search would be justified.

## 1.10 **Case Study 3 (Section 1)**

Derek snatches the handbag of an elderly victim and runs off down the High Street. An accurate description of Derek and the property stolen is quickly circulated and John, a recently recruited PCSO who is nearby, receives the information on his personal radio. Moments later, John sees Derek running towards him and notices that he fits the description of the suspect of a recent theft. John stops Derek and requires him to submit to a search; under his jacket he finds a lady's purse containing cash and credit cards. John then asks Derek for his name and address and is informed by Derek that he lives rough, and has no permanent home. Although Derek is compliant and makes no effort to leave, John informs him that he is being arrested for theft and requests transport to take him and his prisoner to the police station. John is informed by radio that an officer will be with him shortly and a few moments later PC Cobo arrives at the scene. PC Cobo is unsure of the powers held by PCSOs and decides to simply take John and Derek to the station where he explains the circumstances to the custody officer, PS Jones. PS Jones is also unsure of the powers of PCSOs and seeks advice from Inspector Orton.

### Was John entitled to carry out a stop and search?

Inspector Orton should advise PS Jones that PCSOs have limited powers and that these do not extend to the power to search under s 1 PACE; this power is limited to constables. Had John been a constable then the circumstances were such that a search under s 1 could be justified. As a PCSO, however, John had no power to require Derek to submit to a search.

Because John had reasonable grounds to believe that Derek had committed a relevant offence (loss of property), he had good reason to carry out a 'stop and account' and was entitled to ask Derek to provide his name and address.

### Was John entitled to arrest Derek?

As John had grounds to suspect that Derek had committed a relevant offence, and as Derek had failed to comply with the requirement to provide details of his name and address, John could have required Derek to remain with him for a period of up to 30 minutes pending the arrival of a police officer and could have used reasonable force to detain Derek for this purpose if necessary. John had no power however to arrest Derek. Neither is it likely that John would be able to rely on the 'citizen's power' of arrest provided for by s 24A PACE; whilst theft is an indictable offence and therefore the first condition of s 24A is met, John would also have to show that it appeared to him that it was not reasonably practicable for a constable to make the arrest instead. In view of the compliant nature of Derek and the imminent arrival of PC Cobo it is unlikely that this pre-condition could be made out. The arrest of Derek by John was therefore unlawful.

### What action should PC Cobo have carried out?

When PC Cobo arrived, John should have outlined the facts to him. PC Cobo would then have the responsibility of deciding on any further action. One option would be to carry out a s 1 search. PC Cobo must decide for himself whether there are reasonable grounds to justify a search, but it is likely in this case that the information provided by John together with the original information provided over the radio about the suspect would afford reasonable grounds for suspicion. PC Cobo could then have carried out the search and arrested Derek on suspicion of theft.

### What are likely to be the effects of an unlawful search and arrest?

Inspector Orton should advise PS Jones that PC Cobo should arrest Derek for theft and caution him without delay. The full circumstances should be recorded in the custody record. The purse seized by John in what was in fact an unlawful search is still evidence and could be used as such although the circumstances in which it was found may give rise to an application to exclude the admission of that evidence under s 78 PACE.

The period of detention between the 'arrest' by John and the arrest by PC Cobo is likely to be held to be unlawful; however it is likely that this would give rise to a potential civil action, rather than have any material effect upon any criminal trial.

# Powers of Entry, Search, and Seizure: Part II

**Law and Commentary**

# Law and Commentary

## 2.1 Introduction

Part II of the Act has the title 'Powers of Entry, Search, and Seizure'. The powers and duties covered by the Part are:

**(i) Search warrants and access to material (ss 8–16).**

The Act gives power to issue search warrants both to magistrates (s 8) and to judges (the 'special procedure' under s 9 and Sch 1), reserving to the latter the more complex and sensitive applications. It separates the two by creating special categories of material (ss 11–14) which are used to describe the type of items which can only be obtained by an application to a judge. Under the special procedure, an alternative to a search warrant is provided by Sch 1, para 4 which provides a procedure for compelling a person, by notice, to provide access to material. Legally privileged material (s 10) cannot be obtained by any application. Section 15 provides safeguards, common to both s 8 applications and Sch 1, para 12 applications, as to the form of the application and the form of the warrant. Section 16 sets out the requirements and procedure, common to both s 8 applications and Sch 1, para 12 applications, for the execution of warrants. Extensive guidance is contained in Code B.

**(ii) Entry for particular purposes, including arrest; and entry and search after arrest (s 18).**

**(iii) General provisions relating to seizure, retention, and rights and duties with respect to seized things (ss 19–22).**

## 2.2 The Two New Types of Warrants: 'Specific Premises Warrants' and 'All Premises Warrants'

The Serious Organised Crime and Police Act 2005 introduces a significant modification to the requirement that the premises should be specified (new s 8(1A), s 8(1B); amendment of s 8(1)(b)). The s 9, Sch 1 procedure is similarly modified: see below. There are now two different types of warrant:

**(i) a 'specific premises warrant'.**

This permits the search of specified premises, including multiple premises.

**(ii) an 'all premises warrant'.**

This permits the search of all the premises under the control of a specified person, including, where it is not reasonably practicable to specify all of them, unspecified premises. The effect is that those premises which can be specified, should be.

Under both types of warrants, authorization may be given for multiple entries, either limited in number or unlimited (ss 8(1C) and 8(1D)).

## 2.3 Power of Magistrates to Issue Warrants to Enter and Search Premises (Section 8)

### 2.3.1 Who may hear the application and issue a warrant under section 8?

Section 8 confers the power to issue search warrants on 'a justice of the peace'. This includes both 'lay' magistrates (non-professional civilian appointees) and 'District Judges (Magistrates' Courts)' (formerly known as 'stipendiary magistrates', legally qualified professional appointees) (Courts Act 2003, Part 2).

### 2.3.2 Who may apply for a warrant under section 8 and to whom may it be issued?

The application must be made by a constable (s 8(1)) or by a civilian designated as an 'investigating officer' under s 38 of the Police Reform Act 2002 (Sch 4, Pt 2, para 16(a)) and the warrant may be issued to both (s 8(1); Police Reform Act 2002, Sch 4, Pt 2, para 16(b)).

### 2.3.3 What are the preconditions to the granting of an application under section 8?

Before granting the application, the magistrate must have reasonable grounds for believing that all of the five preconditions set out in s 8(1) are satisfied:

(i) **An indictable offence has been committed.** The Serious Organised Crime and Police Act 2005 replaced the phrase 'serious arrestable offence' with the phrase 'indictable offence' which represents a loosening of this requirement: an extension from the most serious offences to a wider class of more serious offences. An indictable offence is defined in the Interpretation Act 1978, Sch 1: it includes both 'indictable only' and 'triable either way' offences, ie both offences which are only triable in the Crown Court and offences which are triable in both the Magistrates' Court and in the Crown Court.

(ii) **There is material on the premises mentioned which is likely to be of substantial value (either by itself or together with other material) to the investigation of the offence.**

(iii) **The material is likely to be relevant evidence.** 'Relevant evidence' is anything which would be admissible at a trial for the offence (s 8(4)).

(iv) **The material does not consist of or include 'items subject to legal privilege', 'excluded material' or 'special procedure material'.** These terms are defined in ss 10–14 (see below). The words *'prima facie'* should be read into s 8(1)(e) so that a magistrate faced with a case where he cannot be satisfied that there are reasonable grounds for believing that the material sought does not include any items which are, *prima facie*, subject to legal privilege, or any material which is, *prima facie*, special procedure material, should refuse the application under s 8 and leave the applicant to proceed under s 9: *R v Guildhall Magistrates' Court, ex p Primlaks Holdings Co (Panama) Inc* 89 Cr App R 215, DC at 224.

**(v) It is not practicable to communicate with a person entitled to grant entry and access to the material; or such access would not be granted without a warrant; or the purpose of the search may be frustrated or seriously prejudiced unless immediate access is secured (s 8(1)(e) and s 8(3)).**

What is contemplated by the last of these is the situation where there are reasonable grounds for believing that evidence would be destroyed should the occupier be asked to grant entry.

### 2.3.4 What is the procedure for making an application under section 8?

The application is made *ex parte* and supported by an information in writing s 15(3). Section 15 provides safeguards, common to both s 8 applications and Sch 1, para 12 applications, as to the form of the application and the form of the warrant (see below).

In addition, see the discussion below in relation to the s 9 and Sch 1 procedure, which provides persuasive guidance as to the principles of openness and proactive full disclosure applicable to applications of this type.

### 2.3.5 Who may seize and retain things under section 8?

Things may be seized and retained by a constable (s 8(2)) or a civilian designated as an 'investigating officer' under s 38 of the Police Reform Act 2002 (Sch 4, Pt 2, para 16(c)).

### 2.3.6 What may be seized and retained under section 8?

Anything for which the search is authorized under the warrant may be seized and retained (s 8(2)). There is an extension of the power to require electronic data to be produced in a form in which it is or may readily become intelligible (see s 20 below). Rights to access and copies of things seized are provided (see s 21 below). The length of time that seized things may be retained is set out in s 22 (see below).

### 2.3.7 Execution of warrant under section 8 and conduct of search

Section 16 provides safeguards, common to both s 8 applications and Sch 1, para 12 applications, as to the execution of a warrant and the conduct of the search (see below).

## 2.4 Items Subject to Legal Privilege (Section 10), Excluded Material (Section 11), and Special Procedure Material (Section 14)

### 2.4.1 The significance of the categories under sections 10, 11, and 14

These categories are referred to throughout this Part of the Act. Their significance is:

- any item which falls within these categories cannot be the subject of a search warrant issued by a magistrate under s 8 (see s 8(1)(d));
- 'excluded material' (s 11) and certain types of 'special procedure material' (s 14) can, however, be the subject of a warrant issued by a judge under s 9 and Sch 1;
- 'items subject to legal privilege' (s 10) cannot be the subject of a warrant by either a magistrate or a judge; nor can they be the object of entry and search after arrest (s 18(1)); nor can they be seized by a constable exercising his general power of seizure under s 19 or under any statutory power of seizure (s 19(6)); nor can they be the subject of an order under the Terrorism Act 2000, Sch 5, Pt I.

However, this basic position is now subject to an important qualification introduced by the Criminal Justice and Police Act 2001, Pt 2. Items which an officer has no power to seize, including items subject to legal privilege, excluded material, and special procedure material, may now be removed in accordance with the 'seize and sift powers' contained in that Part (see below).

### 2.4.2 Items subject to legal privilege (section 10)

Subject to the exceptions set out below, 'items subject to legal privilege' are:

(i) (by s 10(1)(a) and (c)) communications (or items enclosed with or referred to in such communications) *made in connection with the giving of legal advice to a client* between:

- a lawyer and client; or
- a lawyer and a person representing the client; and

(ii) (by s 10(1)(b) and (c)) communications (or items enclosed with or referred to in such communications) *made in connection with or in contemplation of legal proceedings and for the purpose of such proceedings* between:

- a lawyer and client; or
- a lawyer and a person representing the client; and
- a lawyer and any other person; and
- the client and any other person (which, as a matter of principle, would include a person representing the client, although this is not stated); and
- the person representing the client and any other person.

The communications covered are represented in the diagrams below

**(i) Communications made in connection with the giving of legal advice to a client, protected by legal privilege**

**(ii) Communications made in connection with or in contemplation of legal proceedings and for the purpose of such proceedings, protected by legal privilege**

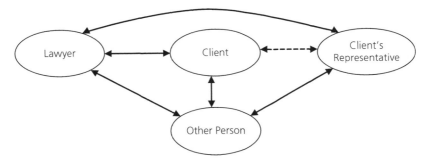

The exceptions are:

(i)  items enclosed with or referred to in such communications where they are not in the possession of a person who is entitled to possession of them (s 10(1)(c)); and

(ii)  items held with the intention of furthering a criminal purpose (s 10(2)).

The phrase 'held with the intention of furthering a criminal purpose' contained in s 10(2) should be given a purposive rather than a literal construction so as to include not just the intentions of the person holding the item but also the intentions of any other person (regardless of whether the holder was aware of such intention): *R v Central Criminal Court, ex p Francis and Francis (a Firm)* [1989] AC 346. In that case, documents held innocently by a solicitor on behalf of an innocent client did not attract privilege because of the intentions of a third party to which the documents related.

The types of items not covered by legal privilege include:

• documents sent by a client to a lawyer, for the purpose of obtaining advice, if they were pre-existing documents which do not themselves fall within the definition of privileged material: *R v Guildhall Magistrates' Court, ex p Primlaks Holdings Co (Panama) Inc* 89 Cr App R 215, DC at 225. (The enclosures do not fall within s 10(1)(c). They would, however, be, *prima facie*, 'special procedure material'. Technically, the covering letter would be privileged as falling within s 10(1)(a).);

- documents created by a lawyer which are formal instruments or administrative records such as conveyancing and financing documents (*R v Inner London Crown Court, ex p Baines and Baines (a Firm)* (1988) 87 Cr App R 111, CA) or a solicitor's attendance note or other record of time devoted to a case (*R v Manchester Crown Court, ex p Rogers* [1999] 2 Cr App R 267, DC);
- forgeries made to support a civil claim since the phrase 'made in connection with or in contemplation of legal proceedings' in s 10(1)(b) should be read as meaning 'lawfully made': *R v Leeds Magistrates' Court, ex p Dumbleton* [1993] Crim LR 866, DC.

### 2.4.3 Excluded material (section 11)

'Excluded material' is material held by a 'person' (ie either an individual or an organization: Sch 1, Interpretation Act 1978) in confidence owed to a third party.

It takes three forms and the nature of the confidence required differs as between the first two, on the one hand, and the last, on the other.

**(i) personal records.**

Essentially, they are the most private records. They consist of records which:

(a) are acquired or created by a person in the course of any trade, business, profession, or other occupation, or for the purposes of any paid or unpaid office (s 11(1)(a)); and

(b) are held by that person in confidence in the sense that they are held either (1) subject to an express or implied undertaking to hold them in confidence or (2) subject to a statutory obligation imposing a restriction on disclosure or an obligation of secrecy (s 11(1)(a) and s 11(2)); and

(c) concern identifiable individuals (living or dead); and are either: (1) records relating to an individual's physical or mental health, or spiritual counselling or assistance (whether given or to be given); or (2) records relating to counselling or assistance for the purposes of an individual's personal welfare (whether given or to be given) by a voluntary organization or individual who, by reason of his office or occupation, or an order of a court, has responsibilities for the first individual's personal welfare (s 12).

The result is that all records relating to the core private categories of an individual's physical, mental, or spiritual welfare are within the definition whereas records relating to counselling or assistance for 'personal welfare' (a wider but undefined term) will only be within the definition if the person giving the counselling or assistance has some special responsibility for such counselling or assistance. Counselling or assistance by priests and probation officers would fall within the definition whereas counselling or assistance by obliging accountants or mortgage brokers would not.

**(ii) human tissue or tissue fluid,** taken for the purposes of diagnosis or medical treatment and held in confidence in the sense that they are held either (1) subject to an express or implied undertaking to hold it in confidence, or (2) subject to a statutory obligation imposing a restriction on disclosure or an obligation of secrecy (s 11(1)(b) and s 11(2)).

**(iii) journalistic material held in confidence, consisting of documents or records other than documents.**

This is material which:

(a)  consists of documents or records other than documents (s 11(1)(c)); and
(b)  is held in confidence in the sense of being subject to an undertaking, restriction, or obligation, and it must have been continuously so held by one or more persons since first acquired or created for the purposes of journalism (s 11(1)(c) and s 11(3)); and
(c)  is 'journalistic material', ie material in the possession of a person who acquired or created it for the purposes of journalism (and a person who receives material from someone who intends that the recipient shall use it for the purposes of journalism shall be taken to have acquired it for the purposes of journalism) (s 13).

The result of (b) above is that material which initially falls within the definition of journalistic material will cease to do so if there is any time during which nobody holds it in confidence. The result of (c) above is that material will remain journalistic material only when in the possession of someone who acquires or creates it for the purposes of journalism (in effect, someone who is a journalist); but if he acquires it without that purpose (for example, if it is dropped through his letter-box) it may nonetheless be regarded as journalistic material (if the provider of the material intended that the recipient should use it for the purposes of journalism). The effect of the two is that, in order for such material to remain excluded material, there must be a continuous chain, from the creation or acquisition of the material for the purposes of journalism, of journalists holding it in confidence, although they can pass it from one to another.

### 2.4.4 **Special procedure material (section 14)**

This is a sweeping-up category of material meriting special protection but falling outside of the categories of 'items subject to legal privilege' (s 10) and 'excluded material' (s 11). It is broken up into two categories.

**(i) material created or acquired by a person in their work and held by them in confidence.**

This is material which:

(a)  is other than items subject to legal privilege and excluded material (s 14(2)); and

(b) is in the possession of a person who acquired or created it in the course of any trade, business, profession, or other occupation, or for the purpose of any paid or unpaid office (s 14(2) and s 14(2)(a)); and

(c) is held by that person subject either (1) to an express or implied undertaking to hold it in confidence, or (2) subject to a statutory obligation imposing a restriction on disclosure or an obligation of secrecy (s 14(2)(b)).

### (ii) 'journalistic material' other than 'excluded material' (s 14(1)(b)).

This is material which:

(a) is 'journalistic material', ie material in the possession of a person who acquired or created it for the purposes of journalism (and a person who receives material from someone who intends that the recipient shall use it for the purposes of journalism shall be taken to have acquired it for the purposes of journalism) (s 13); and

(b) is not 'excluded material' within s 11.

What remains for category (ii), given the scope of journalistic material falling within s 11, is either (1) journalistic material which consists of material which is not in the form of either 'documents' or 'records other than documents', and (2) journalistic material which is not held 'in confidence' (as defined in s 11(3)). The former might include items of real evidence created or acquired for the purposes of journalism.

The section extends to 'material' generally and is not confined to documents.

The remaining parts of the section, s 14(3)–(6), have the effect of preventing an employer or group of companies artificially creating a duty of confidence internally within the business or group for the purposes of the section and thereby gaining the protection of a special procedure material classification: the duty of confidence only arises with respect to a true third party individual or company. The obvious application of these subsections is to the first rather than the second (journalistic material) category of special procedure material; and the wording of s 14(1) and s 14(2) suggest that it is only the first category which is qualified by s 14(3) to s 14(6).

## 2.5 Search Warrant and Other Orders Issued by Judge under the 'Special Procedure' (Section 9 and Schedule 1)

Section 9(1) provides that a constable may, for the purposes of a criminal investigation, obtain access to 'excluded material' and 'special procedure material' (but not 'items subject to legal privilege') by making an application under and in accordance with Sch 1. The Schedule provides for two forms of access: (1) an order requiring a person to surrender or grant access to material (para 4); and (2) a warrant authorizing a constable to enter and search premises (para 12), and to seize and retain things (para 13). In contrast to applications for warrants to search for evidence outside of these categories of material, which can be made to a magistrate (s 8), Sch 1 provides that the application must be made to a judge, reflecting the added seriousness, sensitivity, and complexity of such applications.

### 2.5.1  Who may hear the special procedure application and make the order or issue the warrant?

The provisions presently state that a 'Circuit Judge' may make the order or issue the application (Sch 1, paras 1, 4, 12); and it is clear that Recorders have no jurisdiction (*R v Central Criminal Court, ex p Francis and Francis (a Firm)* [1989] AC 346, HL, at 368 and 382). Prospective amendments provided for under the Courts Act 2003, s 65, Sch 4, para 6(1), which would add a new para 17 to Sch 1 of the Act extending the jurisdiction to a High Court Judge, Circuit Judge, Recorder and District Judge, have never been brought into force.

### 2.5.2  Who may apply for a special procedure warrant or order; and with respect to whom may an order be made; and to whom may a warrant be issued?

The application must be made by a constable (s 9(1)) or by a civilian designated as an 'investigating officer' under s 38 of the Police Reform Act 2002 (Sch 4, Pt 2, para 17(a) and (b)); and the order may be made with respect to both; and the warrant may be issued to both (ibid).

### 2.5.3  Understanding the preconditions to the granting of special procedure applications: the 'access conditions' of Schedule 1

The scheme of the schedule is to employ, for the purposes of describing the preconditions to both applications, sets of requirements described as 'access conditions'.

(i) **The first set of access conditions.** This is the wider gateway but to a narrower class of material: it permits access to important evidence relating to serious offences but cannot include 'excluded material' (as defined in s 11). It requires the judge to be satisfied as to all of the following (Sch 1, para 2):

(a)  that there are reasonable grounds for believing that (1) an indictable offence has been committed; and (2) that there is material on any premises specified in the application or, in the case of an 'all premises' warrant, premises occupied or controlled by the person specified, which consists of or includes 'special procedure material' and does not also include 'excluded material'; and (3) that the material is likely to be of 'substantial value' (which is further defined) to the investigation; and (4) that the material is likely to be relevant evidence; and

(b) other methods of obtaining the material have been tried without success or have not been tried because it appeared that they were bound to fail; and

(c) it is in the public interest, having regard to the likely benefit to the investigation and the circumstances under which the person holds the material, that it should be produced or that access should be granted.

**(ii) The second set of access conditions.** This is the narrower gateway but to a wider class of material. It permits access to both 'excluded material' (as defined in s 11) and 'special procedure material' (as defined in s 14) in circumstances in which historically a search warrant could have been issued. Such historical powers cease to have effect, by virtue of s 9(2), in so far as they relate to the authorization of searches for 'items subject to legal privilege', 'excluded material', or, with respect to documents or other records, 'special procedure material'. This set requires the judge to be satisfied as to all of the following (Sch 1, para 3):

(a) that there are reasonable grounds for believing that there is material which consists of or includes 'excluded material' or 'special procedure material' on any premises specified in the application, or, in the case of an 'all premises' warrant, premises occupied or controlled by the person specified; and

(b) that such a warrant could have been issued under one of the historical statutory provisions; and

(c) that the issue of such a warrant would have been appropriate.

### 2.5.4 What are the preconditions to the granting of a special procedure application requiring a person to surrender or grant access to material (Schedule 1, paragraph 4)?

If the judge is satisfied that one or other of the sets of access conditions is fulfilled, he may make an order (Sch 1, para 1).

### 2.5.5 What is the procedure for special procedure applications under Schedule 1, paragraph 4 or 12?

**(i) General: para 12 applications to be made exceptionally; presumption in favour of para 4 applications.** Recognizing that para 12 applications, which are made *ex parte*, are a serious inroad into the liberty of the subject, the courts have emphasized that applications should normally be made *inter partes* (ie by way of a para 4 application) unless to do so would frustrate the purpose of the application. All the circumstances had to be considered, including the seriousness of the matter being investigated, evidence already available to the police, and the extent to which the person in possession already knew of the interest in his affairs such as might have caused him to destroy or interfere with documents: *R v Southampton Crown Court, ex p J and P* [1993] Crim LR 961, DC. See also *R v Central Criminal Court, ex p A J D Holdings Limited* [1992] Crim LR 669.

### (ii) applications for order to surrender or grant access to material (Sch 1, para 4):

- *Applications made on notice, inter partes.* The application is made *inter partes* (with notice to the affected party and that party's ability to appear) by the service of a notice on the person believed to be in possession of the material (Sch 1, paras 7–10). The person served is under an obligation to preserve the material until the application is determined (subject to certain exceptions) (Sch 1, para 11).
- *No notice to suspect.* There is no requirement to give notice, in addition, to any accused person or suspected party since the purpose of the Act is to permit the police to seek access to special procedure material before they had identified anyone as a likely perpetrator of the crime being investigated: *R v Leicester Crown Court, ex p DPP* [1988] 86 Cr App R 254.
- *In chambers or open court.* The application may be made, at the judge's discretion and in the light of submissions made, in chambers or in open court: *R v Central Criminal Court, ex p DPP*, DC (1988) The Times, 1 April.
- *Application particularized in writing.* The police should set out in writing in the application or in a supporting document what is sought and must bear the risk that the provision of such detail to the person who is the subject of the application will lead to the destruction of evidence: *R v Central Criminal Court ex p Adegbesan* (1987) 84 Cr App R 219, CA, at 224 and 226. However, a failure to do so is not fatal where the information was given orally before the notice was given and the recipient of the notice was specifically referred to the officer to whom that information was given orally (*R v Crown Court at Manchester ex p Taylor* (1988) 87 Cr App R 358 at 370). The notice should set out the general nature of the offence (ibid). Anything served on the court must be served on the person against whom the application is made: *R v Inner London Crown Court ex p Baines and Baines (a firm)* (1988) 87 Cr App R 111, DC at 117. However, it is a matter for the judgment of the police, having regard to any special features of the investigation, whether to disclose evidence relied upon in advance of the hearing, although the omission to do so may justify the granting of an adjournment (ibid).
- *Duty of openness on the police.* The police have a duty to be open handed and to set out all the material in their hands, whether it assisted the applications or militated against them; and the Crown has a duty to make a clear revelation to the Court of all appropriate material in their possession so the judge could safely decide whether the access conditions were fulfilled: *R v Acton Crown Court, ex p Layton* [1993] Crim LR 459. However, where on an *inter partes* application, the respondent had the material in question, a failure by the applicant to reveal the material to the judge was not fatal to the legality of the order. However, as stated above, there is a discretion in the police as to when to disclose evidence relied upon in support.

### (iii) warrant issued by a judge (Sch 1, para 12):

- Safeguards as to the form of the application and the form of the warrant, common to both s 8 applications and Sch 1, para 12 applications. See s 15 below.

- *Application made ex parte.* Although Sch 1 is silent as to the form of the application, s 15(3) states that the application shall be made *ex parte* (without notice to or argument from the affected person).
- *Duty to assist judge.* An officer making an application should draw the judge's attention to material arguably subject to legal privilege and provide him with sufficient information to reach a decision on the question of privilege. Where there is doubt, legal advice should be obtained to assist the judge (*R v Southampton Crown Court ex p J and P* [1993] Crim LR 962, DC.)
- *Judge's reasons should be stated if not apparent.* If it is apparent from the record that the judge had given the matter cursory consideration and allowed the application to go through on the nod, the warrant is liable to be quashed (*R v Southwark Crown Court, ex p Sorsky Defries* [1996] Crim LR 195).

### 2.5.6 What order may be made on a special procedure application requiring a person to surrender or grant access to material (Schedule 1, paragraph 4)?

The order is for the person who appears to the judge to be in possession of the material, within seven days or such longer period as may be specified, either to (a) produce it to a constable for him to take it away or (b) give a constable access to it (Sch 1, para 4). Specific provision is made for the viewing and printing out of electronic data (Sch 1, para 5).

### 2.5.7 What are the consequences of failing to comply with a special procedure order requiring a person to surrender or grant access to material (Schedule 1, paragraph 4)?

If a person fails to comply with such an order, the judge may deal with him as if he had committed a contempt of the Crown Court (Sch 1, para 15). In addition, such a failure leads naturally to an application under para 12 for a warrant since it is one of the conditions for one of the routes to the granting of a warrant (para 12(b)(ii)).

### 2.5.8 What are the preconditions for the issue of a warrant by a judge under the special procedure (Schedule 1, paragraph 12)?

There are two alternative routes:

(i) *The first route.* The judge must be satisfied (Sch 1, para 12, 14) that:
    (a) either set of access conditions is fulfilled; and

(b) any of the following apply: (1) access could not practicably be granted by a person entitled to grant entry to the premises or access to the material; or (2) the material contains information which is likely to be disclosed in breach of a statutory restriction on disclosure or obligation of secrecy if a warrant is not issued; or (3) the service of notice of an application under Sch 1, para 4 may seriously prejudice the investigation.

(ii) *The second route.* The judge must be satisfied (Sch 1, para 12, 14) that:
   (a) the second set of access conditions is fulfilled; and
   (b) an order under Sch 1, para 4 has not been complied with.

### 2.5.9 What may be seized under a warrant issued by a judge under the special procedure (Schedule 1, paragraph 12)?

A constable may seize and retain anything for which a search has been authorized by the judge (Sch 1, para 13). There is an extension of the power to require electronic data to be produced in a form in which it is or may readily become intelligible (see s 20 below). Rights to access and copies of things seized are provided (see s 21 below). The length of time that seized things may be retained is set out in s 22 (see below).

### 2.5.10 Execution of warrant under the special procedure and conduct of search

Section 16 provides safeguards, common to both s 8 applications and Sch 1, para 12 applications, as to the execution of a warrant and the conduct of the search (see below).

## 2.6 Search Warrant Safeguards (Section 15)

Section 15 provides safeguards, common to both s 8 applications and Sch 1, para 12 applications, as to the form of the application and the form of the warrant. Its reach, together with that of s 16, goes beyond the Act and extends to any statutory power to issue warrants to enter and search premises (s 15(1)). Further guidance as to the specific statutory powers covered is contained in Code B, Note for Guidance 2A.

It is now settled that, despite a lack of clarity in the wording of s 15(1), in order for a search to be lawful, both s 15 and s 16 must be satisfied (*R v Longman* 88 Cr App R 148, CA; *R v Central Criminal Court, ex p AJD Holdings Limited* [1992] Crim LR 669; *R v Chief Constable of Lancashire, ex p Parker and Another* (1993) 97 Cr App R 90, DC, at 95; *R v Chesterfield Justices, ex p Bramley*, [2000] 1 Cr App R 486 at 499).

### 2.6.1 **What are the duties of the officer applicant?**

#### (i) preliminary enquiries.

Requirements in Code B 3 include the following:

- When information appears to justify an application, the officer must take reasonable steps to check the information is accurate, recent, and not provided maliciously or irresponsibly; and an application may not be made on the basis of information from an anonymous source if corroboration has not been sought.
- The officer shall ascertain as specifically as possible the nature of the articles concerned and their location.
- The officer shall make reasonable enquiries to establish: whether anything is known about the likely occupier of the premises and the nature of the premises themselves; whether the premises have been searched previously and how recently; and to obtain any other relevant information.
- Consultation with the local police/community liaison officer should be made if there is reason to believe that a search might have an adverse effect on relations between the police and the community, save in urgent cases when the consultation should be as soon as possible after the search.

#### (ii) matters to be stated in the application.

It is the duty of the officer (s 15(1)–(3)), who must answer under oath any question asked by the magistrate or judge (s 15(4)), to state:

- the ground of the application (however the identity of informants need not be disclosed, although answers may be given as to the reliability of the source: Code B, Note for Guidance 3A);
- the enactment under which the warrant would be issued (including the Act itself);
- where the application is for multiple entries, the grounds for such application; whether he seeks a warrant authorizing an unlimited number of entries, or, if not, the maximum number sought;
- where the application is for a 'specific premises warrant' (under s 8(1A)(a) or Sch 1, para 12), the premises;
- where the application is for an 'all premises warrant' (under s 8(1A)(b) or Sch 1, para 12), as many premises as it is reasonably practicable to specify; why it is necessary to search more than may be specified, and why it is not reasonably practicable to specify them all; the person/s in occupation or control of the premises;
- so far as practicable, the identity of the articles or person sought.

This is supplemented by guidance and requirements in the Code. Additional matters which should be specified in writing, by virtue of Code B 3.6 are:

- how the evidence relates to any investigation;

- the object of the search;
- that there are no reasonable grounds to believe that the material sought (a) in the case of an application to a judge (s 9 and Sch 1), consists of or includes items subject to legal privilege (s 10); and (b) in the case of an application to a magistrate (s 8), consists of or includes excluded material (s 10) or special procedure material (s 14).

Code B, Note for Guidance 3B states that the information supporting a search warrant application should be as specific as possible, particularly in relation to the articles or persons being sought and where in the premises it is suspected they may be found.

### (iii) signed written authority required in application.

Code B 3.4 requires any application to a magistrate (s 8) or to a judge (Sch 1) to be supported by a signed written authority from an officer of at least the rank of inspector; although, in an urgent application, the next most senior officer on duty can give such authority. (In addition, the principle in s 107 and Code B 2.7 applies: sergeants authorized to act as inspectors have a like power.)

### 2.6.2 Formalities and form of a warrant

The warrant must specify (s 15(4)–(6)):

- if it specifies multiple entries, whether they are limited (and, if so, the number) or unlimited;
- the name of the applicant;
- the date issued;
- the enactment under which it is issued;
- the premises to be searched or, in the case of an 'all premises warrant', the person in occupation or control and any premises which can be specified;
- so far as practicable, the identity of the articles or person sought.

Provision is made for the number of copies required (s 15(7)).

## 2.7 Execution of Search Warrants (Section 16)

### 2.7.1 Who may execute a warrant or accompany persons executing warrants?

#### (i) constables or designated persons.

The warrant may be executed by 'any constable' (s 16(1)) or by a civilian designated as an 'investigating officer' under s 38 of the Police Reform Act 2002 (Sch 4, Pt 2, para 16(e)). The effect of s 16(1) was to remove the requirement in certain statutes of limiting the execution of warrants to a constable named in the warrant.

### (ii) persons accompanying.

However, a person authorized by the warrant may accompany any person executing the warrant (s 16(2)) and, so long as he is in the company of and under the supervision of the latter, he has the same powers as the latter with respect to (a) the execution of the warrant, and (b) the seizure of anything to which the warrant relates (s 16(2A) and (2B); Code B 2.11; and Police Reform Act 2002, Sch 4, Pt 2, para 16(e)). Code B, Note for Guidance 3C states that this includes any suitably qualified or skilled person or an expert in a particular field whose presence is needed to help accurately identify the material sought or to advise where certain evidence is most likely to be found and how it should be dealt with. The obvious application is to forensic experts of all types, eg those concerned in the retrieval and preservation of electronic data.

### 2.7.2 Who is in charge of the execution of a warrant?

Code B 2.10 requires that whenever there is a search of premises to which the Code applies, one officer must act as the officer in charge of the search. This should normally be the most senior officer present; but a supervising officer may appoint a person of lower rank; or select an officer where all are of the same rank; otherwise, the officers themselves should nominate one of their number to be in charge (Code B, Note for Guidance 2F).

### 2.7.3 How long does a warrant remain valid?

Any entry and search under a warrant must be within three months from the date of its issue (s 16(3)). (An amendment effected by the Serious Organised Crime and Police Act 2005 extended the period from one month to three months.)

### 2.7.4 What are the conditions for entry and search on more than one occasion?

Multiple entries are now permitted under the two types of warrants introduced by the Serious Organised Crime and Police Act 2005, the 'specific premises warrant' and the 'all premises warrant' (see the discussion at para 2.2 above as to the meaning of these terms). Amendments to s 16 are made by the Serious Organised Crime and Police Act 2005 to introduce additional safeguards into the execution of warrants where either multiple entries are to be made or entry is to be made to premises not specified in an 'all premises warrant'.

Written authorization by a police officer of at least the rank of inspector is required:

(i) entry and search of premises not specified in an 'all premises warrant' (s 16(3A); Code B 6.3B); or

(ii) entry and search of premises entered on a second or any subsequent time under a warrant authorizing multiple searches (s 16(3B); Code B 6.3A).

There is provision for sergeants to perform the role of the authorizing inspector, if so authorized by an officer of at least the rank of superintendent (s 107; Code B 2.7). (In addition, as stated above, there is a requirement in Code B 3.4—although not the Act—for all applications to magistrates or judges to be authorized in writing by a senior officer.)

### 2.7.5 Are there restrictions on when in the day a warrant may be executed?

Entry and search under a warrant must be at a reasonable hour unless it appears to the constable executing it that the purpose of a search may be frustrated on an entry at that time (s 16(4); Code B 6.3).

### 2.7.6 What is meant by 'premises'?

Section 23 defines 'premises' as 'any place', including:

(a)   any vehicle, vessel, aircraft or hovercraft;
(b)   any offshore installation;
(ba) any renewable energy installation;
(c)   any tent or movable structure.

The entire premises may be seized where it is necessary and physically possible to do so—for example, where the premises is a vehicle, tent or caravan (Code B, Note for Guidance 7B).

Despite the wide definition that can be attached to the word 'premises', the powers of entry search and seizure conferred by a warrant are strictly limited to those premises that are identified within that warrant. In *Wood v North Avon Magistrates Court* [2009] EWHCA 3614 (Admin), the seizure of a Mercedes car from a car park to a block of flats was held to be unlawful where the warrant was limited to one of the flats in the block. The 'premises' was the flat and any common parts necessary to gain access to those premises. The court found that the terms and scope of the warrant are so important that it would be wrong and dangerous to assume that the warrant covered the car park to the flat.

### 2.7.7 What are the formalities at entry and search and when is the use of force permissible?

**(i) where premises are occupied or person entitled to grant access is present:**

(a)  The statutory requirements are stated in s 16(5) and s 16(6) which do not, however, state anything about timing. The constable must:
  • identify himself to the occupier or other person entitled to grant access and, if not in uniform, produce to him documentary evidence that he is a constable;
  • produce the warrant to him; and
  • supply him with a copy of it.

**39**

(b) Code B sets out the timing of these steps.

- Prior to entry, an attempt should ordinarily be made to secure entry by agreement. The officer in charge should first attempt to communicate with the occupier or any other person entitled to grant access to the premises and explain the authority under which he seeks entry to the premises and ask the occupier to allow him to enter. However, this is unnecessary where there are reasonable grounds for believing that to alert the occupier or any other person entitled to grant access by attempting to communicate with him would frustrate the object of the search or endanger the officers concerned or other people (Code B 6.4). An example of this proviso is where there is a search for small disposable items, such as drugs, which could readily be flushed down the lavatory.
- Prior to search, the officer should: identify himself and, if not in uniform, show his warrant card; state the purpose of and grounds for the search; and identify any person accompanying the officer and describe their role in the process (Code B 6.5). However, in terrorism cases or where officers reasonably believe that recording or disclosing their names might put them in danger, warrant and identification numbers and the name of their police station may be used for identification (Code B 2.9). The names of persons accompanying the officers may be withheld in like cases (ibid).

(c) Use of force. Reasonable and proportionate force may be used to effect entry where the occupier or other person entitled to grant access has refused entry or it is impossible to communicate with such persons (Code B 6.6).

**(ii) where premises are unoccupied and no one entitled to grant access is present.**

The officer is relieved of the formalities of introduction (Code B 6.4) and reasonable and proportionate force may be used to effect entry (Code B 6.6).

### 2.7.8 How should a search be conducted?

**(i) the extent of the search permitted by a warrant.**

The search may only be to the extent required for the purpose for which the warrant was issued (s 16(5)). Further guidance is provided by Code B 6.9, 6.9A, and 6.9B: regard is to be had to the size and nature of whatever is sought; a search may not continue once everything specified in the warrant is found or the officer in charge is satisfied that whatever is being sought is not on the premises.

**(ii) Guidance as to the conduct of the search.**

Guidance in Code B includes these important points.

- Searches must be conducted with due consideration for the property and privacy of the occupier and with no more disturbance than necessary; and reasonable force may be used only when necessary and proportionate because the cooperation of the occupier cannot be obtained or is insufficient for the purpose (Code B 6.10).

- If the occupier wishes, a friend or neighbour of the occupier may witness the search, subject to certain exceptions (Code B 6.11).
- Questions solely necessary for the purpose of furthering the effective and proper conduct of the search may be asked of a person without first cautioning them but questioning which goes beyond that, is likely to constitute an interview within Code C (Code B 6.12 and 12A).

### 2.7.9 Documents used in a search or recording a search

**(i) Notice of powers and rights.**

Unless impracticable, such a notice should be provided to the occupier (Code B 6.7). It should ordinarily be provided before the search begins (Code B 6.8).

**(ii) The warrant.**

A copy should ordinarily be provided to the occupier before the search begins (Code B 6.8). Where there is no occupier present or other person in charge of the premises, the warrant should be left in a prominent place on the premises and endorsed with certain details (s 16(7); Code B 6.8). The original of the warrant must be endorsed with a record of what was found and seized (s 16(9); Code B 8.2). It must be returned to the appropriate person at the issuing court when it has been executed or within three months of the date of its issue (s 16(10) and (10A); and Code B 8.3) where it must be retained for 12 months (s 16(11)) during which the occupier has the right to inspect it (s 16(12)).

**(iii) Search records and search registers.**

A detailed record must be made by the officer in charge of the search of specified details relating to the execution of the warrant (Code B 8.1). A search register, in which all search records for the area are made, copied, or referred to must be maintained at specified police stations (Code B 9.1).

### 2.7.10 How should premises entered by force be left?

Before leaving the officer in charge of the search must make sure they are secure by arranging for the occupier or their agent to be present or by any other appropriate means (Code B 6.13).

## 2.8 Alternative Powers of Search and Seizure, Supplementary to PACE

### 2.8.1 Powers of seize and sift under Criminal Justice and Police Act 2001, Part 2 (Code B 7)

These provisions apply to all the powers of seizure in Part II of the Act.

Where it is not reasonably practicable to determine whether things on premises fall, in whole or part, within the class of things which a person is entitled to seize, or where it is not reasonably practicable to separate seizable things from things that the person has no power to seize, he may nonetheless remove the whole of it. It thus permits the removal of items subject to legal privilege, excluded material, and special procedure material.

The power is conferred on a person lawfully on any premises and extends to a constable, a civilian designated as a 'community support officer' under s 38 of the Police Reform Act 2002 (Sch 4, Pt 1, para 24), and a person authorized to accompany them under s 16.

Provision is made, amongst other things, for the service of notices, access to the material, and the return of things which the person has no power to seize following the sift process.

### 2.8.2 Powers of access, search, and seizure under Terrorism Act 2000, Schedule 5, Part I (Code B 6.14 and 6.15)

A modified version of PACE, s 8 and Sch 1 procedures is provided in this schedule applicable to terrorist investigations. Applications may be made to a magistrate for a search warrant with respect to material which does not include material subject to legal privilege, excluded material, or special procedure material (PACE, ss 10, 11, and 14). Applications may be made to a Crown Court judge for orders requiring production of or access to or for a search warrant with respect to material which includes excluded material or special procedure material. There are additional exceptional powers such as: the power to require a person to state the location of material to which a production order relates; the power to require a person to provide an explanation for material seized or produced; and the power, in urgent cases, of an officer of at least the rank of superintendent to give written authorization for the (above-mentioned) powers normally granted only by magistrates and judges.

PACE, ss 15 and 16 apply to search warrants issued to and executed under Sch 5: Code B, Note for Guidance 2A and guidance is contained in the Code at B 6.14 and 6.15. The powers in question are exercisable by a constable.

## 2.9 Power of Entry for Specified Purposes, Including Arrest (Section 17)

As the Code states, s 17 does not create or confer any powers of arrest (Code B 4.1). It abolishes some powers and imposes conditions on the exercise of others. It abolishes all common law powers of a constable to enter premises without a warrant, save the power of entry to deal with or prevent a breach of the peace (s 17(5) and (6)). (A breach of the peace is an act done or threatened to be done which either actually harms a person, or, in his presence, his property, or is likely to cause such harm or which puts someone in fear of such harm being done.) It does not affect statutory powers, save those expressly mentioned. Nor does it apply to an officer invited into premises (*Hobson v Chief Constable of Cheshire* [2003] EWHC 3011).

### 2.9.1  Who may exercise the power under section 17?

The full extent of the power may be exercised by a constable (s 17(1)). A civilian designated as a 'community support officer' under s 38 of the Police Reform Act 2002 may exercise one limited component of the full power: the power to enter and search any premises in the relevant police area for the purpose of saving life or limb or preventing serious damage to property, ie that contained in s 17(1)(e) (Sch 4, Pt 1, para 8).

### 2.9.2  What are the preconditions to the exercise of the power under section 17?

Entry and search of premises is permitted by s 17 for the following purposes and subject to the following conditions:

**(i) executing specified powers of arrest or recapture, where the constable has reasonable grounds for believing that the person whom he is seeking is on the premises.**

Section 17(1) lists a wide range of powers of arrest or recapture for which purpose a constable may enter and search premises. They fall within the following categories:

- the execution of a warrant of arrest in criminal proceedings or a 'warrant of commitment' (relating to the failure to pay a sum arising from conviction or order in a Magistrates' Court);
- the arrest of a person for an 'indictable offence';
- the arrest of a person for a wide range of specified particular offences (two of which are stated to be exercisable only by an officer in uniform (s 17(3)));
- the arrest of a child or young person remanded or committed to local authority accommodation;
- the recapturing of a person unlawfully at large, consisting either of (1) persons 'unlawfully at large' whom the officer is 'pursuing' (s 17(1)(d)), or (2) persons who have escaped from a specified category of places of detention, ie prisons etc, whether or not they are being pursued (s 17(1)(cb)). The phrase 'unlawfully at large' is used in many statutes. It denotes that a person is subject to lawful detention of any kind and has either absconded or escaped or failed to surrender.

**(ii) for the purpose of saving life or limb or preventing serious damage to property (s 17(1)(e)).**

For this purpose, it is not necessary for the person exercising the power to have reasonable grounds for believing that the person whom he is seeking is on the premises (s 17(2)).

There is no express requirement that the dangers giving rise to the power should relate to the property entered. However, in view of the need to protect a person's rights under Article 8 of the European Convention on Human Rights (right to respect for private and family life, home, and correspondence) it must be demonstrated that the purpose requirement stated in s 17(1)(e) is strictly satisfied. In *R v Veneroso* [2002] Crim LR 306 (Crown Ct (Inner London)), a search of the home of a seriously injured person to ascertain his identity and next of kin, which resulted in the discovery of drugs, was held by the trial judge to be outside of the purpose in s 17(1)(e) and in breach of Article 8, with the result that the evidence was excluded under s 78.

### 2.9.3 What is the extent of the search permitted by the power under section 17?

The power of search conferred by the section is limited to the extent that is reasonably required for the purpose for which the power of entry is exercised (s 17(4)).

Except for searches under s 17(1)(e) (ie the second of the two categories described above), where the premises consist of two or more separate dwellings, the search is limited to common parts and any dwelling in which the constable has reasonable grounds for believing that the person whom he is seeking is on (s 17(2)).

### 2.9.4 In what circumstances may force be used under section 17?

The constable may use reasonable force, if necessary, in the exercise of the power (s 117). However, before doing so, he should, unless it was impossible, impracticable, or undesirable to do so, give the occupant of the property reasons for his seeking to gain access. This is because Parliament clearly had that common law obligation in mind when conferring the power of entry on the police under the Act: *O'Loughlin v Chief Constable of Essex* [1998] 1 WLR 374, CA (Civ Div).

## 2.10 Entry and Search after Arrest (Section 18)

### 2.10.1 Who may exercise the power under section 18?

The power may be exercised by a constable (s 18(1)) or by a civilian designated as an 'investigating officer' under s 38 of the Police Reform Act 2002 (Sch 4, Pt 2, para 18(a)).

### 2.10.2 **What are the preconditions to the exercise of the power under section 18?**

A constable may enter and search premises under s 18 if the following conditions are satisfied:

(i) the premises are occupied or controlled by a person under arrest for indictable offence (s 18(1)); and ...

'Controlled' is a wider notion than 'occupied': it will embrace premises which the person manages in the sense that he runs, organizes, and plans them even if he has no legal right to be in them.

(ii) the constable has reasonable grounds for suspecting that there is on the premises evidence, other than items subject to legal privilege (as defined in s 10), that relates either (1) to the offence for which the person was arrested or (2) to some other indictable offence, connected with or similar to that offence (s 18(1)); and ...

The word 'offence' means a domestic (rather than foreign) offence, although there is a surviving common law power of search and seizure with respect to the investigation of foreign offences: *R (Rottman) v Metropolitan Police Comr* [2002] 2 WLR 1315 (HL).

(iii) either the search has been authorized in writing by an officer of the rank of inspector or above (or a sergeant authorized to exercise that power under s 107) or that, before the arrested person has been taken to a police station or released on bail, his presence at a place other than a police station is necessary for the effective investigation of the offence (in which case no written authorization is required) (s 18(4)–(5A)).

Where a search is conducted in the circumstances which permit a search without authorization, an officer of the rank of inspector or above (or a sergeant authorized to exercise that power under s 107) must be informed of the search as soon as practicable after it has been made. Authority should only be given if the authorizing officer is satisfied that the necessary grounds exist (Code B 4.3).

### 2.10.3 **What is the extent of the search permitted by the power under section 18?**

The power of search conferred by the section is limited to the extent that is reasonably required for the purpose of discovering such evidence (s 17(3)).

### 2.10.4 **In what circumstances may force be used under section 18?**

The constable may use reasonable force, if necessary, in the exercise of the power (s 117). However, before doing so, he should, unless it was impossible, impracticable, or undesirable to do so, give the occupant of the property reasons for his seeking to gain access. This is because Parliament clearly had that common law obligation in mind when conferring the power of entry on the police under the Act (*O'Loughlin v Chief Constable of Essex* [1998] 1 WLR 374, CA (Civ Div)) and because of the mandatory language in Code B (*Linehan v DPP* [2000] Crim LR 861, DC).

### 2.10.5  What may be seized and retained under section 18?

'Anything' for which he may search under the section may be seized and retained, (ie, evidence, other than items subject to legal privilege (as defined in s 10), that relates either (1) to the offence for which the person was arrested, or (2) to some other indictable offence, connected with or similar to that offence (s 18(1)); s 18(2)).

A movable vehicle may be seized as 'anything' within the section, notwithstanding that the vehicle itself amounts to 'premises' within the meaning of the Act (s 23) since 'anything' includes 'everything' (*Cowan v Condon* [2000] 1 WLR 254, CA (Civ Div)). See Code B, Note for Guidance 7B: the principle extends to tents and caravans.

There is an extension of the power to require electronic data to be produced in a form in which it is or may readily become intelligible (see s 20 below). Rights to access and copies of things seized are provided (see s 21 below). The length of time that seized things may be retained is set out in s 22 (see below).

### 2.10.6  What records must be kept of the search under section 18?

The authorizing officer, or the officer informed of the search, must make a record in writing of the grounds for the search and the nature of the evidence sought (s 18(7)); and, where the arrested person is in police detention at the time of the making of the record, it should be made in that person's custody record (s 18(8)). If there is no custody record, it should be made in the authorizing officer's pocket book or the search record (Code B 4.3).

## 2.11  General Power of Seizure (Section 19)

### 2.11.1  Who may exercise the power under section 19?

The power may be exercised by a constable (s 19(1)) or by a civilian designated as an 'investigating officer' under s 38 of the Police Reform Act 2002 (Sch 4, Pt 2, para 19(a)).

### 2.11.2  What are the preconditions to the exercise of the power under section 19?

The officer may seize items in premises under s 19 if the following conditions are satisfied.

(i) he is lawfully on the premises (s 19(1)); and

(ii) he has reasonable grounds for believing:

(a) that the item seized is either (1) a thing which has been obtained in consequence of the commission of an offence (s 19(2): eg stolen items or the proceeds of crime) or (2) that it is evidence in relation to an offence he is investigating or any other offence (s 19(3)); and

(b) that it is necessary to seize it in order to prevent it being concealed, lost, damaged, altered or destroyed (s 19(2)(b) and s 19(3)(b)); and ...

In fact, the word 'damaged' is omitted from s 19(3)(b) (which is otherwise in identical form to s 19(2)(b)) but this is probably an inadvertent drafting error. It would appear that, unlike the use of the phrase 'relevant evidence' in s 8, 'evidence' may here include material which would be inadmissible at trial. The word 'offence' means a domestic (rather than foreign) offence, although there is a surviving common law power of search and seizure with respect to the investigation of foreign offences (*R (Rottman) v Metropolitan Police Comr* [2002] 2 WLR 1315 (HL)). The section supplements without repealing existing powers of seizure (s 19(5)). (An example of such a power in a different statute is s 26(3) of the Theft Act 1968.)

(iii) the item is not one which he has reasonable grounds for believing to be subject to legal privilege (as defined in s 10) (s 19(6)).

### 2.11.3 How may an officer seize electronic data under the general section 19 power?

There is a special rule for electronic data in s 19(4). The officer may require it to be produced in a form in which it can be taken away and is either a form (1) in which it is visible or legible, or (2) from which it can readily be produced in a visible and legible form. This would include print-outs and copies of data processed so as to be intelligible. It may include a whole computer.

The conditions are similar to the general seizure conditions but tailored to deal with electronic data. In that respect, they are narrower than the extension of specific powers of seizure to electronic data effected by s 20. The conditions are:

(i) he is lawfully on the premises (s 19(1)); and

(ii) electronic information is accessible from the premises; and ...

This would include electronic information which is stored off the premises but is accessible, for example, through a network.

(iii) he has reasonable grounds for believing:

(a) that the electronic information either (1) has been obtained in consequence of the commission of an offence or (2) is evidence in relation to an offence he is investigating or any other offence; and

(b) that it is necessary to seize it in order to prevent it being concealed, lost, tampered with or destroyed; and

(iv) the information is not information which he has reasonable grounds for believing to be subject to legal privilege (as defined in s 10) (s 19(6)).

Section 19(6) speaks of an 'item' but, from the context, this must include electronic data.

### 2.11.4 How long may seized things be retained?

See s 22 below.

## 2.12 Extension of Powers of Seizure to Computerized Information (Section 20)

### 2.12.1 Who may exercise the power under section 20?

The power may be exercised by a constable (s 20(1)) or by a civilian designated as an 'investigating officer' under s 38 of the Police Reform Act 2002 (Sch 4, Pt 2, para 16(g)).

### 2.12.2 How may an officer seize electronic data under the extension in section 20?

The power is framed in similar terms to that in s 19 but without the require- ment that the officer must fear for the destruction, etc of the electronic data. Under s 20, the officer may require it to be produced in a form in which it can be taken away and is either a form (1) in which it is visible or legible, or (2) from which it can readily be produced in a visible and legible form. This would include print-outs and copies of data processed so as to be intelligible. It may include a whole computer.

The officer may seize items in premises under s 20 if the following conditions are satisfied.

(i) he has entered premises under any statutory power; and

(ii) he is exercising a statutory power of seizure in any Act (whether passed before or after PACE) or the powers of seizure contained in PACE in (1) s 8 (magistrates' search warrant) or (2) Sch 1 (judge's search warrant) or (3) s 18 (entry and search after arrest).

### 2.12.3 How long may seized things be retained?

See s 22 below.

## 2.13 **Rights to Access and Copies or Photographs of Seized Material (Section 21)**

Rights are extended to persons with respect to seized material. In the case of companies, the person possessing the statutory right is the company itself and not its directors (*Re DPR Futures Limited* [1989] 1 WLR 778, Ch D).

### 2.13.1 **Record of seizure (Section 21(1), (2), and (9); Code B 7.16)**

- A record of what is seized
- by a constable or by a civilian designated as an 'investigating officer' under s 38 of the Police Reform Act 2002 (Sch 4, Pt 2, para 16(h)) or by a person authorized (under s 16(2)) to accompany a person executing a warrant
- acting under any statutory power
- if required by the occupier or person having custody or control immediately before seizure
- must be provided by the constable etc within a reasonable time of the request.

Unlike the rights to access etc, this is an absolute right, unqualified by s 21(8).

## 2.14 **Access to Seized Material (Section 21(3), (8), and (9); Code B 7.17)**

- Access under the supervision of a constable or by a civilian designated as an 'investigating officer' under s 38 of the Police Reform Act 2002 (Sch 4, Pt 2, para 16(i))
- to anything seized and retained for the purpose of investigating an offence by a constable or by a civilian designated as an 'investigating officer' under s 38 of the Police Reform Act 2002 (Sch 4, Pt 2, para 16(i)) or by a person authorized (under s 16(2)) to accompany a person executing a warrant
- must be allowed to a person having custody or control of the thing immediately before seizure or someone acting on their behalf if he requests such access
- unless the officer in charge of the investigation for the purposes of which it was seized has reasonable grounds for believing that granting access would prejudice that investigation or the investigation of another offence or the criminal investigations into those offences.

There is no requirement that such access should be provided within a reasonable time. Given the general scheme of the section, this is probably an oversight and should be read into the section. Persons are to be provided, on request, with photographs or copies 'at their own expense' (Code B 7.17). When access is denied, a record of the grounds shall be made (ibid). The paragraph provides another reason for refusing access: when such access might lead to the commission of an offence by providing access to unlawful material such as pornography.

## 2.15 **Photographs or Copies (Section 21(3)–(9))**

- Access to, under the supervision of a constable or by a civilian designated as an 'investigating officer' under s 38 of the Police Reform Act 2002 (Sch 4, Pt 2, para 16(i)), for the purpose of photographing and copying, or, in the alternative, the provision of photographs or copies of
- anything seized and retained for the purpose of investigating an offence by a constable or by a civilian designated as an 'investigating officer' under s 38 of the Police Reform Act 2002 (Sch 4, Pt 2, para 16(i)) or by a person authorized (under s 16(2)) to accompany a person executing a warrant
- must be allowed to a person having custody or control of the thing immediately before seizure or someone acting on their behalf if he requests a photograph or copy; and a photograph or copy may be made without such a request and, if so, must be provided to the person who made the request; and, in the case of photographs or copies, must be provided within a reasonable time of a request
- unless the officer in charge of the investigation for the purposes of which it was seized has reasonable grounds for believing that granting access would prejudice that investigation or the investigation of another offence or the criminal investigations into those offences.

There is no requirement that such access (as opposed to photographs or copies) should be provided within a reasonable time. Given the general scheme of the section, this is probably an oversight and should be read into the section. Strictly speaking, the duty is not triggered by a request for access to the material but only by a request for a photograph or copy but this, no doubt, is an academic distinction.

## 2.16 **The Duration of Retention of Seized Items (Section 22)**

Anything seized by a constable or by a civilian designated as an 'investigating officer' under s 38 of the Police Reform Act 2002 (Sch 4, Pt 2, para 16(i)) or by a person authorized (under s 16(2)) to accompany a person executing a warrant may be retained for the following periods:

(i) **in the case of (1) anything lawfully seized, whether justified by statute or common law, or (2) electronic data taken following a requirement under** s 19 (general power of seizure) or s 20 (extension to electronic data), for so long as is necessary in all the circumstances (s 22(1); Code B 7.14 and 7.15).

See *R v Chief Constable of Lancashire, ex p Parker* 97 Cr App R 90, DC at 98.

(ii) in the case of anything falling within (i) but seized for the purpose of a criminal investigation, unless a photograph or copy would suffice, for the time required for its use either (1) as evidence at a trial or (2) for forensic examination in connection with an offence or (3) for investigation in connection with an offence (s 22(2)(a) and (4); Code B 7.14 and 7.15).

The wording of this section was wrestled with by the Court of Appeal in *R v Chief Constable of Lancashire, ex p Parker* 97 Cr App R 90, DC at 98. In rejecting the suggestion that s 22(2)(a) permitted the retention of unlawfully obtained items, the Court held that s 22(2)(a) gave specific examples of matters falling within s 22(1).

(iii) in the case of anything for which there are reasonable grounds for believing that it has been obtained in consequence of the commission of an offence, unless a photograph or copy would suffice, for the time required to establish its lawful owner (s 22(2)(b) and (4)).

(iv) in the case of an item seized on the ground that it may be used to cause physical injury or to damage property or to interfere with evidence or to assist in the escape of a person lawfully detained, until the person from whom it was seized is released from the custody of the police or the court on bail or otherwise (s 22(3)).

# Practical Guidance

## 2.17 **Case Study 1 (Sections 18 and 19)**

Smith, a well-known thief, is arrested for stealing a car radio from an unattended vehicle in an area where numerous other thefts from vehicles have recently taken place. Smith occupies a bed sit in a large house that is separated into several rooms where residents share a communal kitchen. At the station, the arresting officer applies to his inspector for written authority to search Smith's room under s 18 of PACE. This is granted and officers attend the address to carry out the search. At the house, other residents have no objection to Smith's room being searched but refuse access to the communal kitchen. A search of Smith's room reveals no stolen property but a substance is discovered hidden under a mattress believed to be a controlled drug.

*Was the inspector correct to authorize a search of Smith's house?*

Smith is under arrest for an indictable offence and his address is known. He is a well known thief and there have been other thefts from vehicles in the same area. Therefore, there are reasonable grounds to suspect that stolen property from other vehicle thefts may be found at his address and the authority was fully justified.

*Have the searching officers the right to search more than Smith's room?*

The officers have the right to search those parts of the premises occupied or controlled by Smith. This includes those communal areas to which Smith has access such as the kitchen.

*Do the searching officers have any power to seize the substance suspected of being a controlled drug?*

Although the substance is not directly connected with or similar to the offence for which Smith was arrested, the general power of seizure under s 19 is relevant. The officers are lawfully on the premises and may seize anything if there are reasonable grounds to believe the item in question has been obtained in consequence of the commission of an offence (and that it is necessary to seize it in order to prevent it being destroyed etc).

## 2.18  Case Study 2 (Sections 17, 18, and 19 [and Section 32])

PC Brown lawfully arrests Jones for interfering with a motor vehicle. Whilst waiting for the police van and before being searched, Jones breaks away and runs to his house, closely pursued by the officer, and goes inside. Having received no response to repeated knocking, PC Brown forces the door open, searches the premises, and finds Jones hiding in the loft.

*Did PC Brown have lawful authority to use force to enter the premises?*

Although Jones was not under arrest for an arrestable offence he was unlawfully at large and was being pursued by police. In these circumstances PC Brown had a right to enter the premises by virtue of s 17(1)(d) of PACE. He was entitled to use reasonable force in the exercise of the power by virtue of s 117.

*Could PC Brown have carried out a search under section 18 or section 32 PACE whilst on the premises?*

In this case, the offence for which Jones was arrested is 'summary only'. Under s 18, PC Brown can only search premises occupied or controlled by a person under arrest for an indictable offence. Under s 32, a search of premises is only permitted where the person is arrested for an indictable offence and was in premises when arrested, or immediately before being arrested (s 32(1)(b)).

Accordingly, PC Brown had no power, in these circumstances, to search under either s 18 or s 32. However, if while searching for Jones, PC Brown found any item that he reasonably suspected had been obtained as a result of a criminal offence (and that it was necessary to seize it to prevent it being concealed etc) then the officer could seize this as well by virtue of s 19.

## 2.19 **Case Study 3 (Search Warrants)**

*DC Potts has received information from an informant that stolen goods are hidden in the house of a man known to the officer to have previous convictions for burglary. DC Potts is unsure about the best way to respond to this information. What advice should DC Potts be given?*

DC Potts should be advised that obtaining a search warrant may be the best way forward but he must first take reasonable steps to check the information is correct. The credibility of the informant is very important and it would be relevant that the person has on a number of previous occasions provided accurate information. Even if the informant is tried and tested, DC Potts should still take steps to verify the accuracy of the information, for example, by obtaining a description of the stolen goods and their location in the house. This may connect the goods to a recent theft or burglary in the area and add more credence to the information. In addition, DC Potts should make reasonable enquiries to establish if anything is known about the premises and the occupier and obtain any other information that may be relevant (Code B 3.1 to 3.3(i)–(ii)). Having taken steps to verify the information, DC Potts should then seek the written authority of an officer of at least Inspector rank to proceed with the application.

*Inspector North is approached by DC Potts and requested to provide written authority for him to apply for a search warrant. What should Inspector North establish before complying with this request?*

Inspector North should establish that DC Potts has indeed taken reasonable steps to check the accuracy of the information and properly carried out the steps as listed in the Code of Practice. He should also satisfy himself that the criteria under s 8 are present. The execution of a search warrant is a serious infringement of an individual's liberty and the role of the inspector is vital to ensure that applications for search warrants are both necessary and reasonable.

*DS Cooper has obtained an 'all premises' search warrant under s 8(1A)(b). He has identified a house that is controlled by a suspect who was specified in the application. DS Cooper is unsure how to proceed and asks Inspector North for advice*

Inspector North should advise DS Cooper that if the identified premises are not specified on the search warrant then they may not be searched unless the prior written authority of an officer of at least inspector rank is obtained. Providing Inspector North is not involved in the investigation himself he may give the necessary authorization. Inspector North should ensure the search warrant is with respect to 'all premises' and that there are reasonable grounds to believe that a person who was specified in the application controls the premises DS Cooper wishes to search. If so satisfied, Inspector North should prepare a written authorization (s 16(3A); Code B 6.3B).

*DS Cooper informs Inspector North that there is likely to be a considerable quantity of documentary material at the premises, only a small part of which will be of substantial value to the investigation. He suggests that the most efficient method would be to seize all the documents and bring them to the station for examination. Any not connected with the investigation can then be returned to the owner. What advice should Inspector North give DS Cooper?*

Inspector North should advice DS Cooper that before any item is seized there must be reasonable grounds for believing the item in question is likely to be relevant evidence, of substantial value to the investigation, and not subject to legal privilege or excluded or special procedure material. Therefore, the wholesale seizure of large amounts of documents to be sifted through later is not allowed under the Act. DS Cooper should be advised that he has two alternatives: either the documents should be examined at the premises and only those that come within the above criteria seized; or the material may now be removed in accordance with the 'seize and sift powers' contained in Criminal Justice and Police Act 2001, Pt 2.

*DS Cooper carries out the search and subsequently discovers that a letter from the suspect's solicitor, addressed to the suspect and giving legitimate legal advice was inadvertently seized. Having examined the document he considers that it may provide some evidence of the offence he is investigating. DS Cooper asks Inspector North if he can use the document as evidence against the suspect*

Inspector North should advise DS Cooper that the letter is subject to legal privilege and despite being seized in good faith cannot be used as evidence against the suspect. DS Cooper should be advised to destroy any copies made of the letter and return it to the suspect.

## 2.20 **Case Study 4**

DC Brown is the investigating officer in a case where a male suspect is believed to have used his laptop computer to access sites containing indecent images of children and to download them. Intelligence indicated that the suspect had been tipped off about the enquiry and DC Brown therefore swiftly obtained a warrant under s 8 PACE to search the suspect's home address for the computer. No computer was found; however DC Brown was in possession of sufficient other evidence to provide reasonable grounds to arrest the suspect who, on arrival at the station, requested the attendance of a local solicitor.

In the course of the interview, the suspect submitted a pre-prepared statement in which he admitted that he did get wind of the fact that the police suspected him of downloading images. Although maintaining innocence, he further states that he did not trust the police to carry out a fair examination of his computer and so took the laptop to the office of his solicitor, Mr Green, for safe-keeping.

Mr Green confirms to DC Brown that he does have the computer in his possession and is arranging for its examination. Further, Mr Green informs DC Brown that he cannot hand over the laptop to the police without his client's permission, but is willing to confirm in writing that his firm has the laptop, that arrangements are being made expeditiously to have it examined by an independent expert, and that all relevant content, including any that is adverse to his client will be passed to the police. Solicitor Green adds that in view of his client's mistrust of the police this would be the most appropriate way forward, and one that would ensure his client maintained confidence in the integrity of the investigative process.

DC Brown however is keen to obtain a search warrant to search Mr Green's office for the laptop and believes that it would be appropriate to make an application under the Special Procedure provisions of Sch 1 PACE. In accordance with Code B, para 3.4, DC Brown seeks written authority from an inspector to apply to a circuit judge for a search warrant and approaches Inspector Orton with this request.

### Into which category does the laptop fall?

Inspector Orton should consider whether the laptop can be placed in the category of excluded material under s 11(1) (personal records, human tissue or journalistic material), or special procedure material under s 14(1), (2) (material acquired by a trade, business or profession and held in confidence subject to an express or implied undertaking to that effect). Under these circumstances the laptop is unlikely to fit into the former category but is very likely to come within the latter. Indeed, it is difficult to conceive of circumstances where material passed by a client to a solicitor would not constitute special procedure material, and it would be sensible to apply a generous interpretation and err on the side of caution.

### What factors should be considered by Inspector Orton in deciding whether to authorize an application and by the judge in deciding whether to issue a search warrant?

As only special procedure material is sought, it is only necessary to pass through the first set of access conditions (Sch 1, para 2). Inspector Orton should therefore consider whether there are reasonable grounds to believe that:

- an indictable offence has been committed (possession of indecent images of a person under 18 is an indictable offence);
- there is material consisting of special procedure material on the relevant premises (the laptop is such material and Mr Green has stated that the laptop is in his possession);
- the material is likely to be of substantial value to the matter under investigation and relevant evidence (any indecent images found on the laptop would be primary evidence);
- other methods of obtaining the laptop have been tried without success, or would be bound to fail if tried (Mr Green has been asked to hand over the laptop and has refused);
- it is in the public interest that access to the laptop is granted (possession of indecent images of children is a serious offence, which it is in the public interest to investigate).

Inspector Orton could be satisfied that he should authorize DC Brown to apply to a circuit judge for an order compelling Mr Green to produce the laptop to him within seven days from the date the order was made. However, to obtain a search warrant it would be necessary to satisfy the judge of one or more further conditions.

### What further conditions must the judge be satisfied of?

Under Sch 1, para 14, it would be necessary to satisfy the judge of one or more of the following:

- It was not practicable to communicate with Mr Green or other persons regarding access to the premises or the material ('practicable' bears a wider meaning than 'feasible' or 'physically possible', nevertheless, in this case it would be difficult to suggest that this condition applies).
- Material subject to a statutory restriction on disclosure is likely to be disclosed unless a search warrant is issued (not applicable here).
- The service of a notice of application of an order would seriously prejudice the investigation (because, eg, the laptop, or any evidence on it, would be removed or destroyed).

### If none of the further conditions are satisfied, what alternative options are available?

It is unlikely in the circumstances of this case that any of the further conditions would be made out. As indicated above, the appropriate course of action in such circumstances would be to apply to the Judge for a production order directing Mr Green to hand over the laptop to the police.

### What if it is believed that the solicitor will not comply with such an order?

The application for a production order should take place *inter partes* and on notice; once notice has been served on Mr Green then no steps can be taken to conceal, destroy, alter or dispose of the material without the leave of the judge or written authority from the police. Failure to comply with the order can be dealt with as a contempt of court (Sch 1, para 15). A solicitor is not to be regarded as somehow tainted or unreliable simply because he has acted for someone charged or convicted of a criminal offence; however it may be appropriate to obtain a search warrant whether the solicitor's firm itself is being investigated—*R (Faisaltex Ltd) v Preston Crown Court* [2009] 1 Cr App R 549. In addition, a subsequent application for a search warrant could of course be made on the grounds that the production order has not been complied with—Sch 1, para 12(b)(i), (ii).

## 2.21 **Decision-making Chart for Obtaining Material on Premises by Warrant etc**

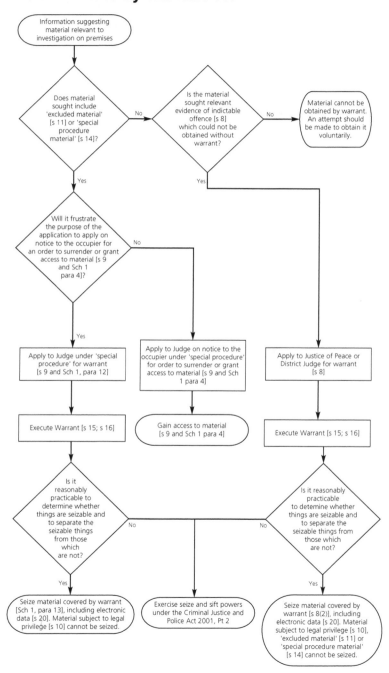

# 3

# Arrest: Part III

---

# Law and Commentary

## 3.1 Introduction

Part III of the Act has the title 'Arrest'. The powers and duties are:

(i) Arrest without warrant by constables (s 24) and other persons (s 24A)

(ii) Requirement for offenders to attend for fingerprinting and arrest in default (s 27)

(iii) Information to be given on arrest (s 28)

(iv) Powers and procedures with respect to persons arrested elsewhere than at police station (s 30)

(v) The bail of persons arrested elsewhere than at police station ('street bail') (ss 30A–D)

(vi) The arrest of persons at police stations, attending voluntarily (s 29) or by arrest for further offence (s 31)

(vii) Search of persons and search and entry of premises upon arrest at a place other than a police station (s 32)

## 3.2 Arrest without Warrant by Constables (Section 24) and Other Persons (Section 24A)

The Serious Organised Crime and Police Act 2005 has reformed this general power, splitting it into two sections which cover separately, first, arrests effected by constables and, secondly, those effected by other persons.

Analogous powers to the general arrest conditions contained in the old s 25, now repealed, are absorbed into the new s 24.

The new sections retain the division which existed in the old s 24 between arrests for which 'reasonable grounds to suspect' are necessary and arrests for which such grounds are not necessary. Essentially, if it is established that the right person has been arrested, the arrest is regarded as lawful without more; otherwise, its lawfulness will depend upon the arresting person having such grounds.

Under both sections, the arresting person must have reasonable grounds for believing that a power of summary arrest is necessary for one of a number of specified reasons.

As one would expect, the constable's powers are wider than that of other persons in a number of respects:

• the constable's powers extend to arrest for *any offence* whereas the powers of other persons are confined to arrest for the more serious category of *indictable offences*;

- even then, the other person may only make the arrest where it is not reasonably practicable for a constable to make it;
- the constable has a broader list of reasons which can make out the necessity for the arrest (extending to such matters as highway obstruction, public decency, and child protection, in addition to the ascertaining of the person's identity);
- the constable may arrest persons for future offences (which are about to occur) whereas other persons can only arrest for present offences (which are occurring) or past offences (which have occurred).

### 3.2.1 Arrest without warrant by constables (section 24)

A constable may arrest without warrant for any offence where:

(i)  he has reasonable grounds for believing that it is necessary to arrest the person for any of these reasons:
- to ascertain the person's name or address (including where he has reasonable grounds for doubting that he has been provided with real details);
- to prevent the person causing physical injury to himself or another or suffering it;
- to prevent the person causing loss or damage to property;
- to prevent the person committing an offence against public decency (although this is confined to cases where members of the public going about their normal business cannot reasonably be expected to avoid the person);
- to protect a child or vulnerable person from the person in question;
- to allow the prompt and effective investigation of the offence or conduct of the person;
- to prevent any prosecution for the offence being hindered by the disappearance of the person; *and*
(ii)  the person is, in fact, about to commit an offence, or is in the act of committing an offence, or has committed an offence (whether or not the constable has reasonable grounds to suspect those matters); *or*
(iii)  the constable has reasonable grounds for suspecting that the person is about to commit an offence, or is in the act of committing an offence, or has committed an offence (whether or not the person, in fact, is guilty of such misconduct).

Guidance is contained in Code G as to the statutory power of arrest and, in particular:

- the interpretation of the grounds and the meaning of the 'necessity criteria' set out in (i) above (Code G 2.4–2.9);
- the meaning of the phrase 'reasonable grounds for suspecting' in (iii) above. Code G, Note for Guidance 2 states: 'There must be some reasonable, objective grounds for the suspicion, based on known facts or information which are relevant to the likelihood the offence has been committed and the person

to be questioned committed it' (See also Code C, Note for guidance 10A and the parallel terrorism provision at Code H, Note for guidance 10A; both in the same form as Code G, Note for guidance 2 but relate to cautions);

• records to be made of arrest in the arresting officer's pocket book or by other methods (Code G 4).

Note that the arrest must be 'necessary' for one of the reasons stated above. There have in recent years been a slew of cases in which it has been successfully argued that an arrest was unnecessary, and therefore unlawful, because the suspect was prepared voluntarily to assist the police with their investigations: see eg *C, R (on the application of) v 'A' Magistrates' Court* [2006] EWHC 2352 (Admin).

### 3.2.2 Arrest without warrant by other persons (section 24A)

A person other than a constable may arrest without warrant another person for an indictable offence where:

(i)   he has reasonable grounds for believing that it is necessary to arrest the person for any of these reasons:
   • to prevent the person causing physical injury to himself or another or suffering it;
   • to prevent the person causing loss or damage to property;
   • to prevent the person making off before a constable can assume responsibility for him; *and*

(ii)  it appears to the person making the arrest that it is not reasonably practicable for a constable to make it instead; *and*

(iii) that other person is in the act of committing an indictable offence or has committed an indictable offence (whether or not the arresting person has reasonable grounds to suspect those matters); *or*

(iv)  the arresting person has reasonable grounds for suspecting that the other person is in the act of committing an indictable offence, or has committed an indictable offence (whether or not that other person, in fact, is guilty of such misconduct). An indictable offence is defined in the Interpretation Act 1978, Sch 1: it includes both 'indictable only' and 'triable either way', ie both offences (a) which are only triable in the Crown Court and (b) offences which are triable in both the Magistrates' Court and in the Crown Court.

### 3.2.3 The meaning of 'reasonable grounds to suspect' in sections 24 and 24A

#### The three part test

The meaning of this phrase was explained by Woolf LJ in *Castorina v The Chief Constable of Surrey* The Times, 15 June 1988; Local Government Reports, 30 March 1996, 241 (where it is fully reported) at p 248 (in a passage quoted in part in *Chapman v Director of Public Prosecutions* 89 Cr App R 190 at p 198):

I suggest that, in a case where it is alleged that there has been an unlawful arrest, there are three questions to be answered:

(1) Did the arresting officer suspect that the person who was arrested was guilty of the offence? The answer to this question depends entirely on the findings of fact as to the officer's state of mind.

(2) Assuming the officer had the necessary suspicion, was there reasonable cause for that suspicion? This is a purely objective requirement to be determined by the judge if necessary on facts found by a jury.

(3) If the answer to the two previous questions is in the affirmative, then the officer has a discretion which entitled him to make an arrest and in relation to that discretion the question arises as to whether the discretion has been exercised in accordance with the principles laid down by Lord Greene MR in *Associated Provincial Picture Houses Ltd v Wednesbury Corporation* [1948] 1 KB 223.

In *Associated Provincial Picture Houses Ltd v Wednesbury Corporation* [1948] 1 KB 223, Lord Greene MR described the concept which has become known as 'Wednesbury reasonableness':

a person entrusted with a discretion must, so to speak, direct himself properly in law. He must call his own attention to the matters which he is bound to consider. He must exclude from his consideration matters which are irrelevant to what he has to consider. If he does not obey those rules, he may truly be said, and often is said, to be acting 'unreasonably'. Similarly, there may be something so absurd that no sensible person could ever dream that it lay within the powers of the authority. Warrington LJ in *Short v Poole Corporation* ([1926] Ch 66 at p 901) gave the example of the red-haired teacher, dismissed because she had red hair. That is unreasonable in one sense. In another sense it is taking into consideration extraneous matters. It is so unreasonable that it might almost be described as being done in bad faith; and, in fact, all these things run into one another (at p 229).

## The meaning of suspicion

The classic statement of the meaning of the word suspicion in the context of the phrase 'reasonable suspicion' is that of Lord Devlin in *Hussein v Chong Fook Kam* [1970] AC 942, (PC) at p 948:

Suspicion in its ordinary meaning is a state of conjecture or surmise where proof is lacking: 'I suspect but I cannot prove'. Suspicion arises at or near the starting-point of an investigation of which the obtaining of prima facie proof is the end. When such proof has been obtained, the police case is complete; it is ready for trial and passes on to its next stage. It is indeed desirable as a general rule that an arrest should not be made until the case is complete. But if arrest before that were forbidden, it could seriously hamper the police. To give power to arrest on reasonable suspicion does not mean that it is always or even ordinarily to be exercised. It means that there is an executive discretion. In the exercise of it many factors have to be considered besides the strength of the case.

*Hussein* was considered in *Metropolitan Police Comr v Raissi* [2008] EWCA Civ 1237, in which it was stated that the threshold for the existence of reasonable grounds for suspicion is low.

## The duty to make preliminary enquiries

Purchas LJ in *Castorina* said this (at p 246):

> There is ample authority for the proposition that courses of inquiry which may or may not be taken by an investigating officer before arrest are not relevant to the consideration whether, on the information available to him at the time of the arrest, he had reasonable grounds for suspicion. Of course, failure to follow an obvious course in exceptional circumstances may well be grounds for attacking the executive exercise of that power under the *Wednesbury* principle.

The courts have been slow to find such exceptional circumstances: see the unreported cases referred to in R Clayton and H Tomlinson, *Civil Actions Against the Police* (3rd edn, 2003), para 5-072. It follows that, save in the most striking case where a simple enquiry is capable of verifying an explanation tendered by a person, an officer is entitled to form a reasonable suspicion on the information presently within his knowledge.

## Reliance on information or instructions provided by another

The important distinction is between information upon which an independent judgment can be made (which will suffice) and a mere instruction to arrest (which will not).

An officer's reasonable grounds to suspect did not have to be based on the officer's own observations but could arise from information he had received, even if it was subsequently shown to be false, provided that a reasonable man, having regard to all the surrounding circumstances, would regard them as reasonable grounds for suspicion; but a mere order by a superior officer to arrest would be insufficient to afford reasonable grounds for suspicion (*O'Hara v Chief Constable of RUC* (HL (NI)) 1997 AC 286).

An entry in the police national computer was capable of constituting sufficient objective justification for an arrest since an officer was clearly entitled to base the grounds for his suspicion upon information received via a police informer or from the public; although, in certain other circumstances, such as where the situation was not so urgent, the arresting officer was likely to be subject to a duty to make additional enquiries before a reasonable suspicion could be founded (*Hough v Chief Constable of Staffordshire* (CA (Civ Div)) [2001] EWCA Civ 39; (2001) 98(14) LSG 41; The Times, 14 February 2001.

In the case of information provided by others such as informants or members of the public, the reasonableness of a suspicion founded solely on such information will depend upon the reputation and reliability of the source (*Lister v Perryman* (1870) LR 4 HL 521 (HL) ('information given by one person of whom the party knows nothing, would be regarded very differently from information given by one whom he knows to be a sensible and trustworthy person')).

### Assisting another officer in detaining a suspect

In a 'hot pursuit' or public order situation, an officer may form reasonable grounds to suspect as an inference derived from the conduct of a fellow officer: see the unreported cases referred to in R Clayton and H Tomlinson, *Civil Actions Against the Police* (3rd edn, 2003), para 5-082.

### 3.2.4 Repeal of earlier statutory powers of arrest without warrant or order of court (section 26)

Any statutory powers of arrest without warrant or order of court contained in Acts preceding the passing of the Act are repealed except for preserved powers specified in Sch 2 (those in particular Acts concerned with such matters as the Armed Forces).

## 3.3 Requirement for Offenders to Attend for Fingerprinting; and Arrest in Default (Section 27)

Section 27(1)–(3) is to be repealed by the Crime and Security Act 2010, s 6 when that Act comes into force. The current s 27 applies only to those convicted, cautioned or warned for a recordable offence, and confers a power to require them, in certain circumstances, to attend for fingerprinting and to arrest them if they fail to do so. The new amendments will extend the powers to cover both those arrested or charged as well as those convicted, and provide for the taking of non-intimate samples as well as fingerprints (see further Chapter 6 below).

The law as it currently stands is as set out below.

### 3.3.1 Who may be required to attend a police station for fingerprinting?

The power (s 27(1)) is confined to a person who:

(i) has been convicted of a 'recordable offence' or been cautioned for such an offence (s 27(1B)(a)), or been warned or reprimanded for such an offence under s 65 of the Crime and Disorder Act 1998 (s 27(1B)(b)); *and*

(ii) has not at any time been in police detention for the offence (save for any time during which fingerprints were taken which were incomplete or of insufficient quality s 27(1A)); *and*

(iii) has not already been fingerprinted with respect to the investigation of the offence or the conviction (save for any fingerprints which yielded prints which were incomplete or of insufficient quality s 27(1A)); *and*

(iv)  has been convicted, cautioned, warned, or reprimanded, not longer than one month before the requirement is made (s 27(1)); *and*

(v)  has been given notice of at least seven days of the requirement (s 27(2)).

A 'recordable offence' is defined by s 118(1) as 'any offence to which regulations under section 27 above apply'. Regulations made under s 27(4) are the National Police Records (Recordable Offences) Regulations 2000 (SI 2000/1139) and the National Police Records (Recordable Offences) (Amendment) Regulations 2003 (SI 2003/2823). These specify a large number of offences concerned with such matters as public order, child safety, and licensing. Guidance is given in Code D, Note for Guidance 4A as to the offences covered.

### 3.3.2  Who may exercise the power to require a person to attend a police station for fingerprinting?

The power may be exercised by a constable (s 27(1)) or by a civilian designated as a 'detention officer' under s 38 of the Police Reform Act 2002 (Sch 4, Pt 3, para 25).

### 3.3.3  The use of reasonable force, information to be provided, records

Code D 4.6 makes it plain that (consistent with s 117) reasonable force may be used, if necessary, to take a person's fingerprints without their consent.

Code D 4.7 and D 4.8 set out the information which should be provided to the person and requires the making of a record of the fingerprinting in certain circumstances.

### 3.3.4  The power to arrest for failure to comply with a requirement to attend a police station for fingerprinting (Section 27(3))

The power is confined to constables.

## 3.4  Information to be Given on Arrest (Section 28)

Regardless of whether the fact of the purported arrest or the grounds thereof is obvious, the arrest of a person is not lawful unless, either at the time of the arrest or as soon as is practicable thereafter, the person is informed:

(i)  that he is under arrest, and

(ii)  the grounds of the arrest.

It follows that the failure to comply with this section, even when such failure appears to be inconsequential, has highly significant consequences in law. The arrest is rendered unlawful. The allegation of failure to comply with this requirement is often a feature of civil actions for false imprisonment.

Section 28(5) makes it explicit that if a person escapes before it is reasonably practicable for him to be informed of these matters, there is no requirement for the information to be given. (Presumably, the purpose is to relieve the constable of the obligation which might otherwise arise of tracking down apprehended absconders in order to render the original incomplete apprehension a lawful arrest.)

Guidance is contained in Code G as to information to be given on arrest. (Guidance in the same form, but specific to cautions, may be found in both Code C and Code H. See Code C 10.3; Code H 10.2; Code C, Note for Guidance 10B; Code H, Note for Guidance 10B).

- Code G 3.3 states the requirements of s 28. (G 3 is mostly concerned with the interrelated requirement to caution.)
- Code G, Note for Guidance 3 states: 'An arrested person must be given sufficient information to enable them to understand they have been deprived of their liberty and the reason they have been arrested, eg when a person is arrested on suspicion of committing an offence they must be informed of the suspected offence's nature, when and where it was committed. The suspect must also be informed of the reason or reasons why arrest is considered necessary. Vague or technical language should be avoided.'

The courts have provided guidance which similarly emphasizes that, provided that the gist of the important matters is conveyed, that will suffice.

- *Christie v Leachinsky* [1947] AC 573 (HL) (the case establishing the common law principle from which s 28 was derived) at p 587: 'technical or precise language' need not be used, 'the matter is a matter of substance'.
- *Chapman v DPP* (1989) 89 Cr App R 190 (DC) at p 197: 'It is not of course to be expected that a police constable in the heat of an emergency, or while in hot pursuit of a suspected criminal, should always have in mind specific statutory provisions, or that he should mentally identify specific offences with technicality or precision. He must, in my judgment, reasonably suspect the existence of facts amounting to an arrestable offence of a kind which he has in mind. Unless he can do that he cannot comply with s 28(3) of the Act by informing the suspect of grounds which justify the arrest.'

## 3.5 Powers and Procedures with Respect to Persons Arrested Elsewhere than at Police Station (Section 30)

### 3.5.1 What are the powers and procedures?

A 'designated police station' is one which, by virtue of s 35, the chief officer designates in that area to be used for the purpose of detaining arrested persons. The effect of s 30 is that there is a presumption in favour of bringing the person to a designated police station speedily but that it can be displaced either where the person can properly be released or bailed, or where the circumstances justify taking him, in the alternative, to any police station or to some other place to carry out immediate investigations. If displaced, he must be taken to a designated police station soon thereafter unless released or bailed.

The effect of s 30 may be summarized as follows.

(i) Where, at any place other than a police station, a person is arrested by a constable or taken into custody by a constable after being arrested by a person other than a constable, the person must be taken by a constable to a police station as soon as practicable after arrest (s 30(1) and (1A)) unless (a) the person is released on bail under s 30A, or (b) released without bail under s 30(7) and (7A) (ie where there are no grounds for keeping him under arrest or releasing him on bail under s 30A), or (c) a delay is necessary in order to carry out such investigations as it is reasonable to carry out immediately (s 30(10) and s 30(10A)).

(ii) The police station to which he must be taken must be a designated police station (s 30(2)) unless the following conditions apply, in which case he may be taken to any police station:

(a) in the case of a constable who works in a locality covered by a police station which is not a designated police station or a constable who is maintained by an authority other than a police authority, where it does not appear to the constable that it may be necessary to keep the person in police detention for more than six hours (s 30(3) and (4));

(b) in the case of any lone constable (who has arrested or taken the person into custody without assistance and who thereafter has no assistance available), where it appears to the constable that he will be unable to take the person to a designated police station without the person injuring either himself, the constable, or some other person (s 30(5)).

(iii) Where (in accordance with the above) the person is taken to a police station which is not designated, he must be taken to a designated police station within six hours unless he is first released (s 30(6)).

(iv) The release of a person or any delay in releasing him or taking him to a police station must be recorded (s 30(8) and (11)).

(v) Exceptions to the application of the procedures are specified in s 30(12) and (13). They include certain immigration and terrorism cases.

### 3.5.2 To whom do the provisions apply?

The provisions of s 30 apply to a constable and, subject to certain exceptions (eg the 'lone constable' provisions and the release without bail provisions) by a civilian designated as an 'escort officer' under s 38 of the Police Reform Act 2002 (Sch 4, Pt 4, para 34).

## 3.6 **The Bail of Persons Arrested Elsewhere than at Police Station ('Street Bail') (Sections 30A, 30B, and 30C)**

The Criminal Justice Act 2003 introduced a new power to release arrested persons elsewhere than at police stations, referred to in Code C as 'street bail'.

The power is free of the normal bail framework contained in the Bail Act 1976 (s 30C(3)). A person released on street bail may nonetheless be re-arrested without a warrant 'if new evidence justifying a further arrest has come to light since his release'.

### 3.6.1 **What are the terms and conditions of the power?**

(i)   The power applies to persons who, at any place other than a police station, are arrested by a constable or taken into custody by a constable after being arrested by a person other than a constable (s 30A(1)).

(ii)  Such a person may be released on bail at any time before he arrives at a police station.

(iii) A person released on bail must be subject to a requirement to attend any police station (whether designated or not) (s 30A(3), (5)).

(iv)  A person released on bail may be made subject to such conditions as the constable who releases that person on bail deems necessary:

   (a)  to secure that the person surrenders to custody;

   (b)  to secure that the person does not commit an offence on bail;

   (c)  to secure that the person does not interfere with witnesses or obstruct justice;

   (d)  for the person's own protection or interests, or, if under 17, for the person's own welfare (s 30A(3B)).

(v)   Bail conditions cannot include a requirement of a surety, security or recognizance; neither can a requirement be made that the person reside in a bail hostel (s 30A(3A)).

(vi)  The person must be given a notice in writing before he is released stating (s 30B):

   (a)  the offence for which he is arrested;

   (b)  the ground on which he is arrested;

   (c)  that he is required to attend a police station;

   (d)  any requirements imposed by any conditions of bail,

   (e)  the opportunities to vary the conditions of bail.

(vii) the police station and the time he is required to attend must be specified either (s 30B):

   (a)  in the original notice in writing; or, if it is not,

   (b)  in a further notice in writing; or, if those requirements are altered,

   (c)  in a further notice or notices in writing of any changes in the requirements.

### 3.6.2 **Who may exercise the power?**

The power may be exercised by a constable (s 30A and s 30B).

### 3.6.3 **What are the possible ultimate outcomes of street bail?**

The possibilities are (s 30C(1)):

(i) that the person is given further notice in writing that he is no longer required to attend a police station; or

(ii) in the case of a person who is bailed to a non-designated police station, that he is, within six hours, either released or taken to a designated police station; or

(iii) in the case of a person who is bailed to a designated police station, there are no further restrictions as to the way in which he is dealt with.

### 3.6.4 **How may conditions of bail be varied?**

A person who has been released on bail subject to conditions may make a request to vary those conditions to a relevant officer at the police station at which he is required to attend (the custody officer) or, where no notice specifying that police station has been given, to a relevant officer at the police station specified in the notice as that to which he may apply for the variation of those conditions (an officer not involved in the investigation unless such an officer is not readily available, in which case an officer other than the officer who granted bail unless such an officer is not readily available).

There is no restriction on the number of requests to vary conditions that may be made; however any subsequent request must be based on new information. The restrictions on the types of conditions that may be attached, and the purpose of conditions attached are as before.

Conditions may also be varied by a magistrates' court (s 30CB).

## 3.7 **The Arrest of Persons at Police Stations, Attending Voluntarily (Section 29) or by Arrest for Further Offence (Section 31)**

These sections deal with two situations in which a person already at a police station may come to be arrested:

(i) A person who has attended voluntarily at a police station without having been arrested is entitled to leave unless he is arrested; and, if a decision has been taken to prevent him from leaving at will, he must be informed 'at once' that he is under arrest (s 29).

(ii) A person at a police station as a result of being arrested must be further arrested at the police station for any other offence for which he would be liable for arrest if released (s 31).

The safeguards afforded to persons at police stations by these provisions are limited in important respects.

### 3.7.1 Persons attending voluntarily

The right to be informed of an arrest under s 29 is only triggered by the decision of an officer to stop the person from leaving the police station or, in practical terms, by a determination on the part of the person to leave. (See also Code C 3.21 which supports this view.) Up until that time, the converse does not apply: he is not entitled to be told that he is not under arrest and is entitled to leave.

However, if he is cautioned whilst not under arrest, he must at the same time be told that he is not under arrest and is free to leave (Code C 10.2).

Code D does not apply to persons attending a police station voluntarily unless they are arrested (Code C 1.10); although guidance is provided in that Code as to how they should be dealt with and their rights to legal advice and communication (Code C, Note for Guidance 1A; C 3.22). Code H treats persons attending police stations voluntarily in connection with terrorism cases in the same way (Code H, Note for Guidance 1A).

When a person attending voluntarily at a police station is arrested, the rights and obligations contained in Code C (with respect to the custody officer, a custody record, legal rights, and legal advice) become engaged (C 2.1A, 2.1, 3.1, 3.21, 3.22). Parallel provisions apply to persons attending police stations voluntarily in connection with terrorism cases under Code H (Code H 2.1, 2.2, 3.1).

### 3.7.2 Arrest for further offences

The purpose and limitations of the duty to arrest for further offences under s 31 were described in *R v Samuel* [1988] QB 615 (CA) at p 622:

> It seems to this court that the obvious purpose of that section is to prevent the release and immediate re-arrest of an alleged offender. Nor does the section impose any duty on the constable to arrest immediately. We see nothing in the section which would prevent the constable delaying arresting him until the time (if it ever arrived) when his release was imminent.

A person further arrested must be informed at the time, or as soon as practicable thereafter, that they are under arrest and the grounds for their arrest (Code C 10.3); and, unless they have already been cautioned immediately prior to arrest, they must be cautioned on being arrested unless it is impracticable to do so by reason of their condition or behaviour (Code C 10.4). Parallel provisions appear in Code H with respect to persons further arrested in terrorism cases (Code H 10.2 and 10.3.)

## 3.8 Search of Persons and Search and Entry of Premises Upon Arrest at a Place Other than a Police Station (Section 32)

This is one of the most important and frequently employed provisions permitting the search of persons or premises.

### 3.8.1 Who may exercise the powers under section 32?

The powers may be exercised by:

(i) in their entirety, by a constable; or
(ii) by a civilian designated as a 'Community Support Officer' under s 38 of the Police Reform Act 2002 (Sch 4, Pt 1, para 2A) but only with respect to the power to search the person and only with respect to a person upon whom the Community Support Officer has imposed a 'requirement to wait' under that schedule.

### 3.8.2 What power is there to search a person on arrest at a place other than a police station?

A person arrested at a place other than a police station may be searched:

(i) if the constable has reasonable grounds for believing that the arrested person may present a danger to himself or others (s 32(1)); or
(ii) if the constable has reasonable grounds for believing that the person may have concealed on him anything (a) which the person might use to assist him to escape from lawful custody, or (b) which might be evidence relating to an offence, to the extent which is reasonably required for the purpose of discovering those things (s 32(2)(a), (3), and (5)).

Code A 2.2 to 2.11 contains extensive guidance on powers of search of the person requiring reasonable grounds for suspicion. Code A 3.8 to 3.11 and 4 sets out requirements in relation to steps to be taken prior to a search (including information to be given) and recording of searches.

### 3.8.3 What is the extent of the search of the person permitted under section 32?

In the course of the search (s 32(4)):

(i) the person may be required to remove in public only the following items of clothing: an outer coat, jacket, or gloves; and
(ii) the constable is authorized to search the person's mouth.

Code A 3.5 states:

> ... A search in public of a person's clothing which has not been removed must be restricted to superficial examination of outer garments. This does not, however, prevent an officer from placing his or her hand inside the pockets of the outer clothing, or feeling round the inside of collars, socks and shoes if this is reasonably necessary in the circumstances to look for the object of the search or to remove and examine any item reasonably suspected to be the object of the search. For the same reasons, subject to the restrictions on the removal of headgear, a person's hair may also be searched in public ...

The power is limited to the extent which is reasonably required for the purpose of discovering those things (s 32(3)).

The words 'in public' imply a corollary: if taken to a place out of the public eye, the person can be required to remove items of clothing other than those specified in s 32(4).

Reasonable force may be used, if necessary, in the exercise of the power (s 117).

### 3.8.4 What may be seized or retained in the course of a search of the person under section 32?

(i) An item found following a search of the person (under s 32(1)) on the ground that the person may present a danger to himself or others may be seized and retained if the constable has reasonable grounds for believing that the person may use it to cause physical injury to himself or to any other person (s 32(8)).

(ii) An item found, other than an item subject to legal privilege (see s 10), following a search of the person (under s 32(2)(a), ie on the ground that that the person may have concealed on him anything (a) which the person might use to assist him to escape from lawful custody, or (b) which might be evidence relating to an offence), may be seized and retained if the constable has reasonable grounds for believing (a) that the person might use it to assist him to escape from lawful custody, or (b) that it is evidence of an offence or has been obtained in consequence of an offence (s 32(9)).

### 3.8.5 What power is there to enter and search premises under section 32?

Where a person is arrested at a place other than a police station for an indictable offence, any premises in which he was when arrested or immediately before he was arrested may be searched for evidence relating to the offence if the constable has reasonable grounds for believing that such evidence is in the premises (s 32(2)(b) and s 32(6)).

An indictable offence is defined in the Interpretation Act 1978, Sch 1: it includes both 'indictable only' and 'triable either way', ie both offences (a) which are only triable in the Crown Court, and (b) offences which are triable in both the Magistrates' Court and in the Crown Court.

Code B applies to searches under s 32 (see Code B 2.3(b)). In particular, the guidance contained in Code B 6 'searching premises—general considerations' is of importance. The procedural and record-keeping requirements of Code B in relation to searches (considered in greater detail in relation to Part II of the Act) apply.

### 3.8.6 What is the extent of the search of the premises permitted under section 32?

The power is limited to:

(i) in all cases, the extent which is reasonably required for the purpose of discovering any evidence relating to the indictable offence for which the person was arrested (s 32(2) and (3)); and

(ii) in the case of multi-occupational dwellings, to the search of the premises in which the arrest took place or in which the person arrested was immediately before his arrest and the common parts of the premises used by the occupier of that dwelling (whether or not the occupier is the person arrested) (s 32(7)).

Reasonable force may be used, if necessary, in the exercise of the power (s 117).

# Practical Guidance

## 3.9 Case Study 1 (Section 24 [and Section 1])

PC Smith has reasonable grounds to carry out a search under s 1 of PACE on Jones. His attempts to gain Jones' cooperation fail and PC Smith uses reasonable force to carry out the search. Jones resists and punches PC Smith in the lip causing minor bleeding. Jones finally calms down and the subsequent search reveals no unlawful or prohibited articles.

*How should PC Smith deal with the assault on him?*

Prior to 1 January 2006 the arrest of Jones would have been virtually automatic and detention authorized merely for the purpose of charging. How PC Smith will have to deal with the above scenario demonstrates the profound changes introduced by the Serious Organised Crime and Police Act 2005. Whatever the offence, the power to arrest is underpinned by necessity. Under s 24, PC Smith must have reasonable grounds to believe that one or more of the reasons specified in s 24(5) are made out. In many instances the necessity criteria will be obvious, for example where it is not possible to establish the suspect's identity or where it is clear the suspect will have to be interviewed at the station. In the above scenario, if Jones confirms his identity and is no longer violent then the most obvious necessity criteria are not present. However, it may be that Jones' arrest is necessary to allow the prompt and effective investigation of the offence. Jones may have injured his own hand or have traces of PC Smith's blood on his clothing. His arrest for the purposes of having his hand examined by a Forensic Medical Examiner and the taking of photographs and or swabs may provide PC Smith with reasonable grounds to believe arrest is necessary. The Code of Practice provides useful examples of when arrest may be necessary to allow the prompt and effective investigation of an offence (Code G 2.9(e)(i) and (ii)).

## 3.10 **Case Study 2 (Section 24)**

PC Smith is on mobile patrol and sees White driving a car along the High Street.

PC Smith was present in court three months before when White, a youth well known to local police, was disqualified for a period of 12 months for a drink-drive offence. PC Smith stops the vehicle and questions White, who adopts an aggressive and rude manner, refusing to answer questions and shouting out that he is not disqualified, his name is Clark, and he is being harassed by police.

*Can PC Smith arrest White for driving whilst disqualified?*

PC Smith must first have reasonable grounds to suspect White is committing an offence and additionally must have reasonable grounds to believe that arrest is necessary for any of the reasons mentioned in s 24(5). Police officers must bear in mind that the provisions relating to arrestable offences have been repealed and, whatever the offence, one or more of the reasons in s 24(5) must be made out.

In this case it is three months since the conviction and PC Smith should carry out checks on the Police National Computer to ensure the disqualification is still current. White may have successfully appealed against conviction or had the disqualification period reduced. Once satisfied the disqualification is current, PC Smith has reasonable grounds to suspect White of committing an offence but now, in addition, must be able to show at least one of the reasons to arrest is present. As White is known to local police, the name and address provisions provided by s 24(5)(a) and (b) are unlikely to be relevant; but in many instances, where it is not possible to establish the address and or identity of the suspect, this part of the section would provide the reason necessary to arrest.

In cases where none of the s 24(5) reasons to arrest exist, the correct procedure is to report the suspect for summons. However, in the circumstances outlined there is an identity issue. White is denying his identity and the taking of his fingerprints to compare with those when he was arrested would provide conclusive evidence that he was in fact White. Therefore, White's arrest in order to take fingerprints for the prompt and effective investigation of the offence would provide a reason to arrest (s 24(5)(e)).

4

# Detention: Part IV

---

**Law and Commentary**

**Practical Guidance**

# Law and Commentary

## 4.1 Introduction

Sections 34 to 51, which make up Part IV of the Act, set out the conditions under which a person can be held in police detention and when they must be released, the role and responsibilities of the custody officer, and importantly sets out a timetable within which decisions relating to detention and charge must be made.

Code of Practice C applies to this Part.

## 4.2 Police Detention

### 4.2.1 What is police detention?

Section 118(2) states that a person is in police detention for the purposes of the Act if he has been taken to a police station following arrest, or is arrested at the police station after attending there voluntarily and is detained there or elsewhere (other than at court following charge) in the charge of a constable.

A person is in addition to be treated as under arrest for an offence (and therefore in police detention) where he returns to a police station to answer bail (save where that bail is live link bail (s 46ZA(2)) or is arrested for failing to answer bail (s 34(7)).

Under the Police Reform Act 2002, paragraphs 22 and 34(1) and 35(3) of Sch 4 to that Act, a person is also in police detention where they have been transferred into the lawful custody of an investigating officer, or are being escorted to a police station or to any other place authorized by the custody officer.

Once in police detention, a person cannot be released except on the authority of a custody officer at the station where his detention was last authorized (s 34(3)). That custody officer must, however, release a detainee (other than one who was unlawfully at large on arrest) once he is aware that the grounds for detention have ceased to apply and that there are no other grounds on which continued detention could be justified (s 34(2)).

Section 34(1) specifies that a person arrested for an offence shall not be kept in police detention except in accordance with the provisions of the Act. The relevant provisions must be read together with Code C of the Codes of Practice. With the exception of identified classes of people set out in Code C 1.12, and those detained under the Terrorism Act, Code C 1.10 makes it clear that the Code applies to people in custody at police stations in England and Wales *whether or not they have been arrested*, as well as to those who have been removed to a police station as a place of safety under ss 135 and 136 of the Mental Health Act 1983.

Code C, Note for guidance 1A states:

> Although certain sections of this Code apply specifically to people in custody at police stations, those there voluntarily to assist with an investigation should be treated with no less consideration, eg offered refreshments at appropriate times, and enjoy an absolute right to obtain legal advice or communicate with anyone outside the police station.

It should be noted that even for the excepted classes under Code 1.12 there are minimum standards of treatment to be applied which are set out at ss 8 and 9 of Code C.

### 4.2.2 Where can a person be detained?

The primary rule is that a detained person should be held at a 'designated police station', that is, a station designated by the chief officer of police for each police area as one that appears to him to provide sufficient accommodation for the purpose of detaining arrested persons in that area (s 35(1)–(2)).

In certain circumstances, set out in s 30(4) and (5), an arrested person can be taken to and detained at a police station that is not a designated police station; however, where that occurs, the detainee must be transferred to a station that is a designated police station not more than six hours after his first arrival at a police station unless he is earlier released (s 30(6)).

All police stations are designated for the purposes of detention of a person arrested under s 41 of the Terrorism Act 2000, however such a detainee must be taken to the police station considered by the arresting officer to be 'most appropriate' (Code H Note for Guidance 1M).

## 4.3 The Custody Officer (Sections 36–40A)

### 4.3.1 Who may perform the functions of the Custody Officer?

The chief officer (or such other officer as the chief officer may direct) for the area in which the designated police station is situated must appoint one or more custody officers for each designated police station (s 36(1)–(2)). Following the implementation of the Policing and Crime Act 2009, the custody officer must be a police officer of at least the rank of sergeant; a return to the position that existed before the Serious Organised Crime and Police Act came into force, which allowed for civilians to take on this important role. Even so, circumstances may arise where an officer of any rank may have to take on the functions of the custody officer. In *Vince v Chief Constable of Dorset Police* [1993] 1 WLR 415 it was held that there was no duty to ensure that an appointed custody officer was on duty at all times. If therefore the circumstances are such that a custody officer at a designated police station cannot be readily available without undue delay, an officer of any rank may perform the functions of a custody officer (s 36(4)). However, as it is the clear intention of the Act that the roles of the custody officer and the investigating officer should be kept separate, whoever takes on the role of the custody officer should not be involved in the investigation of the offence for which the person is in police detention (s 36(5)).

Another situation that might arise is where the arrested person has been taken to a police station that is not a designated police station. There any officer who is not involved in the investigation of the offence for which he is in police detention can carry out the functions of a custody officer. If no such officer is readily available, then the officer who took the arrested person to the station or any other officer (including an investigating officer) can act as the custody officer (s 36(7)). This would clearly be a matter of last resort, however, and where this is going to occur an officer of at least the rank of inspector and who is attached to a designated police station must be informed as soon as practicable (s 36(9), (10)).

Even where a custody officer is available and on duty, some procedures such as fingerprinting or searches may be delegated to other specified persons designated under the Police Reform Act 2002; however, whoever in fact carries out the procedures, the responsibility for ensuring that all procedures are carried out correctly and in accordance with the Codes of Practice rests with the custody officer (Code C 1.13–1.16).

### 4.3.2 What are the duties of the custody officer before charge?

Whenever a person is brought to a police station under arrest, is arrested at the police station, or attends a police station to answer bail, they must be brought before the custody officer as soon as practicable (Code C 2.1A).

Code C 1.1 states that:

> All persons in custody must be dealt with expeditiously, and released as soon as the need for detention no longer arises.

The tasks of dealing with all such persons is that of the custody officer who must perform the functions attributed to him by the Act and Code C as soon as practical. Should delays occur, a note should be made in the custody record detailing the fact of the delay and the reason for it. Provided that all reasonable steps are taken to prevent unnecessary delays, and provided that any delay that does occur can be justified, then there will not be a breach of the Code.

In respect of each person in police detention, the custody officer must:

- open a custody record;
- ensure that the detainee is given his rights;
- assess whether the detainee may be a juvenile, suffer from a mental disorder, or have difficulties in communication;
- determine whether there is sufficient evidence to charge or whether the detainee needs to be kept in custody in order to secure, preserve, or obtain such evidence;

- make decisions on charging and on bail;
- ensure that the detainee is treated in accordance with the Act and the Codes.

Each of these duties is dealt with in turn below.

### 4.3.3 **The custody record**

A custody record must be opened for each person in police detention. This is an extremely important document. All information that must be recorded in accordance with the provisions of the Act and Code must be recorded as soon as practicable within it (Code C 2.1).

It should be borne in mind that the custody record is an 'open' document that must be made available to the defence. A solicitor is entitled to consult a detainee's custody record as soon as practicable after his arrival at the police station (Code C 2.4), the detainee and his legal representative must be given a copy of the record on request at any time within 12 months after he has left police detention or has been taken before a court (Code C 2.4A), and shall in addition be permitted to inspect the original custody record on giving reasonable notice (Code C 2.5).

All entries in the custody record must be timed and signed by the maker unless he reasonably believes that to disclose a name might put him in danger (Code C 2.6, 2.6A), or the case is linked to the investigation of terrorism (Code H 2.8). In either case it is sufficient for the maker to use a warrant or other identification number.

It is the custody officer's responsibility to ensure that the custody record is accurate and complete (Code C 2.3).

### 4.3.4 **Rights of detainees**

All detainees have three basic rights under Code C which can be exercised at any time. They are:

- the right to have someone informed of their arrest;
- the right to consult privately with a solicitor and the provision of free legal advice;
- the right to consult the Codes of Practice.

The detainee must be told about these rights in clear terms at the outset of their detention, and must also be served with a written notice setting out in addition to those rights the arrangements for obtaining legal advice, their right to a copy of the custody record, and the caution (Code C 3.2). A further written notice setting out the detainee's 'entitlements whilst in custody' should also be served. Those entitlements are detailed in the Notes for Guidance at 3A and B.

In certain circumstances, set out in Annex B to Code C and considered in more detail in Chapter 5 below, a detainee's right to have someone informed of their arrest and the right to obtain free legal advice may be delayed for up to 36 hours.

Where a person has attended the police station voluntarily to assist the police they are entitled to leave at will unless subsequently arrested. They must be told that they are not under arrest and are not obliged to remain at the police station, but that if they do so then they are entitled to free and independent legal advice (Code C 3.21).

### 4.3.5 Assessment of the detainee

The first task of the custody officer is to assess the arrested person. The custody officer is required to carry out an assessment of any potential risks that the detainee may pose, whether to himself or to the custody staff. In order to discharge this function properly the custody officer may need to consult with others, for example the arresting officer or a health care professional, should carry out a check on the Police National Computer, and should consult Home Office Circular 32/2000 which provides detailed guidance on the conduct of a risk assessment. The custody officer is responsible not only for initiating the assessment, but also for implementing any measures required as a consequence (Code C 3.6–3.10).

Persons arrested under s 41 Terrorism Act 2000 may present special risks, not only to custody staff but to any individual who comes into contact with the detainee. Code H 3.6 imposes a duty on the custody officer to obtain information from the investigation team in order to be able properly to assess and minimize any such risk.

Where it appears to the officer that the person may:

- be mentally disordered or otherwise mentally vulnerable;
- be under the age of 17; or
- have difficulty hearing, speaking, or understanding English,

then that person will fall within a special group of detained persons for whom there are additional provisions that must be complied with whilst they are in police detention. These are considered as a separate topic in Chapter 7.

### 4.3.6 Charging

As soon as practicable after an arrested person arrives at the police station, or in the case of a person arrested at the police station, as soon as practicable after his arrest, the custody officer must determine whether he has before him sufficient evidence to charge that person with the offence for which he was arrested, and may detain him at the police station for such period as is necessary to enable him to do so (s 37(1), (10)). In making that determination the custody officer will invariably rely on the information given to him by the arresting officer; he is entitled to do so, and to assume that the arrest was a lawful one.

Where the custody officer considers that there is insufficient evidence to charge, the detained person must be released (either with or without bail) unless the custody officer has reasonable grounds for believing that detention without charge is necessary in order to 'secure or preserve evidence relating to an offence for which he is under arrest or to obtain such evidence by questioning him' (s 37(2), (3)). This may include an interview, search, or identification procedure.

Where authorization to detain is given, the custody officer must, as soon as practicable, make a written record of the grounds for the detention (s 37(4)). Unless the person to be detained is incapable of understanding what is being said to him, asleep, violent or likely to become violent, or is in urgent need of medical help or attention, then the record of the grounds for his detention must be made in his presence and he must be informed by the custody officer of those grounds (s 37(5), (6), Code C 3.23).

Where the custody officer determines that he does have sufficient evidence to charge the person arrested with the offence for which he was arrested, then s 37(7) provides the custody officer with five options. They are that the person arrested shall be:

- released without charge and on bail for the purpose of enabling the Director of Public Prosecutions (DPP) to make a decision under s 37B;
- kept in police detention for the purpose of enabling the DPP to make a decision under s 37B;
- released without charge and on bail but not for s 37B purposes;
- released without charge and without bail; or
- charged.

Although s 37(7A) states that the decision as to which of the above routes to follow is that of the custody officer, in making that decision custody officers must comply with guidance issued by the DPP (s 37A(3)).

### What amounts to 'sufficient evidence'?

Paragraph 1.1 of the Director's Guidance on Charging states that the Guidance is to be applied when the custody officer determines that there is sufficient evidence in accordance with the 'Threshold Test'; that is, where in all the circumstances of the case there is at least a reasonable suspicion against the person of having committed an offence and that, based on the information available at the time of charge, it is in the public interest to proceed.

### If there is sufficient evidence in accordance with the threshold test, what must the custody officer do then?

Under the Guidance, Crown Prosecutors will be responsible for deciding whether and what to charge in all indictable only, either way, or summary offences save for those specified within the Guidance which may be charged or cautioned by the police without reference to a Crown Prosecutor (Guidance para 3.1).

The offences which may be charged by the police are set out in para 3.3. Most minor offences under the Road Traffic Acts, Bail Act offences, offences committed under bylaws, and summary offences punishable with a term of imprisonment of three months or less fall within this category.

Pending full implementation of the Guidance, the police may also determine the charge in any either way or summary offence where it appears to the custody officer that a guilty plea is likely and that the case is suitable for sentencing in the magistrates' court (para 3.2(3iii)).

It is probable that there will be amendments to the Guidance before too long in order to give effect to the coalition government's pledge to give power to the police to make the charging decisions in all but the most complex or sensitive of cases; these are likely to include those offences currently set out in Annex A to the Guidance, which must always be referred to a Crown Prosecutor for a decision on charging. They include offences which involve racial, religious, or homophobic aggravation, offences of domestic violence, offences under the Sexual Offences Act 2003 in which either the defendant or the complainant is under 18 years, offences involving persistent young offenders, and certain other specific offences.

Where the Threshold Test has been passed and it appears that the charge will be one which, in accordance with the Guidance, will be determined by a Crown Prosecutor, the custody officer must ensure that the investigating officer consults the Duty Prosecutor as soon as practicable. If the Prosecutor is unable to make an immediate decision on the information available at that time, then where the person is suitable for bail, the custody officer may release the detained person on pre-charge bail, with or without conditions in accordance with s 37(7)(a) to enable the DPP (acting through the Crown Prosecution Service (CPS)) to decide whether and with what offence the person should be charged (s 37B(1); Code C 16.1B; Guidance para 8.4).

Thereafter the custody officer must act in accordance with the decision made by the DPP by either charging the person, issuing a caution, or by giving written notice to the person that he is not to be prosecuted as applicable.

There may be circumstances where, although the custody officer feels that there is sufficient evidence to charge, nevertheless it is not thought appropriate to do so at that stage—where there are outstanding enquiries or investigations to be conducted, for example. In those circumstances, the custody officer may release the detained person under s 37(7)(b). Following the implementation of the Police and Justice Act 2006, conditions may be attached to bail.

Where the police consider that the Threshold Test is met in a case other than an indictable only case and determine that it is in the public interest to administer a caution, reprimand, or final warning, they may do so without referring the case to the Crown Prosecutor, although it would be a sensible precaution to consult with the CPS first (Guidance 9.1, 2).

## (i) Flow diagram on charging decisions

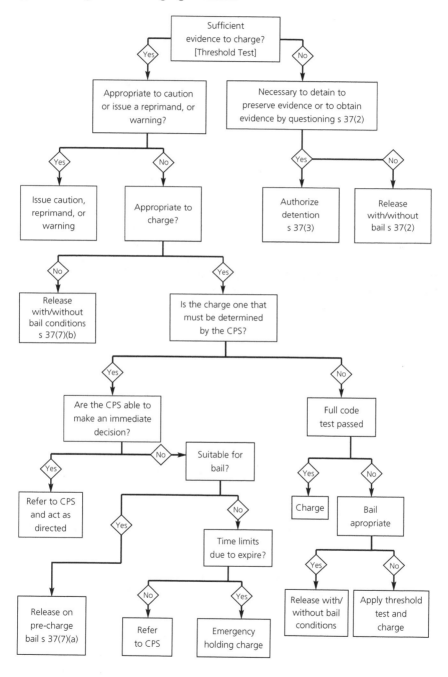

### Additional tests to apply when charging

Where the custody officer makes the charging decision, the 'Full Code Test' must be applied, that is that (following a review of the evidential material provided) there is enough evidence to provide a realistic prospect of conviction and that it is in the public interest to proceed. It may be, however, that the evidential material required to apply the full code test is not yet available. In such circumstances and where it is not proposed to release the detained person on bail after charge, then the threshold test should be applied (Guidance 3.11).

Clearly it takes time to report to, consult with, and obtain a decision from the CPS. Section 37(6) has been amended to enable an arrested person to be kept in detention whilst this takes place. This provision cannot, however, be used to extend the period of time in which a person can be kept in police detention, should be relied upon only where a quick decision on charge can be expected, and only where the release of the person on bail pending a decision has been considered to be inappropriate. Moreover, the custody officer may, on the authority of an inspector, charge in 'emergency cases' where the charging responsibility lies with a Crown Prosecutor, but where it has not been possible to consult with a Crown Prosecutor prior to the expiry of any applicable time limits and where it is proposed to seek a remand into custody (Guidance 3.12).

Any decision by a custody officer to charge will be subject to review by a Crown Prosecutor.

### 4.3.7 **Bail**

Section 38(1) requires that where a person arrested for an offence, otherwise than under a warrant endorsed for bail, is charged with an offence, the custody officer shall order his release from police detention with or without bail.

There are a number of exceptions to this requirement. They are:

- where there is doubt about the arrested person's real name or address;
- where the custody officer has reasonable grounds for believing that the person arrested will fail to answer bail;
- where, in the case of a person arrested for an imprisonable offence, the custody officer has reasonable grounds for believing that detention is necessary to prevent the commission of further offences;
- where detention is necessary to enable a sample to be taken from the arrested person under s 63B (testing for the presence of Class A drugs)—but only for a period of up to six hours after charge;
- where, in the case of a person arrested for an offence which is not an imprisonable offence, the custody officer has reasonable grounds for believing that detention is necessary to prevent physical injury to another person or to prevent loss of or damage to property;

- where the custody officer has reasonable grounds for believing that detention is necessary to prevent the person arrested from interfering with the administration of justice or with the investigation of an offence;
- where the custody officer has reasonable grounds for believing that the detention of the person arrested is necessary for his own protection;
- the offence with which the person is charged where the charge is murder.

An arrested juvenile may additionally be refused bail if the custody officer has reasonable grounds for believing that he ought to be detained in his own interests (s 38(1)(b)(ii)).

In determining whether or not there exist reasonable grounds to believe that the person arrested will fail to answer bail, commit further offences, injure another person, or cause loss or damage to property, or interfere with the administration of justice, the custody officer must have regard to:

- the nature and seriousness of the offence;
- the character, antecedents, associations, and community ties of the arrested person;
- the arrested person's previous bail record;
- the strength of the evidence together with any other relevant consideration (s 38(2A)).

Where a custody officer authorizes the continued detention of a person who has been charged, he shall as soon as practicable make a written record of the grounds for his detention in the presence of the person charged and shall at the same time inform him of those grounds (s 38(3), (4)).

The requirement to inform the person charged of the reasons for his detention and to make a written record of the grounds in his presence does not apply where the person charged is:

- incapable of understanding what is said to him;
- violent or likely to become violent;
- in urgent need of medical attention.

Release on bail from detention may be with, or without conditions which must be both relevant and necessary (see further below). Where the release on bail is pre-charge, the police have no power subsequently to vary those conditions. Where therefore, a person breaches the conditions imposed pre-charge and is again released on bail, any conditions attached must be the same as they were previously.

### 4.3.8 **Treatment**

It is the duty of the custody officer to ensure that all persons in police detention at the police station are treated in accordance with the Act and the Codes, and that all matters which are required by the Act and Codes to be recorded are recorded in the custody records (s 39(1)), save that where the custody of a detained person has been transferred by the custody officer to an investigating officer or to an officer who has charge of that detained person outside the police station, then that other officer will bear the responsibility of ensuring that he is treated in accordance with the provisions of the Act and the Codes, and on returning the detained person to the custody of the custody officer, must confirm that the Act and Codes have been so complied with (s 39(2), (3)).

That the responsibility for the care and treatment of a detained person falls squarely on the custody officer's shoulders is made clear by s 39(6). Where an officer of a higher rank than the custody officer, or in the case of a staff custody officer any police officer or police employee, gives directions relating to a person in police detention which are at variance with any decision made or action taken, or which would have been made or taken by the custody officer in the performance of a duty imposed upon him by the Act, then the custody officer must at once refer the matter to an officer of at least the rank of superintendent or above.

The provisions relating to the care and treatment of detained persons are to be found in Codes C 8 and 9 and are dealt with further in Chapter 5.

## 4.4 Reviews

Periodic reviews of the detention of each person held in police detention in connection with the investigation of an offence must be carried out by a 'review officer' throughout the period in which a person is detained, both before and after charge. In basic terms, the review officer must ask himself is the person's continued detention really necessary? When the review takes place before charge there are essentially two questions: is there sufficient evidence to charge, and if not, is the person's continued detention necessary in order to secure or preserve evidence relating to an offence or to obtain such evidence through questioning?

The identity of the review officer depends upon when the review is carried out, whether pre- or post-charge. Where the detained person has been arrested but not yet charged, an officer of at least the rank of inspector who has not been directly involved in the investigation will carry out the reviews. After charge, the review officer will be the custody officer (s 40(1)).

The importance of the role of the review officer is underlined in s 40(11); if an officer of a higher rank than the custody officer gives directions relating to a person in police detention and those directions are at variance with any decision or action made or which would have been made by the review officer in the performance of his duties, then the review officer must immediately refer the matter to an officer of at least the rank of superintendent.

A separate regime applies to those persons arrested under the Terrorism Act 2000 s 41 which allows such a person to be detained for up to 28 days. Details of the procedures to be followed can be found in Code H, section 14.

### 4.4.1 **How often must a person's detention be reviewed?**

The timetable for reviews of detention is set out at s 40(3):

- the first review shall be no later than six hours after detention was first authorized;
- the second review shall be no later than nine hours after the first;
- subsequent reviews shall take place at intervals of not more than nine hours apart.

A review may be postponed if, in all the circumstances at the time, it is not practicable to carry out the review at the specified time. Section 40(4)(b) provides two examples of when it might not be practicable to carry out a review. The first is where at the time of the review the detained person is being questioned by the police and the review officer considers that to interrupt the questioning for the purposes of a review would prejudice the investigation in connection with which he is being questioned; the second is that there is no review officer readily available at the specified time.

Where any review has been postponed, (whether for one of the reasons described in s 40(4)(b), or for any other reason) the reasons for that postponement must be recorded by the review officer on the custody record (s 40(7)), and the postponed review must take place as soon as practicable thereafter (s 40(5)).

It is important to note, however, that the postponement of a review does not affect the timetable laid down in s 40(3); a subsequent review must take place within the time limit measured from the time when the postponed review should have taken place, not from when it actually did take place.

### 4.4.2 **What tests are applied in a review of detention?**

Where the detention of a person who has not been charged is under review, the review officer applies the same tests as the custody officer under s 37(1)–(6) when first considering the necessity for detention following arrest; that is, whether there is sufficient evidence to charge, and if not, whether his detention without being charged is necessary to secure or preserve evidence relating to an offence for which he is under arrest or to obtain such evidence by questioning him. Where continued detention is authorized, the person whose detention is authorized must be informed of the grounds for that decision and a written record must be made of them in his presence, unless he is incapable of understanding what is being said to him, asleep, violent or likely to become so, or is in urgent need of medical attention (s 40(8)).

Where a person is in police detention under s 37(9) or s 37D(5), that is, where he is unfit, the purpose of the review is to establish whether he is yet in a fit state (s 40(9)).

Where the person whose detention is under review has been charged (s 38(1)–(6B)) 'Duties of custody officer after charge' apply (s 40(10)). As the

**89**

review officer will at this stage be the custody officer, the only effect of s 40(10) is to provide a timetable for the custody officer acting as a review officer to review his original decision under s 38 (whether or not to allow the person charged to be released on bail).

In all cases, the review officer must, before determining whether or not to authorize a person's continued detention, remind the detainee (unless asleep) of his right to free legal advice (Code C 15.4) and give the detained person (unless asleep) or any solicitor available at the time of the review the opportunity to make representations about that continued detention, either orally or in writing (s 40(12), (13)). There is no requirement to contact a solicitor to invite representations or to delay a review in order to allow a solicitor to attend.

The review officer may refuse to hear oral representations from the detained person under review if it appears from his behaviour or because of his condition that he is unfit to make such representations (s 40(14)).

### 4.4.3 **How may reviews be carried out?**

Reviews may be carried out in person, or by telephone, or, where facilities exist and the conditions set out in s 45A are satisfied, by use of video-conferencing.

Under s 45A an officer who is not present in the police station but who has access to the use of video-conferencing facilities enabling him to communicate with persons in that station may use those facilities to carry out:

• the functions of a custody officer under ss 37, 38, or 40 where the arrested person is at a police station that is not a designated police station, provided that the officer is a custody officer at a designated police station; and
• a review under s 40(1)(b)—review of a person arrested but not charged by an officer of at least the rank of inspector.

Where video-conferencing facilities are used for the purpose of carrying out a s 40 review, the detained person or his solicitor must still be given the opportunity to make representations either through the video-conferencing facilities or in writing by fax or e-mail. A record of the review must be made in the custody record, but the obligation for making that record may be delegated to another officer.

Where video-conferencing facilities do not exist or it is not practicable to use them, a review may be carried out by telephone (s 40A). Again, the obligations relating to the making of records are retained but transferred to another officer, and an opportunity for representations to be made must again be provided, either orally over the telephone to the review officer, or in writing where facilities exist for the immediate transmission of those written representations (fax or e-mail).

A record must be made in the custody record of the fact that the detainee was reminded of his right to free legal advice, the grounds for and extent of any delay in a review, the reasons for and details surrounding a telephone review, and the outcome of any review, extension, or application to extend (Code C 15.12–15.16).

## 4.5 **Limits on Detention (Section 41)**

The basic rule set out in s 41 is that no person shall be kept in police detention for longer than 24 hours after the time (referred to as 'the relevant time') at which he arrived at the relevant police station, or the time of arrest, whichever is the earlier. To this basic rule there are a number of variations:

- where a person is arrested outside England and Wales, the 24 hours runs from the time at which he arrives at a police station in England or Wales in the police area in which the offence is being investigated, or 24 hours after his entry into England or Wales, whichever is the earlier (s 41(2)(a));
- where a person attends at a police station either voluntarily or in the company of a constable without having been arrested, and is arrested at the police station, the 24 hours runs from the time of his arrest (s 41(c));
- where a person attends a police station to answer bail under s 30A, the 24 hours runs from the time he arrives at the police station (s 41(ca));
- where a person's arrest is sought in area A but he is arrested in area B although not questioned there, the 24 hours runs from the time at which he arrives in the first police station in area A or from the time 24 hours after the time of his arrest whichever is the earlier (s 41(3));
- where a person is in police detention in area A but his arrest is sought in area B and he is taken to area B for the purposes of investigation without having previously been questioned, the 24 hours runs from the time 24 hours after he leaves the place at which he was detained in area A or the time at which he arrives at the first police station in area B, whichever is the earlier (s 41(5));
- where a person in police detention is removed to hospital for treatment, any time during which he was questioned shall count towards the 24 hours but any other time (whether whilst in hospital or on journeys to and from it) shall not form part of the calculation (s 41(6));
- where a person already under arrest is arrested for a further offence under s 31, any calculations taken from the time of arrest are taken from the time of the original not subsequent arrest (s 41(4)).

On the expiry of the 24-hour limit, a person who is in police detention but who has not been charged must be released, with or without bail, unless an extension of the 24-hour period has been authorized under ss 42 or 43 (s 41(7), (8)).

Where an extension period has been authorized, and a detained person has been released, the time limits cannot be circumvented by re-arresting without a warrant for the original offence unless there is new evidence justifying such a re-arrest or that re-arrest comes as a result of a failure to answer to police bail under s 46A (s 41(9)).

## 4.6 **Extensions of Detention (Sections 42–44)**

The 24-hour period may be extended after the second review to up to 36 hours where an officer of the rank of at least superintendent who is responsible for the police station at which the person is being detained has reasonable grounds for believing that:

- the detention of the person without charge is necessary to secure or preserve evidence relating to an offence for which he is under arrest or to obtain such evidence by questioning him;
- an offence for which he is under arrest is an indictable offence; and
- the investigation is being conducted diligently and expeditiously (s 42(1)).

Where the extension period authorized expires less than 36 hours after the relevant time, a further extension period up to that time limit may be authorized if the authorizing officer is satisfied that the conditions set out above still apply (s 42(2)).

The extension period cannot be authorized retrospectively, neither can it be given in early anticipation that an extended period of time might be needed. Section 42(4) states that no authorization to extend up to 36 hours shall be given more than 24 hours after the relevant time, or before the second review of detention under s 40 has been carried out.

Again, the detained person must be told of his right to free legal advice and he (if fit to do so) or his solicitor (if available) must be given the opportunity to make representations either orally or in writing before the decision to authorize continued detention is made.

A detainee cannot be held incommunicado for longer than 36 hours. Where, therefore, continued detention is authorized, and where the detained person has not previously exercised his right under s 56 to have someone informed of his arrest, or under s 58 to consult with a solicitor, the authorizing officer must:

- inform him of that right;
- decide whether he should be permitted to exercise it;
- record the decision in the custody record; and
- if the authorizing officer has refused to permit the detained person to exercise those rights, record the grounds for that decision in the custody record.

After the expiration of the 36-hour period, if the detained person has not yet been charged he must be released from custody, with or without bail, unless a warrant of further detention has been obtained in accordance with s 43.

If he is released, he cannot be re-arrested without warrant for the same offence unless new evidence justifying such a course of action has come to light, or unless the arrest is carried out under s 46A, failure to answer to or comply with conditions of police bail.

### 4.6.1 **Warrants of further detention**

If further time is required to hold a person in detention in order to secure, preserve, or obtain evidence through questioning for an indictable offence, an application can be made on oath by a constable to a magistrates' court for a warrant of further detention authorizing the keeping of that person in police detention for a further period of up to 36 hours.

The application can only be heard where it is supported by an information, where a copy of that information has been given to the detained person, and where the detained person has been brought before the court for the hearing (s 43(2)).

The information must state:

- the nature of the offence;
- the general nature of the evidence;
- what inquiries have already been carried out and what further inquiries are proposed;
- the reasons for believing that the continued detention of the person is necessary for the purposes of such further inquiries (s 43(14)).

The detained person is entitled to be legally represented at the hearing, although may be kept in police detention during any adjournment of the case necessary in order to obtain that legal representation (s 43(3)).

The application may be made at any time before the expiry of the 36 hours after the relevant time. There is a degree of leeway permitted to cover the situation in which it is not practicable for the court to sit at the time when ordinarily the application would be made; in these circumstances s 43(5)(b) allows a further six hours after the expiry of the 36-hour limit within which the application must be made. The person may be kept in police detention during this extra period but a note must be made in the custody record of that fact and the reasons for it (s 43(6)).

Police must be careful not to regard the extra six hours grace as forming part of the ordinary time limits; if an application is made after the expiry of the 36-hour period and it appears to the magistrates that it would have been reasonable to have made the application prior to the expiry of that period, 'the court shall dismiss the application' (s 43(7)). Regard should be had to Note 15D which states that an application to a magistrates' court for a warrant of further detention or extension under ss 43 or 44 should be made between 10am and 9pm, and if possible during normal court hours.

The task of the magistrates' court is to consider whether they are satisfied that there are reasonable grounds for believing that a person's further detention is justified. To conclude that it is and that a warrant should be issued, they must be satisfied of three things:

- that the detention is necessary to secure or preserve evidence relating to an offence for which he is under arrest or to obtain such evidence by questioning him;

- that the offence is an indictable offence; and
- that the investigation is being conducted diligently and expeditiously (s 43(5)).

Where the magistrates' court is not so satisfied at the time of the application they may adjourn the hearing (although the period of that adjournment must not exceed the expiry of the original 36-hour period) or refuse the application (s 43(8)).

If the application is refused, the person concerned must either be charged or released with or without bail within 24 hours from the relevant time or before the expiry of such longer period of time as has been authorized under s 42 (s 43(15), (16)).

No further application may be made unless supported by new evidence (s 43(17)).

Where the application is granted a warrant of further detention will be issued authorizing the person to be kept in police detention for the period stated in it which shall be for the period that the magistrates' court deems appropriate having regard to the evidence before it, but which shall not exceed 36 hours (s 43(10)–(12)).

Prior to the expiry of the warrant, the person to whom it relates must be charged or released either with or without bail unless the warrant is extended.

### 4.6.2 **Extension of warrants**

Where, having heard an application on oath supported by an information, a magistrates' court is satisfied that there are reasonable grounds for believing that the further detention of a person to whom the application relates is justified, the court may further extend the application of the warrant for such period as it thinks fit, but which shall not be longer than 36 hours or end later than 96 hours after the relevant time.

If a warrant is extended for a period that brings the total period of detention to less than 96 hours, the court may further extend the warrant until that maximum period is reached (s 44(1)–(4)).

## 4.7 **Detention after Charge (Section 46)**

Section 46 sets out the procedure and timetable for bringing a person who has been kept in police detention following charge, or who is detained by a local authority under s 38(6), before a magistrates' court.

The primary aim is that such a person should be brought before the magistrates' court in the same local justice area as the police station at which he was charged as soon as practicable, and in any event no later than the first court sitting after he is charged with the offence.

Where, however, the court is not due to be sitting that day or the following day, or where the person is taken to a magistrates' court in an area other than that in which the police station at which he was charged is situated, then s 46 provides for the 'designated officer' for the relevant local justice area to make arrangements for a magistrates' court to sit.

## 4.8 **Bail and Arrest (Sections 46A and 47)**

Where a person has been released on bail with a duty to re-attend at the police station but fails to do so at the appointed time, that person may be arrested without warrant (s 46A(1)).

Where a person has been released on bail under s 37, s 37C(2)(b), or s 37CA(2)(b), he may be arrested without warrant if a constable has reasonable grounds for suspecting that he has breached his bail conditions.

Conditions may be attached to a grant of bail where a person is released either before charge under s 37—release on bail for a charging decision to be made, or for any other reason, or after charge under s 38(1). Any conditions attached must be relevant and proportionate, and limited to those necessary to secure the person's surrender to custody, prevent reoffending whilst on bail, and to ensure that the person does not interfere with witnesses or otherwise obstruct justice. Where the person is under 17, conditions may also be imposed for that person's welfare or in their own interests. A condition may not be imposed of residence in a bail hostel, neither can any surety, security or recognizance be taken (Explanatory notes to Police and Justice Act 2006). Any conditions that are imposed may, on application, be varied by a magistrates' court (s 47(1E)).

Where bail is granted, that bail may be either to appear before a magistrates' court on a date not later than the first court sitting after he has been charged (unless the case cannot be accommodated until a later date), or to re-attend at the police station, whether for a live link preliminary hearing under s 57C of the Crime and Disorder Act 1998, or for any other reason, unless written notice is given that he need not attend at that time (s 46(3)–(4)).

# **Practical Guidance**

## 4.9 **Case Study**

Jones, a 19-year-old youth, is arrested for burglary by DC Potts and taken to the police station where detention is authorized at 11am by the custody officer, Sergeant Brown.

*It is now 4pm and Jones has been in custody for five hours. What are Sergeant Brown's responsibilities in respect of reviewing Jones's detention?*

As Jones has not at this stage been charged Sergeant Brown should ensure that before the expiry of six hours from when detention was authorized an officer of not less rank than inspector is notified of the need to review Jones's detention.

*Sergeant Brown discovers the duty inspector is engaged at a serious incident and will not be available for some hours. The chief inspector volunteers to carry out the review but must do so immediately as he has to leave the station. How should Sergeant Brown deal with this situation?*

It is not necessary to wait for the expiry of six hours before the first review and Sergeant Brown should use the chief inspector to carry out the initial review of detention. It should be noted that the nine-hour period in respect of the next review commences at the time of the first review and not after six hours. Therefore if Jones's detention is reviewed at 4pm the next review should take place not later than 1am the next day.

*Having completed all his enquiries DC Potts asks Sergeant Brown to charge Jones with burglary. How should Sergeant Brown deal with this request?*

Sergeant Brown should first of all decide whether the 'Threshold Test' is met; that is, whether there is at least a reasonable suspicion against Jones that he has committed an offence and that it is in the public interest to proceed. He must then consider whether or not it would be appropriate to charge Jones or whether in the circumstances of the case the matter could be dealt with by issuing a caution, reprimand or warning. If Sergeant Brown considers that the Threshold Test is met and that it would be appropriate to charge then, even though the decision on charge is a matter for him under s 37(7A) nevertheless, Sergeant Brown must comply with the guidance issued by the DPP under s 37A(3) and given the nature of the offence, he should refer the matter to the CPS for a charging decision and act as directed by them.

*Jones is charged with burglary and DC Potts suggests that bail would not be appropriate as Jones is unlikely to attend court. How should Sergeant Brown deal with the question of bail?*

Sergeant Brown is obliged by s 38 of PACE to release Jones either with or without bail unless one or more of the conditions in s 38(i)–(vi) is satisfied. Sergeant Jones should ascertain from DC Potts on what basis he considers Jones will fail to appear at court and decide whether this and any other relevant information provide him with reasonable grounds to conclude that Jones will indeed fail to appear at court. If so satisfied, then Sergeant Jones may refuse to bail Jones and keep him in custody pending a court appearance.

*If Sergeant Brown decides to bail Jones but is then ordered by the detective chief inspector to keep Jones in custody, how should he deal with this situation?*

This would be a difficult situation for any custody officer to deal with but Sergeant Brown's duties are clear. As the detective chief inspector's order is at variance with a decision made in the performance of Sergeant Brown's duty under the detention provisions of the act, then he should respectfully refuse to carry out the order. Sergeant Brown should then refer the matter to an officer of at least the rank of superintendent responsible for that station (s 39(6)). The superintendent or above will then be responsible for deciding whether Jones is given bail. Sergeant Brown should comply with the superintendent's decision and ensure a full entry is created in the custody record.

*How should Sergeant Brown respond if the detective inspector at the station offered to carry out the review?*

Sergeant Brown should ascertain if the detective inspector has had any direct involvement in the case. If not, then there is no reason why a detective officer of the appropriate rank should not carry out the review. If the detective inspector has had direct involvement then he or she cannot act as a reviewing officer for that particular case.

# 5

# Treatment: Part V

**Law and Commentary**

**Practical Guidance**

# Law and Commentary

## 5.1 Introduction

Sections 53 to 65 form Part V of the Act which is entitled 'Questioning and Treatment of Persons by the Police'. Part V encompasses disparate but important provisions relating to the rights and treatment of detainees, interviews, and identification.

Sections 53 to 55 provide for the detainee to be searched, both to ascertain what items the person searched is in possession of, but also to assist in identifying the detained person. At the end of Part V ss 60 to 64 provide the police with the power to take fingerprints, impressions of footwear, intimate and other samples, photographs, and to test the detainee for the presence of Class A drugs.

In between these two 'bookends' are provisions giving rights to the detainee; notably the right to have someone informed of their arrest and the right to legal advice. The sections of the Act are expanded upon substantially in Code C of the Codes of Practice which also sets out minimum standards for the conditions in which a person is held in police detention. In addition, it is in Code C (rather than in the substantive sections of the Act) that there can be found the extremely important provisions relating to police interviews.

Juveniles and other vulnerable detainees, referred to in the Code as 'special groups' have additional rights and safeguards applicable to their detention.

For ease of reference and convenience the provisions relating to interviews, identification, and vulnerable witnesses are dealt with in separate chapters. This chapter is concerned with the rights and treatment of detainees.

## 5.2 Rights of Detainees

As was seen in Chapter 4 above, all detainees, whether brought to the police station under arrest or arrested at the police station having gone there voluntarily, have the same three basic rights under Code C which can be exercised at any time. They are:

- the right to have someone informed of their arrest;
- the right to consult privately with a solicitor and the provision of free legal advice;
- the right to consult the Codes of Practice (Code C 3.1).

The detainee must be told about these rights in clear terms at the outset of their detention, and must also be served with a written notice which sets out:

- those rights;
- the arrangements for obtaining legal advice;

- the right to a copy of the custody record after leaving police detention; and,
- the caution (Code C 3.2).

Each detainee should also be given a 'notice of entitlements' which lists their entitlements whilst in custody to, for example:

- reasonable standards of physical comfort;
- adequate food and drink;
- access to toilets and washing facilities, clothing, medical attention, and exercise where practicable (Code C 3.2; Note for Guidance 3A).

Foreign nationals or citizens of independent Commonwealth countries must be told that they have the right to communicate at any time with their High Commission, Embassy, or Consulate, and the right to have their High Commission, Embassy, or Consulate informed of their whereabouts and the grounds for their detention (Code C 3.3; Code C 7).

Juveniles, the mentally disordered or otherwise mentally vulnerable, and those who have difficulty communicating (whether because of disability or for any other reason) have a substantial number of additional rights and safeguards. These are covered in detail in Chapter 8.

Although the rights set out in the Act and Codes relate to detainees, Code C 1A makes it clear that those who are not in detention but who are voluntarily present at the police station in order to assist in an investigation 'should be treated with no less consideration'. In particular they should be offered refreshments and have 'an absolute right' to obtain legal advice or to communicate at will with anyone outside the police station. In addition, if they are not arrested but cautioned in accordance with Code C 10, they must be told that they are not under arrest and are not obliged to remain at the police station, and informed that if they do remain, then they are entitled to free and independent legal advice (Code C 3.21).

Code C 8 sets out the standards to be applied for accommodation: cells must be adequately cleaned, heated, and ventilated; clean bedding, toilet and washing facilities, and meals must be provided; where practicable outdoor exercise should be offered; and additional restraints kept to a minimum.

Code C 9 provides for the care and treatment of detainees. All detainees should be visited every hour (more frequently if any risks were identified on risk assessment); clinical attention should be obtained as soon as practicable where requested by the detainee or where it appears to the custody officer that the person appears to be suffering from a physical illness or mental disorder, is injured, or for any other reason appears to need clinical attention; arrangements must be made to provide medication or other treatment as directed; and any complaints made by the detainee must be reported as soon as possible to a senior officer (inspector or above) not connected with the investigation.

Code C does not apply to those detained under the Terrorism Act 2000 (C 1.11). Code H applies to such detainees who, it is recognized, may be held in detention for long periods of time and may have special needs. The provisions emphasize the need to offer appropriate exercise, food, clothing and reading materials as well as the need to provide the detainee with the opportunity to carry out religious observance.

### 5.2.1 **Right to have someone informed when arrested**

Section 56 provides a detainee with the right, if he so requests, to have one friend, relative, or other person 'known to him or who is likely to take an interest in his welfare' told of his arrest and detention.

The right is exercisable by the detainee, not only when first arrested and held in police custody, but if he is transferred from one place to another (eg between different police stations), on each transfer (s 56(8)).

Although the right is only exercisable on request, the detainee must be informed by the custody officer of the existence of the right and asked if he wants to exercise it (Code C 3.5).

If the detainee does choose to exercise his right to have someone informed, his request must be carried out as soon as practicable (s 56(1)).

Code H provides additional entitlements for a person detained following arrest under s 41 of the Terrorism Act 2000. Such persons may be detained for lengthy periods and where possible should be allowed visits from family and friends as well as from 'official visitors' (Code H 5.4, Note for Guidance 5B, 5C).

### What if the named person cannot be contacted?

If the person nominated by the detainee cannot be contacted, then he may name up to two alternative persons. If neither of those are contactable further attempts can be made at the discretion of the custody officer or investigating officer (Code C 5.1).

If the detainee is unable to nominate someone who is readily contactable, Note for Guidance 5C urges the police to themselves consider who may be able to offer advice or support.

### Are there any circumstances in which the exercise of the right can be delayed?

An officer of the rank of at least inspector can authorize a delay for up to 36 hours from the relevant time (as defined in s 41(2)) where the person is in police detention for an indictable offence, and he has reasonable grounds for believing that informing the named person of the arrest will:

- lead to interference with or harm to evidence connected with an indictable offence; or
- lead to interference with or physical injury to other persons; or
- lead to the alerting of other persons suspected of having committed an indictable offence but not yet arrested for it; or

- hinder the recovery of any property obtained as a result of such an offence; or
- hinder the recovery of the value of the property constituting the benefit to a detainee of his criminal conduct (as defined in Part 2 of PACE) (s 56(5), (5A); Annex B 1, 2).

Where a delay for any of the above reasons is authorized, that authorization must be confirmed in writing and the detainee informed of the reasons as soon as practicable. The decision and the reasons for it must also be noted in the detainee's custody record. As soon as the grounds for authorizing delay cease to exist, the detainee must be asked whether he wants to exercise this right and have his custody record noted accordingly (Annex B 6).

## Additional entitlements to contact

In addition to the right conferred by s 56, the detainee is also entitled to himself telephone one person 'for a reasonable time' and must be provided with writing materials if he wishes to write a letter (Code C 5.6).

If necessary, an interpreter should be provided to assist with the translation, either of the phone call or letter (Note for Guidance 5A).

There is no obligation on the custody officer to inform the detainee directly of these entitlements, however they must be set out in the notice of entitlements which must be given to the detainee under Code C 3.2

If the detainee chooses to exercise these privileges he must be informed in advance that the letter may be read or the phone call listened to and the details of any such communication (save where between the detainee and a solicitor) may be given in evidence (Code C 7).

## Can these entitlements be delayed?

The entitlements conferred by Code C 5.6 may not only be delayed but may be refused if the person is detained for any arrestable or indictable offence, and an officer of the rank of inspector or above considers that communication by letter or telephone may result in one of the consequences as set out in s 56(5) and (5A) and repeated in Annex B (hindrance of the investigation of the offence or recovery of the value of the benefit to the detainee of his criminal conduct).

They may also be delayed or refused if the person is detained under the Terrorism Act 2000 and Annex B paras 8 and 9 of Code C applies.

As well as contact made by the detainee with someone outside, it may be that a friend, relative, or any other person interested in his welfare may themselves seek information about the detainee's whereabouts. Unless reasons for withholding this information apply (as above), then the information shall be given if the detainee agrees (Code C 5.5). Moreover, at the custody officer's discretion and subject to practicalities, the detainee may receive visits (Code C 5.4).

A record must be kept of any communications made or refused (Code C 5.8).

## 5.2.2 **Right to legal advice (Section 58)**

Section 58(1) provides every person arrested and held in custody with the right, if he so requests, to consult with a solicitor at any time. The consultation may be in person, by telephone, or in writing, but must be in private (Code C 6.1).

A qualification to this right comes in Code H 6.5 where in certain circumstances an officer of the rank of Commander or Assistant Chief Constable may give a direction that a detainee arrested under s 41 of the Terrorism Act 2000 may only consult with a solicitor within the sight and hearing of a 'qualified officer'. Even for such detainees it is recognized that the right to consult privately with a solicitor is fundamental and would only exceptionally be interfered with (Code H, Note for Guidance 6I).

Note for Guidance 6B2 draws a distinction between the procedure to be followed where a detainee is willing to pay for legal advice, and that where publicly funded advice is sought. However, it was considered that it was inappropriate for the custody officer to enquire of detainees whether they intended to pay privately for legal advice. Consequently the procedure now to be followed is for the detainee to be asked whether they want a named solicitor and for that name to be passed to the Defence Solicitor Call Centre (DSCC) who will, where appropriate, contact that nominee. In all other cases, the DSCC will determine whether legal advice should be limited to telephone advice (non-imprisonable offences, arrests on warrant or for breach of bail, drink-driving allegations) or whether a solicitor should attend in person. Attendance may be appropriate not only in the more serious cases, but where it is proposed to carry out an interview or identification parade, where the detainee is eligible for assistance from an appropriate adult, where the detainee is unable to communicate over the telephone, and where there has been an allegation of serious police maltreatment.

The right to legal advice is of fundamental importance. The custody officer must not only inform the detainee of the right at an early stage, but must provide him with written details of the arrangements for obtaining such advice and ask him whether or not he wishes to exercise that right (Code C 3.5).

Moreover, posters in English, Welsh, and the main minority ethnic or European languages advertising the right to legal advice should be displayed in a prominent position not only in the charging area of each police station as required by Code C 6.3, but wherever such an advertisement is likely to be helpful and it is practicable to do so (Code C, Note for Guidance 6H).

It is important that nothing is said to a detainee to influence his choice of solicitor or to dissuade him from seeking legal advice (Code C 6.4).

If the detainee decides that he does not wish to exercise his right to consult with a solicitor he should be reminded that he can speak to a solicitor on the telephone. If he continues to decline legal advice he should be asked why and any reasons given noted on the custody record (Code C 6.5).

He is not, however, obliged to give any reasons and should not be pressed to do so (Code C, Note for Guidance 6K).

Even if a detainee declines legal advice on being initially offered it, the right continues throughout his time in police detention and can be exercised at any time. He must in addition be reminded of his entitlement at specified points throughout his detention, in particular before interview, and on detention reviews.

If a solicitor attends the police station to see a particular detainee, that person must be advised of that fact and asked if they would like to see the solicitor, even if he has previously waived his right to legal advice (Code C 6.15).

Where such a request is made the fact of the request and the time at which it was made must be noted in the custody record and the request complied with as soon as practicable (s 58(2), (4)).

### Can access to legal advice be delayed?

Compliance with the request may be delayed for the same reasons as set out in s 56 and Code C, Annex B above in relation to the right not to be held incommunicado but only where the officer who authorizes that delay has reasonable grounds for believing that the solicitor will do something which will result in one of those consequences, in which case, the detainee must be allowed to choose another solicitor.

The fact that an authorization to delay notification of arrest under s 56 has been given does not necessarily mean that a delay in access to legal advice will also be authorized.

Code C, Note for Guidance B3 notes that a decision to delay access to a nominated solicitor will be rarely made, and only where it can be shown that the detainee is capable of misleading the solicitor, and that 'there is a more than substantial risk' that the detainee will be able to pass information that will lead to one of the specified consequences.

Delay in providing access to legal advice can only be authorized by an officer of the rank of superintendent or above (s 58(6), (8)).

Where authorization for a delay is given, it must be confirmed in writing and the detainee must be informed of the reasons for the decision which must be noted in his custody record.

The detainee must be informed that he may exercise his right to consult privately with a solicitor as soon as the reason for authorizing the delay has ceased to exist, and in any event within 36 hours of the relevant time as defined in s 41(2) (s 58(11), (5); Code C, Annex B 6).

## 5.3 Searches (Section 54)

### 5.3.1 Searches of detained persons

Section 54(1), supplemented by Code C 4.1, provides that the custody officer 'shall ascertain everything that a person has with him' when in police detention.

This does not, however, mean that the detainee must be searched; s 54(6) makes it clear that a search need only be carried out where the custody officer considers it necessary to do so in order to fulfil his duty under subsection (1). Similarly, the extent of the search should be limited to that which the custody officer considers necessary for the purposes of subsection (1) and may not in any event involve the removal of more than the outer clothing.

Where a search is carried out, it should be conducted by a constable of the same sex as the person to be searched (s 54(8), (9)).

### What can be seized?

Anything found on a search can be seized and retained (s 54(3)). However, clothing and 'personal effects' (defined in Code C 4.3 as 'items a detainee may lawfully need, use or refer to while in detention' but not including cash or valuables) may only be seized where the custody officer believes that the detainee may use them:

- to cause physical injury to himself or another person;
- to damage property;
- to interfere with evidence; or
- to assist him to escape (s 54(4)(a)).

A search for any items that may be used for such purposes may be conducted at any time during which a person is in police detention, whether at a police station or elsewhere (s 54(6A)).

Clothes and personal effects may also be seized where the custody officer has reasonable grounds to believe that they may be evidence relating to an offence (s 54(4)(b)).

In the event that anything is seized, the person searched must be told the reasons for the seizure unless that is impracticable either because the detainee is violent or at risk of becoming violent, or is incapable of understanding what is said (s 54(5)).

If any item of clothing or personal effects is seized, the reason for that seizure must be recorded (Code C 4.5).

There is no mandatory requirement to keep records of any other items seized; however, in practice a record is made, both of property noted to be in possession of the detainee and of the items seized which is usually attached to or forms part of the custody record. Where any record is made, the detainee should be invited to check and sign it (Code C 4.4).

In the event that clothing is seized, whether under this section or for any other reason (eg hygiene), adequate replacement clothing must be provided (Code C 8.5).

Section 43(2) of the Terrorism Act 2000 additionally allows a constable to search a detainee arrested under s 41 of the same Act, for anything that may constitute evidence that he is a terrorist (Code H, Note for Guidance 4D).

Where the person has attended the police station in answer to live link bail, a constable may 'at any time' search that person or any article in that person's possession. No authority appears to be necessary for such a search to take place, neither is there any requirement to record that a search has taken place or that items have been seized as a result, although a record 'may' be made. Where items are found which may:

- jeopardize the maintenance of order in the police station;
- put the safety of any person in the police station at risk;
- be evidence of, or in relation to, an offence,

such items may be seized and retained where necessary

- for use as evidence at trial;
- for forensic examination or for investigation in connection with an offence;
- to establish its lawful owner where there are reasonable grounds for believing that it has been obtained in consequence of the commission of an offence (s 54B).

### 5.3.2 **Intimate searches**

An intimate search is defined in Annex A of Code C of the Codes of Practice as 'the physical examination of a person's body orifices other than the mouth'.

As it is recognized that such searches carry with them inherent risks, Note for Guidance A1 advises that every reasonable effort should be made to persuade the detainee to hand the item over voluntarily and without the need for a search. In such circumstances a registered medical practitioner or nurse should be available to provide assistance to the detainee.

An intimate search can only be carried out where an officer of at least the rank of inspector has reasonable grounds for believing that the detainee has concealed upon him either:

- something which he could use to cause physical injury to himself or others whilst in police detention or the custody of a court; or
- a Class A drug which he intended either to supply to another or to export,

and the officer has reasonable grounds for believing that such an item or drug cannot be found without an intimate search (s 55(1), (2)).

Note for Guidance A2 makes it clear that authorization for an intimate search should only be given where there are real grounds for believing that a relevant item has been concealed and where there is no other alternative to such a search taking place.

### Where can an intimate search be carried out?

An intimate search can only be carried out at:

- a police station (but not where it is a drug search);
- at a hospital;

**107**

- at a registered medical practitioner's surgery; or
- at some other place used for medical purposes (s 55(8)).

## Who may carry out the search?

An intimate search should be carried out by either a registered medical practitioner or a registered nurse unless an officer of at least the rank of inspector considers that this is not practicable, in which case the search can be carried out by a constable of the same sex as the person to be searched (s 55(5)–(7)).

At least two people in addition to the detainee should be present during the search; subject to that, the number of people present should be kept to the minimum necessary and (unless a medical practitioner or nurse) should be of the same sex as the person searched (Annex A6).

Although the Act provides for a constable to carry out a search if it is 'not practicable' for the search to be carried out by a registered medical practitioner or nurse, Note for Guidance A4 states that this should only happen as a matter of last resort and in circumstances where the authorizing officer is satisfied that the detainee might use the article for causing a 'sufficiently severe' injury to himself or another.

Where the intimate search is a search for a Class A drug intended by the suspected person for supply or export, then the search may only be carried out by a registered medical practitioner or nurse at a hospital, surgery, or other medical premises.

Anything found in the course of the search which the custody officer believes may be used by the detainee:

- to cause physical injury to himself or another person;
- to damage property;
- to interfere with evidence; or
- to assist him to escape,

may be seized and retained (s 55(12)(a)).

A custody officer may also cause to be seized anything found which he has reasonable grounds for believing may be evidence relating to an offence (s 55(12)(b)).

The detainee must be told the reason for the seizure unless he is violent, at risk of becoming violent, or is incapable of understanding what is said to him (s 55(13)).

## Records

Authorization for an intimate search must be given or confirmed in writing (s 55(3)).

Section 55(10) states that a record must be made in the custody record of the parts of the body that have been searched and the reason for that search.

Annex A7 expands the requirement for documentation to include details of who carried out the search, who was present, why it was thought that the article could only be removed through an intimate search, and the result.

If the intimate search was carried out by a police officer instead of a registered medical practitioner or nurse, the reasons must be recorded (Code C, Annex A8).

### 5.3.3 X-rays and ultrasound scans

Where an officer of the rank of inspector or above has reasonable grounds for believing that a suspect who has been arrested and is in police detention may have swallowed a Class A drug that he was, prior to his arrest intending either to supply to another or to export, then that officer may authorize either an x-ray and/or an ultrasound scan to be carried out on the suspect (s 55A(1)).

An x-ray or scan authorized under this section must be carried out by a 'suitably qualified person'—that is, a registered nurse or registered medical practitioner, and only at a hospital, surgery or other medical premises.

An x-ray or ultrasound can only be carried out if the suspect gives his consent in writing. However, if he fails to give his consent without good cause, then that refusal can be taken into account by a judge in deciding whether there is a case to answer or to grant an application for dismissal, and a court or jury can draw adverse inferences from the refusal.

The suspect must be warned of these consequences by a police officer or member of police staff; the appropriate words of the warning can be found at Note K2 of Annex K of Code C.

A refusal may be taken into account against the suspect only where that refusal was without good cause. Understandably, perhaps, a suspect may have some concerns about the effects of undergoing an x-ray or ultrasound scan. Note for Guidance K1 therefore suggests that the medical practitioner or nurse should explain the procedure to the suspect to allay any concerns. As well as being good medical practice, following such a course of action may have the added benefit of removing any argument of 'good cause' for refusing to undergo the procedure.

A record must be made in the custody record of the authorization, the grounds upon which it was given, the warning, written consent (or refusal), and details of where the procedure took place, who carried it out, who else was present, and the result.

### 5.3.4 Strip searches

There are no substantive provisions in the Act governing the conduct of strip searches which are instead dealt with only in the Codes of Practice at Code C, Annex A.

A strip search is defined at Annex A9 as 'a search involving the removal of more than outer clothing [which] includes shoes and socks'. The purpose of a strip search is to remove an article which the detainee would not be allowed to keep. A strip search should not be carried out as a matter of routine, but only where it is reasonably considered that such an article might have been concealed.

The Code is silent on the question of authorization although, as with other searches, the authority of the custody officer should be obtained. However, as a strip search may well result in the establishment of reasonable grounds to carry out an intimate search, the safer course may well be to obtain the authority of an Inspector. As with the conduct of an intimate search, a strip search should be carried out quickly and with sensitivity. Annex A11(d) states that 'every effort shall be made to secure the detainee's co-operation and minimise embarrassment'. Accordingly, the detainee should not have to remove all his clothes at once and should be allowed to re-dress as soon as the procedure is complete, the search must be carried out by an officer of the same sex as the detainee, and the search should take place in a private area.

Ordinarily, if the strip search will expose intimate body parts, two people other than the detainee should be present (Annex A11(c)).

Body orifices may be visually inspected but may not be touched. To do so would constitute an intimate search. If, therefore, it appears likely on visual inspection that an article is within a body orifice, then the detainee should be asked to hand the item over (Annex A11(f)). If he refuses to do so, then an intimate search will need to be authorized and conducted in accordance with s 55 and Part A of Annex A.

A record must be made on the custody record detailing the reason for the strip search, the identities of those present, and the result (Annex A12).

### 5.3.5 Searches to establish identity

A detainee may also be searched or examined in order to ascertain whether he has any identifying mark or otherwise to help facilitate identification. The provisions relating to these searches (found at s 54 and in Code D) are dealt with in Chapter 6 below.

## 5.4 Fingerprints

The provisions relating to the taking of fingerprints and impressions of footwear are dealt with in Chapter 6 below.

## 5.5 Samples (Section 63)

There are a number of provisions dealing with the taking of both intimate and non-intimate samples. As these are primarily taken for the purpose of confirming or eliminating the identification of a suspect as the offender they are more conveniently dealt with in Chapter 6, below. The exception is where a sample is taken for the purpose of ascertaining whether a detainee has taken Class A drugs; these provisions are dealt with here.

### 5.5.1 **Drug testing**

In certain circumstances, a non-intimate sample, including a sample of urine may be taken from a person in police detention in order to ascertain whether he has a specified Class A drug in his body (s 63B(1)).

Where by notification by the Secretary of State the relevant arrangements are in place (whether at a specified police station or for a police area as a whole), samples may be requested for these purposes from detainees over the age of 14. Where notification has not been given, they apply to detainees who have reached the age of 18.

The circumstances in which such a sample can be requested are where either:

- the detainee has been charged with a 'trigger offence'; or
- the detainee has been charged with an offence and an officer of at least the rank of inspector has reasonable grounds for suspecting that the misuse of a specified Class A drug caused or contributed to the offence.

'Trigger offences' are defined in Sch 6 of the Criminal Justice and Court Services Act 2000 as:

- theft, robbery, burglary, obtaining property by deception, handling stolen goods, and attempts to commit any of those offences;
- aggravated burglary, taking a motor vehicle or other conveyance without authority, aggravated vehicle taking, going equipped for burglary, theft, or cheat;
- offences under s 4, 5(2) and 5(3) of the Misuse of Drugs Act 1971—that is production, supply, possession and possession with intent to supply where the drug in question is a Class A drug;
- begging, persistent begging.

'Specified Class A drugs' are defined in the Criminal Justice (Specified Class A Drugs) Order 2001 Art 2 as:

- cocaine, its salts and any preparation or other product containing cocaine or its salts; and
- diamorphine, its salts and any preparation or other product containing diamorphine or its salts.

As a non-intimate sample cannot be taken without consent, the police can only request a detainee to give such a sample. However, failure without good cause to give a sample when requested under s 63B is a summary offence punishable with up to 51 weeks imprisonment (s 63B(8); s 63C(1)).

The detainee must be warned of the possible consequences if he fails to give consent before the sample is formally requested (s 63B(5)).

Where a sample has been taken, the information derived from it may be disclosed for the purposes of informing decisions taken about bail, supervision, and sentencing, and to ensure that the person is given appropriate advice and treatment. A non-intimate sample taken for the purposes of drug–testing cannot be used for any other purpose (eg identification).

A record must be made, in the detainee's custody record where applicable, of any authorization given under s 63B(2)(b) and the grounds for suspicion that led to that authorization.

# Practical Guidance

## 5.6 Case Study (Detainee's Rights)

Jones, a 19-year-old youth, is arrested for burglary and taken to the police station where detention is authorized at 11am. DC Potts takes charge of the case and reasonably suspects that some of the property stolen during the burglary may be at Jones's house. Fearing that if allowed to make a phone call Jones will alert others to dispose of the property DC Potts asks the custody officer, Sergeant Brown, not to allow Jones to make a phone call or contact a solicitor until a search of his house has been carried out. Jones requests a solicitor, asks that his brother is informed of his arrest, and that he be allowed to make a phone call.

*Can Sergeant Brown prevent Jones from making a phone call and contacting a solicitor?*

As Jones's brother is a person likely to take an interest in his welfare then Jones is entitled to have notification of his arrest sent to him. He is also entitled to speak on the telephone for a reasonable period and to consult and communicate privately with a solicitor at any time (s 56/58 of PACE). Sergeant Brown has a duty to facilitate these rights unless delay is authorized by the Act. Sergeant Brown cannot authorize delay himself but should ensure the necessary conditions are fully met before seeking authority from an officer of appropriate rank. The offence for which Jones is under arrest is an indictable offence so the first condition is met. Sergeant Brown should ensure that there are reasonable grounds to believe that informing Jones's brother of Jones's whereabouts, allowing Jones to make a phone call, and contacting a solicitor will hinder the recovery of any property obtained as a result of having committed burglary. In the case of preventing Jones from making a phone call and informing his brother, on the facts it is reasonable to delay communication until steps have been taken to search his premises. However, in respect of refusing access to a solicitor this is much harder to justify. There must be reasonable grounds to believe the solicitor Jones wants to contact will inadvertently or otherwise pass on a message or act in some other way that will hinder the recovery of stolen property (Code of Practice C, Annex B3). This is a difficult condition to satisfy. Only on rare occasions will a delay in access to a solicitor be justified. The Code of Practice makes clear that the fact that the grounds for delaying notification of arrest may be satisfied does not automatically mean the grounds for delaying access to legal advice will also be satisfied (Code of Practice C, Annex B5).

Only an officer of at least the rank of inspector may authorize delay in having someone informed of Jones's whereabouts and speaking to someone on the phone. In the case of delay in contacting a solicitor the authority of an officer of at least superintendent rank is required. Sergeant Brown should make a record in the custody record of the request for notification, and request to see a solicitor, and the action taken. If delay is authorized then as soon as practicable a further record should be made in the custody record of the grounds, and Jones informed of them (Code of Practice Code C, Annex B13).

*Assuming the request to delay legal advice is turned down, how should Sergeant Brown deal with a request from Jones to have legal advice from a friend who is a first year student studying law at university?*

Jones has a right to consult and communicate privately with a solicitor. The Code of Practice states that 'solicitor' means, a person holding a current practicing certificate or an accredited or probationary representative. Sergeant Brown should therefore explain this to Jones and refuse the request. He should make an entry in the custody record and remind Jones that free independent legal advice is available from the duty solicitor.

*When informed that notification to his brother is being delayed, Jones states that he is a citizen of the Irish Republic and asks that the embassy be informed of his arrest. How should Sergeant Brown deal with this request?*

Nationals of foreign countries including the Republic of Ireland may communicate at any time with the appropriate High Commission, Embassy, or Consulate. This right may not be interfered with and therefore Sergeant Brown should ensure the appropriate Embassy is informed of Jones's whereabouts and make an entry.

# Identification: Part V, Code D

# Law and Commentary

## 6.1 Introduction

Part V of the Act contains a number of important sections dealing with procedures that can take place in order to help facilitate identification, both to establish the identity of the suspect but also to identify the suspect as the offender. The methods by which a suspect may be identified are varied; searching or examining the suspect for any identifying features, taking fingerprints and footwear impressions to compare with those found at a scene, and taking physical samples (both intimate and non-intimate) from the suspect's person to obtain a DNA profile. As and when the Crime and Security Act 2010 comes into force, ss 2 and 6 of that Act will provide the police with additional powers to take fingerprints and DNA samples from people arrested, charged or convicted of a recordable offence, or who have been convicted overseas of a serious sexual or violent offence.

The comprehensive provisions concerning the identification of a suspect by witnesses are to be found, not in the Act, but in Code D which 'concerns the principal methods used by police to identify people in connection with the investigation of offences and the keeping of accurate and reliable criminal records' (Code D 1.1). Proposals are currently being drawn up to amend Code D to differentiate between the appropriate procedures to be adopted where the identifying witness is an eye-witness, and where the witness is someone who is able to recognize the suspect (eg a police officer viewing CCTV footage). Further amendments will be required to bring the Code into line with the amendments to the Act following the coming into force of the Crime and Security Act.

## 6.2 Searches to Ascertain Identity (Section 54A)

Under s 54A, a detainee (other than one detained at a police station to be searched under a stop and search power) may be searched and/or examined by a constable of the same sex as the person to be searched:

- in order to ascertain whether he has any mark that would tend to identify him as a person involved in the commission of an offence; or
- to facilitate the ascertainment of his identity.

Authority for such a search or examination can only be given by an officer of at least the rank of inspector (s 54(1)). If given orally, the authorization must be confirmed in writing as soon as practicable (s 54(4)).

### 6.2.1 When can authorization be given?

If the purpose of the examination or search is to find an identifying mark, then authorization can only be given if:

- the detainee has refused to consent to such a search or examination; or
- it is not practicable to obtain such consent, for example, where the detainee is unfit to give consent (s 54(2); Code D, Note for Guidance 5D).

If the purpose of the examination or search is to facilitate identification, then authorization can only be given where:

- the detainee has refused to identify himself; or
- the officer has reasonable grounds for suspecting that the detainee is not who he claims to be (s 54(3)).

A 'mark' includes features and injuries. An 'identifying mark' is a mark which either facilitates the ascertainment of the detainee's identity or his identification as a person involved in the commission of an offence (s 54A(12)). Where an identifying mark (as defined) is found, it may be photographed by a constable of the same sex as the person searched, either with or without the consent of the detainee (s 54A(5)–(7)).

The use to which such a photograph (which is defined to include any visual image however produced) can be put is wide. Section 54A(9) and (10) provide that a photograph of the identifying mark can be used by or disclosed to any person for any purpose related to the prevention or detection of crime, the investigation of an offence or the conduct of a prosecution whether in the United Kingdom or abroad. Examples of how a photograph might be used for such purposes are listed in Code D, Note for Guidance 5B.

A photograph taken of an identifying mark under this section may be retained but may only be used for the purposes set out above (Code D 5.6). If a person refuses to cooperate with a search, examination, or photograph, a constable may use reasonable force to search, examine, or photograph the person without his consent (Code D 5.9).

Any search or examination under s 54A should be kept to the minimum necessary to achieve the desired purpose. If it is necessary to remove more than a person's outer clothing to properly search or examine him, then the search must be carried out in accordance with the provisions of Code C, Annex A, 11 (ie strip searches) (Code D 5.10).

## 6.3 **Fingerprints (Sections 61, 63A, and 64)**

A person may give consent in writing at a police station for his fingerprints to be taken.

Fingerprints may only be taken from a person without consent in the following situations.

(a) Where a person has been detained (or, when s 2 of the Crime and Security Act 2010 is in force, is on bail) as a result of his arrest for a recordable offence or has been charged or informed that he will be reported for a recordable offence (see para 3.3.1), and either:

 (i) his fingerprints have not already been taken in the course of the investigation into the offence, or

 (ii) if they have, either they did not amount to a full set, or they were not of sufficient quality for comparison or analysis (s 61(3), (3A)).

(b) Where a person has answered to bail at a court or police station and either the court or an officer of at least the rank of inspector has given authority for them to be taken either because:

 (i) there are reasonable grounds to believe that he is not the same person as the person in whose name he is answering to bail and whose fingerprints were taken on a previous occasion, or

 (ii) the person who answers to bail himself claims to be a different person (s 61(4), (4A)).

(c) Where a person has been:

 (i) convicted of a recordable offence, or

 (ii) given a caution for the offence which he has admitted, or

 (iii) warned or reprimanded under s 65 of the Crime and Disorder Act 1998 (s 61(6)).

When the Crime and Security Act 2010 comes into force, the use of this power will require the authorization of an inspector who must be satisfied that it is necessary to take such prints to assist in the prevention or detection of crime.

Section 27 of the Act provides the police with the power to require such a person who has not previously had his fingerprints taken in the course of the investigation for the offence, or whose fingerprints (if taken) were not satisfactory to attend the police station to have his prints taken, and may arrest without warrant a person who fails to comply with this requirement. (See para 3.3 above.)

Note, however, that s 27(1)–(3) is due to be repealed when the Crime and Security Act 2010 is brought into force. That Act provides for a new Schedule 2A to be inserted into PACE, which sets out the powers to require attendance at a police station for fingerprints and/or other samples to be taken and the time limits within which such powers must be exercised. As at present, a constable may arrest a person who does not comply with the requirement to attend.

(d) Where a constable reasonably suspects that a person is committing or attempting or has committed or attempted to commit an offence and either:

 (i) the name of the person cannot be readily ascertained by the constable, or

 (ii) the constable has reasonable grounds for doubting that the name furnished by the suspect is correct.

Note that fingerprints taken under this section do not count as fingerprints taken in the course of an investigation (s 61(6A)–(6C)), and must be destroyed as soon as they have fulfilled the purpose for which they were taken (s 64(1BA)).

A person whose fingerprints are taken, whether with or without consent, must be told in advance that the prints may be subject to a speculative search (s 61(7A)).

The fact that he has been informed of the above possibility together with the reasons for taking the fingerprints must be recorded. If he is in police detention, the record must be made in the person's custody record (s 61(8)).

A speculative search may be carried out where a person has been arrested on suspicion of being involved in a recordable offence, or has been charged with or informed that he will be reported for such an offence (s 63A(1)), as may prints taken under s 61(6A) (s 63A(1ZA)).

Where a person's fingerprints have been taken in the course of the investigation but otherwise than detailed above, he may give his consent in writing to a speculative search (s 61(1C)).

Where a speculative search takes place, fingerprints or information derived from them may be checked against other fingerprints or information contained in records to which the person carrying out the check has access held by other law-enforcement agencies as listed in s 63A.

The power to take the fingerprints without consent of a person detained at a police station is only exercisable by a constable who may use reasonable force if necessary. (See s 117.)

## 6.4 **Impressions of Footwear (Sections 61A and 63A)**

A new s 61A permitting impressions of a person's footwear to be taken has been inserted by the Serious Organised Crime and Police Act 2005. The provisions mirror subsections (1), (2), (3), (3A), (7A) and (8) of s 61 which deals with fingerprints.

Section 61A(2) states that an impression of a person's footwear may be taken with consent, which must be given in writing if he is at the police station. An impression of footwear can only be taken without consent by a constable and where:

- the person is detained at a police station and has either been
- detained in consequence of his arrest for a recordable offence, or has been charged with or informed that he will be reported for a recordable offence, and either,
- he has not had an impression of his footwear taken previously in the course of the investigation of the offence or if it has, that impression was incomplete or of insufficient quality for comparison or analysis (s 61A(3), (4)).

As with fingerprints, whether the impression is taken with or without consent, the person from whom it is taken must be told in advance that it may be subject to a speculative search as described above and set out at s 63A and a record must be made in his custody record that he has been informed of this possibility (s 61A(5)).

Where the impression is taken without consent, the person must be told the reason why and the reason recorded in his custody record (s 61A(6)).

## 6.5 Samples (Sections 62, 63, 63A, and 65)

### 6.5.1 Intimate samples

An intimate sample is defined in section 65 of the Act as:

- a sample of blood, semen or any other tissue fluid, urine, or pubic hair;
- a dental impression;
- a swab taken from any part of a person's genitals (including pubic hair) or from a person's body orifice other than the mouth.

An intimate sample can only be taken from a person in police detention where the detainee has given written consent, and where the taking of the sample has been authorized by an officer of at least the rank of inspector (s 62(1)).

An intimate sample may also be taken from a person who is not in police detention where he has already in the course of the investigation provided two non-intimate samples for the same means of analysis as it is intended to subject the intimate sample (eg DNA testing), but where those two non-intimate samples have proved to be insufficient.

The person from whom the intimate sample was taken would still need to give written consent and the taking of the sample must be authorized by an officer of at least the rank of inspector (s 62(1A)).

In either case, authorization can only be given where the authorizing officer has reasonable grounds for believing that the person from whom it is to be taken has been involved in a recordable offence (see para 3.3.1 above) and that the sample will tend to prove or disprove his involvement (s 62(2)).

Where consent is sought to take an intimate sample, the person must be informed that authorization has been given, the grounds upon which that authorization has been based, and the nature of the offence in question (s 62(5)). He must also be informed that the sample may be the subject of a speculative search as described above and as set out at s 63A.

Details of the authorization, grounds, notification of the possibility of a speculative search, and consent must all be recorded in the person's custody record as soon as practicable after the sample has been taken (s 62(8)).

### By whom may the sample be taken?

If the sample to be taken is a dental impression, then it must be taken by a registered dentist. In all other cases (save a sample of urine) the sample may only be taken by a registered medical practitioner or other health care professional (s 62(9A)).

### What if consent is withheld?

If consent is refused without good cause, then in any subsequent proceedings adverse inferences may be drawn by a court, judge, or jury (s 62(10)).

The suspect must be made aware of the possible consequences and be reminded of his entitlement to free legal advice (Code D 6.3).

Note that none of the above provisions apply to the taking of a specimen for the purposes of s 4–11 of the Road Traffic Act 1988.

### 6.5.2 **Non-intimate samples**

Section 63 deals with the taking of non-intimate samples.

A non-intimate sample is:

- a sample of hair (other than pubic hair). Hair may be cut or plucked, but if the latter, a sample no bigger than is reasonably necessary. The suspect should be allowed a reasonable choice as to what part of the body the hair is taken from;
- a sample from or under a nail;
- a swab taken from the mouth or any other non-intimate part of the body;
- saliva;
- a skin impression.

Unlike intimate samples which can only be taken if they have been authorized and if the appropriate written consent has been given, a constable can use reasonable force to take a non-intimate sample without consent in a number of situations (see s 117):

(a) where the person is in police detention (or, when s 2 of the Crime and Security Act 2010 is in force, on bail) having been arrested for a recordable offence and either
  (i) he has not had the same type of sample from the same part of the body taken previously in the investigation, or
  (ii) any such sample that was taken was insufficient—(s 63(2C));
(b) where the person has been charged with or informed that he will be reported for a recordable offence and either
  (i) no non-intimate sample has been taken previously in the investigation, or
  (ii) any such sample that was taken was insufficient (s 63(3A));
(c) where a person has been convicted of a recordable offence since 10 April 1995 or is a person to whom s 1 of the Criminal Evidence (Amendment) Act 1997 applies (s 63(3B)), or, following the implementation of the Crime and Security Act 2010, has been cautioned, warned or reprimanded for a recordable offence. Under the same Act, a non-intimate sample may only be taken where a sample has not previously been taken since the conviction, caution, reprimand or warning, or such a sample was insufficient; and where

authorization for the sample has been given by an officer of the rank of inspector who is satisfied that it is necessary for the prevention or detection of crime.

(d) where a person has been detained following acquittal on grounds of insanity or finding of unfitness to plead (s 63(3C)).

A non-intimate sample may also be taken from a person who is being held in custody by the police on the authority of a court and where an officer of at least the rank of inspector has reasonable grounds for suspecting that the person has been involved in a recordable offence and that the sample will tend to prove or disprove his involvement (s 63(3), (4)).

Where a sample is taken under s 63(3B) or (3C), that sample may be taken in any hospital or other place in which he is detained (s 63A(3A), (3B)).

A non-intimate sample authorized under the above sections may not be a skin impression if an impression from the same part of the body has previously been taken in the course of the investigation, unless that previous impression was insufficient (s 63(5A)).

Where a sample is taken without consent, the person must be told the reason why the sample is to be taken, and in a case to which subsection (3) applies, the fact that authorization has been given, the grounds upon which that authorization was based, and the nature of the offence in which it is suspected that the person concerned has been involved (s 63(6)–(8)).

In all cases in which a non-intimate sample is taken, whether with or without consent, the person must in addition be told that the sample may be subject to a speculative search as described above and as set out at s 63A (s 63(8B)).

A record must be made of all the above matters which in the case of a person detained at the police station must be in the person's custody record (s 63(9)).

Where a person has been charged with a recordable offence or informed that he will be reported for such an offence and either has not had a sample taken from him in the course of the investigation, or any such sample that was taken has proved insufficient, a constable may require a person who is not in police detention or otherwise held in custody by the police to attend a police station to have such a sample taken within one month of the date of charge or information, or one month from the date upon which the investigating officer became aware that the sample that had previously been taken was insufficient (s 63(4), (5)).

Where a person has been convicted of a recordable offence and either has not had a sample taken from him since his conviction, or has had a sample taken either before or after his conviction which has proved insufficient, a constable may require such a person not being a person in police detention or custody to attend a police station for a sample to be taken within one month of the date either of his conviction or of the date when the officer in charge of the police station from which the investigation of the offence of which he was convicted became aware that a previous sample was insufficient (s 63A(5)).

Should a person required to attend the police station for a sample to be taken fail to do so, he may be arrested without warrant (s 63A(7)).

New time limits for the exercise of these powers will be provided for in the new Sch 2A to be inserted into the Act when the Crime and Security Act 2010 comes into force.

## 6.6 **Destruction of Fingerprints, Footwear Impressions, and Samples (Section 64)**

Section 14 of the Crime and Security Act 2010 will insert a new s 64 into PACE with 14 new sections following it. These amendments, which set out the framework for the retention and destruction of fingerprints and samples, give effect to the decision in *S and Marper v UK* [2008] ECHR 1581, which held that the retention of fingerprints and DNA samples from those suspected, but not convicted, of offences, was a breach of Art 8.

The law as it currently stands, pending these important changes, is as set out below.

Unless the person from whom they were taken gives his consent in writing to their retention, all fingerprints, footwear impressions, and samples must be destroyed as soon as they have fulfilled the purpose for which they were taken if either:

- they were taken in accordance with s 61(6A) (fingerprints taken from a person whose identity cannot be readily ascertained or confirmed who a constable reasonably believes to have committed or attempted or to be about to commit or attempt to commit an offence), or
- they were taken from a person in connection with the investigation of an offence but where that person is not suspected of having committed the offence, eg where they are taken for elimination purposes (s 64(3)).

As well as destroying the print, impression, or sample, any copies of fingerprints or footwear impressions must also be destroyed and any computer data relating to such prints or impressions must be rendered inaccessible (s 64(5)).

A person whose fingerprints, footwear impressions or copies of either are to be destroyed is entitled to witness their destruction and to be given a certificate confirming that access to computer data relating to them has been made impossible (s 64(6A)).

Where a person gives his consent for fingerprints, impressions, or samples to be retained which would otherwise be destroyed, it is important that that consent is an informed consent. The Notes for Guidance to Annex F of

Code D sets out the form of wording to be employed when written consent is given.

All other fingerprints, impressions of footwear, samples, and information retained from them may be retained but may be used solely for purposes relating to the prevention or detection of crime, the investigation of an offence, or the conduct of a prosecution, including speculative checks under s 63A(1) or (1C) (s 64(1A), (1B)).

## 6.7 **Photographs (Section 64A)**

Section 64A, as amended by the Serious Organised Crime and Police Act, provides the police with wide powers to photograph suspects.

A person may be photographed, with or without their consent, if they have been:

- detained at a police station;
- arrested by a constable for an offence;
- taken into custody by a constable after being arrested for an offence by a person other than a constable;
- made subject to a requirement to wait with a community support officer under para 2(3) or (3A) of Sch 4 to the Police Reform Act 2002;
- required to leave a locality under s 27 of the Violent Crime Reduction Act 2007;
- given certain fixed penalty notices as set out at s 64A(1B)(d)–(e).

The person taking the photograph may require the removal (or may, using reasonable force, remove himself) any item or substance worn on or over the whole or any part of the head or face of the person to be photographed (s 64A(2)).

Consent is not required before taking the photograph and if necessary a photograph may be taken covertly or by the use of reasonable force (Code D 5.14).

Any photograph taken may be retained and disclosed for purposes related to the prevention or detection of (any) crime, or the investigation of (any) offence or conduct of a prosecution (s 64A(4)).

The person photographed must be informed of the purpose of the photograph, the grounds on which authority has been obtained for the photograph if applicable, and the purposes for which the photograph may be used, disclosed, or retained, either before the photograph is taken, or afterwards if it is taken covertly (Code D 5.15).

A record must be made detailing the identity of the officer who took the photograph, the purpose of the photograph, whether the photograph was taken with or without consent, details of any authority given, and details of the circumstances and identities of those present where any force was used.

A person who is suspected on reasonable grounds of involvement in a criminal offence but who is at a police station voluntarily and is therefore not in police detention may also be photographed, but may not be subjected to any force in order to do so (Code D 5.21).

Photographs or other images of a person not detained must be destroyed unless the person is either charged, prosecuted, or informed that they may be prosecuted for a recordable offence; is cautioned, given a warning or a reprimand for a recordable offence (see para 3.3.1 above); or gives 'informed consent' in writing for the photograph to be retained. 'Informed consent' means that they must be fully appraised of the purposes to which that photograph could in future be put (Code D 5.22).

A photograph includes any visual image however recorded, including a video or other film (s 64A(6)).

A photograph may only be taken by a constable (s 64A(3)).

## 6.8 **Identification by Witnesses (Code D)**

The important provisions concerning the practice and procedure of the identification of a suspect by witnesses are contained entirely within Code D. The procedures are intended to test the witness's ability to identify a person they saw on a previous occasion (for example, committing an offence or at the scene of a crime), and to provide safeguards against the dangers of a mistaken identification.

The identification procedure to be adopted depends in the first instance on whether or not the identity of the suspect is known to the police. The identity of the suspect will be 'known' when there is sufficient information known to the police to justify the arrest of a person for suspected involvement in an offence (Code D 3.4).

### 6.8.1 **Identification where the suspect's identity is not known**

Such cases are covered in Code D 3.2 and 3.3 and allow for a witness to be taken to a particular place to see whether they can identify the relevant person, or for the witness to be shown photographs or other images from which an identification might be made.

The first of these situations most commonly occurs where an offence takes place in a particular locality to which the police are called and arrive within a short period of time. The witness may then be driven around that area or any other relevant place in the hope that the offender might be spotted by the witness and an identification made. Whilst Code D 3.2 allows for the fact that the circumstances in which such an identification might be made cannot be controlled in the same way as formal identification procedures, nevertheless, insofar as possible, measures should be adopted to ensure that the witness's identification is independent and to safeguard against the possibility of a mistaken identification.

Where practicable therefore:

- an accurate and legible record should be made of the first description of a suspect given by a witness before the witness is asked to make any identification;
- the witness's attention should not be directed towards any particular person save where it appears that a witness may be in danger of overlooking a possible suspect because they are, for example, only looking in one direction;
- where there is more than one witness, they should be kept separate so that independent identifications can be made;
- a detailed record should be kept by the officer or other member of police staff accompanying the witness of all the circumstances surrounding the identification.

### Photographs

In accordance with Code D 3.3 and Annex E, a witness may be shown up to 12 photographs (including drawings or computerized images) at a time and told that a photograph of the person that they saw may or may not be amongst them. They should further be told that if they cannot make a positive identification they should say so, but that they should not make a decision until they have viewed all 12 photographs.

Where a positive identification is made from photographs then no other witnesses should be asked to view the photographs but instead, as the identity of the suspect is now 'known', formal identification procedures should be held. The suspect and his legal representative must be told before any formal identification procedures that the witness has previously been shown photographs or other similar images.

Again, as with a 'street identification', measures should be put in place to ensure that any identification is made independently. So, prior to being shown any photographs at all, the supervising officer (sergeant or above) must confirm that the first description of the suspect given by the witness has been recorded; the photographs shown should, so far as possible, be of the same type; only one witness at a time should be shown the photographs; witnesses must not be allowed to communicate with each other; the witness must not be prompted or guided in their selection.

All photographs shown must be retained, whether or not a positive identification was made, and a record, signed by the supervising officer, must be kept of all the circumstances surrounding the showing of the photographs and any identification subsequently made.

### 6.8.2 Identification procedures where the identity of the suspect is known

A formal identification procedure in accordance with Code D must be held where:

- the identity of the suspect is known to the police (that is, where there is sufficient information to justify the arrest of an individual on suspicion of involvement in an offence); and
- the suspect is available (that is, available and willing to take part in an identification procedure that it is practicable to arrange within a reasonable period of time); and
- the suspect disputes being the person the witness claims to have seen; and either
- the witness has purported to identify the suspect prior to formal procedures (eg in a street identification or from photographs); or,
- there is a witness available who has not previously been given the opportunity to identify the suspect who may be able to make an identification (Code D 3.12).

An identification procedure may additionally be held where the officer in charge of the investigation considers that it would be useful (Code D 3.13). An example might be where, although not positively raised as an issue by the suspect at the time of the investigation, the circumstances are such that it is clear to the police that identification will be in issue.

Where the witness has only been able to give evidence of a very general nature, whether of appearance or of clothing, but has not been able to describe any facial features, identification procedures need not be held as there would be no reasonable possibility that he would be able to make an identification (*R v Gayle* [1999] EWCA Crim 450).

Where the identifying witness recognizes the offender, and where it is not disputed that the suspect and the witness are known to each other, identification procedures will be of little value and need not be held. Some caution is needed, however, in ascertaining whether or not the purported recognition is accepted. If the suspect disputes the recognition, identification procedures must still be held (*R v Harris* (2003) 147 SJ 237, CA; [2003] EWCA Crim 174).

Proposals are currently under consideration to amend Code D by providing for new procedures to be undertaken where a witness purports to recognize a suspect. These procedures allow for a film, photograph or other medium to be shown to the witness, and for a record to be made of how and why the witness purports to be able to recognize that suspect. The typical situation envisaged appears to be where a police officer claims to be able to recognize a suspect after viewing CCTV images.

### What form can the identification procedure take?

There are three primary forms of identification procedure which in order of preference are:

- video identification;

- identification parade;
- group identification.

Whichever procedure is adopted, the suspect must be informed orally and in writing of:

- the purposes of the procedure;
- their entitlement to free legal advice;
- the conduct of the procedure, including their right to be represented;
- the first description given by any witness who is to attend the procedure;
- whether the witness has previously been shown any photographs or other images by the police.

They must also be warned that:

- they do not need to consent to or cooperate with any procedure but that if they do not their refusal may be given in evidence at court and the police may proceed to make other arrangements to test a witness's ability to identify them which could include an identification from images taken covertly;
- if they significantly alter their appearance prior to the procedure taking place, then evidence of that change may be given in court and other forms of identification considered;
- a moving image or photograph may be taken of them when they attend for the procedure.

A copy of the written notice setting out the above should be signed after reading by the suspect and retained by the officer supervising the identification (the identification officer).

## Who decides which procedure should be used?

The identification officer and the officer in charge of the investigation should consult to determine which form of identification procedure should be offered. Almost invariably, the suspect should be offered a video identification unless it is not practicable in which case the suspect should be offered an identification parade (Code D 3.14).

The suspect and his solicitor may, however, make representations why another form of procedure from that offered should take place, and if appropriate the identification officer should make arrangements for another form of procedure to take place if suitable and practicable (Code D 3.15).

Any representations made and the reasons for any resultant decisions must be recorded (Code D 3.16).

## Who is the identification officer?

The identification officer will be an officer of at least the rank of inspector who will be responsible for the arrangements for and conduct of the identification procedure. The identification officer may delegate some or all of the tasks connected with arrangements and procedures to another officer or police staff; however, he will retain supervisory control and must be able to intervene or to be contacted as necessary.

No officer involved in the investigation of the offence should act as the identification officer or otherwise take part in the procedures except as specifically provided for in the Code (Code D 3.11).

### 6.8.3 Video identification

A video identification will comprise a set of images including the suspect and at least eight other people who resemble the suspect in age, height, and general appearance. As far as possible the images will show the suspect and all other people in the same positions or carrying out the same sequence of movements under identical conditions. If the suspect has any distinctive feature—eg a scar—the feature may be concealed or replicated (electronically or otherwise) by the identification officer. Although the choice is for the identification officer, Annex A, 2A states that where a witness makes reference to a particular feature the feature should, if practicable, be replicated; if the suspect has a feature that the witness has not referred to, however, it should be concealed. The images shown must be moving images, unless the suspect does not consent, or is unavailable, or has a physical feature that can neither be concealed nor replicated. In those circumstances, any suitable still or moving images may be used. In practice the head and shoulders of each individual is shown against a plain background, face on and then, by turning to each side, in profile.

The set of images must be shown to the suspect and his representative prior to being shown to a witness and any objections to the images noted and resolved where practicable.

### Conduct of the video identification

A video identification must be carried out in accordance with the provisions in Annex A of Code D.

The suspect and his solicitor must be given reasonable notification of the time and place of the video identification and the solicitor given the opportunity to be present. If no representative is able to be present, the procedure must itself be recorded on video.

If the suspect refuses to cooperate with identification procedures or is otherwise 'unavailable', a video-identification may still be held using any suitable still or moving images, obtained covertly if necessary.

Only one witness at a time may be shown the images and steps must be taken to ensure that there is no contact or communication between a witness who has seen the images and one who has not that might compromise the independence of any identification made.

The witness must be told before viewing the images that the person they saw on a specified earlier occasion may or may not appear in the images and that if they cannot make a positive identification they should say so.

If the witness is or appears to be mentally disordered or vulnerable or a juvenile, then a 'pre-trial support person', who should not themselves be or be likely to be a witness, should be present (Code D 2.15A; Code D, Note for Guidance 2AB).

Care must be taken not to prompt an identification whether by directing the witness's attention to a particular image, reminding him of his earlier description, or in any other way. A witness may, however, view all or some of the images as many times as they like and may ask to have a particular image frozen for them to study.

All relevant material used in the course of a video identification must be retained and kept securely.

A record must be kept on forms provided for the purpose of the conduct of the video identification procedure and of any identification made.

### 6.8.4 Identification parades

Code D 3.7 defines an identification parade as one where 'the witness sees the suspect in a line of others who resemble the suspect'. Identification procedures must be conducted in accordance with Annex B of Code D.

Before the identification parade begins, the suspect must be given a reasonable opportunity to have a solicitor or friend present, must be reminded of the procedures for the conduct of the identification parade, and must be cautioned.

The parade must be conducted in the presence and hearing of the suspect and his solicitor or friend unless the parade is being conducted in a room with a screen separating the participants in the parade from the identifying witness, in which case everything said to or by any witness at the parade must be said in the solicitor's or friend's presence unless the parade is itself recorded on video.

The parade must consist of at least eight other people in addition to the suspect who shall as closely as possible resemble him in age, height, and general appearance; any identifying features (such as a scar or tattoo) should, with the agreement of the suspect and his solicitor, be concealed (however this can be removed at the request of the viewing witness).

Separate parades should be held for each suspect save that where there are two suspects of a similar appearance they may stand on the same parade with at least 12 other participants.

If there are any objections from the suspect or his solicitor about the arrangements for or composition of the parade, steps should be taken to resolve those objections where practicable; any objections should be formally recorded.

The suspect may choose where in the line to stand and may if he wishes alter his position after each witness has viewed the parade.

### Conduct of the parade

As with any other form of identification procedure, care must be taken to ensure that any identification made is independent. Arrangements must therefore be made to ensure that witnesses do not communicate with each other, see any member of the parade including the suspect, or see or be reminded of any picture or description given of the suspect.

The witness must be told that the person that they saw on a specified earlier occasion may or may not be present, and if they cannot make a positive identification they should say so. They should be asked to look at each person on the parade at least twice before making any identification.

If a witness viewing the parade wishes to hear a participant speak, or see them move, or adopt a particular posture they must be asked whether they can make an identification on the basis of physical appearance alone. They should also be reminded if they ask to hear a particular person speak that participants have been chosen on the basis only of physical appearance. The person may then, however, be asked to speak, move, or adopt the position requested by the witness. They may also be asked to remove anything used to conceal an identifying mark at the request of the witness.

If the witness is mentally disordered, vulnerable, or a juvenile, a pre-trial support person should be present but must take care not to prompt an identification by the witness.

It not infrequently occurs that a witness purports to make an identification after the parade has ended. Where this occurs, the suspect and his solicitor should be informed, and consideration given to allowing the witness a further opportunity to identify the suspect.

A video recording of the conduct of the parade should normally be made and must be made where the parade takes place behind a screen separating the parade from the viewing witness and where no representative of the suspect is present.

A formal record must be made of the details of the conduct of the parade and any comments made by either the witness or the suspect about the parade or identifications.

### 6.8.5 Group identification

A group identification is when the witness sees the suspect in an informal group of people, and may take place either with the suspect's cooperation and consent, or covertly.

Group identifications will usually be carried out in a public place; they should only be conducted in a police station or prison if the group identification involves a prison inmate, or for other reasons of safety, security, or practicability.

A group identification will by its very nature be harder to control than a video identification or identification parade; nevertheless the same principles of fairness and independence apply to group identifications as much as to the more formal procedures. The measures to be adopted to ensure so far as possible that these can be achieved are set out in Annex C to Code D.

## Location

The location chosen for the group identification to take place should be one in which there are likely to be groups of people (whether stationary or moving) that the suspect can join, and where the numbers and types of people that are likely to be present might be reasonably expected to include those of a broadly similar appearance to the defendant. Annex C4 gives as examples of locations that might fit these requirements a shopping centre or a bus or railway station.

Where the identification is to take place covertly, then the choice of location will of necessity be restricted to those public places known to be frequented by the suspect.

## Conduct

The suspect should, unless the procedure is to be conducted covertly, be given a reasonable opportunity to have a solicitor or friend present who will remain with the witness and those conducting the procedure. The witness and others observing the procedure (including a pre-trial support person if applicable) may be concealed from the group they are observing if it assists with the conduct of the identification, or the witness may be asked to himself move among the group and to take a closer look where practicable to confirm any identification made.

The suspect will be told to join a group of people, whether moving or stationary, and may choose and/or change his position within that group.

The person conducting the parade shall remind the witness that the person they saw on a previous specified occasion may or may not be in the group and tell them that if they cannot make a positive identification they should say so. The witness's attention should then be directed towards the group and the witness asked to point out any person they think they saw on the previous occasion.

A witness should be allowed as long as is reasonably necessary to observe and compare members of the group before attempting to make an identification.

If the suspect unreasonably delays joining the group, or deliberately conceals himself from the witness's sight, then his conduct may be treated as a refusal to cooperate.

Only one witness at a time should view a group identification, and arrangements must be made to ensure that there is no contamination between witnesses, or that they are reminded of any picture or description of the suspect.

A video or colour photograph should be taken of the location used for the group identification either during or immediately after the procedure, or at a later date if not practicable to do it at the time.

A formal record must be made of all the details surrounding the group identification.

### 6.8.6 Confrontations

Where the identity of a suspect is known but the suspect is unavailable, for example because he has refused to cooperate, the identification officer may arrange for the suspect to be directly confronted by the witness (Code D 3.23).

A confrontation must be carried out in accordance with Annex D.

The confrontation should normally take place in a police station, and must be in the presence of the suspect's solicitor or friend unless this would cause unreasonable delay. If no representative is present, the confrontation should be recorded on video.

Prior to the confrontation taking place, the witness must be warned that the person he is about to see may or may not be the person that he saw on a previous specified occasion. The witness should then be shown the suspect and asked, 'Is this the person?'

Although the suspect's consent is not required for a confrontation to take place, no force can be used to make the suspect's face visible to the witness.

# Practical Guidance

## 6.9 Case Study 1 (fingerprints, searches, and examinations)

PC Smith is on mobile patrol and sees White driving a car along the High Street. PC Smith was present in court three months before when White, a youth well known to local police, was disqualified for a drink-drive offence. PC Smith stops the vehicle and questions White who refuses to answer questions but states that he is not disqualified and his name is Clark.

*Can PC Smith arrest White for driving whilst disqualified?*

See para 3.10 Case Study above. White's arrest in order to take fingerprints for the prompt and effective investigation of the offence would provide a reason to arrest (s 24(5)(e)).

Once at the station White's fingerprints could be taken without his consent under the provisions of s 61(3)(a) and (b) of PACE and checked against the fingerprints taken when he was arrested in respect of the original offence that led to his disqualification (s 63A(1)(b)).

*Once at the station PC Smith recalls that White, who is still denying his identity, has a distinctive tattoo on his back. When requested by the*

**133**

*custody officer to show his back, White refuses. How should this situation be dealt with?*

As an examination of White's back may facilitate the ascertainment of his identity then authority from an officer of at least the rank of inspector should be sought to carry out such an examination and photograph the tattoo. The examination and taking of the photograph may only be carried out by a police officer of the same sex using reasonable force (ss 54A and 117 PACE). As the examination will require the removal of more than outer clothing then the Code of Practice requires the examination be conducted in a place where White cannot be seen by anyone who does not need to be present or any member of the opposite sex (Code of Practice D 5.10 and C. Annex A11(a)—(g)).

## 6.10 Case Study 2 (footwear impressions)

Jones, a 19-year-old youth, has been arrested for burglary and has been taken to the police station.

*DC Potts has discovered a footprint left at the scene of the burglary and requests permission to take an impression of Jones's footwear. When asked to cooperate Jones refuses. How should Sergeant Brown deal with this situation?*

Sergeant Brown should inform Jones of the reason why an impression is needed and that the impression may be retained and may be the subject of a speculative search. In addition Jones should be informed that if he is subsequently acquitted of the burglary offence the impression will be destroyed and he may witness the destruction (Code of Practice D 4.19(a)–(c)). If Jones refuses to cooperate then as he is in custody for a recordable offence and has not previously had an impression taken of his footwear, a police officer may use reasonable force to take the impression without Jones's consent.

## 6.11 Case Study 3 (non-intimate samples)

*Jan is in custody for grievous bodily harm and gives written authority for a sample of head hair to be taken from her. DC Harley, the officer in the case, takes possession of the sample intending to take it by hand for DNA analysis. The officer misplaces the sample and requests that a further sample be obtained from the prisoner. However, Jan now refuses to give written authority and DC Harley asks Inspector Lister to authorize the use of force to take another sample. How should Inspector Lister deal with this request?*

A sample of hair is a non-intimate sample and can be taken without the appropriate consent and by use of reasonable force if necessary. However, in this case a sample of hair has already been taken and the only occasion a second sample can be taken of the same type and from the same part of the body is where the first proved insufficient. Inspector Lister should advise DC Harley that as the sample of hair was lost then without Jan's written consent no more hair may be taken from her head. He could advise that if another type of non-intimate sample, such as a nail clipping, could be used for the purposes of DNA analysis and this would tend to prove or disprove Jan's involvement in a recordable offence, then the sample can be taken with Jan's consent. If Jan should refuse to give consent Inspector Lister can authorize the taking of the sample using reasonable force (s 63 PACE; Code of Practice D paras 6.5–6.6).

## 6.12 Case Study 4 (fingerprints, use of force)

*Curtis has been charged with theft and refuses to allow his fingerprints to be taken. He has an arm injury and suffers from high blood pressure. He is aggressive and indicates he will do all he can to prevent anyone taking his fingerprints. The Forensic Medical Examiner (FME) has previously certified that Curtis is fit to be detained. PS Simpson, the custody officer, is unsure about how to deal with Curtis and seeks advice from Inspector North. What advice should Inspector North give to PS Simpson?*

Inspector North should advise PS Simpson that as Curtis is in custody and has been charged with a recordable offence then s 61 of PACE provides the power to take his fingerprints without consent. In addition, reasonable force may be used if necessary. Whilst the power is clear the actual taking of the fingerprints by force can provide real difficulties. The first priority should be to use all reasonable persuasion to encourage Curtis to give his authority and allow officers to take his fingerprints. The Codes of Practice require that certain information is given to Curtis before the fingerprints are taken and if video/audio recording facilities are available in the custody area it is sensible to ensure the giving of this information is recorded on tape. If Curtis still refuses to give his consent then in view of his condition it is good practice to call the FME to carry out an examination before any force is used. The FME should also be asked to remain whilst the fingerprints are taken. The taking of the fingerprints by force from a person who is resisting is extremely difficult and great care needs to be taken to avoid causing injury. If possible the use of force should also be recorded on video (Codes of Practice D para 4.3).

## 6.13 Case Study 5 (identification procedures)

Whilst walking home from work late at night, Lyndsey is struck from behind by a man who then steals her handbag from her and runs away across a common towards a residential area. When she has managed to recover from the shock, Lyndsey is able to make her way to a nearby pub from where the landlord calls the police on her behalf.

The police arrive within a matter of minutes and PC Swift asks Lyndsey if she can describe the person who attacked her. She states that he was in his late teens or early 20s, over 6ft, well built and was wearing dark clothing and a green 'beanie' cap; she is unable to describe any facial features. At this stage, there appear to be no other witnesses.

### What should PC Swift do?

At this stage, the identity of the attacker is not known; however Lyndsey has been able to provide a general description of the man together with a description of his clothing. The area towards which he was running is known and thanks to the prompt arrival of the police a very short time has elapsed since the commission of the offence. PC Swift should note the description given by Lyndsey and then take her on a 'drive round' the area towards which the offender made off to see whether she can identify the person who attacked her.

PC Swift puts out details of the attack and the description of the offender over his radio and begins to drive towards the residential area towards which the attacker ran. During the drive, PC Swift receives information from PC Price that a member of the public, Adam King, has observed a man discarding a handbag in Kingston Avenue, which he has handed to the police; the handbag appears to belong to Lyndsey and the detailed description given by Adam matches that given by Lyndsey.

### What should PC Swift do now?

Code D 3.2 permits the police to drive a suspect to a particular locality to see if a witness can identify the person they saw; PC Swift can therefore drive Lyndsey to Kingston Avenue and the surrounding streets in which it would appear that the offender may still be present. However, Code D 3.2(b) states that care must be taken not to direct the witness's attention to any individual unless, taking account of all the circumstances this cannot be avoided. Such an 'unavoidable' situation might exist where a suspect has already been stopped by the police and is standing with them when the witness arrives on the scene.

In a street adjacent to Kingston Avenue, Lyndsey points out a man wearing a green 'beanie' hat and dark clothing as the person who attacked her, telling PC Swift that she recognizes him because of his hat. PC Price arrives at the location moments later and arrests the man, Cyrus on suspicion of robbery.

### What duties does PC Swift have now?

PC Swift should ensure that, in accordance with Code D 3.2(e), a detailed record is made of the time, place and circumstances of the identification made, together with details of the weather, lighting conditions, whether the witness's attention was drawn to the suspect for any reason, and what comments if any were made by either the witness or the suspect.

Cyrus is searched but no stolen property is found on him. He is interviewed by DC Booth and makes no comment; however he does submit a short pre-prepared statement in which he says that he was simply walking home from a night out with friends, he never attacked anyone and is not guilty of any offence.

### What should DC Booth do?

Although he has not said so directly, it is clear from the terms of Cyrus's pre-prepared statement that he disputes that he was correctly identified by Lyndsey. Under Code D 3.12, wherever a witness has purported to identify a suspect, or there is a witness who may reasonably be able to identify a suspect, and where the suspect disputes the correctness of the identification, then an identification procedure 'shall be held'. DC Booth should therefore ask Cyrus whether he is willing to take part in an identification procedure, which should be a video identification unless such a procedure is not practicable.

Cyrus agrees to a video identification, but his solicitor, Mr Atkins, expresses concern that such a procedure may be unfair because Cyrus has a very noticeable scar running across his right cheek.

### What if anything should DC Booth do to take account of the solicitor's objection?

All the images shown on the identification video should be of people who are as like to the suspect in terms of their facial and general physical appearance as possible, and this extends to distinctive physical features. DC Booth should arrange for the images to be modified so that either all the people shown have the same scar replicated on their image, or the scar should be concealed on the image of the defendant. The choice is for DC Booth to make, however Annex A, 2A states that where a feature is referred to by a witness it should be replicated and, where it is not, should be concealed.

### Which witnesses should attend the identification procedure?

There are two potential witnesses; Lyndsey and Adam. Adam gave the police a detailed description of the man he saw discarding Lyndsey's handbag including facial features such as a scar to his cheek. There is therefore a reasonable chance that Adam will be able to make a positive identification and he should be asked to attend the procedure. As he did make a reference to the scar, DC Booth should, as stated above, arrange for all the images shown to be electronically manipulated to replicate the same scar on each person's face. Lyndsey made a street identification of Cyrus before the identification procedure; on an initial reading of Code D 3.12 therefore, she should attend the procedure. However, the same paragraph of the Code states that no identification procedure need be held if it would serve no useful purpose. Although Lyndsey gave a general description to the police and made a street identification, her identification was based upon recognition of clothing, not facial features, which she was unable to describe. Although DC Booth may feel that it is worth a chance asking Lyndsey to attend the identification procedure there is no requirement under the Act or Code for her to do so as it is highly unlikely that she would be able to make a positive identification and thus 'no useful purpose' would be achieved by requiring her to attend.

# Interviews: Part V, Code E

**Law and Commentary**

**Practical Guidance**

# Law and Commentary

## 7.1 Introduction

Perhaps surprisingly, there are no substantive provisions within the Act itself dealing with this important topic. Instead, s 60 imposes a duty on the Secretary of State to make an order requiring that interviews with suspects are tape recorded and to issue a code of practice in connection with such interviews; s 60A provides the Secretary of State with the power (as opposed to a duty) to make a similar order and to issue a code of practice for the visual recording of interviews.

The Code of Practice that applies is Code E although there are also important relevant provisions in Code C, especially Code C 10–14. Code F applies to the audio-visual recording of interviews. Both Codes E and F were updated with effect from 1 May 2010 with amendments in keeping with the advance of technology covering the use of digital recordings.

Officers who conduct interviews should also have regard to Home Office Circular 26/1995 (1995) 159 JPN 303 which provides national guidelines on the preparation of records of interviews in accordance with Code E Note for Guidance 5A.

## 7.2 What is an Interview?

An interview is defined in Code C 11.1A as 'the questioning of a person regarding their involvement or suspected involvement in a criminal offence or offences' which must be carried out under caution.

The basic rules are that:

- the interview should take place at a police station or other authorized place of detention;
- the suspect is entitled to free legal advice before and during his interview;
- the interview must be carried out under caution;
- the interview must be recorded.

It is important to recognize that *any* questioning regarding a person's involvement or suspected involvement in an offence can constitute an interview, however short that questioning may be and wherever it takes place. Accordingly an exchange between a police officer and a suspect at the scene of an offence or during a search may be held to amount to an interview if the questioning is about the suspect's involvement in an offence; the relevant provisions of Code C will therefore apply, breaches of which—in particular the requirement to caution the suspect and to record the contents of the interview—may lead to the exclusion of the interview. Note, however, that the trigger for the application of Code C 11.1 is that the person is a 'suspect'. As was stated in

*Hughes v DPP* [2010] EWHC 515, applying *R (Ridehalgh) v DPP* [2005] EWHC 1100 (Admin):

> Where police officers question people, in any circumstances in the course of possible investigations relating to the commission of a criminal offence, there inevitably comes a time when it begins to occur to them that an offence might have been committed. They need to make further enquiries to establish whether there are grounds for suspecting the particular person, the potential defendant, of committing the offence. If the stage comes when there are such grounds, then the duty to caution arises.

## 7.3 **Interviews at the Police Station (Code C 12)**

A suspect must only be interviewed about an offence in a police station 'or other authorised place of detention' unless that would cause a delay which would be likely to:

- lead to interference with, or harm to, evidence connected with an offence;
- lead to interference with, or physical harm to, other people; or
- serious loss of or damage to property; or
- alert other people suspected of committing an offence but not yet arrested for it; or
- hinder the recovery of property obtained in consequence of the commission of an offence (Code C 11.1).

Once the risk which has necessitated an urgent interview has passed, the questioning must stop.

Where the interview does take place at a police station, then insofar as it is practicable, the interview must take place in a room which is adequately heated, lit, and ventilated (Code C 12.4).

However if a suspect who has been detained before charge in order to obtain evidence by questioning refuses to cooperate by either refusing to leave their cell, or by trying to leave the interview room, the interview can if necessary be conducted in their cell (Code C 12.5).

If an interview room is not used, a record must be made of the reasons why and any consequent actions taken (Code C 12.11).

### 7.3.1 **The role of the custody officer**

If an officer wishes to interview a suspect held in police detention, then he will require the consent of the custody officer who will be responsible for deciding whether or not to transfer custody of the detainee to the interviewing officer (Code C 12.1).

Before making that decision, the custody officer will need to assess whether or not the detainee is fit enough to be interviewed. This will require an assessment of the detainee's mental and physical state carried out if necessary in consultation with the interviewing officer and an appropriate health professional. The custody officer should also, as part of this assessment, consider what safeguards might be appropriate if the interview was permitted to proceed. Annex G provides helpful guidance on the factors to be taken into account when assessing a detainee's fitness to be interviewed.

If, following an assessment, the custody officer considers that an interview would cause significant harm to the detainee's physical or mental state, then he must not permit the interview to proceed.

A vulnerable suspect should always be considered to be at risk. (For consideration of the appropriate provisions relating to such suspects, see Chapter 8.)

A record must be made of the time and reason why the detainee is no longer in the custody of the custody officer and the reason for any refusal to deliver him out of that custody(Code C 12.10).

The custody officer must in addition have in mind Code C 12.2 in deciding when a detainee should be interviewed. Code C 12.2 provides that in every 24-hour period a detainee must be allowed a continuous period of at least eight hours rest free from questioning, travel, or any interruption in connection with the investigation concerned. The rest period may, however, be interrupted or delayed if there are reasonable grounds for believing that not interrupting or delaying the period would:

- involve a risk of harm to people or serious loss of, or damage to, property; or
- delay unnecessarily the person's release from custody; or
- otherwise prejudice the outcome of the investigation.

If the rest period is interrupted or delayed for any of the above reasons, then a new period must be allowed.

The rest period may also be interrupted or delayed:

- at the request of the detainee, his legal representative or appropriate adult; or
- in order to comply with legal obligations or duties under Code C 15 (reviews and extensions of detention); or
- in order to take action required under Code C 9 (provisions relating to the care and treatment of detained persons) or in accordance with medical advice.

As well as determining whether and when an interview can start, the custody officer will also have an important role in determining when questioning should be brought to an end (see below).

Once the interviewing process has commenced, care should be taken to ensure that there are adequate breaks to allow for the provision of meals or other refreshments. Breaks of at least 45 minutes should be taken at mealtimes and short (15-minute) refreshment breaks should be provided at approximately two hour intervals, subject to the interviewing officer's discretion to delay breaks if there are reasonable grounds to believe that it would:

- involve a risk of harm to people or serious loss of, or damage to property;
- unnecessarily delay the detainee's release;
- otherwise prejudice the outcome of the investigation (Code C 12.8).

Any decision to delay a break in the interview must be recorded together with the reasons (Code C 12.12).

If any complaints are made by the suspect in the course of the interview, the interviewer must record those complaints in the interview record and notify the custody officer (Code C 12.9).

## 7.4 **The Conduct of Interviews (Code C and Annex B and C)**

### 7.4.1 **Legal advice**

At the outset of an interview the interviewer must remind the detainee that he has the right to free legal advice and that the interview can be delayed in order to obtain such advice (Code C 11.2).

#### Can an interview take place in the absence of a solicitor if the detainee has requested legal advice?

If a detainee does want legal advice then the basic rule is that he must not be interviewed until he has received it. Or, if in the course of an interview the detainee indicates that he wishes to take legal advice then the interview must stop until such advice has been received.

Despite the apparently absolute terms of the above provision, there are nevertheless a number of situations in which the police may proceed with an interview in the absence of a solicitor, notwithstanding that the detainee has requested legal advice. They are where:

- an officer of the rank of superintendent or above has reasonable grounds for believing that access to a solicitor will result in one of the consequences set out at Annex B1 or 2; or
- an officer of superintendent rank or above has reasonable grounds to believe that the delay occasioned in waiting for a solicitor to arrive might lead to one of the consequences set out in Annex B1; or
- a solicitor has been contacted and agreed to attend but where an officer of the rank of superintendent or above has reasonable grounds to believe that the delay caused in awaiting his arrival would cause unreasonable delay to the process of investigation; or
- the detainee's nominated solicitor cannot be contacted, has indicated that he does not wish to be contacted, or having been contacted declines to attend,

and the detainee has refused the duty solicitor, and an officer of inspector rank or above has agreed to the interview proceeding; or
- the detainee has changed his mind about wanting legal advice but agrees in writing or on tape to proceed without it, and an officer of the rank of inspector or above has enquired about the reasons why the detainee has changed his mind, and being satisfied that it is proper to do so gives his authority for the interview to proceed (Code C 6.6; Note for Guidance 6I).

The consequences set out in Annex B that would permit the appropriate officer to authorize an interview notwithstanding the fact that the suspect has not been permitted to exercise his right to legal advice are when the officer has reasonable grounds to believe that exercising that right would lead to:

- interference with, or harm to, evidence connected with an indictable offence; or
- interference with or physical harm to, other people; or
- alerting other suspects who have yet to be arrested; or
- hindering the recovery of property obtained as a result of the offence;

or where:

- the person detained for an indictable offence has benefited from their criminal conduct; and
- the recovery of the value of the property constituting the benefit will be hindered by the exercise of the right.

In considering whether it would be appropriate to continue or start an interview in the absence of a solicitor where it has been established that a solicitor is willing to attend, the police should obtain from the solicitor an estimate of how long it will take for him to arrive and if it appears that the delay might lead to one of the consequences in Annex B1, or to an unreasonable delay to the investigation, should if necessary give the detainee the opportunity to obtain legal advice from an alternative source (Note for Guidance 6A).

### Are the police obliged to give pre-interview disclosure?

Code C 10.3 states that a person who is arrested must be informed as soon as practicable after their arrest of the fact of their arrest and the grounds for it. Note for Guidance 10B clarifies that this means that the suspect must be informed of the nature of the suspected offence, when and where it was committed and the reasons why arrest is considered necessary. Although there is no requirement to give any additional information prior to interview, in practice some pre-interview disclosure is almost invariably given, although the quality and quantity of that disclosure will depend on the case. The interviewing officer will need to bear in mind that if no or no adequate disclosure is given, the defence could argue that the legal representative was unable to give proper legal advice to the suspect; in those circumstances there is a risk that not only would the suspect be advised to exercise his right to silence in interview, but that no adverse inferences would be drawn from that silence (see *Ward v Police Service of Northern Ireland* [2007] UKHL 50).

### Can the police refuse to allow a solicitor to attend an interview?

A detainee is entitled to have the benefit of the presence of a solicitor throughout their interview unless one of the exceptions outlined above applies (Code C 6.8).

In exceptional circumstances, a solicitor can be required to leave an interview if their conduct is such that the interview cannot be conducted properly.

Where this occurs, the interview should be stopped and the interviewer should consult a senior officer, ideally an officer of the rank of superintendent or above, but if such an officer is not available, then an inspector, not concerned in the investigation, who will subsequently have to report the matter to a superintendent.

As in any of the other possible situations in which an interview could proceed without legal advice being available to a detainee who has requested it, the removal of a solicitor should be a matter of last resort. It should be remembered that the role of a solicitor at the police station, and in interview, is to protect the legal rights of their client. This may involve advice not to answer some or all questions; it may involve intervention to prevent what a solicitor regards as improper questions being put or seeking to stop the interview in order to give his client further advice. None of these would be grounds for seeking the removal of the solicitor, however frustrating his actions may be to the officers conducting the interview. Note 6D states that it is only when the solicitor's conduct 'prevents or unreasonably obstructs proper questions being put to the suspect or the suspect's response being recorded' that consideration should be given to removing the solicitor. Some indication of how serious the conduct would have to be is given in Code C 6.11; that consideration should be given to reporting the solicitor to the Law Society and/or the Legal Services Commission. Even then, the authorizing officer should first speak to the solicitor in question about his conduct and if a decision is made to remove him should give the suspect the opportunity to consult with and have present in interview an alternative solicitor (Code C 6.10).

Where a solicitor is excluded, Note for Guidance 6E points out that the authorizing officer will need to be able to satisfy a court that his decision was appropriate. To do so, he may have himself needed to witness the conduct that led to his decision to exclude.

### 7.4.2 **Cautions**

Before any questions (or further questions) are put to a suspect about his involvement in an offence, he must be cautioned (Code C 10.1).

The words of the caution are:

> You do not have to say anything. But it may harm your defence if you do not mention when questioned something that you later rely on in court. Anything that you do say may be given in evidence. (Code C 10.5)

It is important that the person cautioned understands what this means and the possible implications of it. If necessary, therefore, the meaning of the caution should be explained by the officer who gives it. Moreover, the person being questioned must, under Code C 11.1A, be informed of the true nature of the offence about which he is being questioned so that he can make an informed choice whether or not to answer questions.

Note that the caution is required before there is any questioning about a suspect's involvement in a criminal offence—the same definition as that for an interview. A person need not be cautioned if the questions are 'for other necessary purposes' such as seeking to ascertain someone's identity, or for the proper and effective conduct of a search where those questions fall short of an 'interview' (Code C 10A); so, for example, in *R v Senior* [2004] 2 Cr App R 12, CA, a case involving customs officers (bound by the Codes), no caution was required prior to questioning two suspects in a drug-smuggling operation about the ownership of a suitcase where the identity of the owner was unclear, but was required before any other questions were put.

Moreover, a caution is only required where the person being questioned is suspected—there must therefore be reasonable grounds to suspect a person of involvement in an offence before a caution is required when questioning. Where, objectively, grounds for suspicion are present, a caution should be administered (*R v Hunt* [1992] Crim LR 582, CA; *R v Nelson and Rose* [1998] 2 Cr App R 399, CA).

As the caution must be given before any questions 'or further questions' are put, if there is a break in the course of an interview, the police should on resumption ensure that the suspect understands that he is still under caution; the safest course may well be to give the caution in full again (Code C 10.8).

A failure to give the caution where required is likely to be regarded by the courts as a significant and substantial breach of the Code and may render the evidence inadmissible. The courts will in this regard assess the 'fairness' of the conduct. Although the Code extends beyond those in police custody, the courts have tended to differentiate between a failure to give a caution when a suspect was in the custody of or otherwise vulnerable to pressure from the police, and the situation in which incriminating comments have been given by a suspect to, for example, an undercover police officer, but in circumstances where those comments have been made voluntarily—albeit in ignorance of the person to whom they have been talking (*R v Christou and Wright* [1992] 95 Cr App R 264, CA).

The police cannot, however, take advantage by such a method *in order* to circumvent the Code—if that was the effect of any action by the police, then irrespective of their intention the courts would be likely to regard it as unfair and to exclude the evidence obtained.

### What are the consequences if a suspect interviewed under caution refuses to answer some or all of the questions put to him?

If a suspect who is being interviewed in accordance with the Act and Codes fails, having been cautioned, to mention a fact that he later relies on in his defence, that being a fact that he could reasonably have been expected to mention when questioned, a court or jury may draw 'such inferences from the failure as appear proper' (s 34 Criminal Justice and Public Order Act 1994).

This only applies, however, where the person questioned has been given the opportunity to have legal advice (whether from a nominated solicitor or the duty solicitor). Where access to legal advice has been denied under Annex B, or an interview has commenced in circumstances where the detainee has asked for legal advice but before he has had the opportunity to speak to his solicitor, then no adverse inference can be drawn and a shorter caution should be applied which is:

> You do not have to say anything, but anything you do say may be given in evidence. (Code C, Annex C 1–2)

If the position changes then the person interviewed must be re-cautioned appropriately. So, for example, if a suspect wished to have the benefit of legal advice, but Annex B applied and authority was given to withhold access to legal advice, no adverse inference could be drawn from any failure in the course of that interview to mention facts later relied on in evidence and the shorter caution should be given. If Annex B subsequently ceases to apply and the suspect is permitted then to consult with a solicitor, on resuming the interview the suspect must be re-cautioned in the terms set out in Code 10.5. Note for Guidance C2 sets out some suggested wording to be used when re-cautioning either because the restriction on adverse inferences begins or ceases to apply.

### 7.4.3 Special warnings

If a detainee on being interviewed fails or refuses to answer questions satisfactorily or at all, when asked to account for objects, marks, or substances or marks on objects found:

- on his person; or
- in or on his clothing or footwear; or
- otherwise in his possession; or
- in any place in which he is at the time of his arrest;

or he fails or refuses to answer questions satisfactorily or at all, when asked to account for his presence at a place at or about the time the offence for which he has been arrested is alleged to have been committed and it is reasonably believed that his presence at that time and place may be attributable to his participation in the commission of the offence, then under ss 36 and 37 of the Criminal Justice and Public Order Act 1994, an adverse inference may be drawn, but only where:

- the restriction in Annex C on drawing adverse inferences from silence does not apply (see above);
- the person being questioned is under arrest; and
- the person being questioned has been given a special warning (Code 10.10; Note for Guidance 10F).

In giving the warning, the suspect being interviewed must be told in ordinary language:

- what offence is being investigated;
- what fact they are being asked to account for;
- that this fact may be due to them taking part in the commission of the offence;
- that a court may draw a proper inference if they fail or refuse to account for this fact;
- that a record is being made of the interview and it may be given in evidence if they are brought to trial (Code 10.11).

### 7.4.4 **Content of interviews**

When questioning, Note for Guidance 11B advises the interviewing officer to have in mind para 3.4 of the Criminal Procedure and Investigations Act 1996 Code of Practice which states that the investigator must pursue all reasonable lines of enquiry whether they point towards or away from the suspect. The interviewer must, however, be careful not to do or say anything which might be considered to be an inducement or amount to oppression or anything else that might subsequently render the contents of the interview unsafe and inadmissible. Accordingly, Code C 11.5 states that 'no interviewer may try to obtain answers or elicit a statement by the use of oppression'. Neither, save when explaining the terms of the caution or special warning or otherwise explaining to the suspect the legal consequences of refusing to cooperate or answer questions, should the police indicate what action they will take as a result of anything that the suspect says or does except in answer to a direct question, and only then when the action is itself proper and warranted (Code C 11.5).

So, for example, an interviewer should not indicate to a person being questioned that he will get bail if he cooperates—that could be regarded as an inducement that might result in a finding that any answers given in response were unreliable and therefore inadmissible in evidence. Neither should the interviewer give such an indication in response to a direct question, the question of bail being a matter for the custody officer. The interviewer should bear in mind that he may also have to satisfy a court that nothing was said or done to influence the suspect in any breaks within or between interviews. Accordingly, Note for Guidance 10E suggests that at the beginning of any new or resumed interview, the interviewing officer should summarize the reason for the break and confirm this with the suspect. He would also be well advised following any break to ask the suspect to confirm that no questions or other discussions relating to the offence have taken place in the course of the break.

Before the interview begins the interviewer must identify to the suspect all those present in the interview, and as already stated, remind him of his right to free legal advice (if applicable) and caution or re-caution the suspect.

Following these preliminaries, at the outset of the interview the interviewing officer must put to the suspect any 'significant statement' or silence and ask the suspect whether he confirms or denies that statement or silence and whether he wishes to add anything to it (Code C 11.4).

Any record that has been made of a significant statement or silence should be shown to the suspect in interview and he should be asked to sign it to confirm its accuracy if he has not already done so. Any refusal to sign or disagreement with the contents of any such record should be recorded (Note for Guidance 11E).

A significant statement is defined in Code C 11.4A as 'one which appears capable of being used in evidence against the suspect, in particular a direct admission of guilt'. A significant silence is defined in the same section as 'a failure or refusal to answer a question or answer satisfactorily when under caution' in circumstances which might give rise to an adverse inference under the Criminal Justice and Public Order Act 1994. Comments made outside the context of an interview which do not amount in themselves to a significant statement but which nevertheless might be relevant to an offence should if possible also be recorded and put to a suspect for him to read, sign, and indicate whether and to what extent he agrees or disagrees with its contents (Code C 11.13).

### 7.4.5 Ending the interview

Section 37 of the Act provides that where there is insufficient evidence to charge a suspect, the custody officer may authorize his detention for such period as is necessary (subject to review) to obtain such evidence—*inter alia*, by questioning. When the custody officer has sufficient evidence to charge the person with the offence for which he was arrested that person must either be charged or released with or without bail.

If, in the course of the interview, sufficient evidence has been gained to charge, must the interview immediately be brought to an end? Code C 11.6 states that the interview of a person about an offence with which that person has not been charged must cease when:

- the investigating officer is satisfied that all the questions considered relevant to obtaining accurate and reliable information about the offence have been put to the suspect, including allowing the suspect an opportunity to give an innocent explanation and asking questions to test if the explanation is accurate and reliable;

- the investigating officer has taken account of any other available evidence; and
- the investigating officer or, in the case of a detained suspect, the custody officer, reasonably believes that there is sufficient evidence to provide a realistic prospect of conviction if the person was prosecuted.

Accordingly, once the interviewing officer concludes that he has sufficient evidence for a prosecution to succeed, he should ask the person being interviewed if he has anything further to say, and once he has said all he wishes, the interview should be terminated and the person brought before the custody officer to be charged or otherwise dealt with.

## 7.5 Interview Records (Codes C and E)

An accurate record must be made of every interview, whether it is conducted at a police station or elsewhere (Code C 11.7).

Where the interview takes place at a police station, audio-recording must be used unless the custody officer gives authorization not to audio-record the interview in circumstances where it is not reasonably practicable to do so due to the unavailability of equipment, whether due to equipment failure, or because the person to be interviewed refuses to go into or remain in a suitable interview room and no portable recording equipment is available. In those circumstances the interview must be recorded in writing.

Interviews may be audio-recorded using removable media (audio or audio/visual taping) to which Code E 2 to 6 apply, or via a secure digital network, to which Code E 7 applies. See also Code F in this regard.

### 7.5.1 Tape-recording

Section 60 of the Act imposes on the Secretary of State a duty to issue a code of practice for the tape-recording of interviews with suspects at police stations and to make an order requiring that some or all such interviews as specified are tape-recorded.

The applicable code of practice in this regard is Code E which provides detailed guidance on the audio-recording of interviews from the type of tapes and tape-machines to use, or what to do if a tape breaks, to sections dealing with the maintenance of tape security following an interview. There is substantial overlap with, and indeed repetition of some of the provisions of Code C and the two codes must accordingly be read together.

The primary provision in Code E is E 3.1(a) which states that the interviews of all persons who are interviewed about an indictable offence at a police station, under caution and in accordance with the provisions of Code C must be audio-recorded.

An interview must also be audio-recorded where an officer asks further questions after the suspect has been charged or told that he may be prosecuted for an offence, or where an officer wants to tell such a person about any written statement or interview with another person.

The only exceptions to the above are where either it is not practicable to use audio-recording because the recording equipment or the facilities to use it are not available and the custody officer has reasonable grounds to consider that the interview should not be delayed; or where it is clear from the outset that no prosecution will follow (Code E 3.3). A further possible but highly unusual scenario would be where a suspect will not cooperate with the interview procedure and the custody officer gives authority for the interview to be conducted in the suspect's cell and no portable equipment is available (Code E 3.4).

If the interview is not tape-recorded for one of these reasons, it must nevertheless be recorded in writing, as must the reason for departing from the normal procedure which the authorizing officer may well need to justify in court.

Where an interview is tape-recorded, the recording should be done openly. Two tapes should be used simultaneously, one of which will become the master copy and the other the working copy. The tapes should be clean and unused and should be unwrapped or opened in the presence of the suspect (Code E 4.3).

At the outset the interviewer should ask all persons present, including the suspect, to speak to identify themselves—this will in due course have the very practical effect of aiding voice recognition.

As well as identifying the persons present, reminding the suspect of his entitlement to free legal advice, and cautioning the suspect, the interviewer should in addition at the commencement of a tape-recorded interview state that the interview is being tape-recorded, state the time, date, and place of interview, and tell the suspect that he will be given a notice about what will happen to the tapes (Code E 4.4).

If the suspect objects to the interview being tape-recorded, the interviewer should ask for the suspect to state his objections on tape. When he has done so (or if he refuses to do so) the interviewer has a discretion whether to continue to record the interview or to turn the tape off and record any further questions and answers in writing (Code E 4.8). It might reasonably be supposed, however, that such a course of action would be a risky one to take.

If the reason for wanting the tape turned off is that the suspect wants to tell the interviewer about other matters not directly connected with the offence and that it is these matters that they are unwilling to speak about on tape, then an opportunity should be provided at the conclusion of the interview for this to be done (Code E 4.10).

Where any complaints are made by the suspect in the course of the interview the custody officer must be informed (Code C 12.9). Ideally, the tape should be allowed to run whilst the custody officer speaks to the suspect and deals with the matter of complaint (Note for Guidance 4E). However, if the complaint is about a matter unconnected with the interview then the interviewer may at his discretion continue the interview and bring the matter to the attention of the custody officer as soon as practicable after the interview has concluded (Note for Guidance 4F).

If an interview is suspended for a break to be taken, that fact and the time of the break should be recorded on tape. If the break is a short one and all parties remain in the interview room the tape-recorder can simply be turned off; when the interview recommences it should be recorded on the same tapes. If, however, the suspect leaves the room in the course of a break, then the tapes should be removed and dealt with in the same way as if the interview had concluded (Code E 4.12, 4.13).

At the conclusion of the interview the suspect must be asked whether there is anything he would like to clarify or add, following which the time should be recorded and the tape switched off. The master tape must then be sealed, the suspect and his legal representative or appropriate adult if any asked to sign the seal, and the tape then treated as an exhibit (Code E 4.18).

Once sealed the seal of a master tape required in criminal proceedings may not be broken by a police officer save in the presence of a representative of the Crown Prosecution Service and on notice to the defendant or his legal representative who is entitled to be present (Code E 6.2).

If a suspect is charged or informed that he will be prosecuted, he is entitled to a copy of the tape, and at the conclusion of the interview must be given a notice detailing his entitlement to the tape, the arrangements for access to the tape, and how it is to be used (Code E 4.19).

Whether or not a suspect is ultimately prosecuted, all master tapes of interviews must be kept in secure conditions and treated in the same way as an exhibit (Code E 6.1).

### 7.5.2 **Video recording**

The Secretary of State has a 'duty' under s 60 of the Act to issue a code of practice and to make an order requiring the tape-recording of interviews. Under s 61 he has a 'power' to issue a code of practice in connection with and to make an order requiring the visual recording of interviews. The applicable Code of Practice is Code F which at the outset makes clear that there is no statutory requirement to visually record interviews, but that if an audio-visual recording is made then the contents of the Code should be 'considered'.

The majority of the provisions in Code F mirror those applicable to tape-recorded interviews in Code E, and the provisions in Code C relating to interviews and the drawing of adverse inferences apply equally here as to interviews recorded either on audio tape or in writing.

Although there is no requirement at the present time that interviews should be visually recorded, there are obvious benefits in doing so. In particular,

Code F 3.1(d) and (e) draw attention to the fact that it could be considered appropriate to visually record an interview that takes place with or in the presence of a deaf or deaf/blind or speech impaired person who uses sign language to communicate, or where the interview has taken place with or in the presence of anyone who requires an appropriate adult.

Note: a video-recorded interview must not be used for any identification purpose (Code F, Note for Guidance 2D).

### 7.5.3 **Secure digital network**

The requirements for recording using a secure digital network (which does not involve the use of removable media) are set out at Code E 7 and closely follow the requirements for interviews conducted using other formats.

In the event of an equipment failure that cannot be quickly rectified, the interview should continue using removable media (audio or audio-visual taping) unless such equipment is unavailable, in which case authority should be sought from the custody officer in accordance with Code E 3.3 to complete the interview record in writing.

Code E 7.16, 7.17 contain requirements to ensure the security and integrity of secure digital network interview records, and emphasize the need to strictly control and monitor necessary access to those records.

### 7.5.4 **Writing**

Where an interview is recorded in writing, that record must be made on forms provided for that purpose or in the interviewer's pocket book (Code C 11.7(c)).

The record must be made contemporaneously with the interview unless this would not be practicable or would interfere with the conduct of the interview. If the record is not made in the course of the interview then it must be made as soon as practicable thereafter and must include within it the reason why it could not be made during the interview (Code C 11.8, 11.10).

Where possible the suspect, his legal representative, or appropriate adult if present during the interview should be given the opportunity to read the record of interview and sign it as correct. If the suspect cannot read, then the record should be read over to him (Code C 11.11, 11.12).

The written record should so far as possible be a verbatim transcript of the questions and answers or an adequate and accurate summary

## 7.6 **Written Statements under Caution (Code C, Annex D)**

Annex D1 of Code C states that 'a person shall always be invited to write down what they want to say'. Despite the seemingly mandatory requirement of the provision, in reality it will be little used, as Note for Guidance 12A makes it clear that there would normally be no necessity for a written statement where the interview was recorded or taped contemporaneously and the record signed by the interviewee. A suspect may, however, be asked, or may himself ask to make a statement. Any statement then made must include at the outset a declaration that the writer makes the statement of his own free will and understands that it is under caution, the words of which will follow. The exact wording to be included is set out in full at Annex D2.

If a detainee asks to make a written statement under caution either on or after being charged or informed that they may be prosecuted for an offence then they may do so. Again the appropriate version of the caution must be included at the outset.

If the detainee wishes, they may ask a police officer to write the statement for them. In these circumstances the officer writing the statement must use the exact words spoken by the person making the statement. If any clarification is required the questions and answers concerning the clarification must be included. At the conclusion of the statement taking the person who made the statement must be given the opportunity to read the statement himself, to make any corrections, alterations, and additions, to confirm that it is correct, and to sign a declaration to that effect. If the person cannot or will not read the statement it should be read to him.

# Practical Guidance

## 7.7 Case Study 1

*Green is in custody having been arrested for theft. DC Potts decides to question him and takes Green to the interview room at the police station. Green declines to have a solicitor; and DC Potts, having switched on the audio recording facility, commences questioning him. After about ten minutes Green asks DC Potts not to record the interview on tape. How should DC Potts deal with this request?*

DC Potts should explain to Smith that the Codes of Practice require him to record his objections to the audio recording on tape and ascertain what they are. Once Smith has stated on tape what his objections are or refused to do so, DC Potts should consider whether to continue the recording (Code E 4.8). If he chooses not to do so, he should then turn the recorder off. DC Potts should then commence the interview again and make a contemporaneous written record of the questions and answers. He should caution Smith again, repeat any special warnings, and remind him of his right to free legal advice. If possible, DC Potts should also obtain the assistance of a colleague to record the interview and to act as a witness in case Smith should subsequently dispute the accuracy of the written record. Once the interview has been completed DC Potts should ensure Smith is given the opportunity to read the written account and sign it as correct. It is good practice to go through the record of each question and answer and, if the interviewee agrees with the accuracy, ask him to initial each answer as well as signing the foot of each page (Codes of Practice C, para 11.7–11.11, E 4.8).

## 7.8 **Case Study 2**

PC Smith is called to an address where a burglar alarm has been activated. She sees Dean, a known criminal loitering in the vicinity. PC Smith approaches Dean, who appears to be the worse for wear for drink. She notices that he is carrying a CD player and asks him where he got it from. Dean states that he is keeping it for a friend who he refuses to name. PC Smith then receives further information via her personal radio confirming that a house nearby has been broken into and a CD player stolen. PC Smith then arrests Dean on suspicion of burglary and cautions him. Dean is placed in the rear of PC Smith's police car to await a van to transport him to the police station. While they are waiting, PC Smith again asks Dean where he got the CD player from and Dean admits that he stole it in the course of the burglary. PC Smith, realizing the significance of what has been said, hurriedly makes a note in her notebook and asks Dean to sign it, which he does without reading it.

After being booked into custody, Dean is examined by the forensic medical examiner and is deemed unfit for interview due to alcohol consumption.

After a night's rest, Dean is interviewed by PC Smith. On the advice of his solicitor Dean gives a pre-prepared statement in which he denies any wrongdoing. After the interview, Dean's solicitor makes an official complaint against PC Smith for abusing her authority by interviewing his client away from the police station and whilst he was drunk.

### Did PC Smith's initial questions amount to an interview?

There can be a fine line between questions asked to establish if reasonable grounds to arrest exist and conducting an interview. Any questioning of a *suspect* regarding their involvement in a criminal offence is classified as an interview; but police officers may regularly regard a person as 'suspicious' without having sufficient grounds to regard them as a suspect for an offence and, moreover, are entitled to ask questions of those who are not 'suspects' in the course of their investigations without such questioning amounting to an interview. Here, it is at least arguable that at the time of the initial questioning Dean was not a suspect for an offence and that therefore the questions did not amount to an interview.

*At what point does Dean become a suspect?*

When it is confirmed to PC Smith that a burglary has occurred and that a CD player was stolen, those facts together with Dean's known background, his proximity to the scene of the crime, and his possession of an item that may have been stolen in the course of that burglary, clearly provide reasonable grounds to suspect him of involvement in the offence. At this point, PC Smith quite properly arrested and cautioned him.

*Were PC Smith's subsequent questions an interview?*

As Dean has been arrested as a suspect, no further questioning should take place; any such questioning would be classed as an interview which should take place at the police station and in accordance with the Codes of Practice. PC Smith's actions would probably be viewed as an attempt to circumvent the Codes and any questions and answers would almost certainly be excluded under s 78(1).

*What if Dean had volunteered the information given in the car?*

The position would be different if Dean's 'confession' was made spontaneously rather than as a result of questioning. Had that been the situation, PC Smith's actions of recording the comments made and asking Dean to sign them would be entirely appropriate. PC Smith should then draw those comments to the attention of the custody officer on arrival at the station and they should be raised at the outset of the recorded interview. It may well be that an application would be made to exclude those comments as unreliable due to Dean's inebriated state, but PC Smith's actions could not be criticized.

# The Detention and Treatment of Vulnerable Suspects

# Law and Commentary

## 8.1 Introduction

The law recognizes that there are particular classes of detainee who may have difficulty in understanding the significance of procedures, questioning, and the implication of any replies they make to such questioning. Such detainees, described in Code C 3(b) as 'special groups' are deemed in need of special protection. Code C provides a number of safeguards covering the detention, treatment, and questioning of the members of such groups.

As it is recognized that those who may have limited understanding or be otherwise vulnerable may be liable to give misleading, unreliable, or self-incriminating evidence, consequently it must be recognized that any breach of the safeguards designed to protect their interests may well give rise to a subsequent successful application to exclude any evidence thereafter obtained.

## 8.2 The Special Groups

### 8.2.1 Which detainees form the 'special groups'?

Those for whom special safeguards exist are:

- juveniles;
- the mentally disordered or otherwise mentally vulnerable;
- those who appear to be deaf, or about whom there is doubt about their hearing or speaking ability or ability to understand English;
- those who are blind, seriously visually impaired, or unable to read.

### 8.2.2 Who is a juvenile?

A juvenile is a person under the age of 17. Proof of age is not required, however, and the law errs on the side of caution; accordingly it is sufficient that someone *appears* to be under 17. If they do, then in the absence of clear evidence to the contrary they must be treated as a juvenile (Code C 1.5).

### 8.2.3 What is meant by 'mentally vulnerable or otherwise mentally disordered'?

Again, where there is any uncertainty or room for doubt about the mental state of a detainee then the detainee must be regarded as vulnerable. Therefore, if an officer has any suspicion, or is told in good faith that a person of any age may be mentally disordered or otherwise mentally vulnerable, or is mentally incapable of understanding the significance of questions or their replies, then that person is to be treated as mentally vulnerable in the absence of clear evidence to dispel that suspicion (Code C 1.4; Annex E 1).

A detainee is 'mentally vulnerable' if, because of their mental state or capacity, they may not understand the significance of what is said, of questions, or their replies.

'Mental disorder' is defined in the Mental Health Act 1983 as '... mental illness, arrested or incomplete development of mind, psychopathic disorder and any other disorder or disability of mind' (Code C, Note for Guidance 1G).

## 8.3 **Initial Steps**

### 8.3.1 **What initial steps must be taken when a juvenile is detained?**

Where a juvenile is detained, the custody officer must as soon as practicable inform the appropriate adult of the grounds of the juvenile's detention and whereabouts, and ask them to come to the station to see the detainee (Code C 3.15).

All detainees are entitled under s 56 of PACE to have a friend, relative, or some other person likely to take an interest in his welfare informed of his arrest. Where the person detained is a juvenile, s 57 places the police under an additional duty to take such steps as are practicable to identify the person responsible for the juvenile's welfare (who may or may not be the person acting as the appropriate adult) and inform them of the facts of his arrest.

Section 57 must be read together with Code C 3.13. That provides that where it appears to the custody officer that the detainee is under 17, he must as soon as practicable ascertain the identity of a person responsible for their welfare and inform that person that:

- the juvenile has been arrested;
- why they have been arrested; and
- where they are detained.

The relevant person may be:

- a parent or guardian;
- (if the juvenile is in local authority care, or is being otherwise looked after under the Children Act 1989), a person appointed by that organization to have responsibility for the juvenile's welfare;
- any other person who has for the time being assumed responsibility for the juvenile's welfare.

If the juvenile is under a court order, the 'responsible officer' who supervises or otherwise monitors the juvenile should also be informed; for example a member of the Youth Offending Team or the contractor providing electronic monitoring (Code C 3.14). Consideration should also be given to contacting the juvenile's parents, even where there is no legal obligation to inform them (eg because the juvenile is in local authority care), or where the juvenile is not living with them (Code C, Note for Guidance 3C).

A juvenile therefore has the right, in common with all detainees, to have someone informed of the circumstances of his detention under s 56, and the police have a duty to inform the person responsible for the juvenile's welfare under s 57 and Code 3.13, and to inform and secure the attendance at the police station of an appropriate adult (who may or may not be the person responsible for the juvenile's welfare). Additionally, they should consider informing the juvenile's parents if not already informed under one of the above categories. In practice, however, it is usually a parent who is informed both as the person responsible for the juvenile's welfare and as the appropriate adult.

Note that a juvenile cannot be held incommunicado. Even where Annex B of Code C applies (delay in notifying arrest or allowing access to legal advice in certain specified situations), the appropriate adult and the person responsible for the juvenile detainee's welfare must be contacted, informed of the circumstances of arrest, and asked to attend the police station to see the detainee (Note for Guidance B1).

### 8.3.2 What initial steps must be taken when a suspect who may have a mental or physical disorder is detained?

The custody officer must determine whether the detainee might be in need of medical treatment or attention—whether due to a physical illness or injury, or because of a mental disorder or for any other reason (eg the effects of drink or drugs) appears to need clinical attention. Wherever there is any doubt the custody officer must err on the side of caution and take steps to ensure that the detainee receives appropriate clinical attention as soon as reasonably practicable (Code C 9.5).

This applies irrespective of whether or not the detainee has asked for medical assistance and irrespective of whether he has received clinical attention elsewhere (Code C 9.5A).

Note for Guidance 9C warns that when assessing whether or not a detainee requires clinical attention and if so what, it is important to bear in mind that there may be hidden and serious causes for a detainee's apparent condition. A detainee who appears to be drunk may in fact have sustained an injury, particularly a head injury that might not be immediately obvious; a detainee who is behaving abnormally may have a physical or mental illness; a detainee who is dependent on drink or drugs may experience harmful effects within a short time of being deprived of their supply. Wherever there is any doubt, or where the need is urgent, the police must act immediately to call a health care professional or an ambulance.

A mentally disordered or otherwise mentally vulnerable person who has been detained under s 136 of the Mental Health Act 1983 must be assessed as soon as possible and should whenever practicable be taken to hospital for that purpose (Code 9D). Where the assessment takes place at the police station, an approved social worker and a registered medical practitioner must be called to the police station as soon as possible to interview and examine the detainee. Once the detainee has been interviewed and examined and suitable arrangements have been made for their treatment and care they can no longer be detained under s 136. Neither can their detention continue under s 136 if, having examined them, a registered medical practitioner concludes that they are not mentally disordered within the meaning of the Act (Code C 3.16).

Where the detainee is mentally disordered or otherwise mentally vulnerable, an appropriate adult must be notified, apprised of the circumstances of the person's detention and whereabouts, and asked to come to the station to see the detainee (Code C 3.15).

As with juveniles, the right to have an appropriate adult informed under Code C 3.15 applies even where the police could in the case of a non-vulnerable detainee have delayed notification of arrest or access to legal advice in accordance with Annex B.

### 8.3.3 What initial steps should be taken if the detainee has difficulty communicating?

It is a pre-requisite that a detainee should be able to understand what is taking place and to be able to communicate effectively. Many of the safeguards provided by PACE and Code C are directed to ensure this. The custody officer must therefore check to determine whether a detainee requires help to check documentation or an interpreter in order to facilitate communication (Code C 3.5(c)(ii)).

If the detainee appears to be deaf, or if there is doubt about his hearing or speaking ability, or ability to understand English, and effective communication cannot be established, the custody officer must as soon as practicable call an interpreter for assistance (Code C 3.12).

If the detainee is blind, seriously visually impaired, or unable to read, a person not involved in the investigation (eg a solicitor, relative, or—in the case of a juvenile or mentally vulnerable detainee—an appropriate adult) must be made available to help them check any documentation (Code 3.20).

## 8.4 Who can Act as an Appropriate Adult?

The categories of people who can act as an appropriate adult differ according to whether the detainee is a juvenile or is mentally disordered or otherwise mentally vulnerable.

Where the detainee is a juvenile, the appropriate adult can be:

- the parent, guardian, or, if in local authority or voluntary organization care or is being looked after under the Children Act 1989, a person representing that authority or organization;
- a social worker of a local authority social services department;
- failing these, some other responsible adult aged 18 or over who is not a police officer or employed by the police (Code C 1.7(a)).

A person, including a parent or guardian, should not act as an appropriate adult if they:

- are suspected of involvement in the offence;
- are the victim;
- are a witness;
- are involved in the investigation;
- have received admissions prior to attending to act as the appropriate adult;
- are a parent or guardian estranged from the juvenile and the juvenile expressly and specifically objects to their presence;
- are a social worker or member of a Youth Offending Team in whose presence the juvenile has admitted the offence at a time other than when they are acting as the appropriate adult;
- are a solicitor or independent custody visitor present at the police station in that capacity (Code C, Note for Guidance 1B, C, F);
- (in the case of a detainee arrested under s 41 the Terrorism Act 2000) are suspected of involvement in the commission, preparation or instigation of acts of terrorism (Code H, Note for Guidance 1B).

Where the detainee is mentally disordered or otherwise mentally vulnerable, the appropriate adult can be:

- a relative, guardian, or other person responsible for their care or custody;
- someone experienced in dealing with mentally disordered or mentally vulnerable people but who is not a police officer or employed by the police;
- failing these, some other responsible adult aged 18 or over who is not a police officer or employed by the police (Code C 1.7(b)).

Note for Guidance 1D advises that it may be more satisfactory if the appropriate adult for a mentally disordered or otherwise mentally vulnerable person is someone experienced or trained in their care, rather than a relative lacking such qualifications. Notwithstanding the guidance, if the detainee prefers a relative to a better qualified stranger or objects to a particular person, then their wishes should, if practicable, be respected.

As for juveniles, a solicitor or independent custody visitor who is present at the police station in that capacity cannot also act as the appropriate adult (Note for Guidance 1F).

### 8.4.1 **What is the role of the appropriate adult?**

It is the appropriate adult's role to ensure that a vulnerable detainee understands the procedures and their rights and is able to exercise those rights effectively. Code C identifies various procedures that must be carried out or repeated in the presence of the appropriate adult, gives the appropriate adult certain rights to oversee procedures, and details specific responsibilities that the appropriate adult will have. In particular, the appropriate adult has a responsibility to give the detainee advice and assistance, and this must be made known to the detainee who must in addition be told that they can consult privately with the appropriate adult at any time (Code C 3.18).

### 8.4.2 **What are the rights and responsibilities of the appropriate adult?**

As it is essential that the detainee should understand his rights, those rights (as enshrined in Code C 3.1–3.5) must be given in the presence of the appropriate adult. If those rights were given prior to the appropriate adult's attendance at the police station, they must be given again and in his presence once he has arrived (Code C 3.17).

It is equally important that the vulnerable detainee should understand the implication of matters put to him and his replies (or lack of them). Whenever a caution is given, therefore, it must be given, or repeated, in the presence of an appropriate adult (Code C 10.12).

The appropriate adult must be permitted to inspect a detainee's custody record as soon as practicable after their arrival at the police station, at any other time whilst the person is detained, and (on giving reasonable notice) after the detainee has left police detention (Code C 2.4; 2.5).

Moreover, the detainee, appropriate adult, or legal representative is entitled to be given a copy of the custody record on request within 12 months of the time when the detainee leaves police detention or is brought before a court (Code C 2.4A).

## 8.5 **When is an Interpreter Required?**

An interpreter may be required either for reasons of disability (a speech or hearing impediment) or language. The underlying intention is to ensure that the detainee understands the procedure, what is put to him, and the significance of his replies.

The custody officer should establish at an early stage whether or not a detainee may require an interpreter. Where effective communication cannot be established with a detainee who is or appears to be deaf, or where there are doubts about their ability to hear, speak, or understand English then a suitably qualified interpreter should be made available at public expense. The interpreter will need to explain the offence to the detainee and any information given by the custody officer.

### 8.5.1 Who can act as an interpreter?

Whenever possible, Code 13.1 advises that interpreters should be drawn from the National Register of Public Service Interpreters. A police officer or civilian support staff may, in certain circumstances, interpret, but only if the detainee (and where applicable the appropriate adult) give their consent in writing, or if in the course of an interview that interview is either audio or visually recorded in accordance with Codes E or F.

As the interpreter must be impartial, a police officer or civilian support staff cannot interpret where that interpretation is required for the purpose of obtaining legal advice (Code C 13.9). The requirement of impartiality extends beyond the use of police staff as interpreters. In *R v West London Youth Court, ex p J* [2001] 1 WLR 2368, it was held that it was wrong for a male relative acting as the appropriate adult for an 11-year-old girl to additionally take on the role of an interpreter. The interpreter had to be wholly impartial and an appropriate adult was not impartial as his function was to assist the person being questioned.

## 8.6 Legal Advice

Advising a vulnerable detainee of the right to free and independent legal advice is one of the main roles of the appropriate adult. Where the detainee is a juvenile, the appropriate adult should always consider whether legal advice from a solicitor is required and has the right to ask for a solicitor to attend if this would be in the best interests of the detainee. The decision whether to receive legal advice is, however, ultimately that of the detainee. Accordingly he cannot be forced to see a solicitor if he does not wish to do so (Code C 6.5A).

Where the detainee does agree to see a solicitor he has the right to consult with that solicitor in private which includes, if he wishes, the absence of the appropriate adult (Code C, Note for Guidance 1E).

As referred to above, where the detainee cannot communicate with the solicitor because of language, hearing, or speech difficulties an interpreter must be called. In this situation the interpreter may not be a police officer or civilian support staff.

## 8.7 Interviews

A juvenile or person who is mentally disordered or otherwise mentally vulnerable must not be interviewed regarding their (suspected) involvement in a criminal offence, or be asked to provide or sign a written statement under caution or record of interview in the absence of an appropriate adult.

The only exception to this is where an officer of at least the rank of superintendent considers that delaying the interview will:

- lead to interference with, or harm to, evidence connected with an offence;
- lead to interference with or physical harm to other people;
- lead to serious loss of, or damage to property;
- alert other suspects yet to be arrested;
- hinder the recovery of property obtained as a result of the commission of an offence (Code C 11.1).

Where any of the above risks exists, an urgent interview may be authorized where the authorizing officer is satisfied that carrying out the interview in such circumstances would not significantly harm the detainee's physical or mental state (Code C 11.18). Once sufficient information has been obtained to avert the risks set out above, then the interview must cease (Code C 11.20).

Similarly, any detainee who:

- appears unable to appreciate the significance of questions and their answers;
- appears unable to understand what is happening because of the effects of drink, drugs, or any illness, ailment, or condition;
- has difficulty understanding English or has a hearing disability and who does not have an interpreter present,

may not be interviewed unless the interview is an urgent one and the authorizing officer is satisfied that no significant harm to the detainee will result.

Guidance to assist in the assessment of how a detainee's physical or mental state might be affected in interview is set out at Annex G to Code C.

The reason why there is such a need for caution in interviewing a vulnerable detainee is made clear in Note for Guidance 11C; that whilst a juvenile or mentally vulnerable detainee may well be capable of providing reliable evidence there is an acknowledged risk that the evidence given will instead be unreliable, misleading, or self-incriminating. Special care should therefore be taken. As well as ensuring that an appropriate adult is involved whenever there is any doubt about the detainee's age or mental state or capacity, corroboration of any facts admitted in interview should be obtained whenever possible.

Where the appropriate adult is present in an interview their role is an active one. The appropriate adult shall be informed that they are not expected to act simply as an observer, but are there to:

- advise the person being interviewed;
- observe whether the interview is being conducted properly and fairly; and
- facilitate communication with the person being interviewed (Code C 11.17).

An appropriate adult present at an interview should be given an opportunity to read and sign the interview record or any written statement taken down during interview (Code 11.12).

A 'person capable of interpreting' must be present during interview if:

- the interviewee has difficulty understanding English;
- the interviewer cannot speak the person's own language;
- the interviewee wants an interpreter to be present.

The only exception is where an urgent interview is authorized (Code C 13.2).

Where an interpreter is present, the interviewer must ensure that the interpreter makes a note of the interview at the time, in the person's language, for use in the event of the interpreter being called to give evidence, and certifies its accuracy. Accordingly, the interview should proceed at such a pace as allows sufficient time for the interpreter to note each question and answer after it is put, given, and interpreted. At the conclusion of the interview, the interviewee should be allowed to read the record or have it read to them and should sign it as correct or indicate the respects in which they consider it inaccurate (Code C 13.3).

If the detainee wishes to give a statement to the police (eg a pre-prepared statement instead of answering questions in interview), and that statement is given in a foreign language, the interpreter must record the statement in the language in which it is made, and the detainee be invited to sign it. The statement will at a later date need to be translated into English (Code C 13.4).

If a person appears to be deaf, or there is doubt about their hearing or speaking ability, they can be interviewed in the absence of an interpreter, but only where they agree in writing to such a course, or an urgent interview is authorized as above (Code 13.5).

As with an interview in a foreign language, the interpreter must be given the opportunity to read the interview record and certify its accuracy in the event of the interpreter being called to give evidence (Code 13.7).

An interpreter should also be called if a juvenile is to be interviewed and the appropriate adult appears to be deaf or there is doubt about their hearing or speaking ability, unless they agree in writing to proceeding without one or it is an urgent interview (Code C 13.6). Note that this only applies where the appropriate adult is also the parent or guardian of the juvenile.

Action taken to call an interpreter and any agreement to be interviewed in the absence of an interpreter must be recorded (Code C 13.11).

Code 11.1 states that an interview must be carried out at a police station 'or other authorised place of detention' unless the interview is an urgent one as defined above. Juveniles may be interviewed at their place of education, but only in exceptional circumstances and only when the principal or their nominee agrees. Where this happens, every effort should be made to notify the parent(s) or some other person responsible for the juvenile's welfare, and the appropriate adult (if this is a different person) that the police want to interview the juvenile, and reasonable time should be allowed to enable the appropriate adult to be present at the interview. If awaiting the arrival of the appropriate adult would cause unreasonable delay then the principal or their nominee can act as the appropriate adult for the purposes of the interview unless the offence of which the juvenile is suspected is an offence against the educational establishment (Code C 11.16).

### Wards of court

Where a juvenile is a ward of court and the police wish to interview him, they must act in accordance with the Practice Direction (Criminal Proceedings: Consolidation), para 5 [2002] 1 WLR 2870. Other than in exceptional cases where immediate action is necessary, the police must apply to the wardship court for leave. Paragraph 5.3 of the Practice Direction acknowledges that it would be an exceptional case justifying immediate action where the police wish to interview a ward who is suspected by the police of having committed a criminal act. The police must act in accordance with the relevant provisions of Code C and notify the parent or other appropriate adult and the reporting officer (if applicable) and supply the reporting officer with a copy of any interview or statement made by the ward.

## 8.8 **Detention**

The necessity for continued detention of any detainee must be reviewed periodically throughout the detention period. A review of detention may take place in person or by telephone, or, where facilities exist, by video-conferencing.

In determining how the review should take place, the review officer must take full account of the needs of the person in custody. Where the detainee is:

- a juvenile; or
- mentally vulnerable; or
- has been subject to medical attention (other than for routine minor ailments)

then ordinarily the review should be conducted in person (C 15.3C).

Without a warrant of further detention, under s 42(1) the maximum period for which the police can authorize detention for an indictable offence is 36 hours. However, whether authorization is in fact given for an extension of detention beyond 24 hours will depend upon the circumstances of the case, and in particular:

- the detainee's special vulnerability;
- the legal obligation to provide an opportunity for representations to be made prior to a decision about extending detention;
- the need to consult and consider the views of any appropriate adult; and
- any alternatives to police custody (Code C 15.2A).

Before authorizing the continued detention of a juvenile or mentally vulnerable person, the authorizing officer, who must be of the rank of superintendent or above, must give the detainee, his solicitor if available, the appropriate adult if available, and (at his discretion) any other people having an interest in the detainee's welfare, the opportunity to make representations (Code C 15.3).

### 8.8.1 **What are the standards of treatment for a vulnerable detainee?**

Sections 8 and 9 of Code C set out provisions for the conditions of detention and the care and treatment of detained persons. They cover the provision of accommodation, toilet and washing facilities, clothing, food, and access to healthcare. It is clear from Code C 1.12 that these are to be considered the minimum standards of treatment. Certain of the provisions relate specifically to the treatment of juveniles and other vulnerable detainees.

### Accommodation in cells

A juvenile must not be placed in a police cell unless there is no other secure accommodation available and the custody officer considers either that it is necessary to place them in a cell for the purposes of practical supervision, or that a cell provides more comfortable accommodation than other secure accommodation available (Code C 8.8). If a juvenile is placed in a cell the reason must be recorded (Code C 8.10).

In no circumstances may a juvenile be placed in a cell with a detained adult (Code C 8.8).

### Use of restraints

Restraints may only be used in a locked cell where absolutely necessary. The restraint equipment must be approved for use, reasonable and necessary in the circumstances, and used to ensure the safety of the detainee and others. Particular care must be taken in deciding to use any form of restraint where the detainee is deaf, mentally disordered, or otherwise mentally vulnerable (Code C 8.2).

If any restraint is used, it must be recorded (Code C 8.11).

### Checks

Detainees should normally be visited every hour. Juveniles and mentally vulnerable detainees should, however, be visited more frequently wherever possible (Code 9.3; Note for Guidance 9B).

Unless otherwise directed by a health professional, those detainees suspected of being intoxicated (whether through drink or drugs), or whose level of consciousness raises concern should be visited and roused at least every half hour and their condition assessed (Code C 9.3).

Where there is any doubt about the condition of a detainee, an appropriate healthcare professional should be called.

## Medical treatment

Where a detainee requests a clinical examination, an appropriate health care professional must be called as soon as practicable to assess the detainee's clinical needs (Code C 9.8).

If a health care professional is called to examine or treat a detainee, the custody officer shall ask for their opinion about any risks or problems which the police need to take into account when making decisions about the detainee's continued detention; when to carry out an interview; and the need for safeguards (Code C 9.13).

It is important that the custody officer ensures that he fully understands any directions given by the healthcare professional, particularly in relation to the frequency of visits or need for observation (Code C 9.14; Note for Guidance 9F).

A record must be made in the custody record of:

- arrangements made for an examination by a health care professional due to an allegation of assault or the use of unreasonable force by the police on the detainee;
- any arrangements made to secure clinical attention where the detainee appeared to be suffering from physical illness, mental disorder, was injured, or appeared to need clinical attention;
- any request by the detainee for clinical attention and arrangements made in response;
- the injury, ailment, condition, or other reason which made it necessary to arrange clinical attention;
- any clinical directions and advice given to the police by the health care professional concerning the care and treatment of the detainee;
- the responses received when attempting to rouse a detainee in accordance with the procedures in Annex H (a series of criteria used to measure the detainee's level of rousability) in order to chart any change in the detainee's consciousness level and arrange clinical treatment if appropriate (Code C 9.15).

# 8.9 **Intimate Searches**

### 8.9.1 **What is an 'intimate search'?**

An intimate search is defined in Annex A of Code C as 'the physical examination of a person's body orifices other than the mouth'. Attention is drawn to the risks associated with intrusive searches.

Intimate searches may only take place where authorized by an officer of the rank of inspector or above who has reasonable grounds for believing that the person may have concealed on themselves anything which they could and might use to cause injury to themselves or another, or a Class A drug which they intended to supply or export to another, and where an intimate search is the only way to recover such items (Annex A2).

Ordinarily, the search must be carried out by a registered medical practitioner or registered nurse and may only take place at a hospital, surgery, or other medical premises, or at the police station (Annex A3, 4).

Where the search is for an object that might be used to cause injury and where it is not practicable for a medical practitioner or nurse to carry out the search, then an officer of at least the rank of inspector may authorize a police officer of the same sex as the detainee to carry out the search; but only following a risk assessment and as a matter of last resort (Annex A3, 3A, 6).

Where the person to be searched is a juvenile, or is mentally vulnerable, an appropriate adult of the same sex must be present during the search unless the detainee specifically requests a particular adult of the opposite sex who is readily available. An intimate search of a juvenile may only take place in the absence of the appropriate adult where the juvenile signifies in the presence of the appropriate adult that he does not want the appropriate adult to be present during the search, and the appropriate adult agrees. Where that happens, a record must be made of the juvenile's decision which the appropriate adult must sign (Annex A5).

Any intimate search must be carried out with proper regard to the sensitivity and vulnerability of the detainee (Annex A6).

A record must be made of the details of the search (Annex A7).

## 8.10 Strip Searches

### 8.10.1 What is a strip search?

A strip search is defined in Code C, Annex A9 as 'a search involving the removal of more than outer clothing'. Strip searches are not to be carried out routinely, but may only be carried out where the authorizing officer reasonably believes that a detainee may have concealed an article which the detainee would not be allowed to keep (Code C, Annex B10).

The officer carrying out the strip search must be of the same sex as the detainee; no-one of the opposite sex to the detainee may be present save for an appropriate adult who has been specifically requested by the detainee (Annex B11(b)).

Except in cases of urgency where there is a risk of serious harm to the detainee or others, whenever a strip search involves exposure of intimate body parts, there must be at least two people present other than the detainee, one of whom must be the appropriate adult where the search is of a juvenile or mentally vulnerable person (Annex B11(c)).

Where the person to be searched is a juvenile, then unless urgent, a strip search must take place in the presence of the appropriate adult unless the juvenile signifies in the presence of the appropriate adult that he does not want the adult to be present during the search and the adult agrees. In such circumstances, a record must be made of the juvenile's decision and signed by the appropriate adult (Annex B11(c)).

As with intimate searches, the guidance makes it clear that proper regard must be had to the sensitivity and vulnerability of the detainee (Annex B11(d)).

## 8.11 **Drug Testing**

In some (but not all) police areas or stations within police areas, provisions are in force under s 63B and Code C 17 providing police with the powers to take a sample of urine or a non-intimate sample from a detained person in order to test whether he has Class A drugs in his body. The power is not a blanket one; the detainee must have been charged with a 'trigger offence' (see Part III Criminal Justice and Court Services Act 2000) or any other offence where an officer of at least the rank of inspector has reasonable grounds for suspecting that the misuse by that person of any specified Class A drug caused or contributed to the offence and authorizes the sample to be taken.

The detainee can only be requested to provide the sample; it cannot be taken by force. However, he must be warned before the request is made that if he fails to provide a sample without good cause then he may be liable to prosecution (s 63B(4), (5)).

Section 5(3)(a) of the Criminal Justice Act 2003 reduced the minimum age for drug testing from 18 to 14; however the new minimum age will only apply in those areas where those provisions have been brought into force, and where the relevant chief officer of police has been notified by the Secretary of State that arrangements for the taking of samples from persons under the age of 18 have been made for the police area as a whole, or for a particular police station within that area, and the notice has not been withdrawn. Those areas are set out in Annex J of Code C.

Where the detainee is under 17, the request for the sample, the warning of the consequences of refusal and (where applicable) the grounds for authorization, and the taking of the sample may not take place other than in the presence of an appropriate adult (s 63B(5A)).

An appropriate adult for the purposes of this section means the person's:

- parent or guardian or, if he is in the care of a local authority or voluntary organization, a person representing that authority or organization; or
- a social worker of a local authority social services department; or
- if none of the above is available, any responsible person aged 18 or over who is not a police officer or a person employed by the police.

## 8.12 **Charging**

When the officer in charge of the investigation reasonably believes that there is sufficient evidence to provide a realistic prospect of conviction, he must immediately inform the custody officer who is responsible for considering whether the detainee should be charged.

**171**

Where the detainee is a juvenile or mentally vulnerable, any resulting action shall be taken in the presence of the appropriate adult if they are present at the time, and if they are not, then the provisions must be complied with again in their presence when they arrive unless the detainee has previously been released (Code C 16.1). However, there is no power to detain a person and delay action under the charging procedures solely to await the presence of an appropriate adult. Neither can bail be refused or delayed simply because an appropriate adult is not available (Note for Guidance 16C).

When a juvenile or mentally vulnerable detainee is charged, a written notice showing particulars of the offence, the precise offence in law with which he has been charged, the officer's name, and the case reference number should be given to the appropriate adult (Code C 16.3).

If, after the detainee has been charged with or informed that they may be prosecuted for an offence, an officer wants to tell them about any written statement or interview with another person relating to such an offence, the detainee shall either be handed a copy of the written statement or the content of the interview record brought to their attention. Where the detainee cannot read, the document shall be read to them. Where the detainee is a juvenile, mentally disordered, or otherwise mentally vulnerable, the appropriate adult shall also be given a copy, or the interview record brought to their attention (Code 16.4, 16.4A).

## 8.13 **Bail**

Following charge, a person must be released from police detention either with or without bail. Continued detention can only be authorized if one of the situations set out in s 38(1)(a) applies. For a juvenile detainee there are two further situations in which bail can be refused, and those are where the custody officer has reasonable grounds for believing that the juvenile ought to be detained in his own interests (s 38(1)(b)(ii)), or where the offence with which the person is charged is murder (s 38(1)(c))

Where detention is authorized under this section that detention must be secured in local authority accommodation, not at the police station, unless one of the exceptions set out in s 38(6) applies. They are that:

- it is impracticable (for reasons that the custody officer must certify), or
- the juvenile is over 12 years old, no secure accommodation is available, and keeping him in other local authority accommodation would not be adequate to protect the public from serious harm.

### What is meant by 'serious harm'?

'Serious harm' is not defined in the act, save in relation to a charge for a violent or sexual offence where it is construed as 'death or serious personal injury, whether physical or psychological, occasioned by further such offences committed by him' (s 38(6A)).

### What is meant by 'impracticable'?

Note for Guidance 16D provides some assistance on the meaning of 'impractical' in s 28(6)(a). Neither a juvenile's behaviour, nor the nature of the offence, nor the unavailability of secure local authority accommodation would make a transfer to local authority accommodation 'impracticable'. They may however be relevant factors under s 38(6)(b) where the juvenile is over 12 years of age.

Where bail is granted, the release on bail cannot be delayed pending the arrival of an appropriate adult unless the absence of the appropriate adult gives rise to one of the grounds for continued detention after charge in accordance with s 38.

# Practical Guidance

## 8.14 **Case Study**

*PC Harvey arrest a 14-year-old juvenile for handling stolen goods and takes him before PS Morris, the custody officer. The juvenile refuses to provide any details in respect of his identity but states he is 18 years old. PS Morris considers he looks much younger. How should PS Morris deal with the prisoner?*

As the prisoner appears to be under 17 years then in the absence of clear evidence to the contrary and despite the stated age, PS Morris should treat him as a juvenile for the purpose of the Codes of Practice (Codes of Practice C 1.5).

*PC Harvey wishes to interview the prisoner who still refuses to provide any personal details. The Social Services have indicated there will be a two-hour delay before a social worker can attend to act as an appropriate adult. John, a civilian employee at the station, has experience of working with underprivileged youths and runs a local youth centre. He offers to sit in at the interview as an appropriate adult. How should PS Morris respond to John's offer?*

As John is employed by the police he is specifically excluded from acting in the role of appropriate adult. PS Morris should therefore decline the offer and delay the interview until a social worker can attend the station (Code C 1.7).

*PC Harvey establishes the juvenile's name and his address; he also receives reliable information that other stolen goods can be found at the address.*

*The officer obtains written authority from an inspector to search the premises. The juvenile now gives his personal details and requests that his parents are informed of his whereabouts. PC Harvey requests that notification be delayed pending the search of the premises. How should PC Harvey's request be dealt with?*

The Codes of Practice requires the custody officer to inform the parents of a detained juvenile of the arrest, where the person is detained, and why the person was arrested. This right is in addition to the right not to be held incommunicado and cannot be interfered with. The custody officer should therefore make arrangements for the parents to be informed as soon as practicable. If the address were nearby, an option would be for officers to attend and inform the parents personally. The premises could then be searched under the authority of s 18 of PACE and little opportunity would have been provided for the occupants to dispose of any stolen goods.

# Evidence: Part VIII

**Law and Commentary**

**Practical Guidance**

# Law and Commentary

## 9.1 Introduction

In early versions of the Act, important provisions relating to evidence in criminal proceedings could be found in both Part VII (Documentary Evidence in Criminal Proceedings) and Part VIII (Evidence in Criminal Proceedings—General). Now, however, Part VII is all but obsolete; s 69, which dealt with evidence derived from computer records, has been repealed, and s 68, which concerned the admissibility of documentary evidence, was replaced by ss 23 to 28 of the Criminal Justice Act 1998, which in turn has been replaced by corresponding provisions in the Criminal Justice Act 2003. The only remaining section in Part VII relates to proving the contents of a document by the production of a microfilm copy of it.

Part VIII by contrast retains enormous importance. Arguably, some of the sections contained within it, in particular ss 76 (confessions) and 78 (exclusion of unfair evidence) are among the most significant of the entire Act. Other sections deal with proof of previous convictions and acquittals where that evidence is admissible in evidence (ss 73–75), confessions, by the accused (s 76), a co-accused (s 76A), and special provisions dealing with confessions by the 'mentally handicapped' (s 77), as well as miscellaneous provisions that provide the courts with the power to exclude evidence (s 78), deal with the competence and compellability of the accused's spouse (ss 80–80A), and the necessity to give advance notice of expert evidence.

## 9.2 Convictions and Acquittals

Section 73 provides one way of proving, where it is necessary to do so, that a person has been convicted or acquitted of an offence in the United Kingdom. It is not the only way by which such matters can be proved; s 73(4) makes it clear that:

> the method of proving a conviction or acquittal authorised by this section shall be in addition to and not to the exclusion of any other authorised manner of proving a conviction or acquittal.

All that is required is the production of a signed certificate or memorandum of conviction or acquittal, together with proof that the person named in the certificate is the person whose conviction or acquittal is to be proved.

### 9.2.1 What does a conviction or acquittal prove?

Section 73 is silent as to what a conviction or acquittal may go to prove, or when such evidence may be admissible.

The Act provides no assistance in relation to either the effect of or the admissibility of an acquittal. Following the decided case law, however, it is likely to be rare that evidence of a previous acquittal is judged to be relevant and therefore admissible, being no more than a reflection of the opinion of the fact-finding tribunal in earlier proceedings. For this same reason, an acquittal is not conclusive proof of innocence, nor does it mean that all relevant issues that arose in the previous matter for which the person was acquitted were resolved in his favour (*R v Terry* [2005] 2 Cr App R 7, CA).

Neither does the Act provide any help on when proof of a conviction may be admissible.

It does however deal with the *effect* of the admissibility of evidence of a conviction in s 74. By virtue of that section, where it is admissible to prove the conviction of a person, whether the accused or a person other than the accused, evidence of his conviction by or before a court in the United Kingdom or a Service court (court-martial or Standing Civilian Court) outside the United Kingdom is admissible as proof that he did commit the offence for which he was convicted unless the contrary is proved.

Furthermore, not only can the fact of conviction be proved as set out in s 73, but (where admissible) the facts upon which the conviction was based can be adduced in evidence through either

(a) the contents of any document which is admissible as evidence of the conviction, and
(b) the contents of the information, complaint, indictment or charge-sheet on which the person in question was convicted (s 75(1)).

It is clear from all of the above, that s 74 is designed to be used where it is relevant and admissible evidence to show that a person *committed* the offence in question, and not simply the fact that he was convicted of it (*R v Smith* [2007] EWCA Crim 2105). Proving the conviction is merely the means by which it may be proved that the person committed the offence.

## 9.3 Confessions (Sections 76, 76A, and 77)

Section 76 deals with the important topic of the admissibility of confessions made by an accused person and their exclusion where the prosecution fail to prove that the confession was, or may have been obtained as a result of oppression, or anything else said or done which was likely to render that confession unreliable.

Although the best known, s 76 is not the only provision in the Act that is concerned with confession evidence. A new s 76A inserted by the Criminal Justice Act 2003 sets out parallel grounds for the admission or exclusion of confessions made by an accused person where their admission is sought by a co-accused rather than the prosecution.

Section 77 imposes a duty on the courts to direct themselves or a jury to treat a case that depends wholly or substantially upon the confession of a mentally handicapped person with caution.

### 9.3.1 Section 76

Insofar as it is relevant to a matter in issue in proceedings, the prosecution may adduce in evidence a confession made by an accused person. In order to be admissible, however, two further tests must be met, namely that the confession was not obtained either:

(a) by oppression of the person who made it; or

(b) in consequence of anything said or done which was likely, in the circumstances existing at the time, to render unreliable any confession which might be made in consequence thereof. (s 76(2))

Where there is an issue as to how the confession was obtained, whether that issue is raised by a party to the proceedings or by the court of its own motion, the prosecution are required to prove beyond reasonable doubt that the confession was not obtained in either of the ways set out in s 76(2).

What is perhaps surprising given that s 76(2)(b) is concerned with the reliability or otherwise of the confession, is that the *truth* of the confession is irrelevant to any determination. It may be thought that if a confession is true, then it must also be reliable. The Act is quite specific, however, that if the prosecution are unable to prove to the required standard that the confession has not been obtained through oppression or in consequence of anything said or done likely to render it unreliable then the court 'shall not' allow it to be admitted in evidence 'notwithstanding that it may be true'.

### What is a confession?

A confession is defined in s 82(1) as including 'any statement wholly or partly adverse to the person who made it, whether made to a person in authority or not and whether made in words or otherwise'.

It can be seen from the above definition that a confession for the purposes of ss 76 to 77 does not necessarily mean 'I did it'; rather, any statement, whether made orally or in writing, in which a person amongst other things admits relevant matters that are adverse to him is a confession.

The relevant time to which the court should have regard when determining whether or not the admissions were indeed adverse to the maker's interests, is the time at which the statement was made rather than, for example, the time at which the evidence is sought to be adduced at trial.

### What is meant by oppression?

Section 76(8) states that oppression 'includes torture, inhuman or degrading treatment, and the use or threat of violence (whether or not amounting to torture)', but conduct need not be so extreme to be oppressive; for example, in *R v Paris, Abdullai and Miller* (1993) 97 Cr App R 99, prolonged questioning of the defendant in which accusations were made in a hostile and intimidating way, where the strength of the prosecution evidence was exaggerated to the suspect and where the police made it clear that they would continue to question him until he agreed with their version of events, was found by the Court of Appeal to have amounted to oppression; and in *R v Mushtaq* [2005] 1 WLR 1513, HL, the House of Lords approved the definition of oppression used in *R v Prager* [1972] 1 WLR 260, CA as:

> ... questioning which by its nature, duration or other circumstances (including the fact of custody) excites hopes (such as the hope of release) or fears, or so affects the mind of the subject that his will crumbles and he speaks when otherwise he would have stayed silent.

### What is meant by 'in consequence of anything said or done'?

Two obvious points arise when considering whether a confession should be excluded under s 76(2)(b). Firstly, that the confession must have been obtained 'in consequence' of something said or done by another. In other words, there must be a link between the making of the confession and the thing said or done. Secondly, that whatever the thing said or done, it must have been something which was likely 'in the circumstances existing at the time' to render the subsequent confession unreliable.

This second factor means, of course, that the particular characteristics of the defendant have to be taken into account as well as, for example, the type of offence about which he is being questioned. So, for example, a court may conclude that to tell a suspect that he will have to remain in police custody until a matter is resolved is unlikely to render unreliable a confession subsequently made by a man of reasonable firmness and intelligence who is being questioned about a serious offence, but a different conclusion may be reached where the 'threat' is made to a vulnerable person who is being questioned about something comparatively minor.

It should also be noted that the 'circumstances existing at the time' could include omitting to do something. In particular, a failure to comply with the Codes of Practice may result in the exclusion of evidence; so where an interview takes place ('something said or done') where there had been a failure to caution the defendant or to make him aware of his right to legal advice ('the circumstances existing at the time'), that omission may well be judged likely to render unreliable any confession which is made as a result.

### What is meant by 'likely ... to render unreliable'?

The Act means what is says. The court is only required to look at whether the oppression or the thing said or done was *likely* to make the subsequent confession unreliable. Unreliability is both fact and, indeed, defendant specific.

**179**

It does not have to be shown that the confession was in fact unreliable, or that it was untrue. The truth or otherwise of the confession made is irrelevant to the test that has to be adopted.

### General propositions

The following observations about s 76 can be made;

- the definition of oppression in s 76(8) is not exhaustive; a wider test as set out in *R v Mushtaq* has been approved (see above);
- there must be a link under s 76(2)(b) between the thing said and done and the confession subsequently made;
- the 'circumstances existing at the time' can include the physical and mental characteristics of the defendant—whether or not known to the police at the time—and can include omitting to do something that should have been done under the Act or Codes as well as doing something that the police are prohibited from doing;
- not every breach of the Act or Codes will render a subsequent confession unreliable—all the circumstances existing at the time will be considered;
- the courts are only concerned with whether the conduct is likely to render a confession made as a result unreliable. It is not necessary to show that it did render the confession unreliable neither is it relevant to consider whether or not the confession is or might be true.

Note, however, that a confession may be excluded under s 78 as well as under s 76.

### 9.3.2 Section 76A

This new section, inserted by s 128(1) of the Criminal Justice Act 2003, sets out identical tests governing the admissibility of a confession made by one defendant which a co-defendant wishes to adduce in his own case. The only difference is that whereas under s 76(2) the prosecution must satisfy the tests beyond reasonable doubt, a co-defendant need only do so on the balance of probabilities. In the same case, therefore, a confession may be ruled inadmissible for use by the prosecution, but admissible for a co-defendant. The remedy in such a situation is likely to be either an application by the defendant whose confession it is for a ruling excluding the admission of that evidence under s 78, or an application for separate trials. Note that a co-defendant's confession is not admissible under s 76A where the co-defendant has pleaded guilty and therefore is not party to the trial, although it may be admitted under the hearsay provisions of the Criminal Justice Act 2003 (*R v Finch* [2007] EWCA Crim 36).

### 9.3.3 What are the consequences when a confession is ruled inadmissible?

Where a confession has been ruled inadmissible, no further reference to it can be made in the course of the trial unless made by the person whose confession it is. Subsection 4(a) of both s 76 and s 76A does, however, permit evidence to be given of any facts discovered as a result of the confession. So, for example, if a suspect being questioned about a burglary admits that he committed the offence and tells the police where he has hidden the stolen property, and where that confession is excluded under s 76, evidence may be given that the police went to a particular location and recovered the stolen items, but no evidence can be given to explain how it was that they came to discover that that was the place at which the items would be found, as to do so would be to admit evidence of the confession which has been excluded, and this is inadmissible unless adduced by the defendant himself (s 76(5)).

Subsection 4(b) also allows evidence of an excluded confession to be given where it is relevant to show that the defendant 'speaks, writes or expresses himself in a particular way'. This will, however, be limited to only so much as is strictly necessary. So, for example, it might be relevant and necessary to demonstrate that the defendant speaks with a particular accent; sufficient of a tape-recorded interview which has otherwise been excluded might be played for this purpose, but the early uncontentious introductory comments may be sufficient.

### 9.3.4 Confessions by mentally handicapped persons

Where a case depends 'wholly or substantially' upon a confession made by a mentally handicapped person, and where that confession was not made in the presence of an 'independent person', the judge must warn the jury that there is a special need for caution before convicting the accused in reliance on the confession, and explain why (s 77(1)).

Where there is no jury (eg in summary proceedings before the magistrates or where a judge is sitting without a jury), the court must treat the case as one in which there is a special need for caution before convicting the accused on his confession (s 77(2), (2A)).

### What is meant by 'mentally handicapped'

Mentally handicapped is defined in s 77(3) as ' ... a state of arrested or incomplete development of mind which includes significant impairment of intelligence and social functioning'. It is not clear why the term 'mentally handicapped' was used rather than 'mentally vulnerable' or 'mentally disordered' as in Code C; however, it is likely that someone who met the test of mentally vulnerable or mentally disordered as set out in Code C, Note for Guidance 1G, would equally meet the definition of mentally handicapped in s 77(3).

### What does 'wholly or substantially' mean?

The test to be applied has been held to be whether the prosecution case is substantially less strong without the confession than it is with it (*R v Campbell* [1995] 1 Cr App R 522 CA).

**181**

### Who is 'an independent person'?

The 'independent person' must, for the purposes of the Act, be someone other than the person to whom the confession was made. Where, therefore, a confession was made to a friend, that person cannot be an independent person (*R v Bailey* [1995] 2 Cr App R 262, CA); neither can a police officer or person 'employed for or engaged on, police purposes', who are specifically excluded from the definition by s 77(3). An independent person is most likely to be the appropriate adult. A solicitor can also be an independent person for these purposes when attending the police station in a professional capacity.

## 9.4 Exclusion of Unfair Evidence (Sections 78 and 82(3))

Tucked towards the back of the Act under the heading 'Miscellaneous' is perhaps the best known of all the provisions and arguably the one with the most far-reaching effects. Section 78(1) states that:

> In any proceedings the court may refuse to allow evidence on which the prosecution proposes to rely to be given if it appears to the court that, having regard to all the circumstances, including the circumstances in which the evidence was obtained, the admission of the evidence would have such an adverse effect on the fairness of the proceedings that the court ought not to admit it.

### 9.4.1 When will Section 78 apply?

No hard and fast rules can be applied to the application of this section; nor are there any uniform guidelines. The power to exclude evidence under this section of the Act is entirely a matter for the discretion of the judge in the particular circumstances of the case before him. In each case, the test that the judge has to apply is whether or not the admission of the evidence would have such an adverse effect on the fairness of the case that he ought not to admit the challenged evidence. Unfortunately for the defendant, this produces uncertain results; what is considered unfair by one judge may be considered fair by another. The Court of Appeal will not interfere with the exercise of a judge's discretion under s 78 save where it can be shown that he has failed to exercise his discretion or has otherwise come to a conclusion that no reasonable judge could have reached. Moreover, although there is voluminous case law on s 78, as each case turns on its own facts caution must be applied in seeking to gain any general guidance as to what may or may not be excluded under this section; the same conduct or misconduct may result in different conclusions depending on all the other circumstances in the case. Some general points can, however, be made.

- Section 78 can be invoked in respect of any evidence irrespective of any other powers that the court has to exclude evidence. So, for example, a court may refuse to exclude the evidence of a confession under s 76 but nevertheless exclude it under s 78.

- Evidence is frequently sought to be excluded where it has been obtained in breach of the Act or Codes. Not every breach will, however, result in exclusion; normally the breach must have been significant and substantial. However, it is the effect of the breach that is important rather than the nature of it. So, a failure to caution prior to interviewing a vulnerable person in police detention for the first time may lead to the exclusion of that interview, whereas a court would be less likely to hold that the failure to caution had such an adverse effect on the fairness of proceedings that evidence was required to be excluded where the person interviewed was a career criminal with substantial experience of police interviews.
- Although not designed to penalize officers who fail to act appropriately, s 78 specifically permits a court to look at how evidence was obtained. Evidence may therefore be excluded where it was obtained improperly or through unlawful means. However there is no obligation to exclude such evidence, merely a discretion to do so.
- Although evidence will often be excluded where a police officer has acted in bad faith, there is no requirement for bad faith to be shown although it will undoubtedly form part of the 'circumstances of the case'. The circumstances of the particular case may call for the exclusion of evidence even where the officer has acted entirely properly. So, for example, where a mentally disordered person was interviewed in the absence of an appropriate adult, the evidence obtained therein might be excluded even though the officer had no reason to suspect that the person was mentally disordered.
- The judge must consider fairness to both sides.
- Although no reference is made to the burden or standard of proof, and although the court may raise s 78 of its own motion, almost invariably the issue is raised by the defence. The practical effect is that the burden of persuading the judge first that there is an issue to be decided and then that the issue should be resolved by the exclusion of the evidence rests on the defence.

The court's power to exclude evidence is not, however, limited to that provided by s 78. Indeed, section 82(3) retains the court's common law power to regulate the admission of evidence by providing that:

> Nothing in this Part of this Act shall prejudice any power of a court to exclude evidence (whether by preventing questions from being put or otherwise) at its discretion.

## 9.5 Time for Taking an Accused's Evidence (Section 77)

Section 79 provides that where the defendant is to give evidence and will also be calling one or more further witnesses of fact, then the defendant should give his evidence first 'unless the court in its discretion otherwise directs'.

## 9.6  Evidence from an Accused's Spouse or Civil Partner (Section 80)

Under s 80(2), the husband, wife, or civil partner of a defendant is compellable to give evidence on behalf of his or her spouse or civil partner unless either:

(a)  he or she is also charged in any proceedings, or

(b)  the offence with which his or her spouse or civil partner is charged is a 'specified offence' that is one which:

- involves an assault on, or injury or threat of injury to the wife, husband, or civil partner, or to a person who was under 16 at the material time;
- is a sexual offence alleged to have been committed against a person who was at the material time under 16;
- consists of attempting or conspiring to commit, or of aiding, abetting, counselling, or procuring or inciting the commission of any such offence as set out above.

Where the offence is a 'specified offence' then a spouse or civil partner *is* compellable to give evidence on behalf of any other person charged in the proceedings (that is, not his or her spouse or civil partner), or on behalf of the prosecution.

### What is meant by 'charged in any proceedings'?

This means charged *and* liable to be convicted. So it does not apply where, for example, the person has already pleaded guilty, or where a charge has been subsequently withdrawn (s 80(4A)). Note that the term used in s 80(4) is 'any proceedings', not 'the same proceedings'. So, for example, if for whatever reason separate trials had been ordered of a husband and wife who were each charged with an offence or offences arising out of the same facts, then one spouse could not be compelled to give evidence for or against the other.

The proceedings must be criminal proceedings including those taking place before a court-martial whether in the United Kingdom or elsewhere.

### What is 'the material time'?

The material time is the date upon which the specified offence was alleged to have been committed.

### What is meant by 'a sexual offence'?

Section 80(7) defines a sexual offence as an offence under the Protection of Children Act 1978, or Part I of the Sexual Offences Act 2003.

### Is a spouse compellable if divorced?

Section 80(5) provides that once divorced, a person is treated as if they had never been married and is therefore compellable to give evidence for or against their former spouse. It makes no difference whether the offence about which they are giving evidence occurred before, during or after the end of the marriage. Section 80(5A) sets out an identical rule for civil partners.

Section 80 has no applicability at all to common-law partners or to second or subsequent wives in a polygamous marriage.

Under s 80A, the prosecution are prohibited from making any comment about the failure of a compellable witness to give evidence on behalf of their spouse or civil partner.

## 9.7 **Expert Evidence (Section 81)**

Section 81 provides for the making of rules requiring a party to criminal proceedings to make advance disclosure to the other side of any expert evidence proposed to be adduced, and prohibiting such evidence from being adduced where advance disclosure has not been made as required except with the leave of the court.

The current rules made under this section are to be found in Part 33 of the Criminal Procedure Rules 2010.

# Practical Guidance

## 9.8 **Case Study 1**

DC Potts is investigating a recent theft in which a large amount of cash has been stolen. The owner of the property from where the cash was taken informs DC Potts that he suspects that his 18-year-old son, James, may have been responsible. DC Potts establishes that James has a drug addiction and has stolen from his father in the past, but that the police were not informed on those occasions. James does not live at his father's address but does have keys and visits frequently. DC Potts asks the victim to notify him should he become aware of James' whereabouts.

The next day, the victim attends the police station with James and informs DC Potts that James was indeed responsible for the theft and produces a handwritten note of confession, made by the father but signed by James. DC Potts takes a statement from the victim who explains how he informed James that unless he told the truth he would no longer provide him with financial support, following which James 'broke down' and admitted stealing the money to spend on drugs. DC Potts arrests James, but at a subsequent interview and following advice from his solicitor, James remains silent.

*Is the evidence so far obtained sufficient to found a conviction?*

An admission does not have to be made to a police officer to come within the ambit of s 82(1); the signed note was adverse to James and, therefore, would amount to a confession within the meaning of the Act. However, whilst admissible evidence under s 76(1), the confession would be vulnerable to an application under s 76(2)(b); in this particular case, James' admission appears to have been made under threat of losing the allowance provided by his father; it could be argued that this was the only reason why he made the confession he did and that for this reason it is unreliable and should be excluded. DC Potts would accordingly be well advised to undertake further enquiries to obtain additional evidence—for example a s 18(1) search of James' address.

## 9.9 **Case Study 2**

PC Smith has arrested Vazon, a seasoned criminal with many convictions, for burglary and interviews him on tape. PC Smith properly cautions Vazon at the start of the interview, which is conducted in accordance with the Codes of Practice. Vazon gives 'no comment' answers to all questions asked. After 30 minutes, Vazon asks for a break. On resuming the interview PC Smith introduces all those present, but forgets to remind Vazon that he is still under caution. In this second part of the interview, Vazon has a change of heart and unexpectedly admits the offence. Later, when transcribing the tape, PC Smith realizes his mistake.

*Has there been a breach of the Codes?*

Code E 4.14 states that after any break in an interview the suspect should be reminded that he is under caution, and if there is any doubt the caution must be given in full again. PC Smith's failure to remind Vazon of the caution is a breach of the Code.

*Would the interview be excluded?*

Any breach of the Codes may give rise to an application for the exclusion of evidence thereafter obtained under either s 76 (confessions) or s 78 (fairness); however it is not every breach that would result in such a determination. Determinations in reported cases in which s 76 or s 78 arguments have arisen are very fact specific. Much depends on the nature of the breach, the reason for it, the motivation of the officer and facts known about the offender. Here, Vazon is an experienced criminal who has been interviewed many times before and who could therefore be expected to be well aware of his rights. There is no suggestion that his admissions in this case were made any way other than voluntarily and fully in the knowledge that they could be used against him. It is unlikely therefore that any application to exclude would succeed. The outcome may well be different if the person interviewed is an inexperienced or vulnerable suspect, particularly if they do not have the benefit of legal advice.

As well as reminding the suspect of the caution, it is also good practice for the interviewing officer to demonstrate that nothing untoward has occurred during a break that might encourage a suspect to make admissions, by summarizing on tape the reasons for the break and asking the suspect whether he agrees with the accuracy of the summary given (Code E Note for Guidance 4G).

## 9.10 **Case Study 3**

PC Jones, a relatively inexperienced officer is dealing with Brown who is in custody for burglary. Brown has a large number of convictions and is a prolific offender. PC Jones had reasonable grounds to arrest Brown, but with nothing else the evidence is weak and unlikely to lead to a conviction. PC Jones carries out an interview during which Brown, who is not represented, says nothing. Feeling somewhat frustrated, PC Jones calls a break and decides to apply some pressure. During the break, when the recording equipment is turned off, PC Jones informs Brown that the results of a forensic examination have just been received and that Brown's fingerprints have been identified inside the premises where the burglary occurred. In fact, no forensic evidence to connect Brown to the offence has been obtained. Brown, who did in fact commit the offence, believes that the game is up and makes a full admission during the second part of the interview and identifies where the proceeds of the burglary are hidden; these are subsequently recovered.

*Was PC Jones' tactic justified?*

Whilst there is no obligation to disclose any information pre-interview, it is important that neither the suspect nor his legal representative (if any) are misled. In this case, PC Jones has told a blatant lie. Brown has made a full admission, but only as a consequence of the deceit practised upon him by PC Jones.

*Would the admissions subsequently made be excluded?*

Brown's admissions are adverse to him and accordingly amount to a confession within the meaning of s 76(1). They would be extremely vulnerable to an application under s 76(2) to exclude them in that it could be strongly argued that PC Jones' actions in deceiving Brown would have rendered the resulting confession unreliable. The fact that the proceeds of the burglary were subsequently found at the location stated by Brown would not retrospectively legitimize PC Jones' actions or provide any real grounds to rebut such an application. Moreover, the courts take a dim view of such behaviour by the police, and in this case, where PC Jones has told a deliberate lie, there is likely to be adverse criticism by the court of his actions.

*If the admissions are excluded, would the evidence found as a result of those admissions also be excluded?*

The fact that the admissions are excluded does not automatically render the evidence of the finding of the proceeds of the crime as a result of those admissions inadmissible (s 76(4)(a)); however, no mention could be made of how the police came by the items, and, in the absence of any forensic link to Brown, such evidence would not strengthen the prosecution's case against him.

# Appendix 1

# Police and Criminal Evidence Act 1984

## 1984 Chapter 60

CONTENTS

Act

*Detention—miscellaneous*

PART V

QUESTIONING AND TREATMENT OF PERSONS BY POLICE

PART VI

CODES OF PRACTICE—GENERAL

Act

## Part X
### Police—General

## Part XI
### Miscellaneous and Supplementary

SCHEDULES

# Police and Criminal Evidence Act 1984

## 1984 Chapter 60

An Act to make further provision in relation to the powers and duties of the police, persons in police detention, criminal evidence, police discipline and complaints against the police; to provide for arrangements for obtaining the views of the community on policing and for a rank of deputy chief constable; to amend the law relating to the Police Federations and Police Forces and Police Cadets in Scotland; and for connected purposes.

[31st October 1984]

s.75

BE IT ENACTED by the Queen's most Excellent Majesty, by and with the advice and consent of the Lords Spiritual and Temporal, and Commons, in this present Parliament assembled, and by the authority of the same, as follows:—

PART I

POWERS TO STOP AND SEARCH

### 1 Power of constable to stop and search persons, vehicles etc

(1) A constable may exercise any power conferred by this section—
  (a) in any place to which at the time when he proposes to exercise the power the public or any section of the public has access, on payment or otherwise, as of right or by virtue of express or implied permission; or
  (b) in any other place to which people have ready access at the time when he proposes to exercise the power but which is not a dwelling.
(2) Subject to subsection (3) to (5) below, a constable—
  (a) may search—
    (i) any person or vehicle;
    (ii) anything which is in or on a vehicle,
    for stolen or prohibited articles[, any article to which subsection (8A) below applies or any firework to which subsection (8B) below applies][1]; and
  (b) may detain a person or vehicle for the purpose of such a search.
(3) This section does not give a constable power to search a person or vehicle or anything in or on a vehicle unless he has reasonable grounds for suspecting that he will find stolen or prohibited articles[, any article to which subsection (8A) below applies or any firework to which subsection (8B) below applies][2].
(4) If a person is in a garden or yard occupied with and used for the purposes of a dwelling or on other land so occupied and used, a constable may not search

---

[1] Amended by SOCAPA 2005, s 115(1), (2).
[2] Amended by SOCAPA 2005, s 115(1), (3).

him in the exercise of the power conferred by this section unless the constable has reasonable grounds for believing—

    (a) that he does not reside in the dwelling; and

    (b) that he is not in the place in question with the express or implied permission of a person who resides in the dwelling.

(5)    If a vehicle is in a garden or yard occupied with and used for the purposes of a dwelling or on other land so occupied and used, a constable may not search the vehicle or anything in or on it in the exercise of the power conferred by this section unless he has reasonable grounds for believing—

    (a) that the person in charge of the vehicle does not reside in the dwelling; and

    (b) that the vehicle is not in the place in question with the express or implied permission of a person who resides in the dwelling.

(6)    If in the course of such a search a constable discovers an article which he has reasonable grounds for suspecting to be a stolen or prohibited article[, an article to which subsection (8A) below applies or a firework to which subsection (8B) below applies][3], he may seize it.

(7)    An article is prohibited for the purposes of this Part of this Act if it is—

    (a) an offensive weapon; or

    (b) an article—

        (i)  made or adapted for use in the course of or in connection with an offence to which this sub-paragraph applies; or

        (ii)  intended by the person having it with him for such use by him or by some other person.

(8)    The offences to which subsection (7)(b)(i) above applies are—

    (a) burglary;

    (b) theft;

    (c) offences under section 12 of the Theft Act 1968 (taking motor vehicle or other conveyance without authority); [...][4]

    [(d) fraud (contrary to section 1 of the Fraud Act 2006)];[5] and

    (e) offences under section 1 of the Criminal Damage Act 1971 (destroying or damaging property)][6].

[(8A) This subsection applies to any article in relation to which a person has committed, or is committing or is going to commit an offence under section 139 of the Criminal Justice Act 1988.][7]

[(8B) This subsection applies to any firework which a person possesses in contravention of a prohibition imposed by fireworks regulations.

(8C)  In this section—

    (a) 'firework' shall be construed in accordance with the definition of 'fireworks' in section 1(1) of the Fireworks Act 2003; and

    (b) 'fireworks regulations' has the same meaning as in that Act.][8]

---

[3] Amended by SOCAPA 2005, s 115(1), (4).
[4] Repealed by the Criminal Justice Act 2003, s 332, Sch 37, Pt 1.
[5] Substituted by Fraud Act 2006, Sch 1, para 21 (16 January 2007).
[6] Amended by the Criminal Justice Act 2003, s 1(2).
[7] Amended by the Criminal Justice Act 1988, s 140(1).
[8] Amended by SOCAPA 2005, s 115(1), (5).

(9) In this Part of this Act 'offensive weapon' means any article—
  (a) made or adapted for use for causing injury to persons; or
  (b) intended by the person having it with him for such use by him or by some other person.

## 2 Provisions relating to search under section 1 and other powers

(1) A constable who detains a person or vehicle in the exercise—
  (a) of the power conferred by section 1 above; or
  (b) of any other power—
    (i) to search a person without first arresting him; or
    (ii) to search a vehicle without making an arrest,
  need not conduct a search if it appears to him subsequently—
    (i) that no search is required; or
    (ii) that a search is impracticable.
(2) If a constable contemplates a search, other than a search of an unattended vehicle, in the exercise—
  (a) of the power conferred by section 1 above; or
  (b) of any other power, except the power conferred by section 6 below and the power conferred by section 27(2) of the Aviation Security Act 1982—
    (i) to search a person without first arresting him; or
    (ii) to search a vehicle without making an arrest,
  it shall be his duty, subject to subsection (4) below, to take reasonable steps before he commences the search to bring to the attention of the appropriate person—
    (i) if the constable is not in uniform, documentary evidence that he is a constable; and
    (ii) whether he is in uniform or not, the matters specified in subsection (3) below;
  and the constable shall not commence the search until he has performed that duty.
(3) The matters referred to in subsection (2)(ii) above are—
  (a) the constable's name and the name of the police station to which he is attached;
  (b) the object of the proposed search;
  (c) the constable's grounds for proposing to make it; and
  (d) the effect of section 3(7) or (8) below, as may be appropriate.
(4) A constable need not bring the effect of section 3(7) or (8) below to the attention of the appropriate person if it appears to the constable that it will not be practicable to make the record in section 3(1) below.
(5) In this section 'the appropriate person' means—
  (a) if the constable proposes to search a person, that person; and
  (b) if he proposes to search a vehicle, or anything in or on a vehicle, the person in charge of the vehicle.
(6) On completing a search of an unattended vehicle or anything in or on such a vehicle in the exercise of any such power as is mentioned in subsection (2) above a constable shall leave a notice—
  (a) stating that he has searched it;
  (b) giving the name of the police station to which he is attached;
  (c) stating that an application for compensation for any damage caused by the search may be made to that police station; and
  (d) stating the effect of section 3(8) below.

(7) The constable shall leave the notice inside the vehicle unless it is not reasonably practicable to do so without damaging the vehicle.

(8) The time for which a person or vehicle may be detained for the purposes of such a search is such time as is reasonably required to permit a search to be carried out either at the place where the person or vehicle was first detained or nearby.

(9) Neither the power conferred by section 1 above nor any other power to detain and search a person without first arresting him or to detain and search a vehicle without making an arrest is to be construed—

(a) as authorising a constable to require a person to remove any of his clothing in public other than an outer coat, jacket or gloves; or

(b) as authorising a constable not in uniform to stop a vehicle.

(10) This section and section 1 above apply to vessels, aircraft and hovercraft as they apply to vehicles.

### 3 Duty to make records concerning searches

(1) Where a constable has carried out a search in the exercise of any such power as is mentioned in section 2(1) above, other than a search—

(a) under section 6 below; or

(b) under section 27(2) of the Aviation Security Act 1982,

he shall make a record of it in writing unless it is not practicable to do so.

(2) If—

(a) a constable is required by subsection (1) above to make a record of a search; but

(b) it is not practicable to make the record on the spot,

he shall make it as soon as practicable after the completion of the search.

(3) The record of a search of a person shall include a note of his name, if the constable knows it, but a constable may not detain a person to find out his name.

(4) If a constable does not know the name of the person whom he has searched, the record of the search shall include a note otherwise describing that person.

(5) The record of a search of a vehicle shall include a note describing the vehicle.

(6) The record of a search of a person or a vehicle—

(a) shall state—

(i) the object of the search;

(ii) the grounds for making it;

(iii) the date and time when it was made;

(iv) the place where it was made;

(v) whether anything, and if so what, was found;

(vi) whether any, and if so what, injury to a person or damage to property appears to the constable to have resulted from the search; and

(b) shall identify the constable making it.

(7) If a constable who conducted a search of a person made a record of it, the person who was searched shall be entitled to a copy of the record if he asks for one before the end of the period specified in subsection (9) below.

Act

(8) If—
　　(a) the owner of a vehicle which has been searched or the person who was in charge of the vehicle at the time when it was searched asks for a copy of the record of the search before the end of the period specified in subsection (9) below; and
　　(b) the constable who conducted the search made a record of it,
　　the person who made the request shall be entitled to a copy.
(9) The period mentioned in subsections (7) and (8) above is the period of 12 months beginning with the date on which the search was made.
(10) The requirements imposed by this section with regard to records of searches of vehicles shall apply also to records of searches of vessels, aircraft and hovercraft.

### 4 Road checks

(1) This section shall have effect in relation to the conduct of road checks by police officers for the purpose of ascertaining whether a vehicle is carrying—
　　(a) a person who has committed an offence other than a road traffic offence or a [vehicle]⁹ excise offence;
　　(b) a person who is a witness to such an offence;
　　(c) a person intending to commit such an offence; or
　　(d) a person who is unlawfully at large.
(2) For the purposes of this section a road check consists of the exercise in a locality of the power conferred by [section 163 of the Road Traffic Act 1988]¹⁰ in such a way as to stop during the period for which its exercise in that way in that locality continues all vehicles or vehicles selected by any criterion.
(3) Subject to subsection (5) below, there may only be such a road check if a police officer of the rank of superintendent or above authorises it in writing.
(4) An officer may only authorise a road check under subsection (3) above—
　　(a) for the purpose specified in subsection (1)(a) above, if he has reasonable grounds—
　　　　(i) for believing that the offence is [an indictable offence]¹¹; and
　　　　(ii) for suspecting that the person is, or is about to be, in the locality in which vehicles would be stopped if the road check were authorised;
　　(b) for the purpose specified in subsection (1)(b) above, if he has reasonable grounds for believing that the offence is [an indictable offence]¹²;
　　(c) for the purpose specified in subsection (1)(c) above, if he has reasonable grounds—
　　　　(i) for believing that the offence would be [an indictable offence]¹³; and
　　　　(ii) for suspecting that the person is, or is about to be, in the locality in which vehicles would be stopped if the road check were authorised;

---

⁹ Amended by the Vehicle Excise and Registration Act 1994, s 63, Sch 3, para 19.
¹⁰ Amended by the Road Traffic (Consequential Provisions) Act 1988, s 4, Sch 3, para 27.
¹¹ Amended by SOCAPA 2005, s 111, Sch 7, Pt 3, para 43(1), (2)(a).
¹² ibid.
¹³ Amended by SOCAPA 2005, s 111, Sch 7, Pt 3, para 43(1), (2)(a).

(d) for the purpose specified in subsection (1)(d) above, if he has reasonable grounds for suspecting that the person is, or is about to be, in that locality.

(5) An officer below the rank of superintendent may authorise such a road check if it appears to him that it is required as a matter of urgency for one of the purposes specified in subsection (1) above.

(6) If an authorisation is given under subsection (5) above, it shall be the duty of the officer who gives it—

(a) to make a written record of the time at which he gives it; and

(b) to cause an officer of the rank of superintendent or above to be informed that it has been given.

(7) The duties imposed by subsection (6) above shall be performed as soon as it is practicable to do so.

(8) An officer to whom a report is made under subsection (6) above may, in writing, authorise the road check to continue.

(9) If such an officer considers that the road check should not continue, he shall record in writing—

(a) the fact that it took place; and

(b) the purpose for which it took place.

(10) An officer giving an authorisation under this section shall specify the locality in which vehicles are to be stopped.

(11) An officer giving an authorisation under this section, other than an authorisation under subsection (5) above—

(a) shall specify a period, not exceeding seven days, during which the road check may continue; and

(b) may direct that the road check—

(i) shall be continuous; or

(ii) shall be conducted at specified times,

during that period.

(12) If it appears to an officer of the rank of superintendent or above that a road check ought to continue beyond the period for which it has been authorised he may, from time to time, in writing specify a further period, not exceeding seven days, during which it may continue.

(13) Every written authorisation shall specify—

(a) the name of the officer giving it;

(b) the purpose of the road check; and

(c) the locality in which vehicles are to be stopped.

(14) The duties to specify the purposes of a road check imposed by subsections (9) and (13) above include duties to specify any relevant [indictable offence][14].

(15) Where a vehicle is stopped in a road check, the person in charge of the vehicle at the time when it is stopped shall be entitled to obtain a written statement of the purpose of the road check if he applies for such a statement not later than the end of the period of twelve months from the day on which the vehicle was stopped.

(16) Nothing in this section affects the exercise by police officers of any power to stop vehicles for purposes other than those specified in subsection (1) above.

---

[14] Amended by SOCAPA 2005, s 111, Sch 7, Pt 3, para 43(1), (2)(b).

**Act**

### 5 Reports of recorded searches and of road checks

(1)    Every annual report—
       [(a) under section 22 of the Police Act 1996; or][15]
       (b) made by the Commissioner of Police of the Metropolis,
       shall contain information—
       (i)    about searches recorded under section 3 above which have been carried
              out in the area to which the report relates during the period to which it
              relates; and
       (ii)   about road checks authorised in that area during that period under sec-
              tion 4 above.

(1A)   [...][16]

(2)    The information about searches shall not include information about specific
       searches but shall include—
       (a) the total numbers of searches in each month during the period to which
           the report relates—
           (i)    for stolen articles;
           (ii)   for offensive weapons [or articles to which section 1(8A) above
                  applies][17]; and
           (iii)  for other prohibited articles;
       (b) the total number of persons arrested in each such month in consequence
           of searches of each of the descriptions specified in paragraph (a)(i) to (iii)
           above.

(3)    The information about road checks shall include information—
       (a) about the reason for authorising each road check; and
       (b) about the result of each of them.

### 6 Statutory undertakers etc

(1)    A constable employed by statutory undertakers may stop, detain and search
       any vehicle before it leaves a goods area included in the premises of the statu-
       tory undertakers.

[(1A) Without prejudice to any powers under subsection (1) above, a constable
       employed [by the [British Transport Police Authority][18]][19] may stop, detain and
       search any vehicle before it leaves a goods area which is included in the prem-
       ises of any successor of the British Railways Board and is used wholly or mainly
       for the purposes of a relevant undertaking.][20]

(2)    In this section 'goods area' means any area used wholly or mainly for the stor-
       age or handling of goods[; and 'successor of the British Railways Board' and
       'relevant undertaking' have the same meaning as in the Railways Act 1993
       (Consequential Modifications) Order 1999][21].

---

[15] Amended by the Police Act 1996, s 103, Sch 7, para 34.
[16] Repealed by SOCAPA 2005, ss 59, 174(2), Sch 4, paras 43, 44, Sch 17, Pt 2.
[17] Amended by the Criminal Justice Act 1988, s 140(2).
[18] Amended by SI 2004/1573, art 12(1)(e).
[19] Amended by the Transport Act 2000, s 217, Sch 18, Pt 1, para 5.
[20] Amended by SI 1999/1998, art 5(1).
[21] Amended by SI 1999/1998, art 5(2).

(3) [...][22]

(4) [...][23]

### 7 Part I—supplementary

(1) The following enactments shall cease to have effect—

  (a)  section 8 of the Vagrancy Act 1824;

  (b)  section 66 of the Metropolitan Police Act 1839;

  (c)  section 11 of the Canals (Offences) Act 1840;

  (d)  section 19 of the Pedlars Act 1871;

  (e)  section 33 of the County of Merseyside Act 1980; and

  (f)  section 42 of the West Midlands County Council Act 1980.

(2) There shall also cease to have effect—

  (a)  so much of any enactment contained in an Act passed before 1974, other than—

    (i)  an enactment contained in a public general Act; or

    (ii)  an enactment relating to statutory undertakers,

    as confers power on a constable to search for stolen or unlawfully obtained goods; and

  (b)  so much of any enactment relating to statutory undertakers as provides that such a power shall not be exercisable after the end of a specified period.

(3) In this Part of this Act 'statutory undertakers' means persons authorised by any enactment to carry on any railway, light railway, road transport, water transport, canal, inland navigation, dock or harbour undertaking.

## PART II
## POWERS OF ENTRY, SEARCH AND SEIZURE

### *Search warrants*

### 8 Power of justice of the peace to authorise entry and search of premises

(1) If on an application made by a constable a justice of the peace is satisfied that there are reasonable grounds for believing—

  (a)  that [an indictable offence][24] has been committed; and

  (b)  that there is material on premises [mentioned in subsection (1A) below][25] which is likely to be of substantial value (whether by itself or together with other material) to the investigation of the offence; and

  (c)  that the material is likely to be relevant evidence; and

  (d)  that it does not consist of or include items subject to legal privilege, excluded material or special procedure material; and

  (e)  that any of the conditions specified in subsection (3) below applies [in relation to each set of premises specified in the application][26],

  he may issue a warrant authorising a constable to enter and search the premises.

---

[22] Repealed by the Energy Act 2004, s 197(9), Sch 23, Pt 1.

[23] ibid.

[24] Amended by SOCAPA 2005, s 111, Sch 7, Pt 3, para 43(1), (3).

[25] Amended by SOCAPA 2005, s 113(1), (2), (3)(a).

[26] Amended by SOCAPA 2005, s 113(1), (2), (3)(b).

[(1A)  The premises referred to in subsection (1)(b) above are—

(a)  one or more sets of premises specified in the application (in which case the application is for a 'specific premises warrant'); or

(b)  any premises occupied or controlled by a person specified in the application, including such sets of premises as are so specified (in which case the application is for an 'all premises warrant').

(1B)  If the application is for an all premises warrant, the justice of the peace must also be satisfied—

(a)  that because of the particulars of the offence referred to in paragraph (a) of subsection(1) above, there are reasonable grounds for believing that it is necessary to search premises occupied or controlled by the person in question which are not specified in the application in order to find the material referred to in paragraph (b) of that subsection; and

(b)  that it is not reasonably practicable to specify in the application all the premises which he occupies or controls and which might need to be searched.][27]

[(1C)  The warrant may authorise entry to and search of premises on more than one occasion if, on the application, the justice of the peace is satisfied that it is necessary to authorise multiple entries in order to achieve the purpose for which he issues the warrant.

(1D)  If it authorises multiple entries, the number of entries authorised may be unlimited, or limited to a maximum.][28]

(2)  A constable may seize and retain anything for which a search has been authorised under subsection (1) above.

(3)  The conditions mentioned in subsection (1)(e) above are—

(a)  that it is not practicable to communicate with any person entitled to grant entry to the premises;

(b)  that it is practicable to communicate with a person entitled to grant entry to the premises but it is not practicable to communicate with any person entitled to grant access to the evidence;

(c)  that entry to the premises will not be granted unless a warrant is produced;

(d)  that the purpose of a search may be frustrated or seriously prejudiced unless a constable arriving at the premises can secure immediate entry to them.

(4)  In this Act 'relevant evidence', in relation to an offence, means anything that would be admissible in evidence at a trial for the offence.

(5)  The power to issue a warrant conferred by this section is in addition to any such power otherwise conferred.

[(6)  This section applies in relation to a relevant offence (as defined in section 28D(4) of the Immigration Act 1971) as it applies in relation to [an indictable offence][29][30].

[(7)  Section 4 of the Summary Jurisdiction (Process) Act 1881 (execution of process of English courts in Scotland) shall apply to a warrant issued on the application

---

[27] Amended by SOCAPA 2005, s 113(1), (2), (4).

[28] Amended by SOCAPA 2005, s 114(1), (2).

[29] Amended by SOCAPA 2005, s 111, Sch 7, Pt 3, para 43(1), (3).

[30] Amended by the Immigration and Asylum Act 1999, s 169(1), Sch 14, para 80(1), (2).

of an officer of Revenue and Customs under this section by virtue of section 114 below.][31]

## 9 Special provisions as to access

(1)    A constable may obtain access to excluded material or special procedure material for the purposes of a criminal investigation by making an application under Schedule 1 below and in accordance with that Schedule.

(2)    Any Act (including a local Act) passed before this Act under which a search of premises for the purposes of a criminal investigation could be authorised by the issue of a warrant to a constable shall cease to have effect so far as it relates to the authorisation of searches—

(a)  for items subject to legal privilege; or

(b)  for excluded material; or

(c)  for special procedure material consisting of documents or records other than documents.

[(2A)  Section 4 of the Summary Jurisdiction (Process) Act 1881 (c 24) (which includes provision for the execution of process of English courts in Scotland) and section 29 of the Petty Sessions (Ireland) Act 1851 (c 93) (which makes equivalent provision for execution in Northern Ireland) shall each apply to any process issued by a circuit judge[32] under Schedule 1 to this Act as it applies to process issued by a magistrates' court under the Magistrates' Courts Act 1980 (c 43).][33]

## 10 Meaning of 'items subject to legal privilege'

(1)    Subject to subsection (2) below, in this Act 'items subject to legal privilege' means—

(a)  communications between a professional legal adviser and his client or any person representing his client made in connection with the giving of legal advice to the client;

(b)  communications between a professional legal adviser and his client or any person representing his client or between such an adviser or his client or any such representative and any other person made in connection with or in contemplation of legal proceedings and for the purposes of such proceedings; and

(c)  items enclosed with or referred to in such communications and made—

(i)    in connection with the giving of legal advice; or

(ii)   in connection with or in contemplation of legal proceedings and for the purposes of such proceedings,

when they are in the possession of a person who is entitled to possession of them.

(2)    Items held with the intention of furthering a criminal purpose are not items subject to legal privilege.

---

[31] Added by Finance Act 2007, s 86 (19 July 2007).

[32] Prospectively amended by the Courts Act 2003, s 65, Sch 4, para 5.

[33] Amended by the Criminal Justice and Police Act 2001, s 86(1).

## 11 Meaning of 'excluded material'

(1) Subject to the following provisions of this section, in this Act 'excluded material' means—

    (a) personal records which a person has acquired or created in the course of any trade, business, profession or other occupation or for the purposes of any paid or unpaid office and which he holds in confidence;

    (b) human tissue or tissue fluid which has been taken for the purposes of diagnosis or medical treatment and which a person holds in confidence;

    (c) journalistic material which a person holds in confidence and which consists—

        (i) of documents; or

        (ii) of records other than documents.

(2) A person holds material other than journalistic material in confidence for the purposes of this section if he holds it subject—

    (a) to an express or implied undertaking to hold it in confidence; or

    (b) to a restriction on disclosure or an obligation of secrecy contained in any enactment, including an enactment contained in an Act passed after this Act.

(3) A person holds journalistic material in confidence for the purposes of this section if—

    (a) he holds it subject to such an undertaking, restriction or obligation; and

    (b) it has been continuously held (by one or more persons) subject to such an undertaking, restriction or obligation since it was first acquired or created for the purposes of journalism.

## 12 Meaning of 'personal records'

(1) In this Part of this Act 'personal records' means documentary and other records concerning an individual (whether living or dead) who can be identified from them and relating—

    (a) to his physical or mental health;

    (b) to spiritual counselling or assistance given or to be given to him; or

    (c) to counselling or assistance given or to be given to him, for the purposes of his personal welfare, by any voluntary organisation or by any individual who—

        (i) by reason of his office or occupation has responsibilities for his personal welfare; or

        (ii) by reason of an order of a court has responsibilities for his supervision.

## 13 Meaning of 'journalistic material'

(1) Subject to subsection (2) below, in this Act 'journalistic material' means material acquired or created for the purposes of journalism.

(2) Material is only journalistic material for the purposes of this Act if it is in the possession of a person who acquired or created it for the purposes of journalism.

(3) A person who receives material from someone who intends that the recipient shall use it for the purposes of journalism is to be taken to have acquired it for those purposes.

**14 Meaning of 'special procedure material'**

(1) In this Act 'special procedure material' means—
 (a) material to which subsection (2) below applies; and
 (b) journalistic material, other than excluded material.
(2) Subject to the following provisions of this section, this subsection applies to material, other than items subject to legal privilege and excluded material, in the possession of a person who—
 (a) acquired or created it in the course of any trade, business, profession or other occupation or for the purpose of any paid or unpaid office; and
 (b) holds it subject—
  (i) to an express or implied undertaking to hold it in confidence; or
  (ii) to a restriction or obligation such as is mentioned in section 11(2)(b) above.
(3) Where material is acquired—
 (a) by an employee from his employer and in the course of his employment; or
 (b) by a company from an associated company,
 it is only special procedure material if it was special procedure material immediately before the acquisition.
(4) Where material is created by an employee in the course of his employment, it is only special procedure material if it would have been special procedure material had his employer created it.
(5) Where material is created by a company on behalf of an associated company, it is only special procedure material if it would have been special procedure material had the associated company created it.
(6) A company is to be treated as another's associated company for the purposes of this section if it would be so treated under [section 449 of the Corporation Tax Act 2010].[34]

**15 Search warrants—safeguards**

(1) This section and section 16 below have effect in relation to the issue to constables under any enactment, including an enactment contained in an Act passed after this Act, of warrants to enter and search premises; and an entry on or search of premises under a warrant is unlawful unless it complies with this section and section 16 below.
(2) Where a constable applies for any such warrant, it shall be his duty—
 (a) to state—
  (i) the ground on which he makes the application; [...][35]
  (ii) the enactment under which the warrant would be issued; [and][36]
  [(iii) if the application is for a warrant authorising entry and search on more than one occasion, the ground on which he applies for such a warrant, and whether he seeks a warrant authorising an unlimited number of entries, or (if not) the maximum number of entries desired;][37]

---

[34] Words substituted by Corporation Tax Act 2010, Sch 1, para 193 (1 April 2010, and has effect for corporation tax purposes for accounting periods ending on or after that day, and for income tax and capital gains tax purposes, for the tax year 2010–11 and subsequent tax years, subject to transitional provisions and savings specified in 2010: Sch 2).
[35] Repealed by SOCAPA 2005, ss 114(1), (3), (4)(a), 174(2), Sch 17, Pt 2.
[36] Amended by SOCAPA 2005, s 114(1), (3), (4)(b).
[37] Amended by SOCAPA 2005, s 114(1), (3), (4)(c).

Act

[(b) to specify the matters set out in subsection (2A) below; and][38]

(c) to identify, so far as is practicable, the articles or persons to be sought.

[(2A) The matters which must be specified pursuant to subsection (2)(b) above are—

[(a) if the application relates to one or more sets of premises specified in the application, each set of premises which it is desired to enter and search;][39]

(b) [if the application relates to any premises occupied or controlled by a person specified in the application—] [40]

(i) as many sets of premises which it is desired to enter and search as it is reasonably practicable to specify;

(ii) the person who is in occupation or control of those premises and any others which it is desired to enter and search;

(iii) why it is necessary to search more premises than those specified under sub-paragraph (i); and

(iv) why it is not reasonably practicable to specify all the premises which it is desired to enter and search.][41]

(3) An application for such a warrant shall be made ex parte and supported by an information in writing.

(4) The constable shall answer on oath any question that the justice of the peace or judge hearing the application asks him.

(5) A warrant shall authorise an entry on one occasion only [unless it specifies that it authorises multiple entries][42].

[(5A) If it specifies that it authorises multiple entries, it must also specify whether the number of entries authorised is unlimited, or limited to a specified maximum.][43]

(6) A warrant—

(a) shall specify—

(i) the name of the person who applies for it;

(ii) the date on which it is issued;

(iii) the enactment under which it is issued; and

[(iv) each set of premises to be searched, or (in the case of an all premises warrant) the person who is in occupation or control of premises to be searched, together with any premises under his occupation or control which can be specified and which are to be searched; and][44]

(b) shall identify, so far as is practicable, the articles or persons to be sought.

[(7) Two copies shall be made of a [warrant][45] (see section 8(1A)(a) above) which specifies only one set of premises and does not authorise multiple entries; and as many copies as are reasonably required may be made of any other kind of warrant.][46]

(8) The copies shall be clearly certified as copies.

---

[38] Amended by SOCAPA 2005, s 113(1), (5), (6).

[39] Amended by SI 2005/3496, art 7(1), (2)(a).

[40] Amended by SI 2005/3496, art 7(1), (2)(b).

[41] Amended by SOCAPA 2005, s 113(1), (5), (7).

[42] Amended by SOCAPA 2005, s 114(1), (3), (5).

[43] Amended by SOCAPA 2005, s 114(1), (3), (6).

[44] Amended by SOCAPA 2005, s 113(1), (5), (8).

[45] Amended by SI 2005/3496, art 7(1), (3).

[46] Amended by SOCAPA 2005, s 114(1), (3), (7).

**16 Execution of warrants**

(1)    A warrant to enter and search premises may be executed by any constable.

(2)    Such a warrant may authorise persons to accompany any constable who is executing it.

[(2A) A person so authorised has the same powers as the constable whom he accompanies in respect of—

   (a)  the execution of the warrant, and

   (b)  the seizure of anything to which the warrant relates.

(2B)  But he may exercise those powers only in the company, and under the supervision, of a constable.][47]

(3)    Entry and search under a warrant must be within [three months][48] from the date of its issue.

[(3A) If the warrant is an all premises warrant, no premises which are not specified in it may be entered or searched unless a police officer of at least the rank of inspector has in writing authorised them to be entered.][49]

[(3B) No premises may be entered or searched for the second or any subsequent time under a warrant which authorises multiple entries unless a police officer of at least the rank of inspector has in writing authorised that entry to those premises.][50]

(4)    Entry and search under a warrant must be at a reasonable hour unless it appears to the constable executing it that the purpose of a search may be frustrated on an entry at a reasonable hour.

(5)    Where the occupier of premises which are to be entered and searched is present at the time when a constable seeks to execute a warrant to enter and search them, the constable—

   (a)  shall identify himself to the occupier and, if not in uniform, shall produce to him documentary evidence that he is a constable;

   (b)  shall produce the warrant to him; and

   (c)  shall supply him with a copy of it.

(6)    Where—

   (a)  the occupier of such premises is not present at the time when a constable seeks to execute such a warrant; but

   (b)  some other person who appears to the constable to be in charge of the premises is present,

   subsection (5) above shall have effect as if any reference to the occupier were a reference to that other person.

(7)    If there is no person present who appears to the constable to be in charge of the premises, he shall leave a copy of the warrant in a prominent place on the premises.

(8)    A search under a warrant may only be a search to the extent required for the purpose for which the warrant was issued.

(9)    A constable executing a warrant shall make an endorsement on it stating—

   (a)  whether the articles or persons sought were found; and

---

[47] Amended by the Criminal Justice Act 2003, s 2.
[48] Amended by SOCAPA 2005, s 114(1), (8)(a).
[49] Amended by SOCAPA 2005, s 113(1), (9)(a).
[50] Amended by SOCAPA 2005, s 114(1), (8)(b).

(b)  whether any articles were seized, other than articles which were sought [and, unless the warrant is a [...][51] warrant specifying one set of premises only, he shall do so separately in respect of each set of premises entered and searched, which he shall in each case state in the endorsement][52].

[(10)  A warrant shall be returned to the appropriate person mentioned in subsection (10A) below—
(a)  when it has been executed; or
(b)  in the case of a specific premises warrant which has not been executed, or an all premises warrant, or any warrant authorising multiple entries, upon the expiry of the period of three months referred to in subsection (3) above or sooner.

(10A) The appropriate person is—
(a)  if the warrant was issued by a justice of the peace, the designated officer for the local justice area in which the justice was acting when he issued the warrant;
(b)  if it was issued by a judge, the appropriate officer of the court from which he issued it.][53]

(11)  A warrant which is returned under subsection (10) above shall be retained for 12 months from its return—
(a)  by the [designated officer for the local justice area][54], if it was returned under paragraph (i) of that subsection; and
(b)  by the appropriate officer, if it was returned under paragraph (ii).

(12)  If during the period for which a warrant is to be retained the occupier of [premises][55] to which it relates asks to inspect it, he shall be allowed to do so.

*Entry and search without search warrant*

## 17 Entry for purpose of arrest etc

(1)    Subject to the following provisions of this section, and without prejudice to any other enactment, a constable may enter and search any premises for the purpose—
(a)  of executing—
(i)   a warrant of arrest issued in connection with or arising out of criminal proceedings; or
(ii)  a warrant of commitment issued under section 76 of the Magistrates' Courts Act 1980
(b)  of arresting a person for an [indictable][56] offence;
(c)  of arresting a person for an offence under—
(i)   section 1 (prohibition of uniforms in connection with political objects) [...][57] of the Public Order Act 1936;

---

[51] Repealed by SI 2005/3496, art 8.
[52] Amended by SOCAPA 2005, s 113(1), (9)(b).
[53] Amended by SOCAPA 2005, s 114(1), (8)(c).
[54] Amended by the Courts Act 2003, s 109(1), Sch 8, para 281(1), (3); for transitional provisions see SI 2005/911, arts 2–5.
[55] Amended by SOCAPA 2005, s 113(1), (9)(c).
[56] Amended by SOCAPA 2005, s 111, Sch 7, Pt 3, para 43(1), (4).
[57] Repealed by the Public Order Act 1986, s 40(3), Sch 3.

(ii)    any enactment contained in sections 6 to 8 or 10 of the Criminal Law Act 1977 (offences relating to entering and remaining on property);

[(iii)   section 4 of the Public Order Act 1986 (fear or provocation of violence);][58]

[(iiia)  section 4 (driving etc when under influence of drink or drugs) or 163 (failure to stop when required to do so by constable in uniform) of the Road Traffic Act 1988;

(iiib)  section 27 of the Transport and Works Act 1992 (which relates to offences involving drink or drugs);][59]

[(iv)   section 76 of the Criminal Justice and Public Order Act 1994 (failure to comply with interim possession order);][60]

[(v)    any of sections 4, 5, 6(1) and (2), 7 and 8(1) and (2) of the Animal Welfare Act 2006 (offences relating to the prevention of harm to animals);][61]

[(ca)   of arresting, in pursuance of section 32(1A) of the Children and Young Persons Act 1969, any child or young person who has been remanded or committed to local authority accommodation under section 23(1) of that Act;

[(caa)  of arresting a person for an offence to which section 61 of the Animal Health Act 1981 applies;][62]

(cb)    of recapturing any person who is, or is deemed for any purpose to be, unlawfully at large while liable to be detained—

(i)    in a prison, remand centre, young offender institution or secure training centre, or

(ii)   in pursuance of [section 92 of the Powers of Criminal Courts (Sentencing) Act 2000][63] (dealing with children and young persons guilty of grave crimes), in any other place;][64]

(d)    of recapturing [any person whatever][65] who is unlawfully at large and whom he is pursuing; or

(e)    of saving life or limb or preventing serious damage to property.

(2)    Except for the purpose specified in paragraph (e) of subsection (1) above, the powers of entry and search conferred by this section—

(a)    are only exercisable if the constable has reasonable grounds for believing that the person whom he is seeking is on the premises; and

(b)    are limited, in relation to premises consisting of two or more separate dwellings, to powers to enter and search—

(i)    any parts of the premises which the occupiers of any dwelling comprised in the premises use in common with the occupiers of any other such dwelling; and

---

[58] Amended by the Public Order Act 1986, s 40(2), Sch 2, para 7.

[59] Amended by SOCAPA 2005, s 111, Sch 7, Pt 4, para 58(a).

[60] Amended by the Criminal Justice and Public Order Act 1994, s 168(2), Sch 10, para 53(a).

[61] Added by Animal Welfare Act 2006, s 24 (6 April 2007; SI 2007/499).

[62] Amended by SOCAPA 2005, s 111, Sch 7, Pt 4, para 58(b).

[63] Amended by the Powers of Criminal Courts (Sentencing) Act 2000, s 165(1), Sch 9, para 95.

[64] Amended by the Prisoners (Return to Custody) Act 1995, s 2(1).

[65] ibid.

Act

    (ii)  any such dwelling in which the constable has reasonable grounds for believing that the person whom he is seeking may be.

(3)  The powers of entry and search conferred by this section are only exercisable for the purposes specified in subsection (1)(c)(ii) [or (iv)][66] above by a constable in uniform.

(4)  The power of search conferred by this section is only a power to search to the extent that is reasonably required for the purpose for which the power of entry is exercised.

(5)  Subject to subsection (6) below, all the rules of common law under which a constable has power to enter premises without a warrant are hereby abolished.

(6)  Nothing in subsection (5) above affects any power of entry to deal with or prevent a breach of the peace.

## 18 Entry and search after arrest

(1)  Subject to the following provisions of this section, a constable may enter and search any premises occupied or controlled by a person who is under arrest for an [indictable][67] offence, if he has reasonable grounds for suspecting that there is on the premises evidence, other than items subject to legal privilege, that relates—

    (a)  to that offence; or

    (b)  to some other [indictable][68] offence which is connected with or similar to that offence.

(2)  A constable may seize and retain anything for which he may search under subsection (1) above.

(3)  The power to search conferred by subsection (1) above is only a power to search to the extent that is reasonably required for the purpose of discovering such evidence.

(4)  Subject to subsection (5) below, the powers conferred by this section may not be exercised unless an officer of the rank of inspector or above has authorised them in writing.

[(5)  A constable may conduct a search under subsection (1)—

    (a)  before the person is taken to a police station or released on bail under section 30A, and

    (b)  without obtaining an authorisation under subsection (4),

    if the condition in subsection (5A) is satisfied.

(5A)  The condition is that the presence of the person at a place (other than a police station) is necessary for the effective investigation of the offence.][69]

(6)  If a constable conducts a search by virtue of subsection (5) above, he shall inform an officer of the rank of inspector or above that he has made the search as soon as practicable after he has made it.

(7)  An officer who—

    (a)  authorises a search; or

---

[66] Amended by the Criminal Justice and Public Order Act 1994, s 168(2), Sch 10, para 53(b).

[67] Amended by SOCAPA 2005, s 111, Sch 7, Pt 3, para 43(1), (5).

[68] ibid.

[69] Amended by the Criminal Justice Act 2003, s 12, Sch 1, paras 1, 2.

(b) is informed of a search under subsection (6) above, shall make a record in writing—

    (i)  of the grounds for the search; and

    (ii)  of the nature of the evidence that was sought.

(8) If the person who was in occupation or control of the premises at the time of the search is in police detention at the time the record is to be made, the officer shall make the record as part of his custody record.

*Seizure etc*

## 19 General power of seizure etc

(1) The powers conferred by subsections (2), (3) and (4) below are exercisable by a constable who is lawfully on any premises.

(2) The constable may seize anything which is on the premises if he has reasonable grounds for believing—

    (a) that it has been obtained in consequence of the commission of an offence; and

    (b) that it is necessary to seize it in order to prevent it being concealed, lost, damaged, altered or destroyed.

(3) The constable may seize anything which is on the premises if he has reasonable grounds for believing—

    (a) that it is evidence in relation to an offence which he is investigating or any other offence; and

    (b) that it is necessary to seize it in order to prevent the evidence being concealed, lost, altered or destroyed.

(4) The constable may require any information which is [stored in any electronic form][70] and is accessible from the premises to be produced in a form in which it can be taken away and in which it is visible and legible [or from which it can readily be produced in a visible and legible form][71] if he has reasonable grounds for believing—

    (a) that—

        (i)  it is evidence in relation to an offence which he is investigating or any other offence; or

        (ii)  it has been obtained in consequence of the commission of an offence; and

    (b) that it is necessary to do so in order to prevent it being concealed, lost, tampered with or destroyed.

(5) The powers conferred by this section are in addition to any power otherwise conferred.

(6) No power of seizure conferred on a constable under any enactment (including an enactment contained in an Act passed after this Act) is to be taken to authorise the seizure of an item which the constable exercising the power has reasonable grounds for believing to be subject to legal privilege.

---

[70] Amended by the Criminal Justice and Police Act 2001, s 70, Sch 2, Pt 2, para 13(1)(a), (2)(a).

[71] Amended by the Criminal Justice and Police Act 2001, s 70, Sch 2, Pt 2, para 13(1)(b), (2)(a).

Act

## 20 Extension of powers of seizure to computerised information

(1) Every power of seizure which is conferred by an enactment to which this section applies on a constable who has entered premises in the exercise of a power conferred by an enactment shall be construed as including a power to require any information [stored in any electronic form][72] and accessible from the premises to be produced in a form in which it can be taken away and in which it is visible and legible [or from which it can readily be produced in a visible and legible form][73].

(2) This section applies—

    (a) to any enactment contained in an Act passed before this Act;

    (b) to sections 8 and 18 above;

    (c) to paragraph 13 of Schedule 1 to this Act; and

    (d) to any enactment contained in an Act passed after this Act.

## 21 Access and copying

(1) A constable who seizes anything in the exercise of a power conferred by any enactment, including an enactment contained in an Act passed after this Act, shall, if so requested by a person showing himself—

    (a) to be the occupier of premises on which it was seized; or

    (b) to have had custody or control of it immediately before the seizure,

    provide that person with a record of what he seized.

(2) The officer shall provide the record within a reasonable time from the making of the request for it.

(3) Subject to subsection (8) below, if a request for permission to be granted access to anything which—

    (a) has been seized by a constable; and

    (b) is retained by the police for the purpose of investigating an offence,

    is made to the officer in charge of the investigation by a person who had custody or control of the thing immediately before it was so seized or by someone acting on behalf of such a person, the officer shall allow the person who made the request access to it under the supervision of a constable.

(4) Subject to subsection (8) below, if a request for a photograph or copy of any such thing is made to the officer in charge of the investigation by a person who had custody or control of the thing immediately before it was so seized, or by someone acting on behalf of such a person, the officer shall—

    (a) allow the person who made the request access to it under the supervision of a constable for the purpose of photographing or copying it; or

    (b) photograph or copy it, or cause it to be photographed or copied.

(5) A constable may also photograph or copy, or have photographed or copied, anything which he has power to seize, without a request being made under subsection (4) above.

(6) Where anything is photographed or copied under subsection (4)(*b*) above, the photograph or copy shall be supplied to the person who made the request.

---

[72] Amended by the Criminal Justice and Police Act 2001, s 70, Sch 2, Pt 2, para 13(1)(a), (2)(a).

[73] Amended by the Criminal Justice and Police Act 2001, s 70, Sch 2, Pt 2, para 13(1)(b), (2)(a).

(7)     The photograph or copy shall be so supplied within a reasonable time from the making of the request.

(8)     There is no duty under this section to grant access to, or to supply a photograph or copy of, anything if the officer in charge of the investigation for the purposes of which it was seized has reasonable grounds for believing that to do so would prejudice—

    (a) that investigation;

    (b) the investigation of an offence other than the offence for the purposes of investigating which the thing was seized; or

    (c) any criminal proceedings which may be brought as a result of—

        (i)  the investigation of which he is in charge; or

        (ii) any such investigation as is mentioned in paragraph (b) above.

[(9)    The references to a constable in subsections (1), (2), (3)(a) and (5) include a person authorised under section 16(2) to accompany a constable executing a warrant.][74]

## 22 Retention

(1)     Subject to subsection (4) below, anything which has been seized by a constable or taken away by a constable following a requirement made by virtue of section 19 or 20 above may be retained so long as is necessary in all the circumstances.

(2)     Without prejudice to the generality of subsection (1) above—

    (a) anything seized for the purposes of a criminal investigation may be retained, except as provided by subsection (4) below—

        (i)  for use as evidence at a trial for an offence; or

        (ii) for forensic examination or for investigation in connection with an offence; and

    (b) anything may be retained in order to establish its lawful owner, where there are reasonable grounds for believing that it has been obtained in consequence of the commission of an offence.

(3)     Nothing seized on the ground that it may be used—

    (a) to cause physical injury to any person;

    (b) to damage property;

    (c) to interfere with evidence; or

    (d) to assist in escape from police detention or lawful custody,

may be retained when the person from whom it was seized is no longer in police detention or the custody of a court or is in the custody of a court but has been released on bail.

(4)     Nothing may be retained for either of the purposes mentioned in subsection (2)(a) above if a photograph or copy would be sufficient for that purpose.

(5)     Nothing in this section affects any power of a court to make an order under section 1 of the Police (Property) Act 1897.

[(6)    This section also applies to anything retained by the police under section 28H(5) of the Immigration Act 1971.][75]

---

[74] Amended by the Criminal Justice Act 2003, s 12, Sch 1, paras 1, 3.

[75] Amended by the Immigration and Asylum Act 1999, s 169(1), Sch 14, para 80(1), (3).

Act

[(7) The reference in subsection (1) to anything seized by a constable includes anything seized by a person authorised under section 16(2) to accompany a constable executing a warrant.][76]

*Supplementary*

### 23 Meaning of 'premises' etc

In this Act—

'premises' includes any place and, in particular, includes—

(a) any vehicle, vessel, aircraft or hovercraft;

(b) any offshore installation;

[(ba) any renewable energy installation;][77]

(c) any tent or movable structure; [...][78]

'offshore installation' has the meaning given to it by section 1 of the Mineral Workings (Offshore Installations) Act 1971;

['renewable energy installation' has the same meaning as in Chapter 2 of Part 2 of the Energy Act 2004][79].

### PART III
### ARREST

### 24 [Arrest without warrant: constables

(1) A constable may arrest without a warrant—

(a) anyone who is about to commit an offence;

(b) anyone who is in the act of committing an offence;

(c) anyone whom he has reasonable grounds for suspecting to be about to commit an offence;

(d) anyone whom he has reasonable grounds for suspecting to be committing an offence.

(2) If a constable has reasonable grounds for suspecting that an offence has been committed, he may arrest without a warrant anyone whom he has reasonable grounds to suspect of being guilty of it.

(3) If an offence has been committed, a constable may arrest without a warrant—

(a) anyone who is guilty of the offence;

(b) anyone whom he has reasonable grounds for suspecting to be guilty of it.

(4) But the power of summary arrest conferred by subsection (1), (2) or (3) is exercisable only if the constable has reasonable grounds for believing that for any of the reasons mentioned in subsection (5) it is necessary to arrest the person in question.

(5) The reasons are—

(a) to enable the name of the person in question to be ascertained (in the case where the constable does not know, and cannot readily ascertain, the person's name, or has reasonable grounds for doubting whether a name given by the person as his name is his real name);

(b) correspondingly as regards the person's address;

---

[76] Amended by the Criminal Justice Act 2003, s 12, Sch 1, paras 1, 4.

[77] Amended by the Energy Act 2004, s 103(2)(a).

[78] Repealed by the Energy Act 2004, s 197(9), Sch 23, Pt 1.

[79] Amended by the Energy Act 2004, s 103(2)(b).

   (c)  to prevent the person in question—
      (i)   causing physical injury to himself or any other person;
      (ii)  suffering physical injury;
      (iii) causing loss of or damage to property;
      (iv) committing an offence against public decency (subject to subsection (6)); or
      (v)  causing an unlawful obstruction of the highway;
   (d)  to protect a child or other vulnerable person from the person in question;
   (e)  to allow the prompt and effective investigation of the offence or of the conduct of the person in question;
   (f)  to prevent any prosecution for the offence from being hindered by the disappearance of the person in question.
(6)  Subsection (5)(c)(iv) applies only where members of the public going about their normal business cannot reasonably be expected to avoid the person in question.][80]

### [24A Arrest without warrant: other persons

(1)  A person other than a constable may arrest without a warrant—
   (a)  anyone who is in the act of committing an indictable offence;
   (b)  anyone whom he has reasonable grounds for suspecting to be committing an indictable offence.
(2)  Where an indictable offence has been committed, a person other than a constable may arrest without a warrant—
   (a)  anyone who is guilty of the offence;
   (b)  anyone whom he has reasonable grounds for suspecting to be guilty of it.
(3)  But the power of summary arrest conferred by subsection (1) or (2) is exercisable only if—
   (a)  the person making the arrest has reasonable grounds for believing that for any of the reasons mentioned in subsection (4) it is necessary to arrest the person in question; and
   (b)  it appears to the person making the arrest that it is not reasonably practicable for a constable to make it instead.
(4)  The reasons are to prevent the person in question—
   (a)  causing physical injury to himself or any other person;
   (b)  suffering physical injury;
   (c)  causing loss of or damage to property; or
   (d)  making off before a constable can assume responsibility for him.][81]
[(5) *This section does not apply in relation to an offence under Part 3 or 3A of the Public Order Act 1986.*[82]]

### 25 General arrest conditions

    [...][83]

---

[80] Amended by SOCAPA 2005, s 110(1).

[81] Inserted by SOCAPA 2005, s 110(1).

[82] New subsection (5) prospectively inserted by the Racial and Religious Hatred Act 2006, s 2 (1 October 2007).

[83] Repealed by SOCAPA 2005, ss 110(2), 174(2), Sch 17, Pt 2.

### 26  Repeal of statutory powers of arrest without warrant or order

(1)    Subject to subsection (2) below, so much of any Act (including a local Act) passed before this Act as enables a constable—
    (a)  to arrest a person for an offence without a warrant; or
    (b)  to arrest a person otherwise than for an offence without a warrant or an order of a court,
    shall cease to have effect.

(2)    Nothing in subsection (1) above affects the enactments specified in Schedule 2 to this Act.

### 27  Fingerprinting of certain offenders

(1)    If a person—
    (a)  has been convicted of a recordable offence;
    (b)  has not at any time been in police detention for the offence; and
    (c)  has not had his fingerprints taken—
        (i)   in the course of the investigation of the offence by the police; or
        (ii)  since the conviction,
    any constable may at any time not later than one month after the date of the conviction require him to attend a police station in order that his fingerprints may be taken.

[(1A)  Where a person convicted of a recordable offence has already had his fingerprints taken as mentioned in paragraph (c) of subsection (1) above, that fact (together with any time when he has been in police detention for the offence) shall be disregarded for the purposes of that subsection if—
    (a)  the fingerprints taken on the previous occasion do not constitute a complete set of his fingerprints; or
    (b)  some or all of the fingerprints taken on the previous occasion are not of sufficient quality to allow satisfactory analysis, comparison or matching.

(1B)   Subsections (1) and (1A) above apply—
    (a)  where a person has been given a caution in respect of a recordable offence which, at the time of the caution, he has admitted, or
    (b)  where a person has been warned or reprimanded under section 65 of the Crime and Disorder Act 1998 (c 37) for a recordable offence,
    as they apply where a person has been convicted of an offence, and references in this section to a conviction shall be construed accordingly.][84]

(2)    A requirement under subsection (1) above—
    (a)  shall give the person a period of at least 7 days within which he must so attend; and
    (b)  may direct him to so attend at a specified time of day or between specified times of day.

(3)    Any constable may arrest without warrant a person who has failed to comply with a requirement under subsection (1) above.

(4)    The Secretary of State may by regulations make provision for recording in national police records convictions for such offences as are specified in the regulations.

---

[84] Amended by the Criminal Justice and Police Act 2001, s 78(1).

(4A)  [...]85
(5)   Regulations under this section shall be made by statutory instrument and
      shall be subject to annulment in pursuance of a resolution of either House
      of Parliament.

### 28 Information to be given on arrest

(1)   Subject to subsection (5) below, where a person is arrested, otherwise than by
      being informed that he is under arrest, the arrest is not lawful unless the
      person arrested is informed that he is under arrest as soon as is practicable after
      his arrest.
(2)   Where a person is arrested by a constable, subsection (1) above applies regard-
      less of whether the fact of the arrest is obvious.
(3)   Subject to subsection (5) below, no arrest is lawful unless the person arrested is
      informed of the ground for the arrest at the time of, or as soon as is practicable
      after, the arrest.
(4)   Where a person is arrested by a constable, subsection (3) above applies regard-
      less of whether the ground for the arrest is obvious.
(5)   Nothing in this section is to be taken to require a person to be informed—
      (a)  that he is under arrest; or
      (b)  of the ground for the arrest,
      if it was not reasonably practicable for him to be so informed by reason of his
      having escaped from arrest before the information could be given.

### 29 Voluntary attendance at police station etc

      Where for the purpose of assisting with an investigation a person attends vol-
      untarily at a police station or at any other place where a constable is present
      or accompanies a constable to a police station or any such other place without
      having been arrested—
      (a)  he shall be entitled to leave at will unless he is placed under arrest;
      (b)  he shall be informed at once that he is under arrest if a decision is taken
           by a constable to prevent him from leaving at will.

### 30 Arrest elsewhere than at police station

[(1)  Subsection (1A) applies where a person is, at any place other than a police
      station—
      (a)  arrested by a constable for an offence, or
      (b)  taken into custody by a constable after being arrested for an offence by
           a person other than a constable.
(1A)  The person must be taken by a constable to a police station as soon as practic-
      able after the arrest.
(1B)  Subsection (1A) has effect subject to section 30A (release on bail) and subsec-
      tion (7) (release without bail).]86
(2)   Subject to subsections (3) and (5) below, the police station to which an arrested
      person is taken under [subsection (1A)]87 above shall be a designated police
      station.

---

85 Repealed by the Criminal Justice and Police Act 2001, s 137, Sch 7, Pt 2(1).
86 Amended by the Criminal Justice Act 2003, s 4(1), (2).
87 Amended by the Criminal Justice Act 2003, s 4(1), (3).

Act

(3)     A constable to whom this subsection applies may take an arrested person to any police station unless it appears to the constable that it may be necessary to keep the arrested person in police detention for more than six hours.

(4)     Subsection (3) above applies—

    (a) to a constable who is working in a locality covered by a police station which is not a designated police station; and

    (b) to a constable belonging to a body of constables maintained by an authority other than a police authority.

(5)     Any constable may take an arrested person to any police station if—

    (a) either of the following conditions is satisfied—

        (i) the constable has arrested him without the assistance of any other constable and no other constable is available to assist him;

        (ii) the constable has taken him into custody from a person other than a constable without the assistance of any other constable and no other constable is available to assist him; and

    (b) it appears to the constable that he will be unable to take the arrested person to a designated police station without the arrested person injuring himself, the constable or some other person.

(6)     If the first police station to which an arrested person is taken after his arrest is not a designated police station, he shall be taken to a designated police station not more than six hours after his arrival at the first police station unless he is released previously.

[(7)    A person arrested by a constable at any place other than a police station must be released without bail if the condition in subsection (7A) is satisfied.

(7A)   The condition is that, at any time before the person arrested reaches a police station, a constable is satisfied that there are no grounds for keeping him under arrest or releasing him on bail under section 30A.][88]

(8)     A constable who releases a person under subsection (7) above shall record the fact that he has done so.

(9)     The constable shall make the record as soon as is practicable after the release.

[(10)   Nothing in subsection (1A) or in section 30A prevents a constable delaying taking a person to a police station or releasing him on bail if the condition in subsection (10A) is satisfied.

(10A)  The condition is that the presence of the person at a place (other than a police station) is necessary in order to carry out such investigations as it is reasonable to carry out immediately.

(11)    Where there is any such delay the reasons for the delay must be recorded when the person first arrives at the police station or (as the case may be) is released on bail.][89]

(12)    Nothing in [subsection (1A) or section 30A][90] above shall be taken to affect—

    (a) paragraphs 16(3) or 18(1) of Schedule 2 to the Immigration Act 1971;

    (b) section 34(1) of the Criminal Justice Act 1972; or

    [(c) any provision of the Terrorism Act 2000.][91]

---

[88] Amended by the Criminal Justice Act 2003, s 4(1), (4).

[89] Amended by the Criminal Justice Act 2003, s 4(1), (5).

[90] Amended by the Criminal Justice Act 2003, s 4(1), (6).

[91] Amended by the Terrorism Act 2000, ss 125(1), Sch 15, para 5(1), (2); for savings see the Terrorism Act 2000, s 129(1)(b) and SI 2001/421, art 2.

(13)    Nothing in subsection (10) above shall be taken to affect paragraph 18(3) of
        Schedule 2 to the Immigration Act 1971.

## [30A  Bail elsewhere than at police station

(1)     A constable may release on bail a person who is arrested or taken into custody
        in the circumstances mentioned in section 30(1).
(2)     A person may be released on bail under subsection (1) at any time before he
        arrives at a police station.
(3)     A person released on bail under subsection (1) must be required to attend
        a police station.
[(3A)   Where a constable releases a person on bail under subsection (1)—
        (a) no recognizance for the person's surrender to custody shall be taken from
            the person,
        (b) no security for the person's surrender to custody shall be taken from the
            person or from anyone else on the person's behalf,
        (c) the person shall not be required to provide a surety or sureties for his
            surrender to custody, and
        (d) no requirement to reside in a bail hostel may be imposed as a condition
            of bail.
(3B)    Subject to subsection (3A), where a constable releases a person on bail under
        subsection (1) the constable may impose, as conditions of the bail, such
        requirements as appear to the constable to be necessary—
        (a) to secure that the person surrenders to custody,
        (b) to secure that the person does not commit an offence while on bail,
        (c) to secure that the person does not interfere with witnesses or otherwise
            obstruct the course of justice, whether in relation to himself or any other
            person, or
        (d) for the person's own protection or, if the person is under the age of 17, for
            the person's own welfare or in the person's own interests.
(4)     Where a person is released on bail under subsection (1), a requirement may be
        imposed on the person as a condition of bail only under the preceding provi-
        sions of this section.][92]
(5)     The police station which the person is required to attend may be any police
        station.][93]

## [30B  Bail under section 30A: notices

(1)     Where a constable grants bail to a person under section 30A, he must give that
        person a notice in writing before he is released.
(2)     The notice must state—
        (a) the offence for which he was arrested, and
        (b) the ground on which he was arrested.
(3)     The notice must inform him that he is required to attend a police station.
(4)     It may also specify the police station which he is required to attend and the
        time when he is required to attend.

---

[92] Section 30A(3A)–(4) substituted for s 30A(4) by Police and Justice Act 2006, Sch 6, para 2 (1 April
2007).
[93] Inserted by the Criminal Justice Act 2003, s 4(1), (7).

Act

[(4A) If the person is granted bail subject to conditions under section 30A(3B), the notice also–

(a) must specify the requirements imposed by those conditions,

(b) must explain the opportunities under sections 30CA(1) and 30CB(1) for variation of those conditions, and

(c) if it does not specify the police station at which the person is required to attend, must specify a police station at which the person may make a request under section 30CA(1)(b).][94]

(5) If the notice does not include the information mentioned in subsection (4), the person must subsequently be given a further notice in writing which contains that information.

(6) The person may be required to attend a different police station from that specified in the notice under subsection (1) or (5) or to attend at a different time.

(7) He must be given notice in writing of any such change as is mentioned in subsection (6) but more than one such notice may be given to him.][95]

[30C **Bail under section 30A: supplemental**

(1) A person who has been required to attend a police station is not required to do so if he is given notice in writing that his attendance is no longer required.

(2) If a person is required to attend a police station which is not a designated police station he must be—

(a) released, or

(b) taken to a designated police station,

not more than six hours after his arrival.

(3) Nothing in the Bail Act 1976 applies in relation to bail under section 30A.

(4) Nothing in section 30A or 30B or in this section prevents the re-arrest without a warrant of a person released on bail under section 30A if new evidence justifying a further arrest has come to light since his release.][96]

[30CA **Bail under section 30A: variation of conditions by police**

(1) Where a person released on bail under section 30A(1) is on bail subject to conditions—

(a) a relevant officer at the police station at which the person is required to attend, or

(b) where no notice under section 30B specifying that police station has been given to the person, a relevant officer at the police station specified under section 30B(4A)(c), may, at the request of the person but subject to subsection (2), vary the conditions.

(2) On any subsequent request made in respect of the same grant of bail, subsection (1) confers power to vary the conditions of the bail only if the request is based on information that, in the case of the previous request or each previous request, was not available to the relevant officer considering that previous request when he was considering it.

---

[94] Added by Police and Justice Act 2006, Sch 6, para 3 (1 April 2007).

[95] Inserted by the Criminal Justice Act 2003, s 4(1), (7).

[96] ibid.

(3) Where conditions of bail granted to a person under section 30A(1) are varied under subsection (1)—

  (a) paragraphs (a) to (d) of section 30A(3A) apply,

  (b) requirements imposed by the conditions as so varied must be requirements that appear to the relevant officer varying the conditions to be necessary for any of the purposes mentioned in paragraphs (a) to (d) of section 30A(3B), and

  (c) the relevant officer who varies the conditions must give the person notice in writing of the variation.

(4) Power under subsection (1) to vary conditions is, subject to subsection (3)(a) and (b), power—

  (a) to vary or rescind any of the conditions, and

  (b) to impose further conditions.

(5) In this section 'relevant officer', in relation to a designated police station, means a custody officer but, in relation to any other police station—

  (a) means a constable [...][97] who is not involved in the investigation of the offence for which the person making the request under subsection (1) was under arrest when granted bail under section 30A(1) , if such a constable [...][98] is readily available, and

  (b) if no such constable [...][99] is readily available—

    (i) means a constable other than the one who granted bail to the person, if such a constable is readily available, and

    (ii) if no such constable is readily available, means the constable who granted bail.][100]

**[30CB  Bail under section 30A: variation of conditions by court**

(1) Where a person released on bail under section 30A(1) is on bail subject to conditions, a magistrates' court may, on an application by or on behalf of the person, vary the conditions if—

  (a) the conditions have been varied under section 30CA(1) since being imposed under section 30A(3B),

  (b) a request for variation under section 30CA(1) of the conditions has been made and refused, or

  (c) a request for variation under section 30CA(1) of the conditions has been made and the period of 48 hours beginning with the day when the request was made has expired without the request having been withdrawn or the conditions having been varied in response to the request.

(2) In proceedings on an application for a variation under subsection (1), a ground may not be relied upon unless—

  (a) in a case falling within subsection (1)(a), the ground was relied upon in the request in response to which the conditions were varied under section 30CA(1), or

  (b) in a case falling within paragraph (b) or (c) of subsection (1), the ground was relied upon in the request mentioned in that paragraph,but this does not

---

[97] Words repealed by Policing and Crime Act 2009, Sch 8, para 1 (12 January 2010).
[98] Words repealed by Policing and Crime Act 2009, Sch 8, para 1 (12 January 2010).
[99] Words repealed by Policing and Crime Act 2009, Sch 8, para 1 (12 January 2010).
[100] Added by Police and Justice Act 2006, Sch 6, para 14 (1 April 2007).

prevent the court, when deciding the application, from considering different grounds arising out of a change in circumstances that has occurred since the making of the application.

(3)   Where conditions of bail granted to a person under section 30A(1) are varied under subsection (1)—

(a)   paragraphs (a) to (d) of section 30A(3A) apply,

(b)   requirements imposed by the conditions as so varied must be requirements that appear to the court varying the conditions to be necessary for any of the purposes mentioned in paragraphs (a) to (d) of section 30A(3B), and

(c)   that bail shall not lapse but shall continue subject to the conditions as so varied.

(4)   Power under subsection (1) to vary conditions is, subject to subsection (3)(a) and (b), power—

(a)   to vary or rescind any of the conditions, and

(b)   to impose further conditions.][101]

## [30D Failure to answer to bail under section 30A

(1)   A constable may arrest without a warrant a person who—

(a)   has been released on bail under section 30A subject to a requirement to attend a specified police station, but

(b)   fails to attend the police station at the specified time.

(2)   A person arrested under subsection (1) must be taken to a police station (which may be the specified police station or any other police station) as soon as practicable after the arrest.

[(2A) A person who has been released on bail under section 30A may be arrested without a warrant by a constable if the constable has reasonable grounds for suspecting that the person has broken any of the conditions of bail.

(2B)   A person arrested under subsection (2A) must be taken to a police station (which may be the specified police station mentioned in subsection (1) or any other police station) as soon as practicable after the arrest.[102]

(3)   In subsection (1), 'specified' means specified in a notice under subsection (1) or (5) of section 30B or, if notice of change has been given under subsection (7) of that section, in that notice.

(4)   For the purposes of—

(a)   section 30 (subject to the obligation in subsection (2) [and (2B)][103], and

(b)   section 31,

an arrest under this section is to be treated as an arrest for an offence.][104]

## 31 Arrest for further offence

(1)   Where—

(a)   a person—

(i)   has been arrested for an offence; and

(ii)   is at a police station in consequence of that arrest; and

---

[101] Added by Police and Justice Act 2006, Sch 6, para 4 (1 April 2007).

[102] Added by Police and Justice Act 2006, Sch 6, para 5(2) (1 April 2007).

[103] Words substituted by Police and Justice Act 2006, Sch 6(2), para 5(3) (1 April 2007).

[104] Added by Criminal Justice Act 2003 c. 44 Pt 1 s.4(7) (January 20, 2004).

    (b)  it appears to a constable that, if he were released from that arrest, he would be liable to arrest for some other offence,

he shall be arrested for that other offence.

### 32 Search upon arrest

(1)  A constable may search an arrested person, in any case where the person to be searched has been arrested at a place other than a police station, if the constable has reasonable grounds for believing that the arrested person may present a danger to himself or others.

(2)  Subject to subsections (3) to (5) below, a constable shall also have power in any such case—

    (a)  to search the arrested person for anything—

        (i)  which he might use to assist him to escape from lawful custody; or

        (ii)  which might be evidence relating to an offence; and

    [(b)  if the offence for which he has been arrested is an indictable offence, to enter and search any premises in which he was when arrested or immediately before he was arrested for evidence relating to the offence][105].

(3)  The power to search conferred by subsection (2) above is only a power to search to the extent that is reasonably required for the purpose of discovering any such thing or any such evidence.

(4)  The powers conferred by this section to search a person are not to be construed as authorising a constable to require a person to remove any of his clothing in public other than an outer coat, jacket or gloves [but they do authorise a search of a person's mouth][106].

(5)  A constable may not search a person in the exercise of the power conferred by subsection (2)(a) above unless he has reasonable grounds for believing that the person to be searched may have concealed on him anything for which a search is permitted under that paragraph.

(6)  A constable may not search premises in the exercise of the power conferred by subsection (2)(b) above unless he has reasonable grounds for believing that there is evidence for which a search is permitted under that paragraph on the premises.

(7)  In so far as the power of search conferred by subsection (2)(b) above relates to premises consisting of two or more separate dwellings, it is limited to a power to search—

    (a)  any dwelling in which the arrest took place or in which the person arrested was immediately before his arrest; and

    (b)  any parts of the premises which the occupier of any such dwelling uses in common with the occupiers of any other dwellings comprised in the premises.

(8)  A constable searching a person in the exercise of the power conferred by subsection (1) above may seize and retain anything he finds, if he has reasonable grounds for believing that the person searched might use it to cause physical injury to himself or to any other person.

---

[105] Amended by SOCAPA 2005, s 111, Sch 7, Pt 3, para 43(1), (6).
[106] Amended by the Criminal Justice and Public Order Act 1994, s 59(2).

Act

(9) A constable searching a person in the exercise of the power conferred by subsection (2)(a) above may seize and retain anything he finds, other than an item subject to legal privilege, if he has reasonable grounds for believing—

(a) that he might use it to assist him to escape from lawful custody; or

(b) that it is evidence of an offence or has been obtained in consequence of the commission of an offence.

(10) Nothing in this section shall be taken to affect the power conferred by [section 43 of the Terrorism Act 2000][107].

## 33 Execution of warrant not in possession of constable

[...][108]

PART IV

DETENTION

*Detention—conditions and duration*

## 34 Limitations on police detention

(1) A person arrested for an offence shall not be kept in police detention except in accordance with the provisions of this Part of this Act.

(2) Subject to subsection (3) below, if at any time a custody officer—

(a) becomes aware, in relation to any person in police detention, that the grounds for the detention of that person have ceased to apply; and

(b) is not aware of any other grounds on which the continued detention of that person could be justified under the provisions of this Part of this Act,

it shall be the duty of the custody officer, subject to subsection (4) below, to order his immediate release from custody.

(3) No person in police detention shall be released except on the authority of a custody officer at the police station where his detention was authorised or, if it was authorised at more than one station, a custody officer at the station where it was last authorised.

(4) A person who appears to the custody officer to have been unlawfully at large when he was arrested is not to be released under subsection (2) above.

(5) A person whose release is ordered under subsection (2) above shall be released without bail unless it appears to the custody officer—

(a) that there is need for further investigation of any matter in connection with which he was detained at any time during the period of his detention; or

[(b) that, in respect of any such matter, proceedings may be taken against him or he may be reprimanded or warned under section 65 of the Crime and Disorder Act 1998,][109]

and, if it so appears, he shall be released on bail.

---

[107] Amended by the Terrorism Act 2000, s 125(1), Sch 15, para 5(1), (3); for savings see the Terrorism Act 2000, s 129(1)(b) and SI 2001/421, art 2.

[108] Repealed by the Access to Justice Act 1999, s 106, Sch 15, Pt V, Table (8); for transitional provisions see SI 2001/168, arts 2(b), 3.

[109] Amended by the Criminal Justice and Court Services Act 2000, s 56(2).

(6)     For the purposes of this Part of this Act a person arrested under [section 6D of the Road Traffic Act 1988][110] [or section 30(2) of the Transport and Works Act 1992 (c 42)][111] is arrested for an offence.

[(7)    For the purposes of this Part a person who—

    (a)  attends a police station to answer to bail granted under section 30A,

    (b)  returns to a police station to answer to bail granted under this Part, or

    (c)  is arrested under section 30D or 46A,

is to be treated as arrested for an offence and that offence is the offence in connection with which he was granted bail.][112]

[(8)    Subsection (7) does not apply in relation to a person who is granted bail subject to the duty mentioned in section 47(3)(b) and who either—

    (a)  attends a police station to answer to such bail, or

    (b)  is arrested under section 46A for failing to do so, (provision as to the treatment of such persons for the purposes of this Part being made by section 46ZA).][113]

### 35  Designated police stations

(1)     The chief officer of police for each police area shall designate the police stations in his area which, subject to [sections 30(3) and (5), 30A(5) and 30D(2)][114], are to be the stations in that area to be used for the purpose of detaining arrested persons.

(2)     A chief officer's duty under subsection (1) above is to designate police stations appearing to him to provide enough accommodation for that purpose.

[(2A)   The Chief Constable of the British Transport Police Force may designate police stations which (in addition to those designated under subsection (1) above) may be used for the purpose of detaining arrested persons.][115]

(3)     Without prejudice to section 12 of the Interpretation Act 1978 (continuity of duties) a chief officer—

    (a)  may designate a station which was not previously designated; and

    (b)  may direct that a designation of a station previously made shall cease to operate.

(4)     In this Act 'designated police station' means a police station designated under this section.

### 36  Custody officers at police stations

(1)     One or more custody officers shall be appointed for each designated police station.

(2)     A custody officer for [a police station designated under section 35(1) above][116] shall be appointed—

---

[110] Amended by the Railways and Transport Safety Act 2003, s 107, Sch 7, para 12.

[111] Amended by the Police Reform Act 2002, s 53(1).

[112] Amended by the Criminal Justice Act 2003, s 12, Sch 1, paras 1, 5.

[113] Added by Police and Justice Act 2006, s 46(2) (1 April 2007 for purposes specified in SI 2007/709, art 3(n); 14 November 2008 for purposes specified in SI 2008/2785, art 2 and not yet in force otherwise).

[114] Amended by the Criminal Justice Act 2003, s 12, Sch 1, paras 1, 6.

[115] Amended by the Anti-terrorism, Crime and Security Act 2001, s 101, Sch 7, paras 11, 12.

[116] Amended by the Anti-terrorism, Crime and Security Act 2001, s 101, Sch 7, paras 11, 13(1).

(a) by the chief officer of police for the area in which the designated police station is situated; or

(b) by such other police officer as the chief officer of police for that area may direct.

[(2A) A custody officer for a police station designated under section 35(2A) above shall be appointed—

(a) by the Chief Constable of the British Transport Police Force; or

(b) by such other member of that Force as that Chief Constable may direct.][117]

(3) No officer may be appointed a custody officer unless he is of at least the rank of sergeant.[118]

(4) An officer of any rank may perform the functions of a custody officer at a designated police station if a custody officer is not readily available to perform them.

(5) Subject to the following provisions of this section and to section 39(2) below, none of the functions of a custody officer in relation to a person shall be performed by an officer who at the time when the function falls to be performed is involved in the investigation of an offence for which that person is in police detention at that time.

(6) Nothing in subsection (5) above is to be taken to prevent a custody officer—

(a) performing any function assigned to custody officers—

(i) by this Act; or

(ii) by a code of practice issued under this Act;

(b) carrying out the duty imposed on custody officers by section 39 below;

(c) doing anything in connection with the identification of a suspect; or

(d) doing anything under [sections 7 and 8 of the Road Traffic Act 1988][119].

(7) Where an arrested person is taken to a police station which is not a designated police station, the functions in relation to him which at a designated police station would be the functions of a custody officer shall be performed—

(a) by an officer who is not involved in the investigation of an offence for which he is in police detention, if such an officer is readily available; and

(b) if no such officer is readily available, by the officer who took him to the station or any other officer.

[(7A) Subject to subsection (7B), subsection (7) applies where a person attends a police station which is not a designated station to answer to bail granted under section 30A as it applies where a person is taken to such a station.

(7B) Where subsection (7) applies because of subsection (7A), the reference in subsection (7)(b) to the officer who took him to the station is to be read as a reference to the officer who granted him bail.][120]

(8) References to a custody officer in the following provisions of this Act include references to an officer other than a custody officer who is performing the functions of a custody officer by virtue of subsection (4) or (7) above.

---

[117] Amended by the Anti-terrorism, Crime and Security Act 2001, s 101, Sch 7, paras 11, 13(1), (3).

[118] Substituted by Policing and Crime Act 2009, Sch 7, para.123(3)(a) (12 January 2010).

[119] Amended by the Road Traffic (Consequential Provisions) Act 1988, s 4, Sch 3, para 27.

[120] Amended by the Criminal Justice Act 2003, s 12, Sch 1, paras 1, 7.

(9)  Where by virtue of subsection (7) above an officer of a force maintained by a police authority who took an arrested person to a police station is to perform the functions of a custody officer in relation to him, the officer shall inform an officer who—

(a)  is attached to a designated police station; and

(b)  is of at least the rank of inspector,

that he is to do so.

(10) The duty imposed by subsection (9) above shall be performed as soon as it is practicable to perform it.

**37 Duties of custody officer before charge**

(1)  Where—

(a)  a person is arrested for an offence—

(i)  without a warrant; or

(ii)  under a warrant not endorsed for bail, [...][121]

(b)  [...][122]

the custody officer at each police station where he is detained after his arrest shall determine whether he has before him sufficient evidence to charge that person with the offence for which he was arrested and may detain him at the police station for such period as is necessary to enable him to do so.

(2)  If the custody officer determines that he does not have such evidence before him, the person arrested shall be released either on bail or without bail, unless the custody officer has reasonable grounds for believing that his detention without being charged is necessary to secure or preserve evidence relating to an offence for which he is under arrest or to obtain such evidence by questioning him.

(3)  If the custody officer has reasonable grounds for so believing, he may authorise the person arrested to be kept in police detention.

(4)  Where a custody officer authorises a person who has not been charged to be kept in police detention, he shall, as soon as is practicable, make a written record of the grounds for the detention.

(5)  Subject to subsection (6) below, the written record shall be made in the presence of the person arrested who shall at that time be informed by the custody officer of the grounds for his detention.

(6)  Subsection (5) above shall not apply where the person arrested is, at the time when the written record is made—

(a)  incapable of understanding what is said to him;

(b)  violent or likely to become violent; or

(c)  in urgent need of medical attention.

(7)  Subject to section 41(7) below, if the custody officer determines that he has before him sufficient evidence to charge the person arrested with the offence for which he was arrested, the person arrested—

[(a) shall be—

(i)  released without charge and on bail, or

---

[121] Repealed by the Criminal Justice and Public Order Act 1994, ss 29(4)(a), 168(3), Sch 11.
[122] ibid.

    (ii) kept in police detention, for the purpose of enabling the Director of
         Public Prosecutions to make a decision under section 37B below][123]
    (b) shall be released without charge and on bail but not for that purpose,
    (c) shall be released without charge and without bail, or
    (d) shall be charged].[124]
[(7A) The decision as to how a person is to be dealt with under subsection (7) above
      shall be that of the custody officer.
(7B)  Where a person is [dealt with under subsection (7)(a)][125] above, it shall be the
      duty of the custody officer to inform him that he is being released[, or (as the
      case may be) detained,][126] to enable the Director of Public Prosecutions to
      make a decision under section 37B below.][127]
(8)   Where—
    (a) a person is released under subsection (7)(b) [or (c)][128] above; and
    (b) at the time of his release a decision whether he should be prosecuted for
        the offence for which he was arrested has not been taken,
      it shall be the duty of the custody officer so to inform him.
[(8A) Subsection (8B) applies if the offence for which the person is arrested is one in
      relation to which a sample could be taken under section 63B below and the
      custody officer—
    (a) is required in pursuance of subsection (2) above to release the person
        arrested and decides to release him on bail, or
    (b) decides in pursuance of subsection (7)(a) or (b) above to release the person
        without charge and on bail.
(8B)  The detention of the person may be continued to enable a sample to be taken
      under section 63B, but this subsection does not permit a person to be detained
      for a period of more than 24 hours after the relevant time.][129]
(9)   If the person arrested is not in a fit state to be dealt with under subsection (7)
      above, he may be kept in police detention until he is.
(10)  The duty imposed on the custody officer under subsection (1) above shall be
      carried out by him as soon as practicable after the person arrested arrives at the
      police station or, in the case of a person arrested at the police station, as soon
      as practicable after the arrest.
(11)–(14) [...][130]
(15)  In this Part of this Act—
      'arrested juvenile' means a person arrested with or without a warrant who
          appears to be under the age of 17 [...][131];
      'endorsed for bail' means endorsed with a direction for bail in accordance with
          section 117(2) of the Magistrates' Courts Act 1980.

---

[123] Section 37(7)(a)(i) and (ii) and words substituted for words by Police and Justice Act 2006, s 11 (15 January 2007).
[124] Amended by the Criminal Justice Act 2003, s 28, Sch 2, para 2(2).
[125] Words substituted by Police and Justice Act 2006, Sch 14, para 9(a) (15 January 2007).
[126] Words inserted by Police and Justice Act 2006, Sch 14, para 9(b) (15 January 2007).
[127] Amended by the Criminal Justice Act 2003, s 28, Sch 2, para 2(3).
[128] Amended by the Criminal Justice Act 2003, s 28, Sch 2, paras 1, 2(1), (4).
[129] Amended by the Drugs Act 2005, s 23(1), Sch 1, paras 1, 2.
[130] Repealed by the Criminal Justice Act 1991, ss 72, 101(2), Sch 13.
[131] Repealed by the Children Act 1989, s 108(7), Sch 15.

**[37A  Guidance**

(1)  The Director of Public Prosecutions may issue guidance—
    (a)  for the purpose of enabling custody officers to decide how persons should be dealt with under section 37(7) above or 37C(2) below, and
    (b)  as to the information to be sent to the Director of Public Prosecutions under section 37B(1) below.

(2)  The Director of Public Prosecutions may from time to time revise guidance issued under this section.

(3)  Custody officers are to have regard to guidance under this section in deciding how persons should be dealt with under section 37(7) above or 37C(2) [or 37CA(2)][132] below.

(4)  A report under section 9 of the Prosecution of Offences Act 1985 (report by DPP to Attorney General) must set out the provisions of any guidance issued, and any revisions to guidance made, in the year to which the report relates.

(5)  The Director of Public Prosecutions must publish in such manner as he thinks fit—
    (a)  any guidance issued under this section, and
    (b)  any revisions made to such guidance.

(6)  Guidance under this section may make different provision for different cases, circumstances or areas.][133]

**[37B  Consultation with the Director of Public Prosecutions**

(1)  Where a person is [dealt with under section 37(7)(a)][134] above, an officer involved in the investigation of the offence shall, as soon as is practicable, send to the Director of Public Prosecutions such information as may be specified in guidance under section 37A above.

(2)  The Director of Public Prosecutions shall decide whether there is sufficient evidence to charge the person with an offence.

(3)  If he decides that there is sufficient evidence to charge the person with an offence, he shall decide—
    (a)  whether or not the person should be charged and, if so, the offence with which he should be charged, and
    (b)  whether or not the person should be given a caution and, if so, the offence in respect of which he should be given a caution.

(4)  The Director of Public Prosecutions [shall give notice][135] of his decision to an officer involved in the investigation of the offence.

[(4A)  Notice under subsection (4) above shall be in writing, but in the case of a person kept in police detention under section 37(7)(a) above it may be given orally in the first instance and confirmed in writing subsequently.][136]

(5)  If his decision is—
    (a)  that there is not sufficient evidence to charge the person with an offence, or

---

[132] Words inserted by Police and Justice Act 2006, Sch 6, para 8(2) (1 April 2007).
[133] Inserted by the Criminal Justice Act 2003, s 28, Sch 2, paras 1, 3.
[134] Words substituted by Police and Justice Act 2006, Sch 14, para 10(2) (15 January 2007).
[135] Words substituted by Police and Justice Act 2006, Sch 14, para 10(3) (15 January 2007).
[136] Added by Police and Justice Act 2006, Sch 14, para 10(4) (15 January 2007).

(b) that there is sufficient evidence to charge the person with an offence but that the person should not be charged with an offence or given a caution in respect of an offence,

a custody officer shall give the person notice in writing that he is not to be prosecuted.

(6)    If the decision of the Director of Public Prosecutions is that the person should be charged with an offence, or given a caution in respect of an offence, the person shall be charged or cautioned accordingly.

(7)    But if his decision is that the person should be given a caution in respect of the offence and it proves not to be possible to give the person such a caution, he shall instead be charged with the offence.[137]

[(8)    For the purposes of this section, a person is to be charged with an offence either—

(a) when he is in police detention after returning to a police station to answer bail or is otherwise in police detention at a police station, or

(b) in accordance with section 29 of the Criminal Justice Act 2003.][138]

(9)    In this section 'caution' includes—

(a) a conditional caution within the meaning of Part 3 of the Criminal Justice Act 2003 [...][139] [...][140]

[(aa) a youth conditional caution within the meaning of Chapter 1 of Part 4 of the Crime and Disorder Act 1998, and][141]

(b) a warning or reprimand under section 65 of that Act].[142]

## [37C  Breach of bail following release under section 37(7)(a)

(1)    This section applies where—

(a) a person released on bail under section 37(7)(a) above or subsection (2)(b) below is arrested under section 46A below in respect of that bail, and

(b) at the time of his detention following that arrest at the police station mentioned in section 46A(2) below, notice under section 37B(4) above has not been given.

(2)    The person arrested—

(a) shall be charged, or

(b) shall be released without charge, either on bail or without bail.

(3)    The decision as to how a person is to be dealt with under subsection (2) above shall be that of a custody officer.

---

[137] New subsection (8) prospectively inserted by the Criminal Justice Act 2003, s 28, Sch 2, paras 1, 3: see below.

[138] Subsection 8 inserted by the Criminal Justice Act 2003, s 28, Sch 2, paras 1, 3 (1 October 2007; SI 2007/2874).

[139] Added by Criminal Justice and Immigration Act 2008, Sch 26(2), para 20(1)(a) (16 November in relation to the areas specified in SI 2009/2780, art 2(2); not yet in force otherwise).

[140] Added by Criminal Justice Act 2003, Sch 2, para 3 (3 July; SI 2004/1629).

[141] Added by Criminal Justice and Immigration Act 2008, Sch 26(2), para 20(1)(a) (16 November 2009 in relation to the areas specified in SI 2009/2780, art 2(2); not yet in force otherwise).

[142] Words substituted by Criminal Justice and Immigration Act 2008, Sch 26(2), para 20(1)(b) (16 November 2009 in relation to the areas specified in SI 2009/2780, art 2(2); not yet in force otherwise).

(4)     A person released on bail under subsection (2)(b) above shall be released on bail subject to the same conditions (if any) which applied immediately before his arrest.][143]

## [37CA   Breach of bail following release under section 37(7)(b)

(1)     This section applies where a person released on bail under section 37(7)(b) above or subsection (2)(b) below—
       (a)  is arrested under section 46A below in respect of that bail, and
       (b)  is being detained following that arrest at the police station mentioned in section 46A(2) below.

(2)     The person arrested–
       (a)  shall be charged, or
       (b)  shall be released without charge, either on bail or without bail.

(3)     The decision as to how a person is to be dealt with under subsection (2) above shall be that of a custody officer.

(4)     A person released on bail under subsection (2)(b) above shall be released on bail subject to the same conditions (if any) which applied immediately before his arrest.][144]

## [37D   Release [on bail] under section 37[145]: further provision

(1)     Where a person is released on bail under section [37, 37C(2)(b) or 37CA(2)(b)][146] above, a custody officer may subsequently appoint a different time, or an additional time, at which the person is to attend at the police station to answer bail.

(2)     The custody officer shall give the person notice in writing of the exercise of the power under subsection (1).

(3)     The exercise of the power under subsection (1) shall not affect the conditions (if any) to which bail is subject.

(4)     Where a person released on bail under section 37(7)(a) or 37C(2)(b) above returns to a police station to answer bail or is otherwise in police detention at a police station, he may be kept in police detention to enable him to be dealt with in accordance with section 37B or 37C above or to enable the power under subsection (1) above to be exercised.

[(4A)  Where a person released on bail under section 37(7)(b) or 37CA(2)(b) above returns to a police station to answer bail or is otherwise in police detention at a police station, he may be kept in police detention to enable him to be dealt with in accordance with section 37CA above or to enable the power under subsection (1) above to be exercised.

(5)     If the person mentioned in subsection (4) or (4A) above is not in a fit state to enable him to be dealt with as mentioned in that subsection or to enable the power under subsection (1) above to be exercised, he may be kept in police detention until he is.][147]

---

[143] Added by Criminal Justice Act 2003, Sch 2, para 3 (29 January 2004; SI 2004/81).
[144] Added by Police and Justice Act 2006, Sch 6, para 8(1) (1 April 2007).
[145] Words substituted by Police and Justice Act 2006, Sch 6, para 9(2) (1 April 2007).
[146] Words substituted by Police and Justice Act 2006, Sch 6(3), para 9(1) (1 April 2007).
[147] Section 37D(4A) and (5) substituted for s 37D(5) by Police and Justice Act 2006, Sch 6, para 10(2) (1 April 2007).

(6) Where a person is kept in police detention by virtue of subsection (4)[(4a)][148] or (5) above, section 37(1) to (3) and (7) above (and section 40(8) below so far as it relates to section 37(1) to (3)) shall not apply to the offence in connection with which he was released on bail under section [37(7), 37C(2)(b) or 37CA(2)(b)][149] above.][150]

## 38 Duties of custody officer after charge

(1) Where a person arrested for an offence otherwise than under a warrant endorsed for bail is charged with an offence, the custody officer shall[, subject to section 25 of the Criminal Justice and Public Order Act 1994,][151] order his release from police detention, either on bail or without bail, unless—

    (a) if the person arrested is not an arrested juvenile—

        (i)   his name or address cannot be ascertained or the custody officer has reasonable grounds for doubting whether a name or address furnished by him as his name or address is his real name or address;

        [(ii)  the custody officer has reasonable grounds for believing that the person arrested will fail to appear in court to answer to bail;

        (iii)  in the case of a person arrested for an imprisonable offence, the custody officer has reasonable grounds for believing that the detention of the person arrested is necessary to prevent him from committing an offence;

        [(iiia) in a case where a sample may be taken from the person under section 63B below, the custody officer has reasonable grounds for believing that the detention of the person is necessary to enable the sample to be taken from him;][152]

        (iv)  in the case of a person arrested for an offence which is not an imprisonable offence, the custody officer has reasonable grounds for believing that the detention of the person arrested is necessary to prevent him from causing physical injury to any other person or from causing loss of or damage to property;

        (v)   the custody officer has reasonable grounds for believing that the detention of the person arrested is necessary to prevent him from interfering with the administration of justice or with the investigation of offences or of a particular offence; or

        (vi)  the custody officer has reasonable grounds for believing that the detention of the person arrested is necessary for his own protection;][153]

    (b) if he is an arrested juvenile—

        (i)   any of the requirements of paragraph (a) above is satisfied [(but, in the case of paragraph (a)(iiia) above, only if the arrested juvenile has attained the minimum age)][154]; or

        (ii)  the custody officer has reasonable grounds for believing that he ought to be detained in his own interests[;][155]

---

[148] Words inserted by Police and Justice Act 2006, Sch 6, para 10(3)(a) (1 April 2007).
[149] Words substituted by Police and Justice Act 2006, Sch 6, para 10(3)(b) (1 April 2007).
[150] Added by Criminal Justice Act 2003, Sch 2, para 3 (29 January 2004; SI 2004/81).
[151] Amended by the Criminal Justice and Public Order Act 1994, s 168(2), Sch 10, para 54.
[152] Amended by the Drugs Act 2005, s 23(1), Sch 1, paras 1, 3(a).
[153] Amended by the Criminal Justice and Public Order Act 1994, s 28(2).
[154] Amended by the Criminal Justice Act 2003, s 5(1), (2)(a)(ii).
[155] Added by Coroners and Justice Act 200, Sch 21, para 77 (1 February 2010).

[(c) the offence with which the person is charged is murder.][156]

(2)      If the release of a person arrested is not required by subsection (1) above, the custody officer may authorise him to be kept in police detention [but may not authorise a person to be kept in police detention by virtue of subsection (1)(a)(iiia) after the end of the period of six hours beginning when he was charged with the offence][157].

[(2A)] The custody officer, in taking the decisions required by subsection (1)(a) and (b) above (except (a)(i) and (vi) and (b)(ii)), shall have regard to the same considerations as those which a court is required to have regard to in taking the corresponding decisions under paragraph [2(1)][158] of Part I of Schedule l to the Bail Act 1976 [(disregarding paragraph 2(2) of that Part) [159].][160]

(3)      Where a custody officer authorises a person who has been charged to be kept in police detention, he shall, as soon as practicable, make a written record of the grounds for the detention.

(4)      Subject to subsection (5) below, the written record shall be made in the presence of the person charged who shall at that time be informed by the custody officer of the grounds for his detention.

(5)      Subsection (4) above shall not apply where the person charged is, at the time when the written record is made—

    (a) incapable of understanding what is said to him;

    (b) violent or likely to become violent; or

    (c) in urgent need of medical attention.

[[(6)     Where a custody officer authorises an arrested juvenile to be kept in police detention under subsection (1) above, the custody officer shall, unless he certifies—

    (a) that, by reason of such circumstances as are specified in the certificate, it is impracticable for him to do so; or

    (b) in the case of an arrested juvenile who has attained the [age of 12 years][161], that no secure accommodation is available and that keeping him in other local authority accommodation would not be adequate to protect the public from serious harm from him,

secure that the arrested juvenile is moved to local authority accommodation.

(6A) In this section—

    'local authority accommodation' means accommodation provided by or on behalf of a local authority (within the meaning of the Children Act 1989);

    ['minimum age' means the age specified in [section 63B(3)(b) below][162][163];

    'secure accommodation' means accommodation provided for the purpose of restricting liberty;

    ['sexual offence' means an offence specified in Part 2 of Schedule 15 to the Criminal Justice Act 2003;

---

[156] Added by Coroners and Justice Act 200, Sch 21, para 77 (1 February 2010).

[157] Amended by the Criminal Justice and Court Services Act 2000, s 57(1), (3)(b).

[158] Amended by the Criminal Justice Act 2003, s 331, Sch 36, Pt 1, para 5(a).

[159] Amended by the Criminal Justice Act 2003, s 331, Sch 36, Pt 1, para 5(b).

[160] Amended by the Criminal Justice and Public Order Act 1994, s 28(3), (4).

[161] Amended by the Criminal Justice and Public Order Act 1994, s 24.

[162] Amended by the Drugs Act 2005, s 23(1), Sch 1, paras 1, 3(b).

[163] Amended by the Criminal Justice Act 2003, s 5(1), (2)(b).

Act

'violent offence' means murder or an offence specified in Part 1 of that Schedule;][164]

and any reference, in relation to an arrested juvenile charged with a violent or sexual offence, to protecting the public from serious harm from him shall be construed as a reference to protecting members of the public from death or serious personal injury, whether physical or psychological, occasioned by further such offences committed by him.][165]

(6B)    Where an arrested juvenile is moved to local authority accommodation under subsection (6) above, it shall be lawful for any person acting on behalf of the authority to detain him.][166]

(7)     A certificate made under subsection (6) above in respect of an arrested juvenile shall be produced to the court before which he is first brought thereafter.

[(7A)   In this section 'imprisonable offence' has the same meaning as in Schedule 1 to the Bail Act 1976.][167]

(8)     In this Part of this Act 'local authority' has the same meaning as in the [Children Act 1989][168].

## 39 Responsibilities in relation to persons detained

(1)     Subject to subsections (2) and (4) below, it shall be the duty of the custody officer at a police station to ensure—

   (a)   that all persons in police detention at that station are treated in accordance with this Act and any code of practice issued under it and relating to the treatment of persons in police detention; and

   (b)   that all matters relating to such persons which are required by this Act or by such codes of practice to be recorded are recorded in the custody records relating to such persons.

(2)     If the custody officer, in accordance with any code of practice issued under this Act, transfers or permits the transfer of a person in police detention—

   (a)   to the custody of a police officer investigating an offence for which that person is in police detention; or

   (b)   to the custody of an officer who has charge of that person outside the police station,

   the custody officer shall cease in relation to that person to be subject to the duty imposed on him by subsection (1)(a) above; and it shall be the duty of the officer to whom the transfer is made to ensure that he is treated in accordance with the provisions of this Act and of any such codes of practice as are mentioned in subsection (1) above.

(3)     If the person detained is subsequently returned to the custody of the custody officer, it shall be the duty of the officer investigating the offence to report to the custody officer as to the manner in which this section and the codes of practice have been complied with while that person was in his custody.

---

[164] Amended by the Criminal Justice Act 2003, s 304, Sch 32, Pt 1, para 44.
[165] Amended by the Criminal Justice Act 1991, s 59.
[166] Amended by the Children Act 1989, s 108(5), Sch 13, para 53(2).
[167] Amended by the Criminal Justice and Public Order Act 1994, s 28(3), (4).
[168] Amended by the Children Act 1989, s 108(5), Sch 13, para 53(3).

(4) If an arrested juvenile is [moved to local authority accommodation][169] under section 38(6) above, the custody officer shall cease in relation to that person to be subject to the duty imposed on him by subsection (1) above.

(5) [...][170]

(6) Where—

    (a) an officer of higher rank than the custody officer[171] [(*or, if the custody officer is a staff custody officer, any police officer or any police employee*)][172] gives directions relating to a person in police detention; and

    (b) the directions are at variance—

        (i) with any decision made or action taken by the custody officer in the performance of a duty imposed on him under this Part of this Act; or

        (ii) with any decision or action which would but for the directions have been made or taken by him in the performance of such a duty,

the custody officer shall refer the matter at once to an officer of the rank of superintendent or above who is responsible for the police station for which the custody officer is acting as custody officer.[173]

[*(7) In subsection (6) above—*

*'police employee' means a person employed under section 15 of the Police Act 1996;*

*'staff custody officer' has the same meaning as in the Police Reform Act 2002.*][174]

### 40 Review of police detention

(1) Reviews of the detention of each person in police detention in connection with the investigation of an offence shall be carried out periodically in accordance with the following provisions of this section—

    (a) in the case of a person who has been arrested and charged, by the custody officer; and

    (b) in the case of a person who has been arrested but not charged, by an officer of at least the rank of inspector who has not been directly involved in the investigation.

(2) The officer to whom it falls to carry out a review is referred to in this section as a 'review officer'.

(3) Subject to subsection (4) below—

    (a) the first review shall be not later than six hours after the detention was first authorised;

    (b) the second review shall be not later than nine hours after the first;

    (c) subsequent reviews shall be at intervals of not more than nine hours.

(4) A review may be postponed—

    (a) if, having regard to all the circumstances prevailing at the latest time for it specified in subsection (3) above, it is not practicable to carry out the review at that time;

---

[169] Amended by the Children Act 1989, s 108(5), Sch 13, para 54.

[170] Repealed by the Children Act 1989, s 108(7), Sch 15.

[171] Prospectively amended by SOCAPA 2005, s 121(7)(a): see below.

[172] The words from '(or, if the' to 'any police employee)' in square brackets inserted by the SOCAPA 2005, s 121(7)(a) on a date to be appointed: see the SOCAPA 2005, s 178(8).

[173] New subsection (7) prospectively inserted by SOCAPA 2005, s 121(7)(b): see below.

[174] Subsection (7) inserted by the SOCAPA 2005, s 121(7)(b) on a date to be appointed: see the SOCAPA 2005, s 178(8).

Act

(b) without prejudice to the generality of paragraph (a) above—

   (i) if at that time the person in detention is being questioned by a police officer and the review officer is satisfied that an interruption of the questioning for the purpose of carrying out the review would prejudice the investigation in connection with which he is being questioned; or

   (ii) if at that time no review officer is readily available.

(5) If a review is postponed under subsection (4) above it shall be carried out as soon as practicable after the latest time specified for it in subsection (3) above.

(6) If a review is carried out after postponement under subsection (4) above, the fact that it was so carried out shall not affect any requirement of this section as to the time at which any subsequent review is to be carried out.

(7) The review officer shall record the reasons for any postponement of a review in the custody record.

(8) Subject to subsection (9) below, where the person whose detention is under review has not been charged before the time of the review, section 37(1) to (6) above shall have effect in relation to him, but with [the modifications specified in subsection (8A)][175].

[(8A) The modifications are—

   (a) the substitution of references to the person whose detention is under review for references to the person arrested;

   (b) the substitution of references to the review officer for references to the custody officer; and

   (c) in subsection (6), the insertion of the following paragraph after paragraph (a)—

      '(aa) asleep;'.][176]

(9) Where a person has been kept in police detention by virtue of section 37(9) [or 37D(5)][177] above, section 37(1) to (6) shall not have effect in relation to him but it shall be the duty of the review officer to determine whether he is yet in a fit state.

(10) Where the person whose detention is under review has been charged before the time of the review, section 38(1) to [(6B)][178] above shall have effect in relation to him, with [the modifications specified in subsection (10A)][179].

[(10A) The modifications are—

   (a) the substitution of a reference to the person whose detention is under review for any reference to the person arrested or to the person charged; and

   (b) in subsection (5), the insertion of the following paragraph after paragraph (a)—

      '(aa) asleep;'.][180]

---

[175] Amended by the Police Reform Act 2002, s 52(1).
[176] Amended by the Police Reform Act 2002, s 52(2).
[177] Amended by the Criminal Justice Act 2003, s 28, Sch 2, paras 1, 4.
[178] Amended by the Police Reform Act 2002, s 52(3)(a).
[179] ibid.
[180] Amended by the Police Reform Act 2002, s 52(4).

(11) Where—
  (a) an officer of higher rank than the review officer gives directions relating to a person in police detention; and
  (b) the directions are at variance—
      (i) with any decision made or action taken by the review officer in the performance of a duty imposed on him under this Part of this Act; or
      (ii) with any decision or action which would but for the directions have been made or taken by him in the performance of such a duty,
  the review officer shall refer the matter at once to an officer of the rank of superintendent or above who is responsible for the police station for which the review officer is acting as review officer in connection with the detention.
(12) Before determining whether to authorise a person's continued detention the review officer shall give—
  (a) that person (unless he is asleep); or
  (b) any solicitor representing him who is available at the time of the review,
  an opportunity to make representations to him about the detention.
(13) Subject to subsection (14) below, the person whose detention is under review or his solicitor may make representations under subsection (12) above either orally or in writing.
(14) The review officer may refuse to hear oral representations from the person whose detention is under review if he considers that he is unfit to make such representations by reason of his condition or behaviour.

**40A [Use of telephone for review under s 40**

[(1) A review under section 40(1)(b) may be carried out by means of a discussion, conducted by telephone, with one or more persons at the police station where the arrested person is held.
(2) But subsection (1) does not apply if—
  (a) the review is of a kind authorised by regulations under section 45A to be carried out using video-conferencing facilities; and
  (b) it is reasonably practicable to carry it out in accordance with those regulations.][181]
(3) Where any review is carried out under this section by an officer who is not present at the station where the arrested person is held—
  (a) any obligation of that officer to make a record in connection with the carrying out of the review shall have effect as an obligation to cause another officer to make the record;
  (b) any requirement for the record to be made in the presence of the arrested person shall apply to the making of that record by that other officer; and
  (c) the requirements under section 40(12) and (13) above for—
      (i) the arrested person, or
      (ii) a solicitor representing him,
      to be given any opportunity to make representations (whether in writing or orally) to that officer shall have effect as a requirement for that person, or such a solicitor, to be given an opportunity to make representations in a manner authorised by subsection (4) below.

---

[181] Amended by the Criminal Justice Act 2003, s 6.

(4) Representations are made in a manner authorised by this subsection—
  (a)   in a case where facilities exist for the immediate transmission of written representations to the officer carrying out the review, if they are made either—
      (i)   orally by telephone to that officer; or
      (ii)  in writing to that officer by means of those facilities;
      and
  (b)   in any other case, if they are made orally by telephone to that officer.
(5) In this section 'video-conferencing facilities' has the same meaning as in section 45A below.][182]

## 41  Limits on period of detention without charge

(1) Subject to the following provisions of this section and to sections 42 and 43 below, a person shall not be kept in police detention for more than 24 hours without being charged.
(2) The time from which the period of detention of a person is to be calculated (in this Act referred to as 'the relevant time')—
  (a)   in the case of a person to whom this paragraph applies, shall be—
      (i)   the time at which that person arrives at the relevant police station; or
      (ii)  the time 24 hours after the time of that person's arrest,
      whichever is the earlier;
  (b)   in the case of a person arrested outside England and Wales, shall be—
      (i)   the time at which that person arrives at the first police station to which he is taken in the police area in England or Wales in which the offence for which he was arrested is being investigated; or
      (ii)  the time 24 hours after the time of that person's entry into England and Wales,
      whichever is the earlier;
  (c)   in the case of a person who—
      (i)   attends voluntarily at a police station; or
      (ii)  accompanies a constable to a police station without having been arrested,
      and is arrested at the police station, the time of his arrest;
  [(ca)  in the case of a person who attends a police station to answer to bail granted under section 30A, the time when he arrives at the police station;][183]
  (d)   in any other case, except where subsection (5) below applies, shall be the time at which the person arrested arrives at the first police station to which he is taken after his arrest.
(3) Subsection (2)(a) above applies to a person if—
  (a)   his arrest is sought in one police area in England and Wales;
  (b)   he is arrested in another police area; and
  (c)   he is not questioned in the area in which he is arrested in order to obtain evidence in relation to an offence for which he is arrested;
and in sub-paragraph (i) of that paragraph 'the relevant police station' means the first police station to which he is taken in the police area in which his arrest was sought.

---

[182] Inserted by the Criminal Justice and Police Act 2001, s 73(1), (2).
[183] Amended by the Criminal Justice Act 2003, s 12, Sch 1, paras 1, 8.

(4) Subsection (2) above shall have effect in relation to a person arrested under section 31 above as if every reference in it to his arrest or his being arrested were a reference to his arrest or his being arrested for the offence for which he was originally arrested.

(5) If—

    (a) a person is in police detention in a police area in England and Wales ('the first area'); and

    (b) his arrest for an offence is sought in some other police area in England and Wales ('the second area'); and

    (c) he is taken to the second area for the purposes of investigating that offence, without being questioned in the first area in order to obtain evidence in relation to it,

the relevant time shall be—

    (i) the time 24 hours after he leaves the place where he is detained in the first area; or

    (ii) the time at which he arrives at the first police station to which he is taken in the second area,

whichever is the earlier.

(6) When a person who is in police detention is removed to hospital because he is in need of medical treatment, any time during which he is being questioned in hospital or on the way there or back by a police officer for the purpose of obtaining evidence relating to an offence shall be included in any period which falls to be calculated for the purposes of this Part of this Act, but any other time while he is in hospital or on his way there or back shall not be so included.

(7) Subject to subsection (8) below, a person who at the expiry of 24 hours after the relevant time is in police detention and has not been charged shall be released at that time either on bail or without bail.

(8) Subsection (7) above does not apply to a person whose detention for more than 24 hours after the relevant time has been authorised or is otherwise permitted in accordance with section 42 or 43 below.

(9) A person released under subsection (7) above shall not be re-arrested without a warrant for the offence for which he was previously arrested unless new evidence justifying a further arrest has come to light since his release[; but this subsection does not prevent an arrest under section 46A below][184].

## 42 Authorisation of continued detention

(1) Where a police officer of the rank of superintendent or above who is responsible for the police station at which a person is detained has reasonable grounds for believing that—

    (a) the detention of that person without charge is necessary to secure or preserve evidence relating to an offence for which he is under arrest or to obtain such evidence by questioning him;

    [(b) an offence for which he is under arrest is an [indictable][185] offence; and][186]

---

[184] Amended by the Criminal Justice and Public Order Act 1994, s 29(4)(b).

[185] Amended by SOCAPA 2005, s 111, Sch 7, Pt 3, para 43(1), (7).

[186] Amended by the Criminal Justice Act 2003, s 7.

(c) the investigation is being conducted diligently and expeditiously,

he may authorise the keeping of that person in police detention for a period expiring at or before 36 hours after the relevant time.

(2) Where an officer such as is mentioned in subsection (1) above has authorised the keeping of a person in police detention for a period expiring less than 36 hours after the relevant time, such an officer may authorise the keeping of that person in police detention for a further period expiring not more than 36 hours after that time if the conditions specified in subsection (1) above are still satisfied when he gives the authorisation.

(3) If it is proposed to transfer a person in police detention to another police area, the officer determining whether or not to authorise keeping him in detention under subsection (1) above shall have regard to the distance and the time the journey would take.

(4) No authorisation under subsection (1) above shall be given in respect of any person—

(a) more than 24 hours after the relevant time; or

(b) before the second review of his detention under section 40 above has been carried out.

(5) Where an officer authorises the keeping of a person in police detention under subsection (1) above, it shall be his duty—

(a) to inform that person of the grounds for his continued detention; and

(b) to record the grounds in that person's custody record.

(6) Before determining whether to authorise the keeping of a person in detention under subsection (1) or (2) above, an officer shall give—

(a) that person; or

(b) any solicitor representing him who is available at the time when it falls to the officer to determine whether to give the authorisation,

an opportunity to make representations to him about the detention.

(7) Subject to subsection (8) below, the person in detention or his solicitor may make representations under subsection (6) above either orally or in writing.

(8) The officer to whom it falls to determine whether to give the authorisation may refuse to hear oral representations from the person in detention if he considers that he is unfit to make such representations by reason of his condition or behaviour.

(9) Where—

(a) an officer authorises the keeping of a person in detention under subsection (1) above; and

(b) at the time of the authorisation he has not yet exercised a right conferred on him by section 56 or 58 below,

the officer—

(i) shall inform him of that right;

(ii) shall decide whether he should be permitted to exercise it;

(iii) shall record the decision in his custody record; and

(iv) if the decision is to refuse to permit the exercise of the right, shall also record the grounds for the decision in that record.

(10) Where an officer has authorised the keeping of a person who has not been charged in detention under subsection (1) or (2) above, he shall be released

from detention, either on bail or without bail, not later than 36 hours after the relevant time, unless—

(a) he has been charged with an offence; or

(b) his continued detention is authorised or otherwise permitted in accordance with section 43 below.

(11) A person released under subsection (10) above shall not be re-arrested without a warrant for the offence for which he was previously arrested unless new evidence justifying a further arrest has come to light since his release[; but this subsection does not prevent an arrest under section 46A below][187].

### 43 Warrants of further detention

(1) Where, on an application on oath made by a constable and supported by an information, a magistrates' court is satisfied that there are reasonable grounds for believing that the further detention of the person to whom the application relates is justified, it may issue a warrant of further detention authorising the keeping of that person in police detention.

(2) A court may not hear an application for a warrant of further detention unless the person to whom the application relates—

(a) has been furnished with a copy of the information; and

(b) has been brought before the court for the hearing.

(3) The person to whom the application relates shall be entitled to be legally represented at the hearing and, if he is not so represented but wishes to be so represented—

(a) the court shall adjourn the hearing to enable him to obtain representation; and

(b) he may be kept in police detention during the adjournment.

(4) A person's further detention is only justified for the purposes of this section or section 44 below if—

(a) his detention without charge is necessary to secure or preserve evidence relating to an offence for which he is under arrest or to obtain such evidence by questioning him;

(b) an offence for which he is under arrest is [an indictable offence][188]; and

(c) the investigation is being conducted diligently and expeditiously.

(5) Subject to subsection (7) below, an application for a warrant of further detention may be made—

(a) at any time before the expiry of 36 hours after the relevant time; or

(b) in a case where—

(i) it is not practicable for the magistrates' court to which the application will be made to sit at the expiry of 36 hours after the relevant time; but

(ii) the court will sit during the 6 hours following the end of that period, at any time before the expiry of the said 6 hours.

(6) In a case to which subsection (5)(b) above applies—

(a) the person to whom the application relates may be kept in police detention until the application is heard; and

---

[187] Amended by the Criminal Justice and Public Order Act 1994, s 29(4)(b).

[188] Amended by SOCAPA 2005, s 111, Sch 7, Pt 3, para 43(1), (8).

Act

    (b) the custody officer shall make a note in that person's custody record—
       (i) of the fact that he was kept in police detention for more than 36 hours after the relevant time; and
      (ii) of the reason why he was so kept.

(7) If—
    (a) an application for a warrant of further detention is made after the expiry of 36 hours after the relevant time; and
    (b) it appears to the magistrates' court that it would have been reasonable for the police to make it before the expiry of that period,
    the court shall dismiss the application.

(8) Where on an application such as is mentioned in subsection (1) above a magistrates' court is not satisfied that there are reasonable grounds for believing that the further detention of the person to whom the application relates is justified, it shall be its duty—
    (a) to refuse the application; or
    (b) to adjourn the hearing of it until a time not later than 36 hours after the relevant time.

(9) The person to whom the application relates may be kept in police detention during the adjournment.

(10) A warrant of further detention shall—
    (a) state the time at which it is issued;
    (b) authorise the keeping in police detention of the person to whom it relates for the period stated in it.

(11) Subject to subsection (12) below, the period stated in a warrant of further detention shall be such period as the magistrates' court thinks fit, having regard to the evidence before it.

(12) The period shall not be longer than 36 hours.

(13) If it is proposed to transfer a person in police detention to a police area other than that in which he is detained when the application for a warrant of further detention is made, the court hearing the application shall have regard to the distance and the time the journey would take.

(14) Any information submitted in support of an application under this section shall state—
    (a) the nature of the offence for which the person to whom the application relates has been arrested;
    (b) the general nature of the evidence on which that person was arrested;
    (c) what inquiries relating to the offence have been made by the police and what further inquiries are proposed by them;
    (d) the reasons for believing the continued detention of that person to be necessary for the purposes of such further inquiries.

(15) Where an application under this section is refused, the person to whom the application relates shall forthwith be charged or, subject to subsection (16) below, released, either on bail or without bail.

(16) A person need not be released under subsection (15) above—
    (a) before the expiry of 24 hours after the relevant time; or
    (b) before the expiry of any longer period for which his continued detention is or has been authorised under section 42 above.

(17) Where an application under this section is refused, no further application shall be made under this section in respect of the person to whom the refusal relates, unless supported by evidence which has come to light since the refusal.

(18) Where a warrant of further detention is issued, the person to whom it relates shall be released from police detention, either on bail or without bail, upon or before the expiry of the warrant unless he is charged.

(19) A person released under subsection (18) above shall not be re-arrested without a warrant for the offence for which he was previously arrested unless new evidence justifying a further arrest has come to light since his release[; but this subsection does not prevent an arrest under section 46A below.][189]

## 44 Extension of warrants of further detention

(1) On an application on oath made by a constable and supported by an information a magistrates' court may extend a warrant of further detention issued under section 43 above if it is satisfied that there are reasonable grounds for believing that the further detention of the person to whom the application relates is justified.

(2) Subject to subsection (3) below, the period for which a warrant of further detention may be extended shall be such period as the court thinks fit, having regard to the evidence before it.

(3) The period shall not—
   (a) be longer than 36 hours; or
   (b) end later than 96 hours after the relevant time.

(4) Where a warrant of further detention has been extended under subsection (1) above, or further extended under this subsection, for a period ending before 96 hours after the relevant time, on an application such as is mentioned in that subsection a magistrates' court may further extend the warrant if it is satisfied as there mentioned; and subsections (2) and (3) above apply to such further extensions as they apply to extensions under subsection (1) above.

(5) A warrant of further detention shall, if extended or further extended under this section, be endorsed with a note of the period of the extension.

(6) Subsections (2), (3), and (14) of section 43 above shall apply to an application made under this section as they apply to an application made under that section.

(7) Where an application under this section is refused, the person to whom the application relates shall forthwith be charged or, subject to subsection (8) below, released, either on bail or without bail.

(8) A person need not be released under subsection (7) above before the expiry of any period for which a warrant of further detention issued in relation to him has been extended or further extended on an earlier application made under this section.

## 45 Detention before charge—supplementary

(1) In sections 43 and 44 of this Act 'magistrates' court' means a court consisting of two or more justices of the peace sitting otherwise than in open court.

---

[189] Amended by the Criminal Justice and Public Order Act 1994, s 29(4)(b).

(2) Any reference in this Part of this Act to a period of time or a time of day is to be treated as approximate only.

**Act**

**[45A Use of video-conferencing facilities for decisions about detention**

(1) Subject to the following provisions of this section, the Secretary of State may by regulations provide that, in the case of an arrested person who is held in a police station, some or all of the functions mentioned in subsection (2) may be performed (notwithstanding anything in the preceding provisions of this Part) by an officer who—

    (a) is not present in that police station; but

    (b) has access to the use of video-conferencing facilities that enable him to communicate with persons in that station.

(2) Those functions are—

    (a) the functions in relation to an arrested person taken to[, or answering to bail at,]¹⁹⁰ a police station that is not a designated police station which, in the case of an arrested person taken to a station that is a designated police station, are functions of a custody officer under section 37, 38 or 40 above; and

    (b) the function of carrying out a review under section 40(1)(b) above (review, by an officer of at least the rank of inspector, of the detention of person arrested but not charged).

(3) Regulations under this section shall specify the use to be made in the performance of the functions mentioned in subsection (2) above of the facilities mentioned in subsection (1) above.

(4) Regulations under this section shall not authorise the performance of any of the functions mentioned in subsection (2)(a) above by such an officer as is mentioned in subsection (1) above unless he is a custody officer for a designated police station.

(5) Where any functions mentioned in subsection (2) above are performed in a manner authorised by regulations under this section—

    (a) any obligation of the officer performing those functions to make a record in connection with the performance of those functions shall have effect as an obligation to cause another officer to make the record; and

    (b) any requirement for the record to be made in the presence of the arrested person shall apply to the making of that record by that other officer.

(6) Where the functions mentioned in subsection (2)(b) are performed in a manner authorised by regulations under this section, the requirements under section 40(12) and (13) above for—

    (a) the arrested person, or

    (b) a solicitor representing him,

to be given any opportunity to make representations (whether in writing or orally) to the person performing those functions shall have effect as a requirement for that person, or such a solicitor, to be given an opportunity to make representations in a manner authorised by subsection (7) below.

---

¹⁹⁰ Amended by the Criminal Justice Act 2003, s 12, Sch 1, paras 1, 9.

(7)  Representations are made in a manner authorised by this subsection—
    (a)  in a case where facilities exist for the immediate transmission of written representations to the officer performing the functions, if they are made either—
        (i)  orally to that officer by means of the video-conferencing facilities used by him for performing those functions; or
        (ii)  in writing to that officer by means of the facilities available for the immediate transmission of the representations;
        and
    (b)  in any other case if they are made orally to that officer by means of the video-conferencing facilities used by him for performing the functions.
(8)  Regulations under this section may make different provision for different cases and may be made so as to have effect in relation only to the police stations specified or described in the regulations.
(9)  Regulations under this section shall be made by statutory instrument and shall be subject to annulment in pursuance of a resolution of either House of Parliament.
(10) Any reference in this section to video-conferencing facilities, in relation to any functions, is a reference to any facilities (whether a live television link or other facilities) by means of which the functions may be performed with the officer performing them, the person in relation to whom they are performed and any legal representative of that person all able to both see and to hear each other.][191]

*Detention—miscellaneous*

## 46 Detention after charge

(1)  Where a person—
    (a)  is charged with an offence; and
    (b)  after being charged—
        (i)  is kept in police detention; or
        (ii)  is detained by a local authority in pursuance of arrangements made under section 38(6) above,
    he shall be brought before a magistrates' court in accordance with the provisions of this section.
(2)  If he is to be brought before a magistrates' court [in the local justice][192] area in which the police station at which he was charged is situated, he shall be brought before such a court as soon as is practicable and in any event not later than the first sitting after he is charged with the offence.
(3)  If no magistrates' court [in that area][193] is due to sit either on the day on which he is charged or on the next day, the custody officer for the police station at which he was charged shall inform the [designated officer][194] for the area that there is a person in the area to whom subsection (2) above applies.

---

[191] Inserted by the Criminal Justice and Police Act 2001, s 73(1), (3).
[192] Amended by the Courts Act 2003, s 109(1), Sch 8, para 282(1), (2); for transitional provisions see SI 2005/911, arts 2–5.
[193] Amended by the Courts Act 2003, s 109(1), Sch 8, para 282(1), (3)(a); for transitional provisions see SI 2005/911, arts 2–5.
[194] Amended by the Courts Act 2003, s 109(1), Sch 8, para 282(1), (3)(b); for transitional provisions see SI 2005/911, arts 2–5.

**Act**

(4) If the person charged is to be brought before a magistrates' court [in a local justice][195] area other than that in which the police station at which he was charged is situated, he shall be removed to that area as soon as is practicable and brought before such a court as soon as is practicable after his arrival in the area and in any event not later than the first sitting of a magistrates' court [in that area][196] after his arrival in the area.

(5) If no magistrates' court [in that area][197] is due to sit either on the day on which he arrives in the area or on the next day—

(a) he shall be taken to a police station in the area; and

(b) the custody officer at that station shall inform the [designated officer][198] for the area that there is a person in the area to whom subsection (4) applies.

(6) Subject to subsection (8) below, where [the designated officer for a local justice][199] area has been informed—

(a) under subsection (3) above that there is a person in the area to whom subsection (2) above applies; or

(b) under subsection (5) above that there is a person in the area to whom subsection (4) above applies, [the designated officer] shall arrange for a magistrates' court to sit not later than the day next following the relevant day.

(7) In this section 'the relevant day'—

(a) in relation to a person who is to be brought before a magistrates' court [in the local justice][200] area in which the police station at which he was charged is situated, means the day on which he was charged; and

(b) in relation to a person who is to be brought before a magistrates' court [in any other local justice][201] area, means the day on which he arrives in the area.

(8) Where the day next following the relevant day is Christmas Day, Good Friday or a Sunday, the duty of the [designated officer][202] under subsection (6) above is a duty to arrange for a magistrates' court to sit not later than the first day after the relevant day which is not one of those days.

(9) Nothing in this section requires a person who is in hospital to be brought before a court if he is not well enough.

---

[195] Amended by the Courts Act 2003, s 109(1), Sch 8, para 282(1), (4)(a); for transitional provisions see SI 2005/911, arts 2–5.

[196] Amended by the Courts Act 2003, s 109(1), Sch 8, para 282(1), (4)(b); for transitional provisions see SI 2005/911, arts 2–5.

[197] Amended by the Courts Act 2003, s 109(1), Sch 8, para 282(1), (5)(a); for transitional provisions see SI 2005/911, arts 2–5.

[198] Amended by the Courts Act 2003, s 109(1), Sch 8, para 282(1), (5)(b); for transitional provisions see SI 2005/911, arts 2–5.

[199] Amended by the Courts Act 2003, s 109(1), Sch 8, para 282(1), (6)(a); for transitional provisions see SI 2005/911, arts 2–5.

[200] Amended by the Courts Act 2003, s 109(1), Sch 8, para 282(1), (7)(a); for transitional provisions see SI 2005/911, arts 2–5.

[201] Amended by the Courts Act 2003, s 109(1), Sch 8, para 282(1), (7)(b); for transitional provisions see SI 2005/911, arts 2–5.

[202] Amended by the Courts Act 2003, s 109(1), Sch 8, para 282(1), (8); for transitional provisions see SI 2005/911, arts 2–5.

**[46ZA  Persons granted live link bail**

(1)  This section applies in relation to bail granted under this Part subject to the duty mentioned in section 47(3)(b) ('live link bail').

(2)  An accused person who attends a police station to answer to live link bail is not to be treated as in police detention for the purposes of this Act.

(3)  Subsection (2) does not apply in relation to an accused person if—

    (a)  [...][203]

    (b)  [at any time before the beginning of proceedings in relation to a live link direction under section 57C of the Crime and Disorder Act 1998 in relation to the accused person,][204] a constable informs him that a live link will not be available for his use for the purposes of that section; [ or]

    (c)  [...][205]

    (d)  the court determines for [any reason][206] not to give such a direction.

(4)  If [paragraph (b) or (d) of subsection (3) applies][207] in relation to a person, he is to be treated for the purposes of this Part—

    (a)  as if he had been arrested for and charged with the offence in connection with which he was granted bail, and

    (b)  as if he had been so charged at the time when that paragraph first applied in relation to him.

(5)  An accused person who is arrested under section 46A for failing to attend at a police station to answer to live link bail, and who is brought to a police station in accordance with that section, is to be treated for the purposes of this Part—

    (a)  as if he had been arrested for and charged with the offence in connection with which he was granted bail, and

    (b)  as if he had been so charged at the time when he is brought to the station.

(6)  Nothing in subsection (4) or (5) affects the operation of section 47(6).][208]

**[46A  Power of arrest for failure to answer to police bail**

(1)  A constable may arrest without a warrant any person who, having been released on bail under this Part of this Act subject to a duty to attend at a police station, fails to attend at that police station at the time appointed for him to do so.

---

[203] Repealed by Coroners and Justice Act 2009, s 107(2)(a)(i) (14 December 2009: repeal has effect on 14 December 2009 as specified in SI 2009/3253, art 3(1)(b) subject to transitional provisions specified in art 4(4)).

[204] Words substituted by Coroners and Justice Act 2009, s 107(2)(a)(ii) (14 December 2009: substitution has effect on 14 December 2009 as specified in SI 2009/3253, art 3(1)(b) subject to transitional provisions specified in art 4(4)).

[205] Repealed by Coroners and Justice Act 2009, Pt 3 c.4 s 107(2)(a)(iii) (14 December 2009: repeal has effect on 14 December 2009 as specified in SI 2009/3253 art 3(1)(b) subject to transitional provisions specified in art 4(4)).

[206] Words substituted by Coroners and Justice Act 2009, s 107(2)(a)(iv) (14 December 2009: substitution has effect on 14 December 2009 as specified in SI 2009/3253 art 3(1)(b) subject to transitional provisions specified in art 4(4)).

[207] Words substituted by Coroners and Justice Act 2009, s 107(2)(b) (14 December 2009: substitution has effect on 14 December 2009 as specified in SI 2009/3253 art 3(1)(b) subject to transitional provisions specified in art 4(4)).

[208] Added by Police and Justice Act 2006, s 46(3) (1 April 2007 for purposes specified in SI 2007/709 art 3(n); 14 November 2008 for purposes specified in SI 2008/2785, art 2 and not yet in force otherwise).

[(1ZA)  The reference in subsection (1) to a person who fails to attend at a police station at the time appointed for him to do so includes a reference to a person who—

(a)  attends at a police station to answer to bail granted subject to the duty mentioned in section 47(3)(b), but

(b)  leaves the police station at any time before the beginning of proceedings in relation to a live link direction under section 57C of the Crime and Disorder Act 1998 in relation to him [...][209]][210]

[(1ZB)  The reference in subsection (1) to a person who fails to attend at a police station at the time appointed for the person to do so includes a reference to a person who—

(a)  attends at a police station to answer to bail granted subject to the duty mentioned in section 47(3)(b), but

(b)  refuses to be searched under section 54B.][211]

[(1A)  A person who has been released on bail under [section 37, 37C(2)(b) or 37CA(2)(b)][212] above may be arrested without warrant by a constable if the constable has reasonable grounds for suspecting that the person has broken any of the conditions of bail.][213]

(2)  A person who is arrested under this section shall be taken to the police station appointed as the place at which he is to surrender to custody as soon as practicable after the arrest.

(3)  For the purposes of—

(a)  section 30 above (subject to the obligation in subsection (2) above), and

(b)  section 31 above,

an arrest under this section shall be treated as an arrest for an offence.][214]

## 47  Bail after arrest

(1)  [Subject to the following provisions of this section][215], a release on bail of a person under this Part of this Act shall be a release on bail granted in accordance with [sections 3, 3A, 5 and 5A of the Bail Act 1976 as they apply to bail granted by a constable][216].

[(1A)  The normal powers to impose conditions of bail shall be available to him where a custody officer releases a person on bail under [section 37 above or section 38(1)][217] (including that subsection as applied by section 40(10) above) but not in any other cases.

---

[209] Words repealed by Coroners and Justice Act 2009, s 107(3) (14 December 2009: repeal has effect on 14 December 2009 as specified in SI 2009/3253, art 3(1)(b) subject to transitional provisions specified in art 4(4)).

[210] Added by Police and Justice Act 2006, s 46(4) (1 April 2007 for purposes specified in SI 2007/709, art 3(n); 14 November 2008 for purposes specified in SI 2008/2785, art 2 and not yet in force otherwise).

[211] Added by Coroners and Justice Act 2009, s 108(2) (14 December 2009 in relation to the relevant local justice areas specified in SI 2009/3253 art 3(2); not yet in force otherwise).

[212] Words substituted by Police and Justice Act 2006, Sch 6, para 7 (1 April 2007).

[213] Amended by the Criminal Justice Act 2003, s 28, Sch 2, paras 1, 5.

[214] Inserted by the Criminal Justice and Public Order Act 1994, s 29(2).

[215] Amended by the Criminal Justice Act 2003, s 28, Sch 2, paras 1, 6(1), (2).

[216] Amended by the Criminal Justice and Public Order Act 1994, s 27(1)(a).

[217] Word substituted by Police and Justice Act 2006, Sch 6, para 6 (1 April 2007).

In this subsection, 'the normal powers to impose conditions of bail' has the meaning given in section 3(6) of the Bail Act 1976.][218]

[(1B) No application may be made under section 5B of the Bail Act 1976 if a person is released on bail under section [37, 37C(2)(b) or 37CA(2)(b)].[219]

(1C) Subsections (1D) to (1F) below apply where a person released on bail under section [37, 37C(2)(b) or 37CA(2)(b)][220] above is on bail subject to conditions.

(1D) The person shall not be entitled to make an application under section 43B of the Magistrates' Courts Act 1980.

(1E) A magistrates' court may, on an application by or on behalf of the person, vary the conditions of bail; and in this subsection 'vary' has the same meaning as in the Bail Act 1976.

(1F) Where a magistrates' court varies the conditions of bail under subsection (1E) above, that bail shall not lapse but shall continue subject to the conditions as so varied.][221]

(2) Nothing in the Bail Act 1976 shall prevent the re-arrest without warrant of a person released on bail subject to a duty to attend at a police station if new evidence justifying a further arrest has come to light since his release.

(3) Subject to [subsections (3A) and (4)][222] below, in this Part of this Act references to 'bail' are references to bail subject to a duty—

[(a) to appear before a magistrates' court at such time and such place as the custody officer may appoint;

(b) to attend at such police station as the custody officer may appoint at such time as he may appoint for the purposes of—

(i) proceedings in relation to a live link direction under section 57C of the Crime and Disorder Act 1998 (use of live link direction at preliminary hearings where accused is at police station); and

(ii) any preliminary hearing in relation to which such a direction is given; or

(c) to attend at such police station as the custody officer may appoint at such time as he may appoint for purposes other than those mentioned in paragraph (b).][223]

[(3A) Where a custody officer grants bail to a person subject to a duty to appear before a magistrates' court, he shall appoint for the appearance—

(a) a date which is not later than the first sitting of the court after the person is charged with the offence; or

(b) where he is informed by the [designated officer for the relevant local justice][224] area that the appearance cannot be accommodated until a later date, that later date.][225]

---

[218] Amended by the Criminal Justice and Public Order Act 1994, s 27(1)(b).

[219] Words substituted by Police and Justice Act 2006, Sch 6, para 11 (1 April 2007).

[220] Words substituted by Police and Justice Act 2006, Sch 6, para 11 (1 April 2007).

[221] Amended by the Criminal Justice Act 2003, s 28, Sch 2, paras 1, 6(1), (4).

[222] Amended by the Crime and Disorder Act 1998, s 46(1).

[223] Section 47(3)(a)–(c) substituted for s 47(3)(a) and (b) and words by Police and Justice Act 2006, s 46(5)(a) (1 April 2007 for purposes specified in SI 2007/709, art 3(n); 14 November 2008 for purposes specified in SI 2008/2785, art 2 and not yet in force otherwise).

[224] Amended by the Courts Act 2003, s 109(1), Sch 8, para 283; for transitional provisions see SI 2005/911, arts 2–5.

[225] Amended by the Crime and Disorder Act 1998, s 46(2).

Act

(4) Where a custody officer has granted bail to a person subject to a duty to appear at a police station, the custody officer may give notice in writing to that person that his attendance at the police station is not required.

(5) [...][226]

(6) Where a person [who has been granted bail [under this Part][227] and either has attended at the police station in accordance with the grant of bail or has been arrested under section 46A above is detained at a police station][228], any time during which he was in police detention prior to being granted bail shall be included as part of any period which falls to be calculated under this Part of this Act.

(7) Where a person who was released on bail [under this Part][229] subject to a duty to attend at a police station is re-arrested, the provisions of this Part of this Act shall apply to him as they apply to a person arrested for the first time[; but this subsection does not apply to a person who is arrested under section 46A above or has attended a police station in accordance with the grant of bail (and who accordingly is deemed by section 34(7) above to have been arrested for an offence)][230] [or to a person to whom section 46ZA(4) or (5) applies][231]

(8) In the Magistrates' Courts Act 1980—

(a) the following section shall be substituted for section 43—

'43 Bail on arrest

(1) Where a person has been granted bail under the Police and Criminal Evidence Act 1984 subject to a duty to appear before a magistrates' court, the court before which he is to appear may appoint a later time as the time at which he is to appear and may enlarge the recognizances of any sureties for him at that time.

(2) The recognizance of any surety for any person granted bail subject to a duty to attend at a police station may be enforced as if it were conditioned for his appearance before a magistrates' court for the petty sessions area in which the police station named in the recognizance is situated.'; and

(b) the following subsection shall be substituted for section 117(3)—

'(3) Where a warrant has been endorsed for bail under subsection (1) above—

(a) where the person arrested is to be released on bail on his entering into a recognizance without sureties, it shall not be necessary to take him to a police station, but if he is so taken, he shall be released from custody on his entering into the recognizance; and

(b) where he is to be released on his entering into a recognizance with sureties, he shall be taken to a police station on his arrest, and the custody officer there shall (subject to his approving any surety tendered in compliance with the endorsement) release him from custody as directed in the endorsement.'.

---

[226] Repealed by the Criminal Justice and Public Order Act 1994, ss 29(4)(c), 168(3), Sch 11.

[227] Amended by the Criminal Justice Act 2003, s 12, Sch 1, paras 1, 10(a).

[228] Amended by the Criminal Justice and Public Order Act 1994, s 29(4)(d).

[229] Amended by the Criminal Justice Act 2003, s 12, Sch 1, paras 1, 10(b).

[230] Amended by the Criminal Justice and Public Order Act 1994, s 29(4)(e).

[231] Words inserted by Police and Justice Act 2006, s 46(5)(b) (1 April 2007 for purposes specified in SI 2007/709, art 3(n); 14 November 2008 for purposes specified in SI 2008/2785, art 2 and not yet in force otherwise).

**[47A Early administrative hearings conducted by justices' clerks**

Where a person has been charged with an offence at a police station, any requirement imposed under this Part for the person to appear or be brought before a magistrates' court shall be taken to be satisfied if the person appears or is brought before [a justices' clerk][232] in order for the clerk to conduct a hearing under section 50 of the Crime and Disorder Act 1998 (early administrative hearings).][233]

## 48 Remands to police detention

In section 128 of the Magistrates' Courts Act 1980—

(a) in subsection (7) for the words 'the custody of a constable' there shall be substituted the words 'detention at a police station';

(b) after subsection (7) there shall be inserted the following subsection—

'(8) Where a person is committed to detention at a police station under subsection (7) above—

(a) he shall not be kept in such detention unless there is a need for him to be so detained for the purposes of inquiries into other offences;

(b) if kept in such detention, he shall be brought back before the magistrates' court which committed him as soon as that need ceases;

(c) he shall be treated as a person in police detention to whom the duties under section 39 of the Police and Criminal Evidence Act 1984 (responsibilities in relation to persons detained) relate;

(d) his detention shall be subject to periodic review at the times set out in section 40 of that Act (review of police detention).'.

## 49 Police detention to count towards custodial sentence

(1) In subsection (1) of section 67 of the Criminal Justice Act 1967 (computation of custodial sentences) for the words from 'period', in the first place where it occurs, to 'the offender' there shall be substituted the words 'relevant period, but where he'.

(2) The following subsection shall be inserted after that subsection—

'(1A) In subsection (1) above 'relevant period' means—

(a) any period during which the offender was in police detention in connection with the offence for which the sentence was passed; or

(b) any period during which he was in custody—

(i) by reason only of having been committed to custody by an order of a court made in connection with any proceedings relating to that sentence or the offence for which it was passed or any proceedings from which those proceedings arose; or

(ii) by reason of his having been so committed and having been concurrently detained otherwise than by order of a court.'.

---

[232] Amended by the Courts Act 2003, s 109(1), Sch 8, para 284; for transitional provisions see SI 2005/911, arts 2–5.

[233] Inserted by the Crime and Disorder Act 1998, s 119, Sch 8, para 62.

(3) The following subsections shall be added after subsection (6) of that section—

'(7) A person is in police detention for the purposes of this section—

(a) at any time when he is in police detention for the purposes of the Police and Criminal Evidence Act 1984; and

(b) at any time when he is detained under section 12 of the Prevention of Terrorism (Temporary Provisions) Act 1984.

(8) No period of police detention shall be taken into account under this section unless it falls after the coming into force of section 49 of the Police and Criminal Evidence Act 1984.'.

## 50 Records of detention

(1) Each police force shall keep written records showing on an annual basis—

(a) the number of persons kept in police detention for more than 24 hours and subsequently released without charge;

(b) the number of applications for warrants of further detention and the results of the applications; and

(c) in relation to each warrant of further detention—

(i) the period of further detention authorised by it;

(ii) the period which the person named in it spent in police detention on its authority; and

(iii) whether he was charged or released without charge.

(2) Every annual report—

[(a) under section 22 of the Police Act 1996; or][234]

(b) made by the Commissioner of Police of the Metropolis,

shall contain information about the matters mentioned in subsection (1) above in respect of the period to which the report relates.

## 51 Savings

Nothing in this Part of this Act shall affect—

(a) the powers conferred on immigration officers by section 4 of and Schedule 2 to the Immigration Act 1971 (administrative provisions as to control on entry etc);

[(b) the powers conferred by virtue of section 41 of, or Schedule 7 to, the Terrorism Act 2000 (powers of arrest and detention);][235]

(c) [...][236]

(d) any right of a person in police detention to apply for a writ of habeas corpus or other prerogative remedy.

## 52 Children

[...][237]

---

[234] Amended by the Police Act 1996, s 103, Sch 7, para 35.

[235] Amended by the Terrorism Act 2000, s 125(1), Sch 15, para 5(1), (4); for savings see the Terrorism Act 2000, s 129(1)(b) and SI 2001/421, art 2.

[236] Repealed by Armed Forces Act 2006, Sch 17, para 1 (31 October 2009; SI 2009/1167).

[237] Repealed by the Children Act 1989, s 108(7), Sch 15.

## PART V
### QUESTIONING AND TREATMENT OF PERSONS BY POLICE

### 53 Abolition of certain powers of constables to search persons

(1)  Subject to subsection (2) below, there shall cease to have effect any Act (including a local Act) passed before this Act in so far as it authorises—

(a)  any search by a constable of a person in police detention at a police station; or

(b)  an intimate search of a person by a constable;

and any rule of common law which authorises a search such as is mentioned in paragraph (a) or (b) above is abolished.

(2)  [...][238]

### 54 Searches of detained persons

(1)  The custody officer at a police station shall ascertain [...][239] everything which a person has with him when he is—

(a)  brought to the station after being arrested elsewhere or after being committed to custody by an order or sentence of a court; or

[(b)  arrested at the station or detained there [, as a person falling within section 34(7), under section 37 above][240].][241] [or as a person to whom section 46ZA(4) or (5) applies].[242]

[(2)  The custody officer may record or cause to be recorded all or any of the things which he ascertains under subsection (1).

(2A)  In the case of an arrested person, any such record may be made as part of his custody record.][243]

(3)  Subject to subsection (4) below, a custody officer may seize and retain any such thing or cause any such thing to be seized and retained.

(4)  Clothes and personal effects may only be seized if the custody officer—

(a)  believes that the person from whom they are seized may use them—

(i)   to cause physical injury to himself or any other person;

(ii)  to damage property;

(iii) to interfere with evidence; or

(iv)  to assist him to escape; or

(b)  has reasonable grounds for believing that they may be evidence relating to an offence.

(5)  Where anything is seized, the person from whom it is seized shall be told the reason for the seizure unless he is—

(a)  violent or likely to become violent; or

(b)  incapable of understanding what is said to him.

---

[238] Repealed by the Prevention of Terrorism (Temporary Provisions) Act 1989, s 25(2), Sch 9, Pt 1.

[239] Repealed by the Criminal Justice Act 2003, ss 8(1), 332, Sch 37, Pt 1.

[240] Amended by the Criminal Justice and Public Order Act 1994, s 168(2), Sch 10, para 55.

[241] Amended by the Criminal Justice Act 1988, s 147(a).

[242] Words inserted by Police and Justice Act 2006, s 46(6) (1 April 2007 for purposes specified in SI 2007/709, art 3(n); 14 November 2008 for purposes specified in SI 2008/2785, art 2 and not yet in force otherwise).

[243] Amended by the Criminal Justice Act 2003, s 8(2).

(6) Subject to subsection (7) below, a person may be searched if the custody officer considers it necessary to enable him to carry out his duty under subsection (1) above and to the extent that the custody officer considers necessary for that purpose.

[(6A) A person who is in custody at a police station or is in police detention otherwise than at a police station may at any time be searched in order to ascertain whether he has with him anything which he could use for any of the purposes specified in subsection (4)(a) above.

(6B) Subject to subsection (6C) below, a constable may seize and retain, or cause to be seized and retained, anything found on such a search.

(6C) A constable may only seize clothes and personal effects in the circumstances specified in subsection (4) above.][244]

(7) An intimate search may not be conducted under this section.

(8) A search under this section shall be carried out by a constable.

(9) The constable carrying out a search shall be of the same sex as the person searched.

## [54A Searches and examination to ascertain identity

(1) If an officer of at least the rank of inspector authorises it, a person who is detained in a police station may be searched or examined, or both—
   (a) for the purpose of ascertaining whether he has any mark that would tend to identify him as a person involved in the commission of an offence; or
   (b) for the purpose of facilitating the ascertainment of his identity.

(2) An officer may only give an authorisation under subsection (1) for the purpose mentioned in paragraph (a) of that subsection if—
   (a) the appropriate consent to a search or examination that would reveal whether the mark in question exists has been withheld; or
   (b) it is not practicable to obtain such consent.

(3) An officer may only give an authorisation under subsection (1) in a case in which subsection (2) does not apply if—
   (a) the person in question has refused to identify himself; or
   (b) the officer has reasonable grounds for suspecting that that person is not who he claims to be.

(4) An officer may give an authorisation under subsection (1) orally or in writing but, if he gives it orally, he shall confirm it in writing as soon as is practicable.

(5) Any identifying mark found on a search or examination under this section may be photographed—
   (a) with the appropriate consent; or
   (b) if the appropriate consent is withheld or it is not practicable to obtain it, without it.

(6) Where a search or examination may be carried out under this section, or a photograph may be taken under this section, the only persons entitled to carry out the search or examination, or to take the photograph, are [constables][245].

---

[244] Amended by the Criminal Justice Act 1988, s 147(b).
[245] Amended by the Police Reform Act 2002, s 107(1), Sch 7, para 9(2).

(7) A person may not under this section carry out a search or examination of a person of the opposite sex or take a photograph of any part of the body of a person of the opposite sex.

(8) An intimate search may not be carried out under this section.

(9) A photograph taken under this section—

(a) may be used by, or disclosed to, any person for any purpose related to the prevention or detection of crime, the investigation of an offence or the conduct of a prosecution; and

(b) after being so used or disclosed, may be retained but may not be used or disclosed except for a purpose so related.

(10) In subsection—

(a) the reference to crime includes a reference to any conduct which—

(i) constitutes one or more criminal offences (whether under the law of a part of the United Kingdom or of a country or territory outside the United Kingdom); or

(ii) is, or corresponds to, any conduct which, if it all took place in any one part of the United Kingdom, would constitute one or more criminal offences;

and

(b) the references to an investigation and to a prosecution include references, respectively, to any investigation outside the United Kingdom of any crime or suspected crime and to a prosecution brought in respect of any crime in a country or territory outside the United Kingdom.

(11) In this section—

(a) references to ascertaining a person's identity include references to showing that he is not a particular person; and

(b) references to taking a photograph include references to using any process by means of which a visual image may be produced, and references to photographing a person shall be construed accordingly.

(12) In this section 'mark' includes features and injuries; and a mark is an identifying mark for the purposes of this section if its existence in any person's case facilitates the ascertainment of his identity or his identification as a person involved in the commission of an offence.

[(13) Nothing in this section applies to a person arrested under an extradition arrest power.][246][247]

### [54B Searches of persons answering to live link bail

(1) A constable may search at any time—

(a) any person who is at a police station to answer to live link bail; and

(b) any article in the possession of such a person.

(2) If the constable reasonably believes a thing in the possession of the person ought to be seized on any of the grounds mentioned in subsection (3), the constable may seize and retain it or cause it to be seized and retained.

---

[246] Amended by the Extradition Act 2003, s 169(1), (2); for savings see SI 2003/3103, arts 2–4.
[247] Inserted by the Anti-terrorism, Crime and Security Act 2001, s 90(1).

Act

(3) The grounds are that the thing—
  (a) may jeopardise the maintenance of order in the police station;
  (b) may put the safety of any person in the police station at risk; or
  (c) may be evidence of, or in relation to, an offence.
(4) The constable may record or cause to be recorded all or any of the things seized and retained pursuant to subsection (2).
(5) An intimate search may not be carried out under this section.
(6) The constable carrying out a search under subsection (1) must be of the same sex as the person being searched.
(7) In this section 'live link bail' means bail granted under Part 4 of this Act subject to the duty mentioned in section 47(3)(b).][248]

### [54C  Power to retain articles seized

(1) Except as provided by subsections (2) and (3), a constable may retain a thing seized under section 54B until the time when the person from whom it was seized leaves the police station.
(2) A constable may retain a thing seized under section 54B in order to establish its lawful owner, where there are reasonable grounds for believing that it has been obtained in consequence of the commission of an offence.
(3) If a thing seized under section 54B may be evidence of, or in relation to, an offence, a constable may retain it—
  (a) for use as evidence at a trial for an offence; or
  (b) for forensic examination or for investigation in connection with an offence.
(4) Nothing may be retained for either of the purposes mentioned in subsection (3) if a photograph or copy would be sufficient for that purpose.
(5) Nothing in this section affects any power of a court to make an order under section 1 of the Police (Property) Act 1897.
(6) The references in this section to anything seized under section 54B include anything seized by a person to whom paragraph 27A of Schedule 4 to the Police Reform Act 2002 applies.][249]

### 55  Intimate searches

(1) Subject to the following provisions of this section, if an officer of at least the rank of [inspector][250] has reasonable grounds for believing—
  (a) that a person who has been arrested and is in police detention may have concealed on him anything which—
    (i) he could use to cause physical injury to himself or others; and
    (ii) he might so use while he is in police detention or in the custody of a court; or

---

[248] Added by Coroners and Justice Act 2009, s 108(1) (14 December 2009 in relation to the relevant local justice areas specified in SI 2009/3253, art 3(2); not yet in force otherwise).
[249] Added by Coroners and Justice Act 2009, s 108(1) (14 December 2009 in relation to the relevant local justice areas specified in SI 2009/3253, art 3(2); not yet in force otherwise).
[250] Amended by the Criminal Justice and Police Act 2001, s 79.

(b) that such a person—
   (i) may have a Class A drug concealed on him; and
   (ii) was in possession of it with the appropriate criminal intent before his arrest,

he may authorise [an intimate search][251] of that person.

(2) An officer may not authorise an intimate search of a person for anything unless he has reasonable grounds for believing that it cannot be found without his being intimately searched.

(3) An officer may give an authorisation under subsection (1) above orally or in writing but, if he gives it orally, he shall confirm it in writing as soon as is practicable.

[(3A) A drug offence search shall not be carried out unless the appropriate consent has been given in writing.

(3B) Where it is proposed that a drug offence search be carried out, an appropriate officer shall inform the person who is to be subject to it—
   (a) of the giving of the authorisation for it; and
   (b) of the grounds for giving the authorisation.][252]

(4) An intimate search which is only a drug offence search shall be by way of examination by a suitably qualified person.

(5) Except as provided by subsection (4) above, an intimate search shall be by way of examination by a suitably qualified person unless an officer of at least the rank of [inspector][253] considers that this is not practicable.

(6) An intimate search which is not carried out as mentioned in subsection (5) above shall be carried out by a constable.

(7) A constable may not carry out an intimate search of a person of the opposite sex.

(8) No intimate search may be carried out except—
   (a) at a police station;
   (b) at a hospital;
   (c) at a registered medical practitioner's surgery; or
   (d) at some other place used for medical purposes.

(9) An intimate search which is only a drug offence search may not be carried out at a police station.

(10) If an intimate search of a person is carried out, the custody record relating to him shall state—
   (a) which parts of his body were searched; and
   (b) why they were searched.

[(10A) If the intimate search is a drug offence search, the custody record relating to that person shall also state—
   (a) the authorisation by virtue of which the search was carried out;
   (b) the grounds for giving the authorisation; and
   (c) the fact that the appropriate consent was given.][254]

---

[251] Amended by the Criminal Justice Act 1988, s 170(1), Sch 15, paras 97, 99.
[252] Amended by the Drugs Act 2005, s 3(1), (2).
[253] Amended by the Criminal Justice and Police Act 2001, s 79.
[254] Amended by the Drugs Act 2005, s 3(1), (3).

(11)    The information required to be recorded by [subsections (10) and (10A)][255] above shall be recorded as soon as practicable after the completion of the search.

(12)    The custody officer at a police station may seize and retain anything which is found on an intimate search of a person, or cause any such thing to be seized and retained—

    (a)  if he believes that the person from whom it is seized may use it—

        (i)   to cause physical injury to himself or any other person;

        (ii)  to damage property;

        (iii) to interfere with evidence; or

        (iv)  to assist him to escape; or

    (b)  if he has reasonable grounds for believing that it may be evidence relating to an offence.

(13)    Where anything is seized under this section, the person from whom it is seized shall be told the reason for the seizure unless he is—

    (a)  violent or likely to become violent; or

    (b)  incapable of understanding what is said to him.

[(13A) Where the appropriate consent to a drug offence search of any person was refused without good cause, in any proceedings against that person for an offence—

    (a)  the court, in determining whether there is a case to answer;

    (b)  a judge, in deciding whether to grant an application made by the accused under paragraph 2 of Schedule 3 to the Crime and Disorder Act 1998 (applications for dismissal); and

    (c)  the court or jury, in determining whether that person is guilty of the offence charged,

may draw such inferences from the refusal as appear proper.][256]

(14)    Every annual report—

    [(a)  under section 22 of the Police Act 1996; or][257]

    (b)  made by the Commissioner of Police of the Metropolis,

shall contain information about searches under this section which have been carried out in the area to which the report relates during the period to which it relates.

(14A)   [...][258]

(15)    The information about such searches shall include—

    (a)  the total number of searches;

    (b)  the number of searches conducted by way of examination by a suitably qualified person;

    (c)  the number of searches not so conducted but conducted in the presence of such a person; and

    (d)  the result of the searches carried out.

(16)    The information shall also include, as separate items—

    (a)  the total number of drug offence searches; and

    (b)  the result of those searches.

---

[255] Amended by the Drugs Act 2005, s 3(1), (4).

[256] Amended by the Drugs Act 2005, s 3(1), (5).

[257] Amended by the Police Act 1996, s 103, Sch 7, para 36.

[258] Repealed by SOCAPA 2005, ss 59, 174(2), Sch 4, paras 43, 45, Sch 17, Pt 2.

Act

(17) In this section—
'the appropriate criminal intent' means an intent to commit an offence under—
(a) section 5(3) of the Misuse of Drugs Act 1971 (possession of controlled drug with intent to supply to another); or
(b) section 68(2) of the Customs and Excise Management Act 1979 (exportation etc with intent to evade a prohibition or restriction);
['appropriate officer' means—
(a) a constable,
(b) a person who is designated as a detention officer in pursuance of section 38 of the Police Reform Act 2002 if his designation applies paragraph 33D of Schedule 4 to that Act[;]
(c) [...][259]]
'Class A drug' has the meaning assigned to it by section 2(1)(b) of the Misuse of Drugs Act 1971;
'drug offence search' means an intimate search for a Class A drug which an officer has authorised by virtue of subsection (1)(b) above; and
'suitably qualified person' means—
(a) a registered medical practitioner; or
(b) a registered nurse.

## [55A X-rays and ultrasound scans

(1) If an officer of at least the rank of inspector has reasonable grounds for believing that a person who has been arrested for an offence and is in police detention—
(a) may have swallowed a Class A drug, and
(b) was in possession of it with the appropriate criminal intent before his arrest,
the officer may authorise that an x-ray is taken of the person or an ultrasound scan is carried out on the person (or both).
(2) An x-ray must not be taken of a person and an ultrasound scan must not be carried out on him unless the appropriate consent has been given in writing.
(3) If it is proposed that an x-ray is taken or an ultrasound scan is carried out, an appropriate officer must inform the person who is to be subject to it—
(a) of the giving of the authorisation for it, and
(b) of the grounds for giving the authorisation.
(4) An x-ray may be taken or an ultrasound scan carried out only by a suitably qualified person and only at—
(a) a hospital,
(b) a registered medical practitioner's surgery, or
(c) some other place used for medical purposes.
(5) The custody record of the person must also state—
(a) the authorisation by virtue of which the x-ray was taken or the ultrasound scan was carried out,
(b) the grounds for giving the authorisation, and
(c) the fact that the appropriate consent was given.

---

[259] Repealed by Policing and Crime Act 2009, Sch 8, para 1 (12 January 2010).

**Act**

(6)  The information required to be recorded by subsection (5) must be recorded as soon as practicable after the x-ray has been taken or ultrasound scan carried out (as the case may be).

(7)  Every annual report—
   (a)  under section 22 of the Police Act 1996, or
   (b)  made by the Commissioner of Police of the Metropolis,
   must contain information about x-rays which have been taken and ultrasound scans which have been carried out under this section in the area to which the report relates during the period to which it relates.

(8)  The information about such x-rays and ultrasound scans must be presented separately and must include—
   (a)  the total number of x-rays;
   (b)  the total number of ultrasound scans;
   (c)  the results of the x-rays;
   (d)  the results of the ultrasound scans.

(9)  If the appropriate consent to an x-ray or ultrasound scan of any person is refused without good cause, in any proceedings against that person for an offence—
   (a)  the court, in determining whether there is a case to answer,
   (b)  a judge, in deciding whether to grant an application made by the accused under paragraph 2 of Schedule 3 to the Crime and Disorder Act 1998 (applications for dismissal), and
   (c)  the court or jury, in determining whether that person is guilty of the offence charged,
   may draw such inferences from the refusal as appear proper.

(10)  In this section 'the appropriate criminal intent', 'appropriate officer', 'Class A drug' and 'suitably qualified person' have the same meanings as in section 55 above.][260]

## 56 Right to have someone informed when arrested

(1)  Where a person has been arrested and is being held in custody in a police station or other premises, he shall be entitled, if he so requests, to have one friend or relative or other person who is known to him or who is likely to take an interest in his welfare told, as soon as is practicable except to the extent that delay is permitted by this section, that he has been arrested and is being detained there.

(2)  Delay is only permitted—
   (a)  in the case of a person who is in police detention for [an indictable offence][261]; and
   (b)  if an officer of at least the rank of [inspector][262] authorises it.

(3)  In any case the person in custody must be permitted to exercise the right conferred by subsection (1) above within 36 hours from the relevant time, as defined in section 41(2) above.

---

[260] Inserted by the Drugs Act 2005, s 5(1).
[261] Amended by SOCAPA 2005, s 111, Sch 7, Pt 3, para 43(1), (9)(a).
[262] Amended by the Criminal Justice and Police Act 2001, s 74.

(4) An officer may give an authorisation under subsection (2) above orally or in writing but, if he gives it orally, he shall confirm it in writing as soon as is practicable.

(5) [Subject to subsection (5A) below][263] an officer may only authorise delay where he has reasonable grounds for believing that telling the named person of the arrest—

(a) will lead to interference with or harm to evidence connected with [an indictable offence][264] or interference with or physical injury to other persons; or

(b) will lead to the alerting of other persons suspected of having committed such an offence but not yet arrested for it; or

(c) will hinder the recovery of any property obtained as a result of such an offence.

[(5A) An officer may also authorise delay where he has reasonable grounds for believing that—

(a) the person detained for [the indictable offence][265] has benefited from his criminal conduct, and

(b) the recovery of the value of the property constituting the benefit will be hindered by telling the named person of the arrest.

(5B) For the purposes of subsection (5A) above the question whether a person has benefited from his criminal conduct is to be decided in accordance with Part 2 of the Proceeds of Crime Act 2002.][266]

(6) If a delay is authorised—

(a) the detained person shall be told the reason for it; and

(b) the reason shall be noted on his custody record.

(7) The duties imposed by subsection (6) above shall be performed as soon as is practicable.

(8) The rights conferred by this section on a person detained at a police station or other premises are exercisable whenever he is transferred from one place to another; and this section applies to each subsequent occasion on which they are exercisable as it applies to the first such occasion.

(9) There may be no further delay in permitting the exercise of the right conferred by subsection (1) above once the reason for authorising delay ceases to subsist.

[(10) Nothing in this section applies to a person arrested or detained under the terrorism provisions.][267]

## 57 Additional rights of children and young persons

The following subsections shall be substituted for section 34(2) of the Children and Young Persons Act 1933—

'(2) Where a child or young person is in police detention, such steps as are practicable shall be taken to ascertain the identity of a person responsible for his welfare.

---

[263] Amended by the Drug Trafficking Offences Act 1986, s 32(1).

[264] Amended by SOCAPA 2005, s 111, Sch 7, Pt 3, para 43(1), (9)(a).

[265] Amended by SOCAPA 2005, s 111, Sch 7, Pt 3, para 43(1), (9)(b).

[266] Amended by the Proceeds of Crime Act 2002, s 456, Sch 11, paras 1, 14(1), (2).

[267] Amended by the Terrorism Act 2000, s 125(1), Sch 15, para 5(1), (5); for savings see the Terrorism Act 2000, s 129(1)(b) and SI 2001/421, art 2.

(3) If it is practicable to ascertain the identity of a person responsible for the welfare of the child or young person, that person shall be informed, unless it is not practicable to do so—
(a) that the child or young person has been arrested;
(b) why he has been arrested; and
(c) where he is being detained.

(4) Where information falls to be given under subsection (3) above, it shall be given as soon as it is practicable to do so.

(5) For the purposes of this section the persons who may be responsible for the welfare of a child or young person are—
(a) his parent or guardian; or
(b) any other person who has for the time being assumed responsibility for his welfare.

(6) If it is practicable to give a person responsible for the welfare of the child or young person the information required by subsection (3) above, that person shall be given it as soon as it is practicable to do so.

(7) If it appears that at the time of his arrest a supervision order, as defined in section 11 of the Children and Young Persons Act 1969, is in force in respect of him, the person responsible for his supervision shall also be informed as described in subsection (3) above as soon as it is reasonably practicable to do so.

(8) The reference to a parent or guardian in subsection (5) above is—
(a) in the case of a child or young person in the care of a local authority, a reference to that authority; and
(b) in the case of a child or young person in the care of a voluntary organisation in which parental rights and duties with respect to him are vested by virtue of a resolution under section 64(1) of the Child Care Act 1980, a reference to that organisation.

(9) The rights conferred on a child or young person by subsections (2) to (8) above are in addition to his rights under section 56 of the Police and Criminal Evidence Act 1984.

(10) The reference in subsection (2) above to a child or young person who is in police detention includes a reference to a child or young person who has been detained under the terrorism provisions; and in subsection (3) above 'arrest' includes such detention.

(11) In subsection (10) above 'the terrorism provisions' has the meaning assigned to it by section 65 of the Police and Criminal Evidence Act 1984'.

## 58 Access to legal advice

(1) A person arrested and held in custody in a police station or other premises shall be entitled, if he so requests, to consult a solicitor privately at any time.

(2) Subject to subsection (3) below, a request under subsection (1) above and the time at which it was made shall be recorded in the custody record.

(3) Such a request need not be recorded in the custody record of a person who makes it at a time while he is at a court after being charged with an offence.

(4) If a person makes such a request, he must be permitted to consult a solicitor as soon as is practicable except to the extent that delay is permitted by this section.

(5)    In any case he must be permitted to consult a solicitor within 36 hours from the relevant time, as defined in section 41(2) above.

(6)    Delay in compliance with a request is only permitted—

    (a) in the case of a person who is in police detention for [an indictable offence][268]; and

    (b) if an officer of at least the rank of superintendent authorises it.

(7)    An officer may give an authorisation under subsection (6) above orally or in writing but, if he gives it orally, he shall confirm it in writing as soon as is practicable.

(8)    [Subject to subsection (8A) below][269] an officer may only authorise delay where he has reasonable grounds for believing that the exercise of the right conferred by subsection (1) above at the time when the person detained desires to exercise it—

    (a) will lead to interference with or harm to evidence connected with [an indictable offence][270] or interference with or physical injury to other persons; or

    (b) will lead to the alerting of other persons suspected of having committed such an offence but not yet arrested for it; or

    (c) will hinder the recovery of any property obtained as a result of such an offence.

[(8A) An officer may also authorise delay where he has reasonable grounds for believing that—

    (a) the person detained for [the indictable offence][271] has benefited from his criminal conduct, and

    (b) the recovery of the value of the property constituting the benefit will be hindered by the exercise of the right conferred by subsection (1) above.

(8B)   For the purposes of subsection (8A) above the question whether a person has benefited from his criminal conduct is to be decided in accordance with Part 2 of the Proceeds of Crime Act 2002.][272]

(9)    If delay is authorised—

    (a) the detained person shall be told the reason for it; and

    (b) the reason shall be noted on his custody record.

(10)   The duties imposed by subsection (9) above shall be performed as soon as is practicable.

(11)   There may be no further delay in permitting the exercise of the right conferred by subsection (1) above once the reason for authorising delay ceases to subsist.

[(12) Nothing in this section applies to a person arrested or detained under the terrorism provisions.][273]

---

[268] Amended by SOCAPA 2005, s 111, Sch 7, Pt 3, para 43(1), (10)(a).

[269] Amended by the Drug Trafficking Offences Act 1986, s 32(2).

[270] Amended by SOCAPA 2005, s 111, Sch 7, Pt 3, para 43(1), (10)(a).

[271] Amended by SOCAPA 2005, s 111, Sch 7, Pt 3, para 43(1), (10)(b).

[272] Amended by the Proceeds of Crime Act 2002, s 456, Sch 11, paras 1, 14(1), (3).

[273] Amended by the Terrorism Act 2000, s 125(1), Sch 15, para 5(1), (6); for savings see the Terrorism Act 2000, s 129(1)(b) and SI 2001/421, art 2.

### 59 Legal aid for persons at police stations

[...][274]

### 60 Tape-recording of interviews

(1) It shall be the duty of the Secretary of State—
   (a) to issue a code of practice in connection with the tape-recording of interviews of persons suspected of the commission of criminal offences which are held by police officers at police stations; and
   (b) to make an order requiring the tape-recording of interviews of persons suspected of the commission of criminal offences, or of such descriptions of criminal offences as may be specified in the order, which are so held, in accordance with the code as it has effect for the time being.

(2) An order under subsection (1) above shall be made by statutory instrument and shall be subject to annulment in pursuance of a resolution of either House of Parliament.

### [60A Visual recording of interviews

(1) The Secretary of State shall have power—
   (a) to issue a code of practice for the visual recording of interviews held by police officers at police stations; and
   (b) to make an order requiring the visual recording of interviews so held, and requiring the visual recording to be in accordance with the code for the time being in force under this section.

(2) A requirement imposed by an order under this section may be imposed in relation to such cases or police stations in such areas, or both, as may be specified or described in the order.

(3) An order under subsection (1) above shall be made by statutory instrument and shall be subject to annulment in pursuance of a resolution of either House of Parliament.

(4) In this section—
   (a) references to any interview are references to an interview of a person suspected of a criminal offence; and
   (b) references to a visual recording include references to a visual recording in which an audio recording is comprised.][275]

### 61 Fingerprinting

(1) Except as provided by this section no person's fingerprints may be taken without the appropriate consent.

(2) Consent to the taking of a person's fingerprints must be in writing if it is given at a time when he is at a police station.

[(3) The fingerprints of a person detained at a police station may be taken without the appropriate consent if—
   (a) he is detained in consequence of his arrest for a recordable offence; and

---

[274] Repealed by the Legal Aid Act 1988, s 45(2), (3), Sch 6.
[275] Inserted by the Criminal Justice and Police Act 2001, s 76(1).

(b) he has not had his fingerprints taken in the course of the investigation of the offence by the police.][276]

[(3A) [Where a person mentioned in paragraph (a) of subsection (3) or (4) has already had his fingerprints taken in the course of the investigation of the offence by the police][277], that fact shall be disregarded for the purposes of that subsection if—

(a) the fingerprints taken on the previous occasion do not constitute a complete set of his fingerprints; or

(b) some or all of the fingerprints taken on the previous occasion are not of sufficient quality to allow satisfactory analysis, comparison or matching (whether in the case in question or generally).][278]

[(4) The fingerprints of a person detained at a police station may be taken without the appropriate consent if—

(a) he has been charged with a recordable offence or informed that he will be reported for such an offence; and

(b) he has not had his fingerprints taken in the course of the investigation of the offence by the police.][279]

[(4A) The fingerprints of a person who has answered to bail at a court or police station may be taken without the appropriate consent at the court or station if—

(a) the court, or

(b) an officer of at least the rank of inspector,

authorises them to be taken.

(4B) A court or officer may only give an authorisation under subsection (4A) if—

(a) the person who has answered to bail has answered to it for a person whose fingerprints were taken on a previous occasion and there are reasonable grounds for believing that he is not the same person; or

(b) the person who has answered to bail claims to be a different person from a person whose fingerprints were taken on a previous occasion.][280]

(5) An officer may give an authorisation under [subsection (4A)][281] above orally or in writing but, if he gives it orally, he shall confirm it in writing as soon as is practicable.

(6) Any person's fingerprints may be taken without the appropriate consent if—

[(a) he has been convicted of a recordable offence;

(b) he has been given a caution in respect of a recordable offence which, at the time of the caution, he has admitted; or

(c) he has been warned or reprimanded under section 65 of the Crime and Disorder Act 1998 (c 37) for a recordable offence][282].[283]

---

[276] Amended by the Criminal Justice Act 2003, s 9(1), (2).

[277] Amended by the Criminal Justice Act 2003, s 9(1), (3).

[278] Amended by the Criminal Justice and Police Act 2001, s 78(3).

[279] Amended by the Criminal Justice Act 2003, s 9(1), (2).

[280] Amended by the Criminal Justice and Police Act 2001, s 78(4).

[281] Amended by the Criminal Justice Act 2003, s 9(1), (4).

[282] Amended by the Criminal Justice and Police Act 2001, s 78(6).

[283] New subsections (6A)–(6C) prospectively inserted by SOCAPA 2005, s 117(1), (2): see below.

[*(6A)   A constable may take a person's fingerprints without the appropriate consent if—*

     *(a)   the constable reasonably suspects that the person is committing or attempting to commit an offence, or has committed or attempted to commit an offence; and*

     *(b)   either of the two conditions mentioned in subsection (6B) is met.*

*(6B)   The conditions are that—*

     *(a)   the name of the person is unknown to, and cannot be readily ascertained by, the constable;*

     *(b)   the constable has reasonable grounds for doubting whether a name furnished by the person as his name is his real name.*

*(6C)   The taking of fingerprints by virtue of subsection (6A) does not count for any of the purposes of this Act as taking them in the course of the investigation of an offence by the police.*][284]

(7)   In a case where by virtue of [subsection (3), (4) or (6)[285]][286] [ , (6) or (6A)][287] above a person's fingerprints are taken without the appropriate consent—

     (a)   he shall be told the reason before his fingerprints are taken; and

     (b)   the reason shall be recorded as soon as is practicable after the fingerprints are taken.

[(7A)   If a person's fingerprints are taken at a police station,[288] [*or by virtue of subsection (6A) at a place other than a police station,*][289] whether with or without the appropriate consent—

     (a)   before the fingerprints are taken, an officer[290] [*(or, in a subsection (6A) case, the constable)*][291] shall inform him that they may be the subject of a speculative search; and

     (b)   the fact that the person has been informed of this possibility shall be recorded as soon as is practicable after the fingerprints have been taken.][292]

(8)   If he is detained at a police station when the fingerprints are taken, the reason for taking them [and, in the case falling within subsection (7A) above, the fact referred to in paragraph (b) of that subsection][293] shall be recorded on his custody record.[294]

---

[284] Subsections (6A)–(6C) inserted by the SOCAPA 2005, s 117(1), (2) on a date to be appointed: see the SOCAPA 2005, s 178(8).

[285] Prospectively amended by SOCAPA 2005, s 117(1), (3).

[286] Amended by the Criminal Justice Act 2003, s 9(1), (5).

[287] The words 'or (6)' repealed and subsequent words in square brackets substituted by the SOCAPA 2005, s 117(1), (3) on a date to be appointed: see the SOCAPA 2005, s 178(8).

[288] Prospectively amended by SOCAPA 2005, s 117(1), (4)(a): see below.

[289] The words from 'or by virtue' to 'a police station,' in square brackets inserted by the SOCAPA 2005, s 117(1), (4)(a) on a date to be appointed: see the SOCAPA 2005, s 178(8).

[290] Prospectively amended by SOCAPA 2005, s 117(1), (4)(b): see below

[291] The words '(or, in a subsection (6A) case, the constable)' in square brackets inserted by the SOCAPA 2005, s 117(1), (4)(b) on a date to be appointed: see the SOCAPA 2005, s 178(8).

[292] Amended by the Criminal Justice and Public Order Act 1994, s 168(2), Sch 10, para 56(a).

[293] Amended by the Criminal Justice and Public Order Act 1994, s 168(2), Sch 10, para 56(b).

[294] New subsection (8A) prospectively inserted by the Criminal Justice and Police Act 2001, s 78(7).

[(8A) *Where a person's fingerprints are taken electronically, they must be taken only in such manner, and using such devices, as the Secretary of State has approved for the purposes of electronic fingerprinting.*][295]

[(8B) The power to take the fingerprints of a person detained at a police station without the appropriate consent shall be exercisable by any constable.][296]

(9)   Nothing in this section—

    (a) affects any power conferred by paragraph 18(2) of Schedule 2 to the Immigration Act 1971[297]; [, *section 141 of the Immigration and Asylum Act 1999 or regulations made under section 144 of that Act*][298] or

    [(b) applies to a person arrested or detained under the terrorism provisions][299].

[(10) Nothing in this section applies to a person arrested under an extradition arrest power.][300]

## 61A [Impressions of footwear

(1)   Except as provided by this section, no impression of a person's footwear may be taken without the appropriate consent.

(2)   Consent to the taking of an impression of a person's footwear must be in writing if it is given at a time when he is at a police station.

(3)   Where a person is detained at a police station, an impression of his footwear may be taken without the appropriate consent if—

    (a) he is detained in consequence of his arrest for a recordable offence, or has been charged with a recordable offence, or informed that he will be reported for a recordable offence; and

    (b) he has not had an impression taken of his footwear in the course of the investigation of the offence by the police.

(4)   Where a person mentioned in paragraph (a) of subsection (3) above has already had an impression taken of his footwear in the course of the investigation of the offence by the police, that fact shall be disregarded for the purposes of that subsection if the impression of his footwear taken previously is—

    (a) incomplete; or

    (b) is not of sufficient quality to allow satisfactory analysis, comparison or matching (whether in the case in question or generally).

(5)   If an impression of a person's footwear is taken at a police station, whether with or without the appropriate consent—

    (a) before it is taken, an officer shall inform him that it may be the subject of a speculative search; and

---

[295] Subsection (8A) inserted by the Criminal Justice and Police Act 2001, s 78(7) on a date to be appointed: see the Criminal Justice and Police Act 2001, s 138(2).

[296] Amended by the Police Reform Act 2002, s 107(1), Sch 7, para 9(3).

[297] Prospectively amended by the Immigration and Asylum Act 1999, s 169(1), Sch 14, para 80(1), (4): see below.

[298] The words from ', section 141' to '144 of that Act' in square brackets inserted by the Immigration and Asylum Act 1999, s 169(1), Sch 14, para 80(1), (4) on a date to be appointed: see the Immigration and Asylum Act 1999, s 170(4).

[299] Amended by the Terrorism Act 2000, s 125(1), Sch 15, para 5(1), (7); for savings see the Terrorism Act 2000, s 129(1)(b) and SI 2001/421, art 2.

[300] Amended by the Extradition Act 2003, s 169(1), (3); for savings see SI 2003/3103, arts 2–4.

Ac1

(b) the fact that the person has been informed of this possibility shall be recorded as soon as is practicable after the impression has been taken, and if he is detained at a police station, the record shall be made on his custody record.

(6) In a case where, by virtue of subsection (3) above, an impression of a person's footwear is taken without the appropriate consent—

(a) he shall be told the reason before it is taken; and

(b) the reason shall be recorded on his custody record as soon as is practicable after the impression is taken.

(7) The power to take an impression of the footwear of a person detained at a police station without the appropriate consent shall be exercisable by any constable.

(8) Nothing in this section applies to any person—

(a) arrested or detained under the terrorism provisions;

(b) arrested under an extradition arrest power.][301]

## 62 Intimate samples

(1) [Subject to section 63B below,][302] an intimate sample may be taken from a person in police detention only—

(a) if a police officer of at least the rank of [inspector][303] authorises it to be taken; and

(b) if the appropriate consent is given.

[(1A) An intimate sample may be taken from a person who is not in police detention but from whom, in the course of the investigation of an offence, two or more non-intimate samples suitable for the same means of analysis have been taken which have proved insufficient—

(a) if a police officer of at least the rank of [inspector][304] authorises it to be taken; and

(b) if the appropriate consent is given.][305]

(2) An officer may only give an authorisation [under subsection (1) or (1A) above][306] if he has reasonable grounds—

(a) for suspecting the involvement of the person from whom the sample is to be taken in a [recordable offence][307]; and

(b) for believing that the sample will tend to confirm or disprove his involvement.

(3) An officer may give an authorisation under subsection (1) [or (1A)][308] above orally or in writing but, if he gives it orally, he shall confirm it in writing as soon as is practicable.

(4) The appropriate consent must be given in writing.

---

[301] Inserted by SOCAPA 2005, s 118(1), (2).

[302] Amended by the Criminal Justice and Court Services Act 2000, s 74, Sch 7, Pt II, paras 76, 78.

[303] Amended by the Criminal Justice and Police Act 2001, s 80(1).

[304] Amended by the Criminal Justice and Police Act 2001, s 80(1).

[305] Amended by the Criminal Justice and Public Order Act 1994, ss 54(2), 168(2), Sch 10, paras 57(a), 62(4)(a).

[306] Amended by the Criminal Justice and Public Order Act 1994, s 54(3).

[307] ibid.

[308] Amended by the Criminal Justice and Public Order Act 1994, s 54(4).

(5)     Where—
         (a)  an authorisation has been given; and
         (b)  it is proposed that an intimate sample shall be taken in pursuance of the authorisation,
         an officer shall inform the person from whom the sample is to be taken—
         (i)   of the giving of the authorisation; and
         (ii)  of the grounds for giving it.

(6)     The duty imposed by subsection (5)(ii) above includes a duty to state the nature of the offence in which it is suspected that the person from whom the sample is to be taken has been involved.

(7)     If an intimate sample is taken from a person—
         (a)  the authorisation by virtue of which it was taken;
         (b)  the grounds for giving the authorisation; and
         (c)  the fact that the appropriate consent was given,
         shall be recorded as soon as is practicable after the sample is taken.

[(7A)  If an intimate sample is taken from a person at a police station—
         (a)  before the sample is taken, an officer shall inform him that it may be the subject of a speculative search; and
         (b)  the fact that the person has been informed of this possibility shall be recorded as soon as practicable after the sample has been taken.][309]

(8)     If an intimate sample is taken from a person detained at a police station, the matters required to be recorded by subsection (7) [or (7A)][310] above shall be recorded in his custody record.

[(9)     In the case of an intimate sample which is a dental impression, the sample may be taken from a person only by a registered dentist.

(9A)  In the case of any other form of intimate sample, except in the case of a sample of urine, the sample may be taken from a person only by—
         (a)  a registered medical practitioner; or
         (b)  a registered health care professional.][311]

(10)   Where the appropriate consent to the taking of an intimate sample from a person was refused without good cause, in any proceedings against that person for an offence—
         (a)  the court, in determining—
             (i)   whether to commit that person for trial; or[312]
             (ii)  whether there is a case to answer; and
         [(aa)  a judge, in deciding whether to grant an application made by the accused under—
             (i)   section 6 of the Criminal Justice Act 1987 (application for dismissal of charge of serious fraud in respect of which notice of transfer has been given under section 4 of that Act); or

---

[309] Amended by the Criminal Justice and Public Order Act 1994, ss 54(2), 168(2), Sch 10, paras 57(a), 62(4)(a).

[310] Amended by the Criminal Justice and Public Order Act 1994, s 168(2), Sch 10, para 57(b).

[311] Amended by the Police Reform Act 2002, s 54(1).

[312] Prospectively repealed by the Criminal Justice Act 2003, ss 41, 332, Sch 3, Pt 2, para 56(1), (2)(a), Sch 37, Pt 4.

Act

(ii) paragraph 5 of Schedule 6 to the Criminal Justice Act 1991 (application for dismissal of charge of violent or sexual offence involving
child in respect of which notice of transfer has been given under
section 53 of that Act); and[313]][314] *[paragraph 2 of Schedule 3 to the Crime
and Disorder Act 1998 (applications for dismissal); and]*[315]

(b) the court or jury, in determining whether that person is guilty of the
offence charged,

may draw such inferences from the refusal as appear proper [...][316]

(11) Nothing in this section [applies to the taking of a specimen for the purposes
of any of the provisions of][317] [sections 4 to 11 of the Road Traffic Act 1988][318]
[or of sections 26 to 38 of the Transport and Works Act 1992][319].

[(12) Nothing in this section applies to a person arrested or detained under the terrorism provisions; and subsection (1A) shall not apply where the non-intimate
samples mentioned in that subsection were taken under paragraph 10 of
Schedule 8 to the Terrorism Act 2000.][320]

### 63 Other samples

(1) Except as provided by this section, a non-intimate sample may not be taken
from a person without the appropriate consent.

(2) Consent to the taking of a non-intimate sample must be given in writing.

[(2A) A non-intimate sample may be taken from a person without the appropriate
consent if two conditions are satisfied.

(2B) The first is that the person is in police detention in consequence of his arrest
for a recordable offence.

(2C) The second is that—

(a) he has not had a non-intimate sample of the same type and from the same
part of the body taken in the course of the investigation of the offence by
the police, or

(b) he has had such a sample taken but it proved insufficient.][321]

(3) A non-intimate sample may be taken from a person without the appropriate
consent if—

(a) he [...][322] is being held in custody by the police on the authority of a court;
and

---

[313] Prospectively amended by the Criminal Justice Act 2003, s 41, Sch 3, Pt 2, para 56(1), (2)(b).

[314] Amended by the Criminal Justice and Public Order Act 1994, s 168(1), Sch 9, para 24.

[315] Subsection (10)(aa)(i) & (ii) repealed and subsequent words in square brackets substituted by the
Criminal Justice Act 2003, s 41, Sch 3, Pt 2, para 56(1), (2)(b) on 9 May 2005 (in relation to cases sent for
trial under the Crime and Disorder Act 1998, ss 51 or 51A(3)(d)): see SI 2005/1267, art 2(1), (2)(a),
Schedule, Pt 1, para 1(1)(l) and for remaining purposes on a date to be appointed: see the Criminal
Justice Act 2003, s 336(3).

[316] Repealed by the Criminal Justice and Public Order Act 1994, s 168(3), Sch 11.

[317] Amended by the Police Reform Act 2002, s 53(2)(a).

[318] Amended by the Road Traffic (Consequential Provisions) Act 1988, s 4, Sch 3, para 27.

[319] Amended by the Police Reform Act 2002, s 53(2)(b).

[320] Amended by the Terrorism Act 2000, s 125(1), Sch 15, para 5(1), (8); for savings see the Terrorism
Act 2000, s 129(1)(b) and SI 2001/421, art 2.

[321] Amended by the Criminal Justice Act 2003, s 10(1), (2).

[322] Repealed by the Criminal Justice Act 2003, ss 10(1), (3), 332, Sch 37, Pt 1.

(b)  an officer of at least the rank of [inspector][323] authorises it to be taken without the appropriate consent.

[(3A)] A non-intimate sample may be taken from a person [(whether or not he is in police detention or held in custody by the police on the authority of a court)[324] without the appropriate consent if—

    (a)  he has been charged with a recordable offence or informed that he will be reported for such an offence; and

    (b)  either he has not had a non-intimate sample taken from him in the course of the investigation of the offence by the police or he has had a non-intimate sample taken from him but either it was not suitable for the same means of analysis or, though so suitable, the sample proved insufficient.

(3B)  A non-intimate sample may be taken from a person without the appropriate consent if he has been convicted of a recordable offence.][325]

[(3C) A non-intimate sample may also be taken from a person without the appropriate consent if he is a person to whom section 2 of the Criminal Evidence (Amendment) Act 1997 applies (persons detained following acquittal on grounds of insanity or finding of unfitness to plead).][326]

(4)  An officer may only give an authorisation under subsection (3) above if he has reasonable grounds—

    (a)  for suspecting the involvement of the person from whom the sample is to be taken in a [recordable offence][327]; and

    (b)  for believing that the sample will tend to confirm or disprove his involvement.

(5)  An officer may give an authorisation under subsection (3) above orally or in writing but, if he gives it orally, he shall confirm it in writing as soon as is practicable.

[(5A) An officer shall not give an authorisation under subsection (3) above for the taking from any person of a non-intimate sample consisting of a skin impression if—

    (a)  a skin impression of the same part of the body has already been taken from that person in the course of the investigation of the offence; and

    (b)  the impression previously taken is not one that has proved insufficient.][328]

(6)  Where—

    (a)  an authorisation has been given; and

    (b)  it is proposed that a non-intimate sample shall be taken in pursuance of the authorisation,

an officer shall inform the person from whom the sample is to be taken—

    (i)  of the giving of the authorisation; and

    (ii)  of the grounds for giving it.

---

[323] Amended by the Criminal Justice and Police Act 2001, s 80(1).

[324] Amended by the Criminal Justice Act 2003, s 10(1), (4).

[325] Amended by the Criminal Justice and Public Order Act 1994, ss 55(2), 168(2), Sch 10, para 58(a).

[326] Amended by the Criminal Evidence (Amendment) Act 1997, s 2(2).

[327] Amended by the Criminal Justice and Public Order Act 1994, s 55(3).

[328] Amended by the Criminal Justice and Police Act 2001, s 80(3).

Act

(7)     The duty imposed by subsection (6)(ii) above includes a duty to state the nature of the offence in which it is suspected that the person from whom the sample is to be taken has been involved.

(8)     If a non-intimate sample is taken from a person by virtue of subsection (3) above—

        (a)  the authorisation by virtue of which it was taken; and

        (b)  the grounds for giving the authorisation,

        shall be recorded as soon as is practicable after the sample is taken.

[(8A)]  In a case where by virtue of [subsection (2A), (3A) [329] [, (3B) or (3C) above][330] a sample is taken from a person without the appropriate consent—

        (a)  he shall be told the reason before the sample is taken; and

        (b)  the reason shall be recorded as soon as practicable after the sample is taken.][331]

[(8B)   If a non-intimate sample is taken from a person at a police station, whether with or without the appropriate consent—

        (a)  before the sample is taken, an officer shall inform him that it may be the subject of a speculative search; and

        (b)  the fact that the person has been informed of this possibility shall be recorded as soon as practicable after the sample has been taken.][332]

(9)     If a non-intimate sample is taken from a person detained at a police station, the matters required to be recorded by subsection (8) [or (8A)][333] [or (8B)][334] above shall be recorded in his custody record.

[(9ZA)  The power to take a non-intimate sample from a person without the appropriate consent shall be exercisable by any constable.][335]

[(9A)   Subsection (3B) above shall not apply to any person convicted before 10th April 1995 unless he is a person to whom section 1 of the Criminal Evidence (Amendment) Act 1997 applies (persons imprisoned or detained by virtue of pre-existing conviction for sexual offence etc).][336]

[(9A)   *Where a non-intimate sample consisting of a skin impression is taken electronically from a person, it must be taken only in such manner, and using such devices, as the Secretary of State has approved for the purpose of the electronic taking of such an impression.*][337]

[(10)   Nothing in this section applies to a person arrested or detained under the terrorism provisions.][338]

[(11)   Nothing in this section applies to a person arrested under an extradition arrest power.][339]

---

[329] Amended by the Criminal Justice Act 2003, s 10(1), (5).

[330] Amended by the Criminal Evidence (Amendment) Act 1997, s 2(2).

[331] Amended by the Criminal Justice and Public Order Act 1994, s 55(4).

[332] Amended by the Criminal Justice and Public Order Act 1994, ss 55(2), 168(2), Sch 10, para 58(a).

[333] Amended by the Criminal Justice and Public Order Act 1994, ss 55(5), 168(2), Sch 10, para 58(b).

[334] ibid.

[335] Amended by the Police Reform Act 2002, s 107(1), Sch 7, para 9(4).

[336] Amended by the Criminal Evidence (Amendment) Act 1997, s 1(2) and new second subsection (9A) prospectively inserted by the Criminal Justice and Police Act 2001, s 80(4).

[337] Subsection (9A): inserted by the Criminal Justice and Police Act 2001, s 80(4) on a date to be appointed: see the Criminal Justice and Police Act 2001, s 138(2).

[338] Amended by the Terrorism Act 2000, s 125(1), Sch 15, para 5(1), (9).

[339] Amended by the Extradition Act 2003, s 169(1), (4); for savings see SI 2003/3103, arts 2–4.

**[63A Fingerprints and samples: supplementary provisions**

[(1)    Where a person has been arrested on suspicion of being involved in a recordable offence or has been charged with such an offence or has been informed
that he will be reported for such an offence, fingerprints[, impressions of
footwear]340 or samples or the information derived from samples taken under
any power conferred by this Part of this Act from the person may be checked
against—

(a)    other fingerprints[, impressions of footwear]341 or samples to which the
person seeking to check has access and which are held by or on behalf of
[any one or more relevant law-enforcement authorities or which]342 are
held in connection with or as a result of an investigation of an offence;

(b)    information derived from other samples if the information is contained
in records to which the person seeking to check has access and which are
held as mentioned in paragraph (a) above.343

[(1ZA) *Fingerprints taken by virtue of section 61(6A) above may be checked against other
fingerprints to which the person seeking to check has access and which are held by or on
behalf of any one or more relevant law-enforcement authorities or which are held in connection with or as a result of an investigation of an offence.*]344

[(1A)] In subsection (1)345 [*and (1ZA)* 346 above 'relevant law-enforcement authority'
means—

(a)    a police force;

[(b)    the Serious Organised Crime Agency;]347

(d)    a public authority (not falling within paragraphs (a) to (c)) with functions
in any part of the British Islands which consist of or include the investigation of crimes or the charging of offenders;

(e)    any person with functions in any country or territory outside the United
Kingdom which—

(i)    correspond to those of a police force; or

(ii)    otherwise consist of or include the investigation of conduct contrary
to the law of that country or territory, or the apprehension of persons
guilty of such conduct;

(f)    any person with functions under any international agreement which consist of or include the investigation of conduct which is—

(i)    unlawful under the law of one or more places,

(ii)    prohibited by such an agreement, or

(iii)    contrary to international law,

or the apprehension of persons guilty of such conduct.

---

340 Amended by SOCAPA 2005, s 118(1), (3)(a).

341 ibid.

342 Amended by the Criminal Justice and Police Act 2001, s 81(1).

343 New subsection (1ZA) prospectively inserted by SOCAPA 2005, s 117(5)(a): see below.

344 Subsection (1ZA) inserted by the SOCAPA 2005, s 117(5)(a) on a date to be appointed: see the
SOCAPA 2005, s 178(8).

345 Prospectively amended by SOCAPA 2005, s 117(5)(b): see below.

346 The words 'and (1ZA)' in square brackets inserted by the SOCAPA 2005, s 117(5)(b) on a date to be
appointed: see the SOCAPA 2005, s 178(8).

347 Amended by SOCAPA 2005, s 59, Sch 4, paras 43, 46.

(1B)   The reference in subsection (1A) above to a police force is a reference to any of the following—

   (a)  any police force maintained under section 2 of the Police Act 1996 (c 16) (police forces in England and Wales outside London);

   (b)  the metropolitan police force;

   (c)  the City of London police force;

   (d)  any police force maintained under or by virtue of section 1 of the Police (Scotland) Act 1967 (c 77);

   (e)  the Police Service of Northern Ireland;

   (f)  the Police Service of Northern Ireland Reserve;

   (g)  the Ministry of Defence Police;

   (h)  the [Royal Navy Police][348];

   (i)  the Royal Military Police;

   (j)  the Royal Air Force Police;

   (k)  [...][349];

   (l)  the British Transport Police;

   (m) the States of Jersey Police Force;

   (n)  the salaried police force of the Island of Guernsey;

   (o)  the Isle of Man Constabulary.

(1C)  Where—

   (a)  fingerprints[, impressions of footwear][350] or samples have been taken from any person in connection with the investigation of an offence but otherwise than in circumstances to which subsection (1) above applies, and

   (b)  that person has given his consent in writing to the use in a speculative search of the fingerprints[, of the impressions of footwear][351] or of the samples and of information derived from them,

   the fingerprints [or impressions of footwear][352] or, as the case may be, those samples and that information may be checked against any of the fingerprints[, impressions of footwear][353], samples or information mentioned in paragraph (a) or (b) of that subsection.

(1D)  A consent given for the purposes of subsection (1C) above shall not be capable of being withdrawn.][354][355]

(2)    Where a sample of hair other than pubic hair is to be taken the sample may be taken either by cutting hairs or by plucking hairs with their roots so long as no more are plucked than the person taking the sample reasonably considers to be necessary for a sufficient sample.

(3)    Where any power to take a sample is exercisable in relation to a person the sample may be taken in a prison or other institution to which the Prison Act 1952 applies.

---

[348] Repealed by Armed Forces Act 2006, Sch 17, para 1 (31 October 2009; SI 2009/1167).

[349] Repealed by Armed Forces Act 2006, Sch 17, para 1 (31 October 2009; SI 2009/1167).

[350] Amended by SOCAPA 2005, s 118(1), (3)(b)(i).

[351] Amended by SOCAPA 2005, s 118(1), (3)(b)(ii).

[352] Amended by SOCAPA 2005, s 118(1), (3)(b)(iii).

[353] Amended by SOCAPA 2005, s 118(1), (3)(b)(iv).

[354] Amended by the Criminal Justice and Police Act 2001, s 81(2).

[355] Amended by the Criminal Procedure and Investigations Act 1996, s 64.

[(3A) Where—
    (a) the power to take a non-intimate sample under section 63(3B) above is exercisable in relation to any person who is detained under Part III of the Mental Health Act 1983 in pursuance of—
       (i) a hospital order or interim hospital order made following his conviction for the recordable offence in question, or
      (ii) a transfer direction given at a time when he was detained in pursuance of any sentence or order imposed following that conviction, or
    (b) the power to take a non-intimate sample under section 63(3C) above is exercisable in relation to any person,
the sample may be taken in the hospital in which he is detained under that Part of that Act.
Expressions used in this subsection and in the Mental Health Act 1983 have the same meaning as in that Act.
(3B)    Where the power to take a non-intimate sample under section 63(3B) above is exercisable in relation to a person detained in pursuance of directions of the Secretary of State under [section 92 of the Powers of Criminal Courts (Sentencing) Act 2000][356] the sample may be taken at the place where he is so detained.][357]
(4)    Any constable may, within the allowed period, require a person who is neither in police detention nor held in custody by the police on the authority of a court to attend a police station in order to have a sample taken where—
    (a) the person has been charged with a recordable offence or informed that he will be reported for such an offence and either he has not had a sample taken from him in the course of the investigation of the offence by the police or he has had a sample so taken from him but either it was not suitable for the same means of analysis or, though so suitable, the sample proved insufficient; or
    (b) the person has been convicted of a recordable offence and either he has not had a sample taken from him since the conviction or he has had a sample taken from him (before or after his conviction) but either it was not suitable for the same means of analysis or, though so suitable, the sample proved insufficient.
(5)    The period allowed for requiring a person to attend a police station for the purpose specified in subsection (4) above is—
    (a) in the case of a person falling within paragraph (a), one month beginning with the date of the charge [or of his being informed as mentioned in that paragraph][358] or one month beginning with the date on which the appropriate officer is informed of the fact that the sample is not suitable for the same means of analysis or has proved insufficient, as the case may be;
    (b) in the case of a person falling within paragraph (b), one month beginning with the date of the conviction or one month beginning with the date on which the appropriate officer is informed of the fact that the sample is not

---

[356] Amended by the Powers of Criminal Courts (Sentencing) Act 2000, s 165(1), Sch 9, para 97.
[357] Amended by the Criminal Evidence (Amendment) Act 1997, s 3.
[358] Amended by the Criminal Evidence (Amendment) Act 1997, s 4.

**Act**

suitable for the same means of analysis or has proved insufficient, as the case may be.

(6)    A requirement under subsection (4) above—

   (a)   shall give the person at least 7 days within which he must so attend; and

   (b)   may direct him to attend at a specified time of day or between specified times of day.

(7)    Any constable may arrest without a warrant a person who has failed to comply with a requirement under subsection (4) above.

(8)    In this section 'the appropriate officer' is—

   (a)   in the case of a person falling within subsection (4)(a), the officer investigating the offence with which that person has been charged or as to which he was informed that he would be reported;

   (b)   in the case of a person falling within subsection (4)(b), the officer in charge of the police station from which the investigation of the offence of which he was convicted was conducted.[359]

**[63B  Testing for presence of Class A drugs**

(1)    A sample of urine or a non-intimate sample may be taken from a person in police detention for the purpose of ascertaining whether he has any specified Class A drug in his body if[—

   (a)   either the arrest condition or the charge condition is met;

   (b)   both the age condition and the request condition are met; and

   (c)   the notification condition is met in relation to the arrest condition, the charge condition or the age condition (as the case may be)][360].

[(1A)  The arrest condition is that the person concerned has been arrested for an offence but has not been charged with that offence and either—

   (a)   the offence is a trigger offence; or

   (b)   a police officer of at least the rank of inspector has reasonable grounds for suspecting that the misuse by that person of a specified Class A drug caused or contributed to the offence and has authorised the sample to be taken.][361]

(2)    [The charge condition is either][362]—

   (a)   that the person concerned has been charged with a trigger offence; or

   (b)   that the person concerned has been charged with an offence and a police officer of at least the rank of inspector, who has reasonable grounds for suspecting that the misuse by that person of any specified Class A drug caused or contributed to the offence, has authorised the sample to be taken.

[(3)    The age condition is—

   (a)   if the arrest condition is met, that the person concerned has attained the age of 18;

   (b)   if the charge condition is met, that he has attained the age of 14.][363]

---

[359] Inserted by the Criminal Justice and Public Order Act 1994, s 56.

[360] Amended by the Drugs Act 2005, s 7(1), (2), (13), (14).

[361] Amended by the Drugs Act 2005, s 7(1), (3), (13), (14).

[362] Amended by the Drugs Act 2005, s 7(1), (4), (13), (14).

[363] Amended by the Drugs Act 2005, s 7(1), (5), (13), (14).

(4)     The [request]³⁶⁴ condition is that a police officer has requested the person concerned to give the sample.

[(4A)  The notification condition is that—

   (a)  the relevant chief officer has been notified by the Secretary of State that appropriate arrangements have been made for the police area as a whole, or for the particular police station, in which the person is in police detention, and

   (b)  the notice has not been withdrawn.

(4B)   For the purposes of subsection (4A) above, appropriate arrangements are arrangements for the taking of samples under this section from whichever of the following is specified in the notification—

   (a)  persons in respect of whom the arrest condition is met;

   (b)  persons in respect of whom the charge condition is met;

   (c)  persons who have not attained the age of 18.]³⁶⁵

(5)     Before requesting the person concerned to give a sample, an officer must—

   (a)  warn him that if, when so requested, he fails without good cause to do so he may be liable to prosecution, and

   (b)  in a case within subsection [(1A)(b) or]³⁶⁶ (2)(b) above, inform him of the giving of the authorisation and of the grounds in question.

[(5A)  In the case of a person who has not attained the age of 17—

   (a)  the making of the request under subsection (4) above;

   (b)  the giving of the warning and (where applicable) the information under subsection (5) above; and

   (c)  the taking of the sample,

may not take place except in the presence of an appropriate adult.]³⁶⁷

[(5B)  If a sample is taken under this section from a person in respect of whom the arrest condition is met no other sample may be taken from him under this section during the same continuous period of detention but—

   (a)  if the charge condition is also met in respect of him at any time during that period, the sample must be treated as a sample taken by virtue of the fact that the charge condition is met;

   (b)  the fact that the sample is to be so treated must be recorded in the person's custody record.

(5C)   Despite subsection (1)(a) above, a sample may be taken from a person under this section if—

   (a)  he was arrested for an offence (the first offence),

   (b)  the arrest condition is met but the charge condition is not met,

   (c)  before a sample is taken by virtue of subsection (1) above he would (but for his arrest as mentioned in paragraph (d) below) be required to be released from police detention,

   (d)  he continues to be in police detention by virtue of his having been arrested for an offence not falling within subsection (1A) above, and

---

³⁶⁴ Amended by the Drugs Act 2005, s 7(1), (6), (13), (14).
³⁶⁵ Amended by the Drugs Act 2005, s 7(1), (7), (13), (14).
³⁶⁶ Amended by the Drugs Act 2005, s 7(1), (8), (13), (14).
³⁶⁷ Amended by the Criminal Justice Act 2003, s 5(1), (3)(b).

**Act**

(e) the sample is taken before the end of the period of 24 hours starting with the time when his detention by virtue of his arrest for the first offence began.

(5D) A sample must not be taken from a person under this section if he is detained in a police station unless he has been brought before the custody officer.][368]

(6) A sample may be taken under this section only by a person prescribed by regulations made by the Secretary of State by statutory instrument.
No regulations shall be made under this subsection unless a draft has been laid before, and approved by resolution of, each House of Parliament.

[[(6A) The Secretary of State may by order made by statutory instrument amend—
(a) paragraph (a) of subsection (3) above, by substituting for the age for the time being specified a different age specified in the order, or different ages so specified for different police areas so specified;
(b) paragraph (b) of that subsection, by substituting for the age for the time being specified a different age specified in the order.][369]

(6B) A statutory instrument containing an order under subsection (6A) above shall not be made unless a draft of the instrument has been laid before, and approved by a resolution of, each House of Parliament.][370]

(7) Information obtained from a sample taken under this section may be disclosed—
(a) for the purpose of informing any decision about granting bail in criminal proceedings (within the meaning of the Bail Act 1976) to the person concerned;
[(aa) for the purpose of informing any decision about the giving of a conditional caution under Part 3 of the Criminal Justice Act 2003 [or a youth conditional caution under Chapter 1 of Part 4 of the Crime and Disorder Act 1998][371] to the person concerned;][372]
(b) where the person concerned is in police detention or is remanded in or committed to custody by an order of a court or has been granted such bail, for the purpose of informing any decision about his supervision;
(c) where the person concerned is convicted of an offence, for the purpose of informing any decision about the appropriate sentence to be passed by a court and any decision about his supervision or release;
[(ca) for the purpose of an assessment which the person concerned is required to attend by virtue of section 9(2) or 10(2) of the Drugs Act 2005;
(cb) for the purpose of proceedings against the person concerned for an offence under section 12(3) or 14(3) of that Act;][373]
(d) for the purpose of ensuring that appropriate advice and treatment is made available to the person concerned.

---

[368] Amended by the Drugs Act 2005, s 7(1), (9), (13), (14).
[369] Amended by the Drugs Act 2005, s 7(1), (10), (13), (14).
[370] Amended by the Criminal Justice Act 2003, s 5(1), (3)(c).
[371] Words inserted by Criminal Justice and Immigration Act 2008, Sch 26(2), para 20(2) (16 November 2009 in relation to the areas specified in SI 2009/2780, art 2(2); not yet in force otherwise).
[372] Amended by the Drugs Act 2005, s 7(1), (11), (13), (14).
[373] Amended by the Drugs Act 2005, s 23(1), Sch 1, paras 1, 4.

(8)    A person who fails without good cause to give any sample which may be taken
       from him under this section shall be guilty of an offence.

[(9)   [...]374

(10)   In this section—

       'appropriate adult', in relation to a person who has not attained the age of 17,
          means—

          (a)  his parent or guardian or, if he is in the care of a local authority or volun-
               tary organisation, a person representing that authority or organisation;
               or

          (b)  a social worker of a local authority [...]375; or

          (c)  if no person falling within paragraph (a) or (b) is available, any
               responsible person aged 18 or over who is not a police officer or
               a person employed by the police;

       'relevant chief officer' means—

          (a)  in relation to a police area, the chief officer of police of the police
               force for that police area; or

          (b)  in relation to a police station, the chief officer of police of the police
               force for the police area in which the police station is situated.]376]377

## 63C [Testing for presence of Class A drugs: supplementary

(1)    A person guilty of an offence under section 63B above shall be liable on sum-
       mary conviction to imprisonment for a term not exceeding three months
       [51 weeks]378, or to a fine not exceeding level 4 on the standard scale, or to both.

(2)    A police officer may give an authorisation under section 63B above orally or in
       writing but, if he gives it orally, he shall confirm it in writing as soon as is
       practicable.

(3)    If a sample is taken under section 63B above by virtue of an authorisation, the
       authorisation and the grounds for the suspicion shall be recorded as soon as is
       practicable after the sample is taken.

(4)    If the sample is taken from a person detained at a police station, the matters
       required to be recorded by subsection (3) above shall be recorded in his cus-
       tody record.

(5)    Subsections (11) and (12) of section 62 above apply for the purposes of section
       63B above as they do for the purposes of that section; and section 63B above
       does not prejudice the generality of sections 62 and 63 above.

(6)    In section 63B above—

       'Class A drug' and 'misuse' have the same meanings as in the Misuse of Drugs
          Act 1971;

       'specified' (in relation to a Class A drug) and 'trigger offence' have the same mean-
          ings as in Part III of the Criminal Justice and Court Services Act 2000.]379

---

374 Repealed by the Drugs Act 2005, ss 7(1), (12)–(14), 23(2), Sch 2.
375 Repealed by the Children Act 2004, s 64, Sch 5, Pt 4.
376 Amended by the Criminal Justice Act 2003, s 5(1), (3)(d).
377 Inserted by the Criminal Justice and Courts Services Act 2000, s 57(1), (2).
378 The words 'three months' repealed and subsequent words in square brackets substituted by the
Criminal Justice Act 2003, s 280(2), (3), Sch 26, para 35 on a date to be appointed: see the Criminal
Justice Act 2003, s 336(3).
379 Inserted by the Criminal Justice and Courts Services Act 2000, s 57(1), (2).

**Act**

## 64 Destruction of fingerprints and samples

[(1A) Where—
- (a) fingerprints[, impressions of footwear][380] or samples are taken from a person in connection with the investigation of an offence, and
- (b) subsection (3) below does not require them to be destroyed, the fingerprints[, impressions of footwear][381] or samples may be retained after they have fulfilled the purposes for which they were taken but shall not be used by any person except for purposes related to the prevention or detection of crime, the investigation of an offence[, the conduct of a prosecution or the identification of a deceased person or of the person from whom a body part came][382].

(1B) In subsection (1A) above—
- (a) the reference to using a fingerprint [or an impression of footwear][383] includes a reference to allowing any check to be made against it under section 63A(1) or (1C) above and to disclosing it to any person;
- (b) the reference to using a sample includes a reference to allowing any check to be made under section 63A(1) or (1C) above against it or against information derived from it and to disclosing it or any such information to any person;
- (c) the reference to crime includes a reference to any conduct which—
  - (i) constitutes one or more criminal offences (whether under the law of a part of the United Kingdom or of a country or territory outside the United Kingdom); or
  - (ii) is, or corresponds to, any conduct which, if it all took place in any one part of the United Kingdom, would constitute one or more criminal offences;

  and
- (d) the references to an investigation and to a prosecution include references, respectively, to any investigation outside the United Kingdom of any crime or suspected crime and to a prosecution brought in respect of any crime in a country or territory outside the United Kingdom.][384] [385]

[(1BA) Fingerprints taken from a person by virtue of section 61(6A) above must be destroyed as soon as they have fulfilled the purpose for which they were taken.][386]

(3) If—
- (a) fingerprints[, impressions of footwear][387] or samples are taken from a person in connection with the investigation of an offence; and
- (b) that person is not suspected of having committed the offence,

---

[380] Amended by SOCAPA 2005, s 118(1), (4)(a).

[381] ibid.

[382] Amended by SOCAPA 2005, s 117(6), (7).

[383] Amended by SOCAPA 2005, s 118(1), (4)(b).

[384] Amended by the Criminal Justice and Police Act 2001, s 82(1), (2), (6).

[385] New subsection (1BA) prospectively inserted by SOCAPA 2005, s 117(6), (8)

[386] Subsection (1BA) inserted by the SOCAPA 2005, s 117(6), (8) on a date to be appointed: see the SOCAPA 2005, s 178(8).

[387] Amended by SOCAPA 2005, s 118(1), (4)(c).

they must[, except as provided in [the following provisions of this section][388,][389] be destroyed as soon as they have fulfilled the purpose for which they were taken.

[(3AA) Samples[, fingerprints and impressions of footwear][390] are not required to be destroyed under subsection (3) above if—

(a) they were taken for the purposes of the investigation of an offence of which a person has been convicted; and

(b) a sample[, fingerprint, (or as the case may be) an impression of footwear][391] was also taken from the convicted person for the purposes of that investigation.

(3AB) Subject to subsection (3AC) below, where a person is entitled under subsection (3)[392] above to the destruction of any fingerprint[, impression of footwear][393] or sample taken from him (or would be but for subsection (3AA) above), neither the fingerprint[, nor the impression of footwear,][394] nor the sample, nor any information derived from the sample, shall be used—

(a) in evidence against the person who is or would be entitled to the destruction of that fingerprint[, impression of footwear][395] or sample; or

(b) for the purposes of the investigation of any offence;

and subsection (1B) above applies for the purposes of this subsection as it applies for the purposes of subsection (1A) above.

(3AC) Where a person from whom a fingerprint[, impression of footwear][396] or sample has been taken consents in writing to its retention—

(a) that[397] [, impression of footwear][398] sample need not be destroyed under subsection (3) above;

(b) subsection (3AB) above shall not restrict the use that may be made of the fingerprint[, impression of footwear][399] or sample or, in the case of a sample, of any information derived from it; and

(c) that consent shall be treated as comprising a consent for the purposes of section 63A(1C) above;

and a consent given for the purpose of this subsection shall not be capable of being withdrawn.[400]

(3AD) For the purposes of subsection (3AC) above it shall be immaterial whether the consent is given at, before or after the time when the entitlement to the destruction of the fingerprint[, impression of footwear][401] or sample arises.][402]

---

[388] Amended by the Criminal Justice and Police Act 2001, s 82(1), (3).
[389] Amended by the Criminal Justice and Public Order Act 1994, s 57(2).
[390] Amended by SOCAPA 2005, s 118(1), (4)(d)(i).
[391] Amended by SOCAPA 2005, s 118(1), (4)(d)(ii).
[392] Prospectively amended by SOCAPA 2005, s 117(1), (9).
[393] Amended by SOCAPA 2005, s 118(1), (4)(e)(i).
[394] Amended by SOCAPA 2005, s 118(1), (4)(e)(ii).
[395] Amended by SOCAPA 2005, s 118(1), (4)(e)(i).
[396] Amended by SOCAPA 2005, s 118(1), (4)(f).
[397] Prospectively amended by SOCAPA 2005, s 117(6), (10)(a).
[398] Amended by SOCAPA 2005, s 118(1), (4)(f).
[399] ibid.
[400] Prospectively amended by SOCAPA 2005, s 117(1), (10)(b).
[401] Amended by SOCAPA 2005, s 118(1), (4)(g).
[402] Amended by the Criminal Justice and Police Act 2001, s 82(1), (4), (6).

Act

(4) [...]⁴⁰³

[(5) If fingerprints [or impressions of footwear]⁴⁰⁴ are destroyed—
  (a) any copies of the fingerprints [or impressions of footwear]⁴⁰⁵ shall also be destroyed; and
  (b) any chief officer of police controlling access to computer data relating to the fingerprints [or impressions of footwear]⁴⁰⁶ shall make access to the data impossible, as soon as it is practicable to do so.]⁴⁰⁷

(6) A person who asks to be allowed to witness the destruction of his fingerprints [or impressions of footwear]⁴⁰⁸ or copies of them shall have a right to witness it.

[(6A) If—
  (a) subsection (5)(b) above falls to be complied with; and
  (b) the person to whose fingerprints [or impressions of footwear]⁴⁰⁹ the data relate asks for a certificate that it has been complied with,
  such a certificate shall be issued to him, not later than the end of the period of three months beginning with the day on which he asks for it, by the responsible chief officer of police or a person authorised by him or on his behalf for the purposes of this section.

(6B) In this section—
  [...]⁴¹⁰
  'the responsible chief officer of police' means the chief officer of police in whose [police]⁴¹¹ area the computer data were put on to the computer.]⁴¹²

(7) Nothing in this section—
  (a) affects any power conferred by paragraph 18(2) of Schedule 2 to the Immigration Act 1971 [or section 20 of the Immigration and Asylum Act 1999 (c 33) (disclosure of police information to the Secretary of State for use for immigration purposes)]⁴¹³; or
  (b) applies to a person arrested or detained under the terrorism provisions.

## [64A Photographing of suspects etc

(1) A person who is detained at a police station may be photographed—
  (a) with the appropriate consent; or
  (b) if the appropriate consent is withheld or it is not practicable to obtain it, without it.

[(1A) A person falling within subsection (1B) below may, on the occasion of the relevant event referred to in subsection (1B), be photographed elsewhere than at a police station—

---

⁴⁰³ Repealed by the Criminal Justice and Police Act 2001, s 137, Sch 7, Pt 2(1).
⁴⁰⁴ Amended by SOCAPA 2005, s 118(1), (4)(h).
⁴⁰⁵ ibid.
⁴⁰⁶ ibid.
⁴⁰⁷ Amended by the Criminal Justice Act 1988, s 148.
⁴⁰⁸ Amended by SOCAPA 2005, s 118(1), (4)(i).
⁴⁰⁹ Amended by SOCAPA 2005, s 118(1), (4)(j).
⁴¹⁰ Repealed by the Police Act 1996, s 103, Sch 7, Pt II, para 37, Sch 9, Pt I.
⁴¹¹ Amended by the Police Act 1996, s 103, Sch 7, Pt II, para 37.
⁴¹² Amended by the Criminal Justice Act 1988, s 148.
⁴¹³ Amended by the Criminal Justice and Police Act 2001, s 82(1), (5).

    (a) with the appropriate consent; or

    (b) if the appropriate consent is withheld or it is not practicable to obtain it, without it.

(1B) A person falls within this subsection if he has been—

    (a) arrested by a constable for an offence;

    (b) taken into custody by a constable after being arrested for an offence by a person other than a constable;

    (c) made subject to a requirement to wait with a community support officer under paragraph 2(3) or (3B) of Schedule 4 to the Police Reform Act 2002 ('the 2002 Act');

    [(ca) given a direction by a constable under section 27 of the Violent Crime Reduction Act 2006;][414]

    (d) given a penalty notice by a constable in uniform under Chapter 1 of Part 1 of the Criminal Justice and Police Act 2001, a penalty notice by a constable under section 444A of the Education Act 1996, or a fixed penalty notice by a constable in uniform under section 54 of the Road Traffic Offenders Act 1988;

    (e) given a notice in relation to a relevant fixed penalty offence (within the meaning of paragraph 1 of Schedule 4 to the 2002 Act) by a community support officer by virtue of a designation applying that paragraph to him; [...][415]

    (f) given a notice in relation to a relevant fixed penalty offence (within the meaning of paragraph 1 of Schedule 5 to the 2002 Act) by an accredited person by virtue of accreditation specifying that that paragraph applies to him.] or;[416]

    [(g) given a notice in relation to a relevant fixed penalty offence (within the meaning of Schedule 5A to the 2002 Act) by an accredited inspector by virtue of accreditation specifying that paragraph 1 of Schedule 5A to the 2002 Act applies to him. ][417]

(2) A person proposing to take a photograph of any person under this section—

    (a) may, for the purpose of doing so, require the removal of any item or substance worn on or over the whole or any part of the head or face of the person to be photographed; and

    (b) if the requirement is not complied with, may remove the item or substance himself.

(3) Where a photograph may be taken under this section, the only persons entitled to take the photograph are [constables][418].

(4) A photograph taken under this section—

    (a) may be used by, or disclosed to, any person for any purpose related to the prevention or detection of crime, the investigation of an offence or the conduct of a prosecution [or to the enforcement of a sentence][419]; and

---

[414] Added by Violent Crime Reduction Act 2006, s 27(7) (22 August 2007).

[415] Word repealed by Police and Justice Act 2006, Sch 15(2), para 1 (1 April 2007; SI 2007/709).

[416] Added by Police and Justice Act 2006, Sch 14, para 11 (1 April 2007).

[417] Amended by SOCAPA 2005, s 116(1), (2).

[418] Amended by the Police Reform Act 2002, s 107(1), Sch 7, para 9(5).

[419] Amended by SOCAPA 2005, s 116(1), (3).

(b) after being so used or disclosed, may be retained but may not be used or disclosed except for a purpose so related.

(5) In subsection (4)—

    (a) the reference to crime includes a reference to any conduct which—

        (i) constitutes one or more criminal offences (whether under the law of a part of the United Kingdom or of a country or territory outside the United Kingdom); or

        (ii) is, or corresponds to, any conduct which, if it all took place in any one part of the United Kingdom, would constitute one or more criminal offences; and

    (b) the references to an investigation and to a prosecution include references, respectively, to any investigation outside the United Kingdom of any crime or suspected crime and to a prosecution brought in respect of any crime in a country or territory outside the United Kingdom[; and

    (c) 'sentence' includes any order made by a court in England and Wales when dealing with an offender in respect of his offence][420].

(6) References in this section to taking a photograph include references to using any process by means of which a visual image may be produced; and references to photographing a person shall be construed accordingly.

(6A) In this section, a 'photograph' includes a moving image, and corresponding expressions shall be construed accordingly.[421]

[(7) Nothing in this section applies to a person arrested under an extradition arrest power.][422][423]

## 65 Part V—supplementary

[(1)][424] In this Part of this Act—

    ['analysis', in relation to a skin impression, includes comparison and matching;][425]

    'appropriate consent' means—

        (a) in relation to a person who has attained the age of 17 years, the consent of that person;

        (b) in relation to a person who has not attained that age but has attained the age of 14 years, the consent of that person and his parent or guardian; and

        (c) in relation to a person who has not attained the age of 14 years, the consent of his parent or guardian;

    [...][426]

    ['extradition arrest power' means any of the following—

        (a) a Part 1 warrant (within the meaning given by the Extradition Act 2003) in respect of which a certificate under section 2 of that Act has been issued;

---

[420] Amended by SOCAPA 2005, s 116(1), (4).

[421] Amended by SOCAPA 2005, s 116(1), (5).

[422] Amended by the Extradition Act 2003, s 169(1), (5); for savings see SI 2003/3103, arts 2–4.

[423] Inserted by the Anti-terrorism, Crime and Security Act 2001, s 92.

[424] Amended by the Criminal Justice and Police Act 2001, s 80(5).

[425] Amended by the Criminal Justice and Police Act 2001, s 80(5)(a).

[426] Repealed by the Proceeds of Crime Act 2002, s 457, Sch 12.

    (b)  section 5 of that Act;

    (c)  a warrant issued under section 71 of that Act;

    (d)  a provisional warrant (within the meaning given by that Act);][427]

['fingerprints', in relation to any person, means a record (in any form and produced by any method) of the skin pattern and other physical characteristics

or

features of—

    (a)  any of that person's fingers; or

    (b)  either of his palms;][428]

['intimate sample' means—

    (a)  a sample of blood, semen or any other tissue fluid, urine or pubic hair;

    (b)  a dental impression;

    [(c)  a swab taken from any part of a person's genitals (including pubic hair) or from a person's body orifice other than the mouth;][429][430]

['intimate search' means a search which consists of the physical examination of a person's body orifices other than the mouth;][431]

['non-intimate sample' means—

    (a)  a sample of hair other than pubic hair;

    (b)  a sample taken from a nail or from under a nail;

    [(c)  a swab taken from any part of a person's body other than a part from which a swab taken would be an intimate sample;][432]

    (d)  saliva;

    [(e)  a skin impression;][433][434]

['registered dentist' has the same meaning as in the Dentists Act 1984;][435]

['registered health care professional' means a person (other than a medical practitioner) who is—

    (a)  a registered nurse; or

    (b)  a registered member of a health care profession which is designated for the purposes of this paragraph by an order made by the Secretary of State;][436]

['skin impression', in relation to any person, means any record (other than a fingerprint) which is a record (in any form and produced by any method) of the skin pattern and other physical characteristics or features of the whole or any part of his foot or of any other part of his body;][437]

---

[427] Amended by the Extradition Act 2003, s 169(1), (6); for savings see SI 2003/3103, arts 2–4.

[428] Amended by the Criminal Justice and Police Act 2001, s 78(8).

[429] Amended by SOCAPA 2005, s 119(1), (2).

[430] Amended by the Criminal Justice and Public Order Act 1994, s 58(1), (2).

[431] Amended by the Criminal Justice and Public Order Act 1994, s 59(1).

[432] Amended by SOCAPA 2005, s 119(1), (3).

[433] Amended by the Criminal Justice and Police Act 2001, s 80(5)(b).

[434] Amended by the Criminal Justice and Public Order Act 1994, s 58(1), (3).

[435] Amended by the Criminal Justice and Public Order Act 1994, s 58(1), (4).

[436] Amended by the Police Reform Act 2002, s 54(2).

[437] Amended by the Criminal Justice and Police Act 2001, s 80(5)(c).

**Act**

['speculative search', in relation to a person's fingerprints or samples, means such a check against other fingerprints or samples or against information derived from other samples as is referred to in section 63A(1) above;][438]

['sufficient' and 'insufficient', in relation to a sample, means [(subject to sub-section (2) below)][439] sufficient or insufficient (in point of quantity or quality) for the purpose of enabling information to be produced by the means of analysis used or to be used in relation to the sample;][440]

['the terrorism provisions' means section 41 of the Terrorism Act 2000, and any provision of Schedule 7 to that Act conferring a power of detention; and 'terrorism' has the meaning given in section 1 of that Act;][441]

[ ... ][442].

[(1A) A health care profession is any profession mentioned in section 60(2) of the Health Act 1999 (c 8) other than the profession of practising medicine and the profession of nursing.

(1B) An order under subsection (1) shall be made by statutory instrument and shall be subject to annulment in pursuance of a resolution of either House of Parliament.][443]

[(2) References in this Part of this Act to a sample's proving insufficient include references to where, as a consequence of—

(a) the loss, destruction or contamination of the whole or any part of the sample,

(b) any damage to the whole or a part of the sample, or

(c) the use of the whole or a part of the sample for an analysis which produced no results or which produced results some or all of which must be regarded, in the circumstances, as unreliable,

the sample has become unavailable or insufficient for the purpose of enabling information, or information of a particular description, to be obtained by means of analysis of the sample.][444]

## PART VI
### CODES OF PRACTICE—GENERAL

### 66 Codes of practice

[(1)][445] The Secretary of State shall issue codes of practice in connection with—

(a) the exercise by police officers of statutory powers—

(i) to search a person without first arresting him; [...][446]

(ii) to search a vehicle without making an arrest; [or

(iii) to arrest a person;][447]

---

[438] Amended by the Criminal Justice and Public Order Act 1994, s 58(1), (4).

[439] Amended by the Criminal Justice and Police Act 2001, s 80(5)(d).

[440] Amended by the Criminal Justice and Public Order Act 1994, s 58(1), (4).

[441] Amended by the Terrorism Act 2000, s 125(1), Sch 15, para 5(1), (10); for savings see the Terrorism Act 2000, s 129(1)(b) and SI 2001/421, art 2.

[442] Repealed by the Criminal Justice Act 1988, s 170(2), Sch 16 and the Proceeds of Crime Act 2002, s 457, Sch 12.

[443] Amended by the Police Reform Act 2002, s 54(3).

[444] Amended by the Criminal Justice and Police Act 2001, s 80(6).

[445] Amended by the Criminal Justice and Court Services Act 2000, s 57(1), (4).

[446] Repealed by SOCAPA 2005, ss 110(3)(a), 174(2), Sch 17, Pt 2.

[447] Amended by SOCAPA 2005, s 110(3)(b).

(b) the detention, treatment, questioning and identification of persons by police officers;

(c) searches of premises by police officers; and

(d) the seizure of property found by police officers on persons or premises.

[(2) Codes shall (in particular) include provision in connection with the exercise by police officers of powers under section 63B above.][448]

## 67 Codes of practice—supplementary

[(1) In this section, 'code' means a code of practice under section 60, 60A or 66.

(2) The Secretary of State may at any time revise the whole or any part of a code.

(3) A code may be made, or revised, so as to—

(a) apply only in relation to one or more specified areas,

(b) have effect only for a specified period,

(c) apply only in relation to specified offences or descriptions of offender.

(4) Before issuing a code, or any revision of a code, the Secretary of State must consult—

[(a) the Association of Police Authorities,

(b) the Association of Chief Police Officers of England, Wales and Northern Ireland,][449]

(c) the General Council of the Bar,

(d) the Law Society of England and Wales,

(e) the Institute of Legal Executives, and

(f) such other persons as he thinks fit.

(5) A code, or a revision of a code, does not come into operation until the Secretary of State by order so provides.

(6) The power conferred by subsection (5) is exercisable by statutory instrument.

(7) An order bringing a code into operation may not be made unless a draft of the order has been laid before Parliament and approved by a resolution of each House.

(7A) An order bringing a revision of a code into operation must be laid before Parliament if the order has been made without a draft having been so laid and approved by a resolution of each House.

(7B) When an order or draft of an order is laid, the code or revision of a code to which it relates must also be laid.

(7C) No order or draft of an order may be laid until the consultation required by subsection (4) has taken place.

(7D) An order bringing a code, or a revision of a code, into operation may include transitional or saving provisions.][450]

(8) [...][451]

(9) Persons other than police officers who are charged with the duty of investigating offences or charging offenders shall in the discharge of that duty have regard to any relevant provision of [...][452] a code.

---

[448] Amended by the Criminal Justice and Court Services Act 2000, s 57(1), (4).

[449] Substituted by Police and Justice Act 2006, Sch 4, para 1 (1 April 2007).

[450] Amended by the Criminal Justice Act 2003, s 11(1).

[451] Repealed by the Police Act 1996, s 103, Sch 9, Pt II.

[452] Repealed by the Criminal Justice Act 2003, s 332, Sch 37, Pt 1.

Act

[(9A) Persons on whom powers are conferred by—

    (a) any designation under section 38 or 39 of the Police Reform Act 2002 (c 30) (police powers for police authority employees), or

    (b) any accreditation under section 41 of that Act (accreditation under community safety accreditation schemes),

shall have regard to any relevant provision of a code [...][453] in the exercise or performance of the powers and duties conferred or imposed on them by that designation or accreditation.][454]

(10) A failure on the part—

    (a) of a police office to comply with any provision of [...][455] a code; [...][456]

    (b) of any person other than a police officer who is charged with the duty of investigating offences or charging offenders to have regard to any relevant provision of [...][457] a code in the discharge of that duty, [or

    (c) of a person designated under section 38 or 39 or accredited under section 41 of the Police Reform Act 2002 (c 30) to have regard to any relevant provision of [...][458] a code in the exercise or performance of the powers and duties conferred or imposed on him by that designation or accreditation,][459]

shall not of itself render him liable to any criminal or civil proceedings.

(11) In all criminal and civil proceedings any [...][460] code shall be admissible in evidence; and if any provision of [...][461] a code appears to the court or tribunal conducting the proceedings to be relevant to any question arising in the proceedings it shall be taken into account in determining that question.

[(12) In subsection (11) 'criminal proceedings' includes service proceedings.

(13) In this section 'service proceedings' means proceedings before a court (other than a civilian court) in respect of a service offence; and 'service offence' and 'civilian court' here have the same meanings as in the Armed Forces Act 2006.][462]

## Part VII

### Documentary Evidence in Criminal Proceedings

## 68 Evidence from documentary records

    [...][463]

## 69 Evidence from computer records

    [...][464]

---

[453] Repealed by the Criminal Justice Act 2003, s 332, Sch 37, Pt 1.

[454] Amended by the Police Reform Act 2002, s 107(1), Sch 7, para 9(7).

[455] Repealed by the Criminal Justice Act 2003, s 332, Sch 37, Pt 1.

[456] Repealed by the Police Reform Act 2002, s 107(2), Sch 8.

[457] Repealed by the Criminal Justice Act 2003, s 332, Sch 37, Pt 1.

[458] ibid.

[459] Amended by the Police Reform Act 2002, s 107(1), Sch 7, para 9(8).

[460] Repealed by the Criminal Justice Act 2003, s 332, Sch 37, Pt 1.

[461] ibid.

[462] Section 67(12)–(13) substituted for s 67(12) by Armed Forces Act 2006, Sch 16, para 101 (31 October 2009).

[463] Repealed by the Criminal Justice Act 1988, s 170(2), Sch 16.

[464] Repealed by the Youth Justice and Criminal Evidence Act 1999, ss 60, 67(3), Sch 6.

## 70  Provisions supplementary to sections 68 and 69

[...][465]

## 71  Microfilm copies

In any proceedings the contents of a document may (whether or not the document is still in existence) be proved by the production of an enlargement of a microfilm copy of that document or of the material part of it, authenticated in such manner as the court may approve.

[Where the proceedings concerned are proceedings before a magistrates 'court inquiring into an offence as examining justices this section shall have effect with the omission of the words 'authenticated in such manner as the court may approve.][466]

## 72  Part VII—supplementary

(1)  In this Part of this Act—

['copy', in relation to a document, means anything onto which information recorded in the document has been copied, by whatever means and whether directly or indirectly, and 'statement' means any representation of fact, however made; and][467]

'proceedings' means criminal proceedings, including [service proceedings].[468]

[(1A)  In subsection (1) 'service proceedings' means proceedings before a court (other than a civilian court) in respect of a service offence; and 'service offence' and 'civilian court' here have the same meanings as in the Armed Forces Act 2006.][469]

(2)  Nothing in this Part of this Act shall prejudice any power of a court to exclude evidence (whether by preventing questions from being put or otherwise) at its discretion.

## PART VIII
### EVIDENCE IN CRIMINAL PROCEEDINGS—GENERAL

*Convictions and acquittals*

## 73  Proof of convictions and acquittals

(1)  Where in any proceedings the fact that a person has in the United Kingdom been convicted or acquitted of an offence otherwise than by a Service court is admissible in evidence, it may be proved by producing a certificate of conviction or, as the case may be, of acquittal relating to that offence, and proving that the person named in the certificate as having been convicted or acquitted of the offence is the person whose conviction or acquittal of the offence is to be proved.

---

[465] Repealed by the Youth Justice and Criminal Evidence Act 1999, s 67(3), Sch 6.

[466] Amended by the Criminal Procedure and Investigations Act 1996, s 47, Sch 1, para 24 and prospectively repealed by the Criminal Justice Act 2003, ss 41, 332, Sch 3, Pt 2, para 56(1), (3), Sch 37, Pt 4.

[467] Amended by the Civil Evidence Act 1995, s 15(1), Sch 1, para 9(2).

[468] Words substituted for paras (a)–(c) in the definition of proceedings by Armed Forces Act 2006, Sch 16, para 102(2) (31 October 2009).

[469] Added by Armed Forces Act 2006, Sch.16, para 102(3) (31 October 2009).

(2) For the purposes of this section a certificate of conviction or of acquittal—

    (a) shall, as regards a conviction or acquittal on indictment, consist of a certificate, signed by the [proper officer][470] of the court where the conviction or acquittal took place, giving the substance and effect (omitting the formal parts) of the indictment and of the conviction or acquittal; and

    (b) shall, as regards a conviction or acquittal on a summary trial, consist of a copy of the conviction or of the dismissal of the information, signed by the [proper officer][471] of the court where the conviction or acquittal took place or by the [proper officer][472] of the court, if any, to which a memorandum of the conviction or acquittal was sent;

and a document purporting to be a duly signed certificate of conviction or acquittal under this section shall be taken to be such a certificate unless the contrary is proved.

[(3) In subsection (2) above 'proper officer' means—

    (a) in relation to a magistrates' court in England and Wales, the [designated officer][473] for the court; and

    (b) in relation to any other court, the clerk of the court, his deputy or any other person having custody of the court record.][474]

(4) The method of proving a conviction or acquittal authorised by this section shall be in addition to and not to the exclusion of any other authorised manner of proving a conviction or acquittal.

## 74 Conviction as evidence of commission of offence

(1) In any proceedings the fact that a person other than the accused has been convicted of an offence by or before any court in the United Kingdom or by a Service court outside the United Kingdom shall be admissible in evidence for the purpose of proving [that that person committed that offence, where evidence of his having done so is admissible][475] is given.

(2) In any proceedings in which by virtue of this section a person other than the accused is proved to have been convicted of an offence by or before any court in the United Kingdom or by a Service court outside the United Kingdom, he shall be taken to have committed that offence unless the contrary is proved.

(3) In any proceedings where evidence is admissible of the fact that the accused has committed an offence, [...][476] if the accused is proved to have been convicted of the offence—

    (a) by or before any court in the United Kingdom; or

    (b) by a Service court outside the United Kingdom,

he shall be taken to have committed that offence unless the contrary is proved.

---

[470] Amended by the Access to Justice Act 1999, s 90(1), Sch 13, paras 125, 128(1), (2).

[471] ibid.

[472] ibid.

[473] Amended by the Courts Act 2003, s 109(1), Sch 8, para 285; for transitional provisions see SI 2005/911, arts 2–5.

[474] Amended by the Access to Justice Act 1999, s 90(1), Sch 13, paras 125, 128(1), (3).

[475] Amended by the Criminal Justice Act 2003, s 331, Sch 36, Pt 5, para 85(1), (2).

[476] Repealed by the Criminal Justice Act 2003, ss 331, 332, Sch 36, Pt 5, para 85(1), (3), Sch 37, Pt 5.

(4) Nothing in this section shall prejudice—
  (a) the admissibility in evidence of any conviction which would be admissible apart from this section; or
  (b) the operation of any enactment whereby a conviction or a finding of fact in any proceedings is for the purposes of any other proceedings made conclusive evidence of any fact.

### 75 Provisions supplementary to section 74

(1) Where evidence that a person has been convicted of an offence is admissible by virtue of section 74 above, then without prejudice to the reception of any other admissible evidence for the purpose of identifying the facts on which the conviction was based—
  (a) the contents of any document which is admissible as evidence of the conviction; and
  (b) the contents of the information, complaint, indictment or charge-sheet on which the person in question was convicted,
  shall be admissible in evidence for that purpose.

(2) Where in any proceedings the contents of any document are admissible in evidence by virtue of subsection (1) above, a copy of that document, or of the material part of it, purporting to be certified or otherwise authenticated by or on behalf of the court or authority having custody of that document shall be admissible in evidence and shall be taken to be a true copy of that document or part unless the contrary is shown.

(3) Nothing in any of the following—
  (a) [section 14 of the Powers of Criminal Courts (Sentencing) Act 2000][477] (under which a conviction leading to probation or discharge is to be disregarded except as mentioned in that section);
  [(aa)  section 187 of the Armed Forces Act 2006 (which makes similar provision in respect of service convictions);][478]
  (b) [section 247 of the Criminal Procedure (Scotland) Act 1995][479] (which makes similar provision in respect of convictions on indictment in Scotland); and
  (c) section 8 of the Probation Act (Northern Ireland) 1950 (which corresponds to section 13 of the Powers of Criminal Courts Act 1973) or any legislation which is in force in Northern Ireland for the time being and corresponds to that section,
  shall affect the operation of section 74 above; and for the purposes of that section any order made by a court of summary jurisdiction in Scotland under [section 228 or section 246(3) of the said Act of 1995][480] shall be treated as a conviction.

(4) Nothing in section 74 above shall be construed as rendering admissible in any proceedings evidence of any conviction other than a subsisting one.

---

[477] Amended by the Powers of Criminal Courts (Sentencing) Act 2000, s 165(1), Sch 9, para 98.

[478] Added by Armed Forces Act 2006, Sch 16, para 103 (31 October 2009).

[479] Amended by the Criminal Procedure (Consequential Provisions) (Scotland) Act 1995, s 5, Sch 4, para 55(a).

[480] Amended by the Criminal Procedure (Consequential Provisions) (Scotland) Act 1995, s 5, Sch 4, para 55(b).

*Confessions*

## 76 Confessions

Ac⸍

(1) In any proceedings a confession made by an accused person may be given in evidence against him in so far as it is relevant to any matter in issue in the proceedings and is not excluded by the court in pursuance of this section.

(2) If, in any proceedings where the prosecution proposes to give in evidence a confession made by an accused person, it is represented to the court that the confession was or may have been obtained—

(a) by oppression of the person who made it; or

(b) in consequence of anything said or done which was likely, in the circumstances existing at the time, to render unreliable any confession which might be made by him in consequence thereof,

the court shall not allow the confession to be given in evidence against him except in so far as the prosecution proves to the court beyond reasonable doubt that the confession (notwithstanding that it may be true) was not obtained as aforesaid.

(3) In any proceedings where the prosecution proposes to give in evidence a confession made by an accused person, the court may of its own motion require the prosecution, as a condition of allowing it to do so, to prove that the confession was not obtained as mentioned in subsection (2) above.

(4) The fact that a confession is wholly or partly excluded in pursuance of this section shall not affect the admissibility in evidence—

(a) of any facts discovered as a result of the confession; or

(b) where the confession is relevant as showing that the accused speaks, writes or expresses himself in a particular way, of so much of the confession as is necessary to show that he does so.

(5) Evidence that a fact to which this subsection applies was discovered as a result of a statement made by an accused person shall not be admissible unless evidence of how it was discovered is given by him or on his behalf.

(6) Subsection (5) above applies—

(a) to any fact discovered as a result of a confession which is wholly excluded in pursuance of this section; and

(b) to any fact discovered as a result of a confession which is partly so excluded, if the fact is discovered as a result of the excluded part of the confession.

(7) Nothing in Part VII of this Act shall prejudice the admissibility of a confession made by an accused person.

(8) In this section 'oppression' includes torture, inhuman or degrading treatment, and the use or threat of violence (whether or not amounting to torture).

[(9) Where the proceedings mentioned in subsection (1) above are proceedings before a magistrates' court inquiring into an offence as examining justices this section shall have effect with the omission of

(a) in subsection (1) the words 'and is not excluded by the court in pursuance of this section', and

(b) subsections (2) to (6) and (8).][481]

---

[481] Amended by the Criminal Procedure and Investigations Act 1996, s 47, Sch 1, para 25 and prospectively repealed by the Criminal Justice Act 2003, ss 41, 332, Sch 3, Pt 2, para 56(1), (4), Sch 37, Pt 4.

### 76A Confessions may be given in evidence for co-accused

(1) In any proceedings a confession made by an accused person may be given in evidence for another person charged in the same proceedings (a co-accused) in so far as it is relevant to any matter in issue in the proceedings and is not excluded by the court in pursuance of this section.

(2) If, in any proceedings where a co-accused proposes to give in evidence a confession made by an accused person, it is represented to the court that the confession was or may have been obtained—

    (a) by oppression of the person who made it; or

    (b) in consequence of anything said or done which was likely, in the circumstances existing at the time, to render unreliable any confession which might be made by him in consequence thereof,

the court shall not allow the confession to be given in evidence for the co-accused except in so far as it is proved to the court on the balance of probabilities that the confession (notwithstanding that it may be true) was not so obtained.

(3) Before allowing a confession made by an accused person to be given in evidence for a co-accused in any proceedings, the court may of its own motion require the fact that the confession was not obtained as mentioned in subsection (2) above to be proved in the proceedings on the balance of probabilities.

(4) The fact that a confession is wholly or partly excluded in pursuance of this section shall not affect the admissibility in evidence—

    (a) of any facts discovered as a result of the confession; or

    (b) where the confession is relevant as showing that the accused speaks, writes or expresses himself in a particular way, of so much of the confession as is necessary to show that he does so.

(5) Evidence that a fact to which this subsection applies was discovered as a result of a statement made by an accused person shall not be admissible unless evidence of how it was discovered is given by him or on his behalf.

(6) Subsection (5) above applies—

    (a) to any fact discovered as a result of a confession which is wholly excluded in pursuance of this section; and

    (b) to any fact discovered as a result of a confession which is partly so excluded, if the fact is discovered as a result of the excluded part of the confession.

(7) In this section 'oppression' includes torture, inhuman or degrading treatment, and the use or threat of violence (whether or not amounting to torture).[482]

### 77 Confessions by mentally handicapped persons

(1) Without prejudice to the general duty of the court at a trial on indictment[483] [with a jury][484] to direct the jury on any matter on which it appears to the court appropriate to do so, where at such a trial—

    (a) the case against the accused depends wholly or substantially on a confession by him; and

---

[482] Inserted by the Criminal Justice Act 2003, s 128; for savings see the Criminal Justice Act 2004, s 141 and SI 2005/950, art 2(1), Sch 1, para 6.

[483] Prospectively amended by the Criminal Justice Act 2003, s 331, Sch 36, Pt 4, para 48(1), (2): see below.

[484] The words 'with a jury' in square brackets inserted by the Criminal Justice Act 2003, s 331, Sch 36, Pt 4, para 48(1), (2) (24 July 2006 in relation to England and Wales; 8 January 2007 otherwise).

(b)  the court is satisfied—

    (i)   that he is mentally handicapped; and

    (ii)  that the confession was not made in the presence of an independent person,

the court shall warn the jury that there is special need for caution before convicting the accused in reliance on the confession, and shall explain that the need arises because of the circumstances mentioned in paragraphs (a) and (b) above.

(2)  In any case where at the summary trial of a person for an offence it appears to the court that a warning under subsection (1) above would be required if the trial were on indictment[485] [with a jury][486], the court shall treat the case as one in which there is a special need for caution before convicting the accused on his confession.

[(2A)  In any case where at the trial on indictment without a jury of a person for an offence it appears to the court that a warning under subsection (1) above would be required if the trial were with a jury, the court shall treat the case as one in which there is a special need for caution before convicting the accused on his confession.][487]

(3)  In this section—

'independent person' does not include a police officer or a person employed for, or engaged on, police purposes;

'mentally handicapped', in relation to a person, means that he is in a state of arrested or incomplete development of mind which includes significant impairment of intelligence and social functioning; and

'police purposes' has the meaning assigned to it by [section 101(2) of the Police Act 1996][488].

*Miscellaneous*

## 78  Exclusion of unfair evidence

(1)  In any proceedings the court may refuse to allow evidence on which the prosecution proposes to rely to be given if it appears to the court that, having regard to all the circumstances, including the circumstances in which the evidence was obtained, the admission of the evidence would have such an adverse effect on the fairness of the proceedings that the court ought not to admit it.

(2)  Nothing in this section shall prejudice any rule of law requiring a court to exclude evidence.

[(3)  This section shall not apply in the case of proceedings before a magistrates' court inquiring into an offence as examining justices.][489]

---

[485] Prospectively amended by the Criminal Justice Act 2003, s 331, Sch 36, Pt 4, para 48(1), (3): see below.

[486] The words 'with a jury' in square brackets inserted by the Criminal Justice Act 2003, s 331, Sch 36, Pt 4, para 48(1), (3) (24 July 2006 in relation to England and Wales; 8 January 2007 otherwise).

[487] New subsection (2A) prospectively inserted by the Criminal Justice Act 2003, s 331, Sch 36, Pt 4, para 48(1), (4) (24 July 2006 in relation to England and Wales; 8 January 2007 otherwise).

[488] Amended by the Police Act 1996, s 103, Sch 7, para 38.

[489] Amended by the Criminal Procedure and Investigations Act 1996, s 47, Sch 1, para 26 and prospectively repealed by the Criminal Justice Act 2003, ss 41, 332, Sch 3, Pt 2, para 56(1), (5), Sch 37, Pt 4.

### 79 Time for taking accused's evidence

If at the trial of any person for an offence—

(a) the defence intends to call two or more witnesses to the facts of the case; and

(b) those witnesses include the accused,

the accused shall be called before the other witness or witnesses unless the court in its discretion otherwise directs.

### 80 [...][490] Compellability of accused's spouse [or civil partner][491]

(1)      [...][492]

[(2)    In any proceedings the [spouse or civil partner][493] of a person charged in the proceedings shall, subject to subsection (4) below, be compellable to give evidence on behalf of that person.

(2A)    In any proceedings the [spouse or civil partner][494] of a person charged in the proceedings shall, subject to subsection (4) below, be compellable—

(a) to give evidence on behalf of any other person charged in the proceedings but only in respect of any specified offence with which that other person is charged; or

(b) to give evidence for the prosecution but only in respect of any specified offence with which any person is charged in the proceedings.

(3)      In relation to the [spouse or civil partner][495] of a person charged in any proceedings, an offence is a specified offence for the purposes of subsection (2A) above if—

(a) it involves an assault on, or injury or a threat of injury to, the [spouse or civil partner][496] or a person who was at the material time under the age of 16;

(b) it is a sexual offence alleged to have been committed in respect of a person who was at the material time under that age; or

(c) it consists of attempting or conspiring to commit, or of aiding, abetting, counselling, procuring or inciting the commission of, an offence falling within paragraph (a) or (b) above.

(4)      No person who is charged in any proceedings shall be compellable by virtue of subsection (2) or (2A) above to give evidence in the proceedings.

(4A)    References in this section to a person charged in any proceedings do not include a person who is not, or is no longer, liable to be convicted of any offence in the proceedings (whether as a result of pleading guilty or for any other reason).][497]

(5)      In any proceedings a person who has been but is no longer married to the accused shall be [...][498] compellable to give evidence as if that person and the accused had never been married.

---

[490] Repealed by the Youth Justice and Criminal Evidence Act 1999, s 67(1), Sch 4, paras 12, 13(1), (4).

[491] Amended by the Civil Partnership Act 2004, s 261(1), Sch 27, para 97(1), (4).

[492] Repealed by the Youth Justice and Criminal Evidence Act 1999, s 67(1), (3), Sch 4, paras 12, 13(1), (2), Sch 6.

[493] Amended by the Civil Partnership Act 2004, s 261(1), Sch 27, para 97(1), (2).

[494] ibid.

[495] ibid.

[496] ibid.

[497] Amended by the Youth Justice and Criminal Evidence Act 1999, s 67(1), Sch 4, paras 12, 13(1), (3).

[498] Repealed by the Youth Justice and Criminal Evidence Act 1999, s 67(1), (3), Sch 4, paras 12, 13(1), (4), Sch 6.

Act

[(5A)  In any proceedings a person who has been but is no longer the civil partner of the accused shall be compellable to give evidence as if that person and the accused had never been civil partners.][499]

(6)     Where in any proceedings the age of any person at any time is material for the purposes of subsection (3) above, his age at the material time shall for the purposes of that provision be deemed to be or to have been that which appears to the court to be or to have been his age at that time.

(7)     In subsection (3)(b) above 'sexual offence' means an offence under the Sexual Offences Act 1956, the Indecency with Children Act 1960, [...][500] the Protection of Children Act 1978 [or Part 1 of the Sexual Offences Act 2003][501].

(8)     [...][502]

(9)     Section 1(d) of the Criminal Evidence Act 1898 (communications between husband and wife) and section 43(1) of the Matrimonial Causes Act 1965 (evidence as to marital intercourse) shall cease to have effect.

## 80A [Rule where accused's spouse [or civil partner][503] not compellable

The failure of the [spouse or civil partner][504] of a person charged in any proceedings to give evidence in the proceedings shall not be made the subject of any comment by the prosecution.][505]

## 81 Advance notice of expert evidence in crown court

(1)     [Criminal Procedure Rules][506] may make provision for—

(a)     requiring any party to proceedings before the court to disclose to the other party or parties any expert evidence which he proposes to adduce in the proceedings; and

(b)     prohibiting a party who fails to comply in respect of any evidence with any requirement imposed by virtue of paragraph (a) above from adducing that evidence without the leave of the court.

(2)     [Criminal Procedure Rules][507] made by virtue of this section may specify the kinds of expert evidence to which they apply and may exempt facts or matters of any description specified in the rules.

## PART VIII—SUPPLEMENTARY

## 82 Part VIII—Interpretation

(1)     In this Part of this Act—

'confession' includes any statement wholly or partly adverse to the person who made it, whether made to a person in authority or not and whether made in words or otherwise;

---

[499] Amended by the Civil Partnership Act 2004, s 261(1), Sch 27, para 97(1), (3).

[500] Repealed by the Sexual Offences Act 2003, s 140, Sch 7.

[501] Amended by the Sexual Offences Act 2003, s 139, Sch 6, para 28(1), (2).

[502] Repealed by the Youth Justice and Criminal Evidence Act 1999, s 67(1), (3), Sch 4, paras 12, 13(1), (2), Sch 6.

[503] Amended by the Civil Partnership Act 2004, s 261(1), Sch 27, para 98(b).

[504] Amended by the Civil Partnership Act 2004, s 261(1), Sch 27, para 98(a).

[505] Inserted by the Youth Justice and Criminal Evidence Act 1999, s 67(1), Sch 4, paras 12, 14.

[506] Amended by the Courts Act 2003, s 109(1), Sch 8, para 286; for savings see SI 2004/2066, art 3.

[507] ibid.

[...][508];

'proceedings' means criminal proceedings, including [service proceedings;][509]
'Service court' means a court-martial or [the Court Martial or the Service Civilian Court].[510]

[(1A) In subsection (1) 'service proceedings' means proceedings before a court (other than a civilian court) in respect of a service offence; and 'service offence' and 'civilian court' here have the same meanings as in the Armed Forces Act 2006.][511]

(2)    [...][512]

(3)    Nothing in this Part of this Act shall prejudice any power of a court to exclude evidence (whether by preventing questions from being put or otherwise) at its discretion.

## PART IX
### POLICE COMPLAINTS AND DISCIPLINE

*The Police Complaints Authority*

## 83 Establishment of the police complaints authority

[...][513]

*Handling of complaints etc.*

## 84 Preliminary

[...][514]

## 85 Investigation of complaints: standard procedure

[...][515]

## 86 Investigation of complaints against senior officers

[...][516]

## 87 References of complaints to authority

[...][517]

## 88 References of other matters to authority

[...][518]

---

[508] Definition repealed by Armed Forces Act 2006, Sch 17, para 1 (31 October 2009; SI 2009/1167).

[509] Words substituted for paras (a)–(c) in the definition of proceedings by Armed Forces Act 2006, Sch 16, para 104(2)(b) (31 October, 2009).

[510] Words substituted by Armed Forces Act 2006, Sch 16, para 104(2)(c) (31 October 2009).

[511] Added by Armed Forces Act 2006, Sch 16, para 104(3) (31 October 2009).

[512] Repealed by Armed Forces Act 2006, Sch 17, para 1 (31 October 2009; SI 2009/1167).

[513] Repealed by the Police Act 1996, s 103, Sch 9, Pt II.

[514] ibid.

[515] ibid.

[516] ibid.

[517] ibid.

[518] ibid.

Act

**89 Supervision of investigations by authority**

[…]519

**90 Steps to be taken after investigation—general**

[…]520

**91 Steps to be taken where accused has admitted charges**

[…]521

**92 Powers of Authority to direct reference of reports etc. to Director of Public Prosecutions**

[…]522

**93 Powers of Authority as to disciplinary charges**

[…]523

**94 Disciplinary tribunals**

[…]524

**95 Information as to the manner of dealing with complaints etc.**

[…]525

**96 Constabularies maintained by authorities other than police authorities**

[…]526

**97 Reports**

[…]527

**98 Restriction on disclosure of information**

[…]528

**99 Regulations**

[…]529

**100 Regulations—supplementary**

[…]530

---

519 ibid.
520 ibid.
521 ibid.
522 ibid.
523 ibid.
524 ibid.
525 ibid.
526 ibid.
527 ibid.
528 ibid.
529 ibid.
530 ibid.

### 101 Discipline regulations

[...][531]

### 102 Representation at disciplinary proceedings

[...][532]

### 103 Disciplinary appeals

[...][533]

### 104 Restrictions on subsequent proceedings

[...][534]

### 105 Guidelines concerning discipline, complaints etc.

[...][535]

PART X

POLICE—GENERAL

### 106 Arrangements for obtaining the views of the community on policing

[...][536]

### 107 Police officers performing duties of higher rank

(1) For the purpose of any provision of this Act or any other Act under which a power in respect of the investigation of offences or the treatment of persons in police custody is exercisable only by or with the authority of a police officer of at least the rank of superintendent, an officer of the rank of chief inspector shall be treated as holding the rank of superintendent if

[(a) he has been authorised by an officer holding a rank above the rank of superintendent to exercise the power or, as the case may be, to give his authority for its exercise, or

(b) he is acting during the absence of an officer holding the rank of superintendent who has authorised him, for the duration of that absence, to exercise the power or, as the case may be, to give his authority for its exercise.][537]

(2) For the purpose of any provision of this Act or any other Act under which such a power is exercisable only by or with the authority of an officer of at least the rank of inspector, an officer of the rank of sergeant shall be treated as holding the rank of inspector if he has been authorised by an officer of at least the rank of [superintendent][538] to exercise the power or, as the case may be, to give his authority for its exercise.

---

[531] ibid.
[532] ibid.
[533] ibid.
[534] ibid.
[535] ibid.
[536] Repealed by the Police Act 1996, s 103(3), Sch 9, Pt I.
[537] Amended by the Police and Magistrates' Courts Act 1994, s 44, Sch 5, Pt II, para 35.
[538] ibid.

**108** [...][539]

**109 Amendments relating to police federations**

[...][540]

**110** [...][541]

**111 Regulations for Police Forces and Police Cadets—Scotland**

(1) In section 26 to the Police (Scotland) Act 1967 (regulations as to government and administration of police forces)—

   (a) after subsection (1) there shall be inserted the following subsection—

      '(1A) Regulations under this section may authorise the Secretary of State, the police authority or the chief constable to make provision for any purpose specified in the regulations.'; and

   (b) at the end there shall be inserted the following subsection—

      '(10) Any statutory instrument made under this section shall be subject to annulment in pursuance of a resolution of either House of Parliament.'.

(2) In section 27 of the said Act of 1967 (regulations for police cadets) in subsection (3) for the word '(9)' there shall be substituted the words '(1A), (9) and (10)'.

**112 Metropolitan police officers**

[...][542]

PART XI

MISCELLANEOUS AND SUPPLEMENTARY

**113 Application of Act to Armed Forces**

[(1) The Secretary of State may by order make provision in relation to—

   (a) investigations of service offences,

   (b) persons arrested under a power conferred by or under the Armed Forces Act 2006,

   (c) persons charged under that Act with service offences,

   (d) persons in service custody, or

   (e) persons convicted of service offences, which is equivalent to that made by any provision of Part 5 of this Act (or this Part of this Act so far as relating to that Part), subject to such modifications as the Secretary of State considers appropriate.][543]

(2) Section 67(9) above shall not have effect in relation to investigations of [service offences][544].

---

[539] Repealed by Statute Law (Repeals) Act 2008, Sch 1, para 1 (21 July 2008).

[540] Repealed by the Police Act 1996, s 103(3), Sch 9, Pt I.

[541] Repealed by Statute Law (Repeals) Act 2008, Sch 1, para 1 (21 July 2008).

[542] Repealed by Police Act 1996 c. 16 Sch 9(I) para 1 (August 22, 1996).

[543] Substituted by Armed Forces Act 2006, Sch 16, para 105(2) (28 March 2009 for the purpose of enabling the Secretary of State to make orders, regulations and rules; 31 October 2009 otherwise).

[544] Words substituted by Armed Forces Act 2006, Sch.16, para 105(3) (31 October 2009).

(3)     The Secretary of State shall issue a code of practice, or a number of such codes, for persons other than police officers who are [concerned with–][545]

        [(a) the exercise of powers conferred by or under Part 3 of the Armed Forces Act 2006; or

        (b) investigations of service offences.][546]

[(3A)   In subsections (4) to (10), 'code' means a code of practice under subsection (3).][547]

(4)     Without prejudice to the generality of subsection (3) above, a code [...][548] may contain provisions, in connection with [the powers mentioned in subsection (3)(a) above or the [investigations][549] mentioned in subsection (3)(b) above][550], as to the following matters—

        (a)  the tape-recording of interviews;

        (b)  searches of persons and premises; and

        (c)  the seizure of things found on searches.

[(5)    The Secretary of State may at any time revise the whole or any part of a code.

(6)     A code may be made, or revised, so as to—

        (a)  apply only in relation to one or more specified areas,

        (b)  have effect only for a specified period,

        (c)  apply only in relation to specified offences or descriptions of offender.

(7)     The Secretary of State must lay a code, or any revision of a code, before Parliament.][551]

(8)     A failure on the part of any person to comply with any provision of a code [...][552] shall not of itself render him liable to any criminal or civil proceedings except those to which this subsection applies.

[(9)    Subsection (8) above applies to proceedings in respect of an offence under a provision of Part 1 of the Armed Forces Act 2006 other than section 42 (criminal conduct).][553]

(10)    In all criminal and civil proceedings any [...][554] code shall be admissible in evidence and if any provision of [...][555] a code appears to the court or tribunal conducting the proceedings to be relevant to any question arising in the proceedings it shall be taken into account in determining that question.

(11)    [...][556]

(12)    Parts VII and VIII of this Act have effect for the purposes of [service proceedings (a)-(c)][557]—

---

[545] Words substituted by Armed Forces Act 2006, Sch 16, para 105(4) (31 October 2009).

[546] Words substituted by Armed Forces Act 2006, Sch 16, para 105(4) (31 October 2009).

[547] Amended by the Criminal Justice Act 2003, s 11(2), (3).

[548] Repealed by the Criminal Justice Act 2003, s 332, Sch 37, Pt 1.

[549] Word substituted by Armed Forces Act 2006, Sch 16, para 105(5) (31 October 2009).

[550] Amended by the Armed Forces Act 2001, s 13(1), (4); for transitional provisions see SI 2003/2268, arts 3, 4.

[551] Amended by the Criminal Justice Act 2003, s 11(2), (4).

[552] Repealed by the Criminal Justice Act 2003, s 332, Sch 37, Pt 1.

[553] Substituted by Armed Forces Act 2006, Sch 16, para 105(6) (31 October 2009).

[554] Words repealed by Criminal Justice Act 2003 c. 44 Sch 37(1) para 1 (January 20, 2004; SI 2004/81).

[555] ibid.

[556] Repealed by Armed Forces Act 2006, Sch 17, para 1 (31 October 2009; SI 2009/1167).

[557] Words substituted for s 113(12)(a)–(c) by Armed Forces Act 2006, Sch 16, para 105(8) (31 October 2009).

subject to any modifications which the Secretary of State may by order specify.

[(12A) In this section–

> 'service offence' has the meaning given by section 50 of the Armed Forces Act 2006;
>
> 'criminal proceedings' includes service proceedings;
>
> 'service proceedings' means proceedings before a court (other than a civilian court) in respect of a service offence; and
>
> 'civilian court' has the meaning given by section 374 of the Armed Forces Act 2006;
>
> and section 376(1) and (2) of that Act (meaning of 'convicted' in relation to summary hearings and the SAC) apply for the purposes of subsection (1)(e) above as they apply for the purposes of that Act.][558]

(13)   An order under this section shall be made by statutory instrument and shall be subject to annulment in pursuance of a resolution of either House of Parliament.

[(14)   Section 373(5) and (6) of the Armed Forces Act 2006 (supplementary provisions) apply in relation to an order under this section as they apply in relation to an order under that Act.][559]

## 114 [Application of Act to Revenue and Customs][560]

(1)   'Arrested', 'arresting', 'arrest' and 'to arrest' shall respectively be substituted for 'detained', 'detaining', 'detention' and 'to detain' wherever in the customs and excise Acts, as defined in section 1(1) of the Customs and Excise Management Act 1979, those words are used in relation to persons.

(2)   The Treasury may by order direct—

> (a)   that any provision of this Act which relates to investigations of offences conducted by police officers or to persons detained by the police shall apply, subject to such modifications as the order may specify, to [investigations conducted by officers of Revenue and Customs][561] or to [persons detained by officers of Revenue and Customs;][562]; and
>
> (b)   that, in relation to [investigations of offences conducted by officers of Revenue and Customs][563]
>
> > (i)   this Act shall have effect as if the following sections[564] were inserted after section 14—
> >
> > '14A Exception for [Revenue and Customs][565]
> >
> > Material in the possession of a person who acquired or created it in the course of any trade, business, profession or other occupation or for the purpose of any paid or unpaid office [and which relates to a

---

[558] Added by Armed Forces Act 2006, Sch 16, para 105(9) (31 October 2009).

[559] Added by Armed Forces Act 2006, Sch 16, para 105(10) (31 October 2009).

[560] Words substituted by Finance Act 2007, s 82(11) (8 November 2007).

[561] Words substituted by Finance Act 2007, s 82(2)(a) (8 November 2007).

[562] Words substituted by Finance Act 2007, s 82(2)(b) (8 November 2007).

[563] Words substituted by Finance Act 2007, s 82(3) (8 November 2007).

[564] Word substituted by Finance Act 2007, s 82(4) (8 November 2007).

[565] Modified by Finance Act 2007, s 82 (8 November 2007).

matter in relation to which Her Majesty's Revenue and Customs have functions,][566] is neither excluded material nor special procedure material for the purposes of any enactment such as is mentioned in section 9(2) above.'

**[14B Revenue and Customs: restriction on other powers to apply for production of documents**

(1) An officer of Revenue and Customs may make an application for the delivery of, or access to, documents under a provision specified in subsection (3) only if the condition in subsection (2) is satisfied.

(2) The condition is that the officer thinks that an application under Schedule 1 would not succeed because the material required does not consist of or include special procedure material.

(3) The provisions are–

   (a) section 20BA of, and Schedule 1AA to, the Taxes Management Act 1970 (serious tax fraud);

   (b) paragraph 11 of Schedule 11 to the Value Added Tax Act 1994 (VAT);

   (c) paragraph 4A of Schedule 7 to the Finance Act 1994 (insurance premium tax);

   (d) paragraph 7 of Schedule 5 to the Finance Act 1996 (landfill tax);

   (e) paragraph 131 of Schedule 6 to the Finance Act 2000 (climate change levy);

   (f) paragraph 8 of Schedule 7 to the Finance Act 2001 (aggregates levy);

   (g) Part 6 of Schedule 13 to the Finance Act 2003 (stamp duty land tax).[567]; and

(ii) section 55 above shall have effect as if it related only to things such as are mentioned in subsection (1)(a) of that section.

[(d) that where an officer of Revenue and Customs searches premises in reliance on a warrant under section 8 of, or paragraph 12 of Schedule 1 to, this Act (as applied by an order under this subsection) the officer shall have the power to search persons found on the premises–

   (i) in such cases and circumstances as are specified in the order, and

   (ii) subject to any conditions specified in the order; and

(e) that powers and functions conferred by a provision of this Act (as applied by an order under this subsection) may be exercised only by officers of Revenue and Customs acting with the authority (which may be general or specific) of the Commissioners for Her Majesty's Revenue and Customs.][568]

---

[566] Modified by Finance Act 2007, s 82 (8 November 2007).
[567] Modified by Finance Act 2007, s 82 (8 November 2007).
[568] Added by Finance Act 2007, s 82(8) (8 November 2007).

**Act**

[(2A)  A certificate of the Commissioners that an officer of Revenue and Customs had authority under subsection (2)(e) to exercise a power or function conferred by a provision of this Act shall be conclusive evidence of that fact.][569]

(3)     [An order under subsection (2)–
 
    (a)  may make provision that applies generally or only in specified cases or circumstances,

    (b)  may make different provision for different cases or circumstances,

    (c)  may, in modifying a provision, in particular impose conditions on the exercise of a function, and

    (d)  shall not be taken to limit a power under section 164 of the Customs and Excise Management Act 1979.][570]

(4)     [...][571]

(5)     An order under this section shall be made by statutory instrument and shall be subject to annulment in pursuance of a resolution of either House of Parliament.

[**114A  Power to apply Act to officers of the Secretary of State etc**

(1)     The Secretary of State may by order direct that—

    (a)  the provisions of Schedule 1 to this Act so far as they relate to special procedure material, and

    (b)  the other provisions of this Act so far as they relate to the provisions falling within paragraph (a) above,

    shall apply, with such modifications as may be specified in the order, for the purposes of investigations falling within subsection (2) as they apply for the purposes of investigations of offences conducted by police officers.

(2)     An investigation falls within this subsection if—

    (a)  it is conducted by an officer of the department of [the Secretary of State for Business, Innovation and Skills][572] or by another person acting on that Secretary of State's behalf;

    (b)  it is conducted by that officer or other person in the discharge of a duty to investigate offences; and

    (c)  the investigation relates to [an indictable offence][573] or to anything which there are reasonable grounds for suspecting has involved the commission of [an indictable offence][574].

(3)     The investigations for the purposes of which provisions of this Act may be applied with modifications by an order under this section include investigations of offences committed, or suspected of having been committed, before the coming into force of the order or of this section.

---

[569] Added by Finance Act 2007, s 82(9) (8 November 2007).

[570] Substituted by Finance Act 2007, s 82(10) (8 November 2007).

[571] Repealed by the Commissioners for Revenue and Customs Act 2005, ss 50(6), 52(2), Sch 4, para 31, Sch 5.

[572] Words substituted by Secretary of State for Business, Innovation and Skills Order 2009, SI 2009/2748, Sch 1, para 3 (13 November 2009).

[573] Amended by SOCAPA 2005, s 111, Sch 7, Pt 3, para 43(1), (11).

[574] ibid.

(4) An order under this section shall be made by statutory instrument and shall be subject to annulment in pursuance of a resolution of either House of Parliament.][575]

## 115 Expenses

Any expenses of a Minister of the Crown incurred in consequence of the provisions of this Act, including any increase attributable to those provisions in sums payable under any other Act, shall be defrayed out of money provided by Parliament.

## 116 Meaning of 'serious arrestable offence'

[...][576]

## 117 Power of constable to use reasonable force

Where any provision of this Act—
(a) confers a power on a constable; and
(b) does not provide that the power may only be exercised with the consent of some person, other than a police officer,
the officer may use reasonable force, if necessary, in the exercise of the power.

## 118 General interpretation

(1) In this Act—

[...][577]

['British Transport Police Force' means the constables appointed under section 53 of the British Transport Commission Act 1949 (c xxix);][578]

'designated police station' has the meaning assigned to it by section 35 above;

'document' [means anything in which information of any description is recorded.][579];

[...][580]

'item subject to legal privilege' has the meaning assigned to it by section 10 above;

'parent or guardian' means—
(a) in the case of a child or young person in the care of a local authority, that authority;[...][581]
(b) [...][582];

'premises' has the meaning assigned to it by section 23 above;

'recordable offence' means any offence to which regulations under section 27 above apply;

'vessel' includes any ship, boat, raft or other apparatus constructed or adapted for floating on water.

---

[575] Inserted by the Criminal Justice and Police Act 2001, s 85.
[576] Repealed by SOCAPA 2005, ss 111, 174(2), Sch 7, Pt 3, para 43(1), (12), Sch 17, Pt 2.
[577] Repealed by SOCAPA 2005, ss 111, 174(2), Sch 7, Pt 1, para 24(1), (2), Sch 17, Pt 2.
[578] Amended by the Anti-terrorism, Crime and Security Act 2001, s 101, Sch 7, paras 11, 14.
[579] Amended by the Civil Evidence Act 1995, s 15(1), Sch 1, para 9(3).
[580] Repealed by the Criminal Justice and Public Order Act 1994, s 168(3), Sch 11.
[581] Repealed by the Children Act 1989, s 108(7), Sch 15.
[582] ibid.

(2)     [Subject to subsection (2A)]583 a person is in police detention for the purposes of this Act if—

[(a) he has been taken to a police station after being arrested for an offence or after being arrested under section 41 of the Terrorism Act 2000, or]584

(b) he is arrested at a police station after attending voluntarily at the station or accompanying a constable to it,

and is detained there or is detained elsewhere in the charge of a constable, except that a person who is at a court after being charged is not in police detention for those purposes.

[(2A) Where a person is in another's lawful custody by virtue of paragraph 22, 34(1) or 35(3) of Schedule 4 to the Police Reform Act 2002, he shall be treated as in police detention.]585

## 119 Amendments and repeals

(1)     The enactments mentioned in Schedule 6 to this Act shall have effect with the amendments there specified.

(2)     The enactments mentioned in Schedule 7 to this Act (which include enactments already obsolete or unnecessary) are repealed to the extent specified in the third column of that Schedule.

(3)     The repeals in Parts II and IV of Schedule 7 to this Act have effect only in relation to criminal proceedings.

## 120 Extent

(1)     Subject to the following provisions of this section, this Act extends to England and Wales only.

(2)     The following extend to Scotland only—

[...]586

section 111;

section 112(1); and

section 119(2), so far as it relates to the provisions of the Pedlars Act 1871 repealed by Part VI of Schedule 7.

(3)     The following extend to Northern Ireland only—

section 6(4), and

section 112(2).

(4)     The following extend to England and Wales and Scotland—

section 6(1) and (2);

section 7;

[...] and587

section 119(2), so far as it relates to section 19 of the Pedlars Act 1871.

(5)     The following extend to England and Wales, Scotland and Northern Ireland—

section 6(3);

---

583 Amended by the Police Reform Act 2002, s 107(1), Sch 7, para 9(9).

584 Amended by the Terrorism Act 2000, s 125(1), Sch 15, para 5(1), (12); for savings see the Terrorism Act 2000, s 129(1)(b) and SI 2001/421, art 2.

585 Amended by the Police Reform Act 2002, s 107(9), Sch 7, para 9(9).

586 Entries repealed by Statute Law (Repeals) Act 2008, Sch 1(6), para 1 (21 July 2008).

587 Entries repealed by Statute Law (Repeals) Act 2008, Sch 1(6), para 1 (21 July 2008).

[section 9(2A);] and [588]
section 114(1).

(6) [Nothing in subsection (1) affects–
  (a) the extent of section 113(1) to (7) and (12) to (14);
  (b) the extent of the relevant provisions so far as they relate to service proceedings.][589]

(8) In this section 'the relevant provisions' means—
  [(a) section 67(11) to (13);][590]
  (c) Parts VII and VIII of this Act, except paragraph 10 of Schedule 3;
  [(d) section 113(8) to (10).][591]

[(8A) In this section 'service proceedings' means proceedings before a court (other than a civilian court) in respect of a service offence; and 'service offence' and 'civilian court' here have the same meanings as in the Armed Forces Act 2006.

(8B) Section 384 of the Armed Forces Act 2006 (Channel Islands, Isle of Man and British overseas territories) applies in relation to the provisions mentioned in subsection (6)(a) and (b) above as it applies in relation to that Act.][592]

[(9A)][593] Section 119(1), so far as it relates to any provision amended by Part II of Schedule 6, extends to any place to which that provision extends.

(10) Section 119(2), so far as it relates—
  (a) to any provision contained in—
    the Army Act 1955;
    the Air Force Act 1955;
    the Armed Forces Act 1981; or
    the Value Added Tax Act 1983;
  (b) to any provision mentioned in Part VI of Schedule 7, other than section 18 of the Pedlars Act 1871,
  extends to any place to which that provision extends.

(11) So far as any of the following—
  section 115;
  in section 118, the definition of 'document';
  this section;
  section 121; and
  section 122,
  has effect in relation to any other provision of this Act, it extends to any place to which that provision extends.

---

[588] Entry repealed by Statute Law (Repeals) Act 2008, Sch 1, para 1 (21 July 2008) and entry inserted by Criminal Justice and Police Act 2001, s 86(2) (1 August 2001).

[589] Section 120(6) substituted for s 120(6) and (7) by Armed Forces Act 2006, Sch 16, para 106(2) (31 October 2009).

[590] Section 120(8)(a) substituted for s 120(8)(a) and (b) by Armed Forces Act 2006, Sch 16, para 106(3)(a) (31 October 2009).

[591] Section 120(8)(d) substituted for s 120(8)(d)–(e) by Armed Forces Act 2006, Sch 16, para 106(3)(b) (31 October 2009).

[592] Section 120(8A)–(8B) substituted for s 120(9) by Armed Forces Act 2006, Sch 16, para 106(4) (31 October 2009).

[593] Amended by the Criminal Justice Act 1988, s 170(1), Sch 15, para 101.

### 121 Commencement

(1) This Act, except section 120 above, this section and section 122 below, shall come into operation on such day as the Secretary of State may by order made by statutory instrument appoint, and different days may be so appointed for different provisions and for different purposes.

(2) Different days may be appointed under this section for the coming into force of section 60 above in different areas.

(3) When an order under this section provides by virtue of subsection (2) above that section 60 above shall come into force in an area specified in the order, the duty imposed on the Secretary of State by that section shall be construed as a duty to make an order under it in relation to interviews in that area.

(4) An order under this section may make such transitional provision as appears to the Secretary of State to be necessary or expedient in connection with the provisions thereby brought into operation.

### 122 Short title

This Act may be cited as the Police and Criminal Evidence Act 1984.

## SCHEDULES

### SCHEDULE 1
### SPECIAL PROCEDURE

Section 9

*Making of orders by circuit judge*

1    If on an application made by a constable a circuit judge[594] [*judge*][595] is satisfied that one or other of the sets of access conditions is fulfilled, he may make an order under paragraph 4 below.

2    The first set of access conditions is fulfilled if—

    (a)  there are reasonable grounds for believing—

        (i)  that [an indictable offence][596] has been committed;

        (ii)  that there is material which consists of special procedure material or also includes special procedure material and does not also include excluded material on premises specified in the application[, or on premises occupied or controlled by a person specified in the application (including all such premises on which there are reasonable grounds for believing that there is such material as it is reasonably practicable so to specify)][597];

        (iii)  that the material is likely to be of substantial value (whether by itself or together with other material) to the investigation in connection with which the application is made; and

        (iv)  that the material is likely to be relevant evidence;

---

[594] Prospectively amended by the Courts Act 2003, s 65, Sch 4, para 6(1): see below.

[595] The words 'circuit judge' repealed and subsequent word in square brackets substituted by the Courts Act 2003, s 65, Sch 4, para 6(1) on a date to be appointed: see the Courts Act 2003, s 110(1).

[596] Amended by SOCAPA 2005, s 111, Sch 7, Pt 3, para 43(1), (13).

[597] Amended by SOCAPA 2005, s 113(1), (10), (11).

(b) other methods of obtaining the material—
   (i) have been tried without success; or
   (ii) have not been tried because it appeared that they were bound to fail; and
(c) it is in the public interest, having regard—
   (i) to the benefit likely to accrue to the investigation if the material is obtained; and
   (ii) to the circumstances under which the person in possession of the material holds it,

that the material should be produced or that access to it should be given.

3    The second set of access conditions is fulfilled if—
   (a) there are reasonable grounds for believing that there is material which consists of or includes excluded material or special procedure material on premises specified in the application[, or on premises occupied or controlled by a person specified in the application (including all such premises on which there are reasonable grounds for believing that there is such material as it is reasonably practicable so to specify)][598];
   (b) but for section 9(2) above a search of [such premises][599] for that material could have been authorised by the issue of a warrant to a constable under an enactment other than this Schedule; and
   (c) the issue of such a warrant would have been appropriate.

4    An order under this paragraph is an order that the person who appears to the circuit judge[600] [judge][601] to be in possession of the material to which the application relates shall—
   (a) produce it to a constable for him to take away; or
   (b) give a constable access to it,

not later than the end of the period of seven days from the date of the order or the end of such longer period as the order may specify.

5    Where the material consists of information [stored in any electronic form][602]—
   (a) an order under paragraph 4(a) above shall have effect as an order to produce the material in a form in which it can be taken away and in which it is visible and legible [or from which it can readily be produced in a visible and legible form][603]; and
   (b) an order under paragraph 4(b) above shall have effect as an order to give a constable access to the material in a form in which it is visible and legible.

6    For the purposes of sections 21 and 22 above material produced in pursuance of an order under paragraph 4(a) above shall be treated as if it were material seized by a constable.

---

[598] ibid.
[599] Amended by SOCAPA 2005, s 113(1), (10), (12).
[600] Prospectively amended by the Courts Act 2003, s 65, Sch 4, para 6(1): see below.
[601] The words 'circuit judge' repealed and subsequent word in square brackets substituted by the Courts Act 2003, s 65, Sch 4, para 6(1) on a date to be appointed: see the Courts Act 2003, s 110(1).
[602] Amended by the Criminal Justice and Police Act 2001, s 70, Sch 2, Pt 2, para 14(a).
[603] Amended by the Criminal Justice and Police Act 2001, s 70, Sch 2, Pt 2, para 14(b).

*Notices of applications for orders*

7    An application for an order under paragraph 4 above shall be made inter partes.

8    Notice of an application for such an order may be served on a person either by delivering it to him or by leaving it at his proper address or by sending it by post to him in a registered letter or by the recorded delivery service.

9    Such a notice may be served—

(a)  on a body corporate, by serving it on the body's secretary or clerk or other similar officer; and

(b)  on a partnership, by serving it on one of the partners.

10   For the purposes of this Schedule, and of section 7 of the Interpretation Act 1978 in its application to this Schedule, the proper address of a person, in the case of secretary or clerk or other similar officer of a body corporate, shall be that of the registered or principal office of that body, in the case of a partner of a firm shall be that of the principal office of the firm, and in any other case shall be the last known address of the person to be served.

11   Where notice of an application for an order under paragraph 4 above has been served on a person, he shall not conceal, destroy, alter or dispose of the material to which the application relates except—

(a)  with the leave of a judge; or

(b)  with the written permission of a constable,

until—

(i)  the application is dismissed or abandoned; or

(ii) he has complied with an order under paragraph 4 above made on the application.

*Issue of warrants by circuit judge*

12   If on an application made by a constable a circuit judge[604] [*judge*][605]—

(a)  is satisfied—

(i)  that either set of access conditions is fulfilled; and

(ii) that any of the further conditions set out in paragraph 14 below is also fulfilled [in relation to each set of premises specified in the application][606]; or

(b)  is satisfied—

(i)  that the second set of access conditions is fulfilled; and

(ii) that an order under paragraph 4 above relating to the material has not been complied with,

he may issue a warrant authorising a constable to enter and search the premises [or (as the case may be) all premises occupied or controlled by the person referred to in paragraph 2(a)(ii) or 3(a), including such sets of premises as are specified in the application (an 'all premises warrant')][607].

---

[604] Prospectively amended by the Courts Act 2003, s 65, Sch 4, para 6(1): see below

[605] The words 'circuit judge' repealed and subsequent word in square brackets substituted by the Courts Act 2003, s 65, Sch 4, para 6(1) on a date to be appointed: see the Courts Act 2003, s 110(1).

[606] Amended by SOCAPA 2005, s 113(1), (10), (13)(a).

[607] Amended by SOCAPA 2005, s 113(1), (10), (13)(b).

[12A The judge may not issue an all premises warrant unless he is satisfied—

    (a)  that there are reasonable grounds for believing that it is necessary to search premises occupied or controlled by the person in question which are not specified in the application, as well as those which are, in order to find the material in question; and

    (b)  that it is not reasonably practicable to specify all the premises which he occupies or controls which might need to be searched.][608]

13    A constable may seize and retain anything for which a search has been authorised under paragraph 12 above.

14    The further conditions mentioned in paragraph 12(a)(ii) above are—

    (a)  that it is not practicable to communicate with any person entitled to grant entry to the premises [...][609];

    (b)  that it is practicable to communicate with a person entitled to grant entry to the premises but it is not practicable to communicate with any person entitled to grant access to the material;

    (c)  that the material contains information which—

        (i)  is subject to a restriction or obligation such as is mentioned in section 11(2)(b) above; and

        (ii)  is likely to be disclosed in breach of it if a warrant is not issued;

    (d)  that service of notice of an application for an order under paragraph 4 above may seriously prejudice the investigation.

15    (1)  If a person fails to comply with an order under paragraph 4 above, a circuit judge[610] [*judge*][611] may deal with him as if he had committed a contempt of the Crown Court.

    (2)  Any enactment relating to contempt of the Crown Court shall have effect in relation to such a failure as if it were such a contempt.

### Costs

16    The costs of any application under this Schedule and of anything done or to be done in pursuance of an order made under it shall be in the discretion of the judge.[612]

### [*Interpretation*

17    *In this Schedule 'judge' means a Circuit judge [a judge of the High Court, a Circuit judge, a Recorder]*[613] *or a District Judge (Magistrates' Courts).*][614]

---

[608] Amended by SOCAPA 2005, s 113(1), (10), (14).

[609] Repealed by SOCAPA 2005, ss 113(1), (10), (15), 174(2), Sch 17, Pt 2.

[610] Prospectively amended by the Courts Act 2003, s 65, Sch 4, para 6(1): see below.

[611] The words 'circuit judge' repealed and subsequent word in square brackets substituted by the Courts Act 2003, s 65, Sch 4, para 6(1) on a date to be appointed: see the Courts Act 2003, s 110(1).

[612] New para 17 prospectively inserted by the Courts Act 2003, s 65, Sch 4, para 6(2) and new para 17 prospectively amended by SOCAPA 2005, s 114(1), (9).

[613] Para 17: words 'a Circuit judge' in italics repealed and subsequent words in square brackets substituted by the SOCAPA 2005, s 114(1), (9). Date in force: to be appointed: see the SOCAPA 2005, s 178(8).

[614] Para 17 inserted by the Courts Act 2003, s 65, Sch 4, para 6(2) on a date to be appointed: see the Courts Act 2003, s 110(1).

## [SCHEDULE 1A

### SPECIFIC OFFENCES WHICH ARE ARRESTABLE OFFENCES][615]

[...][616]

**Act**

## SCHEDULE 2
### PRESERVED POWERS OF ARREST

Section 26

| [...][617] | [...][618] |
|---|---|
| [...][619] | [...][620] |
| [...][621] | [...][622] |
| [...][623] | [...][624] |
| 1952 c 52 | Section 49 of the Prison Act 1952. |
| 1952 c 67 | Section 13 of the Visiting Forces Act 1952. |
| [...][625] | [...][626] |
| 1969 c 54 | [Section][627] 32 of the Children and Young Persons Act 1969. |
| 1971 c 77 | Section 24(2) of the Immigration Act 1971 and paragraphs 17, 24 and 33 of Schedule 2 and paragraph 7 of Schedule 3 to that Act. |
| [...][628] | |
| 1976 c 63 | Section 7 of the Bail Act 1976. |
| [...][629] 1983 c.20. | [...][630] Sections 18, 35(10), 36(8), 38(7), 136(1) and 138 of the Mental Health Act 1983. |
| [...][631] 1984 c.47. | Section 5(5) of the Repatriation of Prisoners Act 1984. |

---

[615] Inserted by the Police Reform Act 2002, s 48(1), (5), Sch 6.

[616] Repealed by SOCAPA 2005, ss 111, 174(2), Sch 7, Pt 1, para 24(1), (3), Sch 17, Pt 2.

[617] Repealed by SOCAPA 2005, ss 111, 174(2), Sch 7, Pt 1, para 24(1), (4), Sch 17, Pt 2.

[618] ibid.

[619] ibid.

[620] ibid.

[621] Repealed by the Civil Contingencies Act 2004, s 32(2), Sch 3.

[622] ibid.

[623] Repealed by SOCAPA 2005, ss 111, 174(2), Sch 7, Pt 1, para 24(1), (4), Sch 17, Pt 2.

[624] ibid.

[625] Entries repealed by Armed Forces Act 2006, Sch 17, para 1 (31 October 2009; SI 2009/1167).

[626] Entries repealed subject to transitory provisions specified in SI 2005/3495 art 2(2) by Serious Organised Crime and Police Act 2005 c. 15 Sch 17(2) para 1 (1 January 2006: repeal has effect subject to transitory provisions specified in SI 2005/3495 art 2(2)).

[627] Amended by the Children Act 1989, s 108(5), (6), Sch 13, para 55.

[628] Repealed by the Road Traffic (Consequential Provisions) Act 1988, s 3(1), Sch 1, Pt 1.

[629] Repealed by SOCAPA 2005, ss 111, 174(2), Sch 7, Pt 1, para 24(1), (4), Sch 17, Pt 2.

[630] Entry repealed by Electoral Administration Act 2006, Sch 2, para 1 (1 January 2007; SI 2006/3412).

[631] Entry relating to the Prevention of Terrorism (Temporary Provisions) Act 1984 repealed by Prevention of Terrorism (Temporary Provisions) Act 1989, s 25(2), Sch 9, Pt I.

SCHEDULE 3
PROVISIONS SUPPLEMENTARY TO SECTIONS 68 AND 69

Section 70

PART I
PROVISIONS SUPPLEMENTARY TO SECTION 68

[...]632

PART II
PROVISIONS SUPPLEMENTARY TO SECTION 69

[...]633

PART III
PROVISIONS SUPPLEMENTARY TO SECTIONS 68 AND 69

13— [...]634

14— [...]635

15— [...]636

SCHEDULE 4
THE POLICE COMPLAINTS AUTHORITY

Section 83

PART I
GENERAL

[...]637

PART II
TRANSITIONAL

[...]638

SCHEDULE 5
SERIOUS ARRESTABLE OFFENCES

Section 116

PART I
OFFENCES MENTIONED IN SECTION 116(2)(A)

[...]639

---

632 Repealed by the Criminal Justice Act 1988, s 170(2), Sch 16.
633 Repealed by the Youth Justice and Criminal Evidence Act 1999, s 67(3), Sch 6.
634 Repealed by the Criminal Justice Act 1988, s 170(2), Sch 16.
635 Repealed by the Youth Justice and Criminal Evidence Act 1999, s 67(3), Sch 6.
636 ibid.
637 Repealed by the Police Act 1996, s 103, Sch 9, Pt II.
638 ibid.
639 Repealed by SOCAPA 2005, ss 111, 174(2), Sch 7, Pt 3, para 43(1), (14), Sch 17, Pt 2.

## PART II
### OFFENCES MENTIONED IN SECTION 116(2)(B)

[…]640

**Act**

## SCHEDULE 6
### MINOR AND CONSEQUENTIAL AMENDMENTS

Section 119

## PART I
### ENGLAND AND WALES

*Game Act 1831 (c. 32)*

1.  The following section shall be inserted after section 31 of the Game Act 1831—
    'Powers of constables in relation to trespassers
    31A. The powers conferred by section 31 above to require a person found on land as mentioned in that section to quit the land and to tell his christian name, surname, and place of abode shall also be exercisable by a police constable.'.

*Metropolitan Police Act 1839 (c. 47)*

2.  In section 39 of the Metropolitan Police Act 1839 (fairs within the metropolitan police district) after the word 'amusement' there shall be inserted the words 'shall be guilty of an offence'.

*Railway Regulation Act 1840 (c. 97)*

3.  In section 16 of the Railway Regulation Act 1840 (persons obstructing officers of railway company or trespassing upon railway) for the words from 'and' in the third place where it occurs to 'justice,' in the third place where it occurs there shall be substituted the words ', upon conviction by a magistrates' court, at the discretion of the court,'.

*London Hackney Carriages Act 1843 (c. 86)*

4.  In section 27 of the London Hackney Carriages Act 1843 (no person to act as driver of carriage without consent of proprietor) for the words after 'constable' there shall be substituted the words 'if necessary, to take charge of the carriage and every horse in charge of any person unlawfully acting as a driver and to deposit the same in some place of safe custody until the same can be applied for by the proprietor.'.

*Town Gardens Protection Act 1863 (c. 13)*

5.  In section 5 of the Town Gardens Protection Act 1863 (penalty for injuring garden) for the words from the beginning to 'district' there shall be substituted the words 'Any person who throws any rubbish into any such garden, or trespasses therein, or gets over the railings or fence, or steals or damages the

---

640 ibid.

flowers or plants, or commits any nuisance therein, shall be guilty of an offence and'.

*Parks Regulation Act 1872 (c. 15)*

6. The following section shall be substituted for section 5 of the Parks Regulation Act 1872 (apprehension of offender whose name or residence is not known)—

'5. Any person who—

   (a) within the view of a park constable acts in contravention of any of the said regulations in the park where the park constable has jurisdiction; and

   (b) when required by any park constable or by any police constable to give his name and address gives a false name or false address,

shall be liable on summary conviction to a penalty of an amount not exceeding level 1 on the standard scale, as defined in section 75 of the Criminal Justice Act 1982.'

*Dogs (Protection of Livestock) Act 1953 (c. 28)*

7. In the Dogs (Protection of Livestock) Act 1953 the following section shall be inserted after section 2—

'Power of justice of the peace to authorise entry and search

2A. If on an application made by a constable a justice of the peace is satisfied that there are reasonable grounds for believing—

   (a) that an offence under this Act has been committed; and

   (b) that the dog in respect of which the offence has been committed is on premises specified in the application,

he may issue a warrant authorising a constable to enter and search the premises in order to identify the dog.'.

*Army Act 1955 (c. 18)*

*Air Force Act 1955 (c. 19)*

8. [...][641]

*Sexual Offences Act 1956 (c. 69)*

9. [...][642]

*Game Laws (Amendment) Act 1960 (c. 36)*

10. In subsection (1) of section 2 of the Game Laws (Amendment) Act 1960 (power of police to enter on land) for the words 'purpose of exercising any power conferred on him by the foregoing section' there shall be substituted the words 'purpose—

   (a) of exercising in relation to him the powers under section 31 of the Game Act 1831 which section 31A of that Act confers on police constables; or

---

[641] Repealed by Armed Forces Act 2006, Sch 17, para 1 (31 October 2009; SI 2009/1167).
[642] Repealed by the Sexual Offences Act 2003, Sch 7, para 1.

**Act**

(b) of arresting him in accordance with section 25 of the Police and Criminal Evidence Act 1984.'.

11. In subsection (1) of section 4 of that Act (enforcement powers) for the words from 'under', in the first place where it occurs, to 'thirty-one' there shall be substituted the words ', in accordance with section 25 of the Police and Criminal Evidence Act 1984, for an offence under section one or section nine of the Night Poaching Act 1828, or under section thirty'.

*Betting, Gaming and Lotteries Act 1963 (c. 2)*

12. [...]643

*Deer Act 1963 (c. 36)*

13. [...]644

*Police Act 1964 (c. 48)*

14. [...]645
15. [...]646
16. [...]647

*Criminal Law Act 1967 (c. 58)*

17. [...]648

*Theatres Act 1968 (c. 54)*

18. In section 15(1) of the Theatres Act 1968 (powers of entry and inspection) for the words 'fourteen days' there shall be substituted the words 'one month'.

*Children and Young Persons Act 1969 (c. 54)*

19. In the Children and Young Persons Act 1969—
    (a) [...]649
    (b) the following section shall be substituted for section 29—
    **29. 'Recognisance on release of arrested child or young person**
    A child or young person arrested in pursuance of a warrant shall not be released unless he or his parent or guardian (with or without sureties) enters into a recognisance for such amount as the custody officer at the police station where he is detained considers will secure his attendance at the hearing of the charge; and the recognisance entered into in pursuance of this section may, if the custody officer thinks fit, be conditioned for the attendance of the parent or guardian at the hearing in addition to the child or young person.'.

---

643 Repealed by Gambling Act 2005, Sch 17, para 1 (1 September 2007; SI 2006/3272).

644 Repealed by the Deer Act 1991, Sch 4, para 1.

645 Repealed by the Police and Magistrates' Courts Act 1994, Sch 9, Pt I, para 1.

646 ibid.

647 Repealed by the Police Officers (Central Service) Act 1989, s 3, Schedule.

648 Repealed by SOCAPA 2005, s 174(2), Sch 17, Pt 2, para 1; for transitional provisions see SI 2005/3495, art 2(2).

649 Repealed by the Children Act 1989, s 108, Sch 15, para 1.

*Immigration Act 1971 (c. 77)*

20. In section 25(3) of the Immigration Act 1971 for the words 'A constable or' there shall be substituted the word 'An'.

*Criminal Justice Act 1972 (c. 71)*

21. In subsection (1) of section 34 of the Criminal Justice Act 1972 (powers of constable to take drunken offender to treatment centre) for the words from the beginning to 'section the' there shall be substituted the words 'On arresting an offender for an offence under—

   (a)  section 12 of the Licensing Act 1872; or

   (b)  section 91(1) of the Criminal Justice Act 1967,

   a'.

*Child Care Act 1980 (c. 5)*

22. [...]650

*Deer Act 1980 (c. 49)*

23. [...]651

*Animal Health Act 1981 (c. 22)*

24. In subsection (5) of section 60 of the Animal Health Act 1981 (enforcement powers) for the words 'a constable or other officer' there shall be substituted the words 'an officer other than a constable'.

*Wildlife and Countryside Act 1981 (c. 69)*

25. In subsection (2) of section 19 of the Wildlife and Countryside Act 1981 (enforcement powers) after the words 'subsection (1)' there shall be inserted the words 'or arresting a person, in accordance with section 25 of the Police and Criminal Evidence Act 1984, for such an offence'.

*Mental Health Act 1983 (c. 20)*

26. In section 135(4) of the Mental Health Act 1983 for the words 'the constable to whom it is addressed', in both places where they occur, there shall be substituted the words 'a constable'.

*Prevention of Terrorism (Temporary Provisions) Act 1984 (c. 8)*

27. [...]652

---

650 ibid.

651 Repealed by the Deer Act 1991, Sch 4, para 1.

652 Repealed by the Prevention of Terrorism (Temporary Provisions) Act 1989, s 25(2), Sch 9, Pt I.

PART II

OTHER AMENDMENTS

*Army Act 1955 (c. 18)*

28. [...]653

*Air Force Act 1955 (c. 19)*

29. [...]654

*Police (Scotland) Act 1967 (c. 77)*

30. In section 6(2) of the Police (Scotland) Act 1967 (constables below rank of assist-ant chief constable) for the words 'an assistant chief constable or a constable holding the office of deputy chief constable' there shall be substituted the words 'a deputy chief constable or an assistant chief constable'.
31. In section 7(1) of that Act (ranks) after the words 'chief constable,' there shall be inserted the words 'deputy chief constable,'.
32. In section 26(7) of that Act (disciplinary authority) immediately before the words 'deputy chief constable' there shall be inserted the word 'any'.
33. In section 31(2) of that Act (compulsory retirement of chief constable etc.) for the words 'the deputy or an assistant chief constable' there shall be substituted the words 'a deputy or assistant chief constable'.

*Courts-Martial (Appeals) Act 1968 (c. 20)*

34. [...]655

*House of Commons Disqualification Act 1975 (c. 24)*

*Northern Ireland Assembly Disqualification Act 1975 (c. 25)*

35. In Part II of Schedule 1 to the House of Commons Disqualification Act 1975 and Part II of Schedule 1 to the Northern Ireland Assembly Disqualification Act 1975 (bodies of which all members are disqualified under those Acts) there shall be inserted at the appropriate place in alphabetical order—
'The Police Complaints Authority'.

*Armed Forces Act 1976 (c. 52)*

36. [...]656

*Customs and Excise Management Act 1979 (c. 2)*

37. The following subsection shall be substituted for section 138(4) of the Customs and Excise Management Act 1979—
'(4) Where any person has been arrested by a person who is not an officer—
(a) by virtue of this section; or

---

653 Repealed by Armed Forces Act 2006, Sch 17, para 1 (31 October 2009; SI 2009/1167).
654 Repealed by Armed Forces Act 2006, Sch 17, para 1 (31 October 2009; SI 2009/1167).
655 Repealed by Armed Forces Act 2001 c. 19 Sch 7(5) para 1 (11 May 2001) ;
656 ibid.

   (b)   by virtue of section 24 of the Police and Criminal Evidence Act 1984 in
         its application to offences under the customs and excise Acts,
         the person arresting him shall give notice of the arrest to an officer at the
         nearest convenient office of customs and excise.'.
38.  In section 161 of that Act—
   (a)   in subsection (3), for the words from 'that officer' to the end of the subsec-
         tion there shall be substituted the words 'any officer and any person accom-
         panying an officer to enter and search the building or place named in the
         warrant within one month from that day'; and
   (b)   in subsection (4), for the words 'person named in a warrant under subsection
         (3) above' there shall be substituted the words 'other person so authorised'.

*Betting and Gaming Duties Act 1981 (c. 63)*

39.  [...][657]

*Car Tax Act 1983 (c. 53)*

40.  [...][658]

*Value Added Tax Act 1983 (c. 55)*

41.  [...][659]

SCHEDULE 7
REPEALS

Section 119

PART I
ENACTMENTS REPEALED IN CONSEQUENCE OF PARTS I TO V

| Chapter | Short Title | Extent of Repeal |
| --- | --- | --- |
| 5 Geo 4 c 83 | Vagrancy Act 1824 | Section 8. |
| | | Section 13. |
| 1 & 2 Will 4 c 32 | Game Act 1831 | In section 31, the words 'or for any police constable'. |
| 2 & 3 Vict c 47 | Metropolitan Police Act 1839 | Section 34. |
| | | In section 38, the words from 'it' to 'and' in the sixth place where it occurs. |
| | | In section 39, the words 'to take into custody'. |
| | | In section 47, the words 'take into custody' and the words ', and every person so found'. |
| | | In section 54, the words from 'And' to the end of the section. |

---

[657] Repealed by Finance Act 2007, Sch 27(5)(1), para 1 (8 November 2007: commencement order SI).
[658] Repealed by the Statute Law (Repeals) Act 2004, Sch 1, Pt 9.
[659] Repealed by the Value Added Tax Act 1994, Sch 15, para 1.

**Act**

| Chapter | Short Title | Extent of Repeal |
|---|---|---|
| | | In section 62, the words from 'may' in the first place where it occurs to 'and' in the second place where it occurs. |
| | | Sections 63 to 67. |
| 3 & 4 Vict c 50 | Canals (Offences) Act 1840 | The whole Act. |
| 5 & 6 Vict c 55 | Railway Regulation Act 1842 | In section 17, the words 'or for any special constable duly appointed,'. |
| 8 & 9 Vict c 20 | Railways Clauses Consolidation Act 1845 | In section 104, the words 'and all constables, gaolers, and police officers,'. |
| 10 & 11 Vict c 89 | Town Police Clauses Act 1847 | In section 15, the words 'may be taken into custody, without a warrant, by any constable, or' and the words from 'Provided' to the end of the section. |
| | | In section 28, the words from 'and' in the first place where it occurs to 'offence' in the second place where it occurs. |
| 14 & 15 Vict c 19 | Prevention of Offences Act 1851 | Section 11. |
| 23 & 24 Vict c 32 | Ecclesiastical Courts Jurisdiction Act 1860 | In section 3, the words 'constable or'. |
| 24 & 25 Vict c 100 | Offences against the Person Act 1861 | In section 65, the words 'in the daytime'. |
| 34 & 35 Vict c 96 | Pedlars Act 1871 | Sections 18 and 19. |
| 35 & 36 Vict c 93 | Pawnbrokers Act 1872 | In section 36, the words, 'within the hours of business,'. |
| 38 & 39 Vict c 17 | Explosives Act 1875 | In section 78, the words 'a constable, or'. |
| 52 & 53 Vict c 18 | Indecent Advertisements Act 1889 | Section 6. |
| 52 & 53 Vict c 57 | Regulation of Railways Act 1889 | In section 5(2), the words 'or any constable'. |
| 8 Edw 7 c 66 | Public Meeting Act 1908 | In section 1, in subsection (3) the words from 'and' in the sixth place where it occurs to the end of the subsection. |
| 1 & 2 Geo 5 c 28 | Official Secrets Act 1911 | In section 9(1) the words 'named therein'. |
| 15 & 16 Geo 5 c 71 | Public Health Act 1925 | Section 74(2) and (3). |
| 23 & 24 Geo 5 c 12 | Children and Young Persons Act 1933 | Section 10(2). |
| | | Section 13(1) and (2). |
| | | In section 40, in subsection (1) the words 'named therein' and in subsection (4) the words 'addressed to and'. |

| Chapter | Short Title | Extent of Repeal |
|---|---|---|
| 11 & 12 Geo 6 c 58 | Criminal Justice Act 1948 | Section 68. |
| 1 & 2 Eliz 2 c 14 | Prevention of Crime Act 1953 | Section 1(3). |
| 3 & 4 Eliz 2 c 28 | Children and Young Persons (Harmful Publications) Act 1955 | In section 3(1), the words 'named therein'. |
| 4 & 5 Eliz 2 c 69 | Sexual Offences Act 1956 | Section 40. |
|  |  | In section 43(1), the word 'named'. |
| 5 & 6 Eliz 2 c 53 | Naval Discipline Act 1957 | In section 106(1), the words from 'may' in the first place where it occurs to 'and'. |
| 7 & 8 Eliz 2 c 66 | Obscene Publications Act 1959 | In section 3(1), the words, 'within fourteen days from the date of the warrant,'. |
| 8 & 9 Eliz 2 c 36 | Game Laws (Amendment) Act 1960 | Section 1. |
| 1963 c 2 | Betting, Gaming and Lotteries Act 1963 | In section 51(1), the words 'at any time within fourteen days from the time of the issue of the warrant' and the words 'arrest and'. |
| 1963 c 36 | Deer Act 1963 | Section 5(1)(c). |
| 1964 c 26 | Licensing Act 1964 | Section 187(5). |
| 1967 c 58 | Criminal Law Act 1967 | Section 2. |
| 1968 c 27 | Firearms Act 1968 | In section 46(1), the words 'named therein'. |
|  |  | Section 50. |
| 1968 c 52 | Caravan Sites Act 1968 | Section 11(5). |
| 1968 c 60 | Theft Act 1968 | Section 12(3). |
|  |  | Section 26(2). |
| 1968 c 65 | Gaming Act 1968 | Section 5(2). |
|  |  | In section 43, in subsection (4), the words 'at any time within fourteen days from the time of the issue of the warrant', and in subsection (5)(b), the words 'arrest and'. |
| 1970 c 30 | Conservation of Seals Act 1970 | Section 4(1)(a). |
| 1971 c 38 | Misuse of Drugs Act 1971 | Section 24. |
| 1971 c 77 | Immigration Act 1971 | In Schedule 2, in paragraph 17(2), the words 'acting for the police area in which the premises are situated,' and the words 'at any time or times within one month from the date of the warrant'. |
| 1972 c 20 | Road Traffic Act 1972 | Section 19(3). |
|  |  | Section 164(2). |
| 1972 c 27 | Road Traffic (Foreign Vehicles) Act 1972 | Section 3(2). |

Act

| Chapter | Short Title | Extent of Repeal |
|---|---|---|
| 1972 c 71 | Criminal Justice Act 1972 | Section 34(3). |
| 1973 c 57 | Badgers Act 1973 | Section 10(1)(b). |
| 1974 c 6 | Biological Weapons Act 1974 | In section 4(1), the words 'named therein'. |
| 1976 c 32 | Lotteries and Amusements Act 1976 | In section 19, the words 'at any time within 14 days from the time of the issue of the warrant'. |
| 1976 c 58 | International Carriage of Perishable Foodstuffs Act 1976 | Section 11(6). |
| 1977 c 45 | Criminal Law Act 1977 | Section 11. |
|  |  | Section 62. |
| 1979 c 2 | Customs and Excise Management Act 1979 | In section 138, in subsections (1) and (2), the words 'or constable'. |
| 1980 c 43 | Magistrates' Courts Act 1980. | Section 49. |
| 1980 c 49 | Deer Act 1980 | Section 4(1)(c). |
| 1980 c 66 | Highways Act 1980 | Section 137(2). |
| 1980 c x | County of Merseyside Act 1980 | Section 33. |
| 1980 c xi | West Midlands County Council Act 1980 | Section 42. |
| 1981 c 14 | Public Passenger Vehicles Act 1981 | Section 25(2). |
| 1981 c 22 | Animal Health Act 1981 | In section 60, subsection (3), in subsection (4) the words 'or apprehending', and in subsection (5) the words 'constable or', in the second place where they occur. |
| 1981 c 42 | Indecent Displays (Control) Act 1981 | Section 2(1). |
|  |  | In section 2(3), the words 'within fourteen days from the date of issue of the warrant'. |
| 1981 c 47 | Criminal Attempts Act 1981 | Section 9(4). |
| 1981 c 69 | Wildlife and Countryside Act 1981 | Section 19(1)(c). |
| 1982 c 48 | Criminal Justice Act 1982 | Section 34. |
| 1983 c 2 | Representation of the People Act 1983 | In section 97(3), the words from 'and' in the fifth place where it occurs to 'him' in the third place where it occurs. |
|  |  | [...][660] |
| 1983 c 20 | Mental Health Act 1983 | In section 135, in subsections (1) and (2), the words 'named in the warrant'. |

---

[660] Repealed by the Representation of the People Act 1985, s 28, Sch 5.

PART II

ENACTMENTS REPEALED IN RELATION TO CRIMINAL PROCEEDINGS IN
CONSEQUENCE OF PART VII

| Chapter | Short Title | Extent of Repeal |
| --- | --- | --- |
| 1971 c liv | Cornwall County Council Act 1971 | Section 98(4). |
| 1971 c xlvii | Hampshire County Council Act 1972 | Section 86(2). |

PART III

ENACTMENTS REPEALED GENERALLY IN CONSEQUENCE OF PART VII

| Chapter | Short Title | Extent of Repeal |
| --- | --- | --- |
| 3 & 4 Eliz 2 c 18 | Army Act 1955 | In section 198(1), the words 'of this section and of sections 198A and 198B of this Act'. |
| | | Sections 198A and 198B. |
| 3 & 4 Eliz 2 c 19 | Air Force Act 1955 | In section 198(1), the words 'of this section and of sections 198A and 198B of this Act'. |
| | | Sections 198A and 198B. |
| 1965 c 20 | Criminal Evidence Act 1965 | The whole Act. |
| 1969 c 48 | Post Office Act 1969 | In section 93(4), the words 'the Criminal Evidence Act 1965 and'. |
| | | In Schedule 4, paragraph 77. |
| 1981 c 55 | Armed Forces Act 1981 | Section 9. |
| 1981 c xviii | County of Kent Act 1981 | Section 82. |
| 1983 c 55 | Value Added Tax Act 1983 | In Schedule 7, paragraph 7(7) and (8). |

PART IV

ENACTMENTS REPEALED IN RELATION TO CRIMINAL PROCEEDINGS IN
CONSEQUENCE OF PART VIII

| Chapter | Short Title | Extent of Repeal |
| --- | --- | --- |
| 14 & 15 Vict c 99 | Evidence Act 1851 | Section 13. |
| 28 & 29 Vict c 18 | Criminal Procedure Act 1865 | In section 6, the words from 'and a certificate' onwards. |
| 34 & 35 Vict c 112 | Prevention of Crimes Act 1871 | Section 18 except the words 'A previous conviction in any one part of the United Kingdom may be proved against a prisoner in any other part of the United Kingdom'. |

Part V

Enactments Repealed Generally in Consequence of Part VIII

**Act**

| Chapter | Short Title | Extent of Repeal |
|---|---|---|
| 16 & 17 Vict c 83 | Evidence (Amendment) Act 1853 | Section 3. |
| 46 & 47 Vict c 3 | Explosive Substances Act 1883 | Section 4(2). |
| 58 & 59 Vict c 24 | Law of Distress Amendment Act 1895 | Section 5. |
| 61 & 62 Vict c 36 | Criminal Evidence Act 1898 | In section 1, the words 'and the wife or husband, as the case may be, of the person so charged', the words (in paragraph (b)) 'or of the wife or husband, as the case may be, of the person so charged' and paragraphs (c) and (d). |
|  |  | Section 4. |
|  |  | In section 6(1), the words from 'notwithstanding' to the end. |
|  |  | The Schedule. |
| 4 & 5 Geo 5 c 58 | Criminal Justice Administration Act 1914 | Section 28(3). |
| 19 & 20 Geo 5 c 34 | Infant Life (Preservation) Act 1929 | Section 2(5). |
| 23 & 24 Geo 5 c 12 | Children and Young Persons Act 1933 | Section 15. |
|  |  | Section 26(5). |
| 4 & 5 Eliz 2 c 69 | Sexual Offences Act 1956 | Section 12(2) and (3). |
|  |  | Section 15(4) and (5). |
|  |  | Section 16(2) and (3). |
|  |  | Section 39. |
|  |  | In Schedule 3, the entry relating to section 15 of the Children and Young Persons Act 1933. |
| 8 & 9 Eliz 2 c 33 | Indecency with Children Act 1960 | In section 1, subsection (2) and in subsection (3) the words 'except in section 15 (which relates to the competence as a witness of the wife or husband of the accused)'. |
| 1965 c 72 | Matrimonial Causes Act 1965 | Section 43(1). |
| 1968 c 60 | Theft Act 1968 | Section 30(3). |
| 1970 c 55 | Family Income Supplements Act 1970 | Section 12(5). |
| 1973 c 38 | Social Security Act 1973 | In Schedule 23, paragraph 4. |
| 1975 c 14 | Social Security Act 1975 | Section 147(6). |
| 1975 c 16 | Industrial Injuries and Diseases (Old Cases) Act 1975 | Section 10(4). |

| 1975 c 61 | Child Benefit Act 1975 | Section 11(8). |
|---|---|---|
| 1976 c 71 | Supplementary Benefits Act 1976 | Section 26(5). |
| 1977 c 45 | Criminal Law Act 1977 | In section 54(3), the words 'subsection (2) (competence of spouse of accused to give evidence)'. |
| 1978 c 37 | Protection of Children Act 1978 | Section 2(1). |
| 1979 c 18 | Social Security Act 1979 | Section 16. |
| 1980 c 43 | Magistrates' Courts Act 1980 | In Schedule 7, paragraph 4. |
| 1982 c 24 | Social Security and Housing Benefits Act 1982 | Section 21(6). |

## PART VI
### MISCELLANEOUS REPEALS

| Chapter | Short Title | Extent of Repeal |
|---|---|---|
| 2 & 3 Vict c 47 | Metropolitan Police Act 1839 | Section 7. |
| 34 & 35 Vict c 96 | Pedlars Act 1871 | In section 18, the words from 'or' where secondly occurring to 'Act,' and the words from 'and forthwith' to the end of the section. |
| 1964 c 48 | Police Act 1964 | Section 49. |
| | | Section 50. |
| 1967 c 77 | Police (Scotland) Act 1967 | Section 5(3) and section 17(6). |
| 1972 c 11 | Superannuation Act 1972 | In Schedule 1, the reference to the Police Complaints Board. |
| 1975 c 24 | House of Commons Disqualification Act 1975 | In Part II of Schedule 1, the entry relating to the Police Complaints Board. |
| 1975 c 25 | Northern Ireland Assembly Disqualification Act 1975 | In Part II of Schedule 1, the entry relating to the Police Complaints Board. |
| 1976 c 46 | Police Act 1976 | Section 1(1) to (4). |
| | | Sections 2 to 13. |
| | | Section 14(2). |
| | | In the Schedule, paragraphs 1 to 3, in paragraph 4, the words 'remuneration' and 'allowances' and paragraphs 5 to 13. |

# Contents of Appendices 2–9: Codes of Practice

## Appendix 5

**331**

# Appendix 2

## Code A: PACE Code of Practice for the Exercise by Police Officers of Statutory Powers of Stop and Search; Police Officers and Police Staff of Requirements to Record Public Encounters

This code applies to any search by a police officer and the requirement to record public encounters taking place after midnight on 31 December 2008.

### GENERAL

This code of practice must be readily available at all police stations for consultation by police officers, police staff, detained persons and members of the public.

The notes for guidance included are not provisions of this code, but are guidance to police officers and others about its application and interpretation. Provisions in the annexes to the code are provisions of this code.

This code governs the exercise by police officers of statutory powers to search a person or a vehicle without first making an arrest. The main stop and search powers to which this code applies are set out in Annex A, but that list should not be regarded as definitive. [See Note 1]

In addition, it covers requirements on police officers and police staff to record encounters not governed by statutory powers. This code does not apply to:

(a) the powers of stop and search under;
   (i) Aviation Security Act 1982, section 27(2);
   (ii) Police and Criminal Evidence Act 1984, section 6(1) (which relates specifically to powers of constables employed by statutory undertakers on the premises of the statutory undertakers).
(b) searches carried out for the purposes of examination under Schedule 7 to the Terrorism Act 2000 and to which the Code of Practice issued under paragraph 6 of Schedule 14 to the Terrorism Act 2000 applies.

### 1 PRINCIPLES GOVERNING STOP AND SEARCH

1.1 Powers to stop and search must be used fairly, responsibly, with respect for people being searched and without unlawful discrimination. The Race Relations (Amendment) Act 2000 makes it unlawful for police officers to discriminate on the grounds of race, colour, ethnic origin, nationality or national origins when using their powers.

1.2 The intrusion on the liberty of the person stopped or searched must be brief and detention for the purposes of a search must take place at or near the location of the stop.

1.3 If these fundamental principles are not observed the use of powers to stop and search may be drawn into question. Failure to use the powers in the proper manner reduces their effectiveness. Stop and search can play an important role in the detection and prevention of crime, and using the powers fairly makes them more effective.

1.4 The primary purpose of stop and search powers is to enable officers to allay or confirm suspicions about individuals without exercising their power of arrest. Officers may be required to justify the use or authorisation of such powers, in relation both to individual searches and the overall pattern of their activity in this regard, to their supervisory officers or in court. Any misuse of the powers is likely to be harmful to policing and lead to mistrust of the police. Officers must also be able to explain their actions to the member of the public searched. The misuse of these powers can lead to disciplinary action.

1.5 An officer must not search a person, even with his or her consent, where no power to search is applicable. Even where a person is prepared to submit to a search voluntarily, the person must not be searched unless the necessary legal power exists, and the search must be in accordance with the relevant power and the provisions of this Code. The only exception, where an officer does not require a specific power, applies to searches of persons entering sports grounds or other premises carried out with their consent given as a condition of entry.

## 2 EXPLANATION OF POWERS TO STOP AND SEARCH

2.1 This code applies to powers of stop and search as follows:
  (a) powers which require reasonable grounds for suspicion, before they may be exercised; that articles unlawfully obtained or possessed are being carried, or under Section 43 of the Terrorism Act 2000 that a person is a terrorist;
  (b) authorised under section 60 of the Criminal Justice and Public Order Act 1994, based upon a reasonable belief that incidents involving serious violence may take place or that people are carrying dangerous instruments or offensive weapons within any locality in the police area;
  (c) authorised under section 44(1) and (2) of the Terrorism Act 2000 based upon a consideration that the exercise of one or both powers is expedient for the prevention of acts of terrorism;
  (d) powers to search a person who has not been arrested in the exercise of a power to search premises (see Code B paragraph 2.4).

### Searches requiring reasonable grounds for suspicion

2.2 Reasonable grounds for suspicion depend on the circumstances in each case. There must be an objective basis for that suspicion based on facts, information, and/or intelligence which are relevant to the likelihood of finding an article of a certain kind or, in the case of searches under section 43 of the Terrorism Act 2000, to the likelihood that the person is a terrorist. Reasonable suspicion can never be supported on the basis of personal factors. It must rely on intelligence or information about, or some specific behaviour by, the person concerned. For example, other than in a witness description of a suspect, a person's race, age, appearance, or the fact that the person is known to have a previous conviction, cannot be used alone or in combination with any other factor, as the reason for searching that person. Reasonable suspicion cannot be based on generalisations or stereotypical images of certain groups or categories of people as more likely to be involved in criminal activity. A person's religion cannot be considered as reasonable grounds for suspicion and should never be considered as a reason to stop or stop and search an individual.

**Code A**

2.3 Reasonable suspicion can sometimes exist without specific information or intelligence and on the basis of the behaviour of a person. For example, if an officer encounters someone on the street at night who is obviously trying to hide something, the officer may (depending on the other surrounding circumstances) base such suspicion on the fact that this kind of behaviour is often linked to stolen or prohibited articles being carried. Similarly, for the purposes of section 43 of the Terrorism Act 2000, suspicion that a person is a terrorist may arise from the person's behaviour at or near a location which has been identified as a potential target for terrorists.

2.4 However, reasonable suspicion should normally be linked to accurate and current intelligence or information, such as information describing an article being carried, a suspected offender, or a person who has been seen carrying a type of article known to have been stolen recently from premises in the area. Searches based on accurate and current intelligence or information are more likely to be effective. Targeting searches in a particular area at specified crime problems increases their effectiveness and minimises inconvenience to law-abiding members of the public. It also helps in justifying the use of searches both to those who are searched and to the public. This does not however prevent stop and search powers being exercised in other locations where such powers may be exercised and reasonable suspicion exists.

2.5 Searches are more likely to be effective, legitimate, and secure public confidence when reasonable suspicion is based on a range of factors. The overall use of these powers is more likely to be effective when up to date and accurate intelligence or information is communicated to officers and they are well-informed about local crime patterns.

2.6 Where there is reliable information or intelligence that members of a group or gang habitually carry knives unlawfully or weapons or controlled drugs, and wear a distinctive item of clothing or other means of identification to indicate their membership of the group or gang, that distinctive item of clothing or other means of identification may provide reasonable grounds to stop and search a person. [See Note 9]

2.7 A police officer may have reasonable grounds to suspect that a person is in innocent possession of a stolen or prohibited article or other item for which he or she is empowered to search. In that case the officer may stop and search the person even though there would be no power of arrest.

2.8 Under section 43(1) of the Terrorism Act 2000 a constable may stop and search a person whom the officer reasonably suspects to be a terrorist to discover whether the person is in possession of anything which may constitute evidence that the person is a terrorist. These searches may only be carried out by an officer of the same sex as the person searched.

2.9 An officer who has reasonable grounds for suspicion may detain the person concerned in order to carry out a search. Before carrying out a search the officer may ask questions about the person's behaviour or presence in circumstances which gave rise to the suspicion. As a result of questioning the detained person, the reasonable grounds for suspicion necessary to detain that person may be confirmed or, because of a satisfactory explanation, be eliminated. [See Notes 2 and 3] Questioning may also reveal reasonable grounds to suspect the possession of a different kind of unlawful article from that originally suspected. Reasonable grounds for suspicion however cannot be provided retrospectively by such questioning during a person's detention or by refusal to answer any questions put.

2.10 If, as a result of questioning before a search, or other circumstances which come to the attention of the officer, there cease to be reasonable grounds for suspecting that an article is being carried of a kind for which there is a power to stop and search, no search may take place. [See Note 3] In the absence of any other lawful power to detain, the person is free to leave at will and must be so informed.

2.11 There is no power to stop or detain a person in order to find grounds for a search. Police officers have many encounters with members of the public which do not involve detaining people against their will. If reasonable grounds for suspicion emerge during such an encounter, the officer may search the person, even though no grounds existed when the encounter began. If an officer is detaining someone for the purpose of a search, he or she should inform the person as soon as detention begins.

### Searches authorised under section 60 of the Criminal Justice and Public Order Act 1994

2.12 Authority for a constable in uniform to stop and search under section 60 of the Criminal Justice and Public Order Act 1994 may be given if the authorising officer reasonably believes:

(a) that incidents involving serious violence may take place in any locality in the officer's police area, and it is expedient to use these powers to prevent their occurrence, or

(b) that persons are carrying dangerous instruments or offensive weapons without good reason in any locality in the officer's police area.

2.13 An authorisation under section 60 may only be given by an officer of the rank of inspector or above, in writing, specifying the grounds on which it was given, the locality in which the powers may be exercised and the period of time for which they are in force. The period authorised shall be no longer than appears reasonably necessary to prevent, or seek to prevent incidents of serious violence, or to deal with the problem of carrying dangerous instruments or offensive weapons. It may not exceed 24 hours. [See Notes 10-13]

2.14 If an inspector gives an authorisation, he or she must, as soon as practicable, inform an officer of or above the rank of superintendent. This officer may direct that the authorisation shall be extended for a further 24 hours, if violence or the carrying of dangerous instruments or offensive weapons has occurred, or is suspected to have occurred, and the continued use of the powers is considered necessary to prevent or deal with further such activity. That direction must also be given in writing at the time or as soon as practicable afterwards. [See Note 12]

### Powers to require removal of face coverings

2.15 Section 60AA of the Criminal Justice and Public Order Act 1994 also provides a power to demand the removal of disguises. The officer exercising the power must reasonably believe that someone is wearing an item wholly or mainly for the purpose of concealing identity. There is also a power to seize such items where the officer believes that a person intends to wear them for this purpose. There is no power to stop and search for disguises. An officer may seize any such item which is discovered when exercising a power of search for something else, or which is being carried, and which the officer reasonably believes is intended to be used for concealing anyone's identity. This power can only be used if an authorisation under section 60 or an authorisation under section 60AA is in force.

2.16 Authority for a constable in uniform to require the removal of disguises and to seize them under section 60AA may be given if the authorising officer reasonably believes that activities may take place in any locality in the officer's police area that are likely to involve the commission of offences and it is expedient to use these powers to prevent or control these activities.

2.17 An authorisation under section 60AA may only be given by an officer of the rank of inspector or above, in writing, specifying the grounds on which it was given, the locality in which the powers may be exercised and the period of time for which they are in force. The period authorised shall be no longer than appears reasonably necessary to prevent, or seek to prevent the commission of offences. It may not exceed 24 hours. [See Notes 10-13]

2.18 If an inspector gives an authorisation, he or she must, as soon as practicable, inform an officer of or above the rank of superintendent. This officer may direct that the authorisation shall be extended for a further 24 hours, if crimes have been committed, or is suspected to have been committed, and the continued use of the powers is considered necessary to prevent or deal with further such activity. This direction must also be given in writing at the time or as soon as practicable afterwards. [See Note 12]

### Searches authorised under section 44 of the Terrorism Act 2000

2.19 An officer of the rank of assistant chief constable (or equivalent) or above, may give authority for the following powers of stop and search under section 44 of the Terrorism Act 2000 to be exercised in the whole or part of his or her police area if the officer considers it is expedient for the prevention of acts of terrorism:

(a) under section 44(1) of the Terrorism Act 2000, to give a constable in uniform power to stop and search any vehicle, its driver, any passenger in the vehicle and anything in or on the vehicle or carried by the driver or any passenger; and

Code **A**

(b)  under section 44(2) of the Terrorism Act 2000, to give a constable in uniform power to stop and search any pedestrian and anything carried by
the pedestrian.

An authorisation under section 44(1) may be combined with one under section 44(2).

2.20   If an authorisation is given orally at first, it must be confirmed in writing by
the officer who gave it as soon as reasonably practicable.

2.21   When giving an authorisation, the officer must specify the geographical area
in which the power may be used, and the time and date that the authorisation ends (up to a maximum of 28 days from the time the authorisation was
given). [See Notes 12 and 13]

2.22   The officer giving an authorisation under section 44(1) or (2) must cause the
Secretary of State to be informed, as soon as reasonably practicable, that such
an authorisation has been given. An authorisation which is not confirmed by
the Secretary of State within 48 hours of its having been given, shall have
effect up until the end of that 48 hour period or the end of the period specified in the authorisation (whichever is the earlier). [See Note 14]

2.23   Following notification of the authorisation, the Secretary of State may:
(i)   cancel the authorisation with immediate effect or with effect from such
other time as he or she may direct;
(ii)  confirm it but for a shorter period than that specified in the authorisation; or
(iii) confirm the authorisation as given.

2.24   When an authorisation under section 44 is given, a constable in uniform may
exercise the powers:
(a)  only for the purpose of searching for articles of a kind which could be
used in connection with terrorism (see paragraph 2.25);
(b)  whether or not there are any grounds for suspecting the presence of such
articles.

2.24A  When a Community Support Officer on duty and in uniform has been conferred powers under Section 44 of the Terrorism Act 2000 by a Chief Officer
of their force, the exercise of this power must comply with the requirements
of this Code of Practice, including the recording requirements.

2.25   The selection of persons stopped under section 44 of Terrorism Act 2000 should
reflect an objective assessment of the threat posed by the various terrorist
groups active in Great Britain. The powers must not be used to stop and search
for reasons unconnected with terrorism. Officers must take particular care not
to discriminate against members of minority ethnic groups in the exercise of
these powers. There may be circumstances, however, where it is appropriate
for officers to take account of a person's ethnic origin in selecting persons to
be stopped in response to a specific terrorist threat (for example, some international terrorist groups are associated with particular ethnic identities). [See
Notes 12 and 13]

2.26   The powers under sections 43 and 44 of the Terrorism Act 2000 allow a constable to search only for articles which could be used for terrorist purposes.
However, this would not prevent a search being carried out under other
powers if, in the course of exercising these powers, the officer formed reasonable grounds for suspicion.

### Powers to search in the exercise of a power to search premises

2.27 The following powers to search premises also authorise the search of a person, not under arrest, who is found on the premises during the course of the search:

(a) section 139B of the Criminal Justice Act 1988 under which a constable may enter school premises and search the premises and any person on those premises for any bladed or pointed article or offensive weapon; and

(b) under a warrant issued under section 23(3) of the Misuse of Drugs Act 1971 to search premises for drugs or documents but only if the warrant specifically authorises the search of persons found on the premises.

2.28 Before the power under section 139B of the Criminal Justice Act 1988 may be exercised, the constable must have reasonable grounds to believe that an offence under section 139A of the Criminal Justice Act 1988 (having a bladed or pointed article or offensive weapon on school premises) has been or is being committed. A warrant to search premises and persons found therein may be issued under section 23(3) of the Misuse of Drugs Act 1971 if there are reasonable grounds to suspect that controlled drugs or certain documents are in the possession of a person on the premises.

2.29 The powers in paragraph 2.27(a) or (b) do not require prior specific grounds to suspect that the person to be searched is in possession of an item for which there is an existing power to search. However, it is still necessary to ensure that the selection and treatment of those searched under these powers is based upon objective factors connected with the search of the premises, and not upon personal prejudice.

### 3 Conduct of Searches

3.1 All stops and searches must be carried out with courtesy, consideration and respect for the person concerned. This has a significant impact on public confidence in the police. Every reasonable effort must be made to minimise the embarrassment that a person being searched may experience. [See Note 4]

3.2 The co-operation of the person to be searched must be sought in every case, even if the person initially objects to the search. A forcible search may be made only if it has been established that the person is unwilling to co-operate or resists. Reasonable force may be used as a last resort if necessary to conduct a search or to detain a person or vehicle for the purposes of a search.

3.3 The length of time for which a person or vehicle may be detained must be reasonable and kept to a minimum. Where the exercise of the power requires reasonable suspicion, the thoroughness and extent of a search must depend on what is suspected of being carried, and by whom. If the suspicion relates to a particular article which is seen to be slipped into a person's pocket, then, in the absence of other grounds for suspicion or an opportunity for the article to be moved elsewhere, the search must be confined to that pocket. In the case of a small article which can readily be concealed, such as a drug, and which might be concealed anywhere on the person, a more extensive search may be necessary. In the case of searches mentioned in paragraph 2.1(b), (c), and (d), which do not require reasonable grounds for suspicion, officers may make any reasonable search to look for items for which they are empowered to search. [See Note 5]

Code **A**

3.4 The search must be carried out at or near the place where the person or vehicle was first detained. [See Note 6]

3.5 There is no power to require a person to remove any clothing in public other than an outer coat, jacket or gloves except under section 45(3) of the Terrorism Act 2000 (which empowers a constable conducting a search under section 44(1) or 44(2) of that Act to require a person to remove headgear and footwear in public) and under section 60AA of the Criminal Justice and Public Order Act 1994 (which empowers a constable to require a person to remove any item worn to conceal identity). [See Notes 4 and 6] A search in public of a person's clothing which has not been removed must be restricted to superficial examination of outer garments. This does not, however, prevent an officer from placing his or her hand inside the pockets of the outer clothing, or feeling round the inside of collars, socks and shoes if this is reasonably necessary in the circumstances to look for the object of the search or to remove and examine any item reasonably suspected to be the object of the search. For the same reasons, subject to the restrictions on the removal of headgear, a person's hair may also be searched in public (see paragraphs 3.1 and 3.3).

3.6 Where on reasonable grounds it is considered necessary to conduct a more thorough search (e.g. by requiring a person to take off a T-shirt), this must be done out of public view, for example, in a police van unless paragraph 3.7 applies, or police station if there is one nearby. [See Note 6] Any search involving the removal of more than an outer coat, jacket, gloves, headgear or footwear, or any other item concealing identity, may only be made by an officer of the same sex as the person searched and may not be made in the presence of anyone of the opposite sex unless the person being searched specifically requests it. [See Notes 4, 7 and 8]

3.7 Searches involving exposure of intimate parts of the body must not be conducted as a routine extension of a less thorough search, simply because nothing is found in the course of the initial search. Searches involving exposure of intimate parts of the body may be carried out only at a nearby police station or other nearby location which is out of public view (but not a police vehicle). These searches must be conducted in accordance with paragraph 11 of Annex A to Code C except that an intimate search mentioned in paragraph 11(f) of Annex A to Code C may not be authorised or carried out under any stop and search powers. The other provisions of Code C do not apply to the conduct and recording of searches of persons detained at police stations in the exercise of stop and search powers. [See Note 7]

### Steps to be taken prior to a search

3.8 Before any search of a detained person or attended vehicle takes place the officer must take reasonable steps to give the person to be searched or in charge of the vehicle the following information:

(a) that they are being detained for the purposes of a search;

(b) the officer's name (except in the case of enquiries linked to the investigation of terrorism, or otherwise where the officer reasonably believes that giving his or her name might put him or her in danger, in which case a warrant or other identification number shall be given) and the name of the police station to which the officer is attached;

    (c)  the legal search power which is being exercised; and

    (d)  a clear explanation of:

        (i)   the purpose of the search in terms of the article or articles for which there is a power to search; and

        (ii)  in the case of powers requiring reasonable suspicion (see paragraph 2.1(a)), the grounds for that suspicion; or

        (iii) in the case of powers which do not require reasonable suspicion (see paragraph 2.1(b), and (c)), the nature of the power and of any necessary authorisation and the fact that it has been given.

**Code A**

3.9     Officers not in uniform must show their warrant cards. Stops and searches under the powers mentioned in paragraphs 2.1(b), and (c) may be undertaken only by a constable in uniform.

3.10    Before the search takes place the officer must inform the person (or the owner or person in charge of the vehicle that is to be searched) of his or her entitlement to a copy of the record of the search, including his entitlement to a record of the search if an application is made within 12 months, if it is wholly impracticable to make a record at the time. If a record is not made at the time the person should also be told how a copy can be obtained (see section 4). The person should also be given information about police powers to stop and search and the individual's rights in these circumstances.

3.11    If the person to be searched, or in charge of a vehicle to be searched, does not appear to understand what is being said, or there is any doubt about the person's ability to understand English, the officer must take reasonable steps to bring information regarding the person's rights and any relevant provisions of this Code to his or her attention. If the person is deaf or cannot understand English and is accompanied by someone, then the officer must try to establish whether that person can interpret or otherwise help the officer to give the required information.

## 4 RECORDING REQUIREMENTS

4.1     An officer who has carried out a search in the exercise of any power to which this Code applies, must make a record of it at the time, unless there are exceptional circumstances which would make this wholly impracticable (e.g. in situations involving public disorder or when the officer's presence is urgently required elsewhere). If a record is not made at the time, the officer must do so as soon as practicable afterwards. There may be situations in which it is not practicable to obtain the information necessary to complete a record, but the officer should make every reasonable effort to do so. [See Note 21.]

4.2     Except in the circumstances set out in paragraph 4.2A, a copy of a record made at the time must be given immediately to the person who has been searched. In all cases the officer must ask for the name, address and date of birth of the person searched, but there is no obligation on a person to provide these details and no power of detention if the person is unwilling to do so.

4.2A  A receipt of the record rather than a copy of the record may be given immediately to the person who has been searched provided it is produced by electronic means and states how the full record can be accessed. When providing such a receipt, the officer must inform the person that the receipt is in place of a full written record, that the full record is available in electronic or in hard copy format and how the full record can be accessed. The person may request a copy in either format but not both. The full record must comply with paragraph 4.3 of this Code. [See Note 22]

4.3  The following information must always be included in the record of a search even if the person does not wish to provide any personal details:

(i)     the name of the person searched, or (if it is withheld) a description;

(ii)    a note of the person's self-defined ethnic background; [See Note 18]

(iii)   when a vehicle is searched, its registration number; [See Note 16]

(iv)    the date, time, and place that the person or vehicle was first detained;

(v)     the date, time and place the person or vehicle was searched (if different from (iv));

(vi)    the purpose of the search;

(vii)   the grounds for making it, or in the case of those searches mentioned in paragraph 2.1(b) and (c), the nature of the power and of any necessary authorisation and the fact that it has been given; [See Note 17]

(viii)  its outcome (e.g. arrest or no further action);

(ix)    a note of any injury or damage to property resulting from it;

(x)     subject to paragraph 3.8(b), the identity of the officer making the search. [See Note 15]

4.4  Nothing in paragraph 4.3 or 4.10A requires the names of police officers to be shown on the search record or any other record required to be made under this code in the case of enquiries linked to the investigation of terrorism or otherwise where an officer reasonably believes that recording names might endanger the officers. In such cases the record must show the officers' warrant or other identification number and duty station.

4.5  A record is required for each person and each vehicle searched. However, if a person is in a vehicle and both are searched, and the object and grounds of the search are the same, only one record need be completed. If more than one person in a vehicle is searched, separate records for each search of a person must be made. If only a vehicle is searched, the name of the driver and his or her self-defined ethnic background must be recorded, unless the vehicle is unattended.

4.6  The record of the grounds for making a search must, briefly but informatively, explain the reason for suspecting the person concerned, by reference to the person's behaviour and/or other circumstances.

4.7  Where officers detain an individual with a view to performing a search, but the search is not carried out due to the grounds for suspicion being eliminated as a result of questioning the person detained, a record must still be made in accordance with the procedure outlined in Paragraph 4.12.

4.8  After searching an unattended vehicle, or anything in or on it, an officer must leave a notice in it (or on it, if things on it have been searched without opening it) recording the fact that it has been searched.

4.9  Thplication for compensation should be directed.

4.10  The vehicle must if practicable be left secure.

4.10A  When an officer makes a record of the stop electronically and if the officer is able to provide a copy of the record at the time of the stop or stop and search, he or she must do so. This means that if the officer has or has access to a portable printer for use with the electronic recording equipment, then a copy of the record must be provided.

4.10B If the officer is carrying a paper version of the form, then a record must be provided at the time of the incident. [See Note 25] An officer would not be required to produce anything other than a receipt if neither of these two scenarios (4.10A and 4.10B) are met, nor would they be required to provide a full record at the scene in the event that he or she was called to respond to an incident of higher priority. Where the person has been searched, the officer must explain how the person can obtain a full copy of the record of the stop or search and give the person a receipt which contains:

- a unique reference number and guidance on how to obtain a full copy of the stop or search;
- the name of the officer who carried out the stop or search (unless paragraph 4.4 applies); and
- the power used to stop and search them. [See Note 21]

Code A

### Recording of encounters not governed by Statutory Powers

4.11 Not used.

4.12 When an officer requests a person in a public place to account for themselves, ie their actions, behaviour, presence in an area or possession of anything, a record of the encounter as set out in paragraph 4.17 must be completed at the time and a receipt given to the person in accordance with paragraphs 4.12A and 4.17 below. The record must identify the name of the officer who has made the stop and conducted the encounter. This does not apply under the exceptional circumstances outlined in paragraph 4.1 of this Code.

4.12A A receipt can be provided in place of the record of the encounter as set out in paragraph 4.17. The officer conducting the encounter is required to record only the person's self-defined ethnic background [See Notes for Guidance 18 and 24].

4.13 The requirements in paragraph 4.12 and 4.12A do not apply to general conversations such as when giving directions to a place, or when seeking witnesses. It also does not include occasions on which an officer is seeking general information or questioning people to establish background to incidents which have required officers to intervene to keep the peace or resolve a dispute.

4.14 A separate record or receipt need not be completed when:

— stopping a person in a vehicle when an HORT/1 form, a Vehicle Defect Rectification Scheme Notice, or a Fixed Penalty Notice is issued. It also does not apply when a specimen of breath is required under Section 6 of the Road Traffic Act 1988.

— stopping a person when a Penalty Notice is issued for an offence.

4.15 Officers must inform the person of their entitlement to a receipt of the encounter.

4.16 The provisions of paragraph 4.4 of this Code apply equally when the encounters described in 4.12, 4.12A and 4.13 are recorded.

4.17 The following information must be included in the record

(i) a note of the person's self-defined ethnic background; [See Note 18]

4.18 There is no power to require the person questioned to provide personal details. If a person refuses to give their self-defined ethnic background, the record should provide a description of the person's ethnic background. [See Note 18].

4.19 A receipt of an encounter must always be made when the criteria set out in 4.12 have been met. If the criteria are not met but the person requests a receipt, the officer should provide a receipt but record on it that the encounter did not meet the criteria. The officer can refuse to issue the receipt if he or she reasonably believes that the purpose of the request is deliberately aimed at frustrating or delaying legitimate police activity. [See Note 20]

4.20 All references to officers in this section include police staff designated as Community Support Officers under section 38 of the Police Reform Act 2002.

## 5 Monitoring and Supervising the Use of Stop and Search Powers

5.1 Supervising officers must monitor the use of stop and search powers and should consider in particular whether there is any evidence that they are being exercised on the basis of stereotyped images or inappropriate generalisations. Supervising officers should satisfy themselves that the practice of officers under their supervision in stopping, searching and recording is fully in accordance with this Code. Supervisors must also examine whether the records reveal any trends or patterns which give cause for concern, and if so take appropriate action to address this.

5.2 Senior officers with area or force-wide responsibilities must also monitor the broader use of stop and search powers and, where necessary, take action at the relevant level.

5.3 Supervision and monitoring must be supported by the compilation of comprehensive statistical records of stops and searches at force, area and local level. Any apparently disproportionate use of the powers by particular officers or groups of officers or in relation to specific sections of the community should be identified and investigated.

5.4 In order to promote public confidence in the use of the powers, forces in consultation with police authorities must make arrangements for the records to be scrutinised by representatives of the community, and to explain the use of the powers at a local level. [See Note 19].

### Notes for Guidance

**Officers exercising stop and search powers**

1    *This code does not affect the ability of an officer to speak to or question a person in the ordinary course of the officer's duties without detaining the person or exercising any element of compulsion. It is not the purpose of the code to prohibit such encounters between the police and the community with the co-operation of the person concerned and neither does it affect the principle that all citizens have a duty to help police officers to prevent crime and discover offenders. This is a civic rather than a legal duty; but when a police officer is trying to discover whether, or by whom, an offence has been committed he or she may question any person from whom useful information might be obtained, subject to the restrictions imposed by Code C. A person's unwillingness to reply does not alter this entitlement, but in the absence of a power to arrest, or to detain*

*in order to search, the person is free to leave at will and cannot be compelled to remain with the officer.*

2 *In some circumstances preparatory questioning may be unnecessary, but in general a brief conversation or exchange will be desirable not only as a means of avoiding unsuccessful searches, but to explain the grounds for the stop/search, to gain co- operation and reduce any tension there might be surrounding the stop/search.*

3 *Where a person is lawfully detained for the purpose of a search, but no search in the event takes place, the detention will not thereby have been rendered unlawful.*

4. *Many people customarily cover their heads or faces for religious reasons – for example, Muslim women, Sikh men, Sikh or Hindu women, or Rastarfarian men or women. A police officer cannot order the removal of a head or face covering except where there is reason to believe that the item is being worn by the individual wholly or mainly for the purpose of disguising identity, not simply because it disguises identity. Where there may be religious sensitivities about ordering the removal of such an item, the officer should permit the item to be removed out of public view. Where practicable, the item should be removed in the presence of an officer of the same sex as the person and out of sight of anyone of the opposite sex.*

5 *A search of a person in public should be completed as soon as possible.*

6 *A person may be detained under a stop and search power at a place other than where the person was first detained, only if that place, be it a police station or elsewhere, is nearby. Such a place should be located within a reasonable travelling distance using whatever mode of travel (on foot or by car) is appropriate. This applies to all searches under stop and search powers, whether or not they involve the removal of clothing or exposure of intimate parts of the body (see paragraphs 3.6 and 3.7) or take place in or out of public view. It means, for example, that a search under the stop and search power in section 23 of the Misuse of Drugs Act 1971 which involves the compulsory removal of more than a person's outer coat, jacket or gloves cannot be carried out unless a place which is both nearby the place they were first detained and out of public view, is available. If a search involves exposure of intimate parts of the body and a police station is not nearby, particular care must be taken to ensure that the location is suitable in that it enables the search to be conducted in accordance with the requirements of paragraph 11 of Annex A to Code C.*

7 *A search in the street itself should be regarded as being in public for the purposes of paragraphs 3.6 and 3.7 above, even though it may be empty at the time a search begins. Although there is no power to require a person to do so, there is nothing to prevent an officer from asking a person voluntarily to remove more than an outer coat, jacket or gloves (and headgear or footwear under section 45(3) of the Terrorism Act 2000) in public.*

8 *Where there may be religious sensitivities about asking someone to remove headgear using a power under section 45(3) of the Terrorism Act 2000, the police officer should offer to carry out the search out of public view (for example, in a police van or police station if there is one nearby).*

9 *Other means of identification might include jewellery, insignias, tattoos or other features which are known to identify members of the particular gang or group.*

## Authorising officers

10 *The powers under section 60 are separate from and additional to the normal stop and search powers which require reasonable grounds to suspect an individual of carrying an*

*offensive weapon (or other article). Their overall purpose is to prevent serious violence and the widespread carrying of weapons which might lead to persons being seriously injured by disarming potential offenders in circumstances where other powers would not be sufficient. They should not therefore be used to replace or circumvent the normal powers for dealing with routine crime problems. The purpose of the powers under section 60AA is to prevent those involved in intimidatory or violent protests using face coverings to disguise identity.*

11  *Authorisations under section 60 require a reasonable belief on the part of the authorising officer. This must have an objective basis, for example: intelligence or relevant information such as a history of antagonism and violence between particular groups; previous incidents of violence at, or connected with, particular events or locations; a significant increase in knife-point robberies in a limited area; reports that individuals are regularly carrying weapons in a particular locality; or in the case of section 60AA previous incidents of crimes being committed while wearing face coverings to conceal identity.*

12  *It is for the authorising officer to determine the period of time during which the powers mentioned in paragraph 2.1 (b) and (c) may be exercised. The officer should set the minimum period he or she considers necessary to deal with the risk of violence, the carrying of knives or offensive weapons, or terrorism. A direction to extend the period authorised under the powers mentioned in paragraph 2.1(b) may be given only once. Thereafter further use of the powers requires a new authorisation. There is no provision to extend an authorisation of the powers mentioned in paragraph 2.1(c); further use of the powers requires a new authorisation.*

13  *It is for the authorising officer to determine the geographical area in which the use of the powers is to be authorised. In doing so the officer may wish to take into account factors such as the nature and venue of the anticipated incident, the number of people who may be in the immediate area of any possible incident, their access to surrounding areas and the anticipated level of violence. The officer should not set a geographical area which is wider than that he or she believes necessary for the purpose of preventing anticipated violence, the carrying of knives or offensive weapons, acts of terrorism, or, in the case of section 60AA, the prevention of commission of offences. It is particularly important to ensure that constables exercising such powers are fully aware of where they may be used. If the area specified is smaller than the whole force area, the officer giving the authorisation should specify either the streets which form the boundary of the area or a divisional boundary within the force area. If the power is to be used in response to a threat or incident that straddles police force areas, an officer from each of the forces concerned will need to give an authorisation.*

14  *An officer who has authorised the use of powers under section 44 of the Terrorism Act 2000 must take immediate steps to send a copy of the authorisation to the National Joint Unit, Metropolitan Police Special Branch, who will forward it to the Secretary of State. The Secretary of State should be informed of the reasons for the authorisation. The National Joint Unit will inform the force concerned, within 48 hours of the authorisation being made, whether the Secretary of State has confirmed or cancelled or altered the authorisation.*

## Recording

15  *Where a stop and search is conducted by more than one officer the identity of all the officers engaged in the search must be recorded on the record. Nothing prevents an*

*officer who is present but not directly involved in searching from completing the record during the course of the encounter.*

16 *Where a vehicle has not been allocated a registration number (e.g. a rally car or a trials motorbike) that part of the requirement under 4.3(iii) does not apply.*

17 *It is important for monitoring purposes to specify whether the authority for exercising a stop and search power was given under section 60 of the Criminal Justice and Public Order Act 1994, or under section 44(1) or 44(2) of the Terrorism Act 2000.*

18 *Officers should record the self-defined ethnicity of every person stopped according to the categories used in the 2001 census question listed in Annex B. Respondents should be asked to select one of the five main categories representing broad ethnic groups and then a more specific cultural background from within this group. The ethnic classification should be coded for recording purposes using the coding system in Annex B. An additional "Not stated" box is available but should not be offered to respondents explicitly. Officers should be aware and explain to members of the public, especially where concerns are raised, that this information is required to obtain a true picture of stop and search activity and to help improve ethnic monitoring, tackle discriminatory practice, and promote effective use of the powers. If the person gives what appears to the officer to be an "incorrect" answer (e.g. a person who appears to be white states that they are black), the officer should record the response that has been given. Officers should also record their own perception of the ethnic background of every person stopped and this must be done by using the PNC/Phoenix classification system. If the "Not stated" category is used the reason for this must be recorded on the form.*

19 *Arrangements for public scrutiny of records should take account of the right to confidentiality of those stopped and searched. Anonymised forms and/or statistics generated from records should be the focus of the examinations by members of thepublic.*

20 *Where an officer engages in conversation which is not pertinent to the actions or whereabouts of the individual (e.g. does not relate to why the person is there, what they are doing or where they have been or are going) then issuing a form would not meet the criteria set out in paragraph 4.12. Situations designed to impede police activity may arise, for example, in public order situations where individuals engage in dialogue with the officer but the officer does not initiate or engage in contact about the person's individual circumstances.*

21 *In situations where it is not practicable to provide a written record or a full copy of an electronic record or an electronic receipt (in accordance with paragraphs 4.2A and 4.13A above) of the stop or stop and search at that time, the officer should consider providing the person with details of the station to which the person may attend for a record. This may take the form of a simple business card, adding the date of the stop or stop and search.*

22 *The ability to provide an electronic receipt for a stop or stop and search is limited to officers from those British Transport Police (BTP) designated areas set out in Annex D to this Code and to a limited pilot period. The operational nature of BTP policing means that officers from these locations may provide electronic receipts in the course of their duties throughout England and Wales.*

### Definition of Offensive Weapon

23 *'Offensive weapon' is defined as any article made or adapted for use for causing injury to the person, or intended by the person having it with him for such use or by someone else. There are three categories of offensive weapons: those made for causing injury to*

Code **A**

*the person; those adapted for such a purpose; and those not so made or adapted, but carried with the intention of causing injury to the person. A firearm, as defined by section 57 of the Firearms Act 1968, would fall within the definition of offensive weapon if any of the criteria above.*

24 *Under paragraph 4.12A, the officer carrying out the encounter may consider recording the date, time and location of the encounter when the encounter is not recorded electronically. This information is in support of section 5 of this Code and is not required to be provided to the person subject to the encounter.*

25 *Under 4.10B, an officer with an electronic recording device may be carrying a paper version of the record for use as a contingency in the event of a technical breakdown. In these circumstances, where the officer is able to make an electronic record, there would be no requirement to provide a written record.*

## ANNEX A—SUMMARY OF MAIN STOP AND SEARCH POWERS

This table relates to stop and search powers only. Individual statutes below may contain other police powers of entry, search and seizure

| Power | Object of search | Extent of search | Where exercisable |
|---|---|---|---|
| **Unlawful articles general** | | | |
| 1. Public Stores Act 1875, s6 | HM Stores stolen or unlawfully obtained | Persons, vehicles and vessels | Anywhere where the constabulary powers are exercisable |
| 2. Firearms Act 1968, s47 | Firearms | Persons and vehicles | A public place, or anywhere in the case of reasonable suspicion of offences of carrying firearms with criminal intent or trespassing with firearms |
| 3. Misuse of Drugs Act 1971, s23 | Controlled drugs | Persons and vehicles | Anywhere |
| 4. Customs and Excise Management Act 1979, s163 | Goods: (a) on which duty has not been paid; (b) being unlawfully removed, imported or exported; (c) otherwise liable to forfeiture to HM Customs and Excise | Vehicles and vessels only | Anywhere |
| 5. Aviation Security Act 1982, s27(1) | Stolen or unlawfully obtained goods | Airport employees and vehicles carrying airport employees or aircraft or any vehicle in a cargo area whether or not carrying an employee | Any designated airport |

| Power | Object of search | Extent of search | Where exercisable |
|-------|------------------|------------------|-------------------|
| 6. Police and Criminal Evidence Act 1984, s1 | Stolen goods; articles for use in certain Theft Act offences; offensive weapons, including bladed or sharply-pointed articles (except folding pocket knives with a bladed cutting edge not exceeding 3 inches); prohibited possession of a category 4 (display grade) firework, any person under 18 in possession of an adult firework in a public place. | Persons and vehicles | Where there is public access |
| | Criminal Damage: Articles made, adapted or intended for use in destroying or damaging property | Persons and vehicles | Where there is public access |
| Police and Criminal Evidence Act 1984, s6(3) (by a constable of the United Kingdom Atomic Energy Authority Constabulary in respect of property owned or controlled by British Nuclear Fuels plc) | HM Stores (in the form of goods and chattels belonging to British Nuclear Fuels plc) | Persons, vehicles and vessels | Anywhere where the constabulary powers are exercisable |
| 7. Sporting events (Control of Alcohol etc.) Act 1985, s7 | Intoxicating liquor | Persons, coaches and trains | Designated sports grounds or coaches and trains travelling to or from a designated sporting event |
| 8. Crossbows Act 1987, s4 | Crossbows or parts of crossbows (except crossbows with a draw weight of less than 1.4 kilograms) | Persons and vehicles | Anywhere except dwellings |
| 9. Criminal Justice Act 1988 s139B | Offensive weapons, bladed or sharply pointed article | Persons | School premises |
| **Evidence of game and wildlife offences** | | | |
| 10. Poaching Prevention Act 1862, s2 | Game or poaching equipment | Persons and vehicles | A public place |

Code **A**

| Power | Object of search | Extent of search | Where exercisable |
|---|---|---|---|
| 11. Deer Act 1991, s12 | Evidence of offences under the Act | Persons and vehicles | Anywhere except dwellings |
| 12. Conservation of Seals Act 1970, s4 | Seals or hunting equipment | Vehicles only | Anywhere |
| 13. Badgers Act 1992, s11 | Evidence of offences under the Act | Persons and vehicles | Anywhere |
| 14. Wildlife and Countryside Act 1981, s19 | Evidence of wildlife offences | Persons and vehicles | Anywhere except dwellings |
| **Other** | | | |
| 15. Terrorism Act 2000, s43 | *Evidence of liability to arrest under section 41 of the Act* | Persons | Anywhere |
| 16. Terrorism Act 2000, s44(1) | Articles which could be used for a purpose connected with the commission, preparation or instigation of acts of terrorism | *Vehicles, driver and passengers* | Anywhere within the area or locality authorised under subsection (1) |
| 17. Terrorism Act 2000, s44(2) | *Articles which could be used for a purpose connected with the commission, preparation or instigation of acts of terrorism* | *Pedestrians* | Anywhere within the area of locality authorised |
| 18. Paragraphs 7 and 8 of Schedule 7 to the Terrorism Act 2000 | *Anything relevant to determining if a person being examined falls within paragraph 2(1) (a) to (c) of Schedule 5* | Persons, vehicles, vessels etc. | *Ports and airports* |
| 19. Section 60 Criminal Justice and Public Order Act 1994 , *as amended by s8 of the Knives Act 1997* | Offensive weapons or dangerous instruments to prevent incidents of serious violence *or to deal with the carrying of such items* | Persons and vehicles | Anywhere within a locality authorised under subsection (1) |

ANNEX B—SELF-DEFINED ETHNIC CLASSIFICATION CATEGORIES

| White | W |
|---|---|
| A. White—British | W1 |
| B. White—Irish | W2 |
| C. Any other White background | W9 |

| Mixed | M |
|---|---|
| D. White and Black Caribbean | M1 |
| E. White and Black African | M2 |
| F. White and Asian | M3 |
| G. Any other Mixed Background | M9 |
| **Asian/Asian—British** | **A** |
| H. Asian—Indian | A1 |
| I. Asian—Pakistani | A2 |
| J. Asian—Bangladeshi | A3 |
| K. Any other Asian background | A9 |
| **Black/Black—British** | **B** |
| L. Black—Caribbean | B1 |
| M. Black African | B2 |
| N. Any other Black background | B9 |
| **Other** | **O** |
| O. Chinese | O1 |
| P. Any other | O9 |
| **Not Stated** | **NS** |

Code **A**

## ANNEX C—SUMMARY OF POWERS OF COMMUNITY SUPPORT OFFICERS TO SEARCH AND SEIZE

The following is a summary of the search and seizure powers that may be exercised by a community support officer (CSO) who has been designated with the relevant powers in accordance with Part 4 of the Police Reform Act 2002.

When exercising any of these powers, a CSO must have regard to any relevant provisions of this Code, including section 3 governing the conduct of searches and the steps to be taken prior to a search.

### 1. Powers to stop and search not requiring consent

| Designation | Power conferred | Object of Search | Extent of Search | Where Exercisable |
|---|---|---|---|---|
| Police Reform Act 2002, Schedule 4, paragraph 15 | *(a) Terrorism Act 2000, s.44(1)(a) and (d) and 45(2);* | Items intended to be used in connection with terrorism. | (a) Vehicles or anything carried in or on the vehicle and anything carried by driver or passenger. | Anywhere within area of locality authorised and in the company and under the supervision of a constable. |
| | *(b) Terrorism Act 2000, s.44(2)(b) and 45(2).* | | (b) Anything carried by a pedestrian. | |

## 2. Powers to search requiring the consent of the person and seizure

A CSO may detain a person using reasonable force where necessary as set out in Part 1 of Schedule 4 to the Police Reform Act 2002. If the person has been lawfully detained, the CSO may search the person provided that person gives consent to such a search in relation to the following:

| Designation | Powers conferred | Object of Search | Extent of Search | Where Exercisable |
|---|---|---|---|---|
| Police Reform Act 2002, Schedule 4, paragraph 7A | (a) Criminal Justice and Police Act 2001, s12(2) | (a) Alcohol or a container for alcohol | (a) Persons | (a) Designated public place |
| | (b) Confiscation of Alcohol (Young Persons) Act 1997, s1 | (b) Alcohol | (b) Persons under 18 years old | (b) Public place |
| | (c) Children and Young Persons Act 1933, section 7(3) | (c) Tobacco or cigarette papers | (c) Persons under 16 years old found smoking | (c) Public place |

## 3 Powers to search not requiring the consent of the person and seizure

A CSO may detain a person using reasonable force where necessary as set out in Part 1 of Schedule 4 to the Police Reform Act 2002. If the person has been lawfully detained, the CSO may search the person without the need for that person's consent in relation to the following:

| Designation | Power conferred | Object of Search | Extent of Search | Where Exercisable |
|---|---|---|---|---|
| Police Reform Act 2002, Schedule 4, paragraph 2A | Police and Criminal Evidence Act 1984, s.32 | (a) Objects that might be used to cause physical injury to the person or the CSO. | Persons made subject to a requirement to wait. | Any place where the requirement to wait has been made. |
| | | (b) Items that might be used to assist escape. | | |

## 4 Powers to seize without consent

This power applies when drugs are found in the course of any search mentioned above.

| Designation | Power conferred | Object of Seizure | Where Exercisable |
|---|---|---|---|
| Police Reform Act 2002, Schedule 4, paragraph 7B | *Police Reform Act 2002, Schedule 4, paragraph 7B* | Controlled drugs in a person's possession. | Any place where the person is in possession of the drug. |

Annex D – Deleted

Annex E – Deleted

# Appendix 3
## Code B: PACE Code of Practice for Searches of Premises by Police Officers and the Seizure of Property Found by Police Officers on Persons or Premises

Code **B**

This Code applies to applications for warrants made after midnight on 31 January 2008 and to searches and seizures taking place after midnight on 31 January 2008.

### 1 INTRODUCTION

1.1 This Code of Practice deals with police powers to:
- search premises
- seize and retain property found on premises and persons

1.1A These powers may be used to find:
- property and material relating to a crime
- wanted persons
- children who abscond from local authority accommodation where they have been remanded or committed by a court

1.2 A justice of the peace may issue a search warrant granting powers of entry, search and seizure, e.g. warrants to search for stolen property, drugs, firearms and evidence of serious offences. Police also have powers without a search warrant. The main ones provided by the Police and Criminal Evidence Act 1984 (PACE) include powers to search premises:
- to make an arrest
- after an arrest

1.3 The right to privacy and respect for personal property are key principles of the Human Rights Act 1998. Powers of entry, search and seizure should be fully and clearly justified before use because they may significantly interfere with the occupier's privacy. Officers should consider if the necessary objectives can be met by less intrusive means.

1.4 In all cases, police should:
- exercise their powers courteously and with respect for persons and property
- only use reasonable force when this is considered necessary and proportionate to the circumstances

1.5 If the provisions of PACE and this Code are not observed, evidence obtained from a search may be open to question.

## 2 GENERAL

2.1 This Code must be readily available at all police stations for consultation by:
- police officers
- police staff
- detained persons
- members of the public

2.2 The *Notes for guidance* included are not provisions of this Code.

2.3 This Code applies to searches of premises:

  (a) by police for the purposes of an investigation into an alleged offence, with the occupier's consent, other than:
- routine scene of crime searches;
- calls to a fire or burglary made by or on behalf of an occupier or searches following the activation of fire or burglar alarms or discovery of insecure premises;
- searches when *paragraph 5.4* applies;
- bomb threat calls;

  (b) under powers conferred on police officers by PACE, sections 17, 18 and 32;

  (c) undertaken in pursuance of search warrants issued to and executed by constables in accordance with PACE, sections 15 and 16. See *Note 2A*;

  (d) subject to *paragraph 2.6*, under any other power given to police to enter premises with or without a search warrant for any purpose connected with the investigation into an alleged or suspected offence. See *Note 2B*.

For the purposes of this Code, 'premises' as defined in PACE, section 23, includes any place, vehicle, vessel, aircraft, hovercraft, tent or movable structure and any offshore installation as defined in the Mineral Workings (Offshore Installations) Act 1971, section 1. See *Note 2D*

2.4 A person who has not been arrested but is searched during a search of premises should be searched in accordance with Code A. See *Note 2C*

2.5 This Code does not apply to the exercise of a statutory power to enter premises or to inspect goods, equipment or procedures if the exercise of that power is not dependent on the existence of grounds for suspecting that an offence may have been committed and the person exercising the power has no reasonable grounds for such suspicion.

2.6 This Code does not affect any directions of a search warrant or order, lawfully executed in England or Wales that any item or evidence seized under that warrant or order be handed over to a police force, court, tribunal, or other authority outside England or Wales. For example, warrants and orders issued in Scotland or Northern Ireland, see *Note 2B(f)* and search warrants issued under the Criminal Justice (International Co-operation) Act 1990, section 7.

2.7 When this Code requires the prior authority or agreement of an officer of at least inspector or superintendent rank, that authority may be given by a sergeant or chief inspector authorised to perform the functions of the higher rank under PACE, section 107.

2.8 Written records required under this Code not made in the search record shall, unless otherwise specified, be made:
- in the recording officer's pocket book ('pocket book' includes any official report book issued to police officers) or
- on forms provided for the purpose

2.9 Nothing in this Code requires the identity of officers, or anyone accompanying them during a search of premises, to be recorded or disclosed:

    (a) in the case of enquiries linked to the investigation of terrorism; or

    (b) if officers reasonably believe recording or disclosing their names might put them in danger.

In these cases officers should use warrant or other identification numbers and the name of their police station. Police staff should use any identification number provided to them by the police force. See *Note 2E*

2.10 The 'officer in charge of the search' means the officer assigned specific duties and responsibilities under this Code. Whenever there is a search of premises to which this Code applies one officer must act as the officer in charge of the search. See *Note 2F*

2.11 In this Code:

    (a) 'designated person' means a person other than a police officer, designated under the Police Reform Act 2002, Part 4 who has specified powers and duties of police officers conferred or imposed on them. See *Note 2G*

    (b) any reference to a police officer includes a designated person acting in the exercise or performance of the powers and duties conferred or imposed on them by their designation.

    (c) a person authorised to accompany police officers or designated persons in the execution of a warrant has the same powers as a constable in the execution of the warrant and the search and seizure of anything related to the warrant. These powers must be exercised in the company and under the supervision of a police officer. See *Note 3C*.

2.12 If a power conferred on a designated person:

    (a) allows reasonable force to be used when exercised by a police officer, a designated person exercising that power has the same entitlement to use force;

    (b) includes power to use force to enter any premises, that power is not exercisable by that designated person except:

        (i) in the company and under the supervision of a police officer; or

        (ii) for the purpose of:

          • saving life or limb; or

          • preventing serious damage to property.

2.13 Designated persons must have regard to any relevant provisions of the Codes of Practice.

### Notes for guidance

*2A PACE sections 15 and 16 apply to all search warrants issued to and executed by constables under any enactment, e.g. search warrants issued by a:*

    *(a) justice of the peace under the:*

      *• Theft Act 1968, section 26—stolen property;*

      *• Misuse of Drugs Act 1971, section 23—controlled drugs;*

      *• PACE, section 8—evidence of an indictable offence;*

      *• Terrorism Act 2000, Schedule 5, paragraph 1;*

    *(b) Circuit judge under:*

      *• PACE, Schedule 1;*

      *• Terrorism Act 2000, Schedule 5, paragraph 11.*

Code **B**

2B  *Examples of the other powers in paragraph 2.3(d) include:*

    (a) *Road Traffic Act 1988, section 6E(1) giving police power to enter premises under section 6E(1) to:*

        • *require a person to provide a specimen of breath; or*

        • *arrest a person following*

          *—a positive breath test;*

          *—failure to provide a specimen of breath;*

    (b) *Transport and Works Act 1992, section 30(4) giving police powers to enter premises mirroring the powers in (a) in relation to specified persons working on transport systems to which the Act applies;*

    (c) *Criminal Justice Act 1988, section 139B giving police power to enter and search school premises for offensive weapons, bladed or pointed articles;*

    (d) *Terrorism Act 2000, Schedule 5, paragraphs 3 and 15 empowering a superintendent in urgent cases to give written authority for police to enter and search premises for the purposes of a terrorist investigation;*

    (e) *Explosives Act 1875, section 73(b) empowering a superintendent to give written authority for police to enter premises, examine and search them for explosives;*

    (f) *search warrants and production orders or the equivalent issued in Scotland or Northern Ireland endorsed under the Summary Jurisdiction (Process) Act 1881 or the Petty Sessions (Ireland) Act 1851 respectively for execution in England and Wales.*

2C  *The Criminal Justice Act 1988, section 139B provides that a constable who has reasonable grounds to believe an offence under the Criminal Justice Act 1988, section 139A has or is being committed may enter school premises and search the premises and any persons on the premises for any bladed or pointed article or offensive weapon. Persons may be searched under a warrant issued under the Misuse of Drugs Act 1971, section 23(3) to search premises for drugs or documents only if the warrant specifically authorises the search of persons on the premises.*

2D  *The Immigration Act 1971, Part III and Schedule 2 gives immigration officers powers to enter and search premises, seize and retain property, with and without a search warrant. These are similar to the powers available to police under search warrants issued by a justice of the peace and without a warrant under PACE, sections 17, 18, 19 and 32 except they only apply to specified offences under the Immigration Act 1971 and immigration control powers. For certain types of investigations and enquiries these powers avoid the need for the Immigration Service to rely on police officers becoming directly involved. When exercising these powers, immigration officers are required by the Immigration and Asylum Act 1999, section 145 to have regard to this Code's corresponding provisions. When immigration officers are dealing with persons or property at police stations, police officers should give appropriate assistance to help them discharge their specific duties and responsibilities.*

2E  *The purpose of paragraph 2.9(b) is to protect those involved in serious organised crime investigations or arrests of particularly violent suspects when there is reliable information that those arrested or their associates may threaten or cause harm to the officers or anyone accompanying them during a search of premises. In cases of doubt, an officer of inspector rank or above should be consulted.*

*2F   For the purposes of paragraph 2.10, the officer in charge of the search should normally be the most senior officer present. Some exceptions are:*

*(a)   a supervising officer who attends or assists at the scene of a premises search may appoint an officer of lower rank as officer in charge of the search if that officer is:*
- *more conversant with the facts;*
- *a more appropriate officer to be in charge of the search;*

*(b)   when all officers in a premises search are the same rank. The supervising officer if available must make sure one of them is appointed officer in charge of the search, otherwise the officers themselves must nominate one of their number as the officer in charge;*

*(c)   a senior officer assisting in a specialist role. This officer need not be regarded as having a general supervisory role over the conduct of the search or be appointed or expected to act as the officer in charge of the search.*

*Except in (c), nothing in this Note diminishes the role and responsibilities of a supervisory officer who is present at the search or knows of a search taking place.*

*2G   An officer of the rank of inspector or above may direct a designated investigating officer not to wear a uniform for the purposes of a specific operation.*

## 3   Search Warrants and Production Orders

### (a) Before making an application

3.1 When information appears to justify an application, the officer must take reasonable steps to check the information is accurate, recent and not provided maliciously or irresponsibly. An application may not be made on the basis of information from an anonymous source if corroboration has not been sought. See *Note 3A*

3.2 The officer shall ascertain as specifically as possible the nature of the articles concerned and their location.

3.3 The officer shall make reasonable enquiries to:
   (i)   establish if:
   - anything is known about the likely occupier of the premises and the nature of the premises themselves;
   - the premises have been searched previously and how recently;
   (ii)  obtain any other relevant information.

3.4 An application:
   (a)   to a justice of the peace for a search warrant or to a Circuit judge for a search warrant or production order under PACE, Schedule 1 must be supported by a signed written authority from an officer of inspector rank or above:
   Note: If the case is an urgent application to a justice of the peace and an inspector or above is not readily available, the next most senior officer on duty can give the written authority.
   (b)   to a circuit judge under the Terrorism Act 2000, Schedule 5 for
   - a production order;
   - search warrant; or
   - an order requiring an explanation of material seized or produced under such a warrant or production order

Code **B**

must be supported by a signed written authority from an officer of superintendent rank or above.

3.5 Except in a case of urgency, if there is reason to believe a search might have an
adverse effect on relations between the police and the community, the officer in
charge shall consult the local police/community liaison officer:

- before the search; or
- in urgent cases, as soon as practicable after the search

### (b) Making an application

3.6 A search warrant application must be supported in writing, specifying:

  (a) the enactment under which the application is made, see *Note 2A*;

  (b) (i) whether the warrant is to authorise entry and search of:

- one set of premises; or
- if the application is under PACE section 8, or Schedule 1, paragraph 12,
more than one set of specified premises or all premises occupied or
controlled by a specified person, and

    (ii) the premises to be searched;

  (c) the object of the search, see *Note 3B*;

  (d) the grounds for the application, including, when the purpose of the proposed search is to find evidence of an alleged offence, an indication of how
the evidence relates to the investigation;

  (da) where the application is under PACE section 8, or Schedule 1, paragraph 12
for a single warrant to enter and search:

    (i) more than one set of specified premises, the officer must specify each
set of premises which it is desired to enter and search

    (ii) all premises occupied or controlled by a specified person, the officer
must specify;

- as many sets of premises which it is desired to enter and search as it is
reasonably practicable to specify
- the person who is in occupation or control of those premises and any
others which it is desired to search
- why it is necessary to search more premises than those which can be
specified
- why it is not reasonably practicable to specify all the premises which
it is desired to enter and search

  (db) whether an application under PACE section 8 is for a warrant authorising
entry and search on more than one occasion, and if so, the officer must state
the grounds for this and whether the desired number of entries authorised is
unlimited or a specified maximum.

  (e) there are no reasonable grounds to believe the material to be sought, when
making application to a:

    (i) justice of the peace or a Circuit judge consists of or includes items sub-
ject to legal privilege;

    (ii) justice of the peace, consists of or includes excluded material or special
procedure material;

  Note: this does not affect the additional powers of seizure in the Criminal
Justice and Police Act 2001, Part 2 covered in paragraph 7.7, see *Note 3B*;

(f) if applicable, a request for the warrant to authorise a person or persons to accompany the officer who executes the warrant, see *Note 3C*.

3.7 A search warrant application under PACE, Schedule 1, paragraph 12(a), shall if appropriate indicate why it is believed service of notice of an application for a production order may seriously prejudice the investigation. Applications for search warrants under the Terrorism Act 2000, Schedule 5, paragraph 11 must indicate why a production order would not be appropriate.

3.8 If a search warrant application is refused, a further application may not be made for those premises unless supported by additional grounds.

### Notes for guidance

*3A  The identity of an informant need not be disclosed when making an application, but the officer should be prepared to answer any questions the magistrate or judge may have about:*

- *the accuracy of previous information from that source*
- *any other related matters*

*3B  The information supporting a search warrant application should be as specific as possible, particularly in relation to the articles or persons being sought and where in the premises it is suspected they may be found. The meaning of 'items subject to legal privilege', 'excluded material' and 'special procedure material' are defined by PACE, sections 10, 11 and 14 respectively.*

*3C  Under PACE, section 16(2), a search warrant may authorise persons other than police officers to accompany the constable who executes the warrant. This includes, e.g. any suitably qualified or skilled person or an expert in a particular field whose presence is needed to help accurately identify the material sought or to advise where certain evidence is most likely to be found and how it should be dealt with. It does not give them any right to force entry, but it gives them the right to be on the premises during the search and to search for or seize property without the occupier's permission.*

## 4  ENTRY WITHOUT WARRANT—PARTICULAR POWERS

### (a) Making an arrest etc

4.1 The conditions under which an officer may enter and search premises without a warrant are set out in PACE, section 17. It should be noted that this section does not create or confer any powers of arrest. See other powers in *Note 2B(a)*.

### (b) Search of premises where arrest takes place or the arrested person was immediately before arrest

4.2 When a person has been arrested for an indictable offence, a police officer has power under PACE, section 32 to search the premises where the person was arrested or where the person was immediately before being arrested.

### (c) Search of premises occupied or controlled by the arrested person

4.3 The specific powers to search premises occupied or controlled by a person arrested for an indictable offence are set out in PACE, section 18. They may not be exercised, except if section 18(5) applies, unless an officer of inspector rank or above has given written authority. That authority should only be given when the authorising officer is satisfied the necessary grounds exist. If possible the

authorising officer should record the authority on the Notice of Powers and Rights and, subject to *paragraph 2.9*, sign the Notice. The record of the grounds for the search and the nature of the evidence sought as required by section 18(7) of the Act should be made in:
- the custody record if there is one, otherwise
- the officer's pocket book, or
- the search record

## 5 Search with Consent

5.1 Subject to *paragraph 5.4*, if it is proposed to search premises with the consent of a person entitled to grant entry the consent must, if practicable, be given in writing on the Notice of Powers and Rights before the search. The officer must make any necessary enquiries to be satisfied the person is in a position to give such consent. See *Notes 5A* and *5B*

5.2 Before seeking consent the officer in charge of the search shall state the purpose of the proposed search and its extent. This information must be as specific as possible, particularly regarding the articles or persons being sought and the parts of the premises to be searched. The person concerned must be clearly informed they are not obliged to consent and anything seized may be produced in evidence. If at the time the person is not suspected of an offence, the officer shall say this when stating the purpose of the search.

5.3 An officer cannot enter and search or continue to search premises under *paragraph 5.1* if consent is given under duress or withdrawn before the search is completed.

5.4 It is unnecessary to seek consent under *paragraphs 5.1* and *5.2* if this would cause disproportionate inconvenience to the person concerned. See *Note 5C*

### Notes for guidance

5A *In a lodging house or similar accommodation, every reasonable effort should be made to obtain the consent of the tenant, lodger or occupier. A search should not be made solely on the basis of the landlord's consent unless the tenant, lodger or occupier is unavailable and the matter is urgent.*

5B *If the intention is to search premises under the authority of a warrant or a power of entry and search without warrant, and the occupier of the premises co-operates in accordance with paragraph 6.4, there is no need to obtain written consent.*

5C *Paragraph 5.4 is intended to apply when it is reasonable to assume innocent occupiers would agree to, and expect, police to take the proposed action, e.g. if:*
- *a suspect has fled the scene of a crime or to evade arrest and it is necessary quickly to check surrounding gardens and readily accessible places to see if the suspect is hiding*
- *police have arrested someone in the night after a pursuit and it is necessary to make a brief check of gardens along the pursuit route to see if stolen or incriminating articles have been discarded*

## 6 Searching Premises—General Considerations

### (a) Time of searches

6.1 Searches made under warrant must be made within three calendar months of the date of the warrant's issue.

6.2    Searches must be made at a reasonable hour unless this might frustrate the purpose of the search.

6.3    When the extent or complexity of a search mean it is likely to take a long time, the officer in charge of the search may consider using the seize and sift powers referred to in *section 7*.

6.3A   A warrant under PACE, section 8 may authorise entry to and search of premises on more than one occasion if, on the application, the justice of the peace is satisfied that it is necessary to authorise multiple entries in order to achieve the purpose for which the warrant is issued. No premises may be entered or searched on any subsequent occasions without the prior written authority of an officer of the rank of inspector who is not involved in the investigation. All other warrants authorise entry on one occasion only.

6.3B   Where a warrant under PACE section 8, or Schedule 1, paragraph 12 authorises entry to and search of all premises occupied or controlled by a specified person, no premises which are not specified in the warrant may be entered and searched without the prior written authority of an officer of the rank of inspector who is not involved in the investigation.

**(b)  Entry other than with consent**

6.4    The officer in charge of the search shall first try to communicate with the occupier, or any other person entitled to grant access to the premises, explain the authority under which entry is sought and ask the occupier to allow entry, unless:
   (i)   the search premises are unoccupied;
   (ii)  the occupier and any other person entitled to grant access are absent;
   (iii) there are reasonable grounds for believing that alerting the occupier or any other person entitled to grant access would frustrate the object of the search or endanger officers or other people.

6.5    Unless *sub-paragraph 6.4(iii)* applies, if the premises are occupied the officer, subject to *paragraph 2.9*, shall, before the search begins:
   (i)   identify him or herself, show their warrant card (if not in uniform) and state the purpose of and grounds for the search;
   (ii)  identify and introduce any person accompanying the officer on the search (such persons should carry identification for production on request) and briefly describe that person's role in the process.

6.6    Reasonable and proportionate force may be used if necessary to enter premises if the officer in charge of the search is satisfied the premises are those specified in any warrant, or in exercise of the powers described in *paragraphs 4.1* to *4.3*, and if:
   (i)   the occupier or any other person entitled to grant access has refused entry;
   (ii)  it is impossible to communicate with the occupier or any other person entitled to grant access; or
   (iii) any of the provisions of *paragraph 6.4* apply.

**(c)  Notice of Powers and Rights**

6.7    If an officer conducts a search to which this Code applies the officer shall, unless it is impracticable to do so, provide the occupier with a copy of a Notice in a standard format:
   (i)   specifying if the search is made under warrant, with consent, or in the exercise of the powers described in *paragraphs 4.1* to *4.3*. Note: the notice format

Code **B**

     shall provide for authority or consent to be indicated, see *paragraphs 4.3* and *5.1*;

(ii) summarising the extent of the powers of search and seizure conferred by PACE;

(iii) explaining the rights of the occupier, and the owner of the property seized;

(iv) explaining compensation may be payable in appropriate cases for damages caused entering and searching premises, and giving the address to send a compensation application, see *Note 6A*;

(v) stating this Code is available at any police station.

6.8 If the occupier is:

- present, copies of the Notice and warrant shall, if practicable, be given to them before the search begins, unless the officer in charge of the search reasonably believes this would frustrate the object of the search or endanger officers or other people

- not present, copies of the Notice and warrant shall be left in a prominent place on the premises or appropriate part of the premises and endorsed, subject to *paragraph 2.9* with the name of the officer in charge of the search, the date and time of the search

The warrant shall be endorsed to show this has been done.

### (d) Conduct of searches

6.9 Premises may be searched only to the extent necessary to achieve the object of the search, having regard to the size and nature of whatever is sought.

6.9A A search may not continue under:

- a warrant's authority once all the things specified in that warrant have been found

- any other power once the object of that search has been achieved

6.9B No search may continue once the officer in charge of the search is satisfied whatever is being sought is not on the premises. See *Note 6B*. This does not prevent a further search of the same premises if additional grounds come to light supporting a further application for a search warrant or exercise or further exercise of another power. For example, when, as a result of new information, it is believed articles previously not found or additional articles are on the premises.

6.10 Searches must be conducted with due consideration for the property and privacy of the occupier and with no more disturbance than necessary. Reasonable force may be used only when necessary and proportionate because the co-operation of the occupier cannot be obtained or is insufficient for the purpose. See *Note 6C*

6.11 A friend, neighbour or other person must be allowed to witness the search if the occupier wishes unless the officer in charge of the search has reasonable grounds for believing the presence of the person asked for would seriously hinder the investigation or endanger officers or other people. A search need not be unreasonably delayed for this purpose. A record of the action taken should be made on the premises search record including the grounds for refusing the occupier's request.

6.12 A person is not required to be cautioned prior to being asked questions that are solely necessary for the purpose of furthering the proper and effective conduct of a search, see Code C, *paragraph 10.1(c)*. For example, questions to discover the occupier of specified premises, to find a key to open a locked drawer or cupboard or to otherwise seek co-operation during the search or to determine if a particular item is liable to be seized.

6.12A If questioning goes beyond what is necessary for the purpose of the exemption in Code C, the exchange is likely to constitute an interview as defined by Code C, *paragraph 11.1A* and would require the associated safeguards included in Code C, *section 10*.

### (e) Leaving premises

6.13 If premises have been entered by force, before leaving the officer in charge of the search must make sure they are secure by:
- arranging for the occupier or their agent to be present
- any other appropriate means

### (f) Searches under PACE Schedule 1 or the Terrorism Act 2000, Schedule 5

6.14 An officer shall be appointed as the officer in charge of the search, see *paragraph 2.10*, in respect of any search made under a warrant issued under PACE Act 1984, Schedule 1 or the Terrorism Act 2000, Schedule 5. They are responsible for making sure the search is conducted with discretion and in a manner that causes the least possible disruption to any business or other activities carried out on the premises.

6.15 Once the officer in charge of the search is satisfied material may not be taken from the premises without their knowledge, they shall ask for the documents or other records concerned. The officer in charge of the search may also ask to see the index to files held on the premises, and the officers conducting the search may inspect any files which, according to the index, appear to contain the material sought. A more extensive search of the premises may be made only if:
- the person responsible for them refuses to:
  — produce the material sought, or
  — allow access to the index
- it appears the index is:
  — inaccurate, or
  — incomplete
- for any other reason the officer in charge of the search has reasonable grounds for believing such a search is necessary in order to find the material sought

### Notes for guidance

6A *Whether compensation is appropriate depends on the circumstances in each case. Compensation for damage caused when effecting entry is unlikely to be appropriate if the search was lawful, and the force used can be shown to be reasonable, proportionate and necessary to effect entry. If the wrong premises are searched by mistake everything possible should be done at the earliest opportunity to allay any sense of grievance and there should normally be a strong presumption in favour of paying compensation.*

6B *It is important that, when possible, all those involved in a search are fully briefed about any powers to be exercised and the extent and limits within which it should be conducted.*

Code **B**

*6C In all cases the number of officers and other persons involved in executing the warrant should be determined by what is reasonable and necessary according to the particular circumstances.*

## 7 SEIZURE AND RETENTION OF PROPERTY

### (a) Seizure

7.1 Subject to *paragraph 7.2*, an officer who is searching any person or premises under any statutory power or with the consent of the occupier may seize anything:

(a) covered by a warrant

(b) the officer has reasonable grounds for believing is evidence of an offence or has been obtained in consequence of the commission of an offence but only if seizure is necessary to prevent the items being concealed, lost, disposed of, altered, damaged, destroyed or tampered with

(c) covered by the powers in the Criminal Justice and Police Act 2001, Part 2 allowing an officer to seize property from persons or premises and retain it for sifting or examination elsewhere

See *Note 7B*

7.2 No item may be seized which an officer has reasonable grounds for believing to be subject to legal privilege, as defined in PACE, section 10, other than under the Criminal Justice and Police Act 2001, Part 2.

7.3 Officers must be aware of the provisions in the Criminal Justice and Police Act 2001, section 59, allowing for applications to a judicial authority for the return of property seized and the subsequent duty to secure in section 60, see *paragraph 7.12(iii)*.

7.4 An officer may decide it is not appropriate to seize property because of an explanation from the person holding it but may nevertheless have reasonable grounds for believing it was obtained in consequence of an offence by some person. In these circumstances, the officer should identify the property to the holder, inform the holder of their suspicions and explain the holder may be liable to civil or criminal proceedings if they dispose of, alter or destroy the property.

7.5 An officer may arrange to photograph, image or copy, any document or other article they have the power to seize in accordance with *paragraph 7.1*. This is subject to specific restrictions on the examination, imaging or copying of certain property seized under the Criminal Justice and Police Act 2001, Part 2. An officer must have regard to their statutory obligation to retain an original document or other article only when a photograph or copy is not sufficient.

7.6 If an officer considers information stored in any electronic form and accessible from the premises could be used in evidence, they may require the information to be produced in a form:

• which can be taken away and in which it is visible and legible; or

• from which it can readily be produced in a visible and legible form

### (b) Criminal Justice and Police Act 2001: Specific procedures for seize and sift powers

7.7 The Criminal Justice and Police Act 2001, Part 2 gives officers limited powers to seize property from premises or persons so they can sift or examine it elsewhere.

**368**

Officers must be careful they only exercise these powers when it is essential and they do not remove any more material than necessary. The removal of large volumes of material, much of which may not ultimately be retainable, may have serious implications for the owners, particularly when they are involved in business or activities such as journalism or the provision of medical services. Officers must carefully consider if removing copies or images of relevant material or data would be a satisfactory alternative to removing originals. When originals are taken, officers must be prepared to facilitate the provision of copies or images for the owners when reasonably practicable. See *Note 7C*

7.8     Property seized under the Criminal Justice and Police Act 2001, sections 50 or 51 must be kept securely and separately from any material seized under other powers. An examination under section 53 to determine which elements may be retained must be carried out at the earliest practicable time, having due regard to the desirability of allowing the person from whom the property was seized, or a person with an interest in the property, an opportunity of being present or represented at the examination.

**Code B**

7.8A    All reasonable steps should be taken to accommodate an interested person's request to be present, provided the request is reasonable and subject to the need to prevent harm to, interference with, or unreasonable delay to the investigatory process. If an examination proceeds in the absence of an interested person who asked to attend or their representative, the officer who exercised the relevant seizure power must give that person a written notice of why the examination was carried out in those circumstances. If it is necessary for security reasons or to maintain confidentiality officers may exclude interested persons from decryption or other processes which facilitate the examination but do not form part of it. See *Note 7D*

7.9     It is the responsibility of the officer in charge of the investigation to make sure property is returned in accordance with sections 53 to 55. Material which there is no power to retain must be:
  • separated from the rest of the seized property
  • returned as soon as reasonably practicable after examination of all the seized property

7.9A    Delay is only warranted if very clear and compelling reasons exist, e.g. the:
  • unavailability of the person to whom the material is to be returned
  • need to agree a convenient time to return a large volume of material

7.9B    Legally privileged, excluded or special procedure material which cannot be retained must be returned:
  • as soon as reasonably practicable
  • without waiting for the whole examination

7.9C    As set out in section 58, material must be returned to the person from whom it was seized, except when it is clear some other person has a better right to it. See *Note 7E*

7.10    When an officer involved in the investigation has reasonable grounds to believe a person with a relevant interest in property seized under section 50 or 51 intends to make an application under section 59 for the return of any legally privileged, special procedure or excluded material, the officer in charge

**369**

of the investigation should be informed as soon as practicable and the material seized should be kept secure in accordance with section 61. See *Note 7C*

7.11   The officer in charge of the investigation is responsible for making sure property is properly secured. Securing involves making sure the property is not examined, copied, imaged or put to any other use except at the request, or with the consent, of the applicant or in accordance with the directions of the appropriate judicial authority. Any request, consent or directions must be recorded in writing and signed by both the initiator and the officer in charge of the investigation. See *Notes 7F* and *7G*

7.12   When an officer exercises a power of seizure conferred by sections 50 or 51 they shall provide the occupier of the premises or the person from whom the property is being seized with a written notice:

   (i)   specifying what has been seized under the powers conferred by that section;

   (ii)  specifying the grounds for those powers;

   (iii) setting out the effect of sections 59 to 61 covering the grounds for a person with a relevant interest in seized property to apply to a judicial authority for its return and the duty of officers to secure property in certain circumstances when an application is made;

   (iv)  specifying the name and address of the person to whom:

     •  notice of an application to the appropriate judicial authority in respect of any of the seized property must be given;

     •  an application may be made to allow attendance at the initial examination of the property.

7.13   If the occupier is not present but there is someone in charge of the premises, the notice shall be given to them. If no suitable person is available, so the notice will easily be found it should either be:

   •  left in a prominent place on the premises

   •  attached to the exterior of the premises

### (c)  Retention

7.14   Subject to *paragraph 7.15*, anything seized in accordance with the above provisions may be retained only for as long as is necessary. It may be retained, among other purposes:

   (i)   for use as evidence at a trial for an offence;

   (ii)  to facilitate the use in any investigation or proceedings of anything to which it is inextricably linked, see *Note 7H*;

   (iii) for forensic examination or other investigation in connection with an offence;

   (iv)  in order to establish its lawful owner when there are reasonable grounds for believing it has been stolen or obtained by the commission of an offence.

7.15   Property shall not be retained under *paragraph 7.14(i), (ii)* or *(iii)* if a copy or image would be sufficient.

### (d) Rights of owners etc

7.16 If property is retained, the person who had custody or control of it immediately before seizure must, on request, be provided with a list or description of the property within a reasonable time.

7.17 That person or their representative must be allowed supervised access to the property to examine it or have it photographed or copied, or must be provided with a photograph or copy, in either case within a reasonable time of any request and at their own expense, unless the officer in charge of an investigation has reasonable grounds for believing this would:

(i) prejudice the investigation of any offence or criminal proceedings; or

(ii) lead to the commission of an offence by providing access to unlawful material such as pornography;

A record of the grounds shall be made when access is denied.

Code **B**

### Notes for guidance

7A Any person claiming property seized by the police may apply to a magistrates' court under the Police (Property) Act 1897 for its possession and should, if appropriate, be advised of this procedure.

7B The powers of seizure conferred by PACE, sections 18(2) and 19(3) extend to the seizure of the whole premises when it is physically possible to seize and retain the premises in their totality and practical considerations make seizure desirable. For example, police may remove premises such as tents, vehicles or caravans to a police station for the purpose of preserving evidence.

7C Officers should consider reaching agreement with owners and/or other interested parties on the procedures for examining a specific set of property, rather than awaiting the judicial authority's determination. Agreement can sometimes give a quicker and more satisfactory route for all concerned and minimise costs and legal complexities.

7D What constitutes a relevant interest in specific material may depend on the nature of that material and the circumstances in which it is seized. Anyone with a reasonable claim to ownership of the material and anyone entrusted with its safe keeping by the owner should be considered.

7E Requirements to secure and return property apply equally to all copies, images or other material created because of seizure of the original property.

7F The mechanics of securing property vary according to the circumstances; 'bagging up', i.e. placing material in sealed bags or containers and strict subsequent control of access is the appropriate procedure in many cases.

7G When material is seized under the powers of seizure conferred by PACE, the duty to retain it under the Code of Practice issued under the Criminal Procedure and Investigations Act 1996 is subject to the provisions on retention of seized material in PACE, section 22.

7H Paragraph 7.14(ii) applies if inextricably linked material is seized under the Criminal Justice and Police Act 2001, sections 50 or 51. Inextricably linked material is material it is not reasonably practicable to separate from other linked material without prejudicing the use of that other material in any investigation or proceedings. For example, it may not be possible to separate items of data held on computer disk without damaging their evidential integrity. Inextricably linked material must not be examined, imaged, *copied or used for any purpose other than for proving the source and/or integrity of the linked material.*

## 8 ACTION AFTER SEARCHES

8.1 If premises are searched in circumstances where this Code applies, unless the exceptions in *paragraph 2.3(a)* apply, on arrival at a police station the officer in charge of the search shall make or have made a record of the search, to include:
  (i)    the address of the searched premises;
  (ii)   the date, time and duration of the search;
  (iii)  the authority used for the search:
      • if the search was made in exercise of a statutory power to search premises without warrant, the power which was used for the search:
      • if the search was made under a warrant or with written consent;
          —  a copy of the warrant and the written authority to apply for it, see paragraph 3.4; or
          —  the written consent;
              shall be appended to the record or the record shall show the location of the copy warrant or consent.
  (iv)   subject to *paragraph 2.9*, the names of:
      • the officer(s) in charge of the search;
      • all other officers and any authorised persons who conducted the search;
  (v)    the names of any people on the premises if they are known;
  (vi)   any grounds for refusing the occupier's request to have someone present during the search, see *paragraph 6.11*;
  (vii)  a list of any articles seized or the location of a list and, if not covered by a warrant, the grounds for their seizure;
  (viii) whether force was used, and the reason;
  (ix)   details of any damage caused during the search, and the circumstances;
  (x)    if applicable, the reason it was not practicable:
      (a) to give the occupier a copy of the Notice of Powers and Rights, see *paragraph 6.7*;
      (b) before the search to give the occupier a copy of the Notice, see *paragraph 6.8*;
  (xi)   when the occupier was not present, the place where copies of the Notice of Powers and Rights and search warrant were left on the premises, see *paragraph 6.8*.
8.2 On each occasion when premises are searched under warrant, the warrant authorising the search on that occasion shall be endorsed to show:
  (i)    if any articles specified in the warrant were found and the address where found;
  (ii)   if any other articles were seized;

(iii) the date and time it was executed and if present, the name of the occupier or if the occupier is not present the name of the person in charge of the premises;

(iv) subject to paragraph 2.9, the names of the officers who executed it and any authorised persons who accompanied them;

(v) if a copy, together with a copy of the Notice of Powers and Rights was:
  - handed to the occupier; or
  - endorsed as required by paragraph 6.8; and left on the premises and where.

8.3 Any warrant shall be returned within three calendar months of its issue or sooner on completion of the search(es) authorised by that warrant, if it was issued by a:
  - justice of the peace, to the designated officer for the local justice area in which the justice was acting when issuing the warrant; or
  - judge, to the appropriate officer of the court concerned,

Code **B**

## 9 SEARCH REGISTERS

9.1 A search register will be maintained at each sub-divisional or equivalent police station. All search records required under *paragraph 8.1* shall be made, copied, or referred to in the register. See *Note 9A*

### Note for guidance

9A *Paragraph 9.1 also applies to search records made by immigration officers. In these cases, a search register must also be maintained at an immigration office. See also* Note 2D

# Appendix 4

## Code C: PACE Code of Practice for the Detention, Treatment and Questioning of Persons by Police Officers

This Code applies to people in police detention after midnight on 31 January 2008, notwithstanding that their period of detention may have commenced before that time.

### 1 GENERAL

1.1   All persons in custody must be dealt with expeditiously, and released as soon as the need for detention no longer applies.

1.1A  A custody officer must perform the functions in this Code as soon as practicable. A custody officer will not be in breach of this Code if delay is justifiable and reasonable steps are taken to prevent unnecessary delay. The custody record shall show when a delay has occurred and the reason. See *Note 1H*

1.2   This Code of Practice must be readily available at all police stations for consultation by:
- police officers
- police staff
- detained persons
- members of the public.

1.3   The provisions of this Code:
- include the *Annexes*
- do not include the *Notes for guidance.*

1.4   If an officer has any suspicion, or is told in good faith, that a person of any age may be mentally disordered or otherwise mentally vulnerable, in the absence of clear evidence to dispel that suspicion, the person shall be treated as such for the purposes of this Code. See *Note 1G*

1.5   If anyone appears to be under 17, they shall be treated as a juvenile for the purposes of this Code in the absence of clear evidence that they are older.

1.6   If a person appears to be blind, seriously visually impaired, deaf, unable to read or speak or has difficulty orally because of a speech impediment, they shall be treated as such for the purposes of this Code in the absence of clear evidence to the contrary.

1.7   'The appropriate adult' means, in the case of a:
    (a) juvenile:
        (i)  the parent, guardian or, if the juvenile is in local authority or voluntary organisation care, or is otherwise being looked after under

          the Children Act 1989, a person representing that authority or organisation;

          (ii)  a social worker of a local authority;

          (iii) failing these, some other responsible adult aged 18 or over who is not a police officer or employed by the police.

    (b)  person who is mentally disordered or mentally vulnerable: See Note 1D

          (iv) a relative, guardian or other person responsible for their care or custody;

          (v)  someone experienced in dealing with mentally disordered or mentally vulnerable people but who is not a police officer or employed by the police;

          (vi) failing these, some other responsible adult aged 18 or over who is not a police officer or employed by the police.

1.8    If this Code requires a person be given certain information, they do not have to be given it if at the time they are incapable of understanding what is said, are violent or may become violent or in urgent need of medical attention, but they must be given it as soon as practicable.

1.9    References to a custody officer include any:

- police officer; or
- designated staff custody officer acting in the exercise or performance of the powers and duties conferred or imposed on them by their designation, performing the functions of a custody officer. See *Note 1J*

1.9A  When this Code requires the prior authority or agreement of an officer of at least inspector or superintendent rank, that authority may be given by a sergeant or chief inspector authorised to perform the functions of the higher rank under the Police and Criminal Evidence Act 1984 (PACE), section 107.

1.10  Subject to *paragraph 1.12*, this Code applies to people in custody at police stations in England and Wales, whether or not they have been arrested, and to those removed to a police station as a place of safety under the Mental Health Act 1983, sections 135 and 136. *Section 15* applies solely to people in police detention, e.g. those brought to a police station under arrest or arrested at a police station for an offence after going there voluntarily.

1.11  People detained under the Terrorism Act 2000, Schedule 8 and section 41 and other provisions of that Act are not subject to any part of this Code. Such persons are subject to the Code of Practice for detention, treatment and questioning of persons by police officers detained under that Act.

1.12  This Code's provisions do not apply to people in custody:

    (i)   arrested on warrants issued in Scotland by officers under the Criminal Justice and Public Order Act 1994, section 136(2), or arrested or detained without warrant by officers from a police force in Scotland under section 137(2). In these cases, police powers and duties and the person's rights and entitlements whilst at a police station in England or Wales are the same as those in Scotland;

    (ii)  arrested under the Immigration and Asylum Act 1999, section 142(3) in order to have their fingerprints taken;

    (iii) whose detention is authorised by an immigration officer under the Immigration Act 1971;

(iv) who are convicted or remanded prisoners held in police cells on behalf of the Prison Service under the Imprisonment (Temporary Provisions) Act 1980;

(v) not used;

(vi) detained for searches under stop and search powers except as required by Code A.

The provisions on conditions of detention and treatment in *sections 8* and 9 must be considered as the minimum standards of treatment for such detainees.

1.13 In this Code:

(a) 'designated person' means a person other than a police officer, designated under the Police Reform Act 2002, Part 4 who has specified powers and duties of police officers conferred or imposed on them;

(b) reference to a police officer includes a designated person acting in the exercise or performance of the powers and duties conferred or imposed on them by their designation.

1.14 Designated persons are entitled to use reasonable force as follows:-

(a) when exercising a power conferred on them which allows a police officer exercising that power to use reasonable force, a designated person has the same entitlement to use force; and

(b) at other times when carrying out duties conferred or imposed on them that also entitle them to use reasonable force, for example:

- when at a police station carrying out the duty to keep detainees for whom they are responsible under control and to assist any other police officer or designated person to keep any detainee under control and to prevent their escape.
- when securing, or assisting any other police officer or designated person in securing, the detention of a person at a police station.
- when escorting, or assisting any other police officer or designated person in escorting, a detainee within a police station.
- for the purpose of saving life or limb; or
- preventing serious damage to property.

1.15 Nothing in this Code prevents the custody officer, or other officer given custody of the detainee, from allowing police staff who are not designated persons to carry out individual procedures or tasks at the police station if the law allows. However, the officer remains responsible for making sure the procedures and tasks are carried out correctly in accordance with the Codes of Practice. Any such person must be:

(a) a person employed by a police authority maintaining a police force and under the control and direction of the Chief officer of that force;

(b) employed by a person with whom a police authority has a contract for the provision of services relating to persons arrested or otherwise in custody.

1.16 Designated persons and other police staff must have regard to any relevant provisions of the Codes of Practice.

1.17 References to pocket books include any official report book issued to police officers or other police staff.

Code **C**

## Notes for guidance

1A *Although certain sections of this Code apply specifically to people in custody at police stations, those there voluntarily to assist with an investigation should be treated with no less consideration, e.g. offered refreshments at appropriate times, and enjoy an absolute right to obtain legal advice or communicate with anyone outside the police station.*

1B *A person, including a parent or guardian, should not be an appropriate adult if they:*
   - *are*
     - *suspected of involvement in the offence*
     - *the victim*
     - *a witness*
     - *involved in the investigation*
   - received admissions prior to attending to act as the appropriate adult.

   *Note: If a juvenile's parent is estranged from the juvenile, they should not be asked to act as the appropriate adult if the juvenile expressly and specifically objects to their presence.*

1C *If a juvenile admits an offence to, or in the presence of, a social worker or member of a youth offending team other than during the time that person is acting as the juvenile's appropriate adult, another appropriate adult should be appointed in the interest of fairness.*

1D *In the case of people who are mentally disordered or otherwise mentally vulnerable, it may be more satisfactory if the appropriate adult is someone experienced or trained in their care rather than a relative lacking such qualifications. But if the detainee prefers a relative to a better qualified stranger or objects to a particular person their wishes should, if practicable, be respected.*

1E *A detainee should always be given an opportunity, when an appropriate adult is called to the police station, to consult privately with a solicitor in the appropriate adult's absence if they want. An appropriate adult is not subject to legal privilege.*

1F *A solicitor or independent custody visitor (formerly a lay visitor) present at the police station in that capacity may not be the appropriate adult.*

1G *'Mentally vulnerable' applies to any detainee who, because of their mental state or capacity, may not understand the significance of what is said, of questions or of their replies. 'Mental disorder' is defined in the Mental Health Act 1983, section 1(2) as 'mental illness, arrested or incomplete development of mind, psychopathic disorder and any other disorder or disability of mind'. When the custody officer has any doubt about the mental state or capacity of a detainee, that detainee should be treated as mentally vulnerable and an appropriate adult called.*

1H *Paragraph 1.1A is intended to cover delays which may occur in processing detainees e.g. if:*
   - a large number of suspects are brought into the station simultaneously to be placed in custody;
   - interview rooms are all being used;
   - there are difficulties contacting an appropriate adult, solicitor or interpreter.

1I *The custody officer must remind the appropriate adult and detainee about the right to legal advice and record any reasons for waiving it in accordance with section 6.*

1J *The designation of police staff custody officers applies only in police areas where an order commencing the provisions of the Police Reform Act 2002, section 38 and Schedule 4A, for designating police staff custody officers is in effect.*

1K *This Code does not affect the principle that all citizens have a duty to help police officers to prevent crime and discover offenders. This is a civic rather than a legal duty; but when a police officer is trying to discover whether, or by whom, an offence has been committed he is entitled to question any person from whom he thinks useful information can be obtained, subject to the restrictions imposed by this Code. A person's declaration that he is unwilling to reply does not alter this entitlement.*

## 2 CUSTODY RECORDS

2.1A When a person is brought to a police station:
- under arrest;
- is arrested at the police station having attended there voluntarily; or
- attends a police station to answer bail.

they should be brought before the custody officer as soon as practicable after their arrival at the station or, if appropriate, following arrest after attending the police station voluntarily. This applies to designated and non-designated police stations. A person is deemed to be "at a police station" for these purposes if they are within the boundary of any building or enclosed yard which forms part of that police station.

2.1 A separate custody record must be opened as soon as practicable for each person brought to a police station under arrest or arrested at the station having gone there voluntarily or attending a police station in answer to street bail. All information recorded under this Code must be recorded as soon as practicable in the custody record unless otherwise specified. Any audio or video recording made in the custody area is not part of the custody record.

2.2 If any action requires the authority of an officer of a specified rank, subject to *paragraph 2.6A*, their name and rank must be noted in the custody record.

2.3 The custody officer is responsible for the custody record's accuracy and completeness and for making sure the record or copy of the record accompanies a detainee if they are transferred to another police station. The record shall show the:
- time and reason for transfer;
- time a person is released from detention.

2.4 A solicitor or appropriate adult must be permitted to consult a detainee's custody record as soon as practicable after their arrival at the station and at any other time whilst the person is detained. Arrangements for this access must be agreed with the custody officer and may not unreasonably interfere with the custody officer's duties.

2.4A When a detainee leaves police detention or is taken before a court they, their legal representative or appropriate adult shall be given, on request, a copy of the custody record as soon as practicable. This entitlement lasts for 12 months after release.

2.5 The detainee, appropriate adult or legal representative shall be permitted to inspect the original custody record after the detainee has left police detention provided they give reasonable notice of their request. Any such inspection shall be noted in the custody record.

2.6 Subject to *paragraph 2.6A*, all entries in custody records must be timed and signed by the maker. Records entered on computer shall be timed and contain the operator's identification.

Code C

2.6A   Nothing in this Code requires the identity of officers or other police staff to be recorded or disclosed:

      (a)  not used;

      (b)  if the officer or police staff reasonably believe recording or disclosing their name might put them in danger.

      In these cases, they shall use their warrant or other identification numbers and the name of their police station. See *Note 2A*

2.7     The fact and time of any detainee's refusal to sign a custody record, when asked in accordance with this Code, must be recorded.

### Note for guidance

2A     *The purpose of paragraph 2.6A(b) is to protect those involved in serious organised crime investigations or arrests of particularly violent suspects when there is reliable information that those arrested or their associates may threaten or cause harm to those involved. In cases of doubt, an officer of inspector rank or above should be consulted.*

## 3 INITIAL ACTION

### (a) Detained persons—normal procedure

3.1     When a person is brought to a police station under arrest or arrested at the station having gone there voluntarily, the custody officer must make sure the person is told clearly about the following continuing rights which may be exercised at any stage during the period in custody:

      (i)   the right to have someone informed of their arrest as in *section 5*;

      (ii)  the right to consult privately with a solicitor and that free independent legal advice is available;

      (iii) the right to consult these Codes of Practice. See *Note 3D*

3.2     The detainee must also be given:

      • a written notice setting out:

        — the above three rights;

        — the arrangements for obtaining legal advice;

        — the right to a copy of the custody record as in *paragraph 2.4A*;

        — the caution in the terms prescribed in *section 10*.

      • an additional written notice briefly setting out their entitlements while in custody, see *Notes 3A* and *3B*.

     Note: The detainee shall be asked to sign the custody record to acknowledge receipt of these notices. Any refusal must be recorded on the custody record.

3.3     A citizen of an independent Commonwealth country or a national of a foreign country, including the Republic of Ireland, must be informed as soon as practicable about their rights of communication with their High Commission, Embassy or Consulate. See *section 7*

3.4     The custody officer shall:

      • record the offence(s) that the detainee has been arrested for and the reason(s) for the arrest on the custody record. See *paragraph 10.3* and *Code G paragraphs 2.2* and *4.3*.

- note on the custody record any comment the detainee makes in relation to the arresting officer's account but shall not invite comment. If the arresting officer is not physically present when the detainee is brought to a police station, the arresting officer's account must be made available to the custody officer remotely or by a third party on the arresting officer's behalf. If the custody officer authorises a person's detention the detainee must be informed of the grounds as soon as practicable and before they are questioned about any offence;
- note any comment the detainee makes in respect of the decision to detain them but shall not invite comment;
- not put specific questions to the detainee regarding their involvement in any offence, nor in respect of any comments they may make in response to the arresting officer's account or the decision to place them in detention. Such an exchange is likely to constitute an interview as in *paragraph 11.1A* and require the associated safeguards in *section 11*.

See *paragraph 11.13* in respect of unsolicited comments.

3.5 The custody officer shall:
  (a) ask the detainee, whether at this time, they:
      (i)   would like legal advice, see *paragraph 6.5*;
      (ii)  want someone informed of their detention, see *section 5*;
  (b) ask the detainee to sign the custody record to confirm their decisions in respect of (a);
  (c) determine whether the detainee:
      (iii) is, or might be, in need of medical treatment or attention, see *section 9*;
      (iv)  requires:
          - an appropriate adult;
          - help to check documentation;
          - an interpreter;
  (d) record the decision in respect of (c).

3.6 When determining these needs the custody officer is responsible for initiating an assessment to consider whether the detainee is likely to present specific risks to custody staff or themselves. Such assessments should always include a check on the Police National Computer, to be carried out as soon as practicable, to identify any risks highlighted in relation to the detainee. Although such assessments are primarily the custody officer's responsibility, it may be necessary for them to consult and involve others, e.g. the arresting officer or an appropriate health care professional, see *paragraph 9.13*. Reasons for delaying the initiation or completion of the assessment must be recorded.

3.7 Chief officers should ensure that arrangements for proper and effective risk assessments required by *paragraph 3.6* are implemented in respect of all detainees at police stations in their area.

3.8 Risk assessments must follow a structured process which clearly defines the categories of risk to be considered and the results must be incorporated in the detainee's custody record. The custody officer is responsible for making sure those responsible for the detainee's custody are appropriately briefed about the risks. If no specific risks are identified by the assessment, that should be noted in the custody record. See *Note 3E* and *paragraph 9.14*

Code **C**

3.9 The custody officer is responsible for implementing the response to any specific risk assessment, e.g.:
   • reducing opportunities for self harm;
   • calling a health care professional;
   • increasing levels of monitoring or observation.

3.10 Risk assessment is an ongoing process and assessments must always be subject to review if circumstances change.

3.11 If video cameras are installed in the custody area, notices shall be prominently displayed showing cameras are in use. Any request to have video cameras switched off shall be refused.

### (b) Detained persons—special groups

3.12 If the detainee appears deaf or there is doubt about their hearing or speaking ability or ability to understand English, and the custody officer cannot establish effective communication, the custody officer must, as soon as practicable, call an interpreter for assistance in the action under *paragraphs 3.1–3.5*. See *section 13*

3.13 If the detainee is a juvenile, the custody officer must, if it is practicable, ascertain the identity of a person responsible for their welfare. That person:
   • may be:
      — the parent or guardian;
      — if the juvenile is in local authority or voluntary organisation care, or is otherwise being looked after under the Children Act 1989, a person appointed by that authority or organisation to have responsibility for the juvenile's welfare;
      — any other person who has, for the time being, assumed responsibility for the juvenile's welfare.
   • must be informed as soon as practicable that the juvenile has been arrested, why they have been arrested and where they are detained. This right is in addition to the juvenile's right in *section 5* not to be held incommunicado. See *Note 3C*

3.14 If a juvenile is known to be subject to a court order under which a person or organisation is given any degree of statutory responsibility to supervise or otherwise monitor them, reasonable steps must also be taken to notify that person or organisation (the 'responsible officer'). The responsible officer will normally be a member of a Youth Offending Team, except for a curfew order which involves electronic monitoring when the contractor providing the monitoring will normally be the responsible officer.

3.15 If the detainee is a juvenile, mentally disordered or otherwise mentally vulnerable, the custody officer must, as soon as practicable:
   • inform the appropriate adult, who in the case of a juvenile may or may not be a person responsible for their welfare, as in *paragraph 3.13*, of:
      — the grounds for their detention;
      — their whereabouts.
   • ask the adult to come to the police station to see the detainee.

3.16 It is imperative that a mentally disordered or otherwise mentally vulnerable person, detained under the Mental Health Act 1983, section 136, be assessed as soon as possible. If that assessment is to take place at the police station, an approved social worker and a registered medical practitioner shall be called to the station as soon as possible in order to interview and examine the detainee. Once the detainee has been interviewed, examined and suitable arrangements made for their treatment or care, they can no longer be detained under section 136. A detainee must be immediately discharged from detention under section 136 if a registered medical practitioner, having examined them, concludes they are not mentally disordered within the meaning of the Act.

3.17  If the appropriate adult is:
- already at the police station, the provisions of *paragraphs 3.1* to *3.5* must be complied with in the appropriate adult's presence;
- not at the station when these provisions are complied with, they must be complied with again in the presence of the appropriate adult when they arrive.

3.18  The detainee shall be advised that:
- the duties of the appropriate adult include giving advice and assistance;
- they can consult privately with the appropriate adult at any time.

3.19  If the detainee, or appropriate adult on the detainee's behalf, asks for a solicitor to be called to give legal advice, the provisions of *section 6* apply.

3.20  If the detainee is blind, seriously visually impaired or unable to read, the custody officer shall make sure their solicitor, relative, appropriate adult or some other person likely to take an interest in them and not involved in the investigation is available to help check any documentation. When this Code requires written consent or signing the person assisting may be asked to sign instead, if the detainee prefers. This paragraph does not require an appropriate adult to be called solely to assist in checking and signing documentation for a person who is not a juvenile, or mentally disordered or otherwise mentally vulnerable (see *paragraph 3.15*).

## (c)  Persons attending a police station voluntarily

3.21  Anybody attending a police station voluntarily to assist with an investigation may leave at will unless arrested. See *Note 1K*. If it is decided they shall not be allowed to leave, they must be informed at once that they are under arrest and brought before the custody officer, who is responsible for making sure they are notified of their rights in the same way as other detainees. If they are not arrested but are cautioned as in *section 10*, the person who gives the caution must, at the same time, inform them they are not under arrest, they are not obliged to remain at the station but if they remain at the station they may obtain free and independent legal advice if they want. They shall be told the right to legal advice includes the right to speak with a solicitor on the telephone and be asked if they want to do so.

3.22  If a person attending the police station voluntarily asks about their entitlement to legal advice, they shall be given a copy of the notice explaining the arrangements for obtaining legal advice. See *paragraph 3.2*

## (d)  Documentation

3.23  The grounds for a person's detention shall be recorded, in the person's presence if practicable.

3.24  Action taken under *paragraphs 3.12* to *3.20* shall be recorded.

Code **C**

### (e) Persons answering street bail

3.25 When a person is answering street bail, the custody officer should link any documentation held in relation to arrest with the custody record. Any further action shall be recorded on the custody record in accordance with paragraphs 3.23 and 3.24 above.

### Notes for guidance

3A    *The notice of entitlements should:*
- *list the entitlements in this Code, including:*
  - *—visits and contact with outside parties, including special provisions for Commonwealth citizens and foreign nationals;*
  - *—reasonable standards of physical comfort;*
  - *—adequate food and drink;*
  - *—access to toilets and washing facilities, clothing, medical attention, and exercise when practicable.*
- *mention the:*
  - *—provisions relating to the conduct of interviews;*
  - *—circumstances in which an appropriate adult should be available to assist the detainee and their statutory rights to make representation whenever the period of their detention is reviewed.*

3B    *In addition to notices in English, translations should be available in Welsh, the main minority ethnic languages and the principal European languages, whenever they are likely to be helpful. Audio versions of the notice should also be made available.*

3C    *If the juvenile is in local authority or voluntary organisation care but living with their parents or other adults responsible for their welfare, although there is no legal obligation to inform them, they should normally be contacted, as well as the authority or organisation unless suspected of involvement in the offence concerned. Even if the juvenile is not living with their parents, consideration should be given to informing them.*

3D    *The right to consult the Codes of Practice does not entitle the person concerned to delay unreasonably any necessary investigative or administrative action whilst they do so. Examples of action which need not be delayed unreasonably include:*
- *procedures requiring the provision of breath, blood or urine specimens under the Road Traffic Act 1988 or the Transport and Works Act 1992;*
- *searching detainees at the police station;*
- *taking fingerprints, footwear impressions or non-intimate samples without consent for evidential purposes.*

3E    *Home Office Circular 32/2000 provides more detailed guidance on risk assessments and identifies key risk areas which should always be considered.*

## 4 Detainee's Property

### (a) Action

4.1    The custody officer is responsible for:
- (a) ascertaining what property a detainee:
  - (i) has with them when they come to the police station, whether on:
    - arrest or re-detention on answering to bail;

- commitment to prison custody on the order or sentence of a court;
- lodgement at the police station with a view to their production in court from prison custody;
- transfer from detention at another station or hospital;
- detention under the Mental Health Act 1983, section 135 or 136;
- remand into police custody on the authority of a court.

   (ii)  might have acquired for an unlawful or harmful purpose while in custody;

(b)  the safekeeping of any property taken from a detainee which remains at the police station.

The custody officer may search the detainee or authorise their being searched to the extent they consider necessary, provided a search of intimate parts of the body or involving the removal of more than outer clothing is only made as in *Annex A*. A search may only be carried out by an officer of the same sex as the detainee. See *Note 4A*

Code **C**

4.2  Detainees may retain clothing and personal effects at their own risk unless the custody officer considers they may use them to cause harm to themselves or others, interfere with evidence, damage property, effect an escape or they are needed as evidence. In this event the custody officer may withhold such articles as they consider necessary and must tell the detainee why.

4.3  Personal effects are those items a detainee may lawfully need, use or refer to while in detention but do not include cash and other items of value.

## (b) Documentation

4.4  It is a matter for the custody officer to determine whether a record should be made of the property a detained person has with him or had taken from him on arrest. Any record made is not required to be kept as part of the custody record but the custody record should be noted as to where such a record exists. Whenever a record is made the detainee shall be allowed to check and sign the record of property as correct. Any refusal to sign shall be recorded.

4.5  If a detainee is not allowed to keep any article of clothing or personal effects, the reason must be recorded.

### Notes for guidance

*4A  PACE, Section 54(1) and paragraph 4.1 require a detainee to be searched when it is clear the custody officer will have continuing duties in relation to that detainee or when that detainee's behaviour or offence makes an inventory appropriate. They do not require every detainee to be searched, e.g. if it is clear a person will only be detained for a short period and is not to be placed in a cell, the custody officer may decide not to search them. In such a case the custody record will be endorsed 'not searched', paragraph 4.4 will not apply, and the detainee will be invited to sign the entry. If the detainee refuses, the custody officer will be obliged to ascertain what property they have in accordance with paragraph 4.1.*

*4B  Paragraph 4.4 does not require the custody officer to record on the custody record property in the detainee's possession on arrest if, by virtue of its nature, quantity or size, it is not practicable to remove it to the police station.*

*4C  Paragraph 4.4 does not require items of clothing worn by the person be recorded unless withheld by the custody officer as in paragraph 4.2.*

**385**

## 5 Right not to be Held Incommunicado

### (a) Action

5.1 Any person arrested and held in custody at a police station or other premises may, on request, have one person known to them or likely to take an interest in their welfare informed at public expense of their whereabouts as soon as practicable. If the person cannot be contacted the detainee may choose up to two alternatives. If they cannot be contacted, the person in charge of detention or the investigation has discretion to allow further attempts until the information has been conveyed. See *Notes 5C* and *5D*

5.2 The exercise of the above right in respect of each person nominated may be delayed only in accordance with *Annex B*.

5.3 The above right may be exercised each time a detainee is taken to another police station.

5.4 The detainee may receive visits at the custody officer's discretion. See *Note 5B*

5.5 If a friend, relative or person with an interest in the detainee's welfare enquires about their whereabouts, this information shall be given if the suspect agrees and *Annex B* does not apply. See *Note 5D*

5.6 The detainee shall be given writing materials, on request, and allowed to telephone one person for a reasonable time, see *Notes 5A* and *5E*. Either or both these privileges may be denied or delayed if an officer of inspector rank or above considers sending a letter or making a telephone call may result in any of the consequences in:

    (a) *Annex B paragraphs 1* and *2* and the person is detained in connection with an indictable offence; or

    (b) Not used.

Nothing in this paragraph permits the restriction or denial of the rights in *paragraphs 5.1* and *6.1*.

5.7 Before any letter or message is sent, or telephone call made, the detainee shall be informed that what they say in any letter, call or message (other than in a communication to a solicitor) may be read or listened to and may be given in evidence. A telephone call may be terminated if it is being abused. The costs can be at public expense at the custody officer's discretion.

5.7A Any delay or denial of the rights in this section should be proportionate and should last no longer than necessary.

### (b) Documentation

5.8 A record must be kept of any:

    (a) request made under this section and the action taken;

    (b) letters, messages or telephone calls made or received or visit received;

    (c) refusal by the detainee to have information about them given to an outside enquirer. The detainee must be asked to countersign the record accordingly and any refusal recorded.

### Notes for guidance

*5A   A person may request an interpreter to interpret a telephone call or translate a letter.*

*5B   At the custody officer's discretion, visits should be allowed when possible, subject to having sufficient personnel to supervise a visit and any possible hindrance to the investigation.*

5C   If the detainee does not know anyone to contact for advice or support or cannot con-
     tact a friend or relative, the custody officer should bear in mind any local voluntary
     bodies or other organisations who might be able to help. Paragraph 6.1 applies if legal
     advice is required.

5D   In some circumstances it may not be appropriate to use the telephone to disclose infor-
     mation under paragraphs 5.1 and 5.5.

5E   The telephone call at paragraph 5.6 is in addition to any communication under para-
     graphs 5.1 and 6.1.

## 6  RIGHT TO LEGAL ADVICE

**(a) Action**

6.1   Unless *Annex B* applies, all detainees must be informed that they may at any
      time consult and communicate privately with a solicitor, whether in person, in
      writing or by telephone, and that free independent legal advice is available
      from the duty solicitor. See *paragraph 3.1, Notes 6B, 6B1, 6B2* and *Note 6J*

6.2   Not Used.

6.3   A poster advertising the right to legal advice must be prominently displayed in
      the charging area of every police station. See *Note 6H*

6.4   No police officer should, at any time, do or say anything with the intention of
      dissuading a detainee from obtaining legal advice.

6.5   The exercise of the right of access to legal advice may be delayed only as in
      *Annex B*. Whenever legal advice is requested, and unless *Annex B* applies, the
      custody officer must act without delay to secure the provision of such advice.
      If, on being informed or reminded of this right, the detainee declines to speak
      to a solicitor in person, the officer should point out that the right includes the
      right to speak with a solicitor on the telephone. If the detainee continues to
      waive this right the officer should ask them why and any reasons should be
      recorded on the custody record or the interview record as appropriate.
      Reminders of the right to legal advice must be given as in *paragraphs 3.5, 11.2,
      15.4, 16.4, 2B of Annex A, 3 of Annex K* and *16.5* and Code D, *paragraphs 3.17(ii)*
      and *6.3*. Once it is clear a detainee does not want to speak to a solicitor in
      person or by telephone they should cease to be asked their reasons. See *Note 6K*

6.5A  In the case of a juvenile, an appropriate adult should consider whether legal advice
      from a solicitor is required. If the juvenile indicates that they do not want legal
      advice, the appropriate adult has the right to ask for a solicitor to attend if this
      would be in the best interests of the person. However, the detained person cannot
      be forced to see the solicitor if he is adamant that he does not wish to do so.

6.6   A detainee who wants legal advice may not be interviewed or continue to be
      interviewed until they have received such advice unless:

      (a) *Annex B* applies, when the restriction on drawing adverse inferences from
          silence in *Annex C* will apply because the detainee is not allowed an oppor-
          tunity to consult a solicitor; or

      (b) an officer of superintendent rank or above has reasonable grounds for
          believing that:

          (i)  the consequent delay might:
               • lead to interference with, or harm to, evidence connected with an
                 offence;

Code **C**

**387**

- lead to interference with, or physical harm to, other people;
- lead to serious loss of, or damage to, property;
- lead to alerting other people suspected of having committed an offence but not yet arrested for it;
- hinder the recovery of property obtained in consequence of the commission of an offence.

(ii) when a solicitor, including a duty solicitor, has been contacted and has agreed to attend, awaiting their arrival would cause unreasonable delay to the process of investigation.

Note: In these cases the restriction on drawing adverse inferences from silence in *Annex C* will apply because the detainee is not allowed an opportunity to consult a solicitor;

(c) the solicitor the detainee has nominated or selected from a list:

    (i) cannot be contacted;

    (ii) has previously indicated they do not wish to be contacted; or

    (iii) having been contacted, has declined to attend; and

the detainee has been advised of the Duty Solicitor Scheme but has declined to ask for the duty solicitor.

In these circumstances the interview may be started or continued without further delay provided an officer of inspector rank or above has agreed to the interview proceeding.

Note: The restriction on drawing adverse inferences from silence in Annex C will not apply because the detainee is allowed an opportunity to consult the duty solicitor;

(d) the detainee changes their mind, about wanting legal advice.

In these circumstances the interview may be started or continued without delay provided that:

    (i) the detainee agrees to do so, in writing or on the interview record made in accordance with Code E or F; and

    (ii) an officer of inspector rank or above has inquired about the detainee's reasons for their change of mind and gives authority for the interview to proceed.

Confirmation of the detainee's agreement, their change of mind, the reasons for it if given and, subject to *paragraph 2.6A*, the name of the authorising officer shall be recorded in the written interview record or the interview record made in accordance with Code E or F. See *Note 6I*.

Note: In these circumstances the restriction on drawing adverse inferences from silence in *Annex C* will not apply because the detainee is allowed an opportunity to consult a solicitor if they wish.

6.7 If *paragraph 6.6(b)(i)* applies, once sufficient information has been obtained to avert the risk, questioning must cease until the detainee has received legal advice unless *paragraph 6.6(a), (b)(ii), (c)* or *(d)* applies.

6.8 A detainee who has been permitted to consult a solicitor shall be entitled on request to have the solicitor present when they are interviewed unless one of the exceptions in *paragraph 6.6* applies.

Note: In these circumstances the restriction on drawing adverse inferences from silence in *paragraph 6.6* applies.

6.9    The solicitor may only be required to leave the interview if their conduct is such that the interviewer is unable properly to put questions to the suspect. See *Notes 6D and 6E*

6.10   If the interviewer considers a solicitor is acting in such a way, they will stop the interview and consult an officer not below superintendent rank, if one is readily available, and otherwise an officer not below inspector rank not connected with the investigation. After speaking to the solicitor, the officer consulted will decide if the interview should continue in the presence of that solicitor. If they decide it should not, the suspect will be given the opportunity to consult another solicitor before the interview continues and that solicitor given an opportunity to be present at the interview. See *Note 6E*

6.11   The removal of a solicitor from an interview is a serious step and, if it occurs, the officer of superintendent rank or above who took the decision will consider if the incident should be reported to the Law Society. If the decision to remove the solicitor has been taken by an officer below superintendent rank, the facts must be reported to an officer of superintendent rank or above who will similarly consider whether a report to the Law Society would be appropriate. When the solicitor concerned is a duty solicitor, the report should be both to the Law Society and to the Legal Services Commission.

Code **C**

6.12   'Solicitor' in this Code means:
       • a solicitor who holds a current practising certificate;
       • an accredited or probationary representative included on the register of representatives maintained by the Legal Services Commission.

6.12A  An accredited or probationary representative sent to provide advice by, and on behalf of, a solicitor shall be admitted to the police station for this purpose unless an officer of inspector rank or above considers such a visit will hinder the investigation and directs otherwise. Hindering the investigation does not include giving proper legal advice to a detainee as in *Note 6D*. Once admitted to the police station, *paragraphs 6.6 to 6.10* apply.

6.13   In exercising their discretion under *paragraph 6.12A*, the officer should take into account in particular:
       • whether:
         — the identity and status of an accredited or probationary representative have been satisfactorily established;
         — they are of suitable character to provide legal advice, e.g. a person with a criminal record is unlikely to be suitable unless the conviction was for a minor offence and not recent.
       • any other matters in any written letter of authorisation provided by the solicitor on whose behalf the person is attending the police station. See *Note 6F*

6.14   If the inspector refuses access to an accredited or probationary representative or a decision is taken that such a person should not be permitted to remain at an interview, the inspector must notify the solicitor on whose behalf the representative was acting and give them an opportunity to make alternative arrangements. The detainee must be informed and the custody record noted.

6.15 If a solicitor arrives at the station to see a particular person, that person must, unless *Annex B* applies, be so informed whether or not they are being interviewed and asked if they would like to see the solicitor. This applies even if the detainee has declined legal advice or, having requested it, subsequently agreed to be interviewed without receiving advice. The solicitor's attendance and the detainee's decision must be noted in the custody record.

## (b) Documentation

6.16 Any request for legal advice and the action taken shall be recorded.

6.17 A record shall be made in the interview record if a detainee asks for legal advice and an interview is begun either in the absence of a solicitor or their representative, or they have been required to leave an interview.

### Notes for guidance

6A   *In considering if paragraph 6.6(b) applies, the officer should, if practicable, ask the solicitor for an estimate of how long it will take to come to the station and relate this to the time detention is permitted, the time of day (i.e. whether the rest period under paragraph 12.2 is imminent) and the requirements of other investigations. If the solicitor is on their way or is to set off immediately, it will not normally be appropriate to begin an interview before they arrive. If it appears necessary to begin an interview before the solicitor's arrival, they should be given an indication of how long the police would be able to wait before 6.6(b) applies so there is an opportunity to make arrangements for someone else to provide legal advice.*

6B   *A detainee who asks for legal advice should be given an opportunity to consult a specific solicitor or another solicitor from that solicitor's firm or the duty solicitor. If advice is not available by these means, or they do not want to consult the duty solicitor, the detainee should be given an opportunity to choose a solicitor from a list of those willing to provide legal advice. If this solicitor is unavailable, they may choose up to two alternatives. If these attempts are unsuccessful, the custody officer has discretion to allow further attempts until a solicitor has been contacted and agrees to provide legal advice. Apart from carrying out these duties, an officer must not advise the suspect about any particular firm of solicitors. See Notes for Guidance 6B1 and 6B2 below.*

6B1  *With effect from 1 February 2008, Note for Guidance 6B above will cease to apply in the following forces areas:*
*—Greater Manchester Police*
*—West Midlands Police*
*—West Yorkshire Police*
*and the following provisions will apply to those force areas: a detainee who asks for legal advice to be paid for by himself should be given an opportunity to consult a specific solicitor or another solicitor from that solicitor's firm. If this solicitor is unavailable by these means, they may choose up to two alternatives. If these attempts are unsuccessful, the custody officer has discretion to allow further attempts until a solicitor has been contacted and agrees to provide legal advice. Otherwise, publicly funded legal advice shall in the first instance be accessed by telephoning a call centre authorised by the Legal Services Commission (LSC) to deal with calls from the police station. The Defence Solicitor Call Centre will determine whether legal advice should*

*be limited to telephone advice or whether a solicitor should attend. Legal advice will be by telephone if a detainee is:*

- *detained for a non-imprisonable offence,*
- *arrested on a bench warrant for failing to appear and being held for production before the court (except where the solicitor has clear documentary evidence available that would result in the client being released from custody),*
- *arrested on suspicion of driving with excess alcohol (failure to provide a specimen, driving whilst unfit/drunk in charge of a motor vehicle), or*
- *detained in relation to breach of police or court bail conditions.*

*An attendance by a solicitor for an offence suitable for telephone advice will depend on whether limited exceptions apply, such as:*

- *whether the police are going to carry out an interview or an identification parade,*
- *whether the detainee is eligible for assistance from an appropriate adult,*
- *whether the detainee is unable to communicate over the telephone,*
- *whether the detainee alleges serious maltreatment by the police.*

*Apart from carrying out these duties, an officer must not advise the suspect about any particular firm of solicitors. See Note for Guidance 6B2 below.*

6B2 *With effect from 21 April 2008, the contents of Notes for Guidance 6B and 6B1 above will be superseded by this paragraph in all police forces areas in England and Wales by the following. A detainee who asks for legal advice to be paid for by himself should be given an opportunity to consult a specific solicitor or another solicitor from that solicitor's firm. If this solicitor is unavailable by these means, they may choose up to two alternatives. If these attempts are unsuccessful, the custody officer has discretion to allow further attempts until a solicitor has been contacted and agrees to provide legal advice. Otherwise, publicly funded legal advice shall in the first instance be accessed by telephoning a call centre authorised by the Legal Services Commission (LSC) to deal with calls from the police station. The Defence Solicitor Call Centre will determine whether legal advice should be limited to telephone advice or whether a solicitor should attend. Legal advice will be by telephone if a detainee is:*

- *detained for a non-imprisonable offence,*
- *arrested on a bench warrant for failing to appear and being held for production before the court (except where the solicitor has clear documentary evidence available that would result in the client being released from custody),*
- *arrested on suspicion of driving with excess alcohol (failure to provide a specimen, driving whilst unfit/drunk in charge of a motor vehicle), or*
- *detained in relation to breach of police or court bail conditions.*

*An attendance by a solicitor for an offence suitable for telephone advice will depend on whether limited exceptions apply, such as:*

- *whether the police are going to carry out an interview or an identification parade,*
- *whether the detainee is eligible for assistance from an appropriate adult,*
- *whether the detainee is unable to communicate over the telephone,*
- *whether the detainee alleges serious maltreatment by the police.*

*Apart from carrying out these duties, an officer must not advise the suspect about any particular firm of solicitors.*

6C *Not Used.*

6D    A detainee has a right to free legal advice and to be represented by a solicitor. Legal advice by telephone advice may be provided in respect of those offences listed in Note for Guidance 6B1 and 6B2 above. The Defence Solicitor Call Centre will determine whether attendance is required by a solicitor. The solicitor's only role in the police station is to protect and advance the legal rights of their client. On occasions this may require the solicitor to give advice which has the effect of the client avoiding giving evidence which strengthens a prosecution case. The solicitor may intervene in order to seek clarification, challenge an improper question to their client or the manner in which it is put, advise their client not to reply to particular questions, or if they wish to give their client further legal advice. Paragraph 6.9 only applies if the solicitor's approach or conduct prevents or unreasonably obstructs proper questions being put to the suspect or the suspect's response being recorded. Examples of unacceptable conduct include answering questions on a suspect's behalf or providing written replies for the suspect to quote.

6E    An officer who takes the decision to exclude a solicitor must be in a position to satisfy the court the decision was properly made. In order to do this they may need to witness what is happening.

6F    If an officer of at least inspector rank considers a particular solicitor or firm of solicitors is persistently sending probationary representatives who are unsuited to provide legal advice, they should inform an officer of at least superintendent rank, who may wish to take the matter up with the Law Society.

6G    Subject to the constraints of Annex B, a solicitor may advise more than one client in an investigation if they wish. Any question of a conflict of interest is for the solicitor under their professional code of conduct. If, however, waiting for a solicitor to give advice to one client may lead to unreasonable delay to the interview with another, the provisions of paragraph 6.6(b) may apply.

6H    In addition to a poster in English, a poster or posters containing translations into Welsh, the main minority ethnic languages and the principal European languages should be displayed wherever they are likely to be helpful and it is practicable to do so.

6I    Paragraph 6.6(d) requires the authorisation of an officer of inspector rank or above to the continuation of an interview when a detainee who wanted legal advice changes their mind. It is permissible for such authorisation to be given over the telephone, if the authorising officer is able to satisfy themselves about the reason for the detainee's change of mind and is satisfied it is proper to continue the interview in those circumstances.

6J    Whenever a detainee exercises their right to legal advice by consulting or communicating with a solicitor, they must be allowed to do so in private. This right to consult or communicate in private is fundamental. Except as allowed by the Terrorism Act 2000, Schedule 8, paragraph 9, if the requirement for privacy is compromised because what is said or written by the detainee or solicitor for the purpose of giving and receiving legal advice is overheard, listened to, or read by others without the informed consent of the detainee, the right will effectively have been denied. When a detainee chooses to speak to a solicitor on the telephone, they should be allowed to do so in private unless this is impractical because of the design and layout of the custody area or the location of telephones. However, the normal expectation should be that facilities will be available, unless they are being used, at all police stations to enable detainees to speak in private to a solicitor either face to face or over the telephone.

*6K A detainee is not obliged to give reasons for declining legal advice and should not be pressed to do so.*

### 7   CITIZENS OF INDEPENDENT COMMONWEALTH COUNTRIES OR FOREIGN NATIONALS

#### (a) Action

7.1 Any citizen of an independent Commonwealth country or a national of a foreign country, including the Republic of Ireland, may communicate at any time with the appropriate High Commission, Embassy or Consulate. The detainee must be informed as soon as practicable of:
- this right;
- their right, upon request, to have their High Commission, Embassy or Consulate told of their whereabouts and the grounds for their detention. Such a request should be acted upon as soon as practicable.

7.2 If a detainee is a citizen of a country with which a bilateral consular convention or agreement is in force requiring notification of arrest, the appropriate High Commission, Embassy or Consulate shall be informed as soon as practicable, subject to *paragraph 7.4*. The countries to which this applies as at 1 April 2003 are listed in *Annex F*.

7.3 Consular officers may visit one of their nationals in police detention to talk to them and, if required, to arrange for legal advice. Such visits shall take place out of the hearing of a police officer.

7.4 Notwithstanding the provisions of consular conventions, if the detainee is a political refugee whether for reasons of race, nationality, political opinion or religion, or is seeking political asylum, consular officers shall not be informed of the arrest of one of their nationals or given access or information about them except at the detainee's express request.

#### (b) Documentation

7.5 A record shall be made when a detainee is informed of their rights under this section and of any communications with a High Commission, Embassy or Consulate.

#### Note for guidance

*7A The exercise of the rights in this section may not be interfered with even though Annex B applies.*

### 8   CONDITIONS OF DETENTION

#### (a) Action

8.1 So far as it is practicable, not more than one detainee should be detained in each cell.

8.2 Cells in use must be adequately heated, cleaned and ventilated. They must be adequately lit, subject to such dimming as is compatible with safety and security to allow people detained overnight to sleep. No additional restraints shall be used within a locked cell unless absolutely necessary and then only restraint equipment, approved for use in that force by the Chief Officer, which is reasonable

Code C

and necessary in the circumstances having regard to the detainee's demeanour and with a view to ensuring their safety and the safety of others. If a detainee is deaf, mentally disordered or otherwise mentally vulnerable, particular care must be taken when deciding whether to use any form of approved restraints.

8.3   Blankets, mattresses, pillows and other bedding supplied shall be of a reasonable standard and in a clean and sanitary condition. See *Note 8A*

8.4   Access to toilet and washing facilities must be provided.

8.5   If it is necessary to remove a detainee's clothes for the purposes of investigation, for hygiene, health reasons or cleaning, replacement clothing of a reasonable standard of comfort and cleanliness shall be provided. A detainee may not be interviewed unless adequate clothing has been offered.

8.6   At least two light meals and one main meal should be offered in any 24 hour period. See *Note 8B*. Drinks should be provided at meal times and upon reasonable request between meals. Whenever necessary, advice shall be sought from the appropriate health care professional, see *Note 9A*, on medical and dietary matters. As far as practicable, meals provided shall offer a varied diet and meet any specific dietary needs or religious beliefs the detainee may have. The detainee may, at the custody officer's discretion, have meals supplied by their family or friends at their expense. See *Note 8A*

8.7   Brief outdoor exercise shall be offered daily if practicable.

8.8   A juvenile shall not be placed in a police cell unless no other secure accommodation is available and the custody officer considers it is not practicable to supervise them if they are not placed in a cell or that a cell provides more comfortable accommodation than other secure accommodation in the station. A juvenile may not be placed in a cell with a detained adult.

**(b) Documentation**

8.9   A record must be kept of replacement clothing and meals offered.

8.10  If a juvenile is placed in a cell, the reason must be recorded.

8.11  The use of any restraints on a detainee whilst in a cell, the reasons for it and, if appropriate, the arrangements for enhanced supervision of the detainee whilst so restrained, shall be recorded. See *paragraph 3.9*

### Notes for guidance

8A   *The provisions in paragraph 8.3 and 8.6 respectively are of particular importance in the case of a person likely to be detained for an extended period. In deciding whether to allow meals to be supplied by family or friends, the custody officer is entitled to take account of the risk of items being concealed in any food or package and the officer's duties and responsibilities under food handling legislation.*

8B   *Meals should, so far as practicable, be offered at recognised meal times, or at other times that take account of when the detainee last had a meal.*

## 9  CARE AND TREATMENT OF DETAINED PERSONS

**(a) General**

9.1   Nothing in this section prevents the police from calling the police surgeon or, if appropriate, some other health care professional, to examine a detainee for the purposes of obtaining evidence relating to any offence in which the detainee is suspected of being involved. See *Note 9A*

9.2 If a complaint is made by, or on behalf of, a detainee about their treatment since their arrest, or it comes to notice that a detainee may have been treated improperly, a report must be made as soon as practicable to an officer of inspector rank or above not connected with the investigation. If the matter concerns a possible assault or the possibility of the unnecessary or unreasonable use of force, an appropriate health care professional must also be called as soon as practicable.

9.3 Detainees should be visited at least every hour. If no reasonably foreseeable risk was identified in a risk assessment, see *paragraphs 3.6–3.10*, there is no need to wake a sleeping detainee. Those suspected of being intoxicated through drink or drugs or having swallowed drugs, see *Note 9CA*, or whose level of consciousness causes concern must, subject to any clinical directions given by the appropriate health care professional, see *paragraph 9.13*:

- be visited and roused at least every half hour
- have their condition assessed as in *Annex H*
- and clinical treatment arranged if appropriate

See *Notes 9B, 9C* and *9H*

9.4 When arrangements are made to secure clinical attention for a detainee, the custody officer must make sure all relevant information which might assist in the treatment of the detainee's condition is made available to the responsible health care professional. This applies whether or not the health care professional asks for such information. Any officer or police staff with relevant information must inform the custody officer as soon as practicable.

**(b) Clinical treatment and attention**

9.5 The custody officer must make sure a detainee receives appropriate clinical attention as soon as reasonably practicable if the person:

(a) appears to be suffering from physical illness; or
(b) is injured; or
(c) appears to be suffering from a mental disorder; or
(d) appears to need clinical attention.

9.5A This applies even if the detainee makes no request for clinical attention and whether or not they have already received clinical attention elsewhere. If the need for attention appears urgent, e.g. when indicated as in *Annex H*, the nearest available health care professional or an ambulance must be called immediately.

9.5B The custody officer must also consider the need for clinical attention as set out in Note for Guidance 9C in relation to those suffering the effects of alcohol or drugs.

9.6 *Paragraph 9.5* is not meant to prevent or delay the transfer to a hospital if necessary of a person detained under the Mental Health Act 1983, section 136. See *Note 9D*. When an assessment under that Act takes place at a police station, see *paragraph 3.16*, the custody officer must consider whether an appropriate health care professional should be called to conduct an initial clinical check on the detainee. This applies particularly when there is likely to be any significant delay in the arrival of a suitably qualified medical practitioner.

Code **C**

9.7    If it appears to the custody officer, or they are told, that a person brought to a station under arrest may be suffering from an infectious disease or condition, the custody officer must take reasonable steps to safeguard the health of the detainee and others at the station. In deciding what action to take, advice must be sought from an appropriate health care professional. See *Note 9E*. The custody officer has discretion to isolate the person and their property until clinical directions have been obtained.

9.8    If a detainee requests a clinical examination, an appropriate health care professional must be called as soon as practicable to assess the detainee's clinical needs. If a safe and appropriate care plan cannot be provided, the police surgeon's advice must be sought. The detainee may also be examined by a medical practitioner of their choice at their expense.

9.9    If a detainee is required to take or apply any medication in compliance with clinical directions prescribed before their detention, the custody officer must consult the appropriate health care professional before the use of the medication. Subject to the restrictions in *paragraph 9.10*, the custody officer is responsible for the safekeeping of any medication and for making sure the detainee is given the opportunity to take or apply prescribed or approved medication. Any such consultation and its outcome shall be noted in the custody record.

9.10   No police officer may administer or supervise the self-administration of medically prescribed controlled drugs of the types and forms listed in the Misuse of Drugs Regulations 2001, Schedule 2 or 3. A detainee may only self-administer such drugs under the personal supervision of the registered medical practitioner authorising their use. Drugs listed in Schedule 4 or 5 may be distributed by the custody officer for self-administration if they have consulted the registered medical practitioner authorising their use, this may be done by telephone, and both parties are satisfied self-administration will not expose the detainee, police officers or anyone else to the risk of harm or injury.

9.11   When appropriate health care professionals administer drugs or other medications, or supervise their self-administration, it must be within current medicines legislation and the scope of practice as determined by their relevant professional body.

9.12   If a detainee has in their possession, or claims to need, medication relating to a heart condition, diabetes, epilepsy or a condition of comparable potential seriousness then, even though *paragraph 9.5* may not apply, the advice of the appropriate health care professional must be obtained.

9.13   Whenever the appropriate health care professional is called in accordance with this section to examine or treat a detainee, the custody officer shall ask for their opinion about:
   • any risks or problems which police need to take into account when making decisions about the detainee's continued detention;
   • when to carry out an interview if applicable; and
   • the need for safeguards.

9.14   When clinical directions are given by the appropriate health care professional, whether orally or in writing, and the custody officer has any doubts or is in any way uncertain about any aspect of the directions, the custody officer shall ask for clarification. It is particularly important that directions concerning the frequency of visits are clear, precise and capable of being implemented. See *Note 9F*.

### (c) Documentation

9.15 A record must be made in the custody record of:
- (a) the arrangements made for an examination by an appropriate health care professional under *paragraph 9.2* and of any complaint reported under that paragraph together with any relevant remarks by the custody officer;
- (b) any arrangements made in accordance with *paragraph 9.5*;
- (c) any request for a clinical examination under *paragraph 9.8* and any arrangements made in response;
- (d) the injury, ailment, condition or other reason which made it necessary to make the arrangements in (a) to (c), see *Note 9G*;
- (e) any clinical directions and advice, including any further clarifications, given to police by a health care professional concerning the care and treatment of the detainee in connection with any of the arrangements made in (a) to (c), see *Note 9F*;
- (f) if applicable, the responses received when attempting to rouse a person using the procedure in *Annex H*, see *Note 9H*.

9.16 If a health care professional does not record their clinical findings in the custody record, the record must show where they are recorded. See *Note 9G*. However, information which is necessary to custody staff to ensure the effective ongoing care and well being of the detainee must be recorded openly in the custody record, see *paragraph 3.8* and *Annex G, paragraph 7*.

9.17 Subject to the requirements of *Section 4*, the custody record shall include:
- a record of all medication a detainee has in their possession on arrival at the police station;
- a note of any such medication they claim to need but do not have with them.

Code **C**

### Notes for guidance

9A   *A 'health care professional' means a clinically qualified person working within the scope of practice as determined by their relevant professional body. Whether a health care professional is 'appropriate' depends on the circumstances of the duties they carry out at the time.*

9B   *Whenever possible juveniles and mentally vulnerable detainees should be visited more frequently.*

9C   *A detainee who appears drunk or behaves abnormally may be suffering from illness, the effects of drugs or may have sustained injury, particularly a head injury which is not apparent. A detainee needing or dependent on certain drugs, including alcohol, may experience harmful effects within a short time of being deprived of their supply. In these circumstances, when there is any doubt, police should always act urgently to call an appropriate health care professional or an ambulance. Paragraph 9.5 does not apply to minor ailments or injuries which do not need attention. However, all such ailments or injuries must be recorded in the custody record and any doubt must be resolved in favour of calling the appropriate health care professional.*

9CA   *Paragraph 9.3 would apply to a person in police custody by order of a magistrates' court under the Criminal Justice Act 1988, section 152 (as amended by the Drugs Act 2005, section 8) to facilitate the recovery of evidence after being charged with drug possession or drug trafficking and suspected of having swallowed drugs. In the case of the healthcare needs of a person who has swallowed drugs, the custody officer subject to any clinical directions, should consider the necessity for rousing every half hour. This does not negate the need for regular visiting of the suspect in the cell.*

9D    *Whenever practicable, arrangements should be made for persons detained for assessment under the Mental Health Act 1983, section 136 to be taken to a hospital. There is no power under that Act to transfer a person detained under section 136 from one place of safety to another place of safety for assessment.*

9E    *It is important to respect a person's right to privacy and information about their health must be kept confidential and only disclosed with their consent or in accordance with clinical advice when it is necessary to protect the detainee's health or that of others who come into contact with them.*

9F    *The custody officer should always seek to clarify directions that the detainee requires constant observation or supervision and should ask the appropriate health care professional to explain precisely what action needs to be taken to implement such directions.*

9G    *Paragraphs 9.15 and 9.16 do not require any information about the cause of any injury, ailment or condition to be recorded on the custody record if it appears capable of providing evidence of an offence.*

9H    *The purpose of recording a person's responses when attempting to rouse them using the procedure in Annex H is to enable any change in the individual's consciousness level to be noted and clinical treatment arranged if appropriate.*

## 10 Cautions

### (a) When a caution must be given

10.1   A person whom there are grounds to suspect of an offence, see *Note 10A*, must be cautioned before any questions about an offence, or further questions if the answers provide the grounds for suspicion, are put to them if either the suspect's answers or silence, (i.e. failure or refusal to answer or answer satisfactorily) may be given in evidence to a court in a prosecution. A person need not be cautioned if questions are for other necessary purposes, e.g.:

(a)   solely to establish their identity or ownership of any vehicle;

(b)   to obtain information in accordance with any relevant statutory requirement, see *paragraph 10.9*;

(c)   in furtherance of the proper and effective conduct of a search, e.g. to determine the need to search in the exercise of powers of stop and search or to seek cooperation while carrying out a search;

(d)   to seek verification of a written record as in *paragraph 11.13*;

(e)   Not used.

10.2   Whenever a person not under arrest is initially cautioned, or reminded they are under caution, that person must at the same time be told they are not under arrest and are free to leave if they want to. See *Note 10C*

10.3    A person who is arrested, or further arrested, must be informed at the time, or as soon as practicable thereafter, that they are under arrest and the grounds for their arrest, see paragraph 3.4, *Note 10B* and *Code G, paragraphs 2.2 and 4.3*.

10.4    As per *Code G, section 3*, a person who is arrested, or further arrested, must also be cautioned unless:

(a)  it is impracticable to do so by reason of their condition or behaviour at the time;

(b)  they have already been cautioned immediately prior to arrest as in *paragraph 10.1*.

### (b)  Terms of the cautions

10.5    The caution which must be given on:

(a)  arrest;

(b)  all other occasions before a person is charged or informed they may be prosecuted, see *section 16*,

should, unless the restriction on drawing adverse inferences from silence applies, see *Annex C*, be in the following terms:

'You do not have to say anything. But it may harm your defence if you do not mention when questioned something which you later rely on in Court. Anything you do say may be given in evidence.' Where the use of the Welsh Language is appropriate, a constable may provide the caution directly in Welsh in the following terms: 'Does dim rhaid i chi ddweud dim byd. Ond gall niweidio eich amddiffyniad os na fyddwch chi'n sôn, wrth gael eich holi, am rywbeth y byddwch chi'n dibynnu arno nes ymlaen yn y Llys. Gall unrhyw beth yr ydych yn ei ddweud gael ei roi fel tystiolaeth.' See *Note 10G*

**Code C**

10.6    *Annex C, paragraph 2* sets out the alternative terms of the caution to be used when the restriction on drawing adverse inferences from silence applies.

10.7    Minor deviations from the words of any caution given in accordance with this Code do not constitute a breach of this Code, provided the sense of the relevant caution is preserved. See *Note 10D*

10.8    After any break in questioning under caution, the person being questioned must be made aware they remain under caution. If there is any doubt the relevant caution should be given again in full when the interview resumes. See *Note 10E*

10.9    When, despite being cautioned, a person fails to co-operate or to answer particular questions which may affect their immediate treatment, the person should be informed of any relevant consequences and that those consequences are not affected by the caution. Examples are when a person's refusal to provide:

• their name and address when charged may make them liable to detention;

• particulars and information in accordance with a statutory requirement, e.g. under the Road Traffic Act 1988, may amount to an offence or may make the person liable to a further arrest.

### (c)  Special warnings under the Criminal Justice and Public Order Act 1994, sections 36 and 37

10.10   When a suspect interviewed at a police station or authorised place of detention after arrest fails or refuses to answer certain questions, or to answer satisfactorily, after due warning, see *Note 10F*, a court or jury may draw such inferences as appear proper under the Criminal Justice and Public Order Act 1994, sections 36 and 37. Such inferences may only be drawn when:

(a) the restriction on drawing adverse inferences from silence, see *Annex C*, does not apply; and

(b) the suspect is arrested by a constable and fails or refuses to account for any objects, marks or substances, or marks on such objects found:
  • on their person;
  • in or on their clothing or footwear;
  • otherwise in their possession; or
  • in the place they were arrested;

(c) the arrested suspect was found by a constable at a place at or about the time the offence for which that officer has arrested them is alleged to have been committed, and the suspect fails or refuses to account for their presence there.

When the restriction on drawing adverse inferences from silence applies, the suspect may still be asked to account for any of the matters in (b) or (c) but the special warning described in *paragraph 10.11* will not apply and must not be given.

10.11 For an inference to be drawn when a suspect fails or refuses to answer a question about one of these matters or to answer it satisfactorily, the suspect must first be told in ordinary language:

(a) what offence is being investigated;

(b) what fact they are being asked to account for;

(c) this fact may be due to them taking part in the commission of the offence;

(d) a court may draw a proper inference if they fail or refuse to account for this fact;

(e) a record is being made of the interview and it may be given in evidence if they are brought to trial.

## (d) Juveniles and persons who are mentally disordered or otherwise mentally vulnerable

10.12 If a juvenile or a person who is mentally disordered or otherwise mentally vulnerable is cautioned in the absence of the appropriate adult, the caution must be repeated in the adult's presence.

## (e) Documentation

10.13 A record shall be made when a caution is given under this section, either in the interviewer's pocket book or in the interview record.

### Notes for guidance

10A   *There must be some reasonable, objective grounds for the suspicion, based on known facts or information which are relevant to the likelihood the offence has been committed and the person to be questioned committed it.*

10B   *An arrested person must be given sufficient information to enable them to understand that they have been deprived of their liberty and the reason they have been arrested, e.g. when a person is arrested on suspicion of committing an offence they* must be informed of the suspected offence's nature, when and where it was committed. The suspect must also be informed of the reason or reasons why the arrest is considered necessary. Vague or technical language should be avoided.

10C    The restriction on drawing inferences from silence, see Annex C, paragraph 1, does not apply to a person who has not been detained and who therefore cannot be prevented from seeking legal advice if they want, see paragraph 3.21.

10D    If it appears a person does not understand the caution, the person giving it should explain it in their own words.

10E    It may be necessary to show to the court that nothing occurred during an interview break or between interviews which influenced the suspect's recorded evidence. After a break in an interview or at the beginning of a subsequent interview, the interviewing officer should summarise the reason for the break and confirm this with the suspect.

10F    The Criminal Justice and Public Order Act 1994, sections 36 and 37 apply only to suspects who have been arrested by a constable or Customs and Excise officer and are given the relevant warning by the police or customs officer who made the arrest or who is investigating the offence. They do not apply to any interviews with suspects who have not been arrested.

10G    Nothing in this Code requires a caution to be given or repeated when informing a person not under arrest they may be prosecuted for an offence. However, a court will not be able to draw any inferences under the Criminal Justice and Public Order Act 1994, section 34, if the person was not cautioned.

Code **C**

## 11 INTERVIEWS—GENERAL

### (a) Action

11.1A   An interview is the questioning of a person regarding their involvement or suspected involvement in a criminal offence or offences which, under *paragraph 10.1*, must be carried out under caution. Whenever a person is interviewed they must be informed of the nature of the offence, or further offence. Procedures under the Road Traffic Act 1988, section 7 or the Transport and Works Act 1992, section 31 do not constitute interviewing for the purpose of this Code.

11.1    Following a decision to arrest a suspect, they must not be interviewed about the relevant offence except at a police station or other authorised place of detention, unless the consequent delay would be likely to:
   (a)  lead to:
      • interference with, or harm to, evidence connected with an offence;
      • interference with, or physical harm to, other people; or
      • serious loss of, or damage to, property;
   (b)  lead to alerting other people suspected of committing an offence but not yet arrested for it; or
   (c)  hinder the recovery of property obtained in consequence of the commission of an offence.
   Interviewing in any of these circumstances shall cease once the relevant risk has been averted or the necessary questions have been put in order to attempt to avert that risk.

11.2   Immediately prior to the commencement or re-commencement of any interview at a police station or other authorised place of detention, the interviewer should remind the suspect of their entitlement to free legal advice and that the interview can be delayed for legal advice to be obtained, unless one of the exceptions in *paragraph 6.6* applies. It is the interviewer's responsibility to make sure all reminders are recorded in the interview record.

11.3   Not used.

11.4   At the beginning of an interview the interviewer, after cautioning the suspect, see *section 10*, shall put to them any significant statement or silence which occurred in the presence and hearing of a police officer or other police staff before the start of the interview and which have not been put to the suspect in the course of a previous interview. See *Note 11A*. The interviewer shall ask the suspect whether they confirm or deny that earlier statement or silence and if they want to add anything.

11.4A  A significant statement is one which appears capable of being used in evidence against the suspect, in particular a direct admission of guilt. A significant silence is a failure or refusal to answer a question or answer satisfactorily when under caution, which might, allowing for the restriction on drawing adverse inferences from silence, see *Annex C*, give rise to an inference under the Criminal Justice and Public Order Act 1994, Part III.

11.5   No interviewer may try to obtain answers or elicit a statement by the use of oppression. Except as in *paragraph 10.9*, no interviewer shall indicate, except to answer a direct question, what action will be taken by the police if the person being questioned answers questions, makes a statement or refuses to do either. If the person asks directly what action will be taken if they answer questions, make a statement or refuse to do either, the interviewer may inform them what action the police propose to take provided that action is itself proper and warranted.

11.6   The interview or further interview of a person about an offence with which that person has not been charged or for which they have not been informed they may be prosecuted, must cease when:

(a) the officer in charge of the investigation is satisfied all the questions they consider relevant to obtaining accurate and reliable information about the offence have been put to the suspect, this includes allowing the suspect an opportunity to give an innocent explanation and asking questions to test if the explanation is accurate and reliable, e.g. to clear up ambiguities or clarify what the suspect said;

(b) the officer in charge of the investigation has taken account of any other available evidence; and

(c) the officer in charge of the investigation, or in the case of a detained suspect, the custody officer, see *paragraph 16.1*, reasonably believes there is sufficient evidence to provide a realistic prospect of conviction for that offence. See *Note 11B*

This paragraph does not prevent officers in revenue cases or acting under the confiscation provisions of the Criminal Justice Act 1988 or the Drug Trafficking Act 1994 from inviting suspects to complete a formal question and answer record after the interview is concluded.

**(b) Interview records**

11.7 (a) An accurate record must be made of each interview, whether or not the interview takes place at a police station

(b) The record must state the place of interview, the time it begins and ends, any interview breaks and, subject to *paragraph 2.6A*, the names of all those present; and must be made on the forms provided for this purpose or in the interviewer's pocket book or in accordance with the Codes of Practice E or F

(c) Any written record must be made and completed during the interview, unless this would not be practicable or would interfere with the conduct of the interview, and must constitute either a verbatim record of what has been said or, failing this, an account of the interview which adequately and accurately summarises it.

11.8 If a written record is not made during the interview it must be made as soon as practicable after its completion.

11.9 Written interview records must be timed and signed by the maker.

11.10 If a written record is not completed during the interview the reason must be recorded in the interview record.

11.11 Unless it is impracticable, the person interviewed shall be given the opportunity to read the interview record and to sign it as correct or to indicate how they consider it inaccurate. If the person interviewed cannot read or refuses to read the record or sign it, the senior interviewer present shall read it to them and ask whether they would like to sign it as correct or make their mark or to indicate how they consider it inaccurate. The interviewer shall certify on the interview record itself what has occurred. See *Note 11E*

11.12 If the appropriate adult or the person's solicitor is present during the interview, they should also be given an opportunity to read and sign the interview record or any written statement taken down during the interview.

11.13 A written record shall be made of any comments made by a suspect, including unsolicited comments, which are outside the context of an interview but which might be relevant to the offence. Any such record must be timed and signed by the maker. When practicable the suspect shall be given the opportunity to read that record and to sign it as correct or to indicate how they consider it inaccurate. See *Note 11E*

11.14 Any refusal by a person to sign an interview record when asked in accordance with this Code must itself be recorded.

**(c) Juveniles and mentally disordered or otherwise mentally vulnerable people**

11.15 A juvenile or person who is mentally disordered or otherwise mentally vulnerable must not be interviewed regarding their involvement or suspected involvement in a criminal offence or offences, or asked to provide or sign a written statement under caution or record of interview, in the absence of the appropriate adult unless *paragraphs 11.1, 11.18 to 11.20* apply. See *Note 11C*

11.16 Juveniles may only be interviewed at their place of education in exceptional circumstances and only when the principal or their nominee agrees. Every effort should be made to notify the parent(s) or other person responsible for the juvenile's welfare and the appropriate adult, if this is a different person,

Code **C**

that the police want to interview the juvenile and reasonable time should be allowed to enable the appropriate adult to be present at the interview. If awaiting the appropriate adult would cause unreasonable delay, and unless the juvenile is suspected of an offence against the educational establishment, the principal or their nominee can act as the appropriate adult for the purposes of the interview.

11.17 If an appropriate adult is present at an interview, they shall be informed:
- they are not expected to act simply as an observer; and
- the purpose of their presence is to:
  — advise the person being interviewed;
  — observe whether the interview is being conducted properly and fairly;
  — facilitate communication with the person being interviewed.

### (d) Vulnerable suspects—urgent interviews at police stations

11.18 The following persons may not be interviewed unless an officer of superintendent rank or above considers delay will lead to the consequences in *paragraph 11.1(a)* to *(c)*, and is satisfied the interview would not significantly harm the person's physical or mental state (see Annex G):
  (a) a juvenile or person who is mentally disordered or otherwise mentally vulnerable if at the time of the interview the appropriate adult is not present;
  (b) anyone other than in *(a)* who at the time of the interview appears unable to:
    - appreciate the significance of questions and their answers; or
    - understand what is happening because of the effects of drink, drugs or any illness, ailment or condition;
  (c) a person who has difficulty understanding English or has a hearing disability, if at the time of the interview an interpreter is not present.

11.19 These interviews may not continue once sufficient information has been obtained to avert the consequences in *paragraph 11.1(a)* to *(c)*.

11.20 A record shall be made of the grounds for any decision to interview a person under *paragraph 11.18*.

### Notes for guidance

*11A*    *Paragraph 11.4 does not prevent the interviewer from putting significant statements and silences to a suspect again at a later stage or a further interview.*

*11B*    *The Criminal Procedure and Investigations Act 1996 Code of Practice, paragraph 3.4 states 'In conducting an investigation, the investigator should pursue all reasonable lines of enquiry, whether these point towards or away from the suspect. What is reasonable will depend on the particular circumstances.' Interviewers should keep this in mind when deciding what questions to ask in an interview.*

*11C*    *Although juveniles or people who are mentally disordered or otherwise mentally vulnerable are often capable of providing reliable evidence, they may, without knowing or wishing to do so, be particularly prone in certain circumstances to provide information that may be unreliable, misleading or self-incriminating. Special care should always be taken when questioning such a person, and the appropriate adult should be involved if there is any doubt about a person's age, mental state or capacity. Because of the risk of unreliable evidence it is also important to obtain corroboration of any facts admitted whenever possible.*

11D *Juveniles should not be arrested at their place of education unless this is unavoidable. When a juvenile is arrested at their place of education, the principal or their nominee must be informed.*

11E *Significant statements described in paragraph 11.4 will always be relevant to the offence and must be recorded. When a suspect agrees to read records of interviews and other comments and sign them as correct, they should be asked to endorse the record with, e.g. 'I agree that this is a correct record of what was said' and add their signature. If the suspect does not agree with the record, the interviewer should record the details of any disagreement and ask the suspect to read these details and sign them to the effect that they accurately reflect their disagreement. Any refusal to sign should be recorded.*

## 12 INTERVIEWS IN POLICE STATIONS

**(a) Action**

Code **C**

12.1 If a police officer wants to interview or conduct enquiries which require the presence of a detainee, the custody officer is responsible for deciding whether to deliver the detainee into the officer's custody.

12.2 Except as below, in any period of 24 hours a detainee must be allowed a continuous period of at least 8 hours for rest, free from questioning, travel or any interruption in connection with the investigation concerned. This period should normally be at night or other appropriate time which takes account of when the detainee last slept or rested. If a detainee is arrested at a police station after going there voluntarily, the period of 24 hours runs from the time of their arrest and not the time of arrival at the police station. The period may not be interrupted or delayed, except:

(a) when there are reasonable grounds for believing not delaying or interrupting the period would:
   (i) involve a risk of harm to people or serious loss of, or damage to, property;
   (ii) delay unnecessarily the person's release from custody;
   (iii) otherwise prejudice the outcome of the investigation;
(b) at the request of the detainee, their appropriate adult or legal representative;
(c) when a delay or interruption is necessary in order to:
   (i) comply with the legal obligations and duties arising under *section 15*;
   (ii) to take action required under *section 9* or in accordance with medical advice.

If the period is interrupted in accordance with *(a)*, a fresh period must be allowed. Interruptions under *(b)* and *(c)*, do not require a fresh period to be allowed.

12.3 Before a detainee is interviewed the custody officer, in consultation with the officer in charge of the investigation and appropriate health care professionals as necessary, shall assess whether the detainee is fit enough to be interviewed. This means determining and considering the risks to the detainee's physical and mental state if the interview took place and determining what safeguards are needed to allow the interview to take place. See *Annex G.* The custody officer shall not allow a detainee to be interviewed if the custody officer considers it would cause significant harm to the detainee's physical or mental state. Vulnerable suspects listed at *paragraph 11.18* shall be treated as always being at some risk during an interview and these persons may not be interviewed except in accordance with *paragraphs 11.18* to *11.20*.

12.4    As far as practicable interviews shall take place in interview rooms which are adequately heated, lit and ventilated.

12.5    A suspect whose detention without charge has been authorised under PACE, because the detention is necessary for an interview to obtain evidence of the offence for which they have been arrested, may choose not to answer questions but police do not require the suspect's consent or agreement to interview them for this purpose. If a suspect takes steps to prevent themselves being questioned or further questioned, e.g. by refusing to leave their cell to go to a suitable interview room or by trying to leave the interview room, they shall be advised their consent or agreement to interview is not required. The suspect shall be cautioned as in *section 10*, and informed if they fail or refuse to co-operate, the interview may take place in the cell and that their failure or refusal to co-operate may be given in evidence. The suspect shall then be invited to co-operate and go into the interview room.

12.6    People being questioned or making statements shall not be required to stand.

12.7    Before the interview commences each interviewer shall, subject to *paragraph 2.6A*, identify themselves and any other persons present to the interviewee.

12.8    Breaks from interviewing should be made at recognised meal times or at other times that take account of when an interviewee last had a meal. Short refreshment breaks shall be provided at approximately two hour intervals, subject to the interviewer's discretion to delay a break if there are reasonable grounds for believing it would:
- (i)   involve a:
  - risk of harm to people;
  - serious loss of, or damage to, property;
- (ii)   unnecessarily delay the detainee's release;
- (iii) otherwise prejudice the outcome of the investigation.

See *Note 12B*

12.9    If during the interview a complaint is made by or on behalf of the interviewee concerning the provisions of this Code, the interviewer should:
- (i)   record it in the interview record;
- (ii)   inform the custody officer, who is then responsible for dealing with it as in *section 9*.

## (b) Documentation

12.10 A record must be made of the:
- time a detainee is not in the custody of the custody officer, and why
- reason for any refusal to deliver the detainee out of that custody

12.11 A record shall be made of:
- (a) the reasons it was not practicable to use an interview room; and
- (b) any action taken as in *paragraph 12.5*.

The record shall be made on the custody record or in the interview record for action taken whilst an interview record is being kept, with a brief reference to this effect in the custody record.

12.12 Any decision to delay a break in an interview must be recorded, with reasons, in the interview record.

12.13 All written statements made at police stations under caution shall be written on forms provided for the purpose.

12.14 All written statements made under caution shall be taken in accordance with *Annex D*. Before a person makes a written statement under caution at a police station they shall be reminded about the right to legal advice. See *Note 12A*

### Notes for guidance

12A   *It is not normally necessary to ask for a written statement if the interview was recorded in writing and the record signed in accordance with paragraph 11.11 or audibly or visually recorded in accordance with Code E or F. Statements under caution should normally be taken in these circumstances only at the person's express wish. A person may however be asked if they want to make such a statement.*

12B   *Meal breaks should normally last at least 45 minutes and shorter breaks after two hours should last at least 15 minutes. If the interviewer delays a break in accordance with paragraph 12.8 and prolongs the interview, a longer break should be provided. If there is a short interview, and another short interview is contemplated, the length of the break may be reduced if there are reasonable grounds to believe this is necessary to avoid any of the consequences in paragraph 12.8(i) to (iii).*

Code **C**

## 13 Interpreters

### (a) General

13.1   Chief officers are responsible for making sure appropriate arrangements are in place for provision of suitably qualified interpreters for people who:
   • are deaf;
   • do not understand English.
   Whenever possible, interpreters should be drawn from the National Register of Public Service Interpreters (NRPSI) or the Council for the Advancement of Communication with Deaf People (CADCP) Directory of British Sign Language/English Interpreters.

### (b) Foreign languages

13.2   Unless *paragraphs 11.1, 11.18 to 11.20* apply, a person must not be interviewed in the absence of a person capable of interpreting if:
   (a) they have difficulty understanding English;
   (b) the interviewer cannot speak the person's own language;
   (c) the person wants an interpreter present.

13.3   The interviewer shall make sure the interpreter makes a note of the interview at the time in the person's language for use in the event of the interpreter being called to give evidence, and certifies its accuracy. The interviewer should allow sufficient time for the interpreter to note each question and answer after each is put, given and interpreted. The person should be allowed to read the record or have it read to them and sign it as correct or indicate the respects in which they consider it inaccurate. If the interview is audibly recorded or visually recorded, the arrangements in Code E or F apply.

13.4   In the case of a person making a statement to a police officer or other police staff other than in English:

    (a)   the interpreter shall record the statement in the language it is made;

    (b)   the person shall be invited to sign it;

    (c)   an official English translation shall be made in due course.

**(c) Deaf people and people with speech difficulties**

13.5   If a person appears to be deaf or there is doubt about their hearing or speaking ability, they must not be interviewed in the absence of an interpreter unless they agree in writing to being interviewed without one or *paragraphs 11.1, 11.18 to 11.20* apply.

13.6   An interpreter should also be called if a juvenile is interviewed and the parent or guardian present as the appropriate adult appears to be deaf or there is doubt about their hearing or speaking ability, unless they agree in writing to the interview proceeding without one or *paragraphs 11.1, 11.18 to 11.20* apply.

13.7   The interviewer shall make sure the interpreter is allowed to read the interview record and certify its accuracy in the event of the interpreter being called to give evidence. If the interview is audibly recorded or visually recorded, the arrangements in Code E or F apply.

**(d) Additional rules for detained persons**

13.8   All reasonable attempts should be made to make the detainee understand that interpreters will be provided at public expense.

13.9   If *paragraph 6.1* applies and the detainee cannot communicate with the solicitor because of language, hearing or speech difficulties, an interpreter must be called. The interpreter may not be a police officer or any other police staff when interpretation is needed for the purposes of obtaining legal advice. In all other cases a police officer or other police staff may only interpret if the detainee and the appropriate adult, if applicable, give their agreement in writing or if the interview is audibly recorded or visually recorded as in Code E or F.

13.10 When the custody officer cannot establish effective communication with a person charged with an offence who appears deaf or there is doubt about their ability to hear, speak or to understand English, arrangements must be made as soon as practicable for an interpreter to explain the offence and any other information given by the custody officer.

**(e) Documentation**

13.11 Action taken to call an interpreter under this section and any agreement to be interviewed in the absence of an interpreter must be recorded.

## 14   QUESTIONING—SPECIAL RESTRICTIONS

14.1   If a person is arrested by one police force on behalf of another and the lawful period of detention in respect of that offence has not yet commenced in accordance with PACE, section 41 no questions may be put to them about the offence while they are in transit between the forces except to clarify any voluntary statement they make.

14.2    If a person is in police detention at a hospital they may not be questioned without the agreement of a responsible doctor. See *Note 14A*

### Note for guidance

*14A    If questioning takes place at a hospital under paragraph 14.2, or on the way to or from a hospital, the period of questioning concerned counts towards the total period of detention permitted.*

## 15 Reviews and Extensions of Detention

### (a) Persons detained under PACE

15.1    The review officer is responsible under PACE, section 40 for periodically determining if a person's detention, before or after charge, continues to be necessary. This requirement continues throughout the detention period and except as in *paragraph 15.10*, the review officer must be present at the police station holding the detainee. See *Notes 15A* and *15B*

15.2    Under PACE, section 42, an officer of superintendent rank or above who is responsible for the station holding the detainee may give authority any time after the second review to extend the maximum period the person may be detained without charge by up to 12 hours. Further detention without charge may be authorised only by a magistrates' court in accordance with PACE, sections 43 and 44. See *Notes 15C, 15D* and *15E*

15.2A   Section 42(1) of PACE as amended extends the maximum period of detention for indictable offences from 24 hours to 36 hours. Detaining a juvenile or mentally vulnerable person for longer than 24 hours will be dependent on the circumstances of the case and with regard to the person's:
(a) special vulnerability;
(b) the legal obligation to provide an opportunity for representations to be made prior to a decision about extending detention;
(c) the need to consult and consider the views of any appropriate adult; and
(d) any alternatives to police custody.

15.3    Before deciding whether to authorise continued detention the officer responsible under *paragraphs 15.1* or *15.2* shall give an opportunity to make representations about the detention to:
(a) the detainee, unless in the case of a review as in *paragraph 15.1*, the detainee is asleep;
(b) the detainee's solicitor if available at the time; and
(c) the appropriate adult if available at the time.

15.3A   Other people having an interest in the detainee's welfare may also make representations at the authorising officer's discretion.

15.3B   Subject to *paragraph 15.10*, the representations may be made orally in person or by telephone or in writing. The authorising officer may, however, refuse to hear oral representations from the detainee if the officer considers them unfit to make representations because of their condition or behaviour. See *Note 15C*

15.3C   The decision on whether the review takes place in person or by telephone or by video conferencing (see *Note 15G*) is a matter for the review officer. In determining the form the review may take, the review officer must always

**Code C**

take full account of the needs of the person in custody. The benefits of carrying out a review in person should always be considered, based on the individual circumstances of each case with specific additional consideration if the person is:

    (a) a juvenile (and the age of the juvenile); or

    (b) mentally vulnerable; or

    (c) has been subject to medical attention for other than routine minor ailments; or

    (d) there are presentational or community issues around the person's detention.

15.4   Before conducting a review or determining whether to extend the maximum period of detention without charge, the officer responsible must make sure the detainee is reminded of their entitlement to free legal advice, see *paragraph 6.5*, unless in the case of a review the person is asleep.

15.5   If, after considering any representations, the officer decides to keep the detainee in detention or extend the maximum period they may be detained without charge, any comment made by the detainee shall be recorded. If applicable, the officer responsible under *paragraph 15.1* or *15.2* shall be informed of the comment as soon as practicable. See also *paragraphs 11.4* and *11.13*

15.6   No officer shall put specific questions to the detainee:

    • regarding their involvement in any offence; or

    • in respect of any comments they may make:

      —when given the opportunity to make representations; or

      —in response to a decision to keep them in detention or extend the maximum period of detention.

    Such an exchange could constitute an interview as in *paragraph 11.1A* and would be subject to the associated safeguards in *section 11* and, in respect of a person who has been charged, *paragraph 16.5*. See also *paragraph 11.13*

15.7   A detainee who is asleep at a review, see *paragraph 15.1*, and whose continued detention is authorised must be informed about the decision and reason as soon as practicable after waking.

15.8   Not used.

### (b) Telephone review of detention

15.9   PACE, section 40A provides that the officer responsible under section 40 for reviewing the detention of a person who has not been charged, need not attend the police station holding the detainee and may carry out the review by telephone.

15.9A PACE, section 45A(2) provides that the officer responsible under section 40 for reviewing the detention of a person who has not been charged, need not attend the police station holding the detainee and may carry out the review by video conferencing facilities (See *Note 15G*).

15.9B A telephone review is not permitted where facilities for review by video conferencing exist and it is practicable to use them.

15.9C The review officer can decide at any stage that a telephone review or review by video conferencing should be terminated and that the review will be conducted in person. The reasons for doing so should be noted in the custody record. See *Note 15F*

15.10 When a telephone review is carried out, an officer at the station holding the detainee shall be required by the review officer to fulfil that officer's obligations under PACE section 40 or this Code by:

(a) making any record connected with the review in the detainee's custody record;

(b) if applicable, making a record in (a) in the presence of the detainee; and

(c) giving the detainee information about the review.

15.11 When a telephone review is carried out, the requirement in *paragraph 15.3* will be satisfied:

(a) if facilities exist for the immediate transmission of written representations to the review officer, e.g. fax or email message, by giving the detainee an opportunity to make representations:

(i) orally by telephone; or

(ii) in writing using those facilities; and

(b) in all other cases, by giving the detainee an opportunity to make their representations orally by telephone.

**(c) Documentation**

15.12 It is the officer's responsibility to make sure all reminders given under *paragraph 15.4* are noted in the custody record.

15.13 The grounds for, and extent of, any delay in conducting a review shall be recorded.

15.14 When a telephone review is carried out, a record shall be made of:

(a) the reason the review officer did not attend the station holding the detainee;

(b) the place the review officer was;

(c) the method representations, oral or written, were made to the review officer, see *paragraph 15.11*.

15.15 Any written representations shall be retained.

15.16 A record shall be made as soon as practicable about the outcome of each review or determination whether to extend the maximum detention period without charge or an application for a warrant of further detention or its extension. If *paragraph 15.7* applies, a record shall also be made of when the person was informed and by whom. If an authorisation is given under PACE, section 42, the record shall state the number of hours and minutes by which the detention period is extended or further extended. If a warrant for further detention, or extension, is granted under section 43 or 44, the record shall state the detention period authorised by the warrant and the date and time it was granted.

**Notes for guidance**

*15A  Review officer for the purposes of:*

- *PACE, sections 40 and 40A means, in the case of a person arrested but not charged, an officer of at least inspector rank not directly involved in the investigation and, if a person has been arrested and charged, the custody officer;*

*15B  The detention of persons in police custody not subject to the statutory review requirement in paragraph 15.1 should still be reviewed periodically as a matter of good practice. Such reviews can be carried out by an officer of the rank of sergeant or above. The purpose of such reviews is to check the particular power under which a detainee is held continues to apply, any associated conditions are complied with and to make sure appropriate action is taken to deal with any changes. This includes the detainee's prompt release when the power no longer applies, or their transfer if the power requires the detainee be taken elsewhere as soon as the necessary arrangements are made. Examples include persons:*

*(a) arrested on warrant because they failed to answer bail to appear at court;*

*(b) arrested under the Bail Act 1976, section 7(3) for breaching a condition of bail granted after charge;*

*(c) in police custody for specific purposes and periods under the Crime (Sentences) Act 1997, Schedule 1;*

*(d) convicted, or remand prisoners, held in police stations on behalf of the Prison Service under the Imprisonment (Temporary Provisions) Act 1980, section 6;*

*(e) being detained to prevent them causing a breach of the peace;*

*(f) detained at police stations on behalf of the Immigration Service;*

*(g) detained by order of a magistrates' court under the Criminal Justice Act 1988, section 152 (as amended by the Drugs Act 2005, section 8) to facilitate the recovery of evidence after being charged with drug possession or drug trafficking and suspected of having swallowed drugs.*

*The detention of persons remanded into police detention by order of a court under the Magistrates' Courts Act 1980, section 128 is subject to a statutory requirement to review that detention. This is to make sure the detainee is taken back to court no later than the end of the period authorised by the court or when the need for their detention by police ceases, whichever is the sooner.*

15C *In the case of a review of detention, but not an extension, the detainee need not be woken for the review. However, if the detainee is likely to be asleep, e.g. during a period of rest allowed as in paragraph 12.2, at the latest time a review or authorisation to extend detention may take place, the officer should, if the legal obligations and time constraints permit, bring forward the procedure to allow the detainee to make representations. A detainee not asleep during the review must be present when the grounds for their continued detention are recorded and must at the same time be informed of those grounds unless the review officer considers the person is incapable of understanding what is said, violent or likely to become violent or in urgent need of medical attention.*

15D *An application to a Magistrates' Court under PACE, sections 43 or 44 for a warrant of further detention or its extension should be made between 10am and 9pm, and if possible during normal court hours. It will not usually be practicable to arrange for a court to sit specially outside the hours of 10am to 9pm. If it appears a special sitting may be needed outside normal court hours but between 10am and 9pm, the clerk to the justices should be given notice and informed of this possibility, while the court is sitting if possible.*

15E *In paragraph 15.2, the officer responsible for the station holding the detainee includes a superintendent or above who, in accordance with their force operational policy or police regulations, is given that responsibility on a temporary basis whilst the appointed long-term holder is off duty or otherwise unavailable.*

15F *The provisions of PACE, section 40A allowing telephone reviews do not apply to reviews of detention after charge by the custody officer. When video conferencing is not required, they allow the use of a telephone to carry out a review of detention before charge. The procedure under PACE, section 42 must be done in person.*

15G   *The use of video conferencing facilities for decisions about detention under section 45A of PACE is subject to the introduction of regulations by the Secretary of State.*

## 16 CHARGING DETAINED PERSONS

### (a) Action

16.1   When the officer in charge of the investigation reasonably believes there is sufficient evidence to provide a realistic prospect of conviction for the offence (see *paragraph 11.6)*, they shall without delay, and subject to the following qualification, inform the custody officer who will be responsible for considering whether the detainee should be charged. See *Notes 11B and 16A*. When a person is detained in respect of more than one offence it is permissible to delay informing the custody officer until the above conditions are satisfied in respect of all the offences, but see *paragraph 11.6*. If the detainee is a juvenile, mentally disordered or otherwise mentally vulnerable, any resulting action shall be taken in the presence of the appropriate adult if they are present at the time. See *Notes 16B and 16C*.

16.1A  Where guidance issued by the Director of Public Prosecutions under section 37A is in force the custody officer must comply with that Guidance in deciding how to act in dealing with the detainee. See *Notes 16AA and 16AB*.

16.1B  Where in compliance with the DPP's Guidance the custody officer decides that the case should be immediately referred to the CPS to make the charging decision, consultation should take place with a Crown Prosecutor as soon as is reasonably practicable. Where the Crown Prosecutor is unable to make the charging decision on the information available at that time, the detainee may be released without charge and on bail (with conditions if necessary) under section 37(7)(a). In such circumstances, the detainee should be informed that they are being released to enable the Director of Public Prosecutions to make a decision under section 37B.

16.2   When a detainee is charged with or informed they may be prosecuted for an offence, see *Note 16B*, they shall, unless the restriction on drawing adverse inferences from silence applies, see *Annex C*, be cautioned as follows:

'*You do not have to say anything. But it may harm your defence if you do not mention now something which you later rely on in court. Anything you do say may be given in evidence.*' Where the use of the Welsh Language is appropriate, a constable may provide the caution directly in Welsh in the following terms: 'Does dim rhaid i chi ddweud dim byd. Ond gall niweidio eich amddiffyniad os na fyddwch chi'n sôn, yn awr, am rywbeth y byddwch chi'n dibynnu arno nes ymlaen yn y llys. Gall unrhyw beth yr ydych yn ei ddweud gael ei roi fel tystiolaeth.'

*Annex C, paragraph 2* sets out the alternative terms of the caution to be used when the restriction on drawing adverse inferences from silence applies.

16.3   When a detainee is charged they shall be given a written notice showing particulars of the offence and, subject to *paragraph 2.6A*, the officer's name and the case reference number. As far as possible the particulars of the charge shall be stated in simple terms, but they shall also show the precise offence in law with which the detainee is charged. The notice shall begin:

'*You are charged with the offence(s) shown below.*' Followed by the caution.

Code **C**

**413**

If the detainee is a juvenile, mentally disordered or otherwise mentally vulnerable, the notice should be given to the appropriate adult.

16.4    If, after a detainee has been charged with or informed they may be prosecuted for an offence, an officer wants to tell them about any written statement or interview with another person relating to such an offence, the detainee shall either be handed a true copy of the written statement or the content of the interview record brought to their attention. Nothing shall be done to invite any reply or comment except to:

(a) caution the detainee, '*You do not have to say anything, but anything you do say may be given in evidence.*' Where the use of the Welsh Language is appropriate, caution the detainee in the following terms: 'Does dim rhaid i chi ddweud dim byd, ond gall unrhyw beth yr ydych yn ei ddweud gael ei roi fel tystiolaeth.'; and

(b) remind the detainee about their right to legal advice.

16.4A If the detainee:

- cannot read, the document may be read to them
- is a juvenile, mentally disordered or otherwise mentally vulnerable, the appropriate adult shall also be given a copy, or the interview record shall be brought to their attention

16.5    A detainee may not be interviewed about an offence after they have been charged with, or informed they may be prosecuted for it, unless the interview is necessary:

- to prevent or minimise harm or loss to some other person, or the public
- to clear up an ambiguity in a previous answer or statement
- in the interests of justice for the detainee to have put to them, and have an opportunity to comment on, information concerning the offence which has come to light since they were charged or informed they might be prosecuted

Before any such interview, the interviewer shall:

(a) caution the detainee, '*You do not have to say anything, but anything you do say may be given in evidence.*' Where the use of the Welsh Language is appropriate, the interviewer shall caution the detainee, 'Does dim rhaid i chi ddweud dim byd, ond gall unrhyw beth yr ydych yn ei ddweud gael ei roi fel tystiolaeth.';

(b) remind the detainee about their right to legal advice.

See *Note 16B*

16.6    The provisions of *paragraphs 16.2* to *16.5* must be complied with in the appropriate adult's presence if they are already at the police station. If they are not at the police station then these provisions must be complied with again in their presence when they arrive unless the detainee has been released.

See *Note 16C*

16.7    When a juvenile is charged with an offence and the custody officer authorises their continued detention after charge, the custody officer must try to make arrangements for the juvenile to be taken into the care of a local authority to be detained pending appearance in court unless the custody officer certifies it is impracticable to do so or, in the case of a juvenile of at least 12 years old, no secure accommodation is available and there is a risk to the public of serious harm from that juvenile, in accordance with PACE, section 38(6). See *Note 16D*

**(b) Documentation**

16.8   A record shall be made of anything a detainee says when charged.

16.9   Any questions put in an interview after charge and answers given relating to the offence shall be recorded in full during the interview on forms for that purpose and the record signed by the detainee or, if they refuse, by the interviewer and any third parties present. If the questions are audibly recorded or visually recorded the arrangements in Code E or F apply.

16.10  If it is not practicable to make arrangements for a juvenile's transfer into local authority care as *in paragraph 16.7*, the custody officer must record the reasons and complete a certificate to be produced before the court with the juvenile. See *Note 16D*

### Notes for guidance

16A    *The custody officer must take into account alternatives to prosecution under the Crime and Disorder Act 1998, reprimands and warning applicable to persons under 18, and in national guidance on the cautioning of offenders, for persons aged 18 and over.*

16AA   *When a person is arrested under the provisions of the Criminal Justice Act 2003 which allow a person to be re-tried after being acquitted of a serious offence which is a qualifying offence specified in Schedule 5 to that Act and not precluded from further prosecution by virtue of section 75(3) of that Act the detention provisions of PACE are modified and make an officer of the rank of superintendent or above who has not been directly involved in the investigation responsible for determining whether the evidence is sufficient to charge.*

16AB   *Where Guidance issued by the Director of Public Prosecutions under section 37B is in force, a custody officer who determines in accordance with that Guidance that there is sufficient evidence to charge the detainee, may detain that person for no longer than is reasonably necessary to decide how that person is to be dealt with under PACE, section 37(7)(a) to (d), including, where appropriate, consultation with the Duty Prosecutor. The period is subject to the maximum period of detention before charge determined by PACE, sections 41 to 44. Where in accordance with the Guidance the case is referred to the CPS for decision, the custody officer should ensure that an officer involved in the investigation sends to the CPS such information as is specified in the Guidance.*

16B    *The giving of a warning or the service of the Notice of Intended Prosecution required by the Road Traffic Offenders Act 1988, section 1 does not amount to informing a detainee they may be prosecuted for an offence and so does not preclude further questioning in relation to that offence.*

16C    *There is no power under PACE to detain a person and delay action under paragraphs 16.2 to 16.5 solely to await the arrival of the appropriate adult. After charge, bail cannot be refused, or release on bail delayed, simply because an appropriate adult is not available, unless the absence of that adult provides the custody officer with the necessary grounds to authorise detention after charge under PACE, section 38.*

16D    *Except as in paragraph 16.7, neither a juvenile's behaviour nor the nature of the offence provides grounds for the custody officer to decide it is impracticable to arrange the juvenile's transfer to local authority care. Similarly, the lack of secure local authority accommodation does not make it impracticable to transfer the juvenile. The availability of secure accommodation is only a factor in relation to a juvenile*

Code **C**

*aged 12 or over when the local authority accommodation would not be adequate to protect the public from serious harm from them. The obligation to transfer a juvenile to local authority accommodation applies as much to a juvenile charged during the daytime as to a juvenile to be held overnight, subject to a requirement to bring the juvenile before a court under PACE, section 46.*

## 17  TESTING PERSONS FOR THE PRESENCE OF SPECIFIED CLASS A DRUGS

### (a) Action

17.1  This section of Code C applies only in selected police stations in police areas where the provisions for drug testing under section 63B of PACE (as amended by section 5 of the Criminal Justice Act 2003 and section 7 of the Drugs Act 2005) are in force and in respect of which the Secretary of State has given a notification to the relevant chief officer of police that arrangements for the taking of samples have been made. Such a notification will cover either a police area as a whole or particular stations within a police area. The notification indicates whether the testing applies to those arrested or charged or under the age of 18 as the case may be and testing can only take place in respect of the persons so indicated in the notification. Testing cannot be carried out unless the relevant notification has been given and has not been withdrawn. See *Note 17F*

17.2  A sample of urine or a non-intimate sample may be taken from a person in police detention for the purpose of ascertaining whether he has any specified Class A drug in his body only where they have been brought before the custody officer and:

(a)  either the arrest condition, see *paragraph 17.3*, or the charge condition, see *paragraph 17.4* is met;

(b)  the age condition see *paragraph 17.5*, is met;

(c)  the notification condition is met in relation to the arrest condition, the charge condition, or the age condition, as the case may be. (Testing on charge and/or arrest must be specifically provided for in the notification for the power to apply. In addition, the fact that testing of under 18s is authorised must be expressly provided for in the notification before the power to test such persons applies.). See *paragraph 17.1*; and

(d)  a police officer has requested the person concerned to give the sample (the request condition).

17.3  The arrest condition is met where the detainee:

(a)  has been arrested for a trigger offence, see *Note 17E*, but not charged with that offence; or

(b)  has been arrested for any other offence but not charged with that offence and a police officer of inspector rank or above, who has reasonable grounds for suspecting that their misuse of any specified Class A drug caused or contributed to the offence, has authorised the sample to be taken.

17.4  The charge condition is met where the detainee:

(a)  has been charged with a trigger offence, or

(b)  has been charged with any other offence and a police officer of inspector rank or above, who has reasonable grounds for suspecting that the detainee's misuse of any specified Class A drug caused or contributed to the offence, has authorised the sample to be taken.

17.5 The age condition is met where:
- (a) in the case of a detainee who has been arrested but not charged as in *paragraph 17.3*, they are aged 18 or over;
- (b) in the case of a detainee who has been charged as in *paragraph 17.4*, they are aged 14 or over.

17.6 Before requesting a sample from the person concerned, an officer must:
- (a) inform them that the purpose of taking the sample is for drug testing under PACE. This is to ascertain whether they have a specified Class A drug present in their body;
- (b) warn them that if, when so requested, they fail without good cause to provide a sample they may be liable to prosecution;
- (c) where the taking of the sample has been authorised by an inspector or above in accordance with *paragraph 17.3(b)* or *17.4(b)* above, inform them that the authorisation has been given and the grounds for giving it;
- (d) remind them of the following rights, which may be exercised at any stage during the period in custody:
  - (i) the right to have someone informed of their arrest [see section 5];
  - (ii) the right to consult privately with a solicitor and that free independent legal advice is available [see section 6]; and
  - (iii) the right to consult these Codes of Practice [see section 3].

17.7 In the case of a person who has not attained the age of 17—
- (a) the making of the request for a sample under *paragraph 17.2(d)* above;
- (b) the giving of the warning and the information under *paragraph 17.6* above; and
- (c) the taking of the sample,

may not take place except in the presence of an appropriate adult. (see *Note 17G*)

17.8 Authorisation by an officer of the rank of inspector or above within *paragraph 17.3(b)* or *17.4(b)* may be given orally or in writing but, if it is given orally, it must be confirmed in writing as soon as practicable.

17.9 If a sample is taken from a detainee who has been arrested for an offence but not charged with that offence as in *paragraph 17.3*, no further sample may be taken during the same continuous period of detention. If during that same period the charge condition is also met in respect of that detainee, the sample which has been taken shall be treated as being taken by virtue of the charge condition, see *paragraph 17.4*, being met.

17.10 A detainee from whom a sample may be taken may be detained for up to six hours from the time of charge if the custody officer reasonably believes the detention is necessary to enable a sample to be taken. Where the arrest condition is met, a detainee whom the custody officer has decided to release on bail without charge may continue to be detained, but not beyond 24 hours from the relevant time (as defined in section 41(2) of PACE), to enable a sample to be taken.

17.11 A detainee in respect of whom the arrest condition is met, but not the charge condition, see *paragraphs 17.3* and *17.4*, and whose release would be required before a sample can be taken had they not continued to be detained as a result of being arrested for a further offence which does not satisfy the arrest condition, may have a sample taken at any time within 24 hours after the arrest for the offence that satisfies the arrest condition.

Code **C**

### (b) Documentation

17.12 The following must be recorded in the custody record:

    (a) if a sample is taken following authorisation by an officer of the rank of inspector or above, the authorisation and the grounds for suspicion;

    (b) the giving of a warning of the consequences of failure to provide a sample;

    (c) the time at which the sample was given; and

    (d) the time of charge or, where the arrest condition is being relied upon, the time of arrest and, where applicable, the fact that a sample taken after arrest but before charge is to be treated as being taken by virtue of the charge condition, where that is met in the same period of continuous detention. See *paragraph 17.9*

### (c) General

17.13 A sample may only be taken by a prescribed person. See *Note 17C*

17.14 Force may not be used to take any sample for the purpose of drug testing.

17.15 The terms 'Class A drug' and 'misuse' have the same meanings as in the Misuse of Drugs Act 1971. 'Specified' (in relation to a Class A drug) and 'trigger offence' have the same meanings as in Part III of the Criminal Justice and Court Services Act 2000.

17.16 Any sample taken:

    (a) may not be used for any purpose other than to ascertain whether the person concerned has a specified Class A drug present in his body; and

    (b) must be retained until the person concerned has made their first appearance before the court.

### (d) Assessment of misuse of drugs

17.17 Under the provisions of Part 3 of the Drugs Act 2005, where a detainee has tested positive for a specified Class A drug under section 63B of PACE a police officer may, at any time before the person's release from the police station, impose a requirement for them to attend an initial assessment of their drug misuse by a suitably qualified person and to remain for its duration. The requirement may only be imposed on a person if:

    (a) they have reached the age of 18

    (b) notification has been given by the Secretary of State to the relevant chief officer of police that arrangements for conducting initial assessments have been made for those from whom samples for testing have been taken at the police station where the detainee is in custody.

17.18 When imposing a requirement to attend an initial assessment the police officer must:

    (a) inform the person of the time and place at which the initial assessment is to take place;

    (b) explain that this information will be confirmed in writing; and

    (c) warn the person that he may be liable to prosecution if he fails without good cause to attend the initial assessment and remain for its duration

17.19 Where a police officer has imposed a requirement to attend an initial assessment in accordance with *paragraph 17.17*, he must, before the person is released from detention, give the person notice in writing which:

    (a) confirms that he is required to attend and remain for the duration of an initial assessment; and

    (b) confirms the information and repeats the warning referred to in paragraph 17.18.

17.20 The following must be recorded in the custody record:

    (a) that the requirement to attend an initial assessment has been imposed; and

    (b) the information, explanation, warning and notice given in accordance with *paragraphs 17.17* and *17.19*.

17.21 Where a notice is given in accordance with *paragraph 17.19*, a police officer can give the person a further notice in writing which informs the person of any change to the time or place at which the initial assessment is to take place and which repeats the warning referred to in *paragraph 17.18(c)*.

17.22 Part 3 of the Drugs Act 2005 also requires police officers to have regard to any guidance issued by the Secretary of State in respect of the assessment provisions.

Code **C**

### Notes for guidance

*17A*    *When warning a person who is asked to provide a urine or non-intimate sample in accordance with paragraph 17.6(b), the following form of words may be used:*
   *'You do not have to provide a sample, but I must warn you that if you fail or refuse without good cause to do so, you will commit an offence for which you may be imprisoned, or fined, or both'. Where the Welsh language is appropriate, the following form of words may be used: 'Does dim rhaid i chi roi sampl, ond mae'n rhaid i mi eich rhybuddio y byddwch chi'n cyflawni trosedd os byddwch chi'n methu neu yn gwrthod gwneud hynny heb reswm da, ac y gellir, oherwydd hynny, eich carcharu, eich dirwyo, neu'r ddau.'*

*17B*    *A sample has to be sufficient and suitable. A sufficient sample is sufficient in quantity and quality to enable drug-testing analysis to take place. A suitable sample is one which by its nature, is suitable for a particular form of drug analysis.*

*17C*    *A prescribed person in paragraph 17.13 is one who is prescribed in regulations made by the Secretary of State under section 63B(6) of the Police and Criminal Evidence Act 1984. [The regulations are currently contained in regulation SI 2001 No. 2645, the Police and Criminal Evidence Act 1984 (Drug Testing Persons in Police Detention) (Prescribed Persons) Regulations 2001.]*

*17D*    *The retention of the sample in paragraph 17.16(b) allows for the sample to be sent for confirmatory testing and analysis if the detainee disputes the test. But such samples, and the information derived from them, may not be subsequently used in the investigation of any offence or in evidence against the persons from whom they were taken.*

*17E*    *Trigger offences are:*

    *1. Offences under the following provisions of the Theft Act 1968:*

       *section 1*     *(theft)*
       *section 8*     *(robbery)*
       *section 9*     *(burglary)*

|  |  |
|---|---|
| section 10 | *(aggravated burglary)* |
| section 12 | *(taking a motor vehicle or other conveyance without authority)* |
| section 12A | *(aggravated vehicle-taking)* |
| section 15 | *(obtaining property by deception)* |
| section 22 | *(handling stolen goods)* |
| section 25 | *(going equipped for stealing etc.)* |

2.  *Offences under the following provisions of the Misuse of Drugs Act 1971, if committed in respect of a specified Class A drug:—*

|  |  |
|---|---|
| section 4 | *(restriction on production and supply of controlled drugs)* |
| section 5(2) | *(possession of a controlled drug)* |
| section 5(3) | *(possession of a controlled drug with intent to supply)* |

3.  *Offences under the following provisions of the Fraud Act 2006:*

|  |  |
|---|---|
| section 1 | *(fraud)* |
| section 6 | *(possession etc. of articles for use in frauds)* |
| section 7 | *(making or supplying articles for use in frauds)* |

3A.  *An offence under section 1(1) of the Criminal Attempts Act 1981 if committed in respect of an offence under*

    *(a)  any of the following provisions of the Theft Act 1968:*

|  |  |
|---|---|
| section 1 | *(theft)* |
| section 8 | *(robbery)* |
| section 9 | *(burglary)* |
| section 22 | *(handling stolen goods)* |

    *(b)  section 1 of the Fraud Act 2006 (fraud)*

4.  *Offences under the following provisions of the Vagrancy Act 1824:*

|  |  |
|---|---|
| section 3 | *(begging)* |
| section 4 | *(persistent begging)* |

17F   *The power to take samples is subject to notification by the Secretary of State that appropriate arrangements for the taking of samples have been made for the police area as a whole or for the particular police station concerned for whichever of the following is specified in the notification:*

    *(a)  persons in respect of whom the arrest condition is met;*

    *(b)  persons in respect of whom the charge condition is met;*

    *(c)  persons who have not attained the age of 18.*

    *Note: Notification is treated as having been given for the purposes of the charge condition in relation to a police area, if testing (on charge) under section 63B(2) of PACE was in force immediately before section 7 of the Drugs Act 2005 was brought into force; and for the purposes of the age condition, in relation to a police area or police station, if immediately before that day, notification that arrangements had been made for the taking of samples from persons under the age of 18 (those aged 14–17) had been given and had not been withdrawn.*

17G   *Appropriate adult in paragraph 17.7 means the person's—*

    *(a)  parent or guardian or, if they are in the care of a local authority or voluntary organisation, a person representing that authority or organisation; or*

    *(b)  a social worker of, in England, a local authority or, in Wales, a local authority social services department; or*

    *(c)  if no person falling within (a) or (b) above is available, any responsible person aged 18 or over who is not a police officer or a person employed by the police.*

## Annex A—Intimate and Strip Searches

### A Intimate Search

1. An intimate search consists of the physical examination of a person's body orifices other than the mouth. The intrusive nature of such searches means the actual and potential risks associated with intimate searches must never be underestimated.

#### (a) Action

2. Body orifices other than the mouth may be searched only:
   (a) if authorised by an officer of inspector rank or above who has reasonable grounds for believing that the person may have concealed on themselves:
      (i)   anything which they could and might use to cause physical injury to themselves or others at the station; or
      (ii)  a Class A drug which they intended to supply to another or to export; and the officer has reasonable grounds for believing that an intimate search is the only means of removing those items; and
   (b) if the search is under *paragraph 2(a)(ii)* (a drug offence search), the detainee's appropriate consent has been given in writing.

2A. Before the search begins, a police officer, designated detention officer or staff custody officer, must tell the detainee:
   (a) that the authority to carry out the search has been given;
   (b) the grounds for giving the authorisation and for believing that the article cannot be removed without an intimate search.

2B. Before a detainee is asked to give appropriate consent to a search under *paragraph 2(a)(ii)* (a drug offence search) they must be warned that if they refuse without good cause their refusal may harm their case if it comes to trial, see *Note A6*. This warning may be given by a police officer or member of police staff. A detainee who is not legally represented must be reminded of their entitlement to have free legal advice, see *Code C, paragraph 6.5*, and the reminder noted in the custody record.

3. An intimate search may only be carried out by a registered medical practitioner or registered nurse, unless an officer of at least inspector rank considers this is not practicable and the search is to take place under *paragraph 2(a)(i)*, in which case a police officer may carry out the search. See *Notes A1 to A5*

3A. Any proposal for a search under *paragraph 2(a)(i)* to be carried out by someone other than a registered medical practitioner or registered nurse must only be considered as a last resort and when the authorising officer is satisfied the risks associated with allowing the item to remain with the detainee outweigh the risks associated with removing it. See *Notes A1 to A5*

4. An intimate search under:
   • *paragraph 2(a)(i)* may take place only at a hospital, surgery, other medical premises or police station
   • *paragraph 2(a)(ii)* may take place only at a hospital, surgery or other medical premises and must be carried out by a registered medical practitioner or a registered nurse

5. An intimate search at a police station of a juvenile or mentally disordered or otherwise mentally vulnerable person may take place only in the presence of an

appropriate adult of the same sex, unless the detainee specifically requests a particular adult of the opposite sex who is readily available. In the case of a juvenile the search may take place in the absence of the appropriate adult only if the juvenile signifies in the presence of the appropriate adult they do not want the adult present during the search and the adult agrees. A record shall be made of the juvenile's decision and signed by the appropriate adult.

6. When an intimate search under *paragraph 2(a)(i)* is carried out by a police officer, the officer must be of the same sex as the detainee. A minimum of two people, other than the detainee, must be present during the search. Subject to *paragraph 5*, no person of the opposite sex who is not a medical practitioner or nurse shall be present, nor shall anyone whose presence is unnecessary. The search shall be conducted with proper regard to the sensitivity and vulnerability of the detainee.

**(b) Documentation**

7. In the case of an intimate search, the following shall be recorded as soon as practicable, in the detainee's custody record:
   (a) for searches under *paragraphs 2(a)(i)* and *(ii)*;
      • the authorisation to carry out the search;
      • the grounds for giving the authorisation;
      • the grounds for believing the article could not be removed without an intimate search;
      • which parts of the detainee's body were searched;
      • who carried out the search;
      • who was present;
      • the result.
   (b) for searches under paragraph 2(a)(ii):
      • the giving of the warning required by *paragraph 2B*;
      • the fact that the appropriate consent was given or (as the case may be) refused, and if refused, the reason given for the refusal (if any).

8. If an intimate search is carried out by a police officer, the reason why it was impracticable for a registered medical practitioner or registered nurse to conduct it must be recorded.

**B Strip Search**

9. A strip search is a search involving the removal of more than outer clothing. In this Code, outer clothing includes shoes and socks.

**(a) Action**

10. A strip search may take place only if it is considered necessary to remove an article which a detainee would not be allowed to keep, and the officer reasonably considers the detainee might have concealed such an article. Strip searches shall not be routinely carried out if there is no reason to consider that articles are concealed.

*The Conduct of Strip Searches*

11. When strip searches are conducted:
   (a) a police officer carrying out a strip search must be the same sex as the detainee;

(b)  the search shall take place in an area where the detainee cannot be seen by anyone who does not need to be present, nor by a member of the opposite sex except an appropriate adult who has been specifically requested by the detainee;

(c)  except in cases of urgency, where there is risk of serious harm to the detainee or to others, whenever a strip search involves exposure of intimate body parts, there must be at least two people present other than the detainee, and if the search is of a juvenile or mentally disordered or otherwise mentally vulnerable person, one of the people must be the appropriate adult. Except in urgent cases as above, a search of a juvenile may take place in the absence of the appropriate adult only if the juvenile signifies in the presence of the appropriate adult that they do not want the adult to be present during the search and the adult agrees. A record shall be made of the juvenile's decision and signed by the appropriate adult. The presence of more than two people, other than an appropriate adult, shall be permitted only in the most exceptional circumstances;

(d)  the search shall be conducted with proper regard to the sensitivity and vulnerability of the detainee in these circumstances and every reasonable effort shall be made to secure the detainee's co-operation and minimise embarrassment. Detainees who are searched shall not normally be required to remove all their clothes at the same time, e.g. a person should be allowed to remove clothing above the waist and redress before removing further clothing;

(e)  if necessary to assist the search, the detainee may be required to hold their arms in the air or to stand with their legs apart and bend forward so a visual examination may be made of the genital and anal areas provided no physical contact is made with any body orifice;

(f)  if articles are found, the detainee shall be asked to hand them over. If articles are found within any body orifice other than the mouth, and the detainee refuses to hand them over, their removal would constitute an intimate search, which must be carried out as in *Part A*;

(g)  a strip search shall be conducted as quickly as possible, and the detainee allowed to dress as soon as the procedure is complete.

**(b) Documentation**

12. A record shall be made on the custody record of a strip search including the reason it was considered necessary, those present and any result.

### Notes for guidance

*A1  Before authorising any intimate search, the authorising officer must make every reasonable effort to persuade the detainee to hand the article over without a search. If the detainee agrees, a registered medical practitioner or registered nurse should whenever possible be asked to assess the risks involved and, if necessary, attend to assist the detainee.*

*A2  If the detainee does not agree to hand the article over without a search, the authorising officer must carefully review all the relevant factors before authorising an intimate search. In particular, the officer must consider whether the grounds for believing an article may be concealed are reasonable.*

Code **C**

A3 *If authority is given for a search under paragraph 2(a)(i), a registered medical practitioner or registered nurse shall be consulted whenever possible. The presumption should be that the search will be conducted by the registered medical practitioner or registered nurse and the authorising officer must make every reasonable effort to persuade the detainee to allow the medical practitioner or nurse to conduct the search.*

A4 *A constable should only be authorised to carry out a search as a last resort and when all other approaches have failed. In these circumstances, the authorising officer must be satisfied the detainee might use the article for one or more of the purposes in paragraph 2(a)(i) and the physical injury likely to be caused is sufficiently severe to justify authorising a constable to carry out the search.*

A5 *If an officer has any doubts whether to authorise an intimate search by a constable, the officer should seek advice from an officer of superintendent rank or above.*

A6 *In warning a detainee who is asked to consent to an intimate drug offence search, as in paragraph 2B, the following form of words may be used:*
*'You do not have to allow yourself to be searched, but I must warn you that if you refuse without good cause, your refusal may harm your case if it comes to trial.' Where the use of the Welsh Language is appropriate, the following form of words may be used: 'Nid oes rhaid i chi roi caniatâd i gael eich archwilio, ond mae'n rhaid i mi eich rhybuddioos gwrthodwch heb reswm da, y gallai eich penderfyniad i wrthod wneud niwed i'ch achos pe bai'n dod gerbron llys.'*

### ANNEX B—DELAY IN NOTIFYING ARREST OR ALLOWING ACCESS TO LEGAL ADVICE

#### A Persons Detained Under PACE

1. The exercise of the rights in *Section 5* or *Section 6*, or both, may be delayed if the person is in police detention, as in PACE, section 118(2), in connection with an indictable offence, has not yet been charged with an offence and an officer of superintendent rank or above, or inspector rank or above only for the rights in *Section 5*, has reasonable grounds for believing their exercise will:
    (i) lead to:
       • interference with, or harm to, evidence connected with an indictable offence; or
       • interference with, or physical harm to, other people; or
    (ii) lead to alerting other people suspected of having committed an indictable offence but not yet arrested for it; or
    (iii) hinder the recovery of property obtained in consequence of the commission of such an offence.
2. These rights may also be delayed if the officer has reasonable grounds to believe that:
    (i) the person detained for an indictable offence has benefited from their criminal conduct (decided in accordance with Part 2 of the Proceeds of Crime Act 2002); and
    (ii) the recovery of the value of the property constituting that benefit will be hindered by the exercise of either right.
3. Authority to delay a detainee's right to consult privately with a solicitor may be given only if the authorising officer has reasonable grounds to believe the

solicitor the detainee wants to consult will, inadvertently or otherwise, pass on a message from the detainee or act in some other way which will have any of the consequences specified under *paragraphs 1 or 2*. In these circumstances the detainee must be allowed to choose another solicitor. See *Note B3*

4. If the detainee wishes to see a solicitor, access to that solicitor may not be delayed on the grounds they might advise the detainee not to answer questions or the solicitor was initially asked to attend the police station by someone else. In the latter case the detainee must be told the solicitor has come to the police station at another person's request, and must be asked to sign the custody record to signify whether they want to see the solicitor.

5. The fact the grounds for delaying notification of arrest may be satisfied does not automatically mean the grounds for delaying access to legal advice will also be satisfied.

6. These rights may be delayed only for as long as grounds exist and in no case beyond 36 hours after the relevant time as in PACE, section 41. If the grounds cease to apply within this time, the detainee must, as soon as practicable, be asked if they want to exercise either right, the custody record must be noted accordingly, and action taken in accordance with the relevant section of the Code.

7. A detained person must be permitted to consult a solicitor for a reasonable time before any court hearing.

**B  Not Used**

**C  Documentation**

13. The grounds for action under this Annex shall be recorded and the detainee informed of them as soon as practicable.

14. Any reply given by a detainee under *paragraphs 6 or 11* must be recorded and the detainee asked to endorse the record in relation to whether they want to receive legal advice at this point.

**D  Cautions and Special Warnings**

15. When a suspect detained at a police station is interviewed during any period for which access to legal advice has been delayed under this Annex, the court or jury may not draw adverse inferences from their silence.

**Notes for guidance**

*B1  Even if Annex B applies in the case of a juvenile, or a person who is mentally disordered or otherwise mentally vulnerable, action to inform the appropriate adult and the person responsible for a juvenile's welfare if that is a different person, must nevertheless be taken as in paragraph 3.13 and 3.15.*

*B2  In the case of Commonwealth citizens and foreign nationals, see Note 7A.*

*B3  A decision to delay access to a specific solicitor is likely to be a rare occurrence and only when it can be shown the suspect is capable of misleading that particular solicitor and there is more than a substantial risk that the suspect will succeed in causing information to be conveyed which will lead to one or more of the specified consequences.*

Code **C**

ANNEX C—RESTRICTION ON DRAWING ADVERSE INFERENCES
FROM SILENCE AND TERMS OF THE CAUTION WHEN THE
RESTRICTION APPLIES

### (a) The Restriction on Drawing Adverse Inferences from Silence

1. The Criminal Justice and Public Order Act 1994, sections 34, 36 and 37 as amended by the Youth Justice and Criminal Evidence Act 1999, section 58 describe the conditions under which adverse inferences may be drawn from a person's failure or refusal to say anything about their involvement in the offence when interviewed, after being charged or informed they may be prosecuted. These provisions are subject to an overriding restriction on the ability of a court or jury to draw adverse inferences from a person's silence. This restriction applies:

    (a) to any detainee at a police station, see *Note 10C* who, before being interviewed, see *section 11* or being charged or informed they may be prosecuted, see *section 16*, has:
        (i) asked for legal advice, see *section 6, paragraph 6.1*;
        (ii) not been allowed an opportunity to consult a solicitor, including the duty solicitor, as in this Code; and
        (iii) not changed their mind about wanting legal advice, see *section 6, paragraph 6.6(d)*.

    Note the condition in (ii) will
    —apply when a detainee who has asked for legal advice is interviewed before speaking to a solicitor as in *section 6, paragraph 6.6(a)* or *(b)*.
    —not apply if the detained person declines to ask for the duty solicitor,
    —see *section 6, paragraphs 6.6(c)* and *(d)*.

    (b) to any person charged with, or informed they may be prosecuted for, an offence who:
        (i) has had brought to their notice a written statement made by another person or the content of an interview with another person which relates to that offence, see *section 16, paragraph 16.4*;
        (ii) is interviewed about that offence, see *section 16, paragraph 16.5*; or
        (iii) makes a written statement about that offence, see *Annex D paragraphs 4* and *9*.

### (b) Terms of the caution when the restriction applies

2. When a requirement to caution arises at a time when the restriction on drawing adverse inferences from silence applies, the caution shall be:
*'You do not have to say anything, but anything you do say may be given in evidence.'*
Where the use of the Welsh Language is appropriate, the caution may be used directly in Welsh in the following terms: *'Does dim rhaid i chi ddweud dim byd, ond gall unrhyw beth yr ydych chi'n ei ddweud gael ei roi fel tystiolaeth.'*

3. Whenever the restriction either begins to apply or ceases to apply after a caution has already been given, the person shall be re-cautioned in the appropriate terms. The changed position on drawing inferences and that the previous caution no longer applies shall also be explained to the detainee in ordinary language. See *Note C2*

## Notes for guidance

*C1  The restriction on drawing inferences from silence does not apply to a person who has not been detained and who therefore cannot be prevented from seeking legal advice if they want to, see paragraphs 10.2 and 3.15.*

*C2  The following is suggested as a framework to help explain changes in the position on drawing adverse inferences if the restriction on drawing adverse inferences from silence:*

*(a)  begins to apply:*

'*The caution you were previously given no longer applies. This is because after that caution:*

*(i)  you asked to speak to a solicitor but have not yet been allowed an opportunity to speak to a solicitor. See paragraph 1(a); or*

*(ii)  you have been charged with/informed you may be prosecuted.' See paragraph 1(b).*

'*This means that from now on, adverse inferences cannot be drawn at court and your defence will not be harmed just because you choose to say nothing. Please listen carefully to the caution I am about to give you because it will apply from now on. You will see that it does not say anything about your defence being harmed.'*

Code **C**

*(b)  ceases to apply before or at the time the person is charged or informed they may be prosecuted, see paragraph 1(a);*

'*The caution you were previously given no longer applies. This is because after that caution you have been allowed an opportunity to speak to a solicitor. Please listen carefully to the caution I am about to give you because it will apply from now on. It explains how your defence at court may be affected if you choose to say nothing.'*

### Annex D—Written Statements Under Caution

#### (a) Written by a person under caution

1.  A person shall always be invited to write down what they want to say.

2.  A person who has not been charged with, or informed they may be prosecuted for, any offence to which the statement they want to write relates, shall:

(a)  unless the statement is made at a time when the restriction on drawing adverse inferences from silence applies, see Annex C, be asked to write out and sign the following before writing what they want to say:

'*I make this statement of my own free will. I understand that I do not have to say anything but that it may harm my defence if I do not mention when questioned something which I later rely on in court. This statement may be given in evidence.*';

(b)  if the statement is made at a time when the restriction on drawing adverse inferences from silence applies, be asked to write out and sign the following before writing what they want to say;

'*I make this statement of my own free will. I understand that I do not have to say anything. This statement may be given in evidence.*'

3.  When a person, on the occasion of being charged with or informed they may be prosecuted for any offence, asks to make a statement which relates to any such offence and wants to write it they shall:

(a)  unless the restriction on drawing adverse inferences from silence, see *Annex C*, applied when they were so charged or informed they may be prosecuted, be asked to write out and sign the following before writing what they want to say:

*'I make this statement of my own free will. I understand that I do not have to say anything but that it may harm my defence if I do not mention when questioned something which I later rely on in court. This statement may be given in evidence.';*

(b) if the restriction on drawing adverse inferences from silence applied when they were so charged or informed they may be prosecuted, be asked to write out and sign the following before writing what they want to say:

*'I make this statement of my own free will. I understand that I do not have to say anything. This statement may be given in evidence.'*

4. When a person, who has already been charged with or informed they may be prosecuted for any offence, asks to make a statement which relates to any such offence and wants to write it they shall be asked to write out and sign the following before writing what they want to say:

*'I make this statement of my own free will. I understand that I do not have to say anything. This statement may be given in evidence.';*

5. Any person writing their own statement shall be allowed to do so without any prompting except a police officer or other police staff may indicate to them which matters are material or question any ambiguity in the statement.

**(b) Written by a police officer or other police staff**

6. If a person says they would like someone to write the statement for them, a police officer, or other police staff shall write the statement.

7. If the person has not been charged with, or informed they may be prosecuted for, any offence to which the statement they want to make relates they shall, before starting, be asked to sign, or make their mark, to the following:

(a) unless the statement is made at a time when the restriction on drawing adverse inferences from silence applies, see Annex C:

*'I, .............., wish to make a statement. I want someone to write down what I say. I understand that I do not have to say anything but that it may harm my defence if I do not mention when questioned something which I later rely on in court. This statement may be given in evidence.';*

(b) if the statement is made at a time when the restriction on drawing adverse inferences from silence applies:

*'I, .............., wish to make a statement. I want someone to write down what I say. I understand that I do not have to say anything. This statement may be given in evidence.'*

8. If, on the occasion of being charged with or informed they may be prosecuted for any offence, the person asks to make a statement which relates to any such offence they shall before starting be asked to sign, or make their mark to, the following:

(a) unless the restriction on drawing adverse inferences from silence applied, see *Annex C*, when they were so charged or informed they may be prosecuted:

*'I, .............., wish to make a statement. I want someone to write down what I say. I understand that I do not have to say anything but that it may harm my defence*

*if I do not mention when questioned something which I later rely on in court. This statement may be given in evidence.';*

(b) if the restriction on drawing adverse inferences from silence applied when they were so charged or informed they may be prosecuted:

*'I, ............, wish to make a statement. I want someone to write down what I say. I understand that I do not have to say anything. This statement may be given in evidence.'*

9. If, having already been charged with or informed they may be prosecuted for any offence, a person asks to make a statement which relates to any such offence they shall before starting, be asked to sign, or make their mark to:

*'I, ............, wish to make a statement. I want someone to write down what I say. I understand that I do not have to say anything. This statement may be given in evidence.'*

10. The person writing the statement must take down the exact words spoken by the person making it and must not edit or paraphrase it. Any questions that are necessary, e.g. to make it more intelligible, and the answers given must be recorded at the same time on the statement form.

11. When the writing of a statement is finished the person making it shall be asked to read it and to make any corrections, alterations or additions they want. When they have finished reading they shall be asked to write and sign or make their mark on the following certificate at the end of the statement:

*'I have read the above statement, and I have been able to correct, alter or add anything I wish. This statement is true. I have made it of my own free will.'*

12. If the person making the statement cannot read, or refuses to read it, or to write the above mentioned certificate at the end of it or to sign it, the person taking the statement shall read it to them and ask them if they would like to correct, alter or add anything and to put their signature or make their mark at the end. The person taking the statement shall certify on the statement itself what has occurred.

## ANNEX E—SUMMARY OF PROVISIONS RELATING TO MENTALLY DISORDERED AND OTHERWISE MENTALLY VULNERABLE PEOPLE

1. If an officer has any suspicion, or is told in good faith, that a person of any age may be mentally disordered or otherwise mentally vulnerable, or mentally incapable of understanding the significance of questions or their replies that person shall be treated as mentally disordered or otherwise mentally vulnerable for the purposes of this Code. See *paragraph 1.4*

2. In the case of a person who is mentally disordered or otherwise mentally vulnerable, 'the appropriate adult' means:
   (a) a relative, guardian or other person responsible for their care or custody;
   (b) someone experienced in dealing with mentally disordered or mentally vulnerable people but who is not a police officer or employed by the police;
   (c) failing these, some other responsible adult aged 18 or over who is not a police officer or employed by the police.
   See *paragraph 1.7(b) and Note 1D*

3. If the custody officer authorises the detention of a person who is mentally vulnerable or appears to be suffering from a mental disorder, the custody officer

**Code C**

must as soon as practicable inform the appropriate adult of the grounds for detention and the person's whereabouts, and ask the adult to come to the police station to see them. If the appropriate adult:

- is already at the station when information is given as in *paragraphs 3.1* to *3.5* the information must be given in their presence
- is not at the station when the provisions of *paragraph 3.1* to *3.5* are complied with these provisions must be complied with again in their presence once they arrive.

See *paragraphs 3.15* to *3.17*

4.  If the appropriate adult, having been informed of the right to legal advice, considers legal advice should be taken, the provisions of *section 6* apply as if the mentally disordered or otherwise mentally vulnerable person had requested access to legal advice. See *paragraph 3.19* and *Note E1*.

5.  The custody officer must make sure a person receives appropriate clinical attention as soon as reasonably practicable if the person appears to be suffering from a mental disorder or in urgent cases immediately call the nearest health care professional or an ambulance. It is not intended these provisions delay the transfer of a detainee to a place of safety under the Mental Health Act 1983, section 136 if that is applicable. If an assessment under that Act is to take place at a police station, the custody officer must consider whether an appropriate health care professional should be called to conduct an initial clinical check on the detainee. See *paragraph 9.5* and *9.6*

6.  It is imperative a mentally disordered or otherwise mentally vulnerable person detained under the Mental Health Act 1983, section 136 be assessed as soon as possible. If that assessment is to take place at the police station, an approved social worker and registered medical practitioner shall be called to the station as soon as possible in order to interview and examine the detainee. Once the detainee has been interviewed, examined and suitable arrangements been made for their treatment or care, they can no longer be detained under section 136. A detainee should be immediately discharged from detention if a registered medical practitioner having examined them, concludes they are not mentally disordered within the meaning of the Act. See *paragraph 3.16*

7.  If a mentally disordered or otherwise mentally vulnerable person is cautioned in the absence of the appropriate adult, the caution must be repeated in the appropriate adult's presence. See *paragraph 10.12*

8.  A mentally disordered or otherwise mentally vulnerable person must not be interviewed or asked to provide or sign a written statement in the absence of the appropriate adult unless the provisions of *paragraphs 11.1* or *11.18* to *11.20* apply. Questioning in these circumstances may not continue in the absence of the appropriate adult once sufficient information to avert the risk has been obtained. A record shall be made of the grounds for any decision to begin an interview in these circumstances. See *paragraphs 11.1, 11.15* and *11.18* to *11.20*

9.  If the appropriate adult is present at an interview, they shall be informed they are not expected to act simply as an observer and the purposes of their presence are to:

- advise the interviewee

- observe whether or not the interview is being conducted properly and fairly
- facilitate communication with the interviewee

See *paragraph 11.17*

10. If the detention of a mentally disordered or otherwise mentally vulnerable person is reviewed by a review officer or a superintendent, the appropriate adult must, if available at the time, be given an opportunity to make representations to the officer about the need for continuing detention. See *paragraph 15.3*

11. If the custody officer charges a mentally disordered or otherwise mentally vulnerable person with an offence or takes such other action as is appropriate when there is sufficient evidence for a prosecution this must be done in the presence of the appropriate adult. The written notice embodying any charge must be given to the appropriate adult. See *paragraphs 16.1 to 16.4A*

12. An intimate or strip search of a mentally disordered or otherwise mentally vulnerable person may take place only in the presence of the appropriate adult of the same sex, unless the detainee specifically requests the presence of a particular adult of the opposite sex. A strip search may take place in the absence of an appropriate adult only in cases of urgency when there is a risk of serious harm to the detainee or others. See *Annex A, paragraphs 5 and 11(c)*

13. Particular care must be taken when deciding whether to use any form of approved restraints on a mentally disordered or otherwise mentally vulnerable person in a locked cell. See *paragraph 8.2*

**Code C**

### Notes for guidance

E1  *The purpose of the provision at paragraph 3.19 is to protect the rights of a mentally disordered or otherwise mentally vulnerable detained person who does not understand the significance of what is said to them. If the detained person wants to exercise the right to legal advice, the appropriate action should be taken and not delayed until the appropriate adult arrives. A mentally disordered or otherwise mentally vulnerable detained person should always be given an opportunity, when an appropriate adult is called to the police station, to consult privately with a solicitor in the absence of the appropriate adult if they want.*

E2  *Although people who are mentally disordered or otherwise mentally vulnerable are often capable of providing reliable evidence, they may, without knowing or wanting to do so, be particularly prone in certain circumstances to provide information that may be unreliable, misleading or self-incriminating. Special care should always be taken when questioning such a person, and the appropriate adult should be involved if there is any doubt about a person's mental state or capacity. Because of the risk of unreliable evidence, it is important to obtain corroboration of any facts admitted whenever possible.*

E3  *Because of the risks referred to in Note E2, which the presence of the appropriate adult is intended to minimise, officers of superintendent rank or above should exercise their discretion to authorise the commencement of an interview in the appropriate adult's absence only in exceptional cases, if it is necessary to avert an immediate risk of serious harm. See* paragraphs 11.1, 11.18 to 11.20

ANNEX F—COUNTRIES WITH WHICH BILATERAL CONSULAR CONVENTIONS
OR AGREEMENTS REQUIRING NOTIFICATION OF THE ARREST AND
DETENTION OF THEIR NATIONALS ARE IN FORCE AS AT 1 APRIL 2003

| | |
|---|---|
| Armenia | France |
| Austria | Georgia |
| Azerbaijan | German Federal Republic |
| Belarus | Greece |
| Belgium | Hungary |
| Bosnia-Herzegovina | Italy |
| Bulgaria | Japan |
| China* | Kazakhstan |
| Croatia | Macedonia |
| Cuba | Mexico |
| Czech Republic | Moldova |
| Denmark | Mongolia |
| Egypt | Norway |
| Poland | Tajikistan |
| Romania | Turkmenistan |
| Russia | Ukraine |
| Slovak Republic | USA |
| Slovenia | Uzbekistan |
| Spain | Yugoslavia |
| Sweden | |

## ANNEX G—FITNESS TO BE INTERVIEWED

1.  This Annex contains general guidance to help police officers and health care professionals assess whether a detainee might be at risk in an interview.
2.  A detainee may be at risk in a interview if it is considered that:
    (a)  conducting the interview could significantly harm the detainee's physical or mental state;
    (b)  anything the detainee says in the interview about their involvement or suspected involvement in the offence about which they are being interviewed **might** be considered unreliable in subsequent court proceedings because of their physical or mental state.
3.  In assessing whether the detainee should be interviewed, the following must be considered:
    (a)  how the detainee's physical or mental state might affect their ability to understand the nature and purpose of the interview, to comprehend what is being asked and to appreciate the significance of any answers given and make rational decisions about whether they want to say anything;

---

* Police are required to inform Chinese officials of arrest/detention in the Manchester consular district only. This comprises Derbyshire, Durham, Greater Manchester, Lancashire, Merseyside, North South and West Yorkshire, and Tyne and Wear.

(b) the extent to which the detainee's replies may be affected by their physical or mental condition rather than representing a rational and accurate explanation of their involvement in the offence;

(c) how the nature of the interview, which could include particularly probing questions, might affect the detainee.

4.  It is essential health care professionals who are consulted consider the functional ability of the detainee rather than simply relying on a medical diagnosis, e.g. it is possible for a person with severe mental illness to be fit for interview.

5.  Health care professionals should advise on the need for an appropriate adult to be present, whether reassessment of the person's fitness for interview may be necessary if the interview lasts beyond a specified time, and whether a further specialist opinion may be required.

6.  When health care professionals identify risks they should be asked to quantify the risks. They should inform the custody officer:
    - whether the person's condition:
      —is likely to improve
      —will require or be amenable to treatment; and
    - indicate how long it may take for such improvement to take effect

7.  The role of the health care professional is to consider the risks and advise the custody officer of the outcome of that consideration. The health care professional's determination and any advice or recommendations should be made in writing and form part of the custody record.

8.  Once the health care professional has provided that information, it is a matter for the custody officer to decide whether or not to allow the interview to go ahead and if the interview is to proceed, to determine what safeguards are needed. Nothing prevents safeguards being provided in addition to those required under the Code. An example might be to have an appropriate health care professional present during the interview, in addition to an appropriate adult, in order constantly to monitor the person's condition and how it is being affected by the interview.

**Code C**

## ANNEX H—DETAINED PERSON: OBSERVATION LIST

1.  If any detainee fails to meet any of the following criteria, an appropriate health care professional or an ambulance must be called.

2.  When assessing the level of rousability, consider:
    *Rousability*—can they be woken?
    - go into the cell
    - call their name
    - shake gently

    *Response to questions*—can they give appropriate answers to questions such as:
    - What's your name?
    - Where do you live?
    - Where do you think you are?

    *Response to commands*—can they respond appropriately to commands such as:
    - Open your eyes!
    - Lift one arm, now the other arm!

3.  Remember to take into account the possibility or presence of other illnesses, injury, or mental condition, a person who is drowsy and smells of alcohol may also have the following:
    - Diabetes
    - Epilepsy
    - Head injury
    - Drug intoxication or overdose
    - Stroke

## ANNEX I—NOT USED

## ANNEX J—NOT USED

## ANNEX K—X-RAYS AND ULTRASOUND SCANS

### (a) Action

1.  PACE, section 55A allows a person who has been arrested and is in police detention to have an x-ray taken of them or an ultrasound scan to be carried out on them (or both) if:
    (a) authorised by an officer of inspector rank or above who has reasonable grounds for believing that the detainee:
        (i) may have swallowed a Class A drug; and
        (ii) was in possession of that Class A drug with the intention of supplying it to another or to export; and
    (b) the detainee's appropriate consent has been given in writing.
2.  Before an x-ray is taken or an ultrasound scan carried out, a police officer, designated detention officer or staff custody officer must tell the detainee:
    (a) that the authority has been given; and
    (b) the grounds for giving the authorisation.
3.  Before a detainee is asked to give appropriate consent to an x-ray or an ultrasound scan, they must be warned that if they refuse without good cause their refusal may harm their case if it comes to trial, see *Notes K1* and *K2*. This warning may be given by a police officer or member of police staff. A detainee who is not legally represented must be reminded of their entitlement to have free legal advice, see *Code C, paragraph 6.5*, and the reminder noted in the custody record.
4.  An x-ray may be taken, or an ultrasound scan may be carried out, only by a registered medical practitioner or registered nurse, and only at a hospital, surgery or other medical premises.

### (b) Documentation

5.  The following shall be recorded as soon as practicable in the detainee's custody record:
    (a) the authorisation to take the x-ray or carry out the ultrasound scan (or both);
    (b) the grounds for giving the authorisation;
    (c) the giving of the warning required by paragraph 3; and

(d) the fact that the appropriate consent was given or (as the case may be) refused, and if refused, the reason given for the refusal (if any); and

(e) if an x-ray is taken or an ultrasound scan carried out:
- where it was taken or carried out
- who took it or carried it out
- who was present
- the result

6. Paragraphs 1.4–1.7 of this Code apply and an appropriate adult should be present when consent is sought to any procedure under this Annex

### Notes for guidance

K1 *If authority is given for an x-ray to be taken or an ultrasound scan to be carried out (or both), consideration should be given to asking a registered medical practitioner or registered nurse to explain to the detainee what is involved and to allay any concerns the detainee might have about the effect which taking an x-ray or carrying out an ultrasound scan might have on them. If appropriate consent is not given, evidence of the explanation may, if the case comes to trial, be relevant to determining whether the detainee had a good cause for refusing.*

K2 *In warning a detainee who is asked to consent to an x-ray being taken or an ultrasound scan being carried out (or both), as in paragraph 3, the following form of words may be used:*

*'You do not have to allow an x-ray of you to be taken or an ultrasound scan to be carried out on you, but I must warn you that if you refuse without good cause, your refusal may harm your case if it comes to trial.' Where the use of the Welsh Language is appropriate, the following form of words may be provided in Welsh: 'Does dim rhaid i chi ganiatáu cymryd sgan uwchsain neu belydr-x (neu'r ddau) arnoch, ond mae'n rhaid i mi eich rhybuddio os byddwch chi'n gwrthod gwneud hynny heb reswm da, fe allai hynny niweidio eich achos pe bai'n dod gerbron llys.'*

Code C

# Appendix 5
## Code D: PACE Code of Practice for the Identification of Persons by Police Officers

This code has effect in relation to any identification procedure carried out after midnight on 31 January 2008.

### 1 INTRODUCTION

1.1 This Code of Practice concerns the principal methods used by police to identify people in connection with the investigation of offences and the keeping of accurate and reliable criminal records.

1.2 Identification by witnesses arises, e.g., if the offender is seen committing the crime and a witness is given an opportunity to identify the suspect in a video identification, identification parade or similar procedure. The procedures are designed to:
- test the witness' ability to identify the person they saw on a previous occasion
- provide safeguards against mistaken identification.

While this Code concentrates on visual identification procedures, it does not preclude the police making use of aural identification procedures such as a 'voice identification parade', where they judge that appropriate.

1.3 Identification by fingerprints applies when a person's fingerprints are taken to:
- compare with fingerprints found at the scene of a crime
- check and prove convictions
- help to ascertain a person's identity.

1.3A Identification using footwear impressions applies when a person's footwear impressions are taken to compare with impressions found at the scene of a crime.

1.4 Identification by body samples and impressions includes taking samples such as blood or hair to generate a DNA profile for comparison with material obtained from the scene of a crime, or a victim.

1.5 Taking photographs of arrested people applies to recording and checking identity and locating and tracing persons who:
- are wanted for offences
- fail to answer their bail.

1.6 Another method of identification involves searching and examining detained suspects to find, e.g., marks such as tattoos or scars which may help establish their identity or whether they have been involved in committing an offence.

1.7 The provisions of the Police and Criminal Evidence Act 1984 (PACE) and this Code are designed to make sure fingerprints, samples, impressions and photographs are taken, used and retained, and identification procedures carried out, only when justified and necessary for preventing, detecting or investigating crime. If these provisions are not observed, the application of the relevant procedures in particular cases may be open to question.

## 2 GENERAL

2.1   This Code must be readily available at all police stations for consultation by:
  - police officers and police staff
  - detained persons
  - members of the public

2.2   The provisions of this Code:
  - include the *Annexes*
  - do not include the *Notes for guidance.*

2.3   Code C, paragraph 1.4, regarding a person who may be mentally disordered or otherwise mentally vulnerable and the *Notes for guidance* applicable to those provisions apply to this Code.

2.4   Code C, paragraph 1.5, regarding a person who appears to be under the age of 17 applies to this Code.

2.5   Code C, paragraph 1.6, regarding a person who appears blind, seriously visually impaired, deaf, unable to read or speak or has difficulty orally because of a speech impediment applies to this Code.

2.6   In this Code:
  - 'appropriate adult' means the same as in Code C, paragraph 1.7,
  - 'solicitor' means the same as in Code C, paragraph 6.12

and the *Notes for guidance* applicable to those provisions apply to this Code.

2.7   References to custody officers include those performing the functions of custody officer, see *paragraph 1.9* of Code C.

2.8   When a record of any action requiring the authority of an officer of a specified rank is made under this Code, subject to *paragraph 2.18*, the officer's name and rank must be recorded.

2.9   When this Code requires the prior authority or agreement of an officer of at least inspector or superintendent rank, that authority may be given by a sergeant or chief inspector who has been authorised to perform the functions of the higher rank under PACE, section 107.

2.10  Subject to *paragraph 2.18*, all records must be timed and signed by the maker.

2.11  Records must be made in the custody record, unless otherwise specified. References to 'pocket book' include any official report book issued to police officers or police staff.

2.12  If any procedure in this Code requires a person's consent, the consent of a:
  - mentally disordered or otherwise mentally vulnerable person is only valid if given in the presence of the appropriate adult
  - juvenile, is only valid if their parent's or guardian's consent is also obtained unless the juvenile is under 14, when their parent's or guardian's consent is sufficient in its own right. If the only obstacle to an identification procedure in *section 3* is that a juvenile's parent or guardian refuses consent or reasonable efforts to obtain it have failed, the identification officer may apply the provisions of *paragraph 3.21*. See *Note 2A*

2.13 If a person is blind, seriously visually impaired or unable to read, the custody officer or identification officer shall make sure their solicitor, relative, appropriate adult or some other person likely to take an interest in them and not involved in the investigation is available to help check any documentation. When this Code requires written consent or signing, the person assisting may be asked to sign instead, if the detainee prefers. This paragraph does not require an appropriate adult to be called solely to assist in checking and signing documentation for a person who is not a juvenile, or mentally disordered or otherwise mentally vulnerable (see *Note 2B* and Code C *paragraph 3.15*).

2.14 If any procedure in this Code requires information to be given to or sought from a suspect, it must be given or sought in the appropriate adult's presence if the suspect is mentally disordered, otherwise mentally vulnerable or a juvenile. If the appropriate adult is not present when the information is first given or sought, the procedure must be repeated in the presence of the appropriate adult when they arrive. If the suspect appears deaf or there is doubt about their hearing or speaking ability or ability to understand English, and effective communication cannot be established, the information must be given or sought through an interpreter.

2.15 Any procedure in this Code involving the participation of a suspect who is mentally disordered, otherwise mentally vulnerable or a juvenile must take place in the presence of the appropriate adult. See *Code C paragraph 1.4*

2.15A Any procedure in this Code involving the participation of a witness who is or appears to be mentally disordered, otherwise mentally vulnerable or a juvenile should take place in the presence of a pre-trial support person. However, the support-person must not be allowed to prompt any identification of a suspect by a witness. See *Note 2AB*.

2.16 References to:
- 'taking a photograph', include the use of any process to produce a single, still or moving, visual image
- 'photographing a person', should be construed accordingly
- 'photographs', 'films', 'negatives' and 'copies' include relevant visual images recorded, stored, or reproduced through any medium
- 'destruction' includes the deletion of computer data relating to such images or making access to that data impossible.

2.17 Except as described, nothing in this Code affects the powers and procedures:
  (i) for requiring and taking samples of breath, blood and urine in relation to driving offences, etc, when under the influence of drink, drugs or excess alcohol under the:
    - Road Traffic Act 1988, sections 4 to 11
    - Road Traffic Offenders Act 1988, sections 15 and 16
    - Transport and Works Act 1992, sections 26 to 38;
  (ii) under the Immigration Act 1971, Schedule 2, paragraph 18, for taking photographs and fingerprints from persons detained under that Act, Schedule 2, paragraph 16 (Administrative Controls as to Control on Entry etc.); for taking fingerprints in accordance with the Immigration and Asylum Act 1999; sections 141 and 142(3), or other methods for collecting

**Code D**

information about a person's external physical characteristics provided for by regulations made under that Act, section 144;

(iii) under the Terrorism Act 2000, Schedule 8, for taking photographs, fingerprints, skin impressions, body samples or impressions from people:
- arrested under that Act, section 41,
- detained for the purposes of examination under that Act, Schedule 7, and to whom the Code of Practice issued under that Act, Schedule 14, paragraph 6, applies ('the terrorism provisions')

See *Note 2C*;

(iv) for taking photographs, fingerprints, skin impressions, body samples or impressions from people who have been:
- arrested on warrants issued in Scotland, by officers exercising powers under the Criminal Justice and Public Order Act 1994, section 136(2)
- arrested or detained without warrant by officers from a police force in Scotland exercising their powers of arrest or detention under the Criminal Justice and Public Order Act 1994, section 137(2), (Cross Border powers of arrest etc.).

Note: In these cases, police powers and duties and the person's rights and entitlements whilst at a police station in England and Wales are the same as if the person had been arrested in Scotland by a Scottish police officer.

2.18 Nothing in this Code requires the identity of officers or police staff to be recorded or disclosed:
(a) in the case of enquiries linked to the investigation of terrorism;
(b) if the officers or police staff reasonably believe recording or disclosing their names might put them in danger.

In these cases, they shall use warrant or other identification numbers and the name of their police station. See *Note 2D*

2.19 In this Code:
(a) 'designated person' means a person other than a police officer, designated under the Police Reform Act 2002, Part 4, who has specified powers and duties of police officers conferred or imposed on them;
(b) any reference to a police officer includes a designated person acting in the exercise or performance of the powers and duties conferred or imposed on them by their designation.

2.20 If a power conferred on a designated person:
(a) allows reasonable force to be used when exercised by a police officer, a designated person exercising that power has the same entitlement to use force;
(b) includes power to use force to enter any premises, that power is not exercisable by that designated person except:
(i) in the company, and under the supervision, of a police officer; or
(ii) for the purpose of:
- saving life or limb; or
- preventing serious damage to property.

2.21 Nothing in this Code prevents the custody officer, or other officer given custody of the detainee, from allowing police staff who are not designated persons to carry out individual procedures or tasks at the police station if the law allows.

However, the officer remains responsible for making sure the procedures and tasks are carried out correctly in accordance with the Codes of Practice. Any such person must be:

(a) a person employed by a police authority maintaining a police force and under the control and direction of the Chief Officer of that force;

(b) employed by a person with whom a police authority has a contract for the provision of services relating to persons arrested or otherwise in custody.

2.22 Designated persons and other police staff must have regard to any relevant provisions of the Codes of Practice.

### Notes for guidance

2A    *For the purposes of paragraph 2.12, the consent required from a parent or guardian may, for a juvenile in the care of a local authority or voluntary organisation, be given by that authority or organisation. In the case of a juvenile, nothing in paragraph 2.12 requires the parent, guardian or representative of a local authority or voluntary organi-sation to be present to give their consent, unless they are acting as the appropriate adult under paragraphs 2.14 or 2.15. However, it is important that a parent or guardian not present is fully informed before being asked to consent. They must be given the same information about the procedure and the juvenile's suspected involvement in the offence as the juvenile and appropriate adult. The parent or guardian must also be allowed to speak to the juvenile and the appropriate adult if they wish. Provided the consent is fully informed and is not withdrawn, it may be obtained at any time before the procedure takes place.*

Code D

2AB   *The Youth Justice and Criminal Evidence Act 1999 guidance 'Achieving Best Evidence in Criminal Proceedings' indicates that a pre-trial support person should accompany a vulnerable witness during any identification procedure. It states that this support person should not be (or not be likely to be) a witness in the investigation.*

2B    *People who are seriously visually impaired or unable to read may be unwilling to sign police documents. The alternative, i.e. their representative signing on their behalf, seeks to protect the interests of both police and suspects.*

2C    *Photographs, fingerprints, samples and impressions may be taken from a person detained under the terrorism provisions to help determine whether they are, or have been, involved in terrorism, as well as when there are reasonable grounds for suspect-ing their involvement in a particular offence.*

2D    *The purpose of paragraph 2.18(b) is to protect those involved in serious organised crime investigations or arrests of particularly violent suspects when there is reliable information that those arrested or their associates may threaten or cause harm to the officers. In cases of doubt, an officer of inspector rank or above should be consulted.*

## 3 IDENTIFICATION BY WITNESSES

3.1   A record shall be made of the suspect's description as first given by a potential witness. This record must:

(a) be made and kept in a form which enables details of that description to be accurately produced from it, in a visible and legible form, which can be given to the suspect or the suspect's solicitor in accordance with this Code; and

(b)  unless otherwise specified, be made before the witness takes part in any
identification procedures under *paragraphs 3.5 to 3.10, 3.21* or *3.23*.

A copy of the record shall where practicable, be given to the suspect or their
solicitor before any procedures under *paragraphs 3.5 to 3.10, 3.21* or *3.23* are carried out. See *Note 3E*

**(a) Cases when the suspect's identity is not known**

3.2  In cases when the suspect's identity is not known, a witness may be taken to a
particular neighbourhood or place to see whether they can identify the person
they saw. Although the number, age, sex, race, general description and style of
clothing of other people present at the location and the way in which any identification is made cannot be controlled, the principles applicable to the formal
procedures under *paragraphs 3.5 to 3.10* shall be followed as far as practicable.
For example:

(a)  where it is practicable to do so, a record should be made of the witness'
description of the suspect, as in paragraph 3.1(a), before asking the witness
to make an identification;

(b)  care must be taken not to direct the witness' attention to any individual
unless, taking into account all the circumstances, this cannot be avoided.
However, this does not prevent a witness being asked to look carefully at the
people around at the time or to look towards a group or in a particular direction, if this appears necessary to make sure that the witness does not over-
look a possible suspect simply because the witness is looking in the opposite
direction and also to enable the witness to make comparisons between any
suspect and others who are in the area; See *Note 3F*

(c)  where there is more than one witness, every effort should be made to keep
them separate and witnesses should be taken to see whether they can identify a person independently;

(d)  once there is sufficient information to justify the arrest of a particular individual for suspected involvement in the offence, e.g., after a witness makes
a positive identification, the provisions set out from paragraph 3.4 onwards
shall apply for any other witnesses in relation to that individual. Subject to
*paragraphs 3.12* and *3.13*, it is not necessary for the witness who makes such
a positive identification to take part in a further procedure;

(e)  the officer or police staff accompanying the witness must record, in their
pocket book, the action taken as soon as, and in as much detail, as possible.
The record should include: the date, time and place of the relevant occasion
the witness claims to have previously seen the suspect; where any identification was made; how it was made and the conditions at the time (e.g., the
distance the witness was from the suspect, the weather and light); if the witness's attention was drawn to the suspect; the reason for this; and anything
said by the witness or the suspect about the identification or the conduct of
the procedure.

3.3  A witness must not be shown photographs, computerised or artist's composite
likenesses or similar likenesses or pictures (including 'E-fit' images) if the identity of the suspect is known to the police and the suspect is available to take part
in a video identification, an identification parade or a group identification. If the

suspect's identity is not known, the showing of such images to a witness to obtain identification evidence must be done in accordance with *Annex E*.

## (b) Cases when the suspect is known and available

3.4 If the suspect's identity is known to the police and they are available, the identification procedures set out in paragraphs 3.5 to 3.10 may be used. References in this section to a suspect being 'known' mean there is sufficient information known to the police to justify the arrest of a particular person for suspected involvement in the offence. A suspect being 'available' means they are immediately available or will be within a reasonably short time and willing to take an effective part in at least one of the following which it is practicable to arrange:
- video identification;
- identification parade; or
- group identification.

*Video identification*

3.5 A 'video identification' is when the witness is shown moving images of a known suspect, together with similar images of others who resemble the suspect. Moving images must be used unless:
- the suspect is known but not available (see *paragraph 3.21* of this Code); or
- in accordance with *paragraph 2A of Annex A* of this Code, the identification officer does not consider that replication of a physical feature can be achieved or that it is not possible to conceal the location of the feature on the image of the suspect.

The identification officer may then decide to make use of video identification but using still images.

3.6 Video identifications must be carried out in accordance with *Annex A*.

*Identification parade*

3.7 An 'identification parade' is when the witness sees the suspect in a line of others who resemble the suspect.

3.8 Identification parades must be carried out in accordance with *Annex B*.

*Group identification*

3.9 A 'group identification' is when the witness sees the suspect in an informal group of people.

3.10 Group identifications must be carried out in accordance with *Annex C*.

*Arranging identification procedures*

3.11 Except for the provisions in *paragraph 3.19*, the arrangements for, and conduct of, the identification procedures in paragraphs 3.5 to 3.10 and circumstances in which an identification procedure must be held shall be the responsibility of an officer not below inspector rank who is not involved with the investigation, 'the identification officer'. Unless otherwise specified, the identification officer may allow another officer or police staff, see *paragraph 2.21*, to make arrangements for, and conduct, any of these identification procedures. In delegating these procedures, the identification officer must be able to supervise effectively and either intervene or be contacted for advice. No officer or any other person

Code **D**

involved with the investigation of the case against the suspect, beyond the extent required by these procedures, may take any part in these procedures or act as the identification officer. This does not prevent the identification officer from consulting the officer in charge of the investigation to determine which procedure to use. When an identification procedure is required, in the interest of fairness to suspects and witnesses, it must be held as soon as practicable.

*Circumstances in which an identification procedure must be held*

3.12 Whenever:
> (i) a witness has identified a suspect or purported to have identified them prior to any identification procedure set out in paragraphs 3.5 to 3.10 having been held; or
> (ii) there is a witness available, who expresses an ability to identify the suspect, or where there is a reasonable chance of the witness being able to do so, and they have not been given an opportunity to identify the suspect in any of the procedures set out in paragraphs 3.5 to 3.10,

and the suspect disputes being the person the witness claims to have seen, an identification procedure shall be held unless it is not practicable or it would serve no useful purpose in proving or disproving whether the suspect was involved in committing the offence. For example, when it is not disputed that the suspect is already well known to the witness who claims to have seen them commit the crime.

3.13 Such a procedure may also be held if the officer in charge of the investigation considers it would be useful.

*Selecting an identification procedure*

3.14 If, because of paragraph 3.12, an identification procedure is to be held, the suspect shall initially be offered a video identification unless:
> (a) a video identification is not practicable; or
> (b) an identification parade is both practicable and more suitable than a video identification; or
> (c) paragraph 3.16 applies.

The identification officer and the officer in charge of the investigation shall consult each other to determine which option is to be offered. An identification parade may not be practicable because of factors relating to the witnesses, such as their number, state of health, availability and travelling requirements. A video identification would normally be more suitable if it could be arranged and completed sooner than an identification parade.

3.15 A suspect who refuses the identification procedure first offered shall be asked to state their reason for refusing and may get advice from their solicitor and/or if present, their appropriate adult. The suspect, solicitor and/or appropriate adult shall be allowed to make representations about why another procedure should be used. A record should be made of the reasons for refusal and any representations made. After considering any reasons given, and representations made, the identification officer shall, if appropriate, arrange for the suspect to be offered an alternative which the officer considers suitable and practicable. If the officer decides it is not suitable and practicable to offer an alternative identification procedure, the reasons for that decision shall be recorded.

3.16 A group identification may initially be offered if the officer in charge of the investigation considers it is more suitable than a video identification or an identification parade and the identification officer considers it practicable to arrange.

*Notice to suspect*

3.17 Unless *paragraph 3.20* applies, before a video identification, an identification parade or group identification is arranged, the following shall be explained to the suspect:

(i)    the purposes of the video identification, identification parade or group identification;

(ii)   their entitlement to free legal advice; see Code C, *paragraph 6.5*;

(iii)  the procedures for holding it, including their right to have a solicitor or friend present;

(iv)   that they do not have to consent to or co-operate in a video identification, identification parade or group identification;

(v)    that if they do not consent to, and co-operate in, a video identification, identification parade or group identification, their refusal may be given in evidence in any subsequent trial and police may proceed covertly without their consent or make other arrangements to test whether a witness can identify them, see *paragraph 3.21*;

(vi)   whether, for the purposes of the video identification procedure, images of them have previously been obtained, see *paragraph 3.20*, and if so, that they may co-operate in providing further, suitable images to be used instead;

(vii)  if appropriate, the special arrangements for juveniles;

(viii) if appropriate, the special arrangements for mentally disordered or otherwise mentally vulnerable people;

(ix)   that if they significantly alter their appearance between being offered an identification procedure and any attempt to hold an identification procedure, this may be given in evidence if the case comes to trial, and the identification officer may then consider other forms of identification, see *paragraph 3.21* and *Note 3C*;

(x)    that a moving image or photograph may be taken of them when they attend for any identification procedure;

(xi)   whether, before their identity became known, the witness was shown photographs, a computerised or artist's composite likeness or similar likeness or image by the police, see *Note 3B*;

(xii)  that if they change their appearance before an identification parade, it may not be practicable to arrange one on the day or subsequently and, because of the appearance change, the identification officer may consider alternative methods of identification, see *Note 3C*;

(xiii) that they or their solicitor will be provided with details of the description of the suspect as first given by any witnesses who are to attend the video identification, identification parade, group identification or confrontation, see *paragraph 3.1*.

3.18 This information must also be recorded in a written notice handed to the suspect. The suspect must be given a reasonable opportunity to read the notice, after which, they should be asked to sign a second copy to indicate if they are willing to co-operate with the making of a video or take part in the identification

Code **D**

parade or group identification. The signed copy shall be retained by the identification officer.

3.19 The duties of the identification officer under *paragraphs 3.17* and *3.18* may be performed by the custody officer or other officer not involved in the investigation if:

(a) it is proposed to release the suspect in order that an identification procedure can be arranged and carried out and an inspector is not available to act as the identification officer, see *paragraph 3.11*, before the suspect leaves the station; or

(b) it is proposed to keep the suspect in police detention whilst the procedure is arranged and carried out and waiting for an inspector to act as the identification officer, see *paragraph 3.11*, would cause unreasonable delay to the investigation.

The officer concerned shall inform the identification officer of the action taken and give them the signed copy of the notice. See *Note 3C*

3.20 If the identification officer and officer in charge of the investigation suspect, on reasonable grounds that if the suspect was given the information and notice as in *paragraphs 3.17* and *3.18*, they would then take steps to avoid being seen by a witness in any identification procedure, the identification officer may arrange for images of the suspect suitable for use in a video identification procedure to be obtained before giving the information and notice. If suspect's images are obtained in these circumstances, the suspect may, for the purposes of a video identification procedure, co-operate in providing new images which if suitable, would be used instead, see *paragraph 3.17(vi)*.

### (c) Cases when the suspect is known but not available

3.21 When a known suspect is not available or has ceased to be available, see *paragraph 3.4*, the identification officer may make arrangements for a video identification (see *Annex A*). If necessary, the identification officer may follow the video identification procedures but using **still** images. Any suitable moving or **still** images may be used and these may be obtained covertly if necessary. Alternatively, the identification officer may make arrangements for a group identification. See *Note 3D*. These provisions may also be applied to juveniles where the consent of their parent or guardian is either refused or reasonable efforts to obtain that consent have failed (see *paragraph 2.12*).

3.22 Any covert activity should be strictly limited to that necessary to test the ability of the witness to identify the suspect.

3.23 The identification officer may arrange for the suspect to be confronted by the witness if none of the options referred to in paragraphs 3.5 to 3.10 or 3.21 are practicable. A 'confrontation' is when the suspect is directly confronted by the witness. A confrontation does not require the suspect's consent. Confrontations must be carried out in accordance with Annex D.

3.24 Requirements for information to be given to, or sought from, a suspect or for the suspect to be given an opportunity to view images before they are shown to a witness, do not apply if the suspect's lack of co-operation prevents the necessary action.

### (d) Documentation

3.25 A record shall be made of the video identification, identification parade, group identification or confrontation on forms provided for the purpose.

3.26 If the identification officer considers it is not practicable to hold a video identification or identification parade requested by the suspect, the reasons shall be
recorded and explained to the suspect.

3.27 A record shall be made of a person's failure or refusal to co-operate in a video
identification, identification parade or group identification and, if applicable,
of the grounds for obtaining images in accordance with *paragraph 3.20*.

### (e) Showing films and photographs of incidents and information released to the media

3.28 Nothing in this Code inhibits showing films or photographs to the public
through the national or local media, or to police officers for the purposes of
recognition and tracing suspects. However, when such material is shown to
potential witnesses, including police officers, see *Note 3A*, to obtain identification evidence, it shall be shown on an individual basis to avoid any possibility
of collusion, and, as far as possible, the showing shall follow the principles for
video identification if the suspect is known, see *Annex A*, or identification by
photographs if the suspect is not known, see *Annex E*.

3.29 When a broadcast or publication is made, see *paragraph 3.28*, a copy of the
relevant material released to the media for the purposes of recognising or tracing the suspect, shall be kept. The suspect or their solicitor shall be allowed to
view such material before any procedures under *paragraphs 3.5 to 3.10, 3.21 or
3.23* are carried out, provided it is practicable and would not unreasonably
delay the investigation. Each witness involved in the procedure shall be asked,
after they have taken part, whether they have seen any broadcast or published
films or photographs relating to the offence or any description of the suspect
and their replies shall be recorded. This paragraph does not affect any separate
requirement under the Criminal Procedure and Investigations Act 1996 to
retain material in connection with criminal investigations.

Code D

### (f) Destruction and retention of photographs taken or used in identification procedures

3.30 PACE, section 64A, see *paragraph 5.12*, provides powers to take photographs of
suspects and allows these photographs to be used or disclosed only for purposes
related to the prevention or detection of crime, the investigation of offences or
the conduct of prosecutions by, or on behalf of, police or other law enforcement and prosecuting authorities inside and outside the United Kingdom or
the enforcement of a sentence. After being so used or disclosed, they may be
retained but can only be used or disclosed for the same purposes.

3.31 Subject to *paragraph 3.33*, the photographs (and all negatives and copies), of
suspects not taken in accordance with the provisions in *paragraph 5.12* which are
taken for the purposes of, or in connection with, the identification procedures in
*paragraphs 3.5 to 3.10, 3.21 or 3.23* must be destroyed unless the suspect:
 (a) is charged with, or informed they may be prosecuted for, a recordable
 offence;
 (b) is prosecuted for a recordable offence;
 (c) is cautioned for a recordable offence or given a warning or reprimand in
 accordance with the Crime and Disorder Act 1998 for a recordable offence; or

(d) gives informed consent, in writing, for the photograph or images to be retained for purposes described in *paragraph 3.30.*

3.32 When *paragraph 3.31* requires the destruction of any photograph, the person must be given an opportunity to witness the destruction or to have a certificate confirming the destruction if they request one within five days of being informed that the destruction is required.

3.33 Nothing in *paragraph 3.31* affects any separate requirement under the Criminal Procedure and Investigations Act 1996 to retain material in connection with criminal investigations.

### Notes for guidance

*3A Except for the provisions of Annex E, paragraph 1, a police officer who is a witness for the purposes of this part of the Code is subject to the same principles and procedures as a civilian witness.*

*3B When a witness attending an identification procedure has previously been shown photographs, or been shown or provided with computerised or artist's composite likenesses, or similar likenesses or pictures, it is the officer in charge of the investigation's responsibility to make the identification officer aware of this.*

*3C The purpose of paragraph 3.19 is to avoid or reduce delay in arranging identification procedures by enabling the required information and warnings, see sub-paragraphs 3.17(ix) and 3.17(xii), to be given at the earliest opportunity.*

*3D Paragraph 3.21 would apply when a known suspect deliberately makes themself 'unavailable' in order to delay or frustrate arrangements for obtaining identification evidence. It also applies when a suspect refuses or fails to take part in a video identification, an identification parade or a group identification, or refuses or fails to take part in the only practicable options from that list. It enables any suitable images of the suspect, moving or still, which are available or can be obtained, to be used in an identification procedure. Examples include images from custody and other CCTV systems and from visually recorded interview records, see Code F Note for Guidance 2D.*

*3E When it is proposed to show photographs to a witness in accordance with Annex E, it is the responsibility of the officer in charge of the investigation to confirm to the officer responsible for supervising and directing the showing, that the first description of the suspect given by that witness has been recorded. If this description has not been recorded, the procedure under Annex E must be postponed. See Annex E paragraph 2*

*3F The admissibility and value of identification evidence obtained when carrying out the procedure under paragraph 3.2 may be compromised if:*
   *(a) before a person is identified, the witness' attention is specifically drawn to that person; or*
   *(b) the suspect's identity becomes known before the procedure.*

## 4 IDENTIFICATION BY FINGERPRINTS AND FOOTWEAR IMPRESSIONS

### (A) Taking fingerprints in connection with a criminal investigation

#### (a) General

4.1 References to 'fingerprints' means any record, produced by any method, of the skin pattern and other physical characteristics or features of a person's:
   (i) fingers; or
   (ii) palms.

**448**

**(b) Action**

4.2 A person's fingerprints may be taken in connection with the investigation of an offence only with their consent or if *paragraph 4.3* applies. If the person is at a police station consent must be in writing.

4.3 PACE, section 61, provides powers to take fingerprints without consent from any person over the age of ten years:

(a) under section 61(3), from a person detained at a police station in consequence of being arrested for a recordable offence, see Note 4A, if they have not had their fingerprints taken in the course of the investigation of the offence unless those previously taken fingerprints are not a complete set or some or all of those fingerprints are not of sufficient quality to allow satisfactory analysis, comparison or matching.

(b) under section 61(4), from a person detained at a police station who has been charged with a recordable offence, see Note 4A, or informed they will be reported for such an offence if they have not had their fingerprints taken in the course of the investigation of the offence unless those previously taken fingerprints are not a complete set or some or all of those fingerprints are not of sufficient quality to allow satisfactory analysis, comparison or matching.

(c) under section 61(4A), from a person who has been bailed to appear at a court or police station if the person:

  (i) has answered to bail for a person whose fingerprints were taken previously and there are reasonable grounds for believing they are not the same person; or

  (ii) who has answered to bail claims to be a different person from a person whose fingerprints were previously taken;

  and in either case, the court or an officer of inspector rank or above, authorises the fingerprints to be taken at the court or police station;

(d) under section 61(6), from a person who has been:

  (i) convicted of a recordable offence;

  (ii) given a caution in respect of a recordable offence which, at the time of the caution, the person admitted; or

  (iii) warned or reprimanded under the Crime and Disorder Act 1998, section 65, for a recordable offence.

4.4 PACE, section 27, provides power to:

(a) require the person as in *paragraph 4.3(d)* to attend a police station to have their fingerprints taken if the:

  (i) person has not been in police detention for the offence and has not had their fingerprints taken in the course of the investigation of that offence; or

  (ii) fingerprints that were taken from the person in the course of the investigation of that offence, do not constitute a complete set or some, or all, of the fingerprints are not of sufficient quality to allow satisfactory analysis, comparison or matching; and

(b) arrest, without warrant, a person who fails to comply with the requirement.

Code **D**

Note: The requirement must be made within one month of the date the person is convicted, cautioned, warned or reprimanded and the person must be given a period of at least 7 days within which to attend. This 7 day period need not fall during the month allowed for making the requirement.

4.5 A person's fingerprints may be taken, as above, electronically.

4.6 Reasonable force may be used, if necessary, to take a person's fingerprints without their consent under the powers as in *paragraphs 4.3* and *4.4*.

4.7 Before any fingerprints are taken with, or without, consent as above, the person must be informed:

(a) of the reason their fingerprints are to be taken;

(b) of the grounds on which the relevant authority has been given if the power mentioned in *paragraph 4.3 (c) applies*;

(c) that their fingerprints may be retained and may be subject of a speculative search against other fingerprints, see *Note 4B*, unless destruction of the fingerprints is required in accordance with *Annex F, Part (a)*; and

(d) that if their fingerprints are required to be destroyed, they may witness their destruction as provided for in *Annex F, Part (a)*.

### (c) Documentation

4.8 A record must be made as soon as possible, of the reason for taking a person's fingerprints without consent. If force is used, a record shall be made of the circumstances and those present.

4.9 A record shall be made when a person has been informed under the terms of *paragraph 4.7(c)*, of the possibility that their fingerprints may be subject of a speculative search.

### (B) Taking fingerprints in connection with immigration enquiries

### Action

4.10 A person's fingerprints may be taken for the purposes of Immigration Service enquiries in accordance with powers and procedures other than under PACE and for which the Immigration Service (not the police) are responsible, only with the person's consent in writing or if *paragraph 4.11* applies.

4.11 Powers to take fingerprints for these purposes without consent are given to police and immigration officers under the:

(a) Immigration Act 1971, Schedule 2, paragraph 18(2), when it is reasonably necessary for the purposes of identifying a person detained under the Immigration Act 1971, Schedule 2, paragraph 16 (Detention of person liable to examination or removal);

(b) Immigration and Asylum Act 1999, section 141(7)(a), from a person who fails to produce, on arrival, a valid passport with a photograph or some other document satisfactorily establishing their identity and nationality if an immigration officer does not consider the person has a reasonable excuse for the failure;

(c) Immigration and Asylum Act 1999, section 141(7)(b), from a person who has been refused entry to the UK but has been temporarily admitted if an immigration officer reasonably suspects the person might break a condition imposed on them relating to residence or reporting to a police or immigration officer, and their decision is confirmed by a chief immigration officer;

(d) Immigration and Asylum Act 1999, section 141(7)(c), when directions are given to remove a person:
- as an illegal entrant,
- liable to removal under the Immigration and Asylum Act 1999, section 10,
- who is the subject of a deportation order from the UK;

(e) Immigration and Asylum Act 1999, section 141(7)(d), from a person arrested under UK immigration laws under the Immigration Act 1971, Schedule 2, paragraph 17;

(f) Immigration and Asylum Act 1999, section 141(7)(e), from a person who has made a claim:
- for asylum
- under Article 3 of the European Convention on Human Rights; or

(g) Immigration and Asylum Act 1999, section 141(7)(f), from a person who is a dependant of someone who falls into (b) to (f) above.

4.12 The Immigration and Asylum Act 1999, section 142(3), gives a police and immigration officer power to arrest, without warrant, a person who fails to comply with a requirement imposed by the Secretary of State to attend a specified place for fingerprinting.

**Code D**

4.13 Before any fingerprints are taken, with or without consent, the person must be informed:
(a) of the reason their fingerprints are to be taken;
(b) the fingerprints, and all copies of them, will be destroyed in accordance with *Annex F, Part B*.

4.14 Reasonable force may be used, if necessary, to take a person's fingerprints without their consent under powers as in *paragraph 4.11*.

4.15 *Paragraphs 4.1* and *4.8* apply.

## (C) Taking footwear impressions in connection with a criminal investigation

### (a) Action

4.16 Impressions of a person's footwear may be taken in connection with the investigation of an offence only with their consent or if *paragraph 4.17* applies. If the person is at a police station consent must be in writing.

4.17 PACE, section 61A, provides power for a police officer to take footwear impressions without consent from any person over the age of ten years who is detained at a police station:
(a) in consequence of being arrested for a recordable offence, see *Note 4A*; or if the detainee has been charged with a recordable offence, or informed they will be reported for such an offence; and
(b) the detainee has not had an impression of their footwear taken in the course of the investigation of the offence unless the previously taken impression is not complete or is not of sufficient quality to allow satisfactory analysis, comparison or matching (whether in the case in question or generally).

4.18 Reasonable force may be used, if necessary, to take a footwear impression from a detainee without consent under the power in *paragraph 4.17*.

4.19 Before any footwear impression is taken with, or without, consent as above, the person must be informed:

(a) of the reason the impression is to be taken;

(b) that the impression may be retained and may be subject of a speculative search against other impressions, see *Note 4B*, unless destruction of the impression is required in accordance with *Annex F, Part (a)*; and

(c) that if their footwear impressions are required to be destroyed, they may witness their destruction as provided for in *Annex F, Part (a)*.

### (b) Documentation

4.20 A record must be made as soon as possible, of the reason for taking a person's footwear impressions without consent. If force is used, a record shall be made of the circumstances and those present.

4.21 A record shall be made when a person has been informed under the terms of *paragraph 4.19(b)*, of the possibility that their footwear impressions may be subject of a speculative search.

### Notes for guidance

4A *References to 'recordable offences' in this Code relate to those offences for which convictions, cautions, reprimands and warnings may be recorded in national police records. See PACE, section 27(4). The recordable offences current at the time when this Code was prepared, are any offences which carry a sentence of imprisonment on conviction (irrespective of the period, or the age of the offender or actual sentence passed) as well as the non-imprisonable offences under the Vagrancy Act 1824 sections 3 and 4 (begging and persistent begging), the Street Offences Act 1959, section 1 (loitering or soliciting for purposes of prostitution), the Road Traffic Act 1988, section 25 (tampering with motor vehicles), the Criminal Justice and Public Order Act 1994, section 167 (touting for hire car services) and others listed in the National Police Records (Recordable Offences) Regulations 2000 as amended.*

4B *Fingerprints, footwear impressions or a DNA sample (and the information derived from it) taken from a person arrested on suspicion of being involved in a recordable offence, or charged with such an offence, or informed they will be reported for such an offence, may be subject of a speculative search. This means the fingerprints, footwear impressions or DNA sample may be checked against other fingerprints, footwear impressions and DNA records held by, or on behalf of, the police and other law enforcement authorities in, or outside, the UK, or held in connection with, or as a result of, an investigation of an offence inside or outside the UK. Fingerprints, footwear impressions and samples taken from a person suspected of committing a recordable offence but not arrested, charged or informed they will be reported for it, may be subject to a speculative search only if the person consents in writing. The following is an example of a basic form of words:*

*'I consent to my fingerprints, footwear impressions and DNA sample and information derived from it being retained and used only for purposes related to the prevention and detection of a crime, the investigation of an offence or the conduct of a prosecution either nationally or internationally.*

*I understand that my fingerprints, footwear impressions or DNA sample may be checked against other fingerprint, footwear impressions and DNA records held by or on behalf of relevant law enforcement authorities, either nationally or internationally.*

*I understand that once I have given my consent for my fingerprints, footwear impressions or DNA sample to be retained and used I cannot withdraw this consent.'*

*See* Annex F *regarding the retention and use of fingerprints and footwear impressions taken with consent for elimination purposes.*

## 5 EXAMINATIONS TO ESTABLISH IDENTITY AND THE TAKING OF PHOTOGRAPHS

### (A) Detainees at police stations

### (a) Searching or examination of detainees at police stations

5.1 PACE, section 54A (1), allows a detainee at a police station to be searched or examined or both, to establish:

(a) whether they have any marks, features or injuries that would tend to identify them as a person involved in the commission of an offence and to photograph any identifying marks, see *paragraph 5.5*; or

(b) their identity, see *Note 5A*.

A person detained at a police station to be searched under a stop and search power, see Code A, is not a detainee for the purposes of these powers.

5.2 A search and/or examination to find marks under section 54A (1) (a) may be carried out without the detainee's consent, see *paragraph 2.12*, only if authorised by an officer of at least inspector rank when consent has been withheld or it is not practicable to obtain consent, see *Note 5D*.

5.3 A search or examination to establish a suspect's identity under section 54A (1) (b) may be carried out without the detainee's consent, see *paragraph 2.12*, only if authorised by an officer of at least inspector rank when the detainee has refused to identify themselves or the authorising officer has reasonable grounds for suspecting the person is not who they claim to be.

5.4 Any marks that assist in establishing the detainee's identity, or their identification as a person involved in the commission of an offence, are identifying marks. Such marks may be photographed with the detainee's consent, see *paragraph 2.12*; or without their consent if it is withheld or it is not practicable to obtain it, see *Note 5D*.

5.5 A detainee may only be searched, examined and photographed under section 54A, by a police officer of the same sex.

5.6 Any photographs of identifying marks, taken under section 54A, may be used or disclosed only for purposes related to the prevention or detection of crime, the investigation of offences or the conduct of prosecutions by, or on behalf of, police or other law enforcement and prosecuting authorities inside, and outside, the UK. After being so used or disclosed, the photograph may be retained but must not be used or disclosed except for these purposes, see *Note 5B*.

5.7 The powers, as in *paragraph 5.1*, do not affect any separate requirement under the Criminal Procedure and Investigations Act 1996 to retain material in connection with criminal investigations.

Code **D**

5.8    Authority for the search and/or examination for the purposes of *paragraphs 5.2* and *5.3* may be given orally or in writing. If given orally, the authorising officer must confirm it in writing as soon as practicable. A separate authority is required for each purpose which applies.

5.9    If it is established a person is unwilling to co-operate sufficiently to enable a search and/or examination to take place or a suitable photograph to be taken, an officer may use reasonable force to:

(a) search and/or examine a detainee without their consent; and

(b) photograph any identifying marks without their consent.

5.10 The thoroughness and extent of any search or examination carried out in accordance with the powers in section 54A must be no more than the officer considers necessary to achieve the required purpose. Any search or examination which involves the removal of more than the person's outer clothing shall be conducted in accordance with Code C, Annex A, paragraph 11.

5.11 An intimate search may not be carried out under the powers in section 54A.

## (b) Photographing detainees at police stations and other persons elsewhere than at a police station

5.12 Under PACE, section 64A, an officer may photograph:

(a) any person whilst they are detained at a police station; and

(b) any person who is elsewhere than at a police station and who has been:-

     (i)    arrested by a constable for an offence;

     (ii)   taken into custody by a constable after being arrested for an offence by a person other than a constable;

     (iii) made subject to a requirement to wait with a community support officer under *paragraph 2(3) or (3B)* of Schedule 4 to the Police Reform Act 2002;

     (iv) given a penalty notice by a constable in uniform under Chapter 1 of Part 1 of the Criminal Justice and Police Act 2001, a penalty notice by a constable under section 444A of the Education Act 1996, or a fixed penalty notice by a constable in uniform under section 54 of the Road Traffic Offenders Act 1988;

     (v)   given a notice in relation to a relevant fixed penalty offence (within the meaning of paragraph 1 of Schedule 4 to the Police Reform Act 2002) by a community support officer by virtue of a designation applying that paragraph to him;

     (vi) given a notice in relation to a relevant fixed penalty offence (within the meaning of paragraph 1 of Schedule 5 to the Police Reform Act 2002) by an accredited person by virtue of accreditation specifying that that paragraph applies to him; or

     (vii) given a direction to leave and not return to a specified location for up to 48 hours by a police constable (under section 27 of the Violent Crime Reduction Act 2006).

5.12A Photographs taken under PACE, section 64A:

(a) may be taken with the person's consent, or without their consent if consent is withheld or it is not practicable to obtain their consent, see *Note 5E*; and

(b) may be used or disclosed only for purposes related to the prevention or detection of crime, the investigation of offences or the conduct of prosecutions by, or on behalf of, police or other law enforcement and prosecuting authorities inside and outside the United Kingdom or the enforcement of any sentence or order made by a court when dealing with an offence. After being so used or disclosed, they may be retained but can only be used or disclosed for the same purposes. See *Note 5B*.

5.13 The officer proposing to take a detainee's photograph may, for this purpose, require the person to remove any item or substance worn on, or over, all, or any part of, their head or face. If they do not comply with such a requirement, the officer may remove the item or substance.

5.14 If it is established the detainee is unwilling to co-operate sufficiently to enable a suitable photograph to be taken and it is not reasonably practicable to take the photograph covertly, an officer may use reasonable force, see *Note 5F*.

(a) to take their photograph without their consent; and

(b) for the purpose of taking the photograph, remove any item or substance worn on, or over, all, or any part of, the person's head or face which they have failed to remove when asked.

5.15 For the purposes of this Code, a photograph may be obtained without the person's consent by making a copy of an image of them taken at any time on a camera system installed anywhere in the police station.

### (c) Information to be given

5.16 When a person is searched, examined or photographed under the provisions as in *paragraph 5.1* and *5.12*, or their photograph obtained as in *paragraph 5.15*, they must be informed of the:

(a) purpose of the search, examination or photograph;

(b) grounds on which the relevant authority, if applicable, has been given; and

(c) purposes for which the photograph may be used, disclosed or retained.

This information must be given before the search or examination commences or the photograph is taken, except if the photograph is:

(i) to be taken covertly;

(ii) obtained as in *paragraph 5.15*, in which case the person must be informed as soon as practicable after the photograph is taken or obtained.

### (d) Documentation

5.17 A record must be made when a detainee is searched, examined, or a photograph of the person, or any identifying marks found on them, are taken. The record must include the:

(a) identity, subject to paragraph 2.18, of the officer carrying out the search, examination or taking the photograph;

(b) purpose of the search, examination or photograph and the outcome;

(c) detainee's consent to the search, examination or photograph, or the reason the person was searched, examined or photographed without consent;

(d) giving of any authority as in *paragraphs 5.2* and *5.3*, the grounds for giving it and the authorising officer.

Code **D**

**455**

5.18 If force is used when searching, examining or taking a photograph in accordance with this section, a record shall be made of the circumstances and those present.

### (B) Persons at police stations not detained

5.19 When there are reasonable grounds for suspecting the involvement of a person in a criminal offence, but that person is at a police station **voluntarily** and not detained, the provisions of *paragraphs 5.1* to *5.18* should apply, subject to the modifications in the following paragraphs.

5.20 References to the 'person being detained' and to the powers mentioned in *paragraph 5.1* which apply only to detainees at police stations shall be omitted.

5.21 Force may not be used to:
   (a) search and/or examine the person to:
      (i) discover whether they have any marks that would tend to identify them as a person involved in the commission of an offence; or
      (ii) establish their identity, see *Note 5A*;
   (b) take photographs of any identifying marks, see *paragraph 5.4*; or
   (c) take a photograph of the person.

5.22 Subject to *paragraph 5.24*, the photographs of persons or of their identifying marks which are not taken in accordance with the provisions mentioned in *paragraphs 5.1* or *5.12*, must be destroyed (together with any negatives and copies) unless the person:
   (a) is charged with, or informed they may be prosecuted for, a recordable offence;
   (b) is prosecuted for a recordable offence;
   (c) is cautioned for a recordable offence or given a warning or reprimand in accordance with the Crime and Disorder Act 1998 for a recordable offence; or
   (d) gives informed consent, in writing, for the photograph or image to be retained as in *paragraph 5.6*.

5.23 When *paragraph 5.22* requires the destruction of any photograph, the person must be given an opportunity to witness the destruction or to have a certificate confirming the destruction provided they so request the certificate within five days of being informed the destruction is required.

5.24 Nothing in *paragraph 5.22* affects any separate requirement under the Criminal Procedure and Investigations Act 1996 to retain material in connection with criminal investigations.

### Notes for guidance

5A *The conditions under which fingerprints may be taken to assist in establishing a person's identity, are described in Section 4.*

5B *Examples of purposes related to the prevention or detection of crime, the investigation of offences or the conduct of prosecutions include:*
   (a) *checking the photograph against other photographs held in records or in connection with, or as a result of, an investigation of an offence to establish whether the person is liable to arrest for other offences;*
   (b) *when the person is arrested at the same time as other people, or at a time when it is likely that other people will be arrested, using the photograph to help establish who was arrested, at what time and where;*

(c) when the real identity of the person is not known and cannot be readily ascertained or there are reasonable grounds for doubting a name and other personal details given by the person, are their real name and personal details. In these circumstances, using or disclosing the photograph to help to establish or verify their real identity or determine whether they are liable to arrest for some other offence, e.g. by checking it against other photographs held in records or in connection with, or as a result of, an investigation of an offence;

(d) when it appears any identification procedure in section 3 may need to be arranged for which the person's photograph would assist;

(e) when the person's release without charge may be required, and if the release is:

    (i) on bail to appear at a police station, using the photograph to help verify the person's identity when they answer their bail and if the person does not answer their bail, to assist in arresting them; or

    (ii) without bail, using the photograph to help verify their identity or assist in locating them for the purposes of serving them with a summons to appear at court in criminal proceedings;

(f) when the person has answered to bail at a police station and there are reasonable grounds for doubting they are the person who was previously granted bail, using the photograph to help establish or verify their identity;

(g) when the person arrested on a warrant claims to be a different person from the person named on the warrant and a photograph would help to confirm or disprove their claim;

(h) when the person has been charged with, reported for, or convicted of, a recordable offence and their photograph is not already on record as a result of (a) to (f) or their photograph is on record but their appearance has changed since it was taken and the person has not yet been released or brought before a court.

5C There is no power to arrest a person convicted of a recordable offence solely to take their photograph. The power to take photographs in this section applies only where the person is in custody as a result of the exercise of another power, e.g. arrest for fingerprinting under PACE, section 27.

5D Examples of when it would not be practicable to obtain a detainee's consent, see paragraph 2.12, to a search, examination or the taking of a photograph of an identifying mark include:

(a) when the person is drunk or otherwise unfit to give consent;

(b) when there are reasonable grounds to suspect that if the person became aware a search or examination was to take place or an identifying mark was to be photographed, they would take steps to prevent this happening, e.g. by violently resisting, covering or concealing the mark etc and it would not otherwise be possible to carry out the search or examination or to photograph any identifying mark;

(c) in the case of a juvenile, if the parent or guardian cannot be contacted in sufficient time to allow the search or examination to be carried out or the photograph to be taken.

5E Examples of when it would not be practicable to obtain the person's consent, see paragraph 2.12, to a photograph being taken include:

(a) when the person is drunk or otherwise unfit to give consent;

(b) when there are reasonable grounds to suspect that if the person became aware a photograph, suitable to be used or disclosed for the use and disclosure described in

Code D

*paragraph 5.6, was to be taken, they would take steps to prevent it being taken, e.g.*
*by violently resisting, covering or distorting their face etc, and it would not other-*
*wise be possible to take a suitable photograph;*

    *(c) when, in order to obtain a suitable photograph, it is necessary to take it covertly;*
    *and*

    *(d) in the case of a juvenile, if the parent or guardian cannot be contacted in sufficient*
    *time to allow the photograph to be taken.*

5F  *The use of reasonable force to take the photograph of a suspect elsewhere than at a*
*police station must be carefully considered. In order to obtain a suspect's consent and*
*co-operation to remove an item of religious headwear to take their photograph, a con-*
*stable should consider whether in the circumstances of the situation the removal of the*
*headwear and the taking of the photograph should be by an officer of the same sex as*
*the person. It would be appropriate for these actions to be conducted out of public*
*view.*

## 6 IDENTIFICATION BY BODY SAMPLES AND IMPRESSIONS

### (A) General

6.1 References to:

    (a) an 'intimate sample' mean a dental impression or sample of blood, semen or
    any other tissue fluid, urine, or pubic hair, or a swab taken from any part of
    a person's genitals or from a person's body orifice other than the mouth;

    (b) a 'non-intimate sample' means:

        (i) a sample of hair, other than pubic hair, which includes hair plucked
        with the root, see *Note 6A*;

        (ii) a sample taken from a nail or from under a nail;

        (iii) a swab taken from any part of a person's body other than a part from
        which a swab taken would be an intimate sample;

        (iv) saliva;

        (v) a skin impression which means any record, other than a fingerprint,
        which is a record, in any form and produced by any method, of the skin
        pattern and other physical characteristics or features of the whole, or
        any part of, a person's foot or of any other part of their body.

### (B) Action

#### (a) Intimate samples

6.2 PACE, section 62, provides that intimate samples may be taken under:

    (a) section 62(1), from a person in police detention only:

        (i) if a police officer of inspector rank or above has reasonable grounds to
        believe such an impression or sample will tend to confirm or disprove
        the suspect's involvement in a recordable offence, see *Note 4A*, and gives
        authorisation for a sample to be taken; and

        (ii) with the suspect's written consent;

    (b) section 62(1A), from a person not in police detention but from whom two or
    more non-intimate samples have been taken in the course of an investiga-
    tion of an offence and the samples, though suitable, have proved insuffi-
    cient if:

(i) a police officer of inspector rank or above authorises it to be taken; and

(ii) the person concerned gives their written consent. See *Notes 6B* and *6C*

6.3 Before a suspect is asked to provide an intimate sample, they must be warned that if they refuse without good cause, their refusal may harm their case if it comes to trial, see *Note 6D*. If the suspect is in police detention and not legally represented, they must also be reminded of their entitlement to have free legal advice, see Code C, *paragraph 6.5*, and the reminder noted in the custody record. If *paragraph 6.2(b)* applies and the person is attending a station voluntarily, their entitlement to free legal advice as in Code C, *paragraph 3.21* shall be explained to them.

6.4 Dental impressions may only be taken by a registered dentist. Other intimate samples, except for samples of urine, may only be taken by a registered medical practitioner or registered nurse or registered paramedic.

### (b) Non-intimate samples

6.5 A non-intimate sample may be taken from a detainee only with their written consent or if *paragraph 6.6* applies.

6.6 (a) under section 63, a non-intimate sample may not be taken from a person without consent and the consent must be in writing

(aa) A non-intimate sample may be taken from a person without the appropriate consent in the following circumstances:

(i) under section 63(2A) where the person is in police detention as a consequence of his arrest for a recordable offence and he has not had a non-intimate sample of the same type and from the same part of the body taken in the course of the investigation of the offence by the police or he has had such a sample taken but it proved insufficient.

(ii) Under section 63(3) (a) where he is being held in custody by the police on the authority of a court and an officer of at least the rank of inspector authorises it to be taken.

(b) under section 63(3A), from a person charged with a recordable offence or informed they will be reported for such an offence: and

(i) that person has not had a non-intimate sample taken from them in the course of the investigation; or

(ii) if they have had a sample taken, it proved unsuitable or insufficient for the same form of analysis, see *Note 6B*; or

(c) under section 63(3B), from a person convicted of a recordable offence after the date on which that provision came into effect. PACE, section 63A, describes the circumstances in which a police officer may require a person convicted of a recordable offence to attend a police station for a non-intimate sample to be taken.

6.7 Reasonable force may be used, if necessary, to take a non-intimate sample from a person without their consent under the powers mentioned in *paragraph 6.6*.

6.8 Before any intimate sample is taken with consent or non-intimate sample is taken with, or without, consent, the person must be informed:

(a) of the reason for taking the sample;

(b) of the grounds on which the relevant authority has been given;

Code **D**

(c) that the sample or information derived from the sample may be retained and subject of a speculative search, see *Note 6E*, unless their destruction is required as in *Annex F*, Part A.

6.9 When clothing needs to be removed in circumstances likely to cause embarrassment to the person, no person of the opposite sex who is not a registered medical practitioner or registered health care professional shall be present, (unless in the case of a juvenile, mentally disordered or mentally vulnerable person, that person specifically requests the presence of an appropriate adult of the opposite sex who is readily available) nor shall anyone whose presence is unnecessary. However, in the case of a juvenile, this is subject to the overriding proviso that such a removal of clothing may take place in the absence of the appropriate adult only if the juvenile signifies, in their presence, that they prefer the adult's absence and they agree.

## (c) Documentation

6.10 A record of the reasons for taking a sample or impression and, if applicable, of its destruction must be made as soon as practicable. If force is used, a record shall be made of the circumstances and those present. If written consent is given to the taking of a sample or impression, the fact must be recorded in writing.

6.11 A record must be made of a warning given as required by *paragraph 6.3*.

6.12 A record shall be made of the fact that a person has been informed as in *paragraph 6.8(c)* that samples may be subject of a speculative search.

### Notes for guidance

*6A When hair samples are taken for the purpose of DNA analysis (rather than for other purposes such as making a visual match), the suspect should be permitted a reasonable choice as to what part of the body the hairs are taken from. When hairs are plucked, they should be plucked individually, unless the suspect prefers otherwise and no more should be plucked than the person taking them reasonably considers necessary for a sufficient sample.*

*6B (a) An insufficient sample is one which is not sufficient either in quantity or quality to provide information for a particular form of analysis, such as DNA analysis. A sample may also be insufficient if enough information cannot be obtained from it by analysis because of loss, destruction, damage or contamination of the sample or as a result of an earlier, unsuccessful attempt at analysis.*

*(b) An unsuitable sample is one which, by its nature, is not suitable for a particular form of analysis.*

*6C Nothing in paragraph 6.2 prevents intimate samples being taken for elimination purposes with the consent of the person concerned but the provisions of paragraph 2.12 relating to the role of the appropriate adult, should be applied. Paragraph 6.2(b) does not, however, apply where the non-intimate samples were previously taken under the Terrorism Act 2000, Schedule 8, paragraph 10.*

*6D In warning a person who is asked to provide an intimate sample as in paragraph 6.3, the following form of words may be used:*

*'You do not have to provide this sample/allow this swab or impression to be taken, but I must warn you that if you refuse without good cause, your refusal may harm your case if it comes to trial.'*

6E  *Fingerprints or a DNA sample and the information derived from it taken from a person arrested on suspicion of being involved in a recordable offence, or charged with such an offence, or informed they will be reported for such an offence, may be subject of a speculative search. This means they may be checked against other fingerprints and DNA records held by, or on behalf of, the police and other law enforcement authorities in or outside the UK or held in connection with, or as a result of, an investigation of an offence inside or outside the UK. Fingerprints and samples taken from any other person, e.g. a person suspected of committing a recordable offence but who has not been arrested, charged or informed they will be reported for it, may be subject to a speculative search only if the person consents in writing to their fingerprints being subject of such a search. The following is an example of a basic form of words:*

*'I consent to my fingerprints/DNA sample and information derived from it being retained and used only for purposes related to the prevention and detection of a crime, the investigation of an offence or the conduct of a prosecution either nationally or internationally.*

*I understand that this sample may be checked against other fingerprint/DNA records held by or on behalf of relevant law enforcement authorities, either nationally or internationally.*

*I understand that once I have given my consent for the sample to be retained and used I cannot withdraw this consent.'*

*See Annex F regarding the retention and use of fingerprints and samples taken with consent for elimination purposes.*

6F  *Samples of urine and non-intimate samples taken in accordance with sections 63B and 63C of PACE may not be used for identification purposes in accordance with this Code. See Code C note for guidance 17D.*

## ANNEX A—VIDEO IDENTIFICATION

### (a) General

1.  The arrangements for obtaining and ensuring the availability of a suitable set of images to be used in a video identification must be the responsibility of an identification officer, who has no direct involvement with the case.

2.  The set of images must include the suspect and at least eight other people who, so far as possible, resemble the suspect in age, general appearance and position in life. Only one suspect shall appear in any set unless there are two suspects of roughly similar appearance, in which case they may be shown together with at least twelve other people.

2A  If the suspect has an unusual physical feature, e.g., a facial scar, tattoo or distinctive hairstyle or hair colour which does not appear on the images of the other people that are available to be used, steps may be taken to:

(a)  conceal the location of the feature on the images of the suspect and the other people; or

(b)  replicate that feature on the images of the other people.

For these purposes, the feature may be concealed or replicated electronically or by any other method which it is practicable to use to ensure that the images of the suspect and other people resemble each other. The identification officer has discretion to choose whether to conceal or replicate the feature and the method to be used. If an unusual physical feature has been described by the witness, the

Code **D**

**461**

identification officer should, if practicable, have that feature replicated. If it has not been described, concealment may be more appropriate.

2B  If the identification officer decides that a feature should be concealed or replicated, the reason for the decision and whether the feature was concealed or replicated in the images shown to any witness shall be recorded.

2C  If the witness requests to view an image where an unusual physical feature has been concealed or replicated without the feature being concealed or replicated, the witness may be allowed to do so.

3.  The images used to conduct a video identification shall, as far as possible, show the suspect and other people in the same positions or carrying out the same sequence of movements. They shall also show the suspect and other people under identical conditions unless the identification officer reasonably believes:

   (a)  because of the suspect's failure or refusal to co-operate or other reasons, it is not practicable for the conditions to be identical; and

   (b)  any difference in the conditions would not direct a witness' attention to any individual image.

4.  The reasons identical conditions are not practicable shall be recorded on forms provided for the purpose.

5.  Provision must be made for each person shown to be identified by number.

6.  If police officers are shown, any numerals or other identifying badges must be concealed. If a prison inmate is shown, either as a suspect or not, then either all, or none of, the people shown should be in prison clothing.

7.  The suspect or their solicitor, friend, or appropriate adult must be given a reasonable opportunity to see the complete set of images before it is shown to any witness. If the suspect has a reasonable objection to the set of images or any of the participants, the suspect shall be asked to state the reasons for the objection. Steps shall, if practicable, be taken to remove the grounds for objection. If this is not practicable, the suspect and/or their representative shall be told why their objections cannot be met and the objection, the reason given for it and why it cannot be met shall be recorded on forms provided for the purpose.

8.  Before the images are shown in accordance with *paragraph 7*, the suspect or their solicitor shall be provided with details of the first description of the suspect by any witnesses who are to attend the video identification. When a broadcast or publication is made, as in *paragraph 3.28*, the suspect or their solicitor must also be allowed to view any material released to the media by the police for the purpose of recognising or tracing the suspect, provided it is practicable and would not unreasonably delay the investigation.

9.  The suspect's solicitor, if practicable, shall be given reasonable notification of the time and place the video identification is to be conducted so a representative may attend on behalf of the suspect. If a solicitor has not been instructed, this information shall be given to the suspect. The suspect may not be present when the images are shown to the witness(es). In the absence of the suspect's representative, the viewing itself shall be recorded on video. No unauthorised people may be present.

(b)  **Conducting the video identification**

10.  The identification officer is responsible for making the appropriate arrangements to make sure, before they see the set of images, witnesses are not able to

communicate with each other about the case, see any of the images which are to be shown, see, or be reminded of, any photograph or description of the suspect or be given any other indication as to the suspect's identity, or overhear a witness who has already seen the material. There must be no discussion with the witness about the composition of the set of images and they must not be told whether a previous witness has made any identification.

11. Only one witness may see the set of images at a time. Immediately before the images are shown, the witness shall be told that the person they saw on a specified earlier occasion may, or may not, appear in the images they are shown and that if they cannot make a positive identification, they should say so. The witness shall be advised that at any point, they may ask to see a particular part of the set of images or to have a particular image frozen for them to study. Furthermore, it should be pointed out to the witness that there is no limit on how many times they can view the whole set of images or any part of them. However, they should be asked not to make any decision as to whether the person they saw is on the set of images until they have seen the whole set at least twice.

12. Once the witness has seen the whole set of images at least twice and has indicated that they do not want to view the images, or any part of them, again, the witness shall be asked to say whether the individual they saw in person on a specified earlier occasion has been shown and, if so, to identify them by number of the image. The witness will then be shown that image to confirm the identification, see *paragraph 17*.

13. Care must be taken not to direct the witness' attention to any one individual image or give any indication of the suspect's identity. Where a witness has previously made an identification by photographs, or a computerised or artist's composite or similar likeness, the witness must not be reminded of such a photograph or composite likeness once a suspect is available for identification by other means in accordance with this Code. Nor must the witness be reminded of any description of the suspect.

14. After the procedure, each witness shall be asked whether they have seen any broadcast or published films or photographs, or any descriptions of suspects relating to the offence and their reply shall be recorded.

### (c) Image security and destruction

15. Arrangements shall be made for all relevant material containing sets of images used for specific identification procedures to be kept securely and their movements accounted for. In particular, no-one involved in the investigation shall be permitted to view the material prior to it being shown to any witness.

16. As appropriate, *paragraph 3.30* or *3.31* applies to the destruction or retention of relevant sets of images.

### (d) Documentation

17. A record must be made of all those participating in, or seeing, the set of images whose names are known to the police.

18. A record of the conduct of the video identification must be made on forms provided for the purpose. This shall include anything said by the witness about any identifications or the conduct of the procedure and any reasons it was not

Code **D**

practicable to comply with any of the provisions of this Code governing the conduct of video identifications.

ANNEX B—IDENTIFICATION PARADES

**(a) General**

1. A suspect must be given a reasonable opportunity to have a solicitor or friend present, and the suspect shall be asked to indicate on a second copy of the notice whether or not they wish to do so.

2. An identification parade may take place either in a normal room or one equipped with a screen permitting witnesses to see members of the identification parade without being seen. The procedures for the composition and conduct of the identification parade are the same in both cases, subject to *paragraph 8* (except that an identification parade involving a screen may take place only when the suspect's solicitor, friend or appropriate adult is present or the identification parade is recorded on video).

3. Before the identification parade takes place, the suspect or their solicitor shall be provided with details of the first description of the suspect by any witnesses who are attending the identification parade. When a broadcast or publication is made as in *paragraph 3.28*, the suspect or their solicitor should also be allowed to view any material released to the media by the police for the purpose of recognising or tracing the suspect, provided it is practicable to do so and would not unreasonably delay the investigation.

**(b) Identification parades involving prison inmates**

4. If a prison inmate is required for identification, and there are no security problems about the person leaving the establishment, they may be asked to participate in an identification parade or video identification.

5. An identification parade may be held in a Prison Department establishment but shall be conducted, as far as practicable under normal identification parade rules. Members of the public shall make up the identification parade unless there are serious security, or control, objections to their admission to the establishment. In such cases, or if a group or video identification is arranged within the establishment, other inmates may participate. If an inmate is the suspect, they are not required to wear prison clothing for the identification parade unless the other people taking part are other inmates in similar clothing, or are members of the public who are prepared to wear prison clothing for the occasion.

**(c) Conduct of the identification parade**

6. Immediately before the identification parade, the suspect must be reminded of the procedures governing its conduct and cautioned in the terms of Code C, paragraphs 10.5 or 10.6, as appropriate.

7. All unauthorised people must be excluded from the place where the identification parade is held.

8. Once the identification parade has been formed, everything afterwards, in respect of it, shall take place in the presence and hearing of the suspect and any interpreter, solicitor, friend or appropriate adult who is present (unless the identification parade involves a screen, in which case everything said to, or by, any

witness at the place where the identification parade is held, must be said in the hearing and presence of the suspect's solicitor, friend or appropriate adult or be recorded on video).

9. The identification parade shall consist of at least eight people (in addition to the suspect) who, so far as possible, resemble the suspect in age, height, general appearance and position in life. Only one suspect shall be included in an identification parade unless there are two suspects of roughly similar appearance, in which case they may be paraded together with at least twelve other people. In no circumstances shall more than two suspects be included in one identification parade and where there are separate identification parades, they shall be made up of different people.

10. If the suspect has an unusual physical feature, e.g., a facial scar, tattoo or distinctive hairstyle or hair colour which cannot be replicated on other members of the identification parade, steps may be taken to conceal the location of that feature on the suspect and the other members of the identification parade if the suspect and their solicitor, or appropriate adult, agree. For example, by use of a plaster or a hat, so that all members of the identification parade resemble each other in general appearance.

11. When all members of a similar group are possible suspects, separate identification parades shall be held for each unless there are two suspects of similar appearance when they may appear on the same identification parade with at least twelve other members of the group who are not suspects. When police officers in uniform form an identification parade any numerals or other identifying badges shall be concealed.

**Code D**

12. When the suspect is brought to the place where the identification parade is to be held, they shall be asked if they have any objection to the arrangements for the identification parade or to any of the other participants in it and to state the reasons for the objection. The suspect may obtain advice from their solicitor or friend, if present, before the identification parade proceeds. If the suspect has a reasonable objection to the arrangements or any of the participants, steps shall, if practicable, be taken to remove the grounds for objection. When it is not practicable to do so, the suspect shall be told why their objections cannot be met and the objection, the reason given for it and why it cannot be met, shall be recorded on forms provided for the purpose.

13. The suspect may select their own position in the line, but may not otherwise interfere with the order of the people forming the line. When there is more than one witness, the suspect must be told, after each witness has left the room, that they can, if they wish, change position in the line. Each position in the line must be clearly numbered, whether by means of a number laid on the floor in front of each identification parade member or by other means.

14. Appropriate arrangements must be made to make sure, before witnesses attend the identification parade, they are not able to:
    (i) communicate with each other about the case or overhear a witness who has already seen the identification parade;
    (ii) see any member of the identification parade;
    (iii) see, or be reminded of, any photograph or description of the suspect or be given any other indication as to the suspect's identity; or
    (iv) see the suspect before or after the identification parade.

15. The person conducting a witness to an identification parade must not discuss with them the composition of the identification parade and, in particular, must not disclose whether a previous witness has made any identification.

16. Witnesses shall be brought in one at a time. Immediately before the witness inspects the identification parade, they shall be told the person they saw on a specified earlier occasion may, or may not, be present and if they cannot make a positive identification, they should say so. The witness must also be told they should not make any decision about whether the person they saw is on the identification parade until they have looked at each member at least twice.

17. When the officer or police staff (see *paragraph 3.11*) conducting the identification procedure is satisfied the witness has properly looked at each member of the identification parade, they shall ask the witness whether the person they saw on a specified earlier occasion is on the identification parade and, if so, to indicate the number of the person concerned, see *paragraph 28*.

18. If the witness wishes to hear any identification parade member speak, adopt any specified posture or move, they shall first be asked whether they can identify any person(s) on the identification parade on the basis of appearance only. When the request is to hear members of the identification parade speak, the witness shall be reminded that the participants in the identification parade have been chosen on the basis of physical appearance only. Members of the identification parade may then be asked to comply with the witness' request to hear them speak, see them move or adopt any specified posture.

19. If the witness requests that the person they have indicated remove anything used for the purposes of *paragraph 10* to conceal the location of an unusual physical feature, that person may be asked to remove it.

20. If the witness makes an identification after the identification parade has ended, the suspect and, if present, their solicitor, interpreter or friend shall be informed. When this occurs, consideration should be given to allowing the witness a second opportunity to identify the suspect.

21. After the procedure, each witness shall be asked whether they have seen any broadcast or published films or photographs or any descriptions of suspects relating to the offence and their reply shall be recorded.

22. When the last witness has left, the suspect shall be asked whether they wish to make any comments on the conduct of the identification parade.

### (d) Documentation

23. A video recording must normally be taken of the identification parade. If that is impracticable, a colour photograph must be taken. A copy of the video recording or photograph shall be supplied, on request, to the suspect or their solicitor within a reasonable time.

24. As appropriate, *paragraph 3.30* or *3.31*, should apply to any photograph or video taken as in *paragraph 23*.

25. If any person is asked to leave an identification parade because they are interfering with its conduct, the circumstances shall be recorded.

26. A record must be made of all those present at an identification parade whose names are known to the police.

27. If prison inmates make up an identification parade, the circumstances must be recorded.

28. A record of the conduct of any identification parade must be made on forms provided for the purpose. This shall include anything said by the witness or the suspect about any identifications or the conduct of the procedure, and any reasons it was not practicable to comply with any of this Code's provisions.

## ANNEX C—GROUP IDENTIFICATION

### (a) General

1. The purpose of this Annex is to make sure, as far as possible, group identifications follow the principles and procedures for identification parades so the conditions are fair to the suspect in the way they test the witness' ability to make an identification.

2. Group identifications may take place either with the suspect's consent and cooperation or covertly without their consent.

3. The location of the group identification is a matter for the identification officer, although the officer may take into account any representations made by the suspect, appropriate adult, their solicitor or friend.

4. The place where the group identification is held should be one where other people are either passing by or waiting around informally, in groups such that the suspect is able to join them and be capable of being seen by the witness at the same time as others in the group. For example people leaving an escalator, pedestrians walking through a shopping centre, passengers on railway and bus stations, waiting in queues or groups or where people are standing or sitting in groups in other public places.

5. If the group identification is to be held covertly, the choice of locations will be limited by the places where the suspect can be found and the number of other people present at that time. In these cases, suitable locations might be along regular routes travelled by the suspect, including buses or trains or public places frequented by the suspect.

6. Although the number, age, sex, race and general description and style of clothing of other people present at the location cannot be controlled by the identification officer, in selecting the location the officer must consider the general appearance and numbers of people likely to be present. In particular, the officer must reasonably expect that over the period the witness observes the group, they will be able to see, from time to time, a number of others whose appearance is broadly similar to that of the suspect.

7. A group identification need not be held if the identification officer believes, because of the unusual appearance of the suspect, none of the locations it would be practicable to use satisfy the requirements of *paragraph 6* necessary to make the identification fair.

8. Immediately after a group identification procedure has taken place (with or without the suspect's consent), a colour photograph or video should be taken of the general scene, if practicable, to give a general impression of the scene and the number of people present. Alternatively, if it is practicable, the group identification may be video recorded.

Code D

**467**

9. If it is not practicable to take the photograph or video in accordance with *paragraph 8*, a photograph or film of the scene should be taken later at a time determined by the identification officer if the officer considers it practicable to do so.

10. An identification carried out in accordance with this Code remains a group identification even though, at the time of being seen by the witness, the suspect was on their own rather than in a group.

11. Before the group identification takes place, the suspect or their solicitor shall be provided with details of the first description of the suspect by any witnesses who are to attend the identification. When a broadcast or publication is made, as in *paragraph 3.28*, the suspect or their solicitor should also be allowed to view any material released by the police to the media for the purposes of recognising or tracing the suspect, provided that it is practicable and would not unreasonably delay the investigation.

12. After the procedure, each witness shall be asked whether they have seen any broadcast or published films or photographs or any descriptions of suspects relating to the offence and their reply recorded.

**(b) Identification with the consent of the suspect**

13. A suspect must be given a reasonable opportunity to have a solicitor or friend present. They shall be asked to indicate on a second copy of the notice whether or not they wish to do so.

14. The witness, the person carrying out the procedure and the suspect's solicitor, appropriate adult, friend or any interpreter for the witness, may be concealed from the sight of the individuals in the group they are observing, if the person carrying out the procedure considers this assists the conduct of the identification.

15. The person conducting a witness to a group identification must not discuss with them the forthcoming group identification and, in particular, must not disclose whether a previous witness has made any identification.

16. Anything said to, or by, the witness during the procedure about the identification should be said in the presence and hearing of those present at the procedure.

17. Appropriate arrangements must be made to make sure, before witnesses attend the group identification, they are not able to:
    (i) communicate with each other about the case or overhear a witness who has already been given an opportunity to see the suspect in the group;
    (ii) see the suspect; or
    (iii) see, or be reminded of, any photographs or description of the suspect or be given any other indication of the suspect's identity.

18. Witnesses shall be brought one at a time to the place where they are to observe the group. Immediately before the witness is asked to look at the group, the person conducting the procedure shall tell them that the person they saw may, or may not, be in the group and that if they cannot make a positive identification, they should say so. The witness shall be asked to observe the group in which the suspect is to appear. The way in which the witness should do this will depend on whether the group is moving or stationary.

*Moving group*

19. When the group in which the suspect is to appear is moving, e.g. leaving an escalator, the provisions of *paragraphs 20 to 24* should be followed.
20. If two or more suspects consent to a group identification, each should be the subject of separate identification procedures. These may be conducted consecutively on the same occasion.
21. The person conducting the procedure shall tell the witness to observe the group and ask them to point out any person they think they saw on the specified earlier occasion.
22. Once the witness has been informed as in *paragraph 21* the suspect should be allowed to take whatever position in the group they wish.
23. When the witness points out a person as in *paragraph 21* they shall, if practicable, be asked to take a closer look at the person to confirm the identification. If this is not practicable, or they cannot confirm the identification, they shall be asked how sure they are that the person they have indicated is the relevant person.
24. The witness should continue to observe the group for the period which the person conducting the procedure reasonably believes is necessary in the circumstances for them to be able to make comparisons between the suspect and other individuals of broadly similar appearance to the suspect as in *paragraph 6*.

**Code D**

*Stationary groups*

25. When the group in which the suspect is to appear is stationary, e.g. people waiting in a queue, the provisions of *paragraphs 26 to 29* should be followed.
26. If two or more suspects consent to a group identification, each should be subject to separate identification procedures unless they are of broadly similar appearance when they may appear in the same group. When separate group identifications are held, the groups must be made up of different people.
27. The suspect may take whatever position in the group they wish. If there is more than one witness, the suspect must be told, out of the sight and hearing of any witness, that they can, if they wish, change their position in the group.
28. The witness shall be asked to pass along, or amongst, the group and to look at each person in the group at least twice, taking as much care and time as possible according to the circumstances, before making an identification. Once the witness has done this, they shall be asked whether the person they saw on the specified earlier occasion is in the group and to indicate any such person by whatever means the person conducting the procedure considers appropriate in the circumstances. If this is not practicable, the witness shall be asked to point out any person they think they saw on the earlier occasion.
29. When the witness makes an indication as in *paragraph 28*, arrangements shall be made, if practicable, for the witness to take a closer look at the person to confirm the identification. If this is not practicable, or the witness is unable to confirm the identification, they shall be asked how sure they are that the person they have indicated is the relevant person.

*All cases*

30. If the suspect unreasonably delays joining the group, or having joined the group, deliberately conceals themselves from the sight of the witness, this may be treated as a refusal to co-operate in a group identification.

31. If the witness identifies a person other than the suspect, that person should be informed what has happened and asked if they are prepared to give their name and address. There is no obligation upon any member of the public to give these details. There shall be no duty to record any details of any other member of the public present in the group or at the place where the procedure is conducted.

32. When the group identification has been completed, the suspect shall be asked whether they wish to make any comments on the conduct of the procedure.

33. If the suspect has not been previously informed, they shall be told of any identifications made by the witnesses.

### (c) Identification without the suspect's consent

34. Group identifications held covertly without the suspect's consent should, as far as practicable, follow the rules for conduct of group identification by consent.

35. A suspect has no right to have a solicitor, appropriate adult or friend present as the identification will take place without the knowledge of the suspect.

36. Any number of suspects may be identified at the same time.

### (d) Identifications in police stations

37. Group identifications should only take place in police stations for reasons of safety, security or because it is not practicable to hold them elsewhere.

38. The group identification may take place either in a room equipped with a screen permitting witnesses to see members of the group without being seen, or anywhere else in the police station that the identification officer considers appropriate.

39. Any of the additional safeguards applicable to identification parades should be followed if the identification officer considers it is practicable to do so in the circumstances.

### (e) Identifications involving prison inmates

40. A group identification involving a prison inmate may only be arranged in the prison or at a police station.

41. When a group identification takes place involving a prison inmate, whether in a prison or in a police station, the arrangements should follow those in *paragraphs 37 to 39*. If a group identification takes place within a prison, other inmates may participate. If an inmate is the suspect, they do not have to wear prison clothing for the group identification unless the other participants are wearing the same clothing.

### (f) Documentation

42. When a photograph or video is taken as in *paragraph 8* or *9*, a copy of the photograph or video shall be supplied on request to the suspect or their solicitor within a reasonable time.

43. *Paragraph 3.30* or *3.31*, as appropriate, shall apply when the photograph or film taken in accordance with *paragraph 8* or *9* includes the suspect.

44. A record of the conduct of any group identification must be made on forms provided for the purpose. This shall include anything said by the witness or suspect about any identifications or the conduct of the procedure and any reasons why it was not practicable to comply with any of the provisions of this Code governing the conduct of group identifications.

## ANNEX D—CONFRONTATION BY A WITNESS

1. Before the confrontation takes place, the witness must be told that the person they saw may, or may not, be the person they are to confront and that if they are not that person, then the witness should say so.
2. Before the confrontation takes place the suspect or their solicitor shall be provided with details of the first description of the suspect given by any witness who is to attend. When a broadcast or publication is made, as in *paragraph 3.28*, the suspect or their solicitor should also be allowed to view any material released to the media for the purposes of recognising or tracing the suspect, provided it is practicable to do so and would not unreasonably delay the investigation.
3. Force may not be used to make the suspect's face visible to the witness.
4. Confrontation must take place in the presence of the suspect's solicitor, interpreter or friend unless this would cause unreasonable delay.
5. The suspect shall be confronted independently by each witness, who shall be asked 'Is this the person?'. If the witness identifies the person but is unable to confirm the identification, they shall be asked how sure they are that the person is the one they saw on the earlier occasion.
6. The confrontation should normally take place in the police station, either in a normal room or one equipped with a screen permitting a witness to see the suspect without being seen. In both cases, the procedures are the same except that a room equipped with a screen may be used only when the suspect's solicitor, friend or appropriate adult is present or the confrontation is recorded on video.
7. After the procedure, each witness shall be asked whether they have seen any broadcast or published films or photographs or any descriptions of suspects relating to the offence and their reply shall be recorded.

## ANNEX E—SHOWING PHOTOGRAPHS

### (a) Action

1. An officer of sergeant rank or above shall be responsible for supervising and directing the showing of photographs. The actual showing may be done by another officer or police staff, see *paragraph 3.11*.
2. The supervising officer must confirm the first description of the suspect given by the witness has been recorded before they are shown the photographs. If the supervising officer is unable to confirm the description has been recorded they shall postpone showing the photographs.
3. Only one witness shall be shown photographs at any one time. Each witness shall be given as much privacy as practicable and shall not be allowed to communicate with any other witness in the case.
4. The witness shall be shown not less than twelve photographs at a time, which shall, as far as possible, all be of a similar type.

**Code D**

5.  When the witness is shown the photographs, they shall be told the photograph of the person they saw may, or may not, be amongst them and if they cannot make a positive identification, they should say so. The witness shall also be told they should not make a decision until they have viewed at least twelve photographs. The witness shall not be prompted or guided in any way but shall be left to make any selection without help.

6.  If a witness makes a positive identification from photographs, unless the person identified is otherwise eliminated from enquiries or is not available, other witnesses shall not be shown photographs. But both they, and the witness who has made the identification, shall be asked to attend a video identification, an identification parade or group identification unless there is no dispute about the suspect's identification.

7.  If the witness makes a selection but is unable to confirm the identification, the person showing the photographs shall ask them how sure they are that the photograph they have indicated is the person they saw on the specified earlier occasion.

8.  When the use of a computerised or artist's composite or similar likeness has led to there being a known suspect who can be asked to participate in a video identification, appear on an identification parade or participate in a group identification, that likeness shall not be shown to other potential witnesses.

9.  When a witness attending a video identification, an identification parade or group identification has previously been shown photographs or computerised or artist's composite or similar likeness (and it is the responsibility of the officer in charge of the investigation to make the identification officer aware that this is the case), the suspect and their solicitor must be informed of this fact before the identification procedure takes place.

10. None of the photographs shown shall be destroyed, whether or not an identification is made, since they may be required for production in court. The photographs shall be numbered and a separate photograph taken of the frame or part of the album from which the witness made an identification as an aid to reconstituting it.

**(b) Documentation**

11. Whether or not an identification is made, a record shall be kept of the showing of photographs on forms provided for the purpose. This shall include anything said by the witness about any identification or the conduct of the procedure, any reasons it was not practicable to comply with any of the provisions of this Code governing the showing of photographs and the name and rank of the supervising officer.

12. The supervising officer shall inspect and sign the record as soon as practicable.

ANNEX F—FINGERPRINTS, FOOTWEAR IMPRESSIONS AND SAMPLES—
DESTRUCTION AND SPECULATIVE SEARCHES

**(a) Fingerprints, footwear impressions and samples taken in connection with a criminal investigation**

1.  When fingerprints, footwear impressions or DNA samples are taken from a person in connection with an investigation and the person is not suspected of

having committed the offence, see *Note F1*, they must be destroyed as soon as they have fulfilled the purpose for which they were taken unless:

(a) they were taken for the purposes of an investigation of an offence for which a person has been convicted; and

(b) fingerprints, footwear impressions or samples were also taken from the convicted person for the purposes of that investigation.

However, subject to *paragraph 2*, the fingerprints, footwear impressions and samples, and the information derived from samples, may not be used in the investigation of any offence or in evidence against the person who is, or would be, entitled to the destruction of the fingerprints, footwear impressions and samples, see *Note F2*.

2. The requirement to destroy fingerprints, footwear impressions and DNA samples, and information derived from samples, and restrictions on their retention and use in *paragraph 1* do not apply if the person gives their written consent for their fingerprints, footwear impressions or sample to be retained and used after they have fulfilled the purpose for which they were taken, see *Note F1*.

3. When a person's fingerprints, footwear impressions or sample are to be destroyed:

(a) any copies of the fingerprints and footwear impressions must also be destroyed;

(b) the person may witness the destruction of their fingerprints, footwear impressions or copies if they ask to do so within five days of being informed destruction is required;

(c) access to relevant computer fingerprint data shall be made impossible as soon as it is practicable to do so and the person shall be given a certificate to this effect within three months of asking; and

(d) neither the fingerprints, footwear impressions, the sample, or any information derived from the sample, may be used in the investigation of any offence or in evidence against the person who is, or would be, entitled to its destruction.

4. Fingerprints, footwear impressions or samples, and the information derived from samples, taken in connection with the investigation of an offence which are not required to be destroyed, may be retained after they have fulfilled the purposes for which they were taken but may be used only for purposes related to the prevention or detection of crime, the investigation of an offence or the conduct of a prosecution in, as well as outside, the UK and may also be subject to a speculative search. This includes checking them against other fingerprints, footwear impressions and DNA records held by, or on behalf of, the police and other law enforcement authorities in, as well as outside, the UK.

## (b) Fingerprints taken in connection with Immigration Service enquiries

5. Fingerprints taken for Immigration Service enquiries in accordance with powers and procedures other than under PACE and for which the Immigration Service, not the police, are responsible, must be destroyed as follows:

(a) fingerprints and all copies must be destroyed as soon as practicable if the person from whom they were taken proves they are a British or Commonwealth citizen who has the right of abode in the UK under the Immigration Act 1971, section 2(1)(b);

**Code D**

**473**

(b)  fingerprints taken under the power as in *paragraph 4.11(g)* from a dependant of a person in *4.11 (b)* to *(f)* must be destroyed when that person's fingerprints are to be destroyed;

(c)  fingerprints taken from a person under any power as in *paragraph 4.11* or with the person's consent which have not already been destroyed as above, must be destroyed within ten years of being taken or within such period specified by the Secretary of State under the Immigration and Asylum Act 1999, section 143(5).

### Notes for guidance

*F1   Fingerprints, footwear impressions and samples given voluntarily for the purposes of elimination play an important part in many police investigations. It is, therefore, important to make sure innocent volunteers are not deterred from participating and their consent to their fingerprints, footwear impressions and DNA being used for the purposes of a specific investigation is fully informed and voluntary. If the police or volunteer seek to have the fingerprints, footwear impressions or samples retained for use after the specific investigation ends, it is important the volunteer's consent to this is also fully informed and voluntary.*

*Examples of consent for:*

- *DNA/fingerprints/footwear impressions—to be used only for the purposes of a specific investigation;*
- *DNA/fingerprints/footwear impressions—to be used in the specific investigation and retained by the police for future use.*

*To minimise the risk of confusion, each consent should be physically separate and the volunteer should be asked to sign **each consent**.*

*(a)  DNA:*

    *(i)   DNA sample taken for the purposes of elimination or as part of an intelligence-led screening and to be used only for the purposes of that investigation and destroyed afterwards:*

    *'I consent to my DNA/mouth swab being taken for forensic analysis. I understand that the sample will be destroyed at the end of the case and that my profile will only be compared to the crime stain profile from this enquiry. I have been advised that the person taking the sample may be required to give evidence and/or provide a written statement to the police in relation to the taking of it'.*

    *(ii)  DNA sample to be retained on the National DNA database and used in the future:*

    *'I consent to my DNA sample and information derived from it being retained and used only for purposes related to the prevention and detection of a crime, the investigation of an offence or the conduct of a prosecution either nationally or internationally.'*

    *'I understand that this sample may be checked against other DNA records held by, or on behalf of, relevant law enforcement authorities, either nationally or internationally'.*

    *'I understand that once I have given my consent for the sample to be retained and used I cannot withdraw this consent.'*

(b)  Fingerprints:

   (i)   Fingerprints taken for the purposes of elimination or as part of an intelligence-led screening and to be used only for the purposes of that investigation and destroyed afterwards:

   'I consent to my fingerprints being taken for elimination purposes. I understand that the fingerprints will be destroyed at the end of the case and that my fingerprints will only be compared to the fingerprints from this enquiry. I have been advised that the person taking the fingerprints may be required to give evidence and/or provide a written statement to the police in relation to the taking of it.'

   (ii)  Fingerprints to be retained for future use:

   'I consent to my fingerprints being retained and used only for purposes related to the prevention and detection of a crime, the investigation of an offence or the conduct of a prosecution either nationally or internationally'.

   'I understand that my fingerprints may be checked against other records held by, or on behalf of, relevant law enforcement authorities, either nationally or internationally.'

   'I understand that once I have given my consent for my fingerprints to be retained and used I cannot withdraw this consent.'

(c)  Footwear impressions:

   (i)   Footwear impressions taken for the purposes of elimination or as part of an intelligence-led screening and to be used only for the purposes of that investigation and destroyed afterwards:

   'I consent to my footwear impressions being taken for elimination purposes. I understand that the footwear impressions will be destroyed at the end of the case and that my footwear impressions will only be compared to the footwear impressions from this enquiry. I have been advised that the person taking the footwear impressions may be required to give evidence and/or provide a written statement to the police in relation to the taking of it.'

   (ii)  Footwear impressions to be retained for future use:

   'I consent to my footwear impressions being retained and used only for purposes related to the prevention and detection of a crime, the investigation of an offence or the conduct of a prosecution, either nationally or internationally'.

   'I understand that my footwear impressions may be checked against other records held by, or on behalf of, relevant law enforcement authorities, either nationally or internationally.'

   'I understand that once I have given my consent for my footwear impressions to be retained and used I cannot withdraw this consent.'

F2   The provisions for the retention of fingerprints, footwear impressions and samples in paragraph 1 allow for all fingerprints, footwear impressions and samples in a case to be available for any subsequent miscarriage of justice investigation.

Code **D**

# Appendix 6
## Code E: PACE Code of Practice on Audio Recording Interviews with Suspects

This code applies to interviews carried out after midnight on 1 May 2010, notwithstanding that the interview may have commenced before that time.

### 1 GENERAL

1.1   This Code of Practice must be readily available for consultation by:
- police officers
- police staff
- detained persons
- members of the public.

1.2   The *Notes for Guidance* included are not provisions of this Code.

1.3   Nothing in this Code shall detract from the requirements of Code C, the Code of Practice for the detention, treatment and questioning of persons by police officers.

1.4   This Code does not apply to those people listed in Code C, *paragraph 1.12*.

1.5   The term:
- 'appropriate adult' has the same meaning as in Code C, *paragraph 1.7*
- 'solicitor' has the same meaning as in Code C, *paragraph 6.12*.

1.5A  Recording of interviews shall be carried out openly to instil confidence in its reliability as an impartial and accurate record of the interview.

1.6   In this Code:
(aa) 'recording media' means any removable, physical audio recording medium (such as magnetic type, optical disc or solid state memory) which can be played and copied.

(a) 'designated person' means a person other than a police officer, designated under the Police Reform Act 2002, Part 4 who has specified powers and duties of police officers conferred or imposed on them;

(b) any reference to a police officer includes a designated person acting in the exercise or performance of the powers and duties conferred or imposed on them by their designation;

(c) 'secure digital network' is a computer network system which enables an original interview recording to be stored as a digital multi media file or a series of such files, on a secure file server which is accredited by the National Accreditor for Police Information Systems in the National Police Improvement Agency (NPIA) in accordance with the UK Government Protective Marking Scheme. (see section 7 of this Code).

1.7   Sections 2 to 6 of this code set out the procedures and requirements which apply to all interviews together with the provisions which apply only to interviews recorded using removable media. Section 7 sets out the provisions which apply to interviews recorded using a secure digital network and specifies the provisions in sections 2 to 6 which do not apply to secure digital network recording.

1.8   Nothing in this Code prevents the custody officer, or other officer given custody of the detainee, from allowing police staff who are not designated persons to carry out individual procedures or tasks at the police station if the law allows. However, the officer remains responsible for making sure the procedures and tasks are carried out correctly in accordance with this Code. Any such police staff must be:
  (a) a person employed by a police authority maintaining a police force and under the control and direction of the Chief Officer of that force; or
  (b) employed by a person with whom a police authority has a contract for the provision of services relating to persons arrested or otherwise in custody.

1.9   Designated persons and other police staff must have regard to any relevant provisions of the Codes of Practice.

1.10   References to pocket book include any official report book issued to police officers or police staff.

1.11   References to a custody officer include those performing the functions of a custody officer as in *paragraph 1.9* of Code C.

## 2   Recording and Sealing Master Recordings

2.1 Not used.

2.2 One recording, the master recording, will be sealed in the suspect's presence. A second recording will be used as a working copy. The master recording is either of the two recordings used in a twin deck/drive machine or the only recording in a single deck/drive machine. The working copy is either the second/third recording used in a twin/triple deck/drive machine or a copy of the master recording made by a single deck/drive machine. See *Notes 2A* and *2B*. [*This paragraph does not apply to interviews recorded using a secure digital network, see paragraphs 7.4 to 7.6.*]

2.3 Nothing in this Code requires the identity of officers or police staff conducting interviews to be recorded or disclosed:
  (a) in the case of enquiries linked to the investigation of terrorism (see *paragraph 3.2*); or
  (b) if the interviewer reasonably believes recording or disclosing their name might put them in danger.
  In these cases interviewers should use warrant or other identification numbers and the name of their police station. See *Note 2C*

### Notes for guidance

2A   *The purpose of sealing the master recording in the suspect's presence is to show the recording's integrity is preserved. If a single deck/drive machine is used the working copy of the master recording must be made in the suspect's presence and without the master recording leaving their sight. The working copy shall be used for making further copies if needed.*

2B  *Not used.*

2C  *The purpose of paragraph 2.3(b) is to protect those involved in serious organised crime investigations or arrests of particularly violent suspects when there is reliable informa-tion that those arrested or their associates may threaten or cause harm to those involved. In cases of doubt, an officer of inspector rank or above should be consulted.*

### 3  INTERVIEWS TO BE AUDIO RECORDED

3.1  Subject to *paragraphs 3.3* and *3.4*, audio recording shall be used at police stations for any interview:

(a)  with a person cautioned under Code C, *section 10* in respect of any indictable offence, including an offence triable either way; see *Note 3A*

(b)  which takes place as a result of an interviewer exceptionally putting further questions to a suspect about an offence described in *paragraph 3.1(a)* after they have been charged with, or told they may be prosecuted for, that offence, see Code C, *paragraph 16.5*

(c)  when an interviewer wants to tell a person, after they have been charged with, or informed they may be prosecuted for, an offence described in *para-graph 3.1(a)*, about any written statement or interview with another person, see Code C, *paragraph 16.4.*

3.2  The Terrorism Act 2000 makes separate provision for a Code of Practice for the audio recording of interviews of those arrested under Section 41 of, or Schedule 7 to, the 2000 Act. The provisions of this Code do not apply to such interviews. [See *Note 3C*].

Code **E**

3.3  The custody officer may authorise the interviewer not to audio record the inter-view when it is:

(a)  not reasonably practicable because of equipment failure or the unavailabil-ity of a suitable interview room or recorder equipment and the authorising officer considers, on reasonable grounds, that the interview should not be delayed; or

(b)  clear from the outset there will not be a prosecution.

Note: In these cases the interview should be recorded in writing in accordance with Code C, *section 11*. In all cases the custody officer shall record the specific reasons for not audio recording. See *Note 3B*

3.4  If a person refuses to go into or remain in a suitable interview room, see Code C, *paragraph 12.5*, and the custody officer considers, on reasonable grounds, that the interview should not be delayed the interview may, at the custody officer's discretion, be conducted in a cell using portable recording equipment or, if none is available, recorded in writing as in Code C, *section 11*. The reasons for this shall be recorded.

3.5  The whole of each interview shall be audio recorded, including the taking and reading back of any statement.

3.6  A sign or indicator which is visible to the suspect must show when the recording equipment is recording.

### Notes for guidance

3A  *Nothing in this Code is intended to preclude audio recording at police discretion of interviews at police stations with people cautioned in respect of offences not covered by* paragraph 3.1, or responses made by persons after they have been charged with, or told they may be prosecuted for, an offence, provided this Code is complied with.

3B A decision not to audio record an interview for any reason may be the subject of comment in court. The authorising officer should be prepared to justify that decision.

3C If, during the course of an interview under this Code, it becomes apparent that the interview should be conducted under one of the terrorism codes for recording of interviews the interview should only continue in accordance with the relevant code.

## 4 THE INTERVIEW

### (a) General

4.1 The provisions of Code C:
- *sections 10 and 11*, and the applicable *Notes for Guidance* apply to the conduct of interviews to which this Code applies
- *paragraphs 11.7 to 11.14* apply only when a written record is needed.

4.2 Code C, *paragraphs 10.10, 10.11* and Annex C describe the restriction on drawing adverse inferences from a suspect's failure or refusal to say anything about their involvement in the offence when interviewed or after being charged or informed they may be prosecuted, and how it affects the terms of the caution and determines if and by whom a special warning under sections 36 and 37 of the Criminal Justice and Public Order Act 1994 can be given.

### (b) Commencement of interviews

4.3 When the suspect is brought into the interview room the interviewer shall, without delay but in the suspect's sight, load the recorder with new recording media and set it to record. The recording media must be unwrapped or opened in the suspect's presence. [*This paragraph does not apply to interviews recorded using a secure digital network, see paragraphs 7.4 and 7.5.*]

4.4 The interviewer should tell the suspect about the recording process and point out the sign or indicator which shows that the recording equipment is activated and recording. See *paragraph 3.6*. The interviewer shall:
- (a) say the interview is being audibly recorded
- (b) subject to *paragraph 2.3*, give their name and rank and that of any other interviewer present
- (c) ask the suspect and any other party present, e.g. a solicitor, to identify themselves
- (d) state the date, time of commencement and place of the interview
- (e) state the suspect will be given a notice about what will happen to the copies of the recording. [*This sub-paragraph does not apply to interviews recorded using a secure digital network, see paragraphs 7.4 and 7.6 to 7.7.*]

See *Note 4A*

4.5 The interviewer shall:
- caution the suspect, see Code C, *section 10*
- remind the suspect of their entitlement to free legal advice, see Code C, *paragraph 11.2*.

4.6 The interviewer shall put to the suspect any significant statement or silence; see Code C, *paragraph 11.4*.

### (c) Interviews with deaf persons

4.7 If the suspect is deaf or is suspected of having impaired hearing, the interviewer shall make a written note of the interview in accordance with Code C, at the same time as audio recording it in accordance with this Code. See *Notes 4B* and *4C*

### (d) Objections and complaints by the suspect

4.8 If the suspect objects to the interview being audibly recorded at the outset, during the interview or during a break, the interviewer shall explain that the interview is being audibly recorded and that this Code requires the suspect's objections to be recorded on the audio recording. When any objections have been audibly recorded or the suspect has refused to have their objections recorded, the interviewer shall say they are turning off the recorder, give their reasons and turn it off. The interviewer shall then make a written record of the interview as in Code C, *section 11*. If, however, the interviewer reasonably considers they may proceed to question the suspect with the audio recording still on, the interviewer may do so. This procedure also applies in cases where the suspect has previously objected to the interview being visually recorded, see *Code F 4.8*, and the investigating officer has decided to audibly record the interview. See *Note 4D*

4.9 If in the course of an interview a complaint is made by or on behalf of the person being questioned concerning the provisions of this Code or Code C, the interviewer shall act as in Code C, *paragraph 12.9*. See *Notes 4E* and *4F*

4.10 If the suspect indicates they want to tell the interviewer about matters not directly connected with the offence and they are unwilling for these matters to be audio recorded, the suspect should be given the opportunity to tell the interviewer at the end of the formal interview.

### (e) Changing recording media

4.11 When the recorder shows the recording media only has a short time left, the interviewer shall tell the suspect the recording media are coming to an end and round off that part of the interview. If the interviewer leaves the room for a second set of recording media, the suspect shall not be left unattended. The interviewer will remove the recording media from the recorder and insert the new recording media which shall be unwrapped or opened in the suspect's presence. The recorder should be set to record on the new media. To avoid confusion between the recording media, the interviewer shall mark the media with an identification number immediately after they are removed from the recorder. [*This paragraph does not apply to interviews recorded using a secure digital network as this does not use removable media, see paragraphs 1.6 (c), 7.4 and 7.14 to 7.15.*]

### (f) Taking a break during interview

4.12 When a break is taken, the fact that a break is to be taken, the reason for it and the time shall be recorded on the audio recording.

**Code E**

4.12A  When the break is taken and the interview room vacated by the suspect, the recording media shall be removed from the recorder and the procedures for the conclusion of an interview followed, see *paragraph 4.18*.

4.13   When a break is a short one and both the suspect and an interviewer remain in the interview room, the recording may be stopped. There is no need to remove the recording media and when the interview recommences the recording should continue on the same recording media. The time the interview recommences shall be recorded on the audio recording.

4.14   After any break in the interview the interviewer must, before resuming the interview, remind the person being questioned that they remain under caution or, if there is any doubt, give the caution in full again. See *Note 4G*.
       [*Paragraphs 4.12 to 4.14 do not apply to interviews recorded using a secure digital network, see paragraphs 7.4 and 7.8 to 7.10.*]

### (g)  Failure of recording equipment

4.15  If there is an equipment failure which can be rectified quickly, e.g. by inserting new recording media, the interviewer shall follow the appropriate procedures as in *paragraph 4.11*. When the recording is resumed the interviewer shall explain what happened and record the time the interview recommences. If, however, it will not be possible to continue recording on that recorder and no replacement recorder is readily available, the interview may continue without being audibly recorded. If this happens, the interviewer shall seek the custody officer's authority as in *paragraph 3.3*. See *Note 4H*. [*This paragraph does not apply to interviews recorded using a secure digital network, see paragraphs 7.4 and 7.11.*]

### (h)  Removing recording media from the recorder

4.16  When recording media is removed from the recorder during the interview, they shall be retained and the procedures in *paragraph 4.18* followed. [*This paragraph does not apply to interviews recorded using a secure digital network as this does not use removable media, see 1.6 (c), 7.4 and 7.14 to 7.15.*]

### (i)  Conclusion of interview

4.17  At the conclusion of the interview, the suspect shall be offered the opportunity to clarify anything he or she has said and asked if there is anything they want to add.

4.18  At the conclusion of the interview, including the taking and reading back of any written statement, the time shall be recorded and the recording shall be stopped. The interviewer shall seal the master recording with a master recording label and treat it as an exhibit in accordance with force standing orders. The interviewer shall sign the label and ask the suspect and any third party present during the interview to sign it. If the suspect or third party refuse to sign the label an officer of at least inspector rank, or if not available the custody officer, shall be called into the interview room and asked, subject to *paragraph 2.3*, to sign it.

4.19  The suspect shall be handed a notice which explains:
   • how the audio recording will be used
   • the arrangements for access to it

- that if the person is charged or informed they will be prosecuted, a copy of the audio recording will be supplied as soon as practicable or as otherwise agreed between the suspect and the police or on the order of a court.
[*Paragraphs 4.17 to 4.19 do not apply to interviews recorded using a secure digital network, see paragraphs 7.4 and 7.12 to 7.13.*]

### Notes for guidance

4A  *For the purpose of voice identification the interviewer should ask the suspect and any other people present to identify themselves.*

4B  *This provision is to give a person who is deaf or has impaired hearing equivalent rights of access to the full interview record as far as this is possible using audio recording.*

4C  *The provisions of Code C, section 13 on interpreters for deaf persons or for interviews with suspects who have difficulty understanding English continue to apply.*

4D  *The interviewer should remember that a decision to continue recording against the wishes of the suspect may be the subject of comment in court.*

4E  *If the custody officer is called to deal with the complaint, the recorder should, if possible, be left on until the custody officer has entered the room and spoken to the person being interviewed. Continuation or termination of the interview should be at the interviewer's discretion pending action by an inspector under Code C, paragraph 9.2.*

4F  *If the complaint is about a matter not connected with this Code or Code C, the decision to continue is at the interviewer's discretion. When the interviewer decides to continue the interview, they shall tell the suspect the complaint will be brought to the custody officer's attention at the conclusion of the interview. When the interview is concluded the interviewer must, as soon as practicable, inform the custody officer about the existence and nature of the complaint made.*

4G  *The interviewer should remember that it may be necessary to show to the court that nothing occurred during a break or between interviews which influenced the suspect's recorded evidence. After a break or at the beginning of a subsequent interview, the interviewer should consider summarising on the record the reason for the break and confirming this with the suspect.*

4H  *Where the interview is being recorded and the media or the recording equipment fails the officer conducting the interview should stop the interview immediately. Where part of the interview is unaffected by the error and is still accessible on the media, that media shall be copied and sealed in the suspect's presence and the interview recommenced using new equipment/media as required. Where the content of the interview has been lost in its entirety the media should be sealed in the suspect's presence and the interview begun again. If the recording equipment cannot be fixed or no replacement is immediately available the interview should be recorded in accordance with Code C, section 11.*

Code **E**

### 5  After the Interview

5.1  The interviewer shall make a note in their pocket book that the interview has taken place, was audibly recorded, its time, duration and date and the master recording's identification number.

5.2  If no proceedings follow in respect of the person whose interview was recorded, the recording media must be kept securely as in *paragraph 6.1* and *Note 6A*.

*[This section (paragraphs 5.1, 5.2 and Note 5A) does not apply to interviews recorded using a secure digital network, see paragraphs 7.4 and 7.14 to 7.15.]*

### Note for guidance

5A *Any written record of an audibly recorded interview should be made in accordance with national guidelines approved by the Secretary of State, and with regard to the advice contained in the Manual of Guidance for the preparation, processing and submission of prosecution files.*

## 6 MEDIA SECURITY

6.1 The officer in charge of each police station at which interviews with suspects are recorded shall make arrangements for master recordings to be kept securely and their movements accounted for on the same basis as material which may be used for evidential purposes, in accordance with force standing orders. See *Note 6A*

6.2 A police officer has no authority to break the seal on a master recording required for criminal trial or appeal proceedings. If it is necessary to gain access to the master recording, the police officer shall arrange for its seal to be broken in the presence of a representative of the Crown Prosecution Service. The defendant or their legal adviser should be informed and given a reasonable opportunity to be present. If the defendant or their legal representative is present they shall be invited to reseal and sign the master recording. If either refuses or neither is present this should be done by the representative of the Crown Prosecution Service. See *Notes 6B* and *6C*

6.3 If no criminal proceedings result or the criminal trial and, if applicable, appeal proceedings to which the interview relates have been concluded, the chief officer of police is responsible for establishing arrangements for breaking the seal on the master recording, if necessary.

6.4 When the master recording seal is broken, a record must be made of the procedure followed, including the date, time, place and persons present.
*[This section (paragraphs 6.1 to 6.4 and Note 6A to 6C) does not apply to interviews recorded using a secure digital network, see paragraphs 7.4 and 7.14 to 7.15.]*

### Notes for guidance

6A *This section is concerned with the security of the master recording sealed at the conclusion of the interview. Care must be taken of working copies of recordings because their loss or destruction may lead to the need to access master recordings.*

6B *If the recording has been delivered to the crown court for their keeping after committal for trial the crown prosecutor will apply to the chief clerk of the crown court centre for the release of the recording for unsealing by the crown prosecutor.*

6C *Reference to the Crown Prosecution Service or to the crown prosecutor in this part of the Code should be taken to include any other body or person with a statutory responsibility for prosecution for whom the police conduct any audibly recorded interviews.*

## 7 RECORDING OF INTERVIEWS BY SECURE DIGITAL NETWORK

7.1 A secure digital network does not use removable media and this section specifies the provisions which will apply when a secure digital network is used.

7.2 *Not used.*

7.3 The following requirements are solely applicable to the use of a secure digital network for the recording of interviews.

### (a) Application of sections 1 to 6 of Code E

7.4 Sections 1 to 6 of Code E above apply except for the following paragraphs:
- Paragraph 2.2 under 'Recording and sealing of master recordings'
- Paragraph 4.3 under '(b) Commencement of interviews'
- Paragraph 4.4(e) under '(b) Commencement of interviews'
- Paragraphs 4.11–4.19 under '(e) Changing recording media', '(f) Taking a break during interview', '(g) Failure of recording equipment', '(h) Removing recording media from the recorder' and '(i) Conclusion of interview'
- Paragraphs 6.1–6.4 and Notes 6A to 6C under 'Media security'

### (b) Commencement of Interview

7.5 When the suspect is brought into the interview room, the interviewer shall without delay and in the sight of the suspect, switch on the recording equipment and enter the information necessary to log on to the secure network and start recording.

7.6 The interviewer must then inform the suspect that the interview is being recorded using a secure digital network and that recording has commenced.

7.7 In addition to the requirements of paragraph 4.4 (a–d) above, the interviewer must inform the person that:
- they will be given access to the recording of the interview in the event that they are charged or informed that they will be prosecuted but if they are not charged or informed that they will be prosecuted they will only be given access as agreed with the police or on the order of a court; and
- they will be given a written notice at the end of the interview setting out their rights to access the recording and what will happen to the recording.

Code E

### (c) Taking a break during interview

7.8 When a break is taken, the fact that a break is to be taken, the reason for it and the time shall be recorded on the audio recording. The recording shall be stopped and the procedures in paragraphs 7.12 and 7.13 for the conclusion of an interview followed.

7.9 When the interview recommences the procedures in paragraphs 7.5 to 7.7 for commencing an interview shall be followed to create a new file to record the continuation of the interview. The time the interview recommences shall be recorded on the audio recording.

7.10 After any break in the interview the interviewer must, before resuming the interview, remind the person being questioned that they remain under caution or, if there is any doubt, give the caution in full again. See *Note 4G*

### (d) Failure of recording equipment

7.11 If there is an equipment failure which can be rectified quickly, e.g. by commencing a new secure digital network recording, the interviewer shall follow the appropriate procedures as in *paragraphs 7.8 to 7.10*. When the recording is resumed the interviewer shall explain what happened and record the time the interview recommences. If, however, it is not possible to continue recording on the secure digital network the interview should be recorded on removable media as in *paragraph 4.3* unless the necessary equipment is not available.

**485**

If this happens the interview may continue without being audibly recorded and the interviewer shall seek the custody officer's authority as in *paragraph 3.3*. See *Note 4H*.

### (e) Conclusion of interview

7.12 At the conclusion of the interview, the suspect shall be offered the opportunity to clarify anything he or she has said and asked if there is anything they want to add.

7.13 At the conclusion of the interview, including the taking and reading back of any written statement:

    (a) the time shall be orally recorded

    (b) the suspect shall be handed a notice which explains:

        • how the audio recording will be used

        • the arrangements for access to it

        • that if they are charged or informed that they will be prosecuted, they will be given access to the recording of the interview either electronically or by being given a copy on removable recording media, but if they are not charged or informed that they will prosecuted, they will only be given access as agreed with the police or on the order of a court.

        See *Note 7A*.

    (c) the suspect must be asked to confirm that he or she has received a copy of the notice at *paragraph 7.13(b)* above. If the suspect fails to accept or to acknowledge receipt of the notice, the interviewer will state for the recording that a copy of the notice has been provided to the suspect and that he or she has refused to take a copy of the notice or has refused to acknowledge receipt.

    (d) the time shall be recorded and the interviewer shall notify the suspect that the recording is being saved to the secure network. The interviewer must save the recording in the presence of the suspect. The suspect should then be informed that the interview is terminated.

### (f) After the interview

7.14 The interviewer shall make a note in their pocket book that the interview has taken place, was audibly recorded, its time, duration and date and the original recording's identification number.

7.15 If no proceedings follow in respect of the person whose interview was recorded, the recordings must be kept securely as in *paragraphs 7.16* and *7.17*.
    *See Note 5A*

### (g) Security of secure digital network interview records

7.16 Interview record files are stored in read only format on non-removable storage devices, for example, hard disk drives, to ensure their integrity. The recordings are first saved locally to a secure non-removable device before being transferred to the remote network device. If for any reason the network connection fails, the recording remains on the local device and will be transferred when the network connections are restored.

7.17 Access to interview recordings, including copying to removable media, must be strictly controlled and monitored to ensure that access is restricted to those who have been given specific permission to access for specified purposes when this is necessary. For example, police officers and CPS lawyers involved in the preparation of any prosecution case, persons interviewed if they have been charged or informed they may be prosecuted and their legal representatives.

### Note for Guidance

7A *The notice at paragraph 7.13 above should provide a brief explanation of the secure digital network and how access to the recording is strictly limited. The notice should also explain the access rights of the suspect, his or her legal representative, the police and the prosecutor to the recording of the interview. Space should be provided on the form to insert the date and the file reference number for the interview.*

Code **E**

# Appendix 7
# Code F: PACE Code of Practice on Visual Recording with Sound of Interviews with Suspects

The contents of this code should be considered if an interviewing officer decides to make a visual recording with sound of an interview with a suspect after midnight on 1 May 2010.

There is no statutory requirement under PACE to visually record interviews.

## 1 GENERAL

1.1 This code of practice must be readily available for consultation by police officers and other police staff, detained persons and members of the public.

1.2 The notes for guidance included are not provisions of this code. They form guidance to police officers and others about its application and interpretation.

1.3 Nothing in this code shall be taken as detracting in any way from the requirements of the Code of Practice for the Detention, Treatment and Questioning of Persons by Police Officers (Code C). [See *Note 1A*.]

1.4 The interviews to which this Code applies are set out in paragraphs 3.1–3.3.

1.5 In this code, the term 'appropriate adult', 'solicitor' and 'interview' have the same meaning as those set out in Code C. The corresponding provisions and Notes for Guidance in Code C applicable to those terms shall also apply where appropriate.

1.5A The visual recording of interviews shall be carried out openly to instil confidence in its reliability as an impartial and accurate record of the interview.

1.6 Any reference in this code to visual recording shall be taken to mean visual recording with sound and in this code:

(aa) 'recording media' means any removable, physical audio recording medium (such as magnetic tape, optical disc or solid state memory) which can be played and copied;

(a) 'designated person' means a person other than a police officer, designated under the Police Reform Act 2020, Part 4 who has specified powers and duties of police officers conferred or imposed on them;

(b) any reference to a police officer includes a designated person acting in the exercise or performance of the powers and duties conferred or imposed on them by their designation;

(c) 'secure digital network' is a computer network system which enables an original interview recording to be stored as a digital multi media file or a series of such files, on a secure file server which is accredited by the

Code **F**

National Accreditor for Police Information Systems in the National Police Improvement Agency (NPIA) in accordance with the UK Government Protective Marking Scheme. (see section 7 of this Code).

1.7    References to 'pocket book' in this Code include any official report book issued to police officers.

## Note for guidance

*1A    As in paragraph 1.9 of Code C, references to custody officers include those carrying out the functions of a custody officer.*

## 2 RECORDING AND SEALING OF MASTER TAPES

2.1 Not used.

2.2 The camera(s) shall be placed in the interview room so as to ensure coverage of as much of the room as is practicably possible whilst the interviews are taking place. [See *Note 2A*.]

2.3 The certified recording medium will be of a high quality, new and previously unused. When the certified recording medium is placed in the recorder and switched on to record, the correct date and time, in hours, minutes and seconds, will be superimposed automatically, second by second, during the whole recording. [See *Note 2B*.] See section 7 regarding the use of a secure digital network to record the interview.

2.4 One copy of the certified recording medium, referred to in this code as the master copy, will be sealed before it leaves the presence of the suspect. A second copy will be used as a working copy. [See *Note 2C* and *2D*.]

2.5 Nothing in this code requires the identity of an officer to be recorded or disclosed if:

(a)   the interview or record relates to a person detained under the Terrorism Act 2000 (see paragraph 3.2); or

(b)   otherwise where the officer reasonably believes that recording or disclosing their name might put them in danger.

2.6 In these cases, the officer will have their back to the camera and shall use their warrant or other identification number and the name of the police station to which they are attached. Such instances and the reasons for them shall be recorded in the custody record. [See *Note 2E*.]

## Notes for guidance

*2A    Interviewing officers will wish to arrange that, as far as possible, visual recording arrangements are unobtrusive. It must be clear to the suspect, however, that there is no opportunity to interfere with the recording equipment or the recording media.*

*2B    In this context, the certified recording media should be capable of having an image of the date and time superimposed upon them as they record the interview.*

*2C    The purpose of sealing the master copy before it leaves the presence of the suspect is to establish their confidence that the integrity of the copy is preserved.*

*2D    The recording of the interview may be used for identification procedures in accordance with paragraph 3.21 or Annex E of Code D.*

*2E    The purpose of the paragraph 2.5(b) is to protect police officers and others involved in the investigation of serious organised crime or the arrest of particularly violent suspects when there is reliable information that those arrested or their associates may threaten or cause harm to the officers, their families or their personal property.*

## 3 INTERVIEWS TO BE VISUALLY RECORDED

3.1 Subject to paragraph 3.2 below, if an interviewing officer decides to make a visual recording these are the areas where it might be appropriate:

(a) with a suspect in respect of an indictable offence (including an offence triable either way) [see *Notes 3A* and *3B*];

(b) which takes place as a result of an interviewer exceptionally putting further questions to a suspect about an offence described in sub-paragraph (a) above after they have been charged with, or informed they may be prosecuted for, that offence [see *Note 3C*];

(c) in which an interviewer wishes to bring to the notice of a person, after that person has been charged with, or informed they may be prosecuted for an offence described in sub-paragraph (a) above, any written statement made by another person, or the content of an interview with another person [see *Note 3D*];

(d) with, or in the presence of, a deaf or deaf/blind or speech impaired person who uses sign language to communicate;

(e) with, or in the presence of anyone who requires an 'appropriate adult'; or

(f) in any case where the suspect or their representative requests that the interview be recorded visually.

3.2 The Terrorism Act 2000 makes separate provision for a code of practice for the video recording of interviews in a police station of those detained under Schedule 7 or section 41 of the Act. The provisions of this code do not therefore apply to such interviews [see *Note 3E*].

3.3 The custody officer may authorise the interviewing officer not to record the interview visually:

(a) where it is not reasonably practicable to do so because of failure of the equipment, or the non-availability of a suitable interview room, or recorder, and the authorising officer considers on reasonable grounds that the interview should not be delayed until the failure has been rectified or a suitable room or recorder becomes available. In such cases the custody officer may author_ ise the interviewing officer to audio record the interview in accordance with the guidance set out in Code E;

(b) where it is clear from the outset that no prosecution will ensue; or

(c) where it is not practicable to do so because at the time the person resists being taken to a suitable interview room or other location which would enable the interview to be recorded, or otherwise fails or refuses to go into such a room or location, and the authorising officer considers on reasonable grounds that the interview should not be delayed until these conditions cease to apply.

In all cases the custody officer shall make a note in the custody records of the reasons for not taking a visual record. [See *Note 3F*.]

3.4 When a person who is voluntarily attending the police station is required to be cautioned in accordance with Code C prior to being interviewed, the subsequent interview shall be recorded, unless the custody officer gives authority in accordance

Code **F**

with the provisions of paragraph 3.3 above for the interview not to be so recorded.

3.5 The whole of each interview shall be recorded visually, including the taking and reading back of any statement.

3.6 A sign or indicator which is visible to the suspect must show when the visual recording equipment is recording.

### Notes for guidance

*3A Nothing in the code is intended to preclude visual recording at police discretion of interviews at police stations with people cautioned in respect of offences not covered by paragraph 3.1, or responses made by interviewees after they have been charged with, or informed they may be prosecuted for, an offence, provided that this code is complied with.*

*3B Attention is drawn to the provisions set out in Code C about the matters to be considered when deciding whether a detained person is fit to be interviewed.*

*3C Code C sets out the circumstances in which a suspect may be questioned about an offence after being charged with it.*

*3D Code C sets out the procedures to be followed when a person's attention is drawn after charge, to a statement made by another person. One method of bringing the content of an interview with another person to the notice of a suspect may be to play him a recording of that interview.*

*3E If, during the course of an interview under this Code, it becomes apparent that the interview should be conducted under one of the terrorism codes for video recording of interviews the interview should only continue in accordance with the relevant code.*

*3F A decision not to record an interview visually for any reason may be the subject of comment in court. The authorising officer should therefore be prepared to justify their decision in each case.*

### 4 THE INTERVIEW

#### (a) General

4.1 The provisions of Code C in relation to cautions and interviews and the Notes for Guidance applicable to those provisions shall apply to the conduct of interviews to which this Code applies.

4.2 Particular attention is drawn to those parts of Code C that describe the restrictions on drawing adverse inferences from a suspect's failure or refusal to say anything about their involvement in the offence when interviewed, or after being charged or informed they may be prosecuted and how those restrictions affect the terms of the caution and determine whether a special warning under Sections 36 and 37 of the Criminal Justice and Public Order Act 1994 can be given.

#### (b) Commencement of interviews

4.3 When the suspect is brought into the interview room the interviewer shall without delay, but in sight of the suspect, load the recording equipment and set it to record. The recording media must be unwrapped or otherwise opened in the presence of the suspect. [See *Note 4A*.]

4.4 The interviewer shall then tell the suspect formally about the visual recording and point out the sign or indicator which shows that the recording equipment is activated and recording. *See paragraph 3.6*. The interviewer shall:

(a) explain the interview is being visually recorded;

(b) subject to paragraph 2.5, give his or her name and rank, and that of any other interviewer present;

(c) ask the suspect and any other party present (e.g. his solicitor) to identify themselves;

(d) state the date, time of commencement and place of the interview; and

(e) state that the suspect will be given a notice about what will happen to the recording.

4.5 The interviewer shall then caution the suspect, which should follow that set out in Code C, and remind the suspect of their entitlement to free and independent legal advice and that they can speak to a solicitor on the telephone.

4.6 The interviewer shall then put to the suspect any significant statement or silence (i.e. failure or refusal to answer a question or to answer it satisfactorily) which occurred before the start of the interview, and shall ask the suspect whether they wish to confirm or deny that earlier statement or silence or whether they wish to add anything. The definition of a 'significant' statement or silence is the same as that set out in Code C.

## (c) Interviews with the deaf

4.7 If the suspect is deaf or there is doubt about their hearing ability, the provisions of Code C on interpreters for the deaf or for interviews with suspects who have difficulty in understanding English continue to apply.

## (d) Objections and complaints by the suspect

Code **F**

4.8 If the suspect raises objections to the interview being visually recorded either at the outset or during the interview or during a break in the interview, the interviewer shall explain the fact that the interview is being visually recorded and that the provisions of this code require that the suspect's objections shall be recorded on the visual recording. When any objections have been visually recorded or the suspect has refused to have their objections recorded, the interviewer shall say that they are turning off the recording equipment, give their reasons and turn it off. If a separate audio recording is being maintained, the officer shall ask the person to record the reasons for refusing to agree to visual recording of the interview. Paragraph 4.8 of Code E will apply if the person objects to audio recording of the interview. The officer shall then make a written record of the interview. If the interviewer reasonably considers they may proceed to question the suspect with the visual recording still on, the interviewer may do so. See *Note 4G*.

4.9 If in the course of an interview a complaint is made by the person being questioned, or on their behalf, concerning the provisions of this code or of Code C, then the interviewer shall act in accordance with Code C, record it in the interview record and inform the custody officer. [See *4B* and *4C*.]

4.10 If the suspect indicates that they wish to tell the interviewer about matters not directly connected with the offence of which they are suspected and that they are unwilling for these matters to be recorded, the suspect shall be given the opportunity to tell the interviewer about these matters after the conclusion of the formal interview.

### (e) Changing the recording media

4.11 In instances where the recording medium is not of sufficient length to record all of the interview with the suspect, further certified recording medium will be used. When the recording equipment indicates that the recording medium has only a short time left to run, the interviewer shall advise the suspect and round off that part of the interview. If the interviewer wishes to continue the interview but does not already have further certified recording media with him, they shall obtain a set. The suspect should not be left unattended in the interview room. The interviewer will remove the recording media from the recording equipment and insert the new ones which have been unwrapped or otherwise opened in the suspect's presence. The recording equipment shall then be set to record. Care must be taken, particularly when a number of sets of recording media have been used, to ensure that there is no confusion between them. This could be achieved by marking the sets of recording media with consecutive identification numbers.

### (f) Taking a break during the interview

4.12 When a break is to be taken during the course of an interview and the interview room is to be vacated by the suspect, the fact that a break is to be taken, the reason for it and the time shall be recorded. The recording equipment must be turned off and the recording media removed. The procedures for the conclusion of an interview set out in paragraph 4.19, below, should be followed.

4.13 When a break is to be a short one, and both the suspect and a police officer are to remain in the interview room, the fact that a break is to be taken, the reasons for it and the time shall be recorded on the recording media. The recording equipment may be turned off, but there is no need to remove the recording media. When the interview is recommenced the recording shall continue on the same recording media and the time at which the interview recommences shall be recorded.

4.14 When there is a break in questioning under caution, the interviewing officer must ensure that the person being questioned is aware that they remain under caution. If there is any doubt, the caution must be given again in full when the interview resumes. [See *Notes 4D* and *4E.*]

### (g) Failure of recording equipment

4.15 If there is a failure of equipment which can be rectified quickly, the appropriate procedures set out in paragraph 4.12 shall be followed. When the recording is resumed the interviewer shall explain what has happened and record the time the interview recommences. If, however, it is not possible to continue recording on that particular recorder and no alternative equipment is readily available, the interview may continue without being recorded visually. In such circumstances, the procedures set out in paragraph 3.3 of this code for seeking the authority of the custody officer will be followed. [See *Note 4F.*]

**494**

### (h) Removing used recording media from recording equipment

4.16 Where used recording media are removed from the recording equipment during the course of an interview, they shall be retained and the procedures set out in paragraph 4.18 below followed.

### (i) Conclusion of interview

4.17 Before the conclusion of the interview, the suspect shall be offered the opportunity to clarify anything he or she has said and asked if there is anything that they wish to add.

4.18 At the conclusion of the interview, including the taking and reading back of any written statement, the time shall be recorded and the recording equipment switched off. The master tape or CD shall be removed from the recording equipment, sealed with a master copy label and treated as an exhibit in accordance with the force standing orders. The interviewer shall sign the label and also ask the suspect or other third party present during the interview to sign it. If the suspect or third party refuses to sign the label, an officer of at least the rank of inspector, or if one is not available, the custody officer, shall be called into the interview room and asked, subject to paragraph 2.5, to sign it.

4.19 The suspect shall be handed a notice which explains the use which will be made of the recording and the arrangements for access to it. The notice will also advise the suspect that a copy of the tape shall be supplied as soon as practicable if the person is charged or informed that he will be prosecuted.

### Notes for guidance

4A *The interviewer should attempt to estimate the likely length of the interview and ensure that an appropriate quantity of certified recording media and labels with which to seal the master copies are available in the interview room.*

4B *Where the custody officer is called immediately to deal with the complaint, wherever possible the recording equipment should be left to run until the custody officer has entered the interview room and spoken to the person being interviewed. Continuation or termination of the interview should be at the discretion of the interviewing officer pending action by an inspector as set out in Code C.*

4C *Where the complaint is about a matter not connected with this code of practice or Code C, the decision to continue with the interview is at the discretion of the interviewing officer. Where the interviewing officer decides to continue with the interview, the person being interviewed shall be told that the complaint will be brought to the attention of the custody officer at the conclusion of the interview. When the interview is concluded, the interviewing officer must, as soon as practicable, inform the custody officer of the existence and nature of the complaint made.*

4D *In considering whether to caution again after a break, the officer should bear in mind that he may have to satisfy a court that the person understood that he was still under caution when the interview resumed.*

4E *The officer should bear in mind that it may be necessary to satisfy the court that nothing occurred during a break in an interview or between interviews which influenced the suspect's recorded evidence. On the re-commencement of an interview, the officer should consider summarising on the record the reason for the break and confirming this with the suspect.*

Code **F**

4F *If any part of the recording media breaks or is otherwise damaged during the interview, it should be sealed as a master copy in the presence of the suspect and the interview resumed where it left off. The undamaged part should be copied and the original sealed as a master tape in the suspect's presence, if necessary after the interview. If equipment for copying is not readily available, both parts should be sealed in the suspect's presence and the interview begun again.*

4G *The interviewer should be aware that a decision to continue recording against the wishes of the suspect may be the subject of comment in court.*

## 5 AFTER THE INTERVIEW

5.1 The interviewer shall make a note in his or her pocket book of the fact that the interview has taken place and has been recorded, its time, duration and date and the identification number of the master copy of the recording media.

5.2 Where no proceedings follow in respect of the person whose interview was recorded, the recording media must nevertheless be kept securely in accordance with paragraph 6.1 and Note 6A.

### Note for guidance

5A *Any written record of a recorded interview shall be made in accordance with national guidelines approved by the Secretary of State, and with regard to the advice contained in the Manual of Guidance for the preparation, processing and submission of files.*

## 6 MASTER COPY SECURITY

### (a) General

6.1 The officer in charge of the police station at which interviews with suspects are recorded shall make arrangements for the master copies to be kept securely and their movements accounted for on the same basis as other material which may be used for evidential purposes, in accordance with force standing orders. [See *Note 6A.*]

### (b) Breaking master copy seal for criminal proceedings

6.2 A police officer has no authority to break the seal on a master copy which is required for criminal trial or appeal proceedings. If it is necessary to gain access to the master copy, the police officer shall arrange for its seal to be broken in the presence of a representative of the Crown Prosecution Service. The defendant or their legal adviser shall be informed and given a reasonable opportunity to be present. If the defendant or their legal representative is present they shall be invited to reseal and sign the master copy. If either refuses or neither is present, this shall be done by the representative of the Crown Prosecution Service. [See *Notes 6B* and *6C.*]

### (c) Breaking master copy seal: other cases

6.3 The chief officer of police is responsible for establishing arrangements for breaking the seal of the master copy where no criminal proceedings result, or the criminal proceedings, to which the interview relates, have been concluded and it becomes necessary to break the seal. These arrangements should be those which the chief officer considers are reasonably necessary to demonstrate to the person interviewed and any other party who may wish to use or refer to the interview record that the master copy has not been tampered with and that the interview record remains accurate. [See *Note 6D*.]

6.4 Subject to paragraph 6.6, a representative of each party must be given a reasonable opportunity to be present when the seal is broken, the master copy copied and re-sealed.

6.5 If one or more of the parties is not present when the master copy seal is broken because they cannot be contacted or refuse to attend or paragraph 6.6 applies, arrangements should be made for an independent person such as a custody visitor, to be present. Alternatively, or as an additional safeguard, arrangement should be made for a film or photographs to be taken of the procedure.

6.6 Paragraph 6.5 does not require a person to be given an opportunity to be present when:

(a) it is necessary to break the master copy seal for the proper and effective further investigation of the original offence or the investigation of some other offence; and

(b) the officer in charge of the investigation has reasonable grounds to suspect that allowing an opportunity might prejudice any such an investigation or criminal proceedings which may be brought as a result or endanger any person. [See *Note 6E*.]

**(d) Documentation**

6.7 When the master copy seal is broken, copied and re-sealed, a record must be made of the procedure followed, including the date time and place and persons present.

### Notes for guidance

*6A This section is concerned with the security of the master copy which will have been sealed at the conclusion of the interview. Care should, however, be taken of working copies since their loss or destruction may lead unnecessarily to the need to have access to master copies.*

*6B If the master copy has been delivered to the Crown Court for their keeping after committal for trial the Crown Prosecutor will apply to the Chief Clerk of the Crown Court Centre for its release for unsealing by the Crown Prosecutor.*

*6C Reference to the Crown Prosecution Service or to the Crown Prosecutor in this part of the code shall be taken to include any other body or person with a statutory responsibility for prosecution for whom the police conduct any recorded interviews.*

*6D The most common reasons for needing access to master copies that are not required for criminal proceedings arise from civil actions and complaints against police and civil actions between individuals arising out of allegations of crime investigated by police.*

*6E Paragraph 6.6 could apply, for example, when one or more of the outcomes or likely outcomes of the investigation might be: (i) the prosecution of one or more of the original suspects; (ii) the prosecution of someone previously not suspected, including someone who was originally a witness; and (iii) any original suspect being treated as a prosecution witness and when premature disclosure of any police action, particularly through contact with any parties involved, could lead to a real risk of compromising the investigation and endangering witnesses.*

Code **F**

## 7 VISUAL RECORDING OF INTERVIEWS BY SECURE DIGITAL NETWORK

7.1 This section applies if an officer wishes to make a visual recording with sound of an interview mentioned in section 3 of this Code using a secure digital network which does not use removable media (see *paragraph 1.6(c)* above).

7.2 The provisions of sections 1 to 6 of this Code which relate or apply only to removable media will not apply to a secure digital network recording.

7.3 The statutory requirement and provisions for the audio recording of interviews using a secure digital network set out in section 7 of Code E should be applied to the visual recording with sound of interviews mentioned in section 3 of this code as if references to audio recordings of interviews include visual recordings with sound.

# Appendix 8
## Code G: PACE Code of Practice for the Statutory Power of Arrest by Police Officers

This Code applies to any arrest made by a police officer after midnight on 31 December 2005.

### 1 INTRODUCTION

1.1 This Code of Practice deals with statutory power of police to arrest persons suspected of involvement in a criminal offence.

1.2 The right to liberty is a key principle of the Human Rights Act 1998. The exercise of the power of arrest represents an obvious and significant interference with that right.

1.3 The use of the power must be fully justified and officers exercising the power should consider if the necessary objectives can be met by other, less intrusive means. Arrest must never be used simply because it can be used. Absence of justification for exercising the powers of arrest may lead to challenges should the case proceed to court. When the power of arrest is exercised it is essential that it is exercised in a non- discriminatory and proportionate manner.

1.4 Section 24 of the Police and Criminal Evidence Act 1984 (as substituted by section 110 of the Serious Organised Crime and Police Act 2005) provides the statutory power of arrest. If the provisions of the Act and this Code are not observed, both the arrest and the conduct of any subsequent investigation may be open to question.

1.5 This code of practice must be readily available at all police stations for consultation by police officers and police staff, detained persons and members of the public.

1.6 The notes for guidance are not provisions of this code.

### 2 ELEMENTS OF ARREST UNDER SECTION 24 PACE

2.1 A lawful arrest requires two elements:
A person's involvement or suspected involvement or attempted involvement in the commission of a criminal offence;
AND
Reasonable grounds for believing that the person's arrest is necessary.

2.2 Arresting officers are required to inform the person arrested that they have been arrested, even if this fact is obvious, and of the relevant circumstances of the arrest in relation to both elements and to inform the custody officer of these on arrival at the police station. See Code C, *paragraph 3.4*.

Code **G**

### Involvement in the commission of an offence

2.3 A constable may arrest without warrant in relation to any offence, except for the single exception listed in Note for Guidance 1. A constable may arrest anyone:
- who is about to commit an offence or is in the act of committing an offence
- whom the officer has reasonable grounds for suspecting is about to commit an offence or to be committing an offence
- whom the officer has reasonable grounds to suspect of being guilty of an offence which he or she has reasonable grounds for suspecting has been committed
- anyone who is guilty of an offence which has been committed or anyone whom the officer has reasonable grounds for suspecting to be guilty of that offence.

### Necessity criteria

2.4 The power of arrest is only exercisable if the constable has reasonable grounds for believing that it is necessary to arrest the person. The criteria for what may constitute necessity are set out in paragraph 2.9. It remains an operational decision at the discretion of the arresting officer as to:
- what action he or she may take at the point of contact with the individual;
- the necessity criterion or criteria (if any) which applies to the individual; and
- whether to arrest, report for summons, grant street bail, issue a fixed penalty notice or take any other action that is open to the officer.

2.5 In applying the criteria, the arresting officer has to be satisfied that at least one of the reasons supporting the need for arrest is satisfied.

2.6 Extending the power of arrest to all offences provides a constable with the ability to use that power to deal with any situation. However applying the necessity criteria requires the constable to examine and justify the reason or reasons why a person needs to be taken to a police station for the custody officer to decide whether the person should be placed in police detention.

2.7 The criteria below are set out in section 24 of PACE as substituted by section 110 of the Serious Organised Crime and Police Act 2005. The criteria are exhaustive. However, the circumstances that may satisfy those criteria remain a matter for the operational discretion of individual officers. Some examples are given below of what those circumstances may be.

2.8 In considering the individual circumstances, the constable must take into account the situation of the victim, the nature of the offence, the circumstances of the suspect and the needs of the investigative process.

2.9 The criteria are that the arrest is necessary:
- (a) to enable the name of the person in question to be ascertained (in the case where the constable does not know, and cannot readily ascertain, the person's name, or has reasonable grounds for doubting whether a name given by the person as his name is his real name)
- (b) correspondingly as regards the person's address

An address is a satisfactory address for service of summons if the person will be at it for a sufficiently long period for it to be possible to serve him or her with a summons; or, that some other person at that address specified by the person will accept service of the summons on their behalf.

(c) to prevent the person in question—
  (i) causing physical injury to himself or any other person;
  (ii) suffering physical injury;
  (iii) causing loss or damage to property;
  (iv) committing an offence against public decency (only applies where members of the public going about their normal business cannot reasonably be expected to avoid the person in question); or
  (v) causing an unlawful obstruction of the highway;
(d) to protect a child or other vulnerable person from the person in question
(e) to allow the prompt and effective investigation of the offence or of the conduct of the person in question.
  This may include cases such as:
  (i) Where there are reasonable grounds to believe that the person:
    • has made false statements;
    • has made statements which cannot be readily verified;
    • has presented false evidence;
    • may steal or destroy evidence;
    • may make contact with co-suspects or conspirators;
    • may intimidate or threaten or make contact with witnesses;
    • where it is necessary to obtain evidence by questioning; or
  (ii) when considering arrest in connection with an indictable offence, there is a need to:
    • enter and search any premises occupied or controlled by a person;
    • search the person;
    • prevent contact with others;
    • take fingerprints, footwear impressions, samples or photographs of the suspect;
  (iii) ensuring compliance with statutory drug testing requirements.
(f) to prevent any prosecution for the offence from being hindered by the disappearance of the person in question.
  This may arise if there are reasonable grounds for believing that
  • if the person is not arrested he or she will fail to attend court;
  • street bail after arrest would be insufficient to deter the suspect from trying to evade prosecution.

Code **G**

## 3 INFORMATION TO BE GIVEN ON ARREST

### (a) Cautions—when a caution must be given (taken from Code C section 10)

3.1 A person whom there are grounds to suspect of an offence (see *Note 2*) must be cautioned before any questions about an offence, or further questions if the answers provide the grounds for suspicion, are put to them if either the suspect's answers or silence, (i.e. failure or refusal to answer or answer satisfactorily) may be given in evidence to a court in a prosecution. A person need not be cautioned if questions are for other necessary purposes e.g.:
  (a) solely to establish their identity or ownership of any vehicle;
  (b) to obtain information in accordance with any relevant statutory requirement;

(c) in furtherance of the proper and effective conduct of a search, e.g. to determine the need to search in the exercise of powers of stop and search or to seek cooperation while carrying out a search;

(d) to seek verification of a written record as in *Code C paragraph 11.13*;

(e) when examining a person in accordance with the Terrorism Act 2000, Schedule 7 and the Code of Practice for Examining Officers issued under that Act, Schedule 14, paragraph 6.

3.2 Whenever a person not under arrest is initially cautioned, or reminded they are under caution, that person must at the same time be told they are not under arrest and are free to leave if they want to.

3.3 A person who is arrested, or further arrested, must be informed at the time, or as soon as practicable thereafter, that they are under arrest and the grounds for their arrest, see *Note 3*.

3.4 A person who is arrested, or further arrested, must also be cautioned unless:

(a) it is impracticable to do so by reason of their condition or behaviour at the time;

(b) they have already been cautioned immediately prior to arrest as in *paragraph 3.1*;

(c) Terms of the caution (Taken from Code C section 10).

3.5 The caution, which must be given on arrest, should be in the following terms: 'You do not have to say anything. But it may harm your defence if you do not mention when questioned something which you later rely on in Court. Anything you do say may be given in evidence.'
See *Note 5*

3.6 Minor deviations from the words of any caution given in accordance with this Code do not constitute a breach of this Code, provided the sense of the relevant caution is preserved. See *Note 6*

3.7 When, despite being cautioned, a person fails to co-operate or to answer particular questions which may affect their immediate treatment, the person should be informed of any relevant consequences and that those consequences are not affected by the caution. Examples are when a person's refusal to provide:

• their name and address when charged may make them liable to detention;

• particulars and information in accordance with a statutory requirement, e.g. under the Road Traffic Act 1988, may amount to an offence or may make the person liable to a further arrest.

## 4 Records of Arrest

### (a) General

4.1 The arresting officer is required to record in his pocket book or by other methods used for recording information:

• the nature and circumstances of the offence leading to the arrest

• the reason or reasons why arrest was necessary

• the giving of the caution

• anything said by the person at the time of arrest

4.2 Such a record should be made at the time of the arrest unless impracticable to do. If not made at that time, the record should then be completed as soon as possible thereafter.

4.3 On arrival at the police station, the custody officer shall open the custody record (see *paragraph 1.1A* and *section 2 of Code C*). The information given by the arresting officer on the circumstances and reason or reasons for arrest shall be recorded as part of the custody record. Alternatively, a copy of the record made by the officer in accordance with paragraph 4.1 above shall be attached as part of the custody record. See *paragraph 2.2* and *Code C paragraphs 3.4 and 10.3*.

4.4 The custody record will serve as a record of the arrest. Copies of the custody record will be provided in accordance with paragraphs 2.4 and 2.4A of Code C and access for inspection of the original record in accordance with paragraph 2.5 of Code C.

### (b) Interviews and arrests

4.5 Records of interview, significant statements or silences will be treated in the same way as set out in sections 10 and 11 of Code C and in Code E (tape recording of interviews).

### Notes for guidance

1   *The powers of arrest for offences under sections 4(1) and 5(1) of the Criminal Law Act 1967 require that the offences to which they relate must carry a sentence fixed by law or one in which a first time offender aged 18 or over could be sentenced to 5 years or more imprisonment.*

2   *There must be some reasonable, objective grounds for the suspicion, based on known facts or information which are relevant to the likelihood the offence has been committed and the person to be questioned committed it.*

3   *An arrested person must be given sufficient information to enable them to understand they have been deprived of their liberty and the reason they have been arrested, e.g. when a person is arrested on suspicion of committing an offence they must be informed of the suspected offence's nature, when and where it was committed. The suspect must also be informed of the reason or reasons why arrest is considered necessary. Vague or technical language should be avoided.*

4   *Nothing in this Code requires a caution to be given or repeated when informing a person not under arrest they may be prosecuted for an offence. However, a court will not be able to draw any inferences under the Criminal Justice and Public Order Act 1994, section 34, if the person was not cautioned.*

5   *If it appears a person does not understand the caution, the people giving it should explain it in their own words.*

6   *The powers available to an officer as the result of an arrest—for example, entry and search of premises, holding a person incommunicado, setting up road blocks—are only available in respect of indictable offences and are subject to the specific requirements on authorisation as set out in the 1984 Act and relevant PACE Code of Practice.*

Code **G**

# Appendix 9

## Code H: PACE Code of Practice in connection with the Detention, Treatment and Questioning by Police Officers of Persons under Section 41 of, and Schedule 8 to, The Terrorism Act 2000 (Summary)

This new Code H, brought into force at midnight on 24 July 2006, applies to all people in police detention following their arrest under section 41 of the Terrorism Act 2000 (TACT). It should be noted that it applies *only* to such detainees. The provisions contained in Code H do not therefore apply to individuals detained under any other terrorism legislation; Code C will continue to apply in such cases.

Many of the provisions mirror those to be found in Code C. For reasons of space therefore, Code H has not been reproduced in full here; rather the table below sets out the equivalent Code C provisions. Where there is a minor difference, the effect of that difference has been commented upon. Where however there is a significant difference between the Codes, the relevant provision of Code H is set out in full. Direct quotes from Code H are shown italicized.

The full text of Code H can be found on at: http://police.homeoffice.gov.uk/operational-policing/powers-pace-codes/pace-code-intro/

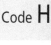

Code H

| Code H | Code C | Text and Commentary |
|---|---|---|
| **1 General** | | |
| 1.1 | | *This Code of Practice applies to, and only to, persons arrested under section 41 of the Terrorism Act 2000 (TACT) and detained in police custody under those provisions and Schedule 8 of the Act. References to detention under this provision that were previously included in PACE Code C—Code for the Detention, Treatment and Questioning of Persons by Police Officers, no longer apply.* |

| Code H | Code C | Text and Commentary |
|---|---|---|
| 1.2 | | *This Code ceases to apply at any point that a detainee is:* <br> *(a) charged with an offence;* <br> *(b) released without charge; or* <br> *(c) transferred to a prison, see section 14.5* |
| 1.3 | | *References to an offence in this Code include being concerned in the commission, preparation or instigation of acts of terrorism.* |
| 1.4 | | *This Code's provisions do not apply to detention of individuals under any other terrorism legislation. This Code does not apply to people:* <br> *(i) detained under section 5(1) of the Prevention of Terrorism Act 2005;* <br> *(ii) detained for examination under TACT Schedule 7 and to whom the Code of Practice issued under that Act, Schedule 14, paragraph 6 applies;* <br> *(iii) detained for searches under stop and search powers.* <br> *The provisions for the detention, treatment and questioning by police officers of persons other than those in police detention following arrest under section 41 TACT, are set out in Code C issued under section 66(1) of the Police and Criminal Evidence Act (PACE) 1984 (PACE Code C).* |
| 1.5 | 1.1 | |
| 1.6 | | Commentary: There is no provision for bail under TACT prior to charge. |
| 1.7 | 1.1A | |
| 1.8 | 1.2 | |
| 1.9 | 1.3 | |
| 1.10 | 1.4 | |
| 1.11 | 1.5 | |
| 1.12 | 1.6 | |
| 1.13 | 1.7 | |
| 1.14 | 1.8 | |

| 1.15 | 1.9 | |
|---|---|---|
| 1.16 | 1.9A | |
| 1.17 | 1.13 | |
| 1.18 | 1.14 | |
| 1.19 | 1.15 | |
| 1.20 | 1.16 | |
| 1.21 | 1.17 | |
| Note 1A | Note 1A | |
| Note 1B | Note 1B | Commentary: Code H adds that a person should not be an appropriate adult if they are suspected of involvement in the offence or involvement in the commission, preparation or instigation of acts of terrorism. |
| Note 1C | Note 1C | |
| Note 1D | Note 1D | |
| Note 1E | Note 1E | |
| Note 1F | Note 1F | |
| Note 1G | Note 1G | |
| Note 1H | Note 1H | |
| Note 1I | Note 1I | |
| Note 1J | Note 1J | |
| Note 1K | Note 1K | |
| Note 1L | | If a person is moved from a police station to receive medical treatment, or for any other reason, the period of detention is still calculated from the time of arrest under section 41 of TACT (or, if a person was being detained under TACT Schedule 7 when arrested, from the time at which the examination under Schedule 7 began). |
| Note 1M | | Under paragraph 1 of Schedule 8 to TACT, all police stations are designated for detention of persons arrested under section 41 of TACT. Paragraph 4 of Schedule 8 requires that the constable who arrests a person under section 41 takes him as soon as practicable to the police station which he considers is 'most appropriate'. |

Code H

| Code H | Code C | Text and Commentary |
|--------|--------|---------------------|
| **2 Custody Records** | | |
| 2.1 | 2.1A | Commentary: The two Codes are the same save that Code H applies to those persons brought to a police station under TACT section 41 arrest or who are arrested at a police station under that provision having gone there voluntarily. |
| 2.2 | 2.1 | |
| 2.3 | 2.2 | |
| 2.4 | 2.3 | |
| 2.5 | 2.4 | Commentary: Code H adds that arrangements for access must not unreasonably interfere with the custody officer's duties *or the justifiable needs of the investigation.* |
| 2.6 | 2.4A | |
| 2.7 | 2.5 | |
| 2.8 | 2.6, 2.6A | Commentary: Code H does not require the identities of officers or other police staff to be recorded or disclosed in the case of enquiries linked to the investigation of terrorism; warrant or other identification numbers should be used instead. See *Note 2A* |
| 2.9 | 2.7 | |
| Note 2A | Note 2A | *The purpose of paragraph 2.8 is to protect those involved in terrorist investigations or arrests of terrorist suspects from the possibility that those arrested, their associates or other individuals or groups may threaten or cause harm to those involved.* |
| **3 Initial Action** | | |
| 3.1 | 3.1 | |
| 3.2 | 3.2 | |
| 3.3 | 3.3 | |
| 3.4 | 3.4 | Commentary: Under Code H, the custody officer must record that the person was arrested under s 41 of the Terrorism Act 2000 rather than recording a specific offence as under the equivalent provision in Code C. Reference is made to paragraph 5.9 of the Code of Practice issued under TACT Schedule 8 paragraph 3 in respect of unsolicited comments. |
| 3.5 | 3.5 | |

| | | |
|---|---|---|
| 3.6 | 3.6 | Commentary: Under Code H 3.6, in carrying out a risk assessment, the custody officer has to consider whether the detainee is likely to present a specific risk not only to the custody staff, but to any individual who may have contact with the detainee (*e.g. legal advisers, medical staff*) or themselves. In making this judgment it *will be necessary for the custody officer to obtain information from other sources, especially the investigation team.* |
| 3.7 | 3.7 | |
| 3.8 | 3.8 | Commentary: Code H and Code C are substantially the same, but Code H adds that *The content of any risk assessment and any analysis of the level of risk relating to the person's detention is not required to be shown or provided to the detainee or any person acting on behalf of the detainee.* |
| 3.9 | 3.9 | Commentary: Code H adds a further example of a response to a specific risk assessment of *reducing the risk to those who come into contact with the detainee.* |
| 3.10 | 3.10 | |
| 3.11 | 3.11 | |
| 3.12 | | *A constable, prison officer or other person authorised by the Secretary of State may take any steps which are reasonably necessary for:*<br>*(a) photographing the detained person;*<br>*(b) measuring him; or*<br>*(c) identifying him.* |
| 3.13 | | *Paragraph 3.12 concerns the power in TACT Schedule 8 paragraph 2. The power in TACT Schedule 8 paragraph 2 does not cover the taking of fingerprints, intimate samples or non-intimate samples, which is covered in TACT Schedule 8 paragraphs 10–15.* |
| 3.14 | 3.12 | |
| 3.15 | 3.13 | |
| 3.16 | 3.14 | |
| 3.17 | 3.15 | |
| 3.18 | 3.17 | |
| 3.19 | 3.18 | |

Code **H**

| Code H | Code C | Text and Commentary |
|---|---|---|
| 3.20 | 3.19 | |
| 3.21 | 3.20 | |
| 3.22 | 3.23 | |
| 3.23 | 3.24 | |
| Note 3A | Note 3A | |
| Note 3B | Note 3B | |
| Note 3C | Note 3C | |
| Note 3D | Note 3D | |
| Note 3E | | *The investigation team will include any officer involved in questioning a suspect, gathering or analysing evidence in relation to the offences of which the detainee is suspected of having committed. Should a custody officer require information from the investigation team, the first point of contact should be the officer in charge of the investigation.* |
| Note 3F | Note 3E. | Commentary: Code H additionally draws attention to the Guidance on Safer Detention & Handling of Persons in Police Custody. |
| Note 3G | | *Arrests under TACT section 41 can only be made where an officer has reasonable grounds to suspect that the individual concerned is a 'terrorist'. This differs from the PACE power of arrest in that it need not be linked to a specific offence. There may also be circumstances where an arrest under TACT is made on the grounds of sensitive information which can not be disclosed. In such circumstances, the grounds for arrest may be given in terms of the interpretation of a 'terrorist' set out in TACT sections 40(1)(a) or 40(1)(b).* |
| Note 3H | | *For the purpose of arrests under TACT section 41, the review officer is responsible for authorising detention (see paragraphs 14.1 and 14.2, and Notes for guidance 14A and 14B). The review officer's role is explained in TACT Schedule 8 Part II. A person may be detained after arrest pending the first review, which must take place as soon as practicable after the person's arrest.* |
| **4  Detainee's Property** | | |
| 4.1 | 4.1 | Commentary: Code H adds that the custody officer has responsibility for ascertaining what property a detainee has with them *either on first arrival at the police station or on any subsequent arrivals at a police station in connection with that detention.* |
| 4.2 | 4.2 | |
| 4.3 | 4.3 | |

| | |
|---|---|
| 4.4 | |
| 4.5 | |
| Note 4A | |
| Note 4B | |
| Note 4C | |
| Note 4D | *Section 43(2) of TACT allows a constable to search a person who has been arrested under section 41 to discover whether he has anything in his possession that may constitute evidence that he is a terrorist.* |

## 5 Right not to be Held Incommunicado

| | |
|---|---|
| 5.1 | Commentary: Code H slightly alters the mirror provision in Code C. Code C permits the detainee to request that a person 'known to them' be informed of his arrest; Code H refers to a *named person who is a friend, relative or a person known to them.* |
| 5.2 | |
| 5.3 | |
| 5.4 | *If the detainee agrees, they may receive visits from friends, family or others likely to take an interest in their welfare, at the custody officer's discretion. Custody Officers should liaise closely with the investigation team (see Note 3E) to allow risk assessments to be made where particular visitors have been requested by the detainee or identified themselves to police. In circumstances where the nature of the investigation means that such requests cannot be met, consideration should be given, in conjunction with a representative of the relevant scheme, to increasing the frequency of visits from independent visitor schemes. See Notes 5B and 5C:* |
| 5.5 | |
| 5.6 | Commentary: Code H 5.6 together with Note 5G draws attention to the possibility that a detainee might seek to pass information detrimental to public safety or the investigation, and the need to carefully consider whether the detainee should be permitted to make a telephone call where that call is made in a language that cannot be readily understood. |
| 5.7 | |
| 5.7A | |
| 5.8 | |
| 5.9 | |
| Note 5A | |

Code H

| Code H | Code C | Text and Commentary |
|---|---|---|
| Note 5B | Note 5B | At the custody officer's discretion (and subject to the detainee's consent), visits from friends, family or others likely to take an interest in the detainee's welfare, should be allowed when possible, subject to sufficient personnel being available to supervise a visit and any possible hindrance to the investigation. Custody Officers should bear in mind the exceptional nature of prolonged TACT detention and consider the potential benefits that visits may bring to the health and welfare of detainees who are held for extended periods. |
| Note 5C | | Official visitors should be given access following consultation with the officer who has overall responsibility for the investigation provided the detainee consents, and they do not compromise safety or security or unduly delay or interfere with the progress of an investigation. Official visitors should still be required to provide appropriate identification and subject to any screening process in place at the place of detention. Official visitors may include:<br>• An accredited faith representative<br>• Members of either House of Parliament<br>• Public officials needing to interview the prisoner in the course of their duties<br>• Other persons visiting with the approval of the officer who has overall responsibility for the investigation<br>• Consular officials visiting a detainee who is a national of the country they represent subject to Annex F<br>Visits from appropriate members of the Independent Custody Visitors Scheme should be dealt with in accordance with the separate Code of Practice on Independent Custody Visiting. |
| Note 5D | Note 5C | |
| Note 5E | Note 5D | |
| Note 5F | Note 5E | Commentary: Code H permits further calls to be made at the custody officer's discretion. |
| Note 5G | | The nature of terrorism investigations means that officers should have particular regard to the possibility of suspects attempting to pass information which may be detrimental to public safety, or to an investigation. |
| 6 Right to Legal Advice | | |
| 6.1 | 6.1 | Commentary: Under Code H an appropriate adult if present must be told of the right to legal advice as well as the detainee. |
| 6.2 | 6.3 | |
| 6.3 | 6.4 | |
| 6.4 | 6.5 | Commentary: Under Code H, access to legal advice may be delayed only exceptionally. |

| | | |
|---|---|---|
| 6.5 | *An officer of the rank of Commander or Assistant Chief Constable may give a direction under TACT Schedule 8 paragraph 9 that a detainee may only consult a solicitor within the sight and hearing of a qualified officer. Such a direction may only be given if the officer has reasonable grounds to believe that if it were not, it may result in one of the consequences set out in TACT Schedule 8 paragraphs 8(4) or 8(5)(c). See Annex B paragraph 3 and Note 6I. A 'qualified officer' means a police officer who:*<br>*(a) is at least the rank of inspector;*<br>*(b) is of the uniformed branch of the force of which the officer giving the direction is a member; and*<br>*(c) in the opinion of the officer giving the direction, has no connection with the detained person's case.*<br>*Officers considering the use of this power should first refer to Home Office Circular 40/2003.* | 6.5A |
| 6.6 | | 6.6 |
| 6.7 | | 6.7 |
| 6.8 | | 6.8 |
| 6.9 | | 6.9 |
| 6.10 | | 6.10 |
| 6.11 | | 6.11 |
| 6.12 | | 6.12 |
| 6.13 | | 6.12A |
| 6.14 | | 6.13 |
| 6.15 | | 6.14 |
| 6.16 | | 6.15 |
| 6.17 | | 6.16 |
| 6.18 | | 6.17 |
| 6.19 | | |
| Note 6A | Commentary: At the end of Note 6A, Code H adds that *Nothing within this section is intended to prevent police from ascertaining immediately after the arrest of an individual whether a threat to public safety exists.* | Note 6A |
| Note 6B | | Note 6B |
| Note 6C | | Note 6D |

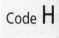

Code **H**

| Code H | Code C | Text and Commentary |
|---|---|---|
| Note 6D | Note 6E | |
| Note 6E | Note 6F | |
| Note 6F | Note 6G | |
| Note 6G | Note 6H | |
| Note 6H | Note 6I | |
| Note 6I | Note 6J | Commentary: Code H reiterates that even for detainees arrested under s 41 TACT, the right to consult privately with a solicitor is fundamental, unless a direction has been given under Schedule 8, paragraph 9 of the Terrorism Act 2000. |
| Note 6J | Note 6K | |
| **7 Citizens of Independent Commonwealth Countries or Foreign Nationals** | | |
| 7.1 | 7.1 | |
| 7.2 | 7.2 | |
| 7.3 | 7.3 | |
| 7.4 | 7.4 | |
| 7.5 | 7.5 | |
| Note 7A | Note 7A | |
| **8 Conditions of Detention** | | |
| 8.1 | 8.1 | |
| 8.2 | 8.2 | |
| 8.3 | 8.3 | |
| 8.4 | 8.4 | |
| 8.5 | 8.5 | |
| 8.6 | 8.6 | Commentary: Not only should meals meet the dietary and religious needs of the detainee, but, adds Code H, *detainees should also be made aware that the meals offered meet such needs.* |

| | | |
|---|---|---|
| 8.7 | 8.7 | Commentary: Code H adds that *Where facilities exist, indoor exercise shall be offered as an alternative if outside conditions are such that a detainee can not be reasonably expected to take outdoor exercise (e.g. in cold or wet weather) or if requested by the detainee for reasons of security.* |
| 8.8 | | *Where practicable, provision should be made for detainees to practice religious observance. Consideration should be given to providing a separate room which can be used as a prayer room. The supply of appropriate food and clothing, and suitable provision for prayer facilities, such as uncontaminated copies of religious books, should also be considered. See Note 8D* |
| 8.9 | 8.9 | |
| 8.10 | | *Police stations should keep a reasonable supply of reading material available for detainees, including but not limited to, the main religious texts. See Note 8D. Detainees should be made aware that such material is available and reasonable requests for such material should be met as soon as practicable unless to do so would:*<br>*(i) interfere with the investigation; or*<br>*(ii) prevent or delay an officer from discharging his statutory duties, or those in this Code.*<br>*If such a request is refused on the grounds of (i) or (ii) above, this should be noted in the custody record and met as soon as possible after those grounds cease to apply.* |
| 8.11 | 8.9 | |
| 8.12 | 8.11 | |
| Note 8A | Note 8A | Commentary: Code H adds that *If an officer needs to examine food or other items supplied by family and friends before deciding whether they can be given to the detainee, he should inform the person who has brought the item to the police station of this and the reasons for doing so.* |
| Note 8B | Note 8B | |
| Note 8C | | *In light of the potential for detaining individuals for extended periods of time, the overriding principle should be to accommodate a period of exercise, except where to do so would hinder the investigation, delay the detainee's release or charge, or it is declined by the detainee.* |
| Note 8D | | *Police forces should consult with representatives of the main religious communities to ensure the provision for religious observance is adequate, and to seek advice on the appropriate storage and handling of religious texts or other religious items.* |

## 9 Care and Treatment of Detained Persons

| | | |
|---|---|---|
| 9.1 | | *Notwithstanding other requirements for medical attention as set out in this section, detainees who are held for more than 96 hours must be visited by a healthcare professional at least once every 24 hours.* |
| 9.2 | 9.1 | |

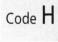

Code **H**

| Code H | Code C | Text and Commentary |
| --- | --- | --- |
| 9.3 | 9.2 | |
| 9.4 | 9.3 | |
| 9.5 | 9.4 | |
| 9.6 | 9.5 | |
| 9.7 | 9.5A | |
| 9.8 | 9.5B | |
| 9.9 | 9.7 | |
| 9.10 | 9.8 | |
| 9.11 | 9.9 | |
| 9.12 | 9.10 | |
| 9.13 | 9.11 | |
| 9.14 | 9.12 | |
| 9.15 | 9.13 | |
| 9.16 | 9.14 | |
| 9.17 | 9.15 | |
| 9.18 | 9.16 | |
| 9.19 | 9.17 | |
| Note 9A | Note 9A | |
| Note 9B | Note 9B | |
| Note 9C | Note 9C | |
| Note 9D | Note 9E | |
| Note 9E | Note 9F | |

| | | |
|---|---|---|
| Note 9F | Note 9G | |
| Note 9G | Note 9H | |
| **10 Cautions** | | |
| 10.1 | 10.1 | Commentary: The examples given in Code C 10.1 of when a person need not be cautioned are not included in the mirror provision in Code H. |
| 10.2 | 10.3 | |
| 10.3 | 10.4 | |
| 10.4 | 10.5 | |
| 10.5 | 10.6 | |
| 10.6 | 10.7 | |
| 10.7 | 10.8 | |
| 10.8 | 10.9 | |
| 10.9 | 10.10 | |
| 10.10 | 10.11 | |
| 10.11 | 10.12 | |
| 10.12 | 10.13 | |
| Note 10A | Note 10A | |
| Note 10B | Note 10B | |
| Note 10C | Note 10D | |
| Note 10D | Note 10E | |
| Note 10E | Note 10F | |
| Note 10F | Note 10G | |

Code **H**

517

| Code H | Code C | Text and Commentary |
|---|---|---|
| **11 Interviews** | | |
| 11.1 | 11.1A | An interview in this Code is the questioning of a person arrested on suspicion of being a terrorist which, under paragraph 10.1, must be carried out under caution. Whenever a person is interviewed they must be informed of the grounds for arrest; see Note 3G |
| 11.2 | 11.1 | Commentary: Under Code H, a suspect arrested under s 41 TACT must not be interviewed except at a place designated for detention under Schedule 8 paragraph 1 of the Terrorism Act 2000 unless it is an urgent interview as in Code C. |
| 11.3 | 11.2 | |
| 11.4 | 11.4 | |
| 11.5 | 11.4A | |
| 11.6 | 11.5 | |
| 11.7 | 11.6 | |
| 11.8 | | Interview records should be made in accordance with the Code of Practice issued under Schedule 8 paragraph 3 to the Terrorism Act 2000 where the interview takes place at a designated place of detention. |
| 11.9 | 11.15 | |
| 11.10 | 11.17 | Commentary: Code H adds that The appropriate adult may be required to leave the interview if their conduct is such that the interviewer is unable properly to put questions to the suspect. This will include situations where the appropriate adult's approach or conduct prevents or unreasonably obstructs proper questions being put to the suspect or the suspect's responses being recorded. If the interviewer considers an appropriate adult is acting in such a way, they will stop the interview and consult an officer not below superintendent rank, if one is readily available, and otherwise an officer not below inspector rank not connected with the investigation. After speaking to the appropriate adult, the officer consulted will decide if the interview should continue without the attendance of that appropriate adult. If they decide it should not, another appropriate adult should be obtained before the interview continues, unless the provisions of paragraph 11.11 below apply. |
| 11.11 | 11.18 | |
| 11.12 | 11.19 | |
| 11.13 | 11.20 | |
| Note 11A | Note 11A | |
| Note 11B | Note 11B | |
| Note 11C | Note 11C | |

| | | |
|---|---|---|
| Note 11D | | *Consideration should be given to the effect of extended detention on a detainee and any subsequent information they provide, especially if it relates to information on matters that they have failed to provide previously in response to similar questioning; see Annex G* |
| Note 11E | Note 11E | |

**12 Interviews in Police Stations**

| | | |
|---|---|---|
| 12.1 | 12.1 | |
| 12.2 | 12.2 | |
| 12.3 | 12.3 | |
| 12.4 | 12.4 | |
| 12.5 | 12.5 | |
| 12.6 | 12.6 | |
| 12.7 | 12.7 | |
| 12.8 | 12.8 | |
| 12.9 | | *During extended periods where no interviews take place, because of the need to gather further evidence or analyse existing evidence, detainees and their legal representative shall be informed that the investigation into the relevant offence remains ongoing. If practicable, the detainee and legal representative should also be made aware in general terms of any reasons for long gaps between interviews. Consideration should be given to allowing visits, more frequent exercise, or for reading and writing materials to be offered; see paragraph 5.4, section 8 and Note 12C.* |
| 12.10 | 12.9 | |
| 12.11 | 12.10 | |
| 12.12 | 12.11 | |
| 12.13 | 12.12 | |
| 12.14 | 12.13 | |
| 12.15 | 12.14 | |
| Note 12A | Note 12A | |
| Note 12B | Note 12B | |

Code **H**

| Code H | Code C | Text and Commentary |
|---|---|---|
| Note 12C | | *Consideration should be given to the matters referred to in paragraph 12.9 after a period of over 24 hours without questioning. This is to ensure that extended periods of detention without an indication that the investigation remains ongoing do not contribute to a deterioration of the detainee's well-being.* |
| **13 Interpreters** | | |
| 13.1 | 13.1 | |
| 13.2 | 13.2 | |
| 13.3 | 13.3 | Commentary: Code H states that *the Code of Practice issued under paragraph 3 of Schedule 8 to the Terrorism Act 2000 will apply to interviews that are recorded audibly or visually with sound.* |
| 13.4 | 13.4 | |
| 13.5 | 13.5 | |
| 13.6 | 13.6 | |
| 13.7 | 13.7 | Commentary: Code H states that *the Code of Practice issued under paragraph 3 of Schedule 8 to the Terrorism Act 2000 will apply to interviews that are recorded audibly or visually with sound.* |
| 13.8 | 13.8 | |
| 13.9 | 13.9 | Commentary: Code H states that *the Code of Practice issued under paragraph 3 of Schedule 8 to the Terrorism Act 2000 will apply to interviews that are recorded audibly or visually with sound.* |
| 13.10 | 13.10 | |
| 13.11 | 13.11 | |
| **14 Reviews and Extensions of Detention** | | |
| 14.1 | | *The powers and duties of the review officer are in the Terrorism Act 2000, Schedule B, Part II. See Notes 14A and 14B. A review officer should carry out his duties at the police station where the detainee is held, and be allowed such access to the detainee as is necessary for him to exercise those duties.* |

| 14.2 | *For the purposes of reviewing a person's detention, no officer shall put specific questions to the detainee:*<br><br>• *regarding their involvement in any offence; or*<br>• *in respect of any comments they may make:*<br>  – *when given the opportunity to make representations; or*<br>  – *in response to a decision to keep them in detention or extend the maximum period of detention.*<br><br>*Such an exchange could constitute an interview as in paragraph 11.1 and would be subject to the associated safeguards in section 11 and, in respect of a person who has been charged see PACE Code C Section 16.8.* |
|---|---|
| 14.3 | *If detention is necessary for longer than 48 hours, a police officer of at least superintendent rank, or a Crown Prosecutor may apply for warrants of further detention under the Terrorism Act 2000, Schedule 8, Part III.* |
| 14.4 | *When an application for a warrant of further or extended detention is sought under paragraph 29 or 36 of Schedule 8, the detained person and their representative must be informed of their rights in respect of the application. These include:*<br><br>*a) the right to a written or oral notice of the warrant. See Note 14G*<br>*b) the right to make oral or written representations to the judicial authority about the application;*<br>*c) the right to be present and legally represented at the hearing of the application, unless specifically excluded by the judicial authority;*<br>*d) their right to free legal advice (see section 6 of this Code)* |
| 14.5 | *Where a warrant is issued which authorises a detention beyond a period of 14 days from the time of arrest (or if a person was being detained under TACT Schedule 7, from the time at which the examination under Schedule 7 began), the detainee must be transferred from detention in a police station to detention in a designated prison as soon as is practicable, unless:*<br><br>*a) the detainee specifically requests to remain in detention at a police station and that request can be accommodated; or*<br>*b) there are reasonable grounds to believe that transferring a person to a prison would:*<br>  *i) significantly hinder a terrorism investigation;*<br>  *ii) delay charging of the detainee or his release from custody; or*<br>  *iii) otherwise prevent the investigation from being conducted diligently and expeditiously.*<br><br>*If any of the grounds in (b)(i) to (iii) above are relied upon, these must be presented to the judicial authority as part of the application for the warrant that would extend detention beyond a period of 14 days from the time of arrest (or if a person was being detained under TACT Schedule 7, from the time at which the examination under Schedule 7 began). See Note 14J* |
| 14.6 | *If a person remains in detention at a police station under a warrant of further detention as described at section 14.5, they must be transferred to a prison as soon as practicable after the grounds at (b)(i) to (iii) of that section cease to apply.* |

Code H

| Code H | Code C | Text and Commentary |
|---|---|---|
| 14.7 | | *Police should maintain an agreement with the National Offender Management Service (NOMS) that stipulates named prisons to which individuals may be transferred under this section. This should be made with regard to ensuring detainees are moved to the most suitable prison for the purposes of the investigation and their welfare, and should include provision for the transfer of male, female and juvenile detainees. Police should ensure that the Governor of a prison to which they intend to transfer a detainee is given reasonable notice of this. Where practicable, this should be no later than the point at which a warrant is applied for that would take the period of detention beyond 14 days.* |
| 14.8 | | *Following a detained person's transfer to a designated prison, their detention will be governed by the terms of Schedule 8 and Prison Rules, and this Code of Practice will not apply during any period that the person remains in prison detention. The Code will once more apply if a detained person is transferred back from prison detention to police detention. In order to enable the Governor to arrange for the production of the detainee back into police custody, police should give notice to the Governor of the relevant prison as soon as possible of any decision to transfer a detainee from prison back to a police station. Any transfer between a prison and a police station should be conducted by police, and this Code will be applicable during the period of transit; see Note 14K. A detainee should only remain in police custody having been transferred back from a prison, for as long as is necessary for the purpose of the investigation.* |
| 14.9 | | *The investigating team and the custody officer should provide as much information as necessary to enable the relevant prison authorities to provide appropriate facilities to detain an individual. This should include, but not be limited to:*<br>*i) medical assessments*<br>*ii) security and risk assessments*<br>*iii) details of the detained person's legal representatives*<br>*iv) details of any individuals from whom the detained person has requested visits, or who have requested to visit the detained person.* |
| 14.10 | | *Where a detainee is to be transferred to prison, the custody officer should inform the detainee's legal adviser beforehand that the transfer is to take place (including the name of the prison). The custody officer should also make all reasonable attempts to inform:*<br>*• family or friends who have been informed previously of the detainee's detention; and*<br>*• the person who was initially informed of the detainee's detention as at paragraph 5.1.* |
| 14.11 | 15.12 | |
| 14.12 | 15.13 | |
| 14.13 | 15.15 | |

| | | |
|---|---|---|
| 14.14 | 15.16 | Commentary: Code H simply states that a record shall be made as soon as practicable about the outcome of each review, determination or application. |
| 14.15 | | *Any decision not to transfer a detained person to a designated prison under paragraph 14.5 must be recorded, along with the reasons for this decision. If a request under paragraph 14.5(a) is not accommodated, the reasons for this should also be recorded.* |
| Note 14A | | *TACT Schedule 8 Part II sets out the procedures for review of detention up to 48 hours from the time of arrest under TACT section 41(or if a person was being detained under TACT Schedule 7, from the time at which the examination under Schedule 7 began). These include provisions for the requirement to review detention, postponing a review, grounds for continued detention, designating a review officer, representations, rights of the detained person and keeping a record. The review officer's role ends after a warrant has been issued for extension of detention under Part III of Schedule 8.* |
| Note 14B | | *Section 24(1) of the Terrorism Act 2006, amended the grounds contained within the 2000 Act on which a review officer may authorise continued detention. Continued detention may be authorised if it is necessary—*<br>*a) to obtain relevant evidence whether by questioning him or otherwise*<br>*b) to preserve relevant evidence*<br>*c) while awaiting the result of an examination or analysis of relevant evidence*<br>*d) for the examination or analysis of anything with a view to obtaining relevant evidence*<br>*e) pending a decision to apply to the Secretary of State for a deportation notice to be served on the detainee, the making of any such application, or the consideration of any such application by the Secretary of State*<br>*f) pending a decision to charge the detainee with an offence.* |
| Note 14C | | *Applications for warrants to extend detention beyond 48 hours, may be made for periods of 7 days at a time (initially under TACT Schedule 8 paragraph 36), up to a maximum period of 28 days from the time of arrest (or if a person was being detained under TACT Schedule 7, from the time at which the examination under Schedule 7 began). Applications may be made for shorter periods than 7 days, which must be specified. The judicial authority may also substitute a shorter period if he feels a period of 7 days is inappropriate.* |
| Note 14D | | *Unless Note 14F applies, applications for warrants that would take the total period of detention up to 14 days or less should be made to a judicial authority, meaning a District Judge (Magistrates' Court) designated by the Lord Chancellor to hear such applications.* |
| Note 14E | | *Any application for a warrant which would take the period of detention beyond 14 days from the time of arrest (or if a person was being detained under TACT Schedule 7, from the time at which the examination under Schedule 7 began), must be made to a High Court Judge.* |
| Note 14F | | *If an application has been made to a High Court Judge for a warrant which would not take detention beyond 14 days, and the High Court Judge instead issues a warrant for a period of time which would not take detention beyond 14 days, further applications for extension of detention must also be made to a High Court Judge, regardless of the period of time to which they refer.* |

Code **H**

| Code H | Code C | Text and Commentary |
|---|---|---|
| Note 14G | | TACT Schedule 8 Paragraph 31 requires a notice to be given to the detained person if a warrant is sought for further detention. This must be provided before the judicial hearing of the application for that warrant and must include:<br>a) notification that the application for a warrant has been made<br>b) the time at which the application was made<br>c) the time at which the application is to be heard<br>d) the grounds on which further detention is sought.<br>A notice must also be provided each time an application is made to extend an existing warrant. |
| Note 14H | | An officer applying for an order under TACT Schedule 8 Paragraph 34 to withhold specified information on which he intends to rely when applying for a warrant of further detention, may make the application for the order orally or in writing. The most appropriate method of application will depend on the circumstances of the case and the need to ensure fairness to the detainee. |
| Note 14I | | Where facilities exist, hearings relating to the extension of detention under Part III of Schedule 8 may take place using video conferencing facilities provided that the requirements set out in Schedule 8 are still met. However, if the judicial authority requires the detained person to be physically present at any hearing, this should be complied with as soon as practicable. Paragraphs 33(4) to 33(9) of TACT Schedule 8 govern the relevant conduct of hearings. |
| Note 14J | | Transfer to prison is intended to ensure that individuals who are detained for extended periods of time are held in a place designed for longer periods of detention than police stations. Prison will provide detainees with a greater range of facilities more appropriate to longer detention periods. |
| Note 14K | | The Code will only apply as is appropriate to the conditions of detention during the period of transit. There is obviously no requirement to provide such things as bed linen or reading materials for the journey between prison and police station. |
| **15  Charging** | | |
| 15.1 | | Charging of detained persons is covered by PACE and guidance issued under PACE by the Director of Public Prosecutions. General guidance on charging can be found in section 16 of PACE Code C. |
| **16  Testing Persons for the Presence of Specified Class A Drugs** | | |
| 16.1 | | The provisions for drug testing under section 63B of PACE (as amended by section 5 of the Criminal Justice Act 2003 and section 7 of the Drugs Act 2005), do not apply to detention under TACT section 41 and Schedule 8. Guidance on these provisions can be found in section 17 of PACE Code C. |

**Annex A—Intimate and Strip Searches**

| | | |
|---|---|---|
| 1 | 1 | |
| 2 | 2 | Commentary: The difference between Annex A 2 in Codes C and H is that under Code H, an intimate search can only be authorized where there are reasonable grounds for believing that the detainee may have something concealed upon them that could be used to cause physical injury, whereas under Code C, an intimate search can additionally be authorized in respect of Class A drugs. |
| 3 | 2A | |
| 4 | 3 | |
| 5 | 3A | |
| 6 | 5 | |
| 7 | 6 | |
| 8 | 7 | |
| 9 | 8 | |
| 10 | 9 | |
| 11 | 10 | |
| 12 | 11 | |
| 13 | 12 | |
| Note A1 | Note A1 | |
| Note A2 | Note A2 | |
| Note A3 | Note A3 | |
| Note A4 | Note A4 | |
| Note A5 | Note A5 | |

Code **H**

525

| Code H | Code C | Text and Commentary |
|---|---|---|
| Annex B—Delay in Notifying Arrest or Allowing Access to Legal Advice for Persons Detained Under the Terrorism Act 2000 | | |
| 1 | 1 | *New* Commentary: Note that Code H refers to a 'serious offence' rather than an indictable offence. |
| 2 | 2 | *New* |
| 3 | 3 | |
| 4 | 4 | |
| 5 | 5 | |
| 6 | 6 | |
| 7 | 7 | |
| 8 | 13 | |
| 9 | 14 | |
| 10 | 15 | |
| Note B1 | Note B1 | |
| Note B2 | Note B2 | |
| Note B3 | Note B3 | |
| Annex C—Restriction on Drawing Adverse Inferences from Silence and the Terms of the Caution when the Restriction Applies | | |
| 1 | 1 | |
| 2 | 2 | |
| Note C1 | Note C1 | |
| Annex D—Written Statements Under Caution | | |
| 1 | 1 | |
| 2 | 2 | |
| 3 | 3 | |

## Annex E—Summary of Provisions Relating to Mentally Disordered and Otherwise Mentally Vulnerable People

| | |
|---|---|
| 4 | 4 |
| 5 | 5 |
| 6 | 6 |
| 7 | 7 |
| 8 | 8 |
| 9 | 9 |
| 10 | 10 |
| 11 | 11 |
| 12 | 12 |
| 1 | 1 |
| 2 | 2 |
| 3 | 3 |
| 4 | 4 |
| 5 | 5 |
| 7 | 6 |
| 8 | 7 |
| 9 | 8 |
| 11 | 9 |
| 12 | 11 |
| 13 | 12 |
| Note E1 | 13 |
| Note E2 | Note E1 |
| Note E3 | Note E2 |
| | Note E3 |

Code H

| Code H | Code C | Text and Commentary |
|---|---|---|
| Annex F—Countries with which Bilateral Consular Conventions or Agreements Requiring Notification of the Arrest and Detention of their Nationals are in Force | | |
| Annex G—Fitness to be Interviewed | | |
| 1 | 1 | |
| 2 | 2 | |
| 3 | 3 | |
| 4 | 4 | |
| 5 | 5 | |
| 6 | 6 | |
| 7 | 7 | |
| 8 | 8 | |
| Annex H—Detained Person: Observation List | | |
| 1 | 1 | |
| 2 | 2 | |
| 3 | 3 | |

# Index